Cinema of the Philippines

ALSO BY BRYAN L. YEATTER
AND FROM MCFARLAND

———————

*Joe Namath, Game by Game:
The Complete Professional Football Career* (2012)

Cinema of the Philippines

A History and Filmography, 1897–2005

Bryan L. Yeatter

McFarland & Company, Inc., Publishers
Jefferson, North Carolina, and London

> *The present work is a reprint of the library bound edition of* Cinema of the Philippines: A History and Filmography, 1897–2005, *first published in 2007 by McFarland.*

LIBRARY OF CONGRESS CATALOGUING-IN-PUBLICATION DATA

Yeatter, Bryan L., 1964–
Cinema of the Philippines : a history and filmography, 1897–2005 / Bryan L. Yeatter.
  p.   cm.
Includes bibliographical references and index.

ISBN: 978-0-7864-7524-7
softcover : 50# alkaline paper ∞

1. Motion pictures—Philippines—History.
I. Title.

PN1993.5.P5Y43   2013   791.4309599—dc22   2007016737

BRITISH LIBRARY CATALOGUING DATA ARE AVAILABLE

© 2007 Bryan L. Yeatter. All rights reserved

No part of this book may be reproduced or transmitted in any form or by any means, electronic or mechanical, including photocopying or recording, or by any information storage and retrieval system, without permission in writing from the publisher.

On the cover: Celia Rodriguez and Ronald Remy in the 1964 film *Kulay Dugo ang Gabi*, directed by Gerardo de Leon

Manufactured in the United States of America

McFarland & Company, Inc., Publishers
Box 611, Jefferson, North Carolina 28640
www.mcfarlandpub.com

Table of Contents

Preface 1
Introduction 3

    One. 1897–1930 5
    Two. 1931–1941 18
    Three. 1942–1945 41
    Four. 1946–1956 51
    Five. 1957–1967 79
    Six. 1968–1973 103
    Seven. 1974–1985 129
    Eight. 1986–1997 166
    Nine. 1998–2005 197

Filmography 241
Chapter Notes 403
Bibliography 407
Index 413

Preface

Somebody once said that Filipino film is better read than watched. If that's true, then this should be the ideal book. Most probably the comment referred to the reading *of* film rather than *about* film, but either way it doesn't seem like a fair statement. Cinema in the Philippines has a very long history dating to the early 20th century, and is the oldest such industry in the region. Documenting its history from its inception should therefore be of immense importance to film historians. Unfortunately, virtually all of the cinematic output of the Philippines from the pre-war period is lost, seemingly irretrievably (only a handful of films from the pre-war period are known to have survived, the oldest dating to 1937). This loss makes it all the more important to record what is known of its history.

In the Philippines such documentation has been undertaken by men like Arsenio "Boots" Bautista, Ed Cabagnot, Mario A. Hernando, Bienvenido Lumbera and Agustin V. Sotto, all of whose work shed much needed light on the most obscure period of the Filipino film industry. In the West, however, the industry's history has remained almost entirely hidden from view; many seem to believe that the Filipino film industry began in the 1950s, and information on its history is frequently garbled and unreliable. If you were to look up filmmaker Luis Nepomuceno on the internet, for instance, you would frequently find him fallaciously referred to as a mere nom de plume for filmmaker Cirio Santiago. Nepomuceno was, in fact, a prominent filmmaker in the Philippines whose family had started the very first film studio owned by Filipinos, Malayan Motion Pictures, which began operating in 1917.

In the course of researching this book I have watched a lot of Filipino films—probably more than many Filipinos themselves have seen—and while I have doubtless endured more hokum than I have encountered pearls of the East, I imagine that I would have had much the same experience had I surveyed the collective artistic output of any nation (perhaps some more than others). Truth is, though, that Filipinos have seemed a little surprised that I have taken such an interest in this particular aspect of their culture. That needn't be a negative reflection on Philippine cinema as much as it is a reflection of America's tendency to ignore the country that it once tried to fashion in its own image, as Stanley Karnow has put it.

Art is, naturally, an important expression of the identity of any culture, and throughout the course of the 20th century film emerged as perhaps the most dominant art form (music being the other most notable expressive outlet that shapes cultural identity). What is most important about Filipino cinema is, therefore, how Philippine culture documents itself through film. It tends to record both the positive and negative aspects of colonialism, of which the Philippines has some not inconsiderable experience. There is the often beautiful melding of influences, which can sometimes be strikingly harmonious, creating a uniquely textured and colorful mix.

There is, on the other hand, the very palpable confusion over national identity, which sometimes almost borders on schizophrenia, the culture often exhibiting a mixture of love and hate toward those who were alternately its tutors and oppressors. The Philippines seems to be a nation eager to assert its identity, and yet concurrently on an endless quest to discover itself. Within is a fascinating and complex amalgam of styles and artistic modes that have always tended to set Philippine cinema apart, often making it seem like a culture vying against itself, between two worlds, too Asian to be thoroughly Westernized, too Westernized to be thoroughly Asian. In this age of modern media, as cultural divides seem to be lessening this kind of cultural osmosis may no longer seem particularly unusual (Asian gangster films drew heavily from vintage American gangster films, and now filmmakers like Quentin Tarantino have in turn begun to draw influence from Asian gangster films). The truth, however, is that Philippine cinema, like Philippine culture itself, has always exhibited this type of mimicry. No nation seems to have as genuine an affection for American popular culture as the Philippines, which somewhat paradoxically may account for much of the nation's more recent disenchantment with the U.S.

When I first started on this project, I sought to rent some Filipino movies from a small Filipino grocer in Ocala, Florida. The proprietor of the store looked at me a bit quizzically and asked, "Why do you like Filipino movies?" I wasn't exactly sure how to respond. "I don't know," I said. "Why do *you* like them?"

Throughout the years there has been a growing resentment among Filipinos, a sense of having been somehow slighted by the West, America in particular. Well, we all know through life experience how painful unreciprocated affections can be. In the Philippines there is the unmistakable impression of having been somehow neglected—perhaps even discarded—by the West; it sometimes expresses itself with a very discernible indignation.

But mostly I have found Filipinos to be kind and helpful, sometimes flattered by my interest, sometimes perhaps a bit bewildered. I have discovered some fascinating stories while poring over crumbling newspapers and frayed old movie magazines. Most are stories completely unknown in the West, and many probably forgotten even in the Philippines. I must take a moment to thank my friend Dr. Anacleto Paras, Jr., Ph.D., for his help in translating many old Tagalog articles. It saved me an enormous amount of time, as translating them myself was both time-consuming and somewhat dicey (Tagalog can be a *very* foreign language).

I would also like to thank Joy and Michael Marshall at Premier Copy Center in Ocala, Florida, for their help in putting the manuscript all together; my father David Yeatter for his help in facilitating the last few months of my work; Sergio Galloza for some needed computer assistance; and John Keyloun for a little research assistance.

But mostly I am grateful and deeply indebted to my brother Alan Yeatter, without whose research assistance this would be a considerably lesser work. He helped me immeasurably in finding research materials, including old film periodicals from the Philippines.

This is really more than the story of a film industry. It's the story of a people and a nation, longing to break free of paternal entities, yet somehow clinging to them, and how a popular art form came to be something much more than a means of expression or mere idle amusement; how those who entertain the people and those who govern the nation eventually became inseparable—one and the same—and how the cult of celebrity reached such proportions that fantasy and reality blended and became increasingly indistinguishable.

My hope is that this book will fill a void in the West as regards documentation of one of the most active and colorful film industries in the world, and that, given the current state of decline of the Filipino film industry, the book might in some small way contribute to stirring some interest in the work of Filipino filmmakers, whose efforts seem to be too frequently overlooked and underappreciated.

Introduction

In 1989 a memorial award was set up in honor of the late Filipino actor Vic Silayan. The award was to be given annually to a member of the Filipino acting community who had achieved recognition in at least two of four categories (film, television, stage and radio). Recipients would be required to have had a career spanning at least twenty years, and to have also received notice for public service or charity works of some sort.

Silayan was a very well respected actor in the Philippines, yet very few outside of his own country have ever heard of him. Those who have probably know him from U.S. co-productions, drive-in and exploitation fare like *Blood Thirst* (1965), *Night of the Cobra Woman* and *Daughters of Satan* (both 1972), and *Too Hot to Handle* (1976). As Silayan once explained, "There are many times in the life of an actor when he cannot make a choice—you are dependent on what the producers want you to do."*

The first Vic Silayan Memorial Award was given at the 1989 Star Awards in the fabled Manila Film Center. The recipient was another fine actor—Ruben Rustia. In his acceptance speech, Rustia recounted a remark made to him by an Australian producer after the making of the film *A Dangerous Life* in 1988. The producer told Rustia, "I have been receiving so [much] favorable feedback from the executives of Home Box Office of America, and [producers in] England. They were all surprised! This is the first time that they have known that the Filipinos have a high degree of acting!"

Both Silayan and Rustia were superb actors, very serious in their craft, yet their best work has remained, by and large, within the confines of their own domestic market. Both appeared in their fair share of international co-productions, but their work in international films, like that of so many of their fellow Filipino thespians, was usually limited to fairly insubstantial supporting roles. Unlike many nations throughout the world with active film industries, the Philippines has not received a great deal of notice from the rest of the world for its film work. Cineastes may know a good deal about the films of France, Italy, Germany, Britain, Spain, Mexico, Japan, China, or even countries normally more isolated from the West, such as Russia or Czechoslovakia; the Philippines, however, has remained something of a blank screen to international film fans. Look through any home video or DVD reference source and you will find very few Filipino films among the listings, even while other countries throughout the world seem fairly well represented. This is most unfortunate, for film fans have been missing out on some very interesting work.

Despite its relatively small size, the Philippines has always had a very robust film indus-

---

*Taken from a videotape interview segment played at the 1989 Star Awards as part of a tribute to Silayan.

try, which had for many years (until very recently) been one of the most active in the world. It would likely come as quite a surprise to most people to learn that Philippine film production dates back to the silent era in the earliest part of the 20th century. Of course, the American presence had much to do with that, and Americans were very involved in getting the Filipino film industry up and running. Nevertheless, Filipinos needed no encouragement to run with it.

Filipinos are storytellers: always have been, and maybe it's this love of storytelling that has made the film medium so immensely popular in the islands. It also might account for the rather longwinded nature of so much of Philippine cinema. It sometimes seems that Filipinos hate to see a story end. But, whatever the reason, Filipinos love movies. The *Guinness Book of World Records* once listed the Philippines as the nation with the world's most avid filmgoing public, averaging a very impressive nineteen trips to the cinema per year, per person! Think about that. Imagine if everyone in the United States went to the movies as often. Even a comparable average in the U.S. would have the moneymen in Hollywood drooling. That impressive average illustrates just how much the Philippine public has always enjoyed films, and there was a time when their own industry held its own on the islands, even standing toe to toe with Hollywood. Manila's film industry created its own superstars and produced its own blockbusters. Sadly, this doesn't seem to be the case anymore, as the Philippine film industry is limping toward the cemetery, victimized by a number of factors, including its inability to compete with the elaborate Hollywood blockbusters of the modern era, the growth of the cable and satellite industries (Filipinos may love movies, but now they can stay home and enjoy them much cheaper), the inability to eradicate film piracy (DVDs of new movies can be purchased easily for about $2 before the films even hit the theaters), and even the shortsighted and inept actions of its own government with its absurd tax policies.

Only time will tell if the Filipino film industry can find a way to survive it all, but whether it reawakens and once more thrives, limps along indefinitely like a wounded dog, or dies tomorrow, the fact remains that the film industry in the Philippines has a very rich and colorful history worth recounting. My hope is that this book will give the reader a glimpse into a cinematic landscape too long ignored and deserving of its due.

1

1897–1930

A Filipino wag is said to have once summed up Philippine history with the remark "Three centuries in a convent, fifty years in Hollywood."[1] The three centuries of Spanish rule brought the Catholicism that would come to dominate the outlook and mindset of the culture. The fifty years in Hollywood is perhaps no less significant. Representing America's brief imperialist experiment, the mention of Hollywood is not insignificant, for it points to the allure of American popular culture. The supplanting of Hollywood for the United States may be no more than a humorist's contrivance, but one can't help feeling that it suggests an inclination to identify America in terms of popular culture rather than ideological beliefs. Similarly, the identification of Spain with a convent is suggestive of repression of sorts.

The Filipinos' embracing of American popular culture seems, on its surface anyway, to be more enthusiastic than the nation's embrace of the ideal of democratic rule. Corruption and self-interest may be a concern in any political system, but in the Philippines, where the people were never weaned of their tribal mindset, the less fortunate characteristics embedded within the political landscape—greed, corruption, the lust for power, and, yes, even nepotism—can effortlessly bound into the realm of caricature. The Spanish had neglected to truly unify the people, feeling that their only genuine duty to the natives was converting them to Christianity. The Americans sought to introduce Filipinos to the concept of Western democracy, believing falsely that this in and of itself would be sufficient to transform the culture. In the Filipinos' earnest desire to emulate the United States, the popular culture of the U.S. seems to take a backseat to nothing, including the concept of democracy itself. In fact, one might well argue that Filipino mimicry of U.S. popular culture has been more successful, for the most part, than their fashioning of a constitutional republic modeled after that of the United States. Democracy in the Philippines has a checkered past that reveals the tribalism that was never eradicated from the national consciousness, although it needs to be said that the two People Power revolutions show that, ultimately, democracy in the Philippines is stronger than many know.

But the United States' longstanding position of influence over Philippine society notwithstanding, as well as the easy identification of the U.S. by way of Hollywood, it was not Americans who first introduced motion pictures to the archipelago. The projected image first appeared in the islands in the twilight of the Spanish colonial era. In fact, electricity had scarcely been introduced in the country when a Spaniard named Pertierra used a salon on Manila's trendy Escolta Street to hold a chronographic showing. Salon de Pertierra had opened in 1896 as a phonograph parlor. Outfitted with a 60 mm Gaumont chronophotograph projector and four titles imported from France, Pertierra held his showing on New Year's Day of

1897. Advertised as "*Espetaculo Cientifico de Pertierra*" (*Pertierra's Scientific Spectacle*), the lineup consisted of *Un Homme au Chapeau* (*Man with a Hat*), *Une Scene de Dansa Japonaise* (*Scene from a Japanese Dance*), *Les Boxers* (*The Boxers*), and *La Place de L'Opera* (*The Place L'Opera*).² The films were necessarily brief; little more than a curiosity, and certainly not anything capable of displacing the popular live entertainment of the day, the *vod-a-vil* shows (a Filipino spelling of vaudeville) and, most especially, the *sarswelas* (from the Spanish *zarzuela*). But from such humble beginnings....

In August of the same year, two Swiss businessmen named Leibman and Peritz offered financial backing to Antonio Ramos, a Spanish soldier with the *Batallon de Cazadores*, who had procured a Lumiere cinematograph. He was also able to import thirty titles for viewing. Some titles known to have been among them are *The Czar's Carriage Passing Place de la Concorde*, *An Arabian Cortege*, *Snow Games*, *Card Players* and *A Train's Arrival*.³ Once again, Escolta Street was the place where this new amusement could be seen. Leibman and Peritz had a private showing for a small number of invited guests at Number 31 Escolta on August 28, 1897, and on August 29 the viewing hall was opened to the general public.⁴ But even with thirty titles, there wasn't enough to build a business on. The films were run every hour in groups of ten from 6–10 P.M., and it wasn't long before audiences dwindled. After three months, business had fallen off to the extent that Leibman and Peritz closed the Escolta hall and moved to a warehouse in Plaza Goiti. Shorn of the Escolta address, the price of admission was lowered accordingly, but in just a few weeks the *warehouse-cum-movie hall* was also closed.⁵

Leibman and Peritz may have been shortsighted regarding the possibilities of this fledgling technology, but Ramos was determined to take it further, and he knew that attracting repeat customers was as valuable as attracting new customers; therefore new films were needed.

Escolta Street in the earliest part of the 20th century. It was Manila's business district and the place where film exhibition in the Philippines first began.

But rather than buying more films from overseas, Ramos used his Lumiere as a camera and shot a series of films locally, all of them documenting life in and around Manila, and not a one of them as long as a minute. The titles included *Escenas Callejeras* (Street Scenes), *Panorama de Manila* (Manila Landscape), *Fiesta de Quiapo* (Quiapo Fiesta) and *Puwente de Espana* (Bridge of Spain).[6] They may have been short and simple, but they were historic: the year was 1898, and suddenly a Spanish military officer from Alhama de Aragon became the first person to shoot motion pictures in the Philippines.

Something else historic was happening in the islands in 1898. On April 11, the U.S. Congress passed a resolution that gave President William McKinley the power to use U.S. military might to end Spanish rule in Cuba. As the Spanish-American War commenced, Assistant Secretary of the Navy Theodore Roosevelt ordered Commodore George Dewey to the Philippines. Arriving in Manila Bay on May 1, Dewey's fleet made short work of the Spanish armada. Eleven of Spain's twelve ships were sunk, the only one left being damaged beyond hope, and some 200 Spanish soldiers were dead. Conversely, the U.S. fleet suffered no damage at all and only one casualty—a soldier who succumbed to the heat.[7] It was the first time that U.S. troops had been deployed overseas, and it marked the beginning of the role of the U.S. as a global power.

In 1898, the other side of the globe was much farther away, and infinitely foreign. The idea of sending back a film document of this new world that the U.S. was inheriting seemed only natural, and so when Dewey came to the Philippines he arrived with a cameraman in tow. The footage is rumored to still exist in the U.S. Library of Congress.[8]

With the U.S. presence came more documentary filmmakers. In 1899 Burton Holmes shot *Battle of Baliwag*. Holmes traveled the world shooting documentary footage and is credited with coining the term "travelogue" in 1904. He produced weekly travelogues for Paramount that ran in the studio's theaters between 1908 and 1922. In 1913 he was back in the Philippines shooting footage in Baguio and some of the southern regions.

At the turn of the century there were others: Raymond Ackerman of American Biography and Mutoscope shot *Filipino Cockfight* and *Battle of Mount Arayat*, and Kimwood Peters filmed *Banawe Rice Terraces*.[9] In the early 1900s Herbert Wyndom visited the Philippines for Edison Biograph and filmed the Manila Fire Department at work in Tanduay.[10] Beyond simple documentaries, the film business was about to change. Film exhibition was attracting businessmen and was catching on with entrepreneurs, if not quite yet with the public.

With the turn of the century came the opening of movie houses; in 1900 Cine Walgrah opened at Number 60 Calle Santa Rosa in Intramuros; in 1902 Spaniard Samuel Rebarber opened the Gran Cinematografo Parisien at Number 80 Calle Crespo in Quiapo,[11] and in 1903 the first movie house to be owned by a Filipino was established when Jose Jimenez opened the Cinematograpo Rizal on Azcarraga Street.[12] Even so, business was not especially brisk at these early movie houses, and, for the most part, movies at that time were little more than a side attraction or time-filler used in-between vaudeville acts.

But the business progressed rapidly and in 1909 there came a flood of movie theaters: The Zorrilla Theater, a venue that staged opera and *sarswela* productions, made the transition to film exhibition. The Zorrilla is where, in 1905, the first opera was performed in the Philippines, that being Pedro Paterno's *Magdapio*. There was also the Cine Anda, Empire, Apollo, Ideal, Luz, Majestic, Gaity, Comedis—genuine movie theaters, unlike their predecessors.[13] The venues were changing as were the movies themselves. The burgeoning number of movie houses was a direct result of the plentiful supply of films. Filmmakers seemed eager to provide a photographic record of anything and everything—festivals, parades and carnivals, religious processions, races, small-town life, airplane flyovers, city construction projects, and of course, the standard street scenes.

Also in 1909 film in the Philippines took a turn for the dramatic ... maybe. Filipino television writer Arsenio Bautista has written that Carl Laemmle's Independent Moving Picture Company, the seedling out of which grew Universal Pictures, may have shot the eight-minute film *Rose of the Philippines* on location in Manila in 1909. The film was released theatrically in the U.S. in January of 1910, but would not be screened in the Philippines until a year later. When it was, the *Manila Times*, an American newspaper that began publishing in 1900, touted the film as being "among the first films produced locally," and promoted it as "a dramatic story from the days of the empire."[14] Whether the film was truly shot on location in the Philippines is viewed with a high degree of skepticism by many film historians, however. After all, feigned locations were ever a part of motion pictures. For instance, one film document shot by Americans circa 1898 purported to show U.S. soldiers engaged in combat with Filipino rebels. It turned out to be a staged scene shot in the U.S. with African Americans portraying the Filipinos.[15]

In 1910, the Grand Opera House in Sta. Cruz, Manila began to show films in between *vod-a-vil* acts. While there had always been audio accompaniment during the showing of films in the Philippines, it usually came in the form of a gramophone or a live pianist. The Manila Grand Opera House took the rather extraordinary step of employing a 200-man choir to accompany film showings.[16] But, as early as 1910, experimentation with sound and film was taking place via the chronophone. It would be close to twenty years, however, before true talking pictures would reach the Philippines.

By 1912, Manila was replete with movie venues and, as a result, foreign distributors seized the opportunity to fill the heavy demand for new product. Being that the country was a U.S. colony, there was no shortage of distribution companies based out of New York and California. Simple street scenes and festival footage was getting to be passé, and there was a need for dramatic presentations, so U.S. and European films were popular beyond their expected appeal as glimpses of a far-off land that most would never see. It was only a matter of time before somebody would film a dramatic feature in the Philippines; a group of Americans resolved to do just that, and chose as their subject the nation's greatest hero, Jose Rizal.

Dr. Jose Rizal (1861–1896), considered the greatest of national heroes in the Philippines. His life and his literary works have been source material for Filipino films since the very beginning of Philippine cinema.

Executed by the Spanish in 1896, Rizal was a man who wore many hats: There is no more revered figure in the nation's history. His father was a Chinese *mestizo* (a Filipino of Chinese descent) who leased land that he farmed through sharecroppers, and the family became prosperous and prominent—suspiciously so to authorities, who viewed any well-to-do Filipinos with caution. Still, Spanish officials were frequent guests in the Rizal home. In 1882 Rizal traveled to Spain to attend the University of Madrid, where he studied medicine. He was 21 years old, and life in Madrid proved to be a real eye-opener for the young Rizal. Intellectual and political debate abounded everywhere, it seemed, and Rizal was struck by the openness of it all—something strongly discouraged in his homeland. Rizal wondered how it was that as a foreigner in Madrid he was afforded rights that were denied him in his own land. He joined with other young wealthy Filipinos in Madrid in forming a group that lobbied politicians in Spain for reforms back home. Living on money from their families in the Philippines, they enjoyed the high-life in Madrid and Barcelona, but there was no hypocrisy in their earnest goals to affect change in the Philippines. Toward that end they published their own newspaper and magazine to trumpet their cause.

Rizal would eventually travel to Paris and Heidelberg to further his medical education, and while there he would set about writing his first novel, *Noli Me Tangere* (*Touch Me Not*), which was published in Berlin. The story's protagonist is widely believed to have been a romanticized version of Rizal himself, a young man who returns home from Europe only to face the harsh realities of life under colonial rule and incur the wrath of a Spanish friar. With its unflattering (to say the least) portrayal of the friars and its obvious admonition that revolution was inevitable unless reforms were initiated in the colonial system, it should come as no surprise that the book was banned by authorities in the Philippines, and Rizal himself branded a heretic by the Catholic Church. But the book was smuggled into the country and Filipinos eagerly snatched up black market copies. Rizal became something more than a celebrity: he became a figurehead for the growing nationalist movement. The irony is that Rizal never advocated secession from Spain, but merely reforms that would bring more equality to Filipinos. Buoyed by his instant celebrity, Rizal followed up with a second novel, *El Filibusterismo* (*The Subversive*), which all the more harshly indicted the friars.

Upon his return to Manila, Rizal founded the *Liga Filipina*, a society dedicated to bringing about change. The society was promptly outlawed and Rizal banished to Dapitan in the southern Philippines. Though beautifully picturesque, it was primitive and far away from the hub of the heart of the country. In 1896, fervent nationalist Andres Bonifacio tried to convince Rizal to participate in an attempt at revolution. Although Rizal declined, when the uprising was put down the Spanish authorities seized the opportunity to lay the blame on Rizal, put him on trial and be done with him once and for all. Rizal was arrested aboard a ship bound for Cuba, where he was headed after volunteering to help fight an epidemic of yellow fever. After being extradited to Manila, Rizal was put on trial, if one can call it that. The Spanish Inquisition serves as a good reminder of the ability of the Spanish to extract, not so much information, but rather desired results. Fifteen witnesses were tortured into testifying that Rizal was the mastermind of the uprising, and the authorities labeled him the "living soul of the insurrection." Although he publicly denounced the uprising, it did no good. Rizal was condemned and was executed by firing squad on December 30, 1896. His place was forever sealed as the nation's greatest martyr, and he would become an almost Christ-like figure in Philippine history.[17]

In 1912, a trio of Americans set out to film the first feature-length motion picture in the Philippines. *La Vida de Jose Rizal* (*The Life of Jose Rizal*), produced by Harry Brown, was written by Dr. Edward Meyer Gross, who adapted the screenplay from his own stage play of the life of the martyred Filipino. Brown and Gross had started their own production company, the Rizalina Film Company. Reportedly 5,000 feet in length, the film told its story in 22 scenes, and was filmed by cinematographer Charles Martin.[18] Martin was the principal photographer for the Philippine Bureau of Science, and when the Bureau decided to purchase motion picture equipment from Pathé in 1909, they sent Martin to France for a year of train-

The majestic Mayon Volcano in Albay on the island of Luzon. Its eruption in 1911 was filmed by American filmmaker and Manila theater owner Albert Yearsley.

ing in how to use the equipment. Martin returned to the Philippines and set about documenting as much of the nation's customs as he could on film. In 1911 he shot what would be some of the most interesting and valuable footage to come out of the Philippines when he happened to be on the scene in Batangas when the Taal Volcano erupted. The footage was viewed around the world.[19]

When word got around that a film about the life of Rizal was in the works, it piqued the interest of one individual in particular. Albert Yearsley was an American theater owner and filmmaker in Manila. His films were, up to 1912, of the documentary variety, and were shot to keep his theater, the Empire, supplied with enough new product to keep the public coming in. The wide variety of subject matter, some of it of great historic significance, would be fascinating to see had any of it managed to survive the years. In 1909 Yearsley filmed *Rizal Day Celebration* and in 1910 *Manila Carnival*. His 1911 titles included *Eruption of Mayon Volcano* and *Airplane Flight Over Manila*, which captured the historic first over flight of the city, accomplished by American pilot Bud Mars. Yearsley also managed to film footage of the fires in Tondo, Pandacan and Paco in 1911. In 1912 he shot footage of the aftermath of the Typhoon in Cebu, and *Departure of the Igorots to Barcelona*.[20]

After hearing that a feature film about Rizal's life was in the works and nearing completion, Yearsley's competitive nature came to the fore, and he determined to beat Brown and company to the punch. In 1909, Yearsley had bought the Orpheum Theater, an old *vod-a-vil* palace, and converted it into a movie theater. He renamed it the Empire and hoped to have a glorious grand opening for what he dreamed would be the most spectacular cinema in the country. But just one day before the Empire was scheduled to open, another movie theater, the Cine Anda, was opened by Eddie Teague and Frank H. Goulette, two Americans working in Manila as policemen who somewhat stole Yearsley's glory.[21]

Yearsley apparently made up his mind not to be bested again, and although he did not have sufficient time to attempt a feature, he did have time to shoot a short film entitled *El*

Fusilamiento de Dr. Jose Rizal (*The Shooting of Dr. Jose Rizal*), which was filmed in one day. Consisting of only one scene, the film, true to its title, depicted Rizal's execution and reportedly ran for approximately 500 feet.[22] Just as Teague and Goulette had beaten Yearsley by only a day, Yearsley managed to rush his Rizal film out and screen it at the Empire the day before Brown's production had its debut in August of 1912. Both films were said to be successful.[23]

Successful, perhaps, but not popular with everybody: It would seem that some Chinese *mestizos* took exception to the black eye given to the Spanish in both films. Considering the fact that it was the Spanish who banned Rizal's books, banished him to Dapitan, put him on trial for an uprising that he had both refused to endorse, and publicly repudiated, and finally executed him, one could reasonably ask how anyone could hope to buttress Spain's reputation while engaged in telling Rizal's story. The Chinese *mestizo* loyalty to the Spanish is not easy to understand. On the one hand, after taking control of the Philippines, the Spanish came to rely heavily on the Chinese immigrants to the islands. The Chinese were highly skilled laborers who constructed the churches, cathedrals and various public buildings that the Spaniards required. As the Chinese were integrated into Philippine society and began intermarrying, they remained close to the Spanish as *mestizos*, garnering both economic and political power. Lighter skinned Filipinos were traditionally more favored by the Spanish, which meant that both Spanish and Chinese *mestizos* were better off than the darker tribes of Malay descent.

On the other hand, the Spanish had a desire to keep *all* of their colonial subjects in their place. They sought to keep the Chinese from feeling too empowered by forcing them to live in ghettos, over-taxing them, and with periodic threats of deportation. Under the circumstances, one could hardly fault the Chinese for the occasional uprising, but when such incidents occurred, the Spanish exercised their authority in no uncertain terms—some thirty thousand Chinese were massacred in the 17th century.

Still, the Chinese *mestizo* population grew in size and prosperity through the Spanish policy of allowing Chinese men to move out of the slums and into rural areas to farm, provided they marry a Filipino woman. As this caught on, the *mestizo* population blossomed and the Chinese became more of an economic force in the country.[24] This may account for the Chinese *mestizo* loyalty to the Spanish, but, whatever the reason, there was a group of *mestizos* in 1912 who sought to improve the image of the Spaniards with their own film. The group was headed by Carlos Palanca, who, despite his Hispanic-sounding name, was said to be of pure Chinese lineage. The other producers—Francis Lauchengco, Ramon Teongson, Fernando Teotico—were Chinese *mestizos*.[25] The film, *La Conquista de Filipinas* (*The Conquest of the Philippines*), was apparently a romanticized version of Miguel Lopez de Legazpi's colonization of the Philippines. Although Ferdinand Magellan had claimed the islands for Spain some forty years prior, it was not until 1564 that the Spanish sought to make the islands something more than an outpost for their empire in the region. The islands were named in honor of King Philip II of Spain when he was still crown prince, and it was Philip's obsession with the growing influence of the Portuguese in the orient that prompted his decision to send Legazpi to the Philippines to fortify Spain's claim. Arriving in Cebu in February of 1565, Legazpi found the local chief, Tupas, recalcitrant, and had to resort to force.

It is not known how much of this the filmmakers bothered to portray in their telling, but it seems likely that Legazpi's pious character would have been considered useful as evidence of the misrepresentation of Spain's conduct in the Philippines. When Tupas, likely intimidated by the display of Spanish force, sought to make nice by offering a niece to Legazpi for his own pleasure, Legazpi unwittingly offended the chief by having the girl baptized and marrying her to one of his crewmen, thereby exacerbating his own precarious situation. Somehow, amid hostile natives, constant threats of mutiny, and Portuguese ships menacingly close by, Legazpi managed to prevail. In time, Philip would send help, and Spanish settlers would travel from Mexico, another Spanish colony, to populate the empire's newest possession.[26]

Legazpi's importance to the confluent history of Spain and the Philippines cannot be overestimated. Aside from solidifying Spain's hold on the islands, it was Legazpi who would eventually mark Manila for the nation's capitol city. All of which makes him a good candidate for canonization in a pro-Spanish film. There is also the possibility that the filmmakers may have been Christians, which in itself would go a long way toward explaining the desire to defend the Spanish; after all, they did bring Catholicism to the archipelago, making it the only predominantly Christian nation in Asia, which it remains to this day.

If the Chinese *mestizos* behind *La Conquista de Filipinas* viewed the Rizal films as being an attempt by Americans—still the new kids on the block—to malign the image of the Spanish, they were doubtless further perturbed by the next film venture by Brown, Gross and Martin. The Spanish could not have come out looking too good when the trio set out to tell the story of Jose Burgos, Mariano Gomez and Jacinto Zamora, three dissident priests executed in February of 1872 for complicity in an uprising. Like the charges that Rizal himself would face little more than a decade later, the accusations were largely absurd, alleging that the priests, in complicity with the United States, had sought to bring autonomy to the Philippines.

Burgos was a Spanish *criollo* (a Spaniard born in one of the empire's colonial territories) born in Luzon, who had in fact been outspoken to an extent about the prejudicial system designed to keep Filipinos out of the clergy. These views had him branded early as a troublemaker. Again like Rizal, Burgos did not advocate Philippine independence from Spain, but rather more equity for Filipinos. Little matter to General Rafael de Izquierdo, the appointed governor of Manila: to Izquierdo it was all the same, and any talk of equality was part of a larger syndrome with the ultimate goal being secession. But it was Izquierdo's heavy-handed governance that brought on the rebellion, which came from within his own ranks. Feeling that *criollos* would necessarily be of divided loyalty, Izquierdo revoked their privileges in the army. It was a *criollo* sergeant in Izquierdo's own army who instigated the uprising and then lost his life when the revolt was quickly put down. Although it was really only a minor uprising, the Spanish authorities felt the need to make a show trial of it for referencing by future would-be revolutionaries. Burgos was high on the list of undesirables who the colonial bureaucracy could do without, and with the Church's influence and dislike of reformers within the clergy, Gomez and Zamora were added to the list of defendants. Gomez had indeed been in favor of reforms, but Zamora seems to have been guilty of little more than being too Filipino in his ways, despite his Spanish lineage.

The trial was a classic farce of bribed witnesses and concocted evidence, which eventually led to the barbaric execution of the three priests, as they were slowly choked by garrote until their necks snapped. But such bestial injustice, witnessed by an estimated 40,000 spectators in what is today Manila's Luneta (the same place where Rizal would one day be killed), would only backfire on the Spanish, as it would feed the growing nationalist mindset.[27]

It appears that the Chinese *mestizos* who had sought to defend Spain's honor with the production of *La Conquista de Filipinas* did not likewise produce an answer to Brown, Gross and Martin's film version of the ill-fated priests, but *somebody* didn't like it. The film's execution sequence was ordered removed by censors, who saw the potential for fomentation of unrest,[28] as the islands were still under colonial rule, albeit by Americans. In the earliest years of film exhibition in the Philippines, the duty of film review and, if necessary, censorship, fell on local civil and sometimes military authorities. It was rather an informal arrangement, however, with the censors principally concerned with the printed word and the dissemination of political ideas. General Arthur MacArthur, for instance, acted as chief censor from 1899–1900, when he held the position of military governor of the islands.[29] Of course, during the time that MacArthur held the position, it would have been largely meaningless from the perspective of the film business, still so much in its infancy. But by 1912 motion pictures had matured enough to be artistically and even ideologically expressive rather than simple documentaries, and so the government felt compelled to establish a board of censorship.[30]

Spain's defenders may not have been moved (or able, as the case may be) to produce a response to Brown's production about the martyrdom of the three priests, but there is evidence to suggest that Brown, Gross and Martin responded to the rose-colored portrayal of Legazpi's arrival. Brown produced *La Conquista de Filipinas de Legazpi* (*The Conquest of the Philippines by Legazpi*) in 1913, once more with Gross writing and Martin serving as cinematographer. Unfortunately, Filipino films of the era no longer exist, and what little information about them that there is makes it very difficult to know the intent of the films or filmmakers, but the extreme similarity between the title of Brown's film and the *mestizos'* production of the previous year does seem to suggest that it may have been intended as something of a historical rebuttal, if not a retaliation. It apparently did not skimp on portraying Spanish brutality, as the film was threatened with censorship due to its violence.[31]

Some may feel that historical reckoning was not a consideration for Americans producing films in the Philippines. Filipino critic and television host Mario A. Hernando has suggested that, since the films produced by Americans were made by businessmen, their motives were not especially to advocate the nationalist cause, but merely to cash in on nationalist sentiments that had been growing. That might sound cynical, but it makes perfect sense. American businessmen in the Philippines would have been well aware of the growing sense of nationalism among Filipinos, especially since it was the Americans who, quite contrary to the Spanish, encouraged such feelings among the people. Although initially Filipino nationalism had been just as strongly discouraged under U.S. colonial rule as it had been under the Spanish, by the time that Brown and Gross were producing their nationalist epics, Francis Burton Harrison was taking his position as governor of Manila, having been appointed by President Woodrow Wilson in 1913. Upon arriving and taking up his appointment, Harrison got started by dismissing Americans serving in the colonial bureaucracy and replacing them with Filipinos.[32]

Clearly, the atmosphere under U.S. rule would have been conducive to a growing sense of nationalism, and it would have been only natural for any entrepreneur to seek to capitalize on it, but Hernando's assessment may not be fair to at least one member of Manila's early filmmaking community: in his keynote address at the Silliman University Symposium on Film and Literature in November of 2002, Bienvenido Lumbera brought up the fact that Edward Meyer Gross was married to Filipino *sarswela* star Titay Molina.[33] Since this was the case, Gross no doubt had a genuine affection of sorts for the country through his wife. Then again, Lumbera mentioned it by way of suggesting that Gross had written the film adaptation of Rizal's *Noli Me Tangere* in order to provide a starring vehicle for his wife.

It would only make sense that if Brown and Gross really wanted to portray the problems and harsh treatment endured by Filipinos during the Spanish colonial era, then they should turn to the era's most articulate martyr, Rizal himself. In 1915 they offered the first film adaptation of Rizal's first novel, *Noli Me Tangere*, and they followed with an adaptation of Rizal's *El Filibusterismo* in 1916. These were big-budget pictures (over 25,000 pesos was spent on each),[34] and with the subsequent tendency in Philippine cinema toward longwinded epics, it is significant to note that each film had a running time that exceeded two hours. Cinema in the Philippines had come of age.

There seem to have been no problems for Brown and Gross with the censors on their two Rizal adaptations. As for Albert Yearsley, well, he seems to have avoided problems with the censors by simply shelving his films when trouble loomed. He had withdrawn his screen adaptation of the *sarswela Walang Sugat* (*Unscathed*), although it isn't clear what the problem might have been. Whatever it was, it may have made Yearsley gun-shy when in 1914 he filmed the story of Eusebio Borja, an infamous bandit and murderer. The local press was harsh in their condemnation of the decision to portray the notorious criminal in this popular new art form, and Yearsley subsequently cancelled exhibition of the film.[35]

Although cinema was gaining in popularity in the first two decades of the 20th century, some of the foreigners who had been involved in the business began divesting their interests in the islands and seeking greener pastures elsewhere. Perhaps they felt that the Philippines had served as a good training ground and they were now ready to try their luck in more lucrative markets. Whatever their reasons, Brown, Gross, Martin—they all seem to have exited the scene. As for Yearsley, he went bankrupt when a fire gutted his theater.[36] The market was now opened for more enterprising Filipinos to move in and fill the void. Thus, in 1917, the first Filipino film studio was born. Using equipment purchased from Brown and Gross,[37] Malayan Motion Pictures was begun by two brothers, Jose and Jesus Nepomuceno. Although they began, predictably enough, by shooting documentary footage of various types (carnivals, for instance), some of it used as newsreel footage in the U.S., by 1919 they were ready to attempt their first feature. They chose the *sarswela Dalagang Bukid* (*Country Girl*) by Hermogenes Ilagan and Leon Ignacio. A musical comedy may strike one as an odd choice for a silent film, but odder still is the fact that Jose Nepomuceno even chose to film the musical numbers. When it came time to show the film, the performers were on hand to sing along to the image being projected on the screen.[38]

Jose Nepomuceno is regarded by most as the first true Filipino filmmaker. He has even been dubbed the "Father of Philippine Movies." Nepomuceno was a photographer, and that being the case, he would have had a natural interest in pursuing the new photographic medium of motion pictures. He was owner of a successful Manila photo studio called *Electro-Fotografia-Parhelio*, which he sold in order to raise capital for his career as a filmmaker.[39] Nepomuceno's production company was the standard bearer for the local film industry during the silent era as it struggled for an audience in the midst of competition from foreign imports, principally Hollywood productions. Money may have been no obstacle for Hollywood, but it was ever a concern for Filipino filmmakers, who struggled with under-capitalization and the technical problems that it brought (increasingly outdated equipment and the like). Circumstances being what they were, Nepomuceno found himself manufacturing the transformers for his arc lamps out of scrap iron. All of which made it difficult for filmmakers in the Philippines to compete with the allure of lavish productions from overseas. They did have one advantage with local audiences, however: Filipino filmmakers knew how better to relate to their audience. Hollywood films may have been popular as spectacles, but outside of Manila there was a large segment of the population that was, to a large extent, not familiar with Western ways, and therefore incapable of truly grasping much of the content. Filipino filmmakers could carve out a niche for themselves by concentrating on more indigenous themes. With that in mind, Nepomuceno sought to make his own version of Rizal's *Noli Me Tangere* in 1930. While regrettably no prints of the film are known to exist today, it is still regarded as one of the most significant Filipino films of the silent era.

Although Manila was obviously taking center stage as the nation's filmmaking capital, the central and southern Philippines were not oblivious to the new medium. Not far behind the mainland, the first cinema in Cebu had opened in 1902 when a man named Pedro Alario had converted a warehouse on Magallanes Street into a moviehouse, naming it *Cinematografo Electro-Optico Luminoso Walgrah*. By 1910, *Teatro Junquera*, Cebu's oldest playhouse, which had been established in 1895, began the conversion from playhouse to moviehouse, and in 1911 *Cine Ideal* was constructed, a venue specifically built for film exhibition. By 1922 filmgoing had become popular enough in Cebu that *Cine Auditorium* was built, an impressive venue that could capacitate 10,000 patrons.

With such patronage it was inevitable that somebody would begin to produce films locally, and in 1922 a group of Cebuano businessmen got together to finance the first Cebuano film, *El Hijo Disobediente* (*The Disobedient Son*). The primary producer was a local doctor named Max Borromeo, and the film was directed by Florentino Borromeo, presumably a relative, perhaps a brother. Florentino Borromeo was a Cebuano playwright born in Cebu City on May 24, 1881, who wrote in both Cebuano and Spanish. His works became important to the local community, being used in local fiestas. He was also very busy in local civics, serving at various times as the Chief Clerk of the provincial governor, Chief Fiscal Clerk, Provincial Warden of Cebu, and Municipal Secretary of Catmon, Cebu.

The personnel involved in *El Hijo Disobediente* were all artists from the local stage, and so it isn't hard to imagine that the film was the brainchild of those working in the theater and that Florentino approached Max with the idea of helping finance the project, as Max Borromeo was prominent in the community and well off. The film was written by local playwright Celestino Rodriguez, and the entire cast was made up of Cebuanos: Buenaventura Rodriguez (also a well known local playwright), Eulalia Hernandez, Jose Rosales—performers from local theater. The cinematographer was a man named Prudencio Irairte, who apparently had little knowledge or background in cinematography as the film is remembered as much for its poor technical execution as it is for being the first Cebuano feature. Some scenes, for instance, ran backwards, both confusing and amusing to patrons. But all of its gaffes and flaws notwithstanding, the Visayan film industry had begun.

The Filipino film industry may have been exceedingly indigenous, but much more so for the nascent Visayan industry, which was inherently regional. Their films tended to play only in the Visayas, and sometimes Mindanao in the extreme south of the nation, and consequently were far more restricted in every way—production capital, venues, financial returns, production capital: it was a vicious cycle. Under such circumstances, the Visayan industry was destined to stay small, and therefore could not truly compete with the Manila-based industry. Even so, from its inception in 1922, the Visayan industry was able to grow through the years, and even to thrive for a brief period after World War II.

If Nepomuceno had a rival for supremacy in the early years of the Filipino film industry it was Vicente Salumbides. But there was no real rivalry between the men—they were friends, and actually worked together from time to time. After spending time studying acting and filmmaking in America, Salumbides served with American forces in France during World War I. His film studies in the U.S. served him well, as he introduced sophisticated filmmaking technique into Filipino films: prior to his 1926 film *Miracles of Love*, Filipino filmmakers had not employed close-ups, and his use of quick-cuts in film editing was also revolutionary to the local industry. In 1927 Salumbides married Rosario Panganiban, a beauty queen from Pampanga who was chosen Miss Centro Escolar University in 1924, Miss Philippines Free Press in 1925 and Miss Pampanga in 1926. She reportedly won the Miss Philippines Free Press title by having her picture chosen from among 2,000 as being the loveliest.[40]

One can hardly fault Salumbides for being willing to sacrifice to keep his marriage to such a beautiful creature, but Panganiban's demands were rather extreme. She had co-starred with her husband in his film *The Soul Saver* in 1927, a true-life account of their own love affair. But in the film *Fate or Consequence* Salumbides had a different leading lady, Sofia Lota, a former school teacher from Jolo and *vod-a-vil* dancing girl at the Savoy.[41] It seems to have been more than Rosario Panganiban could bear when she saw the man she loved on the movie screen kissing another woman. She asked him to leave the film business lest she suffer another debilitating attack of jealousy. In 1929, Salumbides relented and walked away from his film career.

Screen kisses were no simple novelty at the time; Elizabeth "Dimples" Cooper, who had starred in both *Miracles of Love* and *Fate or Consequence* with Salumbides, had caused quite a stir indeed when she allowed herself to be kissed by Luis Tuason in Jose Nepomuceno's *Tatlong Hambog (The Three Braggarts)* in 1926. It was the first screen kiss in Philippine cinema, and to some it was scandalous. But Cooper was not fated to be a stranger to scandal.

Elizabeth Cooper (also known as Isabel Rosario Cooper) was born of a Scottish father and Chinese *mestizo* mother. She became famous as a *vod-a-vil* star under the stage name "Dimples," and she was so charmingly beautiful that it was only natural that she be in motion pictures once the medium began to take shape as the preeminent entertainment of the masses. Miss Cooper's participation in the first screen kiss in Philippine cinema assured her a place in Filipino history, but she would also soon rate a footnote in U.S. history. In 1930, Cooper met U.S. General Douglas MacArthur and became his mistress. By then a middle-aged divorcee, MacArthur doesn't seem to have been particularly worried about the gossip that floated around Manila about himself and the pretty movie queen. He was apparently madly in love with Cooper to the point that he supplied her with a steady stream of embarrassingly syrupy love letters. So embarrassing that to this day the MacArthur estate will not allow direct quotation from the letters.

When MacArthur was appointed Chief of Staff by President Hoover, the lovesick General could not bear to leave his sweetie behind, and so arranged for her to come to the U.S. where he put her up in a comfortable apartment in Washington D.C. But his expectation that she would pass the time alone in her apartment awaiting his every visit proved unrealistic. It would have been so for most any young woman, but particularly for one so beautiful and used to attention. In time, Cooper grew bored and enrolled in school to study law, with MacArthur paying her way. When MacArthur eventually tired of the whole arrangement in 1934, he offered to pay her way back to the Philippines, but Cooper declined. Without MacArthur's money, however, Cooper's fortunes declined quickly. She ventured to Hollywood to try and start a film career in the U.S., but had no luck beyond a few bit roles. It seems that her only good luck would come when MacArthur made the mistake of trying to sue newspaper columnist Drew Pearson for comments that MacArthur considered defamatory. The comments had nothing at all to do with Cooper, but when Pearson learned of her, he couldn't help but want to meet with her, and after discovering that she had kept MacArthur's love letters to her, Pearson used it to his advantage; merely announcing that Cooper would be called as a witness in the case was enough. The whole episode got messier and messier, until MacArthur decided to drop the case. He paid Cooper the considerable sum of $15,000 for the return of his letters, and also paid Pearson's legal expenses. Had she taken that $15,000 and returned to the Philippines, Elizabeth Cooper could have lived out her years quite comfortably. Instead, she stayed in America where the money too soon ran out, and she existed in poverty and obscurity. In 1960, by then a middle-aged woman with no expectations of a bright future, Elizabeth Cooper took her own life with an overdose of barbiturates.[42]

Through the years, the story of Elizabeth Cooper and her love affair with General Douglas MacArthur has undergone the expected embellishments and misreporting. For instance, there are those who have written that Cooper was a 16-year-old girl when she began her affair with MacArthur. She was, in fact, a woman in her early twenties—young enough, to be sure, but hardly the naïve teenage girl that some may believe, and already being a star of stage and screen, she was probably far more worldly than others of her age.

Elizabeth Cooper may have been the first figure of controversy in the Philippine film industry, but she would hardly be the last. Movies were catching on with the public in a big way, and as they quickly grew to become the 20th century's predominant means of both artistic expression and mass entertainment the world over, in the Philippines, where the need to escape the harsh realities of everyday life and live vicariously through others was perhaps more pronounced than in the West, movies would become a national obsession.

2

1931–1941

When Jose Nepomuceno's production *Dalagang Bukid* was premiered on September 25th of 1919—musical numbers and all—leading actress Atang de la Rama was on hand to sing *Nabasag ang Banga* (*The Clay Pot Broke*) in time with her performance of the song on screen. Born Honorata de la Rama in 1903, Atang de la Rama began appearing on the stage in sarswelas at the age of seven. She was very popular with audiences of the day, teary-eyed theatergoers sometimes tossing silver coins onto the stage at the conclusion of her performances. She also wrote sarswelas herself. She was 15 when she appeared in Nepomuceno's film. Accompanied by a three-piece band consisting of a pianist, violinist and trumpeter,[1] it must have been an odd marriage of the two art forms: on the one hand, there was the popular form of live entertainment in the form of the sarswela, and on the other, the new form of entertainment, motion pictures. Having the performers there to recreate their roles live even as they were being played out on the screen would seem to make the film itself somewhat superfluous; after all, since the actors were there, why not just stage a traditional sarswela? But there was something—somewhat intangible, perhaps—that captivated audiences in the flickering image; more so, it would seem, than the familiar spectacle of a live performance. The human imagination seemed riveted by the celluloid image and its ability to transcend time and place. The only element it lacked was the audio component to complete the fantasy. Without it there was something somewhat more distant in the events taking place on the screen; sound would more intimately draw the viewer into the experience.

As did their contemporaries around the world, Filipino filmmakers struggled with this missing element, and sought to overcome the disconnect in the experience by using a gramophone. Then there were some exhibitors who hired musicians to play live in the theater while the film rolled. Music might satisfy the sensory need for some form of audio accompaniment, but it could not truly complete the experience. It was the showing of the American film *Pennsylvania Syncopation* on August 3rd of 1929 at the Radio Theater, complete with dialogue on a phonograph synchronized to the picture,[2] which inspired Filipino filmmakers to begin the race for the first sound picture in the Philippines.

Perhaps the earliest attempt at a sound picture in the Philippines was Araw Movies' 1930 production *Collegian Love* starring Gregorio Fernandez and Naty Fernandez (the two were not related). The producers attempted to synchronize the film with an accompanying phonograph.[3] With no surviving prints, nor known copies of the phonographs, it's difficult to assess just how successful the attempt may have been, or how much of the film may have been in sound. Nor is it easy to say whether the sound was recorded at the same time as the picture or afterward in an early experiment in the concept of dubbing.

But the December 8, 1932, edition of the Filipino periodical *Graphic* heralded the horror film *Ang Aswang* (*The Vampire*) as the first Filipino sound film. Shot by George Musser in a combination of Spanish and English for an outfit called Manila Talkaton Pictures, the film had its premiere on January 1, 1933, at the Lyric Theater on Escolta. The film's sound was handled by William P. Smith, who would provide the sound for many of the films of the post-silent 1930s. Smith's importance to the Filipino film industry's transition into the sound era cannot be overestimated. Born on February 12, 1913, in Echague, Isabela, Smith seems to have had a natural gift for electronics. He was still in his teens when he found employment as a sound technician, installing audio equipment in movie theaters in the early 1930s. Sound being new to the industry, there was an immediate and pressing need for individuals with Smith's know-how, and in 1934 he went to work for a new production company called Filippine Films, a company started by Americans George F. Harris and Edward Tait in 1932. They had originally intended to help the progress of the local industry by employing American technicians, but found that unnecessary after becoming acquainted with Smith. After helping Filippine Films get their sound department up and running, Smith went to do the same for Parlatone Hispano-Filipino in 1935. In 1937 he likewise went to Sampaguita Pictures, another new company, for which he manufactured the studio's sound equipment: "Recorded by Smith Sound System" became a standard credit at the opening of every Sampaguita film of the era. Smith was even instrumental in choosing the location where the studio's facilities would be built, helping to pick out a spot where the terrain would minimize outside noise interference during filming. The sound equipment that Smith developed for Sampaguita would be in service for decades.

Smith's technical orientation was not limited to sound gadgetry: he also developed an interest in film processing, setting up Sampaguita's processing lab. Once color cinematography had been introduced to the local industry, he set up the first color processing lab in the country for LVN Studios in 1951, which was widely regarded as the best color lab facility in that part of the world. He also went on to pioneer film reduction in the Philippines, and through his company, Smith Sound Systems Laboratories, was responsible for the reduction of many 35mm Tagalog film prints to 16mm for television distribution in the 1960s.

While most sources credit *Ang Aswang* as the first sound feature shot in the Philippines, this may be only partially true. Although the film *was* feature length, citing unnamed individuals who recall the film, Arsenio Bautista has written that the film was only partially sound.[4] If this is the case, then that would make Jose Nepomuceno's 1933 film *Punyal na Ginto* (*The Golden Dagger*) the first completely sound production, making its debut some three months later, also at the Lyric Theater.[5] Irrespective of where exactly the truth lies, *Ang Aswang* can take its place as the first Philippine film to utilize sound without the problematic method of synchronizing the picture with an independent sound source. The technology was crude, but there was no turning back. The chasm had been bridged.

In Cebu, the Visayan film industry sought to keep pace, producing its first sound feature in 1938. *Bertoldo-Balodoy* was written and directed by Piux Kabahar, and produced by Estudio Americo-Filipino, the first Cebuano film production company. The company was started by Dr. Virgilio R. Gonzalez, a native of Pampanga who had settled in Cebu in 1919 after marrying a local girl. When he decided to go into the film business, he was apparently very committed to the idea, having two studios built and ordering his film production equipment from the United States. He further showed his desire to put out quality product by sending Kabahar, along with assistant director S. Alvarez Villarino and cinematographer Prudencio Iriarte to Manila to observe and learn about film production at Sampaguita and Parlatone Hispano-Filipino, and to receive schooling from director Carlos Vander Tolosa, not a bad idea if one were to recall the technical defects of the Cebuano industry's first silent feature, *El Hijo Disobediente*, on which Irairte had also served as cinematographer. The schooling may have been in vain: as the film's producers sat down to watch the initial footage that had been shot, they found themselves looking at a blank screen. The cameraman had neglected to remove the lens cap before shooting. Was it Irairte? Sources differ as to who the film's cinematographer was, some listing the film as having been shot by a man named Luis Chiong. This raises the question of whether or not Irairte may have been replaced. That may not be fair to Irairte, but how else to account for the disparate credit?

Piux Kabahar was born Pio A. Cabajar on October 11, 1892, in San Nicolas. He was the son of a well-known Cebuano musician named Justo Cabajar, an organist and former revolutionary who had fought the colonial powers under both Spain and the United States. Piux Kabahar inherited his father's musical talent, writing songs that became local favorites to Cebuanos in his day, who eagerly purchased phonographs of his compositions at the Odeon Palace in Cebu City. He dabbled in many fields, working as a teacher and a journalist; he worked for various journals, for some as a writer, for others as editor. But theater was his true calling, where he was both a director and stage actor, sometimes performing in troupes that ventured to other provinces. More than anything, Kabahar was a prolific playwright. In fact, he adapted *Bertoldo-Balodoy* from his own stage play, a drama about two Siamese twins.

Bertoldo-Balodoy had its premiere at Cebu's Vision Theater on Colon Street in 1938, but although it would even play as widely as Hawaii, the film failed to make a profit for Dr. Gonzalez and his company. It would be another two years before another sound feature in Cebuano would be produced, that being *Gugmang Talagsaon*, co-directed by S. Alvarez Villarino (also a musical composer) and Fernando Alfon. A third sound film, *Bulak sa Lunangan*, a film that was being shot by Florentino Borromeo, was in production when the war broke out and production ceased.

With Hollywood serving as its model, a studio system began to emerge in the Philippines in the 1930s. In 1933 Nepomuceno had revamped Malayan Pictures Corporation into Parlatone Hispano-Filipino. The emerging studio system was also aided by Americans like Harris and Tait at Filippine Films. They had big plans for the company; they hoped to make Manila the filmmaking capitol of Asia and to export films throughout the region to Indonesia, China and Malaya.[6] It was not an unrealistic ambition, as the filmmaking industry in Manila was already well ahead of the rest of Asia. The film industry was profit-driven from its inception— a kind of modern carnival of sorts for the senses—and what was needed to attract attention in an increasingly crowded market was a barker's sensibility. Having been so long under the control of Westerners, and having incorporated their way of thinking into their own regional consciousness, it should come as no surprise that the Philippines would have had a quicker start with the new medium of motion pictures. The initial production from Filippine Films was a 1933 adventure film titled *Ang mga Ulila* (*The Orphans*) about a shipwrecked family.[7] It took a little time, but by 1937 Harris and Tait were assured enough of their product to set their sights on the U.S. and they released the film *Zamboanga*, which played in the U.S. before having its premier in the Philippines. The film's story concerned two Moro tribes living on neighboring islands in the Southern Philippines. One tribe made its living pearl diving, while the other tribe was apparently less industrious and basically subsisted through piracy. One day while the young men of the good tribe are off pearl diving, their women are abducted by the pirates, thus assuring a showdown.

The film's director, Eduardo de Castro, was an American mestizo who was born Marvin Edward Gardner on July 7, 1907, in Manila. He was the son of William Henry Gardner, an American soldier who hailed from Tennessee who decided to stay on in Manila to work as a

Zamboanga (1937/Filippine Films-Grand National Pictures) was the first Filipino film to play U.S. theaters.

police officer after serving in the U.S. military during the American-Philippine War. William Henry Gardner married Ceferina de Castro, who bore him eight children, and the family lived in quarters adjoining the police station. When Marvin Edward Gardner entered the film business as an actor in the early part of the 1930s he took his mother's surname and became Eduardo de Castro. As an actor he came to be known as the "Rudolph Valentino of the Philippines," but his matinee idol looks notwithstanding, he seems to have preferred working from behind the camera and, after marrying Florence Little, one of his leading ladies, he soon made the transition to director. Although he built a reputation as a formidable director, he also had a drinking problem that hurt his career to the point that he died broke at the age of 47 after suffering a stroke, and days later a cerebral hemorrhage in Baguio City on November 17, 1955.

Zamboanga became the first Filipino film to play theaters in the United States. Distributed in the U.S. by Edward L. Alperson's Grand National, the film premiered at the Strand Theater in Pasadena, California, and a number of prominent invited guests were encouraged to give their opinions, which were subsequently used in the film's promotional campaign. Frank Capra described it as "the most exciting and beautiful picture of native life I have ever seen," and went on to say "I was thrilled by it." Ernst Lubitsch at Paramount wrote, "I was much impressed by the way you captured the idealistic feeling of native life in the South of the Philippine Islands, and you have succeeded admirably in portraying it on the screen in a very interesting story."[8] But perhaps more than the praise of industry luminaries, the promotional campaign dreamt up by the advertising department at Grand National tended to rely on the naïveté of film audiences of the era and staked itself on rather fanciful tales of the hazardous conditions under which the film was made. *Zamboanga* was shot on the Southern Philippine island of Basilan, which, like the rest of the nation's islands, is not without its perils (sharks, snakes, and the like), but the Grand National promotional campaign spun some rather tall tales indeed regarding certain scenes in the film. For instance, at one point in the film a pearl diver is caught in the clutches of the shell of a giant 300-pound mollusk. One press release for the film read as follows: "During the filming of the sensational picture 'Zamboanga' ... one of the native divers accidentally stepped into one of [the] trap-like shells. In a twinkling the huge jaws of the clam clapped shut on the leg of the unfortunate diver, literally anchoring him beneath the sea. Fortunately this occurred in the range of the underwater cameras. The alarm to the surface was quickly sounded and divers, armed with spears, rushed to the diver's rescue. This entire scene, from the time the diver was captured by the big clam to the thrilling rescue, though entirely unplanned, was filmed in its entirety by quick-witted cinematographers." Fortunate, indeed.

Still another press release tried to convince that a scene in which one of the film's villains grapples with a python was also a happenstance of location shooting. The release read like a penny dreadful: "With the presence of mind, the cameraman kept his instrument in motion, while the terrified native writhed in agony as the python's coil tightened about his slender body. In the nick of time rescuers dashed forward and extricated the Moro warrior from the 'coils of death' which were squeezing the breath from his body." In order to head skeptics off at the pass, the piece added in conclusion: "Thus was a much doubted tale indisputably verified and the proof recorded on celluloid."

Finally, the promotional campaign included a press release that read in part: "During the months of filming, many accidents and a few fatalities occurred among the Moro actors. One pearl diver was trapped by a giant mollusk, weighing over three hundred pounds. Others were dangerously hurt [due to] too much enthusiasm in the battle scenes on their part, [as they] swung their kris or barong too lustily and their opponents paid dearly for it. The production unit was forced to set up a field hospital to take care of the wounded."

Of all of the campaign's fantastic tales (and leaving aside the reiteration of the monster mollusk story), this piece may have something of the truth in it. There were doubtless accidents, and quite possibly even a fatality or two. Many years later, director Eddie Romero confirmed in an interview that it was not uncommon for stunt men to be killed during the filming of sequences in the earlier years of Philippine filmmaking, and even as late as the 1950s, though he hastened to point out that such incidents did not occur on any of his films.[9] Even major stars were sometimes put in rather perilous circumstances. While portraying *komiks* super heroine Darna in the early 1950s, Rosa del Rosario was suspended from a helicopter for the scenes in which she was supposed to fly through the air, as super heroes are wont to do. It seems incredible that a studio would take such an enormous risk with one of their leading stars, but del Rosario was taken quite high; at one point, barely high enough, as she almost ran into the roof of a church in Quiapo. She also claimed that the suspension caused her back pains for life.[10] It would seem likely that there was also some medical person or persons on hand during the filming of *Zamboanga*, though it may be an exaggeration to say that a field hospital needed to be set up.

Harris and Tait must surely have been encouraged by the early reviews, particularly the review in *The Film Daily*, which pointed out that the film marked "the first definite invasion of the international distribution field by any Asiatic company." This was, after all, their ambition. Other reviews were enthusiastic, with cinematographer William H. Jansen often being singled out for his superb work. Reviewing for *Hollywood Spectator*, Edward Le Veque wrote, "The cameraman understands the secrets of his lenses, and paints with gray pigments what poets strive to describe in words." In *The Los Angeles Times*, Grace Kingsley wrote, "The deep-sea photography is perhaps the best that has been revealed on the screen," and *The Hollywood Reporter* wrote, "William Jansen uses his camera as a brush in many scenes." Film editor Ralph Dixon was also praised in the same review.[11]

The film was at least partially in English, though how much so apparently depends on personal opinion. The reviewer for *The Hollywood Reporter* wrote, "The picture is almost wholly in native dialog, with only an occasional explanatory subtitle and not more than a dozen short speeches in English, yet the details of the story are never in doubt." In contrast, the reviewer for *Motion Picture Daily* wrote, "Most of the dialogue is in English and that which is in the native dialect is interpreted by subtitles." Confusion over what language dominated may have been a box office hindrance, since foreign language films have traditionally kept many patrons away from theaters. This was probably far truer then than now. Filippine Films may have been further ill-served by their Stateside distributor, Grand National, whose insistence on trying to create buzz about the film with ballyhoo about true brushes with death by giant snakes and mollusks seems to have failed to get much attention. *Zamboanga* played briefly in California, and otherwise enjoyed only a limited playdate in New York before disappearing for over half a century. The film had a nine-month shooting schedule—lengthy even for Hollywood pictures of the time—that would have necessitated considerable expense even in the Philippines, and its failure to turn even a minimal profit put Harris and Tait on thin ice economically. They probably would have been satisfied to break even, but they wound up broke instead and eventually sold the company.

One of the campaign's problems may have been its failure to name a single performer in the film, and indeed the film itself credited none of its cast. The logic was, of course, that American audiences would have been completely unfamiliar with the entire cast, and while this is certainly the case, it might have been wiser to at least list the leading players. The filmmakers could then claim to have discovered some new ingénue, which might have helped promotion since the romantic leads were singled out for praise in Kingsley's review, which stated, "Handsome and clever are the actors who interpret the sweethearts." The film's romantic leads were Fernando Poe and Rosa del Rosario.

Allan Fernando Poe was a tall, strapping, handsome Spanish *criollo* born in 1916. His father was Lorenzo Pou (Fernando changed the spelling of the surname when he went into show business),[12] a Spanish playwright from Mallorca, Spain. As a youth, Fernando Poe looked every bit the athlete, and in high school he participated in most every sport available. But his rugged, muscular appearance belied a body dogged by nagging health problems. In 1932, at the age of 16, Poe was participating in a swimming meet when it became necessary to pull him from the pool. Profusely bleeding from the nose and ears, Poe was diagnosed with a severe case of sinusitis that required surgery. It was a problem that would plague him through the years, even making a recurrence during the filming of *Zamboanga*. Another of his films in the 1930s had to shut down production when Poe was hospitalized for nine days with pneumonia.[13]

Fernando Poe was one of the great screen idols of the 1930s. He had a successful career as an actor, producer and director right up to the time of his death in 1951 of rabies.

After leaving high school, Poe found himself living the harsh life of a miner, working in the coalmines outside of Manila. That hard life made a deep impression on him, and after becoming a film star, he seemed suspicious of such an easy existence and forever in fear of losing it. Poe had originally been hired by Filippine Films to do some construction work on a film set, and seeing the leisurely, pampered existence of the film actors, he decided to try his luck. It was his physique and good looks that brought him good fortune in the business rather than any genuine ability as a performer, and Poe knew it. "I do not even have any histrionic background," he quipped.[14] But even after becoming one of the nation's biggest stars in the 1930s and '40s, Poe seemed somehow ill at ease with it all. He took up chemistry, and in June of 1941, by then one of the biggest of film stars in the Philippines, Poe enrolled in the Philippine Dental College. His suspicion of the easy life of a film star soon manifested itself as contemptuousness for the business. "It is a very fickle profession," he said. "Today a star might be a big box-office attraction, then suddenly he hurtles down like an ambushed bird. And people who have had just such luck are a sorry sight. They try valiantly to come back. They fail. They try again. Fail again. They keep on trying until they wind up in the hands of gripping, selfish producers who give them roles at starving pay."[15]

Although he needn't have been, Poe

was clearly fearful of losing his status, and while he felt both respect for, and gratitude toward George Harris, who gave him his start at Filippine Films, by the early 1940s, and now working for X'Otic Films, Poe was very weary of the businessmen behind the scenes. He tried to organize a movie artists' guild in order to create some security for people in the business, and he attempted to enlist the help of actor/filmmaker Gregorio Fernandez in that respect. Fernandez had been a popular actor in the 1920s, and by the early 1940s was one of the nation's most respected directors. Citing his longevity and high degree of respect in the business, Poe encouraged Fernandez by opining, "If anybody can do it, you can."[16] Fernandez doesn't seem to have been especially interested in the idea, however, and he soon let it drop.

Perhaps it was Poe's admiration for Fernandez that occasioned him to enroll in dental school. Fernandez was a Pampanga dentist who made his film debut at the age of 24 in Nepomuceno's *Anak sa Ligaw* (*Stray Child*) in 1928. Nine Years later in 1937 Fernandez made his directorial debut with *Asahar at Kabaong* (*Bad Luck and the Coffin*), which was produced and released through Filippine Films.[17]

Poe never did become a dentist. He would eventually overcome his insecurity by branching out as a producer and director himself. By the postwar 1940s he was producing and directing all of his own films. He was still one of the most popular actors, as well as successful producers, in 1951 when he suffered one of the cruelest of fates: Poe cut his foot on a seashell while filming a movie and, knowing that animals licked their wounds in order to keep them clean and help them heal faster, he allowed his pet dog to lick the wound. Unfortunately, the dog was carrying the rabies virus. Poe died of rabies at the age of 35.[18]

It was Filippine Films that put up the first fight against film censorship in the Philippines. Although a Board of Censors had been established by the government in 1912, it was not until 1929 that legislation was introduced to formally institute and define a Board of Censorship for Moving Pictures. On November 27, 1929, the Philippine Legislature passed Act No. 3582, titled "An Act to Create a Board of Censorship for Moving Pictures and Define its Functions." Consisting of fifteen members appointed by the Governor-General, the Board was to be made up of both government officials and private citizens. The legislation described the Board's function as being "to examine all films, spoken or silent, imported or produced in the Philippine Islands, and prohibit the introduction and exhibition in this country of films, which in their judgment are immoral or contrary to law and good customs or injurious to the prestige of the Government or People of the Philippine Islands." That might sound somewhat draconian by today's standards, but owing to the era, and the generally innocuous nature of film entertainment at the time, when the Board got to work they found little to be disturbed about. Convening for the first time in the office of Secretary of the Interior Honorio Ventura on May 16, 1930, and with Teodoro M. Kalaw as its president (a position he would hold from 1930–1939), they approved 1,249 films during the course of the year while banning only two. Of the 1,249 approved films, only six required any cuts be made in order to meet with the Board's approval.[19]

By 1937, however, films were becoming more adventurous, and in the eyes of some, more provocative. A showdown over content was inevitable. The Board of Censors had a number of objections to Filippine Films' *Batang Tulisan* (*Boy Bandit*): the use of a priest as a villainous character, the use of a hypodermic needle and syringe filled with poison as a murder weapon, a love scene (however innocent) between a ten-year-old boy and girl, various scenes of seduction. Those grievances may have been predictable, given the times, but far less tolerable to a liberal temperament would be the Board's objection to the film's title, which they reasoned "might give our young folk certain subversive ideas."[20]

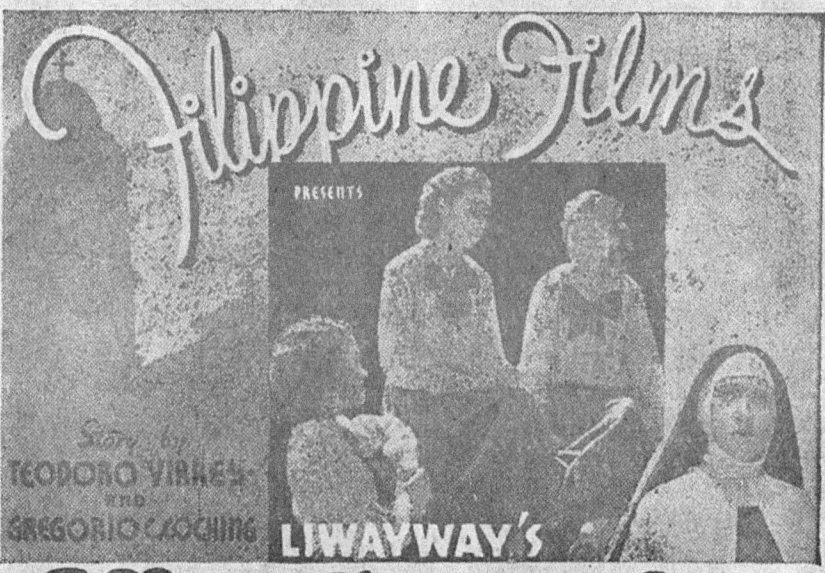

Via Crucis (1936/Filippine Films) was one of the earliest starring roles for Leopoldo Salcedo, who would become one of the great icons of Philippine cinema.

George Harris was not pleased. At the then considerable sum of 16,000 pesos, the film was not inexpensive to make, and Filippine Films fought the Board's order that the film be withdrawn from its scheduled exhibition. The studio objected that foreign films were judged far less stringently than local pictures, a bone of contention that would become a familiar refrain through the years as filmmakers tried to compete with foreign imports. But as a U.S. colonial territory in the 1930s, the Philippine government was necessarily limited in the amount of control it exercised over U.S. imports of any kind. Still, the obstinacy of the problem long after the U.S. had ceded the islands to Filipino sovereignty suggests that there was far more to it than the imposition of an outside ruling power. The censors seem to have been more interested in seeing to it that the local industry maintain some sense of decorum than in making unruly foreigners behave respectably. Ultimately, Filippine Films lost in their valiant struggle for artistic expression. All in all, the dispute served to make other film studios mindful of the cost of straying beyond certain parameters. But provocation was not a staple of the Filipino film industry during the era. The films by-and-large were simple: weepy romance sagas mostly.

The 1930s would birth some of the film studios that would dominate Philippine cinema for the next quarter century. Sampaguita Pictures was founded in 1937 by two brothers with a background in politics, Congressman Pedro Vera and Judge Jose O. Vera, who was a former senator. In 1938 LVN Pictures was founded in a partnership between Dona Narcisa Buencamino de Leon, Carmen Villongco and Eleuterio Navoa. Both studios would be at the top of their game in the postwar years of the '40s and '50s. As for Parlatone Hispano-Filipino, they had begun when Nepomuceno, looking for more capital to increase production values, took on partners and transformed Malayan Pictures Corporation. That proved to be Nepomuceno's undoing, as he eventually lost control of the company and was forced out by his erstwhile partners, and the company came under the ownership of Raymundo Navarro. It was a small matter for Nepomuceno, as he established a pattern of founding film production companies one after another. In 1939 he joined with Jesus Cacho and Julian Sagado in forming X'Otic Films.[21]

As the studio system took shape, it began to define who the power brokers in the industry were. Given the number of popular actors who owed their careers to Jose Nepomuceno, it is easy to see why he came to be known as the "Father of Philippine Movies," aside from the fact that for years many credited him with making the first Filipino film proper (in fact, many still do). But his business acumen may have been lacking. Just as he had lost Parlatone Hispano-Filipino to the partners that he had invited in, Nepomuceno was prone to seeing the stars he created lured away to other studios. Among others, Gregorio Fernandez left, accepting an offer to work for Faustino Lichauco's Mayon Photoplay Corporation, although he would periodically return to work for Nepomuceno. But contrary to the emerging trend, Fernandez was not one to be tied to any one outfit, and particularly after becoming a director, he would continue to freelance, making films for many different companies, including X'Otic Films, Excelsior and Sampaguita. Such independence was an increasingly uncommon thing.

Of course, in any competitive industry it is not always possible to keep people on board indefinitely, but it wasn't only film stars that jumped ship on Nepomuceno. Prior to starting Nolasco Brothers Pictures in 1941, Luis Nolasco had begun his career in the film business as Nepomuceno's publicity manager during the silent era. He left Nepomuceno's employ to join the fledgling Sampaguita Pictures in 1937, becoming the company's first production manager, as well as managing the publicity department. Nolasco was a well-regarded poet and playwright who began writing at the age of 14. Spanish was his language of choice as a writer, and he authored two novels in the language, as well as a collection of poems. Nolasco became very important at Sampaguita, and was credited with being one of those most responsible for the studio's initial success. Perhaps much of the company's subsequent success as well, since Nolasco set the tone for the studio's daily operations, which would remain in effect even after his departure. As production manager he ran a tight ship, making sure that the personnel were disciplined and stuck to schedule. His organizational skills created a demand for his services, and in 1939 he left Sampaguita for Filippine Films, which Harris and Tait had sold to J. Amando Araneta and Placido Mapa, Sr. Araneta was becoming one of the country's major media moguls, having previously bought two radio stations in 1927 from their American owners, and also acquiring a chain of English language newspapers. As production manager at Filippine Films, Nolasco became instrumental in reorganizing the company under its new ownership, and he was responsible for choosing the company's personnel. It was through Nolasco that young directors like Lamberto Avellana and Ramon Estella, who would become very prominent in the industry during the era, would get their first opportunities in the business. In 1940 his services as production manager were acquired by Excelsior Studios, and that company likewise prospered under his supervision.

The success that he was bringing to each company that employed him kindled the fire in Nolasco to start his own company, and so in 1941 he started Nolasco Brothers Pictures. Unfortunately, WW II came to the Philippines shortly afterward, and like all other studios, Nolasco Brothers was closed down. But Nolasco successfully restarted the company after the war. Like Nepomuceno, Nolasco had an eye for talent, and was responsible for the discovery of some of the era's more popular stars, like Rosa Rosal, Leila Morena and Lilia Dizon. Apparently very prolific in his work, Nolasco also worked as a screenwriter, as well as serving as editor of film periodicals of the pre-war era, like *Song-Movie Magazine* and *Manila Movies Magazine*.

One of the more interesting aspects to emerge within the film industry as it evolved was

Buenavista (1938/Filippine Films), an early attempt at making a socially relevant film.

how quickly women were to gain a degree of parity in the business. Of course, many of the biggest stars were women, going back to the industry's inception, including Atang de la Rama, the *sarswela* star who is generally considered to have been the first Filipino film star. It should come as no surprise to anyone that women would figure prominently as performers, especially given the representation of women in the arts historically in the Philippines. Women had always held their place in the country's arts community, not merely as singers and stage performers, but in many artistic endeavors, including painting, where women like sisters Paz and Adelaida Paterno made names for themselves, as well as Carmen Zaragosa, who at the age of 16 took first prize for painting in the 1892 Columbus Quadricentennial Art Contest. That same year a woman named Pelagia Mendoza y Gotianquin took the prize for sculpting in the same contest for her bust of Christopher Columbus.[22]

In the film industry, it wasn't just that women were popular as performers, or even that women like Brigida Perez Villanueva were directing films as early as 1933 (Villanueva, incidentally, directed *Pendulum of Fate*, the last silent Filipino film), and Carmen Concha was directing and producing pictures in the 1930s, but that women were taking the reins of power *within* the business, and a trend toward studio matriarchies began to develop. It seems to have begun in 1938 with the founding of LVN Studios. Though she had founded the studio in a partnership, Dona Narcisa Buencamino de Leon would emerge not only as the leader of the studio, but as one of the main power players in the entire industry. So much so that she came to be known as "The Grand Old Lady of Philippine Movies." Born in San Miguel, Bulacan on October 29, 1877, Dona Sisang, as she was fondly called, was a member of a wealthy family with many business interests (real estate and agriculture, in particular). Upon the death of her parents, Dona Sisang took charge of the family property and was responsible for the care of her 12 younger siblings when she was just 16. In 1905 she married a municipal captain named Jose de Leon, well known to the local residents as "Kapitan Pepe," and through the years the family fortune grew into the millions of pesos. When her husband died in 1934, Dona Sisang assumed leadership of the family's businesses, and she added a new business to the family portfolio: in 1938 she purchased a movie theater. Prior to the purchase, she had never even seen a movie. As the business prospered, Dona Sisang decided to go into the production end of the business and she founded LVN studios. She came to be credited as a major contributor to the growth of the nation's film industry. She was also something of a philanthropist who, aside from garnering many awards within the film industry, was awarded for her work in helping to establish the Philippine Mental Health Association and the Quezon City branch of the Red Cross. She also had the distinction of being chosen to be one of the first directors of NARIC (The National Rice and Corn Corporation) in the 1930s under the administration of President Manuel Quezon.[23]

The tendency toward studio matriarchies may seem surprising given the patriarchal nature of Asian societies—indeed, of societies in general—but it is worth remembering that as Americans continue to ponder when the United States will see its first woman chief executive, and who it might be, the Philippines is, as of this writing, into the second term of the administration of its second Madam President. Then again, it should also be noted that many women who achieved power and prominence in the Philippines derived that power in one way or another by way of their husbands. The assassination of Benigno Aquino, Jr., for instance, assured that he would attain a Christ-like status in the eyes of the masses, as Filipino martyrs tend to do, but it also sent his widow on a mission that gave her a Joan of Arc image, and the result was that Corazon Aquino became the first woman to become President of the Philippines.

Likewise, studio matriarchies were headed by women who inherited their wealth and power—and usually their movie studios—from their husbands. They sometimes seemed to have been little more than figureheads, but the images of the studios seemed somehow to depend on them and the aura of authority that they projected. Although Sampaguita Pictures was founded by the Vera brothers, Dolores H. Vera, the wife of Judge Jose Vera, would become very prominent within the company. Born in Camalig, Albay on the 9th of November in 1896, Dolores Vera was a former beauty queen, having been chosen Miss Albay in 1916.[24] When Judge Vera's health declined in the 1950s and he found it necessary to pass the torch, he may have handed it to his son-in-law, Dr. Jose Perez, whose instincts he came to greatly trust during the studio's bleakest time, but Dolores Vera appears to have had the final say in studio matters. Affectionately known as "Mommy Vera" (a nickname echoed a generation later when Regal Films matriarch Lily Monteverde would come to be known as "Mother Lily"), Dolores Vera was ever a woman of class and taste, making certain that the personnel at the studio were always courteous and respectful. She encouraged a familial atmosphere at the studio, and while the directors would always be addressed more formally by the cast and crew as "Mister" so-and-so, Dolores Vera was greeted with a cheerful "Buenas dias, Mommy Vera." She was mother indeed to the young stars at Sampaguita, even admonishing them about bad posture should she catch any of them slouching. Vera was determined that Sampaguita product would always maintain a certain standard, and she would not allow the studio's product to become distasteful or vulgar, whatever modern mores or market trends might dictate. Years later, her grandson, Gregorio "Cocoy" Perez, recalled that when the wave of sex films, known as "bombas," began to deluge the industry in the early 1970s, Dolores Vera would not permit the studio to follow that trend, irrespective of how lucrative it may have been.[25] Regardless of who was doing the day-to-day job of officially running the studio, be it her son-in-law Dr. Perez or, later, her granddaughter Marichu Maceda, Mommy Vera seems to have been the final word at Sampaguita Pictures until her passing in 1980.

Dona Narcissa Buencamino Vda. De Leon, affectionately called Dona Sisang. Founder and matriarch of LVN Studios, she came to be known as the "Grand Old Lady of Philippine Movies."

Dona Sisang and Mommy Vera were only the most notable women on the production end of the business. There were others: director Susana de Guzman helped found Premiere Productions with Dr. Ciriaco Santiago in 1946. When Santiago died his wife Adela took over as head of the company. Women do not seem to have been particularly hampered by any glass ceiling in the industry. To this day, the uninitiated might be surprised to observe the preponderance of women listed as producers in the credits of Filipino films.

Well established with the public as a source of entertainment, *sarswelas* were a natural source of material when Filipino filmmakers went looking for source material. With the American presence, other forms of entertainment became popular with the public, and inevitably served as fodder for film producers looking for stories to film. One popular American amusement that caught on quickly with Filipinos was the comic strip. Dubbed *komiks* in Tagalog, Filipino magazines began to run dramatic illustrated serials, which were quickly seized upon by film studios. There were also serialized novels that ran in weekly publications like *Liwayway* (*Beautiful Morning*), from which *Batang Tulisan* had been taken. Radio serials also became a staple of Filipino life. The *sarswela* not only had to contend with competition from motion pictures, but was also already facing stiff competition from another fairly new form of entertainment from America, the vaudeville shows. Known in the Philippines as *vod-a-vil* (or sometimes *bod-a-bil*), it was another form of live entertainment that seemed to be fazing out with the increasing popularity of cinema, but many entertainers, particularly comedians, made the transition to film.

After optically recorded sound had been introduced to Filipino filmmakers, and sound films began to become the norm, the question arose as to what language should be spoken. During the silent era, film intertitles were usually bilingual (English and Tagalog), or sometimes trilingual (English, Tagalog and Spanish).

Dolores Vera, the wife of Sampaguita Pictures cofounder Judge Jose Vera. As Sampaguita matriarch, she was lovingly called "Mommy Vera" by Sampaguita personnel.

The truth is that the Philippines had no national language. Indeed, prior to the arrival of the Spanish there was no nation of the Philippines. What there were were some 7,000 islands populated by numerous tribes, speaking many different languages, adhering to their own beliefs, observing their own customs. Many tribes were large extended families that were isolated. It was the Spanish who grouped them all together for the first time under one banner, a grouping that has remained somewhat fragile through the generations, Filipino loyalty often remaining more familial and parochial than national. Spanish friars were obstinate in their refusal to teach the Spanish language to Filipinos, convinced that if they did learn Spanish it would encourage Filipinos to feel equal to the Spaniards.[26] But with three centuries under Spanish rule, a certain amount of the language was bound to become interwoven with the local dialects. Mutated forms of Spanish words can still be found in Tagalog today, as well as many other regional dialects. There is also the fact that many upper-class Filipinos were educated in Spain, attending universities in Madrid and Barcelona, where they necessarily

Alipin ng Palad (*Slave of Destiny*; 1938/Sampaguita Pictures), one of Sampaguita's earlier titles.

would have had to speak Spanish. Spanish also found its way into indigenous languages by way of the arts, as Spanish forms of music and theater were incorporated into local customs.

The Americans had a different approach. When the United States took over the Philippines, it was considered very important to form a bond of sorts with the local people: a shared language was the fastest way of accomplishing this. The earliest teachers sent to the Philippines found the people more than willing to learn the English language, and proficiency in English became a matter of pride for many Filipinos. In 1942 Filipino journalist Carlos Romulo won a Pulitzer Prize for a series of articles about Asia. It was Romulo who had concocted MacArthur's famous "I shall return" declaration. In his acceptance of the Pulitzer, Romulo paid tribute to Hattie Grove, an American teacher sent to the Philippines, whom Romulo said "taught a small pupil to value the beauty of the English language."[27] If one were to calculate the percentage of the population that spoke Tagalog, which would have been a minority, and the percentage of the population that spoke various other regional tongues, and were then to compute what percentage of the population also spoke English, one would find that English would have been among the most widely spoken languages in the country.

Having English spoken so widely may have been a great convenience for Americans living in the Philippines, but the truth is that the nation needed its own language. In reality, the proliferation of English had prevented the emergence of a native tongue as a national dialect. Americans had encouraged a sense of nationalism in the Philippines by allowing Filipinos to govern over their own affairs, but that nationalist pride necessitated the country to settle on a unifying language. Thus, in 1937, Philippine commonwealth President Manuel Quezon declared Tagalog—his own tongue—to be the national language, this despite the fact that Tagalogs made up less than a quarter of the nation's overall population and there were some 80 languages spoken throughout the islands.

The problem for the film industry was that many performers did not speak the language. It remained a problem for years to come. When Eddie Romero was asked by director Gerardo de Leon to write the story for the film *Ang Maestra* (*The Teacher*) in 1941, the young Romero—still a teenager—cautioned de Leon that he did not speak Tagalog. De Leon was undisturbed, telling Romero that they would merely have somebody translate his work into Tagalog afterward.[28] In 1947 Romero made his own directorial debut with the film *Ang Kamay ng Diyos* (*The Hand of God*), still without benefit of speaking the national language. He would direct a half-dozen more Tagalog films before eventually learning the language. Although his friends chided him for years about his poor Tagalog, he was hardly alone. Premiere Productions would become one of the major production companies of the 1950s, and even at that time still found it necessary to hire actor Ruben Rustia to tutor their actors on proper Tagalog pronunciation.[29]

The problem continued to persist into the late–1960s, when Pilar Pilapil, the Philippines' entry in the 1968 Miss Universe pageant in Miami, embarked on a film career after receiving many offers. In the May 1969 edition of *Movie Confidential* one writer felt compelled, after writing of Pilapil's beauty and charm, to say, "At least she's improving her delivery of Tagalog," and went on to write, "She's got her own share of shortcomings. Foremost is her difficulty with the Tagalog language. Her Cebuano accent is so thick that she stumbles on the simplest Tagalog words."[30]

Settling on a unifying language was only a part of the search for some sort of national identity. Through the centuries the islands had come to incorporate quite a diverse racial blend as well. A good number of enduring film stars would begin to emerge in the 1930s, but in what would appear to be a lingering caste prejudice, the biggest stars were usually *mestizos* with de-emphasized Asian features. Leading actresses like Naty Fernandez and Mary Walter could easily pass for Latinos. Walter, for instance, was a pretty *mestiza* of Spanish and German her-

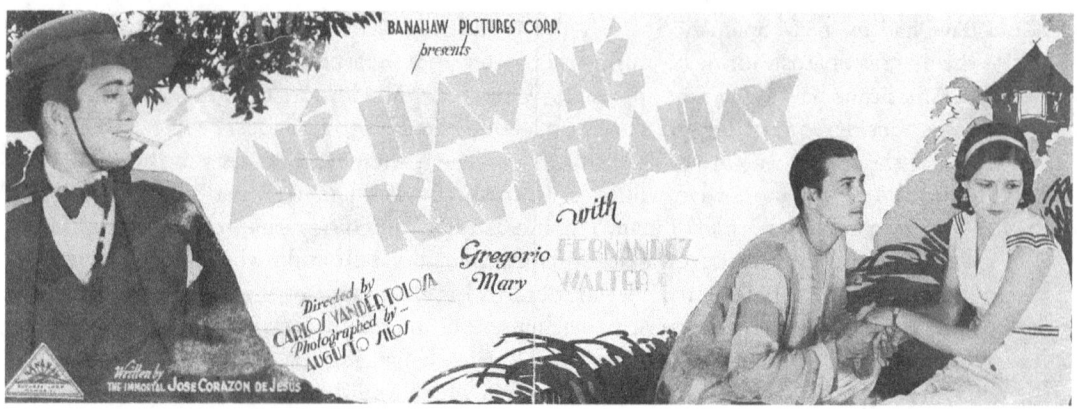

Ang Ilaw ng Kapitbahay (*The Light of the Neighbor*; 1932/Banahaw Pictures) starred Mary Walter, who had the longest career in Philippine cinema, lasting from the silent era until the time of her death in the 1990s.

itage, a *Bicolana* from the southeastern Luzon region. Another of Nepomuceno's discoveries, she was spotted by the director among a crowd that had gathered to watch a film shoot, and Nepomuceno invited her to appear in a dance sequence in the film. Walter made her actual acting debut in the silent film *Ang Lumang Simbahan* (*The Old Church*) in 1928 at the age of 15, playing the role of daughter to Gregorio Fernandez and Sofia Lota. Just a year later she was playing Fernandez's wife in the film *Desperation*. Obviously, she was given diverse roles, and she could be seen playing a tribal princess in *Moro Pirates* in 1931, a victimized young maiden in *Ang Gayuma* (*The Love Potion*) in 1932, and a corpse-devouring ghoul in *Mang Tano: Nuno ng mga Aswang* (*Mang Tano: Descendant of Vampires*), also in 1932, all Nepomuceno films. She eventually transitioned into character roles and in time would achieve the greatest longevity in Philippine cinema, with a career lasting until the time of her death in the 1990s.

And then there was Rosa del Rosario, whose real name was Rose Stagner. She was an American *mestiza* who had been discovered by Jose Nepomuceno's wife, who took notice of del Rosario as she was touring the Malayan Motion Pictures studio lot. Del Rosario was only twelve years old at the time, but Mrs. Nepomuceno was so taken by the enchanting young girl that she asked del Rosario's older sister if her younger sibling might be interested in being in movies. The offer was readily accepted, and the following day a car was sent to pick her up at her home and drive her to the set of her first film, *Ligaw na Bulaklak* (*Wild Flower*) in 1929, in which she was cast as the daughter of actor Jose Padilla. She was promptly renamed Rosa del Rosario, taking her mother's surname.[31] She was very popular in Philippine films during the era, but after marrying American Andrew Cobb, del Rosario left the country and sailed for the United States in September of 1941. Cobb was an actor who was scheduled to star in a film for Filippine Films, but it was said that a film role at MGM brought about his hasty return to the United States.[32] Whether or not he ever did make a picture for MGM, or any other American production company for that matter, is not easy to verify. If he did, he doesn't seem to have had any significant roles. The move back to the U.S. could not have been better-timed, however, as it came less than three months before the first attack on the Philippines by Japan, and it allowed both Cobb and del Rosario to be spared the subsequent Japanese occupation. After the war del Rosario would return to the Philippines, however, to resume her film career with great success.

The caste system has a long history in the Philippines, not surprisingly dating to the Spanish colonial era, when Spaniards were at the top rung of the ladder, with *criollos* (Spaniards born in one of Spain's colonial territories) occupying the next rung. Spanish *mestizos* and mixed Chinese rated above the darker skinned Malays. As far as the caste system's extension into the film industry, aside from being a reflection of the culture, this was at least partially due to the desire to emulate Hollywood and the look of its stars. Seeing the attractive young *mestizos* who were becoming stars, it is interesting to take note of the men who were discovering, casting and essentially creating them, for there is no taking Jose Nepomuceno or Judge Vera for anything other than full-on Asian, whatever ethnic blend their respective backgrounds might include. Both men were dignified and attractive in their way, yet they were obviously not the type that they themselves would have chosen for anything other than supporting or character roles, which are what non-*mestizos* seem to have been limited to: and all of this despite the fact that Spanish *mestizos* made up no more than 1% of the nation's population. Aside from the popular leading ladies, leading men seem also to have been cast largely on the same consideration, many having the appearance of Latin Lotharios. Aside from Fernando Poe, there were popular leading men like Leopoldo Salcedo and, perhaps most popular of all, Rogelio dela Rosa.

Rosa del Rosario in the 1930s. Born Rose Stagner, she was an American mestiza who would enjoy a long film career in the Philippines.

When Jose Nepomuceno was looking for fresh faces for his films he turned for help to Gregorio Fernandez, who suggested Nepomuceno take a look at a nephew of his.[33] Fernandez's nephew was a teenager named Regidor dela Rosa, and after renaming him Rogelio dela Rosa, Nepomuceno cast him in *Ligaw na Bulaklak*. Born in Lubao, Pampanga on November 12, 1916*, dela Rosa was a student who excelled in athletics, captaining an undefeated season for his school's basketball team in Central Luzon. Even after embarking on his acting career, dela Rosa would simultaneously attend Far Eastern University, where he was an inter-collegiate welterweight boxing champion. But his interests were many, and he also excelled at intellectual pursuits, winning debate and oratorical contests in the early 1930s.[34] He had also appeared on the stage in *sarswelas*, singing and specializing in villainous roles. But his villainous stage persona notwithstanding, dela Rosa's six-foot athletic build and boyish good looks made him an ideal leading man for the type of romance sagas that were taking shape as Filipino cinema's most popular genre.

There were some silent film stars in Hollywood who disappeared into oblivion with the advent of talking pictures, their voices sometimes ill suited to sound pictures, sometimes unbe-

---

*While most sources list Rogelio dela Rosa as being born in 1916, some list his birth date as being in 1914, which would seem more likely if his first film was in 1929.

coming of their screen image. In the Philippines sound pictures presented performers with their own set of problems. Nepomuceno was forthright in telling dela Rosa that he didn't feel that the young man had a future in sound pictures: his mastery of Tagalog was lacking. Although dela Rosa spoke impeccable English, and would later become fluent in other languages, he spoke Tagalog with a thick accent that often made it difficult to understand him.[35] But dela Rosa determined to overcome this hurdle, and just as he spoke English with nary a wisp of an accent, and would years later become fluent in French, speaking it with all the effortlessness of a first language, he conquered Tagalog as well, eventually annunciating with ease. No one could have been more pleased than Nepomuceno, who had no desire to see the handsome young man that he himself had groomed for superstardom forced out of the business, and so Nepomuceno gave dela Rosa a chance in a Tagalog feature and cast him in *Diwata sa Karagatan* (*Goddess in Karagatan*). Dela Rosa became the ideal of the Filipino leading man: tall, charming, boyishly handsome, strumming his ukulele or guitar and crooning love songs to the pretty starlets of the day. Nepomuceno's teaming of dela Rosa with Rosa del Rosario cemented the formula of screen love teams, and like Astaire and Rodgers or Gable and Lombard, screen tandems would become a popular draw with the masses. As the 1930s wore on dela Rosa's popularity grew, and he was eventually wooed by Sampaguita Pictures where he was cast in the studio's maiden title, *Bituing Marikit* (*Bright Star*) in 1937. At Sampaguita, dela Rosa would be teamed with other lovely starlets, like singer Elsa Oria, and more popularly with Carmen Rosales, referred to in fan publications of the day as the "Dorothy Lamour of the East."[36] The teaming of dela Rosa and Rosales would last well beyond the '30s, into the postwar years of the 1940s, and finally the 1950s when dela Rosa would abandon his film career in favor of politics.

Rosales was first teamed with dela Rosa in 1939 in the film *Takipsilim* (*Twilight*). Rosales had been a star on radio prior to embarking on her film career, and was called the "Radio Queen." Her husband, Ramon Novales, was also a prominent radio personality who would die fighting against the Japanese during World War II.[37] Although Carmen Rosales may have been his most favored co-star with the movie-going public, dela Rosa's personal favorite co-star and leading lady was indisputably Lota Delgado: dela Rosa married her.

Another interesting residual effect of the Spanish colonial era can be seen in the practice of choosing screen names, which invariably tended to be of the Spanish variety. By way of the Spanish, Filipinos were introduced—or more precisely, converted—to the Christian faith, Catholicism, to be precise. It has been estimated that better than 80% of the country's population has been

Rogelio dela Rosa was the original Philippine matinee idol through the 1930s and '40s. He left show business behind in 1957 when he was elected to the Philippine senate.

baptized into the Church. If the Spanish succeeded at nothing else in the Philippines, they can certainly claim to have made true believers of the majority of the Filipino population. Not even the egregious excesses of the Spanish, or of the friars who came to the islands to disciple the populace, after a fashion, could put the Filipino people off of their Christian faith. As they came to Christianity, many Filipinos came to adopt Spanish surnames appropriate to the faith, resulting in an over-abundance of people with names like del Rosario, Santos, de los Santos, de la Cruz, and any number of other names with a religious connotation. This tended to confuse the Spanish authorities when tax time came, and it was decided that in order to better keep track of the populace, the natives should choose a surname from a list of officially approved choices. In 1849 Governor General Narciso Claveria issued a catalog of approved names for the people to pick from. Most were Spanish names; many were not, but even those of non–Spanish origin took on a distinctly Hispanic flavor. For instance, a Chinese name like "Luk Xin" became "Locsin." By the time the Americans arrived Claveria's decree was fifty years old and the nation was replete with de Leons, del Castillos, Fernandezes and Villas, and just as *mestizos* were favored for leads in motion pictures, there seems also to have been a preference for Hispanic names. Thus, American mestiza Rose Stagner became Rosa del Rosario; the rather plain sounding Marvin Gardner became Eduardo de Castro; Dorothy Jones became Nida Blanca; Carolina Straust became Lilia Dizon; Helen Wessner became Cecilia Lopez; John Montgomery became Johnny Monteiro; Oscar Anson became Oscar Moreno; Maria Grytz became Delia Razon; Sweet Williams became Corazon Rivas; Albert Bregendahl became Ric Rodrigo; Lolita Clark became Lolita Rodriguez; Florence Danon became Rosa Rosal; the list goes on and on. The interesting thing is that many of the stars adopting the desired Spanish names may have had a lineage encompassing nations every bit as prestigious (perhaps, by then, more so), including the United States and many European nations, yet the practice continued for years, so deeply ingrained was the custom. In the late 1950s, Ronald Kookoritchkin, descended from Russian ancestors, was renamed Ronald Remy. One can easily understand a film star wanting to drop the problematic surname Kookoritchkin, yet it is very interesting that a Russian Filipino should take a Spanish name.

More traditional-sounding native names were also eschewed in favor of Spanish. For instance, Bobby Sumilang became Romeo Vasquez and Eduardo Magat became Eduardo del Mar. And so, even as Filipinos were busy living out their own version of the Hollywood dream, they still found themselves adhering to the vestiges of Spanish colonialism.

The 1930s had seen tremendous growth in the industry, though frankly, from its humble beginnings, there was really nowhere to go but up. The industry may have been perpetually hamstrung by inadequate equipment and, despite the blossoming studio system, under-capitalization, but there was a great deal of enthusiasm. The marked improvement in the industry did not necessarily manifest itself in any great strides of a technical nature, but rather of technique. There was a small but talented group of directors responsible for advancing the artistry of the craft in the Philippines. Gerardo de Leon, Lamberto Avellana, Carlos Vander Tolosa, Manuel Silos: these were men who were raising the level of creative integrity in Philippine films. It was through these men that film in the Philippines became something more than merely pointing a camera at actors and shooting. Cinematic composition was naturally an important consideration to the visual aspect of the art of filmmaking.

Manuel Silos had been active in films since the silent era when he and his brothers shot a 16mm film in 1927 called *Tres Sangganos* (*Three Hobos*), which was adapted from a Filipino *komik* strip. Silos and his brothers handled everything, from acting, writing and directing to processing and editing. Born on January 1, 1906, Silos developed an early interest in photography, which was not surprising since his father had opened one of Manila's first photographic studios. His father was also a musician—another interest that Silos inherited. The Silos brothers all gravitated toward the film business in one capacity or another: Octavio Silos was also a director, while brother Cesar became a cinematographer, Luis a soundman, and Augusto a film lab technician. In 1930, Manuel Silos went to work for the fledgling Banahaw Pictures before moving on to work for Parlatone Hispano-Filipino, and then Filippine Films, for which he directed his first sound picture, *Mag-inang Mahirap* (*Poor Mother and Child*), in 1934. But like many of the industry's best talents, by the late 1930s he was doing films for Sampaguita Pictures. With his interest and knowledge of photography, Silos was more technically inclined than many of his contemporaries. He devised the first zoom lens to be used in the Philippines, which he called the "synchro lens," and among his other technical contributions to the craft in the Philippines was his use of montage imagery in films.[38] He accomplished this with another of his inventions, which he immodestly dubbed "Siloscope," a lens that held multiple shots together in one frame. With his background in music, it isn't surprising that Silos came to be known largely for directing musicals, often employing innovative techniques: he was one for using split screens and subjective photography. In the film *Tuloy ang Ligaya* (*Let the Good Times Roll*), for instance, he used subjective photography in a scene in which actress Nida Blanca danced with the camera.

Lamberto Avellana came to the film business by the traditional route of the theater. A 1938 graduate of Ateneo de Manila, where he earned a Bachelor of Arts degree, Avellana established the Barangay Theater Guild with his wife, Daisy Hontiveros, in 1939. Avellana also entered the film business that year when he directed *Sakay* (*The Passenger*).[39] While many of the industry's filmmakers tended toward *komiks* adaptations, saccharine romance sagas and escapist fantasy stories, Avellana's theatrical background had developed his interest in more serious dramatic content and he would help to lead Filipino cinema toward more substantive, issue-driven narratives.

When it comes to advancing the craft of filmmaking in the Philippines, mention needs to be made of Richard Abelardo, a filmmaker whose work was notable for its special effects. He was born in Bulacan on September 29, 1902. His father, Juan Abelardo, was a respected artist who provided the painted backdrops for many of the sarswelas performed in Manila. Richard inherited his father's artistic talent, and he too began to work as a scenic artist when he was a teenager. Abelardo's early work in painting backdrops was at a Manila photographic studio, but his work did not go unnoticed, and he was asked to provide the scenic backdrops for a silent film. Although the film was not completed, the experience created the desire in Abelardo to work in the film industry, and he ultimately had dreams of going to Hollywood. He would realize that dream after joining an orchestra as a saxophone player on an ocean liner in 1923. When the ship docked in San Francisco, Abelardo jumped ship and eventually made his way to Hollywood, where he spent ten years learning the craft of filmmaking, working for prestigious Hollywood studios like Universal, Warner Bros., MGM, and Paramount, and was said to have worked with Charlie Chaplin. With his parents in declining health, Abelardo returned to the Philippines in 1936, where his Hollywood experience no doubt proved useful in finding work in Manila's film industry. Abelardo's talents were varied, and he did not merely paint backdrops, mattes or design sets, but even introduced his colleagues to many of the techniques that he had learned in America, such as background projection. He came to be referred to as the "camera wizard" of local movies and he would use the camera itself to create special effects; for instance, he used the technique of forced perspective to create the illusion of somebody in the palm of a giant. Abelardo would eventually become more than a special effects technician or art director; Fernando Poe allowed him the opportunity to direct a film himself in 1948 for Palaris Productions, Poe's company. But although he would occasionally direct pictures, he remained most in demand for his work designing sets, painting mattes of palaces and kingdoms for costume pictures, and for his ingenuity in creating effects, including prosthetics for monster pictures like *Taong Paniki* (*Bat Man*) and the creature suit for the giant monster film *Tuko sa Madre Kakaw* (*Lizard in Madre Kakaw*), a kind of Filipino Godzilla. His work was regarded highly enough that he would be asked to work with Fritz Lang when the director shot the Hollywood production *An American Guerrilla in the Philippines* on location in 1950.

The industry's appreciable growth, both as a business and an art form, was even enough to inspire Vicente Salumbides into coming out of retirement, and in 1941 he directed *Ibong Adarna* (*Adarna Bird*), which was the first Filipino film to utilize color, as well as being the film in which Richard Abelardo introduced the local industry to the concept of background projection. A costume fantasy, the film starred dashing Fred Cortes as the prince of a mythical land bedeviled by sorcerers and giants. It was not a color picture, *per se*, but rather included sequences in which the multi-colored plumage of the fictitious title bird was painstakingly painted by hand onto the film print.[40] An LVN technician named Ramon Monroy was responsible for the film's color, and audiences were joyfully amazed at the moment when the bird revealed its colorful plumage.

Starring with Cortes in *Ibong Adarna* was Mila del Sol. Born Clarita Rivera in Tondo, Manila on May 12, 1920, del Sol was the younger sister of film actress Gloria Imperial, and as a child she would accompany Imperial to the movie set, occasionally appearing on film herself as an extra in her elder sister's films. LVN matriarch Dona Sisang somehow managed to see her and offered her a starring role in LVN's first film, *Giliw Ko*. It was Dona Sisang who renamed the girl Mila del Sol.

Growth notwithstanding, the industry was still far behind those of America and Europe in most every respect, which would probably surprise no one, but one individual who seemed to be ahead of his contemporaries on any continent was Rogelio dela Rosa. In 1941, while under contract to Sampaguita, dela Rosa made the decision to start his own production company, RDR Productions, which he created as a subsidiary of Filippine Films. At a time when the biggest of Hollywood stars were still bound by the studio system and contracts that kept them beholden to their masters, dela Rosa's gambit would have been bold on either side of the Pacific. But it was really more a thinly veiled subterfuge than any genuine yearning for artistic control.

Dela Rosa had first signed with Sampaguita on August 16, 1937 for only 200 pesos per film, with a monthly salary of 100 pesos. With the success of dela Rosa's initial Sampaguita titles, *Bituing Marikit* and *Inang Mahal* (*Dear Mother*), he was able to renegotiate his contract up to the sum of 600 pesos per film with a 150 pesos monthly salary. His ascendancy to superstardom eventually prompted him to threaten to break his contract and leave unless a new agreement could be reached, and on July 15, 1940 he signed a new four-year contract at the princely sum of 3,000 pesos per film, with the stipulation that he was to appear in at least five films per year.[41] It was the highest price demanded by any Philippine actor of the era. But his once friendly relationship with Sampaguita co-founder Pedro Vera quickly soured when Vera demanded that dela Rosa distance himself from Sampaguita starlet Corazon Noble. Vera had claimed to have received an anonymous letter from other personnel at the studio complaining that an improper relationship had developed between dela Rosa and Noble, a piece of gossip that dela Rosa strongly denied, saying that they were merely good friends whose families had become very close. Dela Rosa claimed a special affection for Noble's younger brother Pepe, whom he said looked up to him like a big brother. But Vera always sought to maintain a family-like atmosphere at the studio, and was particularly protective of the image of his young actresses, and wanting to avoid any suggestion of impropriety, he requested that dela Rosa stop socializing with Noble and her family. It was a suggestion that dela Rosa bitterly resented, and the idea that some of his fellow actors may have been behind the anonymous letter was perhaps even more wounding. Dela Rosa even claimed that his final confrontation with Vera over the matter became so boisterous that they had almost come to blows. When he threatened to leave the studio, dela Rosa was reminded by Vera of their contract, and that, under an agreement signed by all of the studios in 1939 with the instigation of the Motion Picture Producers Association of the Philippines, all of the studios had agreed not to pirate actors, directors, technicians or other employees from one another. This meant that, with his contract not due to expire until July of 1944, dela Rosa's career would be effectively halted for the next three years. Still, dela Rosa found Vera's attitude unreasonable and meddling, and was in the midst of shooting a picture, appropriately titled *Ang Tampuhan* (*The Separation*) when, on July 20, 1941, he failed to show up on the set and effectively broke his contract.[42]

With no other studio legally able to hire him under the terms of the Motion Picture Producers Association agreement, dela Rosa could only hope to continue his career by establishing his own company, which he did by initiating RDR Productions. The problem was that he lacked the sufficient start-up capital and facilities for the venture, not to mention that the personnel needed (skilled technicians of every sort) were all being employed under contract by the studios. It was a problem that he solved by starting his company as a sort of loose subsidiary of Filippine Films, operating out of that company's facilities and using their various technicians. The move wasn't fooling any one.

Vera promptly filed a civil suit in the First District Court of Manila in May of 1941, demanding 15,000 pesos from dela Rosa, plus 500 pesos in legal expenses. The suit also demanded 70,000 pesos from Filippine Films general manager J. Amando Araneta, whom Vera accused of encouraging dela Rosa to leave Sampaguita and come to the Filippine Films facilities to begin their joint venture.[43] Although dela Rosa denied that Araneta had enticed him to leave Sampaguita, with the newly-founded RDR Productions operating right on the Filippine Films lot, there was no doubt that the studio was violating the spirit of the Motion Picture Producers Association agreement, however thinly disguised the working relationship between Filippine Films and RDR Productions may have been. With the litigation the Philippine film industry came of age in the bad sense.

But Sampaguita's dispute with dela Rosa was about to become irrelevant. As Japan waged war on other nations in the region, the Philippines remained shielded by the fact that the nation was a U.S. territory; as long as the U.S. stayed out of the war the Philippine Islands were safe. Then came December 7, 1941 and the attack on Pearl Harbor. With the smoke still billowing from Pearl Harbor, Japanese planes entered the airspace over the Philippine mainland and set their sights on the U.S. naval station in Cavite. The following day at noon President Roosevelt denounced the hostilities initiated by Japan and the U.S. Congress promptly declared war. Any illusion that Americans entertained of staying out of the war went up in flames at Pearl Harbor, and with them went the hopes of Filipinos that they might avoid being caught in the middle of a conflict between two powerful nations. The country braced for the worst. The worst is exactly what they got.

3

1942–1945

On December 8, 1941, President Roosevelt, his voice choked by anguish and rage, denounced the actions of the Japanese. The U.S. had been caught flat-footed at Pearl Harbor, no question, which only makes the events of the following day all the more bewildering. For a full week prior to the attack on Pearl Harbor, aircraft—sometimes unidentified, sometimes known to be Japanese—had been sighted at various places over the Philippine mainland, most notably Clark Field. As early as December 1 unidentified craft had over flown Clark, and radar at Iba Field were picking up blips off the coast of Luzon on December 2. Colonel Harold George had surmised that they were reconnoitering to establish data in order to finalize attack plans, and when a formation of Japanese bombers were spotted within twenty miles of the beaches of Lingayen Gulf Major General Lewis Brereton felt that they were familiarizing themselves with the route that they would take in staging their attack.[1] Phoning from Washington, Brigadier Leonard T. Gerow, who was chief of the army's War Plans Division, told MacArthur that he wouldn't be surprised if the Japanese attacked the Philippines in the "near future."[2] Still, General MacArthur remained convinced that the Japanese would not attack before January 1: maybe that was "near future" enough for MacArthur. It doesn't seem to have been a view held by Philippine commonwealth president Manuel Quezon. As dawn broke in the Philippines on December 8, word was reaching Manila that Davao Gulf was under attack by enemy aircraft. Shortly after 7:00 A.M. Quezon had issued a press statement, which was being broadcast over radio station KMZH repeatedly, warning Filipinos that "zero hour has arrived." Quezon implored Filipinos to do their duty, and he concluded by stating "We have pledged our honor to stand by the United States and we shall not fail her, happen what may."[3]

By 9:30 A.M. word was reaching Brereton that the Japanese had launched carrier-based attacks on various installations in northern Luzon. Carriers would not have been sufficient to launch a significant attack on Clark, and perhaps the attacks were misread to mean that a strike on Clark was not eminent. The truth was that the Japanese armada slated to attack Clark was delayed by heavy fog at their base on Formosa. It was something that greatly concerned the Japanese since word of the attack on Pearl Harbor had surely reached the Philippines by then, and they believed that a U.S. attack on Formosa was probably on the way. The Japanese donned their gas masks to await the attack, but as the morning wore on and the fog lifted, with no U.S. attack arriving, they proceeded with their plans.

Shortly past noon, Manila time, on December 8, Japanese planes made their approach at Clark Field in the Philippines. Forty miles to the west at Iba Field a radio operator had been sending desperate messages to Clark to warn them of the impending attack. Unfortunately for that radio operator, he met his fate as the Japanese rained bombs on the Iba base and obliterated it. Unfortunately for everyone, his frantic messages went unheard as the radio operator at Clark was in the mess hall enjoying lunch with everybody else and the radio was left unmanned. There was a disturbingly widespread opinion at the base that the attack on Pearl Harbor was no more than a rumor concocted as a wily attempt to keep the men on their toes. After finishing lunch, the men at Clark heard a commercial radio broadcast announce that their base was under attack. Looking around, they could see that things were peaceful and serene and they laughed. As they continued to laugh about it and relax they began to hear the faint hum of Japanese planes making their final approach. The Japanese could hardly believe their fortunes: there before them on the ground was America's largest overseas air armada, and practically none of them prepared for takeoff, save three B-17s which had taxied in preparation for a Formosa recon mission. It was like shooting fish in a barrel. Within an hour America's air power in the Pacific was as crippled as the previous day's events had left its naval power. The attack on Clark killed some eighty men while destroying 32 of 36 P-40 fighter planes and 14 of 17 B-17 bombers.

The events at Pearl Harbor had been ominous for the Philippines, but at least occurred at a comfortable distance. If there were any doubts left as to whether or not the Philippines would be directly drawn into the conflict, the debacle at Clark definitively settled the matter. For the Philippines, the war was on.

Hoping to insulate the civilian population against an aggressive military campaign, MacArthur declared Manila an "open city" on December 24th, after ordering his troops to retreat to Bataan. MacArthur himself fled to Corregidor, as did Manuel Quezon. While MacArthur may have bitterly resented the lack of support from Washington, he could scarcely have taken it more personally than did Quezon, who railed against Washington's prioritizing the situation in Europe over the Pacific theater. "How typically American," he barked, "to writhe in anguish at the fate of a distant cousin while a daughter is being raped in a back room."[4] Quezon's rant was occasioned by President Roosevelt's decision to send planes to Britain while no such assistance was forthcoming to the Philippines. The description of the British as "distant cousins" is especially peculiar since the U.S. began its existence as a British colony—was indeed *founded* by British settlers.

It must have been a rude awakening for Quezon, and while many might be surprised at how Quezon could imagine that ties to the Philippines could have been more significant to the U.S. than its ties—historical, strategic, and simply practical—to Europe, his tirade underscores the extent to which Filipinos looked to the U.S. as a paternal entity. He sounded rather like a wounded child upon learning that anyone could be more esteemed in his father's eye.

Still, for all of his tirades and bluster, Quezon was also capable of exemplifying the interesting bond between the U.S. and the Philippines. In February of 1942, Quezon prepared to leave Corregidor and sail for the U.S. where he was to set up a government-in-exile. Before leaving, he took MacArthur by the hand and placed his signet ring on the U.S. general's finger. With all of the endearing melodrama so typical of Filipinos, Quezon looked MacArthur in the eye and said, "When they find your body, I want them to know that you fought for my country."[5] Quezon did not see the conclusion of the war, for the tuberculosis that dogged him would claim his life in New York in 1944.

The unique U.S.–Philippine relationship was something the Japanese did not seem altogether prepared to deal with, nor do they seem to have fully comprehended it. Japanese culture tended to be far more homogenous than the multi-layered cultural landscape of the Philippines, which had come to incorporate a wide and varied array of influences. It is likely that the Japanese viewed the American presence as just another colonial ruling power and that they did not entertain the notion of there being any genuine connection or commonality with the native population. During the course of the war, the Japanese had successfully dislodged European colonial powers throughout Asia, capturing territories from the Dutch, British and French, and found the peoples of those colonial territories often very willing to fight against their European masters. Was it a sense of Asian oneness that found them so receptive to the idea, or merely an act of pragmatism? The Japanese were not above using brutality, or the threat thereof, as a means of coercion. Whatever the reason, it did not extend into the Philippines, where the Japanese found that many more Filipinos seemed to be willing to side with the Americans, despite the often-horrific consequences wrought by the Japanese. It says something very interesting about the U.S. colonial experiment that Filipino loyalty to the U.S. should have grown so strong in less than half a century; after all, in the three centuries of Spanish rule of the islands, such loyalty to Spain was still largely absent at the time of the Spanish-American War. In a sense, the Filipino loyalty to America could be seen as somewhat surprising; Americans living in the Philippines—be they soldiers, teachers or businessmen—were, for the most part, not given to socializing with Filipinos, and lived rather insulated from the native population, excluding them from their prominent social circles. Most Americans seemed to view their time in the Philippines as a distasteful chore, and looked down their noses at Filipinos as unruly, dirty and lazy semi-savages. Paradoxically, many Americans who had come to the Philippines to work at remolding the society in one way or another felt stymied as well by the rigid class structure that had been in place, feeling that it prohibited even the notion of upward mobility and therefore discouraged or even nullified any realistic expectation of spurring economic growth by inspiring Filipinos to dream of a better future that could be attained through diligence. And yet, for all their unfortunate prejudices (which, it needs to be said, is a historical part of America's European patrimony), the American policy itself was driven by a genuine—even noble—ideal, that being the propagation of democracy, which was at that time still much more a grand experiment. But it was not so much Americans themselves that many Filipinos encountered that inspired their loyalty (although there were doubtless many who did), as it was the inspiration that they drew from American ideals. A renowned Filipino educator named Francisco Benitez credited the United States with endowing Filipinos with their sense of nationalism and proclaimed that Filipinos could prove their worth only by seeking the ideals that had so richly blessed America.[6]

While many of the earliest Americans to arrive in the Philippines may have been discouraged upon arriving and setting about their tasks, by the time of World War II American ideals had clearly made an impression and taken hold.

On January 2, 1942, the Japanese entered Manila, moving efficiently and expeditiously seizing control of the city. For Filipino society the transformation was immediate and radical. Feeling that Filipinos had become Westernized to an appalling degree, the Japanese immediately set about their own remolding of the culture. Their aim was to wean the people of such American ideals as individualism and material aspirations and to reinstate a sense of Asian nationalism, a more labor-oriented spirit, and education centered on vocational skills. They sought to eradicate the widespread use of English, and made the Japanese language, Niponggo, a co-national language with Tagalog. After taking control of the nation's newspapers and radio stations (most of which were immediately closed down), the Japanese Propaganda Corps, the *Sendenbu* (later the Department of Information, or *Hodobu*, when it was determined that the word "propaganda" had a duplicitous ring to it), began portraying the Americans as cruel but cowardly oppressors, and tried to reawaken a more suitably Asian outlook (Filipino clocks were set to Japan time, Japanese holidays were observed), but for all of their efforts, the Japanese found that Filipinos were not so easily subdued as a culture. As a result of their Westernization they had been well educated (particularly with the U.S. presence), and having been long under the authority of foreigners, Filipinos were far too savvy as to what the Japanese were up to.

Once the proper machinery was in place for monitoring media outlets, the Japanese had allowed certain newspapers and radio stations to resume operations, but the industry that undoubtedly suffered most demonstrably under occupation was the nation's film industry, which was effectively halted. With all of the film studios closed down, the industry's workers had to find some means of subsistence, and so many of them took to working in the theater, a form of entertainment that the Japanese were quicker to allow, although that also had a great deal to do with the shortage of raw nitrate stock during the war. Performers and artists had to put their various talents to use where and when they could. Director Manuel Silos returned to the stage as an actor, and otherwise made extra cash as a xylophone player in Manila nightclubs.[7] But with all of the personnel displaced by the closing of the film studios, there was simply not enough stage work to go around. The most popular actors could find work in theater, as could the more highly respected directors, and some technicians could find jobs in stagecraft of some type, being employed as set dressers or lighting and wardrobe personnel, but there were many more who could not. Some unfortunate actresses found themselves forced by necessity into prostitution just to survive, as were many ordinary housewives.[8]

William P. Smith, the person most responsible for bringing sound to Philippine cinema, busied himself in an altogether different fashion. He worked with the U.S. Army, repairing communications equipment and helping to arrange needed supplies for such equipment. Eventually Smith was captured by the Japanese and sent to Fort Santiago, which the Japanese had set up as a detention center. Another prisoner detained at Fort Santiago was film director Eduardo de Castro, who had left Manila when the Japanese moved in and had gone to the hills to join the resistance.

It didn't take long for the Japanese to realize that, along with cockfighting, cinema was a national pastime immensely popular among Filipinos, and wanting to disrupt the daily lives of the populace as little as possible, they began to allow theaters to reopen. Aside from the deleterious effect that it would have on their own image and what they were trying to accomplish, the Japanese knew that depriving the Filipinos of such a beloved recreation activity would also deny the enormous propaganda value of the medium. They allowed recent Filipino films to run, and otherwise began to import Japanese films into the country, but there was never enough product to fill the theaters, and they found themselves obliged to allow pre-war American films that were already on hand to run on occasion (importing any further American films was strictly prohibited). All films had to be passed by the *Eiga Haikyusha* (Movie Distribution Company), however.

Importing Japanese films would help better acquaint Filipinos with Japanese culture and customs, but the Japanese wanted to cement the relationship more thoroughly, while estranging Filipinos from the Americans. To fully utilize the propaganda potential of film, the Japanese commissioned a film, knowing that the use of popular local stars would make the message more palatable, and was probably even necessary if such an endeavor were to succeed. In 1943 the *Eiga Haikyusha*, in association with Toho Films, produced *The Dawn of Freedom*, which was to be jointly directed by Japan's Abe Yutaka and respected Filipino director Gerardo de Leon. Under the circumstances, the title was more than a little ironic, concocted as it was by an ironfisted conquering power during wartime. Aside from portraying the Americans in as negative a light as possible, the film sought to promote goodwill among the Japanese and Filipinos, while encouraging Filipinos to accept Japan's authority over them, but de Leon inserted nudging signals to his countrymen. He was very deliberate, for instance, in his choice of camera angles, at one point portraying Filipino lead Fernando Poe as towering over his Japanese co-stars.⁹ While Filipinos may not generally be considered as being as cinematically adept as their Japanese counterparts, de Leon had a keen understanding of the power of cinematic imagery, and he effectively got one over on his Japanese colleagues.

Gerardo de Leon was a tall, lean, bespectacled gentleman with a dignified air about him. American actor John Ashley, who worked with de Leon on two films in the 1960s, once described him as the John Huston of Philippine films.¹⁰ There was no whimsy in the comparison; the respect accorded de Leon was great.

Born in Bulacan on September 12th of 1913, de Leon's artistic sensibilities were no doubt nurtured from the start, having been born into a family with a strong inclination toward the arts. De Leon's father was Hermogenes Ilagan, the well-known writer who had co-authored the *sarswela Dalagang Bukid*, which had been adapted to the screen by Jose Nepomuceno in 1919. De Leon's mother, Casiana de Leon, was a singer. Still, it looked like young Gerry might follow another path entirely when as a young man he enrolled as a medical student at the University of Santo Tomas in the 1930s. While pursuing his degree, however, de Leon's interest in drama proved irresistible and he began appearing in films as an actor in 1937. He made his debut that year in the film *Pusong Dakila* (*Foolish Heart*), and he followed up with appearances in a string of features in 1938, including *Ang Pagbabalik* (*The Return*), *Bukang Liwayway* (*Daybreak*), *Isang Halik Lamang* (*Just One Kiss*) and *Mga Sugat ng Puso* (*Wounds of the Heart*). His acting career notwithstanding, de Leon would still go on to complete his education, receiving his degree as a Doctor of Medicine in 1938. He seldom practiced, however, and it was also in 1938 that he began his career as a director with *Bahay-Kubo* (*Hut Dwelling*). In 1939 he directed *Ama at Anak* (*Father and Son*), in which he also appeared as an actor. It was a rare appearance by de Leon in a film that he would also direct.¹¹

De Leon may not have been too enthused about shilling for the Japanese propaganda machine, but his subversive imagery aside (which apparently went unnoticed by the *Sendenbu*), the Japanese authorities were pleased with his work and did feel that they managed to get their message across. At one point in the film, for instance, a fleeing American soldier mows down a Filipino civilian with a jeep and kills him.¹² This was the image of America that the Japanese wanted Filipinos to see—cowardly and callously indifferent.

De Leon was not the only high-profile Filipino involved in the project. Aside from Poe, the cast included a number of other luminaries from the local industry, including Angel Esmeralda, Leopoldo Salcedo, Norma Blancaflor and Rosa Aguirre.

The film's obvious propagandistic bent was easily seen through by most Filipinos, but in the April 29, 2005, edition of the *Philippine Daily Inquirer*, Daniel H. Dizon of the *War History Club of Angeles* wrote a curiously revisionist piece in which he sought to lend credence to the Japanese perspective. While allowing that, at the time, most Filipinos dismissed the film as "naked enemy propaganda," Dizon went on to note what he considered to be the grim reality of Filipino soldiers starving as "the Americans, safe in the rear, ate full daily rations!" Had he been referring to MacArthur and his companions on Corregidor, the point would have been well taken, as MacArthur, his wife and son, and Philippine commonwealth president Manuel Quezon and his wife were among those on the island, which was stocked to feed ten thousand men for six months. Since Dizon clearly comes across as an admirer of Quezon's, this does not seem to be his point. Dizon's sophistry seems driven by the kind of anti-Americanism that, while more in vogue of late, was not common to his own generation (Dizon was around in 1943 and actually viewed *Dawn of Freedom* in its initial run. In fact, he claims to have been shocked himself at the time by the film's depiction of the Americans.). The truth is that the vast majority of U.S. troops were in Bataan starved and disease-ridden with the Filipino army. Major General Jonathan Mayhew Wainwright IV, who was himself in Bataan, would later say, "If we had something in our bellies things would have been a little more endurable."[13]

U.S. soldiers in Bataan became very resentful toward MacArthur as they suffered with dysentery, scurvy and malaria, their rations dissipated to the point that they were killing any animal they could find—lizards, snakes, dogs or cats—for sustenance. The sick and wounded languished in often excruciating pain for lack of medical supplies. Hardly the portrait of "overbearing American soldiers, most of whom were in the safety of the rear lines and had total control over Filipino soldiers, munitions and all food supplies" that was depicted in *Dawn of Freedom*, and that Dizon sought to defend in hindsight. While American troops may have grown embittered toward MacArthur, by contrast, the Filipino soldiers held him in high regard, revering him as an almost god-like figure, as they tend to do with their own homegrown heroes. One need only look at how Filipinos themselves depicted the years under the Japanese occupation in subsequent films made after the war and the granting of full independence by the U.S. to see how Filipinos truly felt about the experience. Philippine cinemas were replete with war films depicting the barbarity of the Japanese, while rancor toward the U.S. does not seem to have been a common sentiment. Nor was de Leon the only one sending out clandestine messages: there were public performances, for instance, of the song *Bakit Hindi Ka Pa Dumarating?* (Why Have You Not Returned?), an allusion to MacArthur's well known promise. Dr. Ricardo T. Jose, Ph.D. of the University of the Philippines has written that some Filipinos, in an open show of contempt for the news disseminated by the Japanese, were known to read the newspapers upside down.[14] Contempt for the Japanese was nowhere in short supply.

Because of his work on *Dawn of Freedom*, de Leon was shown a degree of favor by the Japanese, and they tapped him to direct *Tatlong Maria* (Three Marias) in 1944. They also freed William Smith from detention in order to take advantage of his expertise as a soundman for the project.

Based on a novel by Jose Esperanza Cruz, the film was adapted for the screen by a Japanese screenwriter, Tsutomu Sawamura, and while it did extol the virtues that the Japanese were trying to engender, it was far less a propaganda piece than *Dawn of Freedom*. Starring Carmen Rosales, Norma Blancaflor, Liwayway Arceo and Fernando Poe, the film tried to shore up Filipino values with a rural tale that emphasized a strong work ethic, which the Japanese felt had suffered under Western imperialism, succumbing to the kind of greed that they felt exemplified American values. The Japanese were somewhat dispirited at the lack of moral clarity in Filipino culture and hoped that the film would bolster more traditional values. It isn't easy to say just how well this message went over.

Otherwise, the Japanese had put out another blatant propaganda tract, *Victory Song of the Orient*, which trumpeted Japan's triumphs in Bataan and Corregidor. The film was celebratory in tone, not just for the supremacy of Japanese military might, but also for Asian unity and the bright new future that these victories promised the people of the Philippines.

But as the Japanese were promising a new era of prosperity and freedom under Japanese authority, Filipino resentments simmered. Although the Japanese were intent on promoting Asian nationalism, Philippine nationalism was not on the agenda: the Philippine flag and national anthem were banned. In hushed tones, Filipinos spread word of the rumored rape of Nanking, and the conduct of the Japanese in the Philippines was not inspiring much confidence among the people. All of the propaganda was more than counteracted by Japanese conduct: private property was confiscated; women were rounded-up into groups to serve as "comfort women," sex slaves for the amusement of Japanese soldiers.

The virtual annihilation of the film industry had consequently revitalized Philippine theater, starved as the people were for some form of entertainment to relieve the stresses of their daily lives. While theater was also under the strict and watchful eye of the Japanese, its rejuvenation was still somewhat cathartic not just for the audience, but also its performers. It was not a great leap for some: Lamberto Avellana, for instance, had begun his career in the theater, and was therefore right at home in transitioning back. The Japanese allowed him to run the Philippine Artists' League, which performed plays at the Avenue Theatre. But, ever the maverick, Avellana had a hard time abiding by the requirements of the Japanese. Hired to direct the play *Bukang Liwayway* (*Beautiful Sunrise*), which was written by a Japanese playwright, Avellana balked at presenting what he considered a bit of bald-faced propaganda. His resistance worn down by the realities of the moment, he eventually relented, but still found himself quibbling with the Japanese over the audience response to certain passages. The play starred Leopoldo Salcedo as a Filipino guerrilla fighting in opposition to the Japanese occupation, and when he defends his reasoning upon capture, the audiences responded a might too enthusiastically for Japanese liking. When the Japanese complained that the audience was not getting the message that was intended, Avellana replied that Salcedo was a very popular movie star and that the audience was bound to respond vigorously to any melodramatic moment from him. This was unacceptable, however, and the Japanese authorities ordered Salcedo be promptly replaced. Dr. Jose has also written that, despite Salcedo's firing, the passage was greeted boisterously by Filipinos irrespective of who was delivering it, and that the Japanese were compelled to cancel the play's run altogether.

While it may not have suited their purpose nearly so well, the Japanese were far more willing to allow the citizenry to while away their leisure time laughing at the misadventures of Pugo and Togo, a pair of former *vod-a-vil funnymen-cum-film stars* who had returned to the stage. Even there the Japanese may have outsmarted themselves. Part of the reason that the audiences took such positive affirmation from the stage antics of Pugo and Togo was not just their comedic antics, or the fact that they were nudging the audience with sly and subtle ridicule of the Japanese, but they were said to have been giving their countrymen hidden messages of impending liberation. They even made on-stage references to "Mang Arturo," an affectionate reference to General MacArthur, which was beyond the Japanese ability to comprehend. One legend that has persisted is that Pugo and Togo were even using their stage act to pass coded messages to allied forces through certain audience members. That might sound a bit cloak-and-dagger, but it was an extraordinary time, and while there doesn't seem to be any hard evidence to substantiate it, it is certainly not beyond the realm of possibility.

The audiences may have responded

Leopoldo Salcedo and Mila del Sol in the early 1940s. Salcedo was dubbed "The Great Profile," a moniker lifted from references in America to John Barrymore.

enthusiastically to any actor delivering a monologue with a hint of nationalistic verve, but Avellana was not exaggerating when citing Salcedo's popularity. Born in Cavite on March 13, 1912, Salcedo was a handsome, dignified and eloquently spoken Spanish *mestizo* whose family line was said to run back to Miguel Lopez de Legazpi. His grandfather was said to have been a Spanish provincial military governor in Cavite. Though Spanish, Salcedo's father, Juan Salcedo, chose to live in the Philippines even after his parents and siblings had decided to return to Spain. He met and married a fisherman's daughter from Binakayan, and started a family, Leopoldo being the second of six children. Despite the family's prestigious heritage, they were said to be of modest means. As a 17-year-old boy, Leopoldo Salcedo was drawn to performing and (having dropped out of school, and then left the seminary after a year) he ran off to join Barromeo Lou's *vod-a-vil* troupe. He also had a good singing voice and would sometimes perform a number as an opening act for the main attraction. His initial involvement in the film industry was the somewhat odd job of promoting films by dressing in costumes and riding a horse around town announcing the current titles at local theaters.[15] Upon embarking on a film career, Salcedo's good looks ensured his success, and he was very popular with the ladies. His first break in films came in 1934 with the film *Sawing Palad* (*Misfortune*), which starred Rogelio dela Rosa. Owing to his looks, the Filipino press had dubbed Salcedo "the Great Profile," a moniker lifted from a description previously used in the United States in reference to the famed American actor John Barrymore. Likening Salcedo to Barrymore was more than a matter of a complimentary profile: just as Barrymore was a highly respected thespian, Salcedo came to be regarded by many as the Philippines' greatest actor. Unlike others in the industry with a stage background—particularly those with *vod-a-vil* experience—Salcedo had an understanding of the more subtle nuances of the medium of film and how the camera is better able to more intimately convey smaller moments and emotions even to those sitting at the back of the room. He adjusted his performing style accordingly and as a result his performances tended to be more subdued than the often flamboyant and overwrought performances of his colleagues. Through the years he would give some of the more memorable and acclaimed performances in Philippine cinema, acting in over 200 films. He was also known to be something of a ladies' man, marrying five times and fathering 14 children. Salcedo died of heart failure in Pasig in 1998 at the age of 86.

Many of the musical scores for the stage shows performed during the war were provided by Tito Arevalo, a former actor and film score composer who had left show business before the war. His given name was Eustacio Ilagan, and he was born on March 29, 1911 in Manila. His father was Hermogenes Ilagan, and so he grew up steeped in the world of the theater and the sarswelas. Both Arevalo and his brother, Gerardo de Leon, began their careers in show business as teenagers, working as piano players in Manila movie theaters, providing musical accompaniment for silent films. Somehow, despite the family's tradition of working in the arts, the Ilagans did not view show business as a true career, and whereas brother Gerry went on to study medicine, Arevalo chose law as his profession. But also like his brother, Arevalo was irresistibly drawn to performing and, adopting his mother's maiden name for his show business dabblings, he began appearing in films in minor roles while still a student. It wasn't long before he began receiving starring roles, including leads in films directed by his brother Gerry. But music was his true passion, and he also worked as a musician in many of the most popular nightclubs on Escolta Street.

Having passed the bar exam in 1938, Arevalo left show business to work as a lawyer for the NBI (the National Bureau of Investigation, the Philippine equivalent of the FBI). While the war was responsible for depriving many in the entertainment industry of their livelihood, the opposite was true with Arevalo: in his case, the war brought about his return to show business. As the Japanese had abolished the NBI, Arevalo suddenly found himself unemployed, and so began composing music for theatrical productions. He could have returned to the NBI after the war, but was convinced instead by Fernando Poe to continue composing, as original music was needed for the resuscitating film business.

Arevalo was quite prolific in scoring films, and he would go on to win FAMAS (Filipino Academy of Motion Picture Arts and Sciences) awards for the music he provided for his brother's films *Noli Me Tangere* (1961), *El Filibusterismo* (1962), and *Lilet* (1971). Although he had abandoned his acting career after the war in favor of music, later in life he would do the reverse, and he began appearing in films again as an actor in the 1980s and '90s.

As the war progressed, the tide began to turn and the yearning among Filipinos for MacArthur's return was all the more palpable. Many Filipinos had wept openly as they watched American soldiers being led captive by the Japanese army through the streets of Manila on the last leg of the infamous Bataan Death March. On February 3, 1945, the U.S. First Cavalry entered the northernmost part of Manila and was welcomed by jubilant Filipinos who flooded the streets. But the city's ordeal was far from over. Although General Tomoyuki Yamashita had declared Manila an "open city" and had ordered the Japanese troops to leave the city, one of his underlings, Rear Admiral Sanji Iwabuchi, disregarded Yamashita's order and decided to try and prevent the Americans from taking the Manila harbor, feeling duty bound to oppose the Americans as long as possible, if for no other reason than to delay the U.S. military's movement toward Japan. As the Americans progressed, the fighting became fierce, and the resulting chaos and carnage was just what Yamashita—and MacArthur before him—had sought to avoid.

Mortar and cannon fire rained from both sides, and the people of the city found themselves caught in the middle. In Malate, American Elizabeth Kelly saw her sister-in-law fall dead in the streets, her body ripped by shrapnel. With her daughter Elizabeth and two-year-old son Ronnie, Kelly found herself caught in the congestion of the mass of civilians who had flooded the streets to try and flee the shelling. She was trying to get to Rizal Avenue where her husband, Fernando Poe, was appearing in a play at the Avenue Theatre. It took hours to make their way through the throng of people to the bridge that traversed the Pasig River. Upon finally reaching the other side and arriving at the theater, Kelly learned that her husband had fled in the opposite direction *toward* Malate in a desperate attempt to reach his family.[16] Fortunately, Poe, his wife and their children would all survive the battle of Manila. Not so lucky was actress Rosario Moreno, who was among the more than 100,000 civilians to be killed in the ferocious fighting.

It needs to be said that, while artillery fire from both sides claimed the lives of most of the 100,000, many of the civilian casualties in Manila were the result of wanton slaughter by the Japanese. As American troops drew closer to Manila, the Japanese had gone on a rampage, murdering men, women and children: women were raped; even little babies were speared on bayonets. They set fires that spread quickly through the slums and gunned down whole families in more a·uent residential areas. To top off their sub-human barbarism, the Japanese strapped patients to their beds as the hospitals were set ablaze: so much for the Asian unity that the Japanese had initially sought to promote.

The battle for Manila was one of the war's bloodiest and most hard fought, dragging on for weeks, house-to-house, building-to-building, culminating in the battle for the old walled city of Intramuros. Although Yamashita was willing to relinquish Manila, he still sought to cling to the archipelago in order to slow U.S. progress to Japan. The result was protracted jungle warfare from one island to the next as the Japanese resolved to fight to the bitter end. They found themselves in much the same condition as U.S. and Philippine soldiers had been in Bataan, perhaps even more so: diseased and starving, even to the point that stories would surface of Japanese soldiers cannibalizing one another.[17] On Corregidor, Japanese soldiers committed mass suicide by detonating an underground weapons depot. On Leyte, there were reports of Japanese soldiers being killed by Filipino villagers.

Meanwhile, in Manila, even as the mopping up continued (the city was not secured until early in the month of March), U.S. soldiers were serenaded by a Filipino band playing "God Bless America." It would not be until July 5, 1945, that MacArthur would formally announce the liberation of the Philippines, but life had slowly begun to return to normal in Manila much earlier, as merchants returned to their shops and ordinary commerce began to resume. Citizens who had fled the city were also returning to what remained of their homes. For a scarred society in tatters, the long recuperative process could finally begin.

4

1946–1956

Emerging from the rubble of the war, the nation was eager to move beyond the horrors of the preceding three years. The road to recovery would be difficult, but Filipinos had reason to be hopeful, if not a bit anxious, about their country's future: the U.S. was ready to grant full independence to the Philippines. It was the first time that any imperialist power had willingly ceded territory to a native population.

There was legitimate reason to question whether or not the nation was capable of tackling the responsibility of sovereignty so immediately upon crawling from the wreckage of a devastating war, but naturally politics loomed large in the decision. The U.S. was pledged to granting sovereignty, and was obligated to follow through. Filipino politicians, including president Sergio Osmena, were doubtless reticent to suggest postponing sovereignty, as they knew it would surely be seized upon by political opponents as a sign of weakness, although they likely knew that postponement was more than reasonable under the circumstances. They needn't have been so cautious. Paul McNutt, scheduled to become the U.S. ambassador to the new independent republic, had expressed the idea publicly in a press conference in 1945 that most Filipinos were not particularly desirous of independence.[i] Filipino politicians and civilians alike were weary of losing U.S. patrimony, although, again, they needn't have been so anxious. Although political autonomy came to the islands, dependence on the U.S. did not wane.

With the Philippines set to become an independent nation for the first time in its history, the country was about to enter into a new and exciting era. But the first order of business was the physical and emotional healing, and in that respect, just as entertainment had helped the populace endure the tribulations of the occupation, cinema was a vital component in the process of national recovery. Cinemas in the Philippines had begun to reopen in late 1945, although it would be well into 1946 before new product was being produced at home. Still, Hollywood films provided a well-needed diversion from the arduous process of extricating the country from the trauma of war. Besides, most theaters in the Philippines had exclusive arrangements with U.S. studios: the Avenue Theater in Manila, for instance, showed only Paramount films, while the Lyric Theater was beholden to Warner Brothers.

When the Filipino film studios were again operating, it was only natural that they should participate in the emotional exorcism so badly needed for the national psyche. Filipino film production resumed in 1946 with the film *Orasang Ginto* (*The Golden Clock*) by director Manuel Conde. The film signaled the trend in productions that portrayed both the horrors of the occupation and the bravery of Filipino resistance, in particular the guerrilla fighters. Octavio Silos wrote and directed *Ulilang Watawat* (*The Forlorn Flag*) for Sampaguita, which heralded the production as "Our first picture after the liberation," and ran ads that dedicated the film to "the dead and living heroes of the Philippines." Brother Manuel Silos directed *Victory Joe* for LVN Pictures, a film that took its title from the slogan used by Filipinos to greet American soldiers upon their triumphant return to Manila. The film starred Rogelio dela Rosa, who seems to have been less interested in running his own production company and signed with LVN. Under the direction of his cousin, Dr. Gregorio Fernandez, dela Rosa would also star in *Garrison 13*, which was promoted by LVN as the story of "2 devil-may-care guerrilla brothers—a price on their heads—fighting for their country and the women they love." The two brothers of the story were, in fact, played by real-life brothers as dela Rosa was cast alongside his younger brother Jaime. The promotional ads promised the film to deliver "Atrocities that will make you scream" and depicted the two brothers being tortured by their Japanese captors. Such grim imagery was commonplace in promotional campaigns for Filipino war pictures of the era. The Nolasco Brothers Pictures' production *Fort Santiago*, which starred Leopoldo Salcedo, was promoted with ads that featured the rather jarring depiction of a Filipino woman about to be beheaded by a sword-wielding Japanese soldier. Similarly, the ads for *Walang Kamatayan (Deathless)* showed a Japanese officer, sword raised, amid images of dead Filipino women and children. "At last!" the ads proclaimed, "It is here! This mighty picture of [the] courage and valor of our own guerrillas. A human document of the beastly atrocities committed during the Japanese regime! A picture dedicated to those who have not died in vain!"

Aside from showing images of Japanese brutality, the ads for *Oo, Ako'y Espiya (Yes, I Am a Spy)* also showed Japanese soldiers being punched, flung and manhandled by brave Filipinos. There may be no more telling image, however, than the simple ad for the film *Maynila (Manila)* in 1946. Devoting the top half of the ad to flattering depictions of the film's three attractive *mestizo* stars (handsome Ely Ramos, pretty Corazon Noble, and angelic Tita Duran), the bottom half of the ad is an artist's rendering of a Japanese soldier running, torch in hand, as Manila goes up in flames in the background. The Japanese soldier's face is quite a contrast to the three attractive Filipinos above; it is barely recognizable as human, distorted as it is in an angry, contorted, evil—even demonic—visage.

Noble was herself labeled by the local press as a victim of Japanese atrocities, and was indeed a witness before the War Crimes Commission in the trial of General Yamashita. In fact, she was the first witness called in Yamashita's trial, testifying to how a Japanese soldier had stabbed her baby to death, even as she cradled the child in her arms. Upon completing *Maynila* she was slated to travel to Japan to further testify against Japanese accused of war crimes.

In 1946 it seems that most every filmmaker had to weigh in with their own contribution to the national purgation. As producer, director and star, Fernando Poe made *Dugo ng Bayan (Blood of the People)* for Palaris Films, which promoted the film as its "humble tribute to the Filipino soldier," and otherwise proclaimed the film to be "the authentic story of a people fit to live because they were not afraid to die." Poe also produced, directed and starred in *Intramuros: The Rape of a City* in 1946 for a production outfit known as ABG.

Lamberto Avellana filmed *Death March* for Philippine Pictures, Inc., which starred Leopoldo Salcedo. "A historic portrayal," said the ads, "of the most thrilling episode in a people's struggle for freedom and democracy amidst a reign of terror and oppression." Salcedo also starred in director Luis Nolasco's *Ginoong Patay Gutom (Mr. Destitute)* for Nolasco Brothers, which enticed viewers to "See ... how G. Patay-Gutom treats Japanese snipers." *Ginoong Patay Gutom* had actually started production in 1941 before the war had come to the Philippines, but apparently not wanting to waste what had been shot, Luis Nolasco decided to resume with production in 1946, with obvious revisions to the story.

An interesting glimpse at the high emotion spilling from Filipino culture in the immediate aftermath of the war can be seen in a review of the film *Fort Santiago*. Produced by Nolasco Brothers Pictures in 1946, the film starred Leopoldo Salcedo as a self-interested ne're-do-well trafficker in stolen goods who has no political allegiances, to America, Japan, or even his own countrymen. But after being arrested by the Japanese for buying stolen Japanese supplies, Salcedo is imprisoned at Fort Santiago, where his patriotism is finally awakened upon making the acquaintance of guerrilla fighters being detained there. The film broke box office records in Manila, where it ran for 34 days.

Reviewing the film for the September 1946 issue of *Stars of the Stage and Screen*, Purificacion del Rio described the character being portrayed by the film's female lead, Vida Florante, as being "a staunch believer in the right of the Filipinos to enjoy freedom: freedom of speech, freedom of thought and faith, freedom from want, and freedom from fear of the hated Japs."

After being released from prison, Salcedo's character becomes a leader in the guerrilla movement, for which he is again arrested, about which del Rio wrote "the Japs tortured him with all the barbarism and inhumanity for which the kempeis* became notorious. Fate was, however, still with our hero. He was able to escape and continue his work killing Japs...." After Salcedo's escape, del Rio wrote that "the Japs turned their inhuman wrath upon our heroine ... who subsequently became a victim of amnesia ... due to the brutality of the tortures which she suffered in Fort Santiago."[2] One can easily forgive del Rio's tendency toward demonstrative editorializing as being the very understandable need of Filipinos to vent.

Fort Santiago saw international release in 1948 under the title *Atrocities of Fort Santiago*, as the industry saw the opportunity to capitalize on the universality of the theme of the war. It was not the only local film to receive release abroad in the late–1940s.

Fort Santiago was Florante's first film. Her given name was Lourdez Dominguez, and she was born in Sampaloc, Manila on November 11, 1920. Her father, Salvador Domingo, was a Spanish writer who went by the name of Saldo de Sana. A beautiful model, Florante professed no desire to be an actress, and reportedly turned down film offers from a number of directors and producers, but she was persuaded by Luis Nolasco to star in *Fort Santiago* after the producer-director met her at a photo studio where she was engaged in a pin-up shoot, and Nolasco gave her an impassioned description of the film's story. Florante's reasons for accepting that particular offer were exceedingly personal: she had herself been imprisoned at Fort Santiago, as was her fiancé, who she later declined to name. Florante said that she had offered herself to the chief of the Japanese military police, who she named as Colonel Nagahama, in exchange for the life of her fiancé, but Nagahama declined, and Florante's fiancé was tortured and killed.[3] If she had declined previous film offers out of concerns about her abilities, she obviously had good reason to believe that she could adequately convey the torment that her character would undergo at Fort Santiago, and the role was doubtless therapeutic.

Certainly no less personal—perhaps more so—was Carmen Rosales' starring role in Sampaguita's *Guerilyera* (*Guerrilla Woman*), the true story of her own participation in the resistance. Born Januaria Constantino Keller on March 3, 1917, she was of Swedish-Filipino descent, and began her career in radio as a singer, being voted Miss Radio of 1936. She auditioned as a singer for Excelsior Studios in the 1930s, and although she was reluctant to embark on an acting career, studio executives convinced her to take a screen test. As it turned out, she was a natural in front of the camera, and after making her film debut, she caught the eye of Congressman Pedro Vera at Sampaguita, who promptly bought out her contract. At Sampaguita, Rosales would become one of the great screen icons of Filipino cinema.

During her time on radio, Rosales married her piano player, Ramon Novales, but he would

---

*The kempeitai were the Japanese military police.

be killed fighting the Japanese during the war. Rosales became involved in the resistance movement herself, and after being captured by the Japanese, she was taken to Pangasinan, where legend has it a Japanese officer fell in love with her and, knowing of her fame, requested she appear in a propaganda film. When Rosales refused, the officer was soon enough able to persuade her by threatening to execute citizens in Pangasinan. Under such circumstances, Rosales relented, but the film was never completed owing to the arrival of U.S. troops. After the war, the people of Pangasinan paid tribute to Rosales by naming a town after her.

As Rosales had been dubbed the "Dorothy Lamour of the East," it is interesting to try to imagine Lamour herself as a guerrilla fighter. This is not to suggest that, had the war somehow come to America in the same way that it had the Philippines, Lamour would not have had the fortitude to take up arms and fight, but merely as an interesting exercise in contrasting life on either side of the Pacific during the war.

Not to deny the concept that laughter is the best medicine, comedians Pugo and Togo offered *Multo ni Yamashita* (*Ghost of Yamashita*), a film in which the ghost of the recently executed Japanese general returns to haunt the comic pair. Following the war, Yamashita had been convicted of war crimes, including what came to be known as the "butchery of Lipa," in which some 20,000 Lipenos were said to have been slaughtered.*

The flurry of war films may have been heavily concentrated in 1946, but they continued for years to come. There was Carlos Vander Tolosa's *Sunset Over Corregidor* in 1948, Gerardo de Leon's *Kumander Sundang* (*Commander Dagger*) in 1949 (promoted as "Another story of Filipino heroism!"), Olive la Torre's *Takas sa Bataan* (*Escapee from Bataan*) in 1950, and *He Promised to Return* in 1951, which boasted of being "the most exciting war picture ever presented."

Carmen Rosales, the Philippine Dorothy Lamour. During the war she fought with a guerrilla army until being captured by the Japanese.

Sunset Over Corregidor was made by X'Otic Productions with the intention of international release, and so, while Carlos Vander Tolosa directed the Tagalog version, the crew simultaneously shot an English version, titled *Outrages of the Orient*, under the direction of Eduardo de Castro. The international title obviously sought to sensationalize the subject, much like *Fort Santiago* had seen international release as *Atrocities of Fort Santiago*, an attempt to draw more attention to the product in a very crowded global market. *Outrages of the Orient* had further exploitation potential due to a nude swimming scene by actress Mona Lisa. As discreetly as the scene may have been shot—one could only see Lisa's backside beneath the surface of the water as she swam—it was still

---

*Yamashita was indicted in September of 1945, court-martialed, and convicted by five U.S. generals for the atrocities committed under his command, although the conviction was questionable to some. Yamashita's defense team, consisting of five U.S. Army lawyers, petitioned the U.S. Supreme Court to have the conviction overturned, claiming that the atrocities in question were committed against rather than under Yamashita's orders. The appeal failed and Yamashita was executed on February 23, 1946.

Fort Santiago (1946/Nolasco Brothers) saw international release in 1948 as *Atrocities of Fort Santiago*.

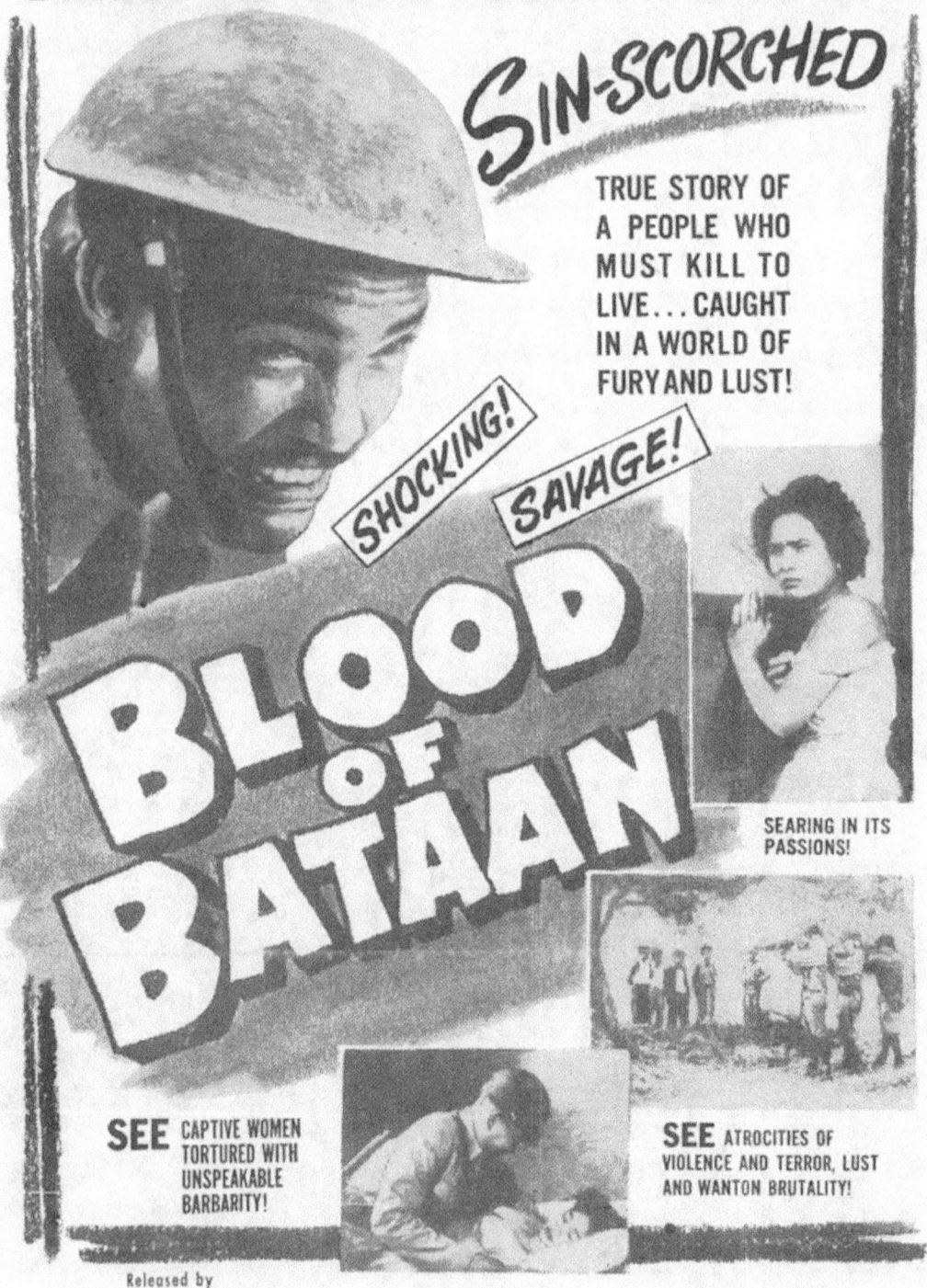

Blood of Bataan (1953/Joseph Brenner Associates) was one of a number of WWII films picked up for international release by American exploitation distributors.

more skin than 1940s audiences were accustomed to seeing, and it probably helped the film appeal to American exploitation market distributor Lloyd Friedgen, who purchased the stateside distribution rights. Friedgen certainly saw his money's worth from the picture, as he continued to periodically re-release it for years to 42nd Street theaters in New York, where the film had something of a cult following among 42nd street patrons who looked forward to its seasonal bookings, as they did likewise for *Beasts of the East* (1950), another Filipino war picture that Friedgen picked up for stateside release.

Lisa was born Gloria Yatco, and she started her film career in the 1930s under the screen name Fleur de Lis. It was de Castro, the father of Lisa's first child, who renamed her Mona Lisa. In *Sunset Over Corregidor* Lisa was cast as a tough guerrilla leader named Eve who joins forces with Captain Corregidor (Fernando Royo) and his men to combat the Japanese. Lisa's tough—at times excessively so—character may have been inspired by real-life accounts of Carmen Rosales' exploits as a guerrilla leader.

Of course, war films were popular in America too, although most Hollywood films dealing with the war in the Pacific were shot on Hollywood back lots. The John Wayne film *Back to Bataan* (1945), for instance, was a stateside shoot. But some American productions were finding their way to the islands. Fritz Lang traveled to the Philippines to shoot *An American Guerrilla in the Philippines* on location in 1950, and even made use of local talent, employing Filipino actors in the film. Unfortunately, no one saw fit to give any of them screen credit. American productions dealing with the war would become far more commonplace in the Philippines during the 1960s. It seemed that the only way that Filipino cast and crew were getting any degree of notice was through the efforts of exploitation distributors.

Friedgen had also acquired a Filipino costume picture in the late 1940s and released it in 1948 as *Forbidden Women*, a film which top-billed Fernando Poe, although the real star was a diminutive teenager named Berting Labra. Poe was cast as the sultan of a nondescript island nation whose scheming, widowed sister-in-law (Mona Lisa) seeks to prevent from turning the kingdom over to his son (Labra). With her lover, Lisa conspires to murder Labra and poison Poe, thereby setting herself up to inherit the kingdom. But as Poe wastes away, Labra flees to a nearby island where he spends his time in a forbidden temple which houses a harem (the forbidden women of the title) being kept for some deity or other. In time, Labra returns home to save his father and foil Lisa's plot. Friedgen tried to juice the film's exploitability by inserting a brief scene of a topless maiden in the temple. Lisa seems to have been getting her fair share of Western exposure during the era.

Lloyd Friedgen was not the only one mining the Philippine market for quick, cheap product to distribute; exploitation film distributor Joseph Brenner, later a specialist in tawdry little sexploitation quickies in the 1960s, picked up *Blood of Bataan*, starring Leopoldo Salcedo and Mona Lisa, for U.S. distribution in 1953, giving it a somewhat garish campaign that promised patrons the opportunity to see "captive women tortured with unspeakable barbarity," and "atrocities of violence and terror, lust and wanton brutality." Such is the art of showmanship.

An interesting example of an early joint U.S.–Philippine production would be the film *No Place to Hide*, produced by Josef Shaftel and Company in 1955 in cooperation with both LVN and Lebran. Along with American leads David Brian and Marsha Hunt, the film featured an impressive cast of Filipino actors, including Celia Flor, Manuel Silos, Alfonso Carvajal, Oscar Keesee, Lou Salvador, Jose (Joseph) de Cordova, Ike Jarlego Jr., and Eddie Infante. Infante was an excellent character actor in the Philippines who also worked as a gossip columnist in the 1950s. He turned in impressive performances in a fair share of international coproductions through the 1950s, '60s and '70s, performing equally capably as priests, military men or peasants. It is very illustrative of the protective nature of the Filipino film industry that they should allow one of their own to provide industry scuttlebutt. Perhaps to avoid a local equivalent to the reign of terror that Hollywood scandal sheets held at that time over stars and studios alike in America, Filipino studio moguls probably wanted to ensure that they had someone that they could trust to disseminate appropriately innocuous gossip that would nonetheless fulfill the public's yearning to read about their idols. Further testament of the cautious nature of the film industry in its relationship with the press can be seen in the fact that film director Susana C. de Guzman was listed as comptroller of one of the era's popular film gossip magazines, *Movie Confidential*, which promoted itself with the slogan "all the news about the movies."

The local industry had been growing in the years prior to the war, producing in the neighborhood of fifty films per year. It managed to pick up again after the war, and with the subsequent granting of independence by the U.S., gathered a full head of steam heading into the 1950s. The ten year period following the war would be productive and lucrative enough that it would come to be known as the Golden Age of Philippine Cinema,* with production eventually reaching close to 100 films per year.

The studio system was back in full swing by 1946. The pre-war giants Sampaguita and LVN managed to survive the war and take up their positions once more as the preeminent film studios in the country. In 1946 they were also joined by Premiere Productions, making up what came to be called the "big three" of the Filipino film industry. Premiere Productions was the result of a partnership between Dr. Ciriaco Santiago, Ricardo Marcelino, and film directors Susana de Guzman and Tony Arnaldo, and the company very quickly rose through the ranks of a plethora of newly formed film companies. Santiago was a surgeon who also owned the Hermoso Drugstore, where his wife Adela worked as a pharmacist. Marcelino, a cinematographer, was a good friend of the family who managed to persuade Santiago to enter into the film business. Premiere took its business seriously, requiring all of its contract players to attend classes on the lot every Monday, Wednesday, and Friday of each week to be schooled in everything from acting, diction and social behavior to dancing and swimming. Moral conduct and appearances were considered extremely important by the studio, and stars who engaged in scan-

Dr. Ciriaco Santiago, the surgeon and drugstore owner who started Premiere Productions in 1946. It quickly grew into one of the "Big Three" studios during the Golden Era of Philippine Cinema.

---

* Some historians, like Ed Cabagnot in his introductory chapter "Notes on the History of Philippine Cinema" in the book Focus on Filipino Films: A Sampling, 1951–1982, refer to the pre-war years of 1934–1941 as the Golden Years, but given the industry's overall growth in both productivity and popularity, the years 1946–1956 seem to be more deserving of the appellation.

dalous behavior were likely to be promptly dismissed. Actors and actresses would also receive fines from the Premiere front office for such offenses as being seen on the boulevard or posing for photographs in a bathing suit. In fact, the studio forbad its contract players from being photographed at all without prior written permission from the studio. When Dr. Santiago died in 1956, his wife Adela took over as president of the studio, while his son Cirio assumed the role of production manager.[4]

Susana C. de Guzman was born on May 24, 1912, in Manila. She was a novelist who also came to be known for writing popular radio serials. She began her film career as a screenwriter for Filippine Films on the picture *Kalapating Puti* (*White Dove*) in 1938, and worked for various production companies as a writer through the remainder of the 1930s and early '40s, including bigger studios like LVN and Sampaguita, and smaller, short-lived outfits like Philippine National Pictures, Plaridel Pictures Corporation, Del Monte Films and Acuna-Zaldariaga Productions. Much of her work during that period was for Excelsior. Her first film as director was also Premiere's maiden offering, *Probinsyana* (*Province Woman*), which starred Carmen Rosales, Jose Padilla, Jr. and Tony Arnaldo. Arnaldo, incidentally, was de Guzman's husband. His real name was Antonio Astudillo, and he had previously worked as a reporter. After changing his name and entering show business, he would star in many of de Guzman's films, and he also became a director himself. *Probinsyana* was a great success that did much to establish Premiere and pave the way for the studio's quick ascendancy to the top ranks of the industry.

Although de Guzman helped put Premiere on the map, she very quickly jumped to LVN, where she both directed and wrote, notably receiving story and screenwriting credits on many of the films that her husband was directing at LVN. She resisted offers to work for Sampaguita, and remained with LVN until the studio ceased production in 1961, and even stayed with the studio in its brief reincarnation as Dalisay Productions in 1961–62.

Premiere may have had early success and had quickly ascended to be listed among the "big three" production companies in the industry, but the good fortune that the studio experienced was fleeting, and as early as 1951 the studio was having serious problems. Claiming to be losing money, the studio filed a petition on October 2, 1951, with the Court of Industrial Relations requesting permission to lay off 44 employees in three of its departments. The presiding judge, Judge Arsenio C. Roldan, took the rather extraordinary step (maybe it was routine in such cases) of going to the studio's facilities to inspect the premises and interview studio personnel. Satisfied that the studio's reasons were sincere, Judge Roldan granted the petition.

Premiere then filed another petition requesting permission to lease its equipment, studios and

Adela Santiago, the wife of Dr. Ciriaco Santiago. When her husband died she took over as studio president.

other facilities to other filmmakers (Eddie Infante among them) in order to get some gain from its dormant facilities. Thinking better of it, the studio quickly withdrew the petition, feeling it unnecessary since the studio was merely exercising its proprietary rights. The motion to withdraw the petition was granted, a decision which drew the ire of the Philippine Movie Pictures Workers' Association. On February 7, 1952, Premiere shipped some of its equipment to a location shoot in Bulacan for the film *Bakas ng Kahapon* (*Trace of Yesterday*), and the workers' guild quickly filed an urgent petition with the Court of Industrial Relations for contempt and injunction, claiming that Premiere had no right to enter into a lease agreement without the court's approval.

Undeterred, and not willing to wait for a decision regarding the guild's petition, Premiere then leased more equipment to be used by Efren Reyes in the filming of *Larawan ng Buhay* (*Picture of Life*), which prompted the guild to file another urgent petition for contempt and injunction. Still undaunted, Premiere continued leasing equipment, and on March 5, 1952, the company leased sound equipment to Manuel Vistan for the film *Troubador* and Artemio Marquez for the film *Boys' Town*. Still more petitions for contempt and injunction were filed by the workers' guild.

It seems more than a little ridiculous that anyone should object to a company leasing idle equipment in order to help reestablish itself financially, but such is the nature of unions. The Philippine Movie Pictures Workers' Association seems to have been of the opinion that Premiere was merely leasing its equipment in order to make money without having to pay its employees.

Premiere's labor troubles continued as their technical crewmen, led by soundman Casimiro Padilla, went on strike in 1952. Sympathizing with the technicians, actresses Anita Linda and Patria Plata offered to act as mediators between the technicians and the studio, taking the workers' list of grievances to Premiere matriarch Adela Santiago, who did not take kindly to the uprising. She also viewed the actions of Linda and Plata as being somewhat traitorous, and after rebuking the actresses she suspended their contracts. They were, however, freed to seek work elsewhere when shortly afterward the studio found it necessary to shut down completely for a period.

LVN matriarch Dona Narcisa de Leon was having labor troubles of a different sort, which centered on exhibition rather than production. Although she owned the Dalisay Theater on Rizal Avenue in Manila, de Leon had leased it in April of 1949 to a company called Filipino Theatrical Enterprises. When the lease ran out in 1951, Filipino Theatrical Enterprises necessarily let their employees go as the lease was not being renewed. Many of the workers seem to have assumed that they would stay on under the new management, but Dona Sisang did not keep them on: in fact, she didn't even keep the theater. Instead, she razed the old Dalisay Theater and built an entirely new one, also called the Dalisay. As the new theater prepared to open, many of those who had been employed by Filipino Theatrical Enterprises might have assumed that they would be rehired to staff the new facility, but when they weren't, they somehow felt justified in getting the National Labor Union involved. When the Dalisay reopened on January 10th of 1952, some thirty protestors were on hand to picket the theater. Since the new management had no history with the former employees of Filipino Theatrical Enterprises, Dona Sisang considered the picketing unjust, and the opening day box office receipts were off enough that the demonstrators did rather appear to have hurt business. Dona Sisang filed suit for damages from the National Labor Union, as well as specific individuals involved in the picketing, although the picketers were merely exercising their constitutional rights. The labor union promptly responded by filing a counter-suit for lost wages, estimating it to collectively be 200 pesos daily, an equally inane waste of time, since the former employees could not reasonably request lost wages from a company that had never employed them to begin with. In a refreshingly sober bit of jurisprudence, the court dismissed both suits, but still feeling wronged at being the target of the picketing, Dona Sisang appealed the decision all the way to the Philippine Supreme Court. It proved to be a singularly ridiculous waste of everybody's time, as the Supreme Court eventually affirmed the original court's ruling in January of 1957.

Despite the troubles that Premiere was experiencing, the explosion of growth in the industry overall can be easily seen in the high number of new production companies. The list includes Palaris Films, Mabuhay Pictures, Oriental Pictures, Sta. Maria Pictures, Philippine Pictures, Philippine Paradise Pictures, Pangilinan Productions, Leyte Motion Pictures, PAL (Philippine Artists League) Productions, SVS Pictures, McLaurin Bros. Productions, Eagle Lion Films, Milagrosa Productions, Bayani Pictures, Lawin Pictures, Filcudoma Pictures, PAR Productions, GLM Productions, and Educational Pictures. There were also industry luminaries who started their own production companies, with eponymous names like Fernando Poe Productions, Manuel Conde Productions and Pedro Vera, Jr. Productions. Some of the companies may have been fly-by-night outfits that wound up with no more than a title or two to their credit before folding, but those that did close shop were replaced soon enough by new companies, so robust had the industry become.

In the 1950s the "big three" became the "big four" as they were joined by Lebran Productions. More companies sprang up in the 1950s: Associated Artists, Filipinas Pictures, Royal Productions, Quezon Memorial Pictures, Benito Bros. Pictures, Fortune Pictures, Far East Films, LGS Productions, Filmakers Productions, Maria Clara Pictures, Palanca Bros. Productions, Deegar Cinema, People's Pictures, Vistan-Chapman Productions, Everlasting Pictures, Tamaraw Studios. Jose Nepomuceno was still at it, starting Jose Nepomuceno Productions.

The film business was also booming off of the mainland in the Visayas. Companies like Lapu-Lapu Pictures were producing films in the late 1940s with popular regional stars, and Azucena Productions began to firmly establish itself in the early 1950s. The studio was started by members of the Arong family, owners of the Liberty Theater in Cebu, and in 1951 they teamed popular Visayan actor Mat Ranillo with Gloria Sevilla in the actress's first lead role. The film was titled *Princesa Tirana* (*Princess Tirana*), and it was a resounding success throughout the Visayas and down south in Mindanao: a screen love team was born. Ranillo and Sevilla became the King and Queen of Visayan films, and, starring in one picture after another, a real-life romance blossomed soon enough. The two married and formed their own production company, S-R Productions, in 1954. Their success was such that just a year later they grew tired of being big fish in a little pond and decided to go to Manila to conquer the Tagalog industry. But they were cautious and sensible enough to keep their Cebuano studio operating, producing films through the remainder of the 1950s and '60s, including Ranillo's final film, *Hain ang Langit* (*Where Is Heaven?*), in 1969. After completing the picture, Ranillo was killed in a plane crash.

Also making a success of itself in the Visayas was a company called VM Productions, started by a Cebuano politician named Natalio Bacalso, who not only ran the company, but was its principal film director as well. Bacalso directed the film *Salingsing sa Kasakit* (*Partner In Pain*) in 1954, which managed to win a FAMAS award in the Best Child Actor category for Undo Juezan, a notable achievement for the smaller industry.

During the 1950s there was also Cebu Stars Productions, which managed to set box office records in the region with the 1953 film *Sangang Nangabali* (*Broken Branches*).

The Golden Era was also a time of artistic growth as the better filmmakers were exploring more than the horrors of war and the occupation, but also the subject of national identity and the ramifications of the emerging new society. Gerardo de Leon directed a picture for Sampaguita in 1946 titled *So Long America*, heralding the new era. The film was subtitled *I'll Be Seeing You Everywhere*, perhaps alluding not merely to America's continued presence as a strong influence over Philippine society, but to its emerging position of global dominance. Unfortunately, no prints of the film seem to have survived the years.

The heavy destruction suffered by Manila wiped out most of Filipino cinema's pre-war heritage: only a handful of films survived (owing to its stateside distribution, a print of the 1937 film *Zamboanga* has been discovered in America in recent years), but neglect and the ravages of time seem to have wiped out the bulk of films from the post-war 1940s and '50s. Many of the titles in Sampaguita's catalog fell victim to a fire that razed the studio's Ortigas Avenue facilities in 1951. The fire swept away film prints and negatives alike—10-million-pesos worth of nitrate stock was lost—and completely destroyed the studio's facilities. It might have brought an end to the prestigious outfit, but Judge Vera was buoyed by the enthusiasm that his employees showed for building things up again, many of them offering to work for free in order to allow the company the opportunity to reestablish itself. Judge Vera turned to his son-in-law, Dr. Jose R. Perez, for help in rescuing the company, but ultimately it was a child that revitalized the studio. With an eye toward keeping production costs low, Doc Perez decided to cast the young daughter of neighbor and professional colleague, Dr. Adriano Agana, in a film adaptation of the Mars Ravelo komik serial *Roberta*. It was the casting of 5-year-old Tessie Agana in the title role that turned the trick.[5] The film was an enormous success, breaking box office records at the time and earning between 10,000–15,000 pesos per day at the Life Theater in Manila, immediately restoring the studio's good fortunes. Directed by Olive la Torre, *Roberta* was the story of a victim of child abuse in the slums, and the studio promoted it with the tag line "The motion picture that will tear your heart to pieces!" Audiences fell in love with Agana and the studio would go on to give her starring roles in films like *Rebecca* and *Ang Prinsesa at ang Pulubi* (*The Princess and the Pauper*), both in 1951, and *Ulila ng Bataan* (*The Orphan of Bataan*) in 1952. Agana was also the daughter of Sampaguita actress Linda Estrella, who had begun her screen career in 1941. Remarkable for a child was Agana's ability to cry on cue, yet she could turn it off just as quickly, asking her directors if she could run off and play after completing a take. In order to keep her in line, the studio frequently bribed her with her favorite food, fried chicken.

Agana's immense popularity was nationwide, and wherever she went throngs of fans clamored to see her. Years later she would recall making a personal appearance in one province where the fans were so enthusiastic that she was quickly taken to her hotel room. The determined fans followed, and when they tried to push their way into her room, those who were trying to protect Agana forced the door shut, closing it on one young girl's hand and severing a finger.

Eventually, desiring some sort of normal life for their child, Agana's parents decided to migrate to the United States, where Agana went on to attend college at De Paul University in Indiana. She was, however, enticed by Doc Perez into returning to the Philippines upon turning 18 to star in the film *Amy, Susie, Tessie* in 1960, alongside popular actresses of the time Amalia Fuentes and Susan Roces. Although she accepted the invitation, and even shot one more feature while there, that being *Love at First Sight*, she had no desire to return to show business, and soon after returned to the United States where two years later she met her husband, Dr. Rodolfo Jao, with whom she would go on to raise a family of nine children in Gary, Indiana.

Sampaguita also found good box office by featuring the husband and wife team of Pancho Magalona and Tita Duran in romantic musical pictures like *Kasintahan sa Pangarap* (*Lover* in *Dream*), *Buhay Pilipino* (*Filipino Life*), *Vod-A-Vil* (*Vaudeville*) and Eddie Romero's *Maria Went to Town*, which the studio promoted as "The biggest musical comedy since musical comedies began!" Magalona's real first name was Enrique, and he was born in Saravia, Negros Occidental. His father, Enrique Magalona Sr., was a former senator, and Magalona had originally planned to pursue a career as a lawyer. He made his screen debut in the 1947 film *Prima Donna*, and his good looks immediately made him stand out as leading man timbre. His wife had gotten an earlier start in the business. Born Teresita Durango in Tondo, Manila, Tita Duran had begun her career in the pre-war era as a child actress. It wasn't until after the war that she began to receive adult roles, her first being in *Guerilyera*.

By the mid-1950s, Sampaguita's bankroll was such that they were able once again to acquire the services of popular screen love team Rogelio dela Rosa and Carmen Rosales, whom they co-billed in a series of romantic tearjerkers like *Ang Tangi Kong Pagibig* (*My Only Love*), *Iyung-Iyo* (*Yours and Yours Alone*), and *Lydia*.

Though occasionally harkening to the Hollywood musicals of the 1930s and '40s, Filipino musicals of the Golden Age seem to have had more in common with opera, the emphasis usually being on heartbreak and tragedy. *Ang Tangi Kong Pagibig* (1954) is very illustrative of the genre, casting Rosales as a popular but unhappy nightclub singer who tries to leave her job, but is prevented from doing so by the tyrannical club owner, who forcibly keeps her there, since business has never been better. Rosales has to resort to knocking her employer over the head and then fleeing to the rural village where her family resides. Once there she meets dela Rosa and the two fall in love and plan to marry, but with his business failing since Rosales' departure, the villainous club owner tracks her down and shows up on her wedding day to drag her back to the city. Dela Rosa gives the club owner a sound beating in a slugfest that looks like it came straight out of a 1940s Hollywood serial, and all would seem to be resolved. But things are never that easy in the world of Philippine melodrama. While nothing spectacular, the film would have been just fine had it ended there, but what can sometimes be exasperating to Westerners about Filipino films is how even the most ordinary of stories are made to drag on interminably, sometimes leaving the viewer feeling that there is no end in sight. The story drags on as the unnecessarily traumatized Rosales runs off and no one is able to find her. Eventually learning that Rosales has become a nun and gone to the city, dela Rosa and his buddy Luis Gonzales set off to find her. They have no

The husband and wife team of Pancho Magalona and Tita Duran were a popular screen tandem for Sampaguita Pictures in the 1950s.

(Left to right) Carmen Rosales, Rogelio dela Rosa and Paraluman were co-stars in the film *Lydia* in 1957.

luck, however, and after a night of heavy drinking they get into a serious car accident. While Gonzales mends quickly, dela Rosa's injuries are more severe, requiring surgery and a lengthy hospital stay. Hearing of the accident, Rosales shows up to tend to dela Rosa as he recuperates, but dela Rosa is frustrated by his inability to convince her to forsake her vows as a nun and return to him. Finally, after a number of teary-eyed scenes, Rosales suddenly comes running back to dela Rosa and all ends happily. Directed by Mar S. Torres and written by Conrado Conde, the film is exceedingly ordinary in both conception and execution, yet is given grand epic treatment, running for more than two hours, though being nothing more than a standard romantic soap.

Rosales and dela Rosa were again teamed under Torres' direction in 1954 in *Maalaala Mo Kaya? (Will You Remember?)*, which cast dela Rosa as an aspiring songwriter who falls in love with Rosales and pens a song in her honor. He travels to the city with his buddy Dolphy to try and pitch the tune, and he is quickly pursued romantically by a pretty music publisher who takes a liking to both him and his song. Dela Rosa falls for her as well, and the two marry. Years later they have a young daughter, but a declining marriage, and dela Rosa again encounters Rosales when she turns up as a music teacher at the school which his daughter attends. It only takes a few chance encounters with Rosales to make dela Rosa's wife insanely jealous, and while arguing one night she pulls a gun on dela Rosa. The two struggle and of course the gun goes off, killing dela Rosa's wife. Accused of murder, dela Rosa stands trial, but he is acquitted after his daughter, who witnessed the accident, testifies on his behalf. The film ends with dela Rosa's daughter playing piano at a school talent show in which she plays the song that her father had written for Rosales all those years ago, which has the effect of bringing dela Rosa and Rosales back together.

Melodramatic soap operas may have been the most popular fare, but the industry covered most every genre imaginable. Costume melodramas proved popular, swashbucklers in particular. Rogelio dela Rosa starred in pictures like *Principeng hindi Tumatawa* (*The Prince Who Does Not Laugh*) in 1946, *Sword of the Avenger* in 1948, *Prinsipe Amante* (*Prince Amante*) in 1950, *Prinsipe Amante sa Rubitanya* (*Prince Amante in Rubitanya*) in 1951, and *El Conde de Monte Carlo* (*The Count of Monte Carlo*) in 1956. Fernando Poe was also starring in costume dramas like *Ali Mudin* and *Awit ni Palaris* (*Song of Palaris*) in 1946 and *Sagur* in 1949. Jaime dela Rosa starred in *Aladin* (1946) and *Satur* (1951), Mario Montenegro starred in *Rodrigo de Villa* in 1952 and *Higit sa Korona* (*More Than a Crown*) in 1956 (both co-starring Delia Razon), Leopoldo Salcedo starred in Eddie Romero's *Huling Mandirigma* (*The Last Warrior*) in 1956. Premiere Productions got into costume pictures with titles like *Kapitan Bagwis* (*Captain Wings*) in 1951, which starred Efren Reyes and Anita Linda, *Agilang Itim* (*The Black Eagle*) in 1953 co-billing Linda with Eduardo del Mar, and *Eskrimador* (*Swordsman*) in 1955 with Efren Reyes, Edna Luna and Juan (Johnny) Monteiro.

But, owing to his partiality to the genre, it was Manuel Conde who came to be referred to as the "king of the swashbucklers." Born Manuel Urbano, Conde studied geological engineering in school, and his initial foray into show business was as a ventriloquist, taking the stage with a dummy named "Kiko." He entered the film business as a lab assistant, later appearing on screen in bit roles and acting as a stunt double. In 1939 he was appearing in the film *Ang Sawing Gantingpala* (*The Unfortunate Reward*) when the director failed to show up to work. Conde volunteered to take over, and apparently desperate not to lose time, the film's producers allowed him the opportunity. He gravitated toward comedy, but forsaking the slapstick brand of humor that dominated the era, he gained respect for raising the comedic bar with more thoughtful humor. For his own company, Manuel Conde Productions, he starred in *Prinsipe Paris* (*Prince Paris*) in 1949 and *Siete Infantes de Lara* (*The Seven Sons of Lara*) in 1950, while also starring in pictures like *Apat na Alas* (*Four Aces*) in 1950 and *Sigfredo* in 1951 (both for Lebran), and *Satur* for LVN in 1951. But it was Conde's essaying the title role in *Genghis Khan* in 1950 that would prove to be a major breakthrough for Filipino cinema. The film is often cited as having been directed by Conde, but it was actually directed by Lou Salvador. Although *Zamboanga* had seen stateside release in 1937, it was not until *Genghis Khan* that a Filipino film would receive wide international recognition. It also received international acclaim, with many critics considering Conde's portrayal to be definitive. United Artists picked up the distribution rights and released the film in a version re-edited by James Agee, a well-known American film critic of the day. Agee otherwise lent his talents by doing a voice-over narration in English. Unfortunately, this altered version seems to be the only one to have survived. *Genghis Khan* became the first Filipino film to be entered in international film festivals, including the 1952 Venice Film Festival.

Conde also produced, wrote and starred in a series of comedies based on a character he created named Juan Tamad (Lazy John), a country bumpkin whose misadventures placed him in various fish-out-of-water scenarios. Conde frequently used the series to voice, with humor, political concerns and discontent. In order not to seem to be targeting any contemporary politicians in particular, the Juan Tamad films were set in the pre–Spanish colonial era. But there was no mistaking the aim of many of the barbs, which were often directed at spendthrift

Genghis Khan (1952/United Artists) was the first Filipino film to play the Venice Film Festival. Shot in 1950, the film received global distribution and acclaim, many considering Manuel Conde's portrayal to be definitive.

politicians lining their pockets with pork barrel programs. The series began in 1947 with *Juan Tamad* (promoted as a "lafterpiece"), and continued for years with titles like *Juan Daldal: Anak ni Juan Tamad* (*Talkative John: Son of Lazy John*), also in 1947, *Juan Tamad Goes to Congress* in 1959, and *Juan Tamad Goest to Society* in 1960. He reprised the role for years, eventually developing a television sitcom based around the character.

Aside from the popular swashbuckler genre, the studios cranked out bizarre comedies, historical epics, including further exaltations of Jose Rizal with films like *Buhay ng Pagibig ni Dr. Jose Rizal* (*The Life and Love of Dr. Jose Rizal*) starring Eduardo del Mar in 1956, dabbled in the classics, like Lebran's production of *Romeo and Juliet* in 1951 and Sampaguita's *Tres Muskiteras* (*The Three Musketeers*) in 1954, and biblical epics including titles like *Kalbaryo ni Hesus* (*Calvary of Jesus*), produced by Lebran in 1952 and starring American Jennings Sturgeon as Christ, and *Ang Pagsilang ng Mesiyas* (*The Birth of the Messiah*), also in 1952. The flipside of the religious films was the Satan genre, which acknowledged the dark side's hand in human events, represented by titles like *El Diablo* (*The Devil*) in 1949, starring Leopoldo Salcedo, and Gerardo de Leon's *Kamay ni Satanas* (*The Hand of Satan*) in 1950, which won top honors for Best Picture, Best Director for de Leon, and Best Actor for Reynaldo Dante at the initial Maria Clara Awards, the first film awards body to be organized in the Philippines. There were other horror offerings as well: *Berdugo ng mga Anghel* (*Executioner of Angels*) in 1951, *Taong Paniki* (*Bat*

Manuel Conde (right) in *Juan Tamad Goes to Congress* (*Lazy John Goes to Congress*; 1959/MC Pictures). Although set in the pre–Spanish colonial period, the film was seen as a spoof of modern politics, and Conde was praised as having raised the standards of Filipino comedy, which nonetheless remained reliant on slapstick.

Man) in 1952 (not to be confused with the American comic book superhero), and *Taong Putik* (*Mud Man*) in 1956. Filipino filmmakers also continued to draw heavily from komiks serials, including science fiction fare like *Exzur*, adapted by People's Pictures from a *Liwayway Magazine* serial, which promised patrons the spectacle of seeing "city hall, the Quezon Bridge, the Bureau of Posts ... destroyed by an armada of flying saucers!" There was standard superhero fare, like *Kidlat ... Ngayon!* (*Lightning ... Now!*), a kind of Filipino take on *Shazam*, which was adapted to the screen by LVN from a popular radio serial on station DZRM (the radio serial was sponsored by Colgate and Palmolive).

But the most popular superhero films were actually those featuring a superheroine named Darna, a sort of Filipino Wonder Woman created by Mars Ravelo and popularized in *Pilipino Komiks*. The initial offering, *Darna*, was directed by Fernando Poe in 1951 and starred Rosa del Rosario. Del Rosario would return to the role in 1952 in the film *Darna at ang Babaing Lawin* (*Darna and the Hawk Woman*), directed by Carlos Vander Tolosa. The character would prove so popular that the series would continue for decades, with various actresses playing the role; Liza Moreno took the part in *Darna at ang Impakta* (*Darna and the Demon Woman*) and *Isputnik vs Darna*, both in 1963; Eva Montes played the role in *Darna at ang Babaing Tuod* (*Darna and the Tree Woman*) in 1965; Gina Pareno starred in *Darna at ang Planetman* (*Darna and the Planet Man*) in 1969; Vilma Santos would play the part in the 1970s in titles like *Darna and the Giants* (1974), *Darna vs the Planet Women* (1975), and *Darna at Ding* (*Darna and Ding*) in 1978. Other actresses would take on the role in the 1980s and '90s, and the character would eventually be featured in a popular television series in 2005.

Another of Ravelo's *Pilipino Komiks* characters to be adapted to the screen was *Dyesebel* (Jezebel), a lovesick mermaid who falls in love with a mortal man. Gerardo de Leon first brought the character to the screen in 1953, and again, the character would endure for decades, with Santos playing the part in 1973, while Alma Moreno played the role in 1978. At least two other versions were produced in the 1990s, each with a different actress in the lead and each version simply titled *Dyesebel*.

Initially, the part of Dyesebel was played by actress Carol Varga, and it did a lot to help revitalize her film career after a very nasty scandal in which she was involved in 1949. Born Carolina Trinidad, Varga was the daughter of a Spanish engineer named Benjamin Trinidad and a schoolteacher named Maria Vizconde. She had originally planned to attend college and then law school, with an eye on a future in politics, but as fate would have it, at the tender age of 16 she was invited to a party attended by a host of Manila film luminaries, including Leopoldo Salcedo and director Carlos Vander Tolosa. They were struck by her beauty and enticed her into taking a screen test for Don Jesus Cacho at Lebran Productions. Cacho signed her to a two-year contract. Varga wore her hair long, citing Heddy Lamarr as her screen idol, and she was only in the film business seven months when she met American businessman George Murray, whom Varga likened to suave French actor Louis Jourdan. Although Murray was married to a woman named Esther del Rosario, Murray and Varga soon began a passionate love affair that ended in tragedy: when del Rosario discovered the affair, she shot and killed Murray. Del Rosario would eventually receive a life sentence for the murder, and, as protective as Philippine studio moguls could be in guarding the image of their stars, in the ensuing trial it was impossible to prevent the revelation that Varga was the other woman in the ill-fated love triangle. "Fate has played me a cruel trick." Varga would say ten years later. "Ours was a beautiful passion and it ended so abruptly. When the incident occurred, I prayed as I had never prayed before to help me get free from this terrible memory."[6]

Such an unfortunate event might have sunk her career, but Varga had many powerful friends in the film industry that rallied around her and helped her to reinvigorate her career.

Although she would continue to carry a torch for the late Murray for years, by 1955 her career was sufficiently recovered that she was honored with a FAMAS (Filipino Academy of Motion Picture Arts and Sciences) award for Best Supporting Actress for her performance in the 1954 film *Guwapo* (*Handsome*).

The Maria Clara Awards were initiated in 1950, and were largely the brainchild of Alejandro Roces, a columnist for the *Manila Times*, and later Secretary of Education. Aware that Philippine cinema, despite its growth in productivity, was achieving little international recognition, and was indeed producing little of the type of quality product that would show the local industry in a favorable light to the rest of the globe, Roces was among those who hoped that an awards body would inspire filmmakers to more diligently pursue their craft as art. Although the Philippines had a longer cinematic history than most neighboring countries, many felt that the local industry was falling behind in terms of quality. But after two years the Maria Clara Awards gave way to the newly formed Filipino Academy of Motion Picture Arts and Sciences.

Carol Varga in 1955 with her FAMAS Best Supporting Actress award.

Unlike the Maria Clara Awards, the FAMAS was founded by industry personnel. Actress Rosa Rosal and writer Flavio Macaso were the principals who started the idea, but they were soon joined by some of the industry's heavy hitters, Gerardo de Leon and Lamberto Avellana. The first FAMAS awards were held in 1953 (which honored the 1952 crop of films), with Gerardo de Leon's *Ang Sawa sa Lumang Simboryo* (*The Serpent in the Old Dome*) winning the Best Picture award while de Leon himself won Best Director for another of his pictures, *Bagong Umaga* (*New Morning*). It speaks to de Leon's stature that two of his films should be so honored at the inaugural FAMAS awards, although one might cynically suggest that his place of prominence in founding the organization may have come into play. That argument could hardly stand, however, since no one could say that de Leon's work was not always among the most impressive in the industry. One of de Leon's films that might have been awarded had the FAMAS Awards been initiated a year earlier was *Sisa*, which won de Leon the Best Director award at the Maria Clara Awards, and Anita Linda the Best Actress trophy. Based on characters from Rizal's *Noli Me Tangere*, the story concerned two brothers who are accused of stealing from the local church coffers during the Spanish colonial era, although the theft was actually committed by the head sacristan. The brothers are tortured by the parish priest, but rather than extracting a confession, the priest only manages to kill one of the boys. The tragedy continues as the second brother escapes and is pursued by the local militia, and Sisa, mother of the two brothers, is driven insane by the ordeal, as she searches endlessly for her children.

Throughout the 1950s, de Leon would cover a wide variety of genres, with fantasy pictures like *Pedro Penduko* (1954) and *Sanda Wong* (1955), war films like *10th Battalion sa 38th Parallel, Korea* (*10th Battalion in the 38th Parallel, Korea*) in 1951, historical pictures like *Diego Silang*

(1951), an account of a renowned tribal leader in northern Luzon who led a rebellion against the Spanish, and *Ifugao* (1954), and standard romantic soapers like *Mr. And Mrs.* (1956), *Sweethearts* (1957), and *Shirley, My Darling* (1958). After the war, de Leon also made a brief return to acting when his protégé Eddie Romero made his directorial debut with *Ang Kamay ng Diyos* in 1947 and coaxed de Leon into appearing in the film. De Leon must have enjoyed the experience, as he put in another appearance as an actor in 1947 in the film *Latang Asahar (Flaming Orange Blossom)*.

But de Leon was by no means the only Filipino filmmaker receiving accolades in his homeland. Most of the heavy hitters from the pre-war era were making noteworthy offerings, including Lamberto Avellana. As was his wont, Avellana was more interested in the realities of Philippine life than in escapist fare. "I like to see dirt in nobility," Avellana said. "I prefer my audience to sit back and identify with the characters. I also like my characters to mirror human imperfections, speaking down-to-earth dialogue, the way authentic people speak. And sex is the part of the film that pulsates."[7]

Owing to the era, sex was somewhat discreet as presented in film, but Avellana did not shy away from touching on the subject. One of his most acclaimed works during the Golden Era was the 1956 drama *Anak Dalita (Child of Sorrow)*, which he shot for LVN from a screenplay written by Rolf Bayer, and which won the Golden Harvest award at the 1956 Asian Film Festival and was shown at the 1957 Frankfurt International Film Festival. Set in the slums of Intramurous, the film starred Tony Santos as a Filipino soldier who returns from service in Korea after being wounded and losing the use of one of his arms. This handicap severely limits his ability to work for a living, and he finds himself drawn into a life of smuggling. Aside from Santos, the film's other lead was Rosa Rosal, who portrayed a prostitute who plies her trade at a local tavern. Rosal sympathizes with Santos' plight and begins a relationship with him. Rosal was a popular screen siren of the era who came to specialize in bad girl roles, playing vamps, schemers, gold diggers, and hookers. Born Florence Danon, the French-Egyptian-Filipina was a discovery of Luis Nolasco, who had signed her to a contract in 1947 and renamed her Rosa Rosal. Although she got her start with Nolasco Brothers Pictures, it was her work for LVN that won her the most acclaim and lasting fame. Due to her beautiful physique, she was asked to be the model for the FAMAS statuette. After achieving stardom, Rosal wanted to give something back to society and she became very involved in the Philippine National Red Cross, which turned into a lifelong commitment.

Rosal and Santos also starred in another of Avellana's most highly regarded works, *Badjao* (1957), again for LVN, and again with a screenplay by Rolf Bayer, which explored the subject of prejudice. Set in Mindanao, the story concerned a young pearl diver (Santos) of the Badjao tribe who falls in love with a pretty girl (Rosal) of a nearby Muslim tribe. The two tribes being at odds, the love affair is something of a taboo, with both tribes holding each other in low regard, and the marriage is put to the test from all sides. Eventually, Santos delivers a monologue on equality and at least convinces his own tribe to accept his bride.

Aside from the pre-war stars who were still popular, there were a good many new faces that became prominent in films during the Golden Era, but as before, the fairer mestizos were the order of the day. During the mid–1950s, pretty mestizas like Susan Roces, who became the ideal of glamour and beauty, Amalia Fuentes, who had a somewhat more innocent charm, and Rita Gomez became very popular in romantic melodramas. There was also Gloria Romero, who was often teamed in romantic films with Luis Gonzales.

Gloria Romero was born Gloria Galla in Denver, Colorado on December 16, 1933. Her father, Pedro Galla, was a Filipino immigrant to the U.S., her mother, Mary Borrego, an American. She would probably have lived her life in America if not for the fact that her family was

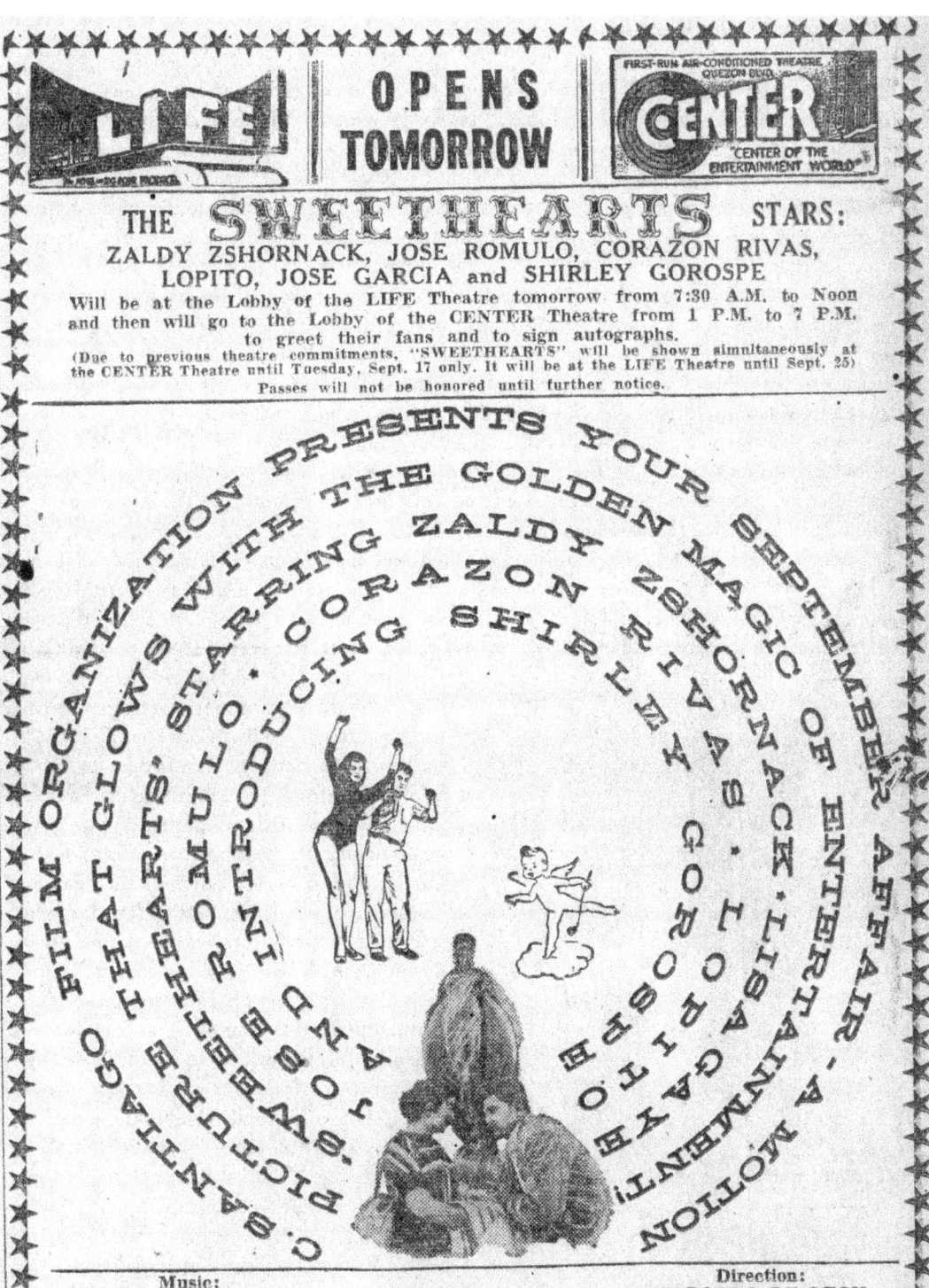

Sweethearts (1957/People's Pictures), one of filmmaker Gerardo de Leon's lighter efforts.

in the Philippines visiting relatives when the war broke out and they found themselves trapped there. After the war they decided to stay. Romero grew up in Mabini, Pangasinan, and as a child she had to go to Alaminos if she wanted to see a movie. She became a fan of some of the popular stars of the day, like Pancho Magalona, Rogelio dela Rosa, Carmen Rosales and Tita Duran, and by the age of 16, she informed her father that she wanted to be an actress. Her father was more than a little supportive: he moved the family from Pangasinan to Manila, knowing that if Gloria wanted to be an actress, that was the place where it could happen. Romero wasn't sure herself why her father didn't hesitate to make such an extraordinary move on nothing more than a young girl's dream of stardom: maybe he knew that young Gloria, being a mestiza, had the right look for the movies, and that she was certainly beautiful enough; perhaps he was himself stymied by life in Pangasinan. Whatever the reason, once the family arrived in Manila, Gloria wasted no time in visiting the offices of Premiere Productions. Premiere was willing to give her a small role in the film *Prinsipe Don Juan* (*Prince Don Juan*), which starred Efren Reyes and Anita Linda, but when it came time for her to deliver her only line, the teen-aged girl—already star struck—was nervous and barely audible. The film's director, Ramon Estella, promptly dismissed her.

Gloria had gone to Premiere first on the advice of actor Jaime Castelvi, who had visited Pangasinan for a stage performance, and had taken the time to encourage her after she approached him about her ambition. The truth is that she had a better connection that she could have followed up on: her uncle, Nario Rosales, was a film editor at Sampaguita. Rosales introduced her to Dolores Vera and Doc Perez, who agreed to give her work in bit parts, and she made her screen debut as an extra in *Kasintahan sa Pangarap*, a musical directed by Eddie Romero. After continuing in bit roles for a few more titles, Romero finally got a speaking part in the film *Ramon Selga*, which starred one of her childhood idols, Pancho Magalona. She only had a single line, but years later she bemusedly recalled it as her big breakthrough role. It was the film *Madame X*, however, in which she got her first significant part. Portraying the daughter of Cesar Ramirez and Alicia Vergel, the role was substantial enough that, for the first time she would receive screen billing. The only problem was that the studio's top brass were not very enthusiastic about Gloria's surname, Galla, and, recalling that her first film for Sampaguita was directed by Eddie Romero, Doc Perez promptly renamed her Gloria Romero. Things happened pretty fast for her after that, and she was soon top-billing romantic tearjerkers and comedies, at which she excelled, although, frankly, she had a tendency to mug rather shamelessly in comedic roles. Still, the public seemed to take to her portrayals of zany characters.

Lovely Rosa Rosal, whose figure was said to have been the model for the FAMAS statuette. She became popular as one of the great screen vamps of the 1950s.

A good example of how the studio tried

to take advantage of her glamour, dramatic abilities, and her comedic talent would be the 1954 film *Kurdapya*. Directed by Tony Cayado, the musical/comedy/melodrama cast Romero in dual roles: as the title character, she portrayed a homely and rather weird girl with a crush on local boy Ramon Revilla. But Romero also played the part of Joana, a beautiful college student from a wealthy family. Joanna winds up pregnant by way of a brief romance with Ric Rodrigo, and in order to conceal this from her grandmother (Etang Discher), Joanna arranges a drastic makeover for Kurdapya, who emerges as Joana's doppelganger. The zany antics ensue when Rodrigo mistakes Kurdapya for Joana and continues trying to romance her. Revilla, who had previously ignored Kurdapya, also takes a sudden interest. There is further zaniness by way of comedian Dolphy and Joana's evil, scheming cousin Eddie Garcia, who is out to cheat Joana of her share of Discher's will. Zaniness can only go so far, but could certainly not sustain a running time that exceeded *two-and-a-half hours*!

In later years Romero began to specialize in villainous roles before moving on to television in the mid-1980s, co-starring in a string of popular sitcoms through the '90s, and up to 2005 as one of the stars of the program *OK, Fine, Whatever*. All the while she continued her film work.

Another of the most popular and enduring stars to emerge during the Golden Era was Charito Solis. Somewhat more exotic in appearance than many of her contemporaries, though perhaps not regarded as comparably beautiful, Solis lacked the glamour of stars like Susan Roces and Rita Gomez, yet she exuded a charm that captivated Filipino audiences. Like so many others in the film industry, she came into her career by way of familial connections, her uncle being director F.H. Constantino, who introduced her to LVN matriarch Dona Narcisa de Leon. It was Constantino who would direct Solis in her film debut, *Nina Bonita (Pretty Nina)* in 1955.

Born in Santa Cruz in 1935, Solis was said to have possessed a world-weary countenance at a young age, having lived through the horrors of the Japanese occupation as a young girl, and her timid demeanor somewhat set her apart from other screen actresses of the time. Whatever unhappy childhood memories she may have had, they no doubt served as fuel for the powerful performances that earned her acclaim, and while she occasionally branched out into comedy and other lighter fare, it was as a dramatic actress that she came to be known and highly regarded. Solis won her first FAMAS Best Actress

Gloria Romero in the 1950s. Born Gloria Galla in Denver, Colorado to a Filipino father and American mother, her family visited relatives in the Philippines in 1942 and found themselves trapped there when the Japanese invaded. After the war they decided to stay.

award in 1959 for her performance in *Kundiman ng Lahi* (*Song of the People*), and she became the first actress to win the award back-to-back when she was honored in 1960 for her performance in the film *Emily*. Solis would continue to garner awards through the 1960s, '70s and '80s.

Nina Bonita had made Solis in instant star. So much so that a year later she starred in a film that bore her name. *Charito, I Love You* was a romantic comedy that was an instant hit, as was the film's title song, composed by Juan Silos, Jr. But whereas many of her contemporaries were considered stars, Solis was regarded more as an actress, and she did not crave the attention that stars typically do. She apparently never married, and refused to indulge gossip columnists by either confirming or denying rumors about affairs she may have had with prominent men, including politicians.

During the Golden Era, censorship remained a minor concern. There were a few exceptions, however. Gerardo de Leon's *Si Eva at si Adan* (*Eve and Adam*) raised a few eyebrows in 1954, however discreet the presentation, but more notable was the consternation censors felt over Ramon Estella's film *Ako Raw Ay Huk* (*They Say I Am a Huk*) in 1947. The concern was that the film might both encourage and romanticize the rebel movement, which the government was engaged in trying to quash.

The Huks (or *Hukbalahap*, a contraction of "Hukbong Bayan Laban sa Hapon," meaning "People's Army Against Japan") were a band of guerrilla fighters who, as the name states, had formed to combat the Japanese during the occupation. Made up of socialists and communists, the group did not disband after the war, but merely re-fixed their sights on the Philippine government with an eye toward exacting the changes that they desired in their country. It was reasonable to imagine that, with such a predominant underclass, portraying the movement in such a highly patronized medium as film might help to popularize the movement.

Although Luis Taruc, the Huk leader, had allowed his forces to be trained by a Chinese communist, and U.S. intelligence was convinced that the aim of the movement was to set up a communist govern-

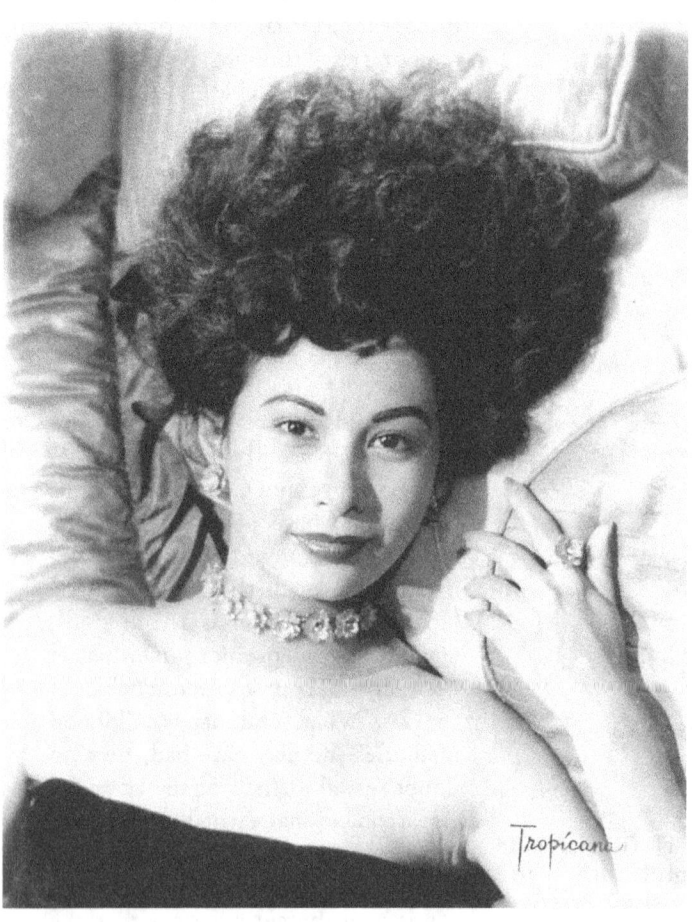

Charito Solis, one of the most respected and enduring stars in the history of Philippine cinema.

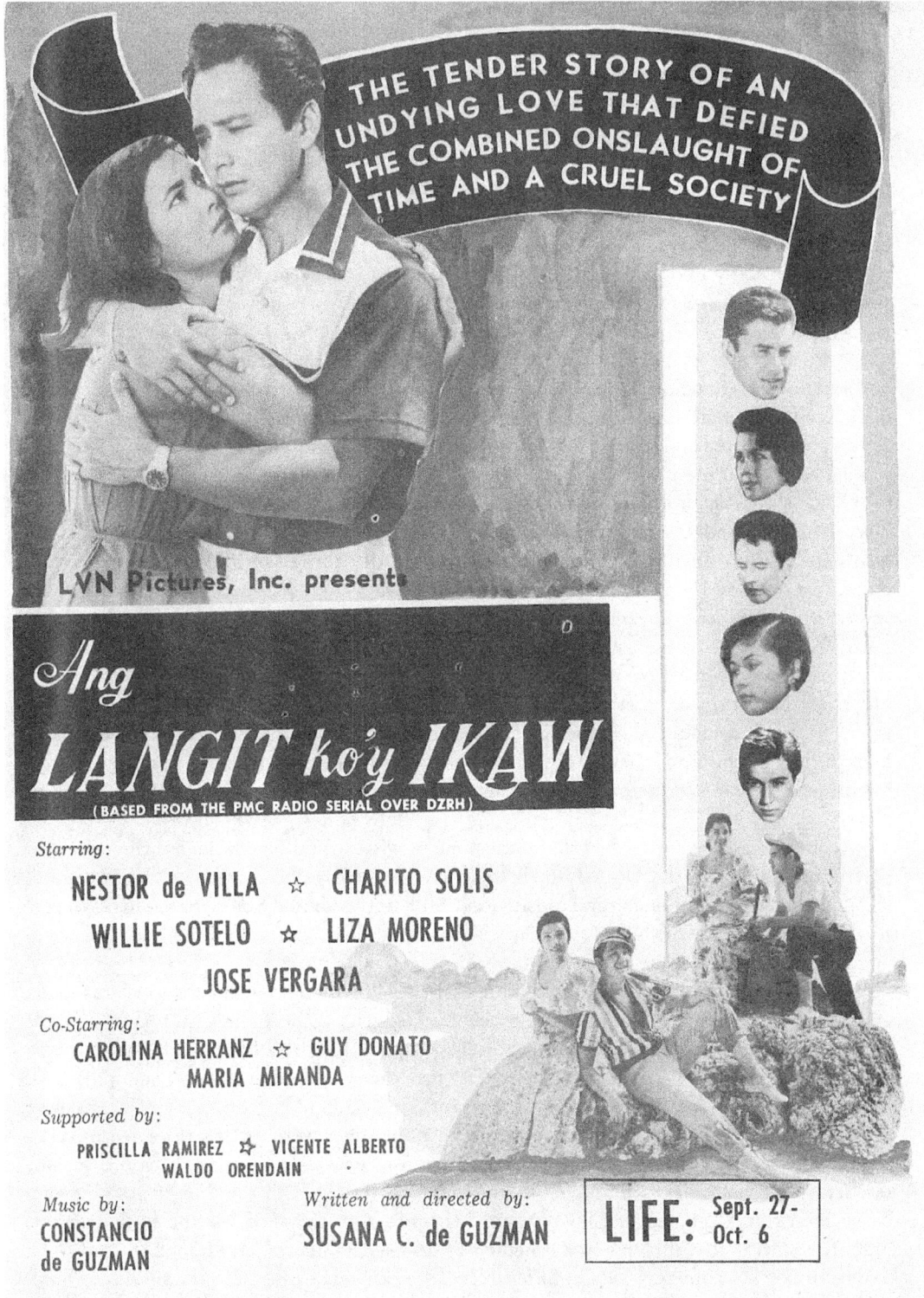

Ang Langit Ko'y Ikaw (*You Are the Only One for Me*; 1959/LVN Pictures) teamed Charito Solis with popular leading man Nestor de Villa. Adapted from a radio serial, the film is a good example of the popular romantic soaps that became a staple of Philippine cinema.

ment in the Philippines modeled after that in Russia, the Huks were not anti–American—at least, not during the war. In their struggle against the Japanese occupation, the Huks were willing to work with the Americans had they been able to remain independent of U.S. authority (although this was surely a simple matter of convenience), and indeed were known to have freed Americans from Japanese prison camps. Unlike the usual gaggle of communist intellectuals around the world, including those in Manila, who saw the U.S. as a wicked capitalist behemoth, the Huks were poor sharecroppers who, for the most part, held the U.S. in high regard, particularly upon the U.S. defeat of Japan. But, concerned with communist expansion, the U.S. refused to formally acknowledge the movement and set about disarming the Huks after the war. The U.S. had legitimate reason for concern, as the Bolsheviks had speculated that one way to bring about the collapse of Western capitalism was by the spreading of communism throughout Asia, which they envisioned as depriving the West of much needed markets and raw materials. After the war, with the communist revolution in China, followed by the wars in Korea and, later, Vietnam, this dream was moving toward realization. The U.S. was determined to prevent this in the Philippines, as was the Philippine government.

With all of this in mind, the concern of the censors over screen depictions of the movement is understandable. In democratized societies, censorship is viewed as a thoroughly distasteful option, but one obviously needs to consider things within the context of the times. Not only was the country recovering from a painful three-year occupation, but also was at last operating as a sovereign nation. The added burden of having to combat rebel insurgents made it an even more delicate period, and one could make the argument that the censors would have been foolish in not considering the ramifications of releasing a film that could turn a guerrilla army into a full-blown populist movement. Years later it would be another matter altogether when censorship would be used as a tool by Ferdinand Marcos, but in the immediate aftermath of the war, censorship was under consideration for the proposed preservation of the society rather than to help a megalomaniac cling to power.

It should also be considered that even some of what would be considered the tamest of entertainment fare in the United States today could not have been made in the 1940s and '50s, such is the erosion of cultural sensitivities. Still, in the United States, problems with censorship were far more likely to be focused on perceived moral corrosion than political ideology. In the Philippines, the two were necessarily given equal weight.

Years later in 1953 the subject was more easily dealt with when Lamberto Avellana made *Huk sa Bagong Pamumuhay* (*Rebels Under a New Life*), which was honored with FAMAS awards for Best Picture, Director (Avellana), Actor (Jose Padilla, Jr.), and Supporting Actor (Leroy Salvador). Of course, by then the difference was that the Huks had been largely marginalized. In 1951, the Huks had tried to induce the peasant population to boycott that year's legislative elections, but they were dismayed by a record turnout. They were further thwarted in creating mischief at the polls by military troops on hand to provide polling security and various teachers and civic leaders who served as poll watchers to safeguard the integrity of the vote. Taruc, who seems to have been a realist, was loath to set his sights on leading a full-scale revolution, knowing that such a grand scheme was doomed to failure, and hoped instead to be a thorn in the government's side in order to exact reforms. His pragmatism was seen by hardcore communists as a lack of commitment or will, and they ousted him, which prompted him to transmit secret messages on the movement to legislator Ramon Magsaysay. Magsaysay was a shrewd politician who knew that his career could be greatly enhanced by courting American favor. "What do you know about Filipinos?" he once said, "They like Americans. They like to see me with Americans."[8] Aside from his own personal ambition, Magsaysay's tendency to keep company with Americans probably also had a lot to do with the fact that he truly saw his own country's betterment as being inexorably linked to its relationship with the U.S., and said that, with America's help, the Philippines could "become the head of a family of democratic nations in this part of the globe."[9] With strong U.S. backing, he would run for the presidency in 1953, and his opponents foolishly labeled him an American puppet, which only increased his standing in the public's eye, and a curious and unlikely turn of events that year would help him go down as the man who brought down the Huks. Actually, actress Nida Blanca probably deserved more of the credit.

Born Dorothy Jones on January 6th of 1936, Blanca was the illegitimate daughter of a U.S. serviceman named John William Jones II and a Filipina mother, Inocencia Acueza. She had begun her film career with LVN in 1951 with the film *Reyna Elena* (*Queen Elena*), and she quickly became a star when teamed with romantic lead Nestor de Villa. She won the FAMAS Best Supporting Actress trophy in 1953 for her performance in the film *Korea*, and with the fame and acclaim came attitude. Known for playing tough-talking tomboys in her films, her screen persona seemed to mirror her public image. Just 17 years of age, she already had a reputation as a temperamental brat, and like many film stars of her age during that time, she entertained ideas of another career beyond movie stardom. With that in mind, she was studying pre-law at the University of Santo Tomas, and while rushing to attend class one day she got into a minor auto accident with a jeepney driver, who clipped her car. When the accident occurred, Blanca lost her temper and jumped from her car to give the jeepney driver a piece of her mind. After the jeepney driver responded in kind, berating Blanca as an arrogant and conceited actress, she wound up slapping him several times. It was the kind of unseemly behavior that would likely have gotten her dismissed had she been with Premiere, but fortunately for Blanca she was under contract with LVN, whose executives seemed to indulge her temperamental and frequently independent spirit. But the whole episode made national headlines the following day when the jeepney driver went on a popular Manila radio program to tell his side of events. The program's host, Rafael Yabut, famous for his opinionated diatribes and lambasting of local politicians, joined the driver in condemning Blanca's behavior, and the event was quickly turning into a public relations nightmare. It was one thing for studio moguls to try and control the trade press by having industry personnel work as magazine publishers or columnists, but the broadcast media proved more unruly, the difference being that many broadcast personalities were stars in their own right; perhaps none more so than Yabut, who was quite popular indeed. People might go to the cinema and see a particular film star every month or so, but they listened to Yabut in the comfort of their own homes every day: Yabut was said to have the power to make or break a career.* With public opinion going against her, damage control was needed and needed quickly, and so Blanca herself appeared on Yabut's program to tell her side of the story.

So where is all of this going? What does any of this have to do with President Magsaysay or the Huks? Well, it happened that as Blanca was pleading her case on Yabut's program and imploring the public to be understanding, her words were being heard in the Laguna mountains by Huk leaders in their jungle camp. Apparently tired of putting up a fight, the Huks were looking for a way to reconcile with the government. They also seem to have sympathized with Blanca's on-air pleas for forgiveness, and they had an idea of how to gain favorable publicity for themselves and Blanca too. Blanca was certainly in need of good publicity. The Huk leadership had a letter delivered to Blanca inviting her to meet with them to mediate talks regarding their surrender. The talks were secret—Blanca did not even inform the studio

---

Yabut would later tone down his on-air persona after being shot in the face and being permanently disfigured.

executives at LVN about what she was up to—and for two months Blanca went to the Huk camp in the mountains of Laguna on weekends to work out the terms of the rebellion's surrender. Her efforts paid off, and more than two-dozen rebels, including some Huk leaders, agreed to surrender to the government. Blanca was a national heroine.

As for Magsaysay, he won a landslide election victory in 1953, and in 1954 he further persuaded Taruc to surrender, but, although he came into the presidency riding a wave of almost cult-like popularity, his presidency proved anticlimactic. Still, being in office at the right time created the circumstance by which he would always be credited more than any other as the man who brought down the Huks, although some say that incompetence within the rebellion's ranks was probably just as much a factor, if not more.

Even American filmmakers used the insurrection as the impetus of the 1956 film *Huk*, an adventure yarn that starred George Montgomery as an American trying to defend his family's plantation against attacks orchestrated by Huk leader Mario Barri. It was Montgomery's first film in the Philippines, but he would return in the early 1960s to produce, direct, and star in a string of features.

Nida Blanca in the 1950s. Blanca's persona was that of a plucky tomboy, which she lived up to, negotiating the surrender of leaders of a communist rebel movement in the 1950s.

One other advancement during the Golden Era that should be mentioned is the introduction of color films to Philippine cinema. Although the pre-war film *Ibong Adarna* had been the industry's first experiment in color, it was limited to partial color in a few sequences. It was not until 1949 that the first full color features were made in the Philippines with the release of LVN's *Battalion XIII* and Premiere's *Ang Lumang Bahay sa Gulod*. The color processing for both films was done in Hollywood. Lacking the facilities to process color, and with the expense involved, black and white remained the norm throughout the 1950s, and even well into the 1960s.

Overall, the first ten years of the postwar period had been very productive in the Filipino film industry, showing the industry to be gaining tremendously in popularity at home, holding its own against foreign competition; but it had made very little progress internationally, and the glory days were not to last. Although production numbers would remain high, the industry was about to enter into a long and trying season.

5

1957–1967

By the late 1950s the Golden Era had drawn to a close and the industry was suddenly on shaky ground. As if to announce the end of the Golden Era, Rogelio dela Rosa left show business to run for the Philippine senate in 1957. The timing was merely a matter of coincidence, of course, but it had something of a symbolic quality about it, as the industry showed signs of contraction.

Dela Rosa did not enter politics on a lark: he was a very committed and erudite man who made a new career of it. In July of 1957 it was announced that prominent residents and civic leaders of dela Rosa's native province of Pampanga had organized a Rogelio dela Rosa-for-senator movement.[1] After more than twenty years in the film business, dela Rosa seemed eager to move into a career that was more substantive, and after being elected, his success seemed to light the fire of political ambition in his former show business colleagues. Suddenly, there were scores of film stars entertaining the idea of a political career, among them dela Rosa's longtime co-star Carmen Rosales. "The election of Roger has become an inspiration to us," Rosales said.[2] Friends and fans alike were hopeful that Rosales would run for the senate herself, and many of the workers at Sampaguita Pictures expressed a desire to help organize her campaign. Rosales said that she was giving the matter a lot of thought. "There are many women in the country who have done well in the political arena," she said, adding "I wish to duplicate their achievement if the people wish me to serve." Despite the support and her apparent willingness to run for office, the elections were too close to start a formidable campaign, and Rosales postponed her political aspirations.

There was also talk of Pancho Magalona (whose father, Enrique Magalona, was a former senator) running for governor of Negros Occidental, but the enthusiastic prodding of that province's Liberal Party notwithstanding, Magalona declined. More willing to entertain the idea of gubernatorial bids were Oscar Moreno and Leopoldo Salcedo. Moreno, whose real surname was Anson, was being courted to run for governor of Albay, and his wife, Belen Anson, seemed pleased by the prospect. "I have faith in Oscar," she said, "I am sure he will do good for the province, because my husband [always has] Albay in his heart."[3]

Salcedo was being pursued by the Liberal Party as a viable candidate to run against Delfin Montano, the incumbent governor of Cavite. Salcedo had toyed with the idea of politics before, having entertained the thought of running for mayor of Manila against incumbent Arsenio Lacson, but in the end seems to have been content to remain in show business.

Part of the natural inclination of political parties to pursue celebrities, no doubt, had much to do with popularity and name recognition. But dela Rosa's election to the senate had also created in its wake an almost giddy enthusiasm in the film industry that had many entertainers considering the prospects: actor Ben Rubio and comedian Miniong Alvarez were among the others expressing an interest in politics, but the enthusiasm was not boundless, and soon waned. Perhaps as studio revenues began to decline, studio executives saw no benefit in watching their box office attractions leaving to pursue higher ambitions, and stopped being so supportive of the idea. Or, for some, it may have been the realization that the soft life of cinematic celebrity was preferable to the more demanding work of a politico. All of the talk notwithstanding, it was more likely at that time for a politician to become a film actor than the reverse. Former Bulacan governor Jose Padilla, Sr., for instance, became a film actor, as did Rene Aboleda, a former vice mayor.

For dela Rosa, however, the commitment was real. After serving his term in the senate, he decided to run for the presidency in 1961. But as election day—November 14th—neared, dela Rosa found his campaign in dire straits financially, somewhat curious for a candidate of his stature, being still fresh in the public's mind as "Roger the matinee idol," and having a loyal Pampanga constituency that saw him as a champion of the common man. Dela Rosa was looking to unseat incumbent president Carlos Garcia, as was Liberal Party candidate Diosdado Macapagal. Dela Rosa and Macapagal both came from the same region—indeed, from the same town of Lubao—where they grew up together. As children they were the best of friends, getting into mischief together, as little boys do. There was that between them and more: dela Rosa's sister Purita was Macapagal's first wife; she died during the war. "It nearly broke my heart," Macapagal told some of his confidants, "that the one closest to me should be the one to oppose my bid for the presidency."[4]

Beyond straining an old friendship, it appeared that the competition between dela Rosa and Macapagal, both being from the same region, would only manage to split the Central Luzon vote, while Garcia would take a plurality of the vote from the southern Philippines, from which he hailed. It is not certain who suggested that for the good of the cause—defeating Garcia—dela Rosa withdraw from the race, but two other Pampangans who had grown up with dela Rosa and Macapagal conducted initial talks in October of 1961. Saddened to see two lifelong friends feuding in the dog eat dog world of politics, former Pampanga governor Jose Lingad spoke with dela Rosa's legal advisor, attorney Antonio Ybarra, and the subject of the financial state of dela Rosa's campaign soon turned the subject to the possibility of his withdrawing from the race and endorsing Macapagal. From there things progressed to secret negotiations and, ultimately, a clandestine plan to make an announcement of dela Rosa's withdrawal on November 4th. The choice of date was a politically catty move: it was Garcia's birthday.

With everything in place, dela Rosa and Macapagal finally met face-to-face at Ybarra's house on November 1st to finalize the agreement. Upon seeing each other again, they embraced and wept together. But their intention of spoiling Garcia's birthday with a bombshell announcement on the 4th was itself spoiled a day early. Somebody leaked the story, and on November 3rd enraged radio commentator Rafael Yabut let the nation know that evil political designs were afoot. Pounding his fist and audibly choking back sobs, Yabut announced that one of the candidates—he didn't name him—was withdrawing from the race as part of a duplicitous plot, and that the candidate's wife was so disturbed by the decision that she had attempted suicide.

The following day, President Garcia's Press Secretary, Jose Nable, was even more damning in his comments on what was about to transpire, accusing dela Rosa—again, without using names—of dropping out of the race in exchange for a 500,000-peso bribe. More than that, Nable said that the withdrawing candidate was promised absolute control of the Central Bank, the Commission of Customs, and the right to fill any three cabinet positions. Nable further said that this same candidate had earlier approached President Garcia with the same offer but been turned away. Nable also repeated the story of the candidate's wife being distraught to the point of attempting suicide, adding that she had been taken to a private hospital.

Nable's assessment may not have been as flamboyant as Yabut's, but it was no less scathing, and probably more creative, labeling dela Rosa's withdrawal a "great conspiracy" against "the entire Filipino people." His diatribe reached its pinnacle in a Biblical analogy: "The Judas in Philippine politics, who has all the time campaigned and posed as the champion of the common people, will betray the very masses whom he swore to defend and protect. The Biblical sale of Christ for thirty pieces of silver has found its counterpart in the 20th century."[5]

Such absolute hysteria in response to a candidate dropping out of the race could only mean that Garcia's party—the Nacionalistas—was genuinely concerned that dela Rosa's votes would indeed go to Macapagal. But there were those who wondered if Macapagal really would be the one to reap the benefit of dela Rosa's standing aside. Hordes of angry supporters showed up at dela Rosa's house on the 3rd, and by the early morning hours of the 4th, they were arriving from all over and gathering at the front gate. They demanded to be let in, and when dela Rosa's people complied, the crowd parked themselves on the front lawn, vowing not to leave until dela Rosa came out and addressed them. It was all in vain as dela Rosa was not even there. He was with Macapagal preparing to make his announcement in a joint press conference. Shortly after 4:00 P.M. on the 4th, dela Rosa and Macapagal appeared together before reporters at the ABS television studios in Manila. One rumor that dela Rosa wanted to dispel was the story that Malacanang (the Presidential Palace) had paid him to run, but that the money stopped when it became evident that dela Rosa was taking more votes away from Garcia than from Macapagal. Dela Rosa went on to announce his withdrawal and the reasoning behind it. He noted that, divided, opposition to Garcia would fail, but in uniting they were sure to triumph. "I will not stoop low," he said, "to answer at this solemn moment the malicious and evil propaganda that are [sic] being spread about this decision I have taken. Suffice it to say that my conscience is absolutely and clearly satisfied that this is the best thing that could be done for our fatherland. Let our people and history be the ultimate judge."[6]

Dela Rosa's brother Jaime stood behind him as he made his announcement, as did his sisters, Africa and Gloria. The three of them wept openly as their brother spoke. But drawing the most attention by her presence was dela Rosa's wife, Lota Delgado. Rumors had been broadcast that she had attempted suicide, and after her husband and Macapagal had finished speaking, Delgado said that she would like an opportunity to say something. She said that she was fully supportive of her husband's decision, and condemned the "ugly rumors" that she was opposed to it. "Some people," she said, "in their evil desire to destroy us have spread the yarn that I have tried to take my life because of this decision. This is nothing but a lie—a monstrous, evil lie."[7] She went on to explain that her recent hospitalization was due to the fatigue and exhaustion that had been brought about by constant campaigning, and a considerable drop in her blood pressure. She portrayed those behind the rumors of her attempting suicide as malicious individuals desperate to cling to power.

Many of dela Rosa's supporters were not at all accepting of his decision. Some, who had gathered at his house prior to the official announcement, proclaimed to reporters at the scene that they were not merely disappointed, but enraged, even to the point of feeling betrayed. Many told reporters that they would indeed be switching sides and voting for Garcia, dela Rosa's endorsement of Macapagal notwithstanding. But in the end the decision seems to have paid off, as Macapagal did indeed reap the benefit of dela Rosa's withdrawal and defeated Garcia for the presidency. In reality, dela Rosa's conditions for dropping out were far less demanding than Nable had suggested. He had wanted Macapagal do adopt some of his policies and he wanted to be something of a conduit between the government and the people, although that stipulation was a bit nebulous. But, more specifically, he did request to be given a position of higher standing within the Liberal Party, although that request also seemed somewhat non-specific. In time, Macapagal would appoint dela Rosa ambassador to Cambodia in 1965. Unless it were for the sake of appearances, it's uncertain why Macapagal should have waited four years to give dela Rosa such a position. Following his service as ambassador to Cambodia, dela Rosa would continue his diplomatic career under the presidency of Ferdinand Marcos, who appointed him ambassador to the Hague. Dela Rosa completed his diplomatic career in Sri Lanka in 1984. He died in 1986.

Dela Rosa may have been the darling of the Liberal Party for his decision to step aside in 1961, so rarely magnanimous a gesture in the politics of any country, but he did take something of a beating in the trade press in 1959, however, for distancing himself from the film industry's mounting troubles. The local industry had indeed been struggling through 1957 and '58, with a combined 400,000-peso loss in revenues, and a proposed 40% tax on all national industry threatened to kill the business off altogether. It was estimated that the enacting of the tax would have increased the film industry's overall deficit to somewhere in the neighborhood of a million pesos. Many film stars testified before the Philippine senate to lobby for the industry's exemption from the potentially fatal levy, but dela Rosa was strangely absent from the session, and was subsequently quiet when asked to comment on it. Particularly hostile to dela Rosa was an individual who wrote the "Screen Sidelights" column for *Literary Song-Movie Magazine* under the name "Snooper." In the magazine's July 1, 1959 edition, Snooper wrote, "Even the supposed champion of the movies, Big Man Rogelio dela Rosa, chose the peace and quiet rather than stick his neck out for a cause that once nurtured him."[8] Snooper even blamed dela Rosa for Oscar Moreno's dwindling prospects to become governor of Albay. "Roger just about loused up his chances," he wrote.

The slump in the film industry was serious enough, and the possibility of its eminent death should the 40% tax bill pass without excluding the industry, that many film stars were talking openly about seeking other careers. Glamorous actress Paraluman said that she would get by as landlady to the two apartment buildings that she and her husband owned; actor Van de Leon thought he might raise gamecocks, what with cockfighting being the nation's most popular sport; Barbara Perez and Rita Gomez both thought about becoming writers, while Susan Roces toyed with the idea of becoming a businesswoman. She doesn't seem to have had a particular business in mind. Perhaps strangest of all among ambitions for a second career was actor Ric Rodrigo's idea that he would work as chauffeur for Sampaguita matriarch Mommy Vera. But Vera dismissed the suggestion, as she said that, should the studio go belly-up, she would be getting rid of her cars. Maybe Rodrigo was only being amusing: maybe they all were, or maybe it was a grand sympathy play.

Dela Rosa may have taken all of the adverse publicity to heart, and the idea that his friends and former colleagues in the film industry might consider him indifferent to their plight was probably something that he did not relish. Whatever his motivations, dela Rosa was prompted to act on the industry's behalf, and by later in the month of July, *Movie Confidential* was proclaiming him and his senatorial colleague Roseller Lim as saviors of the film business. An editorialist in the magazine wrote that the industry's exemption to the tax could be credited to "the unrelenting endeavors exerted in [the industry's] behalf by their heroes in congress, led by senators Rogelio dela Rosa and Roseller Lim. The gentlemen from Pampanga and Zamboanga del Sur, perhaps unwittingly, have been not only the local movies' guardian angels but they are their literal saviours as well from what could have been the catastrophic end of their enterprise. More so, the gentlemen have saved thousands of employees and personnel in the industry from the dire consequences of the law, and ultimately from a future of misery and more suffering for them and their families."⁹ Somewhat melodramatic, perhaps, but definitely a considerable difference from the tone the trade press had been taking earlier in the month. Whatever his motivation to act at last, dela Rosa was apparently vindicated in the circles within which he once moved.

Levy or no levy, the industry was still in sore shape, and the studio system was clearly on the outs. The days of the contract players were quickly becoming a thing of the past, as many actors were taking to freelancing once their contracts were up, accepting work from whoever offered the best pay. It isn't that freelancing was unheard of in the business, but it was quickly becoming the norm.

Another example of the industry's disarray was the absence of its participation in the 9th International Film Festival in Berlin in 1959. Despite entries from other Asian countries (Japan, China, Korea, India, Pakistan, Thailand, Vietnam), there was not a single Filipino film entered. It must have seemed odd, since for years the industry in the Philippines was among the most productive and thriving in the region. "We are not ready," said filmmaker Eddie Romero. "We lack the talent, the money, and besides there's a complete lack of professionalism among movie people in our country!"¹⁰

That statement might have seemed harsh to some, but who would know better than Romero, who had been working in the industry since 1941? Romero was born in Negros Oriental on July 7, 1924, which would have made him only 17 when he was asked by Gerardo de Leon to write the screenplay for the film *Ang Maestra* in 1941. Under de Leon's tutelage Romero had become a formidable director himself. He had been writing for years, and in fact had his first short story published in the *Philippine Free Press* when he was only twelve years old. Years later, Romero joked to an interviewer that the story probably sold *because* he was twelve years old.¹¹ It could have been that, but more than likely the fact that the magazine's American publisher was a friend of Romero's father had more than a little to do with it. In fact, it was Romero's father who took him to the publisher's office to pitch the piece. The publisher bought the piece then and there, handing Romero five pesos, a nice sum in the 1930s, particularly for a twelve-year-old boy. A piece of perhaps fanciful studio publicity stated that Romero's passion for writing nearly cost him his life during World War II when the Japanese put a price on his head for publishing an underground newspaper.¹² It isn't hard to imagine that such should have been the case, since Romero's uncle was a magazine publisher for whom young Eddie began writing at the age of 14, and Romero followed a journalistic career after the war as managing editor of a Manila weekly, but his failure to ever mention his publishing an underground paper during the war in any of a number of interviews in recent years suggests that the story may be apocryphal.

Romero's family had been involved in the film business as owners of two movie theaters—the Luxe and Nepa—in Dumaguete, and as a boy he was watching movies daily. His father, Jose E. Romero, was a former congressman who later served as the Philippine ambassador to England. On his father's suggestion, Romero traveled to London and was able to meet filmmaker David Lean and observe him in the editing process. He also traveled to Italy and met Roberto Rossellini. Romero doubtless learned much about his craft from these men, and he determined that if the Filipino industry was going to truly grow up, than international exposure was the way to do it. There was also the need of upgrading the much-outdated equipment that the studios were working with. The idea was to attract better financing by wooing American backers with the lure of low production costs and an exotic shooting locale. If the industry was ever going to go global, there was also the need of American actors to insure a more saleable product in the lucrative U.S. market.

Bearing all of that in mind, Romero wrote a story about the early years of the U.S. presence in the Philippines and traveled to Hollywood to shop the project around. After the easy way in which he fell into his film career back home, Hollywood proved a rude awakening for Romero. But persistence paid off, and he eventually partnered on the project with Harry Smith, a mixer in the sound department at Columbia Pictures who was looking to branch out. It was through Smith's contacts that Romero was able to put together an impressive cast of American character actors, including Myron Healey, Richard Arlen and Bill Phipps. Fading star John Agar played the American lead in a story detailing the arrival of the U.S. military in a small Philippine village in northern Luzon in 1902, and the difficulty in bridging the cultural and communication gap and engendering trust between the two sides. After the end of Spanish rule, the U.S. had a hard time in some regions getting the local residents to trust their good intentions.

In order to complete financing on the film, titled *Day of the Trumpet*, Romero struck a deal back home with Cirio Santiago at Premiere Productions. The Filipino cast was impressive: Pancho Magalona, Alicia Vergel, Cielito Legaspi, Eddie Infante, and an impish newcomer named Vic Diaz. Though shot in 1957, and being entered in the Asian Film Festival in Manila in 1958, the film did not see U.S. release until 1963 under the title *Cavalry Command* once Romero had gone to court to wrest control of the project from Smith. After haggling with Smith over the rights to *Day of the Trumpet*, Romero found a more agreeable working relationship when he partnered with Kane Lynn, a decorated World War II Navy pilot who had gotten into the business of theatrical distribution.

Also on the forefront of the push to go international was Santiago. Aside from serving as production manager at Premiere, Santiago also started his own branch of the company, shooting features under the banner of C. Santiago Film Organization. He further dabbled in international co-productions in 1957, producing the film *Kim* in South Vietnam with a cast that included French actress Gigi Mariette. Santiago was further inclined to seek some attention from the global filmmaking community in 1959 when he sent his crew to Hawaii to shoot the film *Hawaiian Boy*. While there, he coaxed cameos from U.S. celebrities performing on the islands: singer Roy Hamilton was reportedly paid $3,000 to perform three songs in the film, while rockabilly legend Carl Perkins received $1,000 to perform four songs.[13]

But Romero was making more headway. While in Hollywood cutting *Day of the Trumpet*, Romero had occasion to meet Burgess Meredith, who viewed the film and took an interest in Romero's work. Although the pay was ridiculously paltry compared to what Meredith was making in Hollywood, he volunteered his services for Romero's next project, *Man on the Run*, a noirish action story. Years later Romero remembered Meredith fondly, recalling that, although he often had to send someone to fetch the drunken actor from Bayside, a popular Manila nightspot, during evening shoots, and although the actor was often thoroughly inebriated, the star never missed his mark once the cameras started to roll.

In 1959, Romero also wrote and, with Lynn, co-produced *The Scavengers*, another film noir, which was directed by down-on-his-luck Hollywood veteran John Cromwell and featured a Caucasian leading cast. Shot partly in Hong Kong, the film starred Vince Edwards as an American smuggler who spots his missing wife (Carol Ohmart) in Hong Kong and, with the help of mysterious Vic Diaz, tracks her back to Macao where he discovers that she is involved

Opposite: Eddie Romero teamed up with American Kane W. Lynn to produce the double-bill *Terror Is a Man* and *The Scavengers* in 1959. The two would later partner in forming Hemisphere Pictures, which would bring global exposure for Romero and his mentor, director Gerardo de Leon (1959/Valiant Films).

A UNIQUE Experience in motion picture TERROR!

SO DIFFERENT— a Bell System Has Been Installed For the **SQUEAMISH** and **FAINT-HEARTED!!!** When the Bell Rings we suggest you **CLOSE YOUR EYES!** It will ring again when it's safe to open them!

TERROR IS A MAN

The Doctor — His obsession was driving everyone mad

The Wife — She'd do anything to escape

The Intruder — He knew this was against the laws of nature

starring FRANCIS **LEDERER** • GRETA **THYSSEN** • RICHARD **DERR** • A Lynn Romero Production • Directed by Gerry de Leon • Screenplay by Harry Paul Harber • A Valiant Films Release

Hong Kong, City of Sin and Violence, where Beauties are the Bait and a Bullet is the Pay-off

VINCE **EDWARDS** · CAROL **OHMART** in

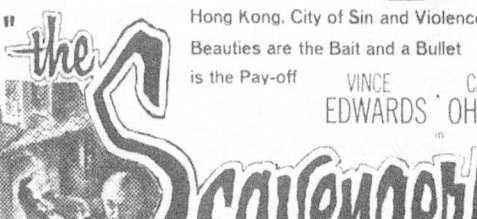

"Scavengers"

THEATRE

in the theft of some bonds and is being pursued by all manner of shady characters. Romero's screenplay showed that he was a good student of low budget Hollywood programmers. Among its Filipino cast the film featured Efren Reyes as a friend of Edwards. Reyes was a superb actor and director who would win the FAMAS Best Actor award in 1960 for the film *Kadenang Putik* (*The Mud Chain*).

The Lynn-Romero partnership proved fairly prolific in 1959, also producing *Terror Is a Man*, an interesting take on *The Island of Dr. Moreau*, directed by Gerardo de Leon and starring Francis Lederer as a scientist cloistered away on a remote Pacific island where he is engaged in experiments aimed at expediting the evolutionary process. With his lab assistant (Oscar Keesee, a two-time FAMAS winner for Best Supporting Actor, in 1960 and '61), he manages to create a leopard-human hybrid that runs amok and kills him in the end. In the meantime, melodrama was provided by a little illicit romance between Lederer's bored and frustrated wife (Greta Thyssen) and Richard Derr, playing the sole survivor of a shipwreck who washes ashore. It was de Leon's first film to receive broad international release.

Other than Romero's efforts, the only other exposure that Filipino films were getting in the U.S. was by way of the exploitation market, which was still wringing all it could out of old Filipino war pictures. In 1959 Social Service Pictures released *Atrocities of the Orient*, a film which was actually cobbled together from two films that had previously seen stateside release through Lloyd Friedgen, 1948's *Outrages of the Orient* and 1950's *Beasts of the East*, both of which had made regular seasonal play dates in New York for years, but neither of which were worth remembering to anyone other than 42nd Street regulars who took joy in their camp value.

One might have expected that the international co-productions might be welcomed by anyone with a genuine concern for the progress of the industry. After all, they were providing Filipino filmmakers with international exposure and, hence, a small but welcome degree of recognition, but it wasn't altogether agreeable to some. In the September 1959 edition of *Songs and Stars Home Magazine*, one writer commented, "The borrowing of foreign film celebrities—such as John Agar, Burgess Meredith, Carol Ohmart, and Richard Garland—has promoted a closer and intenser [sic] brotherhood among nations. But why utilize others' acting talents? What is wrong with ours?"[14]

Still on his soapbox, our friend Snooper went on an excoriating rant, seeing international co-productions as some sort of threat to the always-convoluted sense of national identity. "I understand some foreigners would like to put a finger in the industry." he wrote in *Literary Song-Movie Magazine*. "I understand, too, that they have the raw materials, a booking facilities [sic] and what's more—the capital. They don't intend to come out openly yet, but they will in due time. Is this good? It all depends on which fence you're in. I know a number of us will take it as a slap. But then, we have been used to this kind of indignity, so after a while, it is possible that we shall learn to take it in our stride."[15] He (she?) seemed to see the involvement of foreign producers as some sort of diabolical covert attempt to rob Filipinos of their individuality. The paranoid lament continued: "The 10,000 people or so directly dependent on the industry have very little choice. They will work for anyone under the guise of Art, or any such pretexts, if pretexts they must have.... Yes, there will be movies, but I doubt whether it would be the kind we can call our own."

Most of the Philippine participants in these co-productions were probably more than happy to be working in films that would be screened outside of the islands, regardless of whether or not they were entertaining any notions of "art." As to the question of pretexts, one need not dishonor the motives of individuals who in some cases may have been eager for a chance to give the global community a glimpse of their abilities, and in others, merely may have wanted to keep working, since the Filipino industry was teetering. What, exactly, was the complaint? What was it that was interfering with the concept of a truly Philippine cinema? Was it merely the use of Hollywood actors? Foreign capital? What made a movie uniquely Philippine? The truth is that foreigners had always had a hand in the Philippine film industry, and had, in fact, started it. But those decrying the involvement of foreigners were doubtless compelled to do so by the fact that the Philippines was at last a sovereign nation. With the country asserting its national sovereignty for the first time, the fear in some that their own cultural awareness would be lost by continued outside interference was understandable, to a degree. The confusion over national identity was more acute in the Philippines than in most countries with a colonial past, perhaps because of its prolonged state in the islands, or maybe because Filipinos were somehow more malleable toward outside influences. In reality, Philippine national identity was always intertwined with that of others, either through imperialism or the migration of others (Chinese, for instance) to the islands and intermarrying (sometimes, merely interacting) with others. Filipinos had such a prolonged experience with cultural intermingling that it was always difficult to discern where the influence of others ended and true "Philippinism" (if one can coin a term) began. Other than the stronghold that Catholicism came to have over the population, this perceived encroachment upon the national culture was perhaps most discernible in the arts. Throughout its history, Philippine cinema has resonated strongly the biases and modes of thought that colonialism brought, not merely as traces or lingering impressions left on the culture, but more as defining perspectives that helped shape it, whether the omnipresent considerations that Catholicism introduced into Philippine culture by way of theater and music during the Spanish era, or the conventions of expression derived from Hollywood films and other forms of mass media (radio, comic strips) during the American era. The Philippine arts borrowed liberally from both influences, making it problematic to ascertain what was purely Filipino in expression. If a cinema without outside influences was what Snooper and others were hoping for, it was a bit late in the day for that, since such influences were so deeply embedded in the Philippine consciousness that attempting to extricate them would be futile. Even by the late 1950s, the official use of Tagalog as a national language initiated some twenty years earlier in an attempt to assert a national identity above the American colonial presence, must have seemed odd to some since the language was still spoken by a minority of the people. If Tagalog movies were what Filipinos were supposed to consider their own, what percentage of the populace could truly say so? The 1956 film *Kahariang Bato* (*The Stone Kingdom*) serves as an interesting example of the national mishmash, as it was released in Tagalog, Visayan, and English versions (and was, incidentally, produced by American George L. Joseph and directed by German-American Rolf Bayer, a member in longstanding within the Filipino industry).

During the 1950s, Filipino cinemas were not merely playing films from the U.S. and Europe, but also from countries like Mexico, that had some universal appeal. Exporting Filipino films at the time was largely fantasy. Filmmakers like Eddie Romero understood that if the local industry was to cure what ailed it—principally, under capitalization—then Filipino films needed to be more polished and somehow less indigenous to reach a broader audience. By less indigenous, one can mean not only dealing with less parochial subjects, but also presenting the subject in a certain way; Filipino films have always had a tendency to shift the melodrama into overdrive until it becomes somewhat operatic. Such being the case, adjustments needed to be made since in the post–Golden Era years the industry was, at best, struggling. Even some of the local trade press felt the need to comment on the industry's shortcomings. Echoing Romero's view, *Songs and Stars Home Magazine* admitted the local industry's inadequacies, saying, "Sad to say, the majority of our scenarios are too ingenuous and trite, too full of gaudy trimmings.... Local stories deal too much with outlandish fairy tales,

88 Cinema of the Philippines

fantasies, and sentimental romances.... We are too unprepared. Too green-horned and unprofessional. Our actions are too gruesome, too exaggerated at times. Dramatic thespians are inclined to over-estimate the character portrayed. Comedians perform zany antics much too unnatural."[16]

But Snooper's diatribe against foreign intervention was not without merit. Although international co-productions were giving Philippine talents some greater exposure, the films were necessarily molded to foreign tastes, while not always displaying the local industry to the best of its abilities. Gerry de Leon, for instance, may have gotten his first broad international exposure with *Terror Is a Man*, but few in the local industry saw it as one of his exemplary works. Far more impressive to Filipino critics during the era were de Leon's adaptations of the works of Rizal. In 1961, de Leon filmed an epic adaptation of Rizal's *Noli Me Tangere*, which won him another FAMAS Best Director trophy, while also winning awards for Best Picture, Supporting Actor (Keesee), and Supporting Actress (Lina Carino). De Leon dominated the FAMAS Awards that year, as his picture *The Moises Padilla Story* won the Best Actor award for Leopoldo Salcedo, Best Screenplay for Cesar Amigo, and Best Editing for Teofilo de Leon. The following year, de Leon again dominated the FAMAS Awards with his adaptation of Rizal's *El Filibusterismo*, which again netted him Best Director, with the film also taking Best Picture, Screenplay (de Leon, Jose Flores Sibal and Adrian Cristobal), Cinematography (Mike

Leopoldo Salcedo and Diane Jergens in Eddie Romero's *Lost Battalion* (1961/American International Pictures).

Accion), Filmscore (Tito Arevalo), and Sound (Luis Reyes) honors. As acclaimed as these works were in the Philippines, international exposure was negligible, and for the rest of his life, de Leon's only global attention was largely limited to films considered to be cheesy drive-in fare.

While de Leon's more acclaimed works of the era were exceedingly homegrown, Romero, still courting the international market, sought some commonality with more universal themes. He turned to the WWII genre with pictures like *The Lost Battalion* (1961), a standard war drama notable for the fact that it was a rare chance to see Leopoldo Salcedo as the lead in an international film, playing a hardened resistance fighter. Salcedo had also appeared in Romero's *Raiders of Leyte Gulf* in 1959, eventually released in the U.S. by Hemisphere in 1963, a far more contemplative effort, which starred Michael Parsons as a U.S. Lieutenant sent to a small island near Leyte to rescue captured U.S. Major Jennings Sturgeon. Parsons makes contact with guerrilla leader Salcedo, but finds him reluctant to engage the Japanese, having lived under an unspoken truce with them for some time. But Salcedo finally relents, allowing his men to participate in an attempted rescue of Sturgeon, which fails, prompting Japanese commander Efren Reyes to blame the townspeople. Salcedo gave an excellent performance as the conflicted guerrilla leader, pragmatic to the point of being accused of cowardice by one of his underlings. Oscar Keesee also gave a strong performance as a two-faced tavern owner always looking to earn favor with Reyes' Japanese officer. Romero's screenplay was filled with fascinatingly complex characters.

De Leon got a second shot at international recognition when Romero signed his mentor on as co-director on the impressive World War II picture *The Walls of Hell* for Hemisphere in 1964, a gripping account of the battle for the walled city of Intramuros, which top-billed Hollywood actor Jock Mahoney. Romero followed the film in 1965 by writing and directing another World War II film, *The Ravagers*, which starred John Saxon, also for Hemisphere. Both films featured as their Filipino lead a young actor who had become the number one box office star in the Philippines. He went by the name of Fernando Poe, Jr.

Ronald Allan Poe was born on August 20, 1939, in Manila to Fernando Poe and Elizabeth Kelly. When his father died of rabies in 1951, Ronnie was only 11 years old, but as the

(Left to right) Fernando Poe, Jr., Michael Parsons and Jock Mahoney in *Walls of Hell* (1964/Hemisphere).

90   Cinema of the Philippines

eldest male child it fell on him to become the family breadwinner. Fernando Poe had unfortunately died owing enough debts that his family was forced to sell their plush home on Del Monte Avenue and move into a small apartment, and young Ronnie had to leave school and act as provider. After spending several years working odd jobs, Ronnie decided to follow in his father's footsteps and embarked on a film career. He actually began as a stunt double—for a woman, no less—being dressed to pass for actress Lilia Dizon in a scene where the actress was required to ride a horse (reportedly, a sprained ankle kept Dizon from playing the scene herself). In 1955 he launched his acting career in earnest, starring in the film *Anak ni Palaris* (*Son of Palaris*). Poe's father had played the role of Palaris during his career, and so, with his son now taking on the role, someone—it's a little uncertain who—thought to bill Ronnie as Fernando Poe, Jr., seemingly to increase the film's box office potential by conjuring up images of one of Philippine cinema's biggest stars of the 1930s, '40s and '50s. It didn't work; the film was a failure at the box office.[17] Interestingly, it was Poe's younger brother who had officially been christened Fernando Poe, Jr. But with Ronnie taking the name for show business purposes, his younger brother wound up changing his name to Andy Poe when he subsequently started a film career of his own.

Poe found much more success in 1956 when the Santiagos cast him in Premiere's production *Lo' Waist Gang*, a youth-oriented picture with a cast of young stars like Zaldy Zschor-

The Ravagers (1965/Hemisphere) gave Philippine box office champion Fernando Poe, Jr. a second shot at international exposure.

nack, Berting Labra, Tony Cruz, Boy Francisco and Butch Bautista. The film was a smash hit that spawned a series of sequels through the latter 1950s. Originally cast as delinquents in pictures like *Tough Guy* (1959), Poe would soon evolve into a tough guy of the heroic variety, eventually becoming the Philippines' answer to John Wayne. By 1957, he was earning 3,000 pesos

Early in his career, Fernando Poe, Jr. was cast as young punks and hooligans in films like *Tough Guy* (1959/Larry Santiago productions).

a film. But, his success notwithstanding, Poe's days of odd jobs were not yet behind him. Emboldened by his newfound success, he requested a raise in pay to 4,000 pesos per film and was turned down by Premiere. Although the studio system was disassembling, Poe was under contract, and refusing to honor the contract, he found himself unable to work in the film business for six months, and was forced to take a job as a doorman for 5 pesos a day. When Poe was able to return to work, he was no longer asking for a mere 4,000 pesos per picture, but had upped the price to 8,000 pesos. He found a taker in Hollywood Far East, one of the upstart independent production companies that were springing up in the wake of the declining dominance of the major studios. By the end of the 1950s, he was earning 10,000 pesos per film.

In 1961, Poe started his own production company, FPJ Productions, which released *Batang Maynila* (*Manila Boy*) as its first film. When Poe made *Walls of Hell* and *The Ravagers* for Hemisphere in the mid–1960s he was already renowned as the King of Filipino Films. With Romero and Cesar Amigo writing the screenplay for *The Ravagers*, and Poe being given the romantic lead opposite Maureen O'Hara's daughter Bronwyn Fitzsimmons, Poe managed to steal the film from American lead John Saxon. His status by then had gotten him to a 40,000-pesos-per-film salary. He reportedly received far more—75,000 pesos—to co-star with Mahoney in *The Walls of Hell*.[18]

In 1965, Poe also starred for the first time opposite Susan Roces in the film *Ang Daigdig Ko'y Ikaw* (*You Are My World*). Born Maria Jesusa Purificacion Levy Sonora, Roces was bidding fair as the Queen of Filipino Films, and was considered the exemplification of the classic Filipina beauty. What could be more perfect than for the King and Queen of Filipino cinema

Ang Daigdig Ko'y Ikaw (*You Are My World*; 1965/FPJ Productions) was the first screen team-up for Fernando Poe, Jr. and Susan Roces, the King and Queen of Philippine cinema. The couple would marry in 1968.

to unite on film, and, even better, in real life. In 1964, Sampaguita Pictures had tried to unite the two on film, but Poe, in a move that highlights how the major studios now failed to hold sway, had turned the offer down, saying that if the two did appear in a film together, it would be for his own company, FPJ Productions. After their first film together, the pair starred together in a string of films, like *To Susan with Love*, and did indeed marry in 1968, instantly becoming the First Couple of Filipino Films. Unlike most show business marriages, it was a union that would last a lifetime.

In 1969 Poe and Roces co-starred in *Perlas ng Silangan* (*Pearl of the East*), directed by Pablo Santiago for Poe's FPJ Productions. An impressive historical epic set in the Spanish colonial era, Poe starred as a slave aboard a Spanish galleon who manages to escape the ship and washes ashore an island where he is taken in by the resident Muslim tribe. He falls in love with tribal princess Roces, but must do battle with neighboring tribesman Vic Vargas for the right to wed her. Of course, Poe wins, and he then joins the tribe in their struggle against the Spanish, but in the end the natives are overwhelmed by the enemy and are inevitably forced to surrender to Spanish rule.

The film was well directed by Santiago, and featured some impressive cinematography by Sergio Lobo; it did, however, have one noticeable flaw. Shot in color and widescreen, the film contained no close-ups. For whatever reason, many filmmakers, when first delving into the widescreen format, often neglected the use of close-ups, perhaps being intimidated by the more oblong format, or maybe merely being preoccupied and swept away by the panoramic possibilities that it brought. Either way, the neglect of the use of close-ups squandered the filmmakers' ability to somehow draw the viewer more intimately into the narrative, making them feel more distanced from the events taking place on screen and leaving the film with a sometimes intangibly odd flow. It was not a fatal flaw, however, and the film may have been Santiago's finest work. It was also most probably the most impressive screen pairing of Poe and Roces.

If Poe had a rival during the 1960s for the title of Box Office King, it was Joseph Estrada. At 20,000 pesos per film, Estrada's asking price was, at best, half that of Poe's but was still plenty healthy in comparison to that of his other contemporaries. Even so, his annual income was roughly the same as Poe's by virtue of the fact that he tended to make more films yearly. Born Jose Ejercito on April 19, 1937, in San Juan, outside of Manila, Estrada entered the film business in the mid–1950s with LVN Pictures' *Kandilerong Pilak*. Upon doing so, he changed his name out of respect for his father, Emilio Ejercito, who found the acting profession distasteful and preferred that the family name not be soiled by any association with it. Estrada became a major star in 1962 with the film *Asiong*

Susan Roces in the early 1960s. She was the ideal of the classic Filipina beauty.

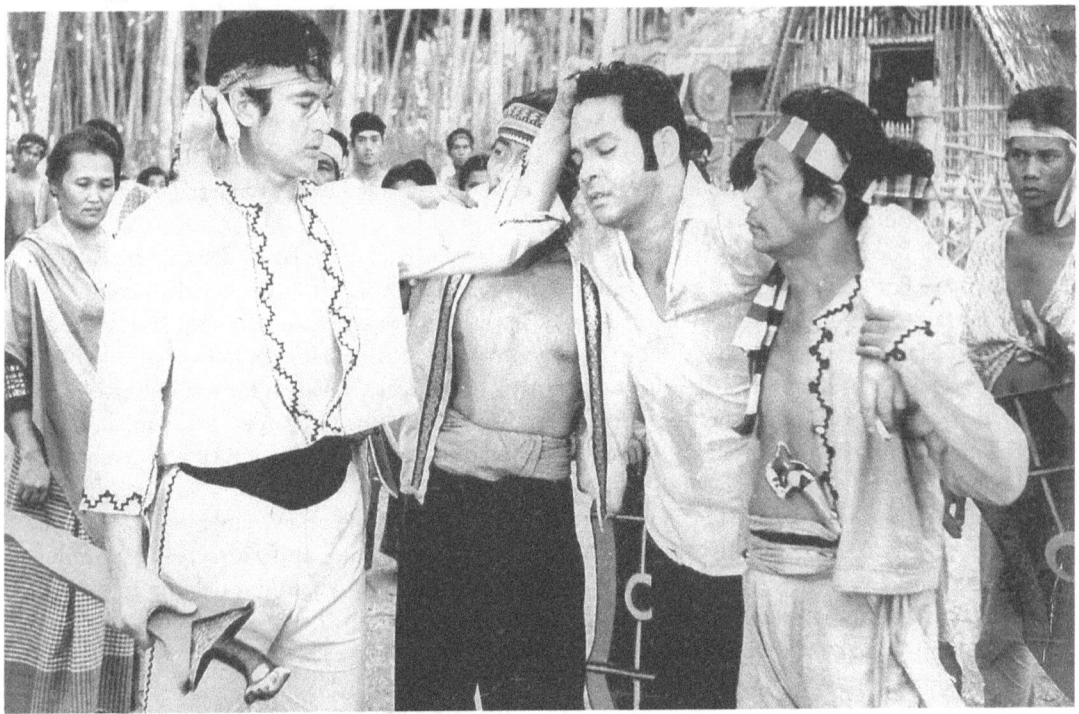

Vic Vargas (left) and Fernando Poe, Jr., in Pablo Santiago's historical epic *Perlas ng Silangan* (1969/FPJ Productions).

Salonga, and he would win the FAMAS Best Actor award that year for his performance in *Markang Rehas*. Estrada's only shot at international exposure came in 1964 with the Lippert-Filipinas co-production *Flight to Fury*, directed by American Monte Hellman. It was a somewhat routine story (written by a young Jack Nicholson) featuring a group of plane crash survivors (including Nicholson) fighting over a cache of stolen diamonds after their plane goes down in the jungle. Estrada portrayed a bandit leader who takes the group captive.

Like Poe, Estrada would start his own production company, JE Productions, and later in the 1970s started a second, EMAR Pictures. But the rivalry between Poe and Estrada was never contentious. They would remain friends for the rest of their lives and together they would dominate Philippine cinema for the next thirty years. Just like in the movies, where Poe and Estrada were larger-than-life heroes unafraid to take on all comers, in 1963 the pair would testify against criminal organizations that were extorting money from film production companies.

Still looking for international exposure, Eddie Romero had served as producer on *Flight to Fury*, and otherwise continued his association with Kane Lynn, who had partnered with Irwin Pizor in New York to form Hemisphere Pictures. Originally, Hemisphere had staked itself on war pictures, with moderate success, but at the suggestion of a young associate in the business, Sam Sherman, they decided to shift gears. Sherman convinced Lynn and Pizor that, on their budget, horror films promised the greatest return. With that in mind, Romero brought Gerry de Leon in again as co-director for *Brides of Blood*, which featured a cast of fading and middling American actors (Kent Taylor, John Ashley, and the improbably named Beverly Hills), and a generally impressive cast of Filipinos (Mario Montenegro, Eva Darren, Bruno Punzalan, Andres Centenera). The film starred Ashley as a U.S. Peace Corps worker who travels with American scientist Taylor and his sexually frustrated wife Hills to Blood Island, where they find the island populated by carnivorous plants and a monster that is quickly depopulating the local community of its young virgin women. Taylor surmises that the island's troubles are the result of atomic mutation caused by the nuclear tests on Bikini and the migration of contaminated sea life to the island.

Lynn devised a kitschy ad campaign involving plastic wedding rings to be given to female patrons in the U.S., which did much to fix the perception of the film as puerile drive-in fodder, as did the film's monster, a rather silly looking blob of a beast. But beneath the exploitation genre trappings, there was a significant underpinning that was revealing of the Filipino experience. The beast in the film turned out to be Montenegro, portraying a wealthy, reclusive mestizo, who periodically transforms into a sexually savage beast, prompting the natives to offer up young women as sacrifices to assuage him. Not surprisingly, the significance of this plot point was lost on Western criticism, which chose only to take notice of the sordid sexual element within the film. When young native girl Eva Darren explains to Ashley that the men on the island will survive the beast's fury, Ashley inquires why. "He wants only women," she explains, "He does not devour his victims; he merely satisfies himself with them." "But they get torn to pieces!" Ashley responds incredulously. "It is his way of satisfying himself," Darren says wanly.

Joseph Estrada in the early 1960s. He was Fernando Poe, Jr.'s closest screen rival, and perhaps closest friend.

It wasn't the only time that a significant bit of commentary in a de Leon film would be lost on Western viewers. In 1964, de Leon filmed *Kulay Dugo ang Gabi* (*The Blood-Colored Night*), an adaptation of a popular komiks serial about an aristocratic vampire named Dr. Marco, another mestizo who terrorizes the populace. Aside from the significance regarding Philippine history of showing the mestizo aristocrat maintaining his power by literally feeding on the blood of the peasantry, the film is also interesting in its depiction of the vampire—normally seen in film as sexually predatory—as a forlorn, tragically romantic figure. Portrayed by Ronald Remy, the character of Dr. Marco is obviously the film's antagonist, but one that engenders a fair share of sympathy, as he is often more of a romantic lead than the story's more traditional heroic lead, Eddie Fernandez. Marco is engaged in trying to save the life of his lover (Amalia Fuentes) by way of a heart transplant, intending to use his lover's twin sister (also portrayed by Fuentes) as the unwilling donor. At one point in the film, Marco is even relieved of his vampirism—albeit briefly—through the power of prayer. It serves as a good example of de Leon's fascination with the potential redemption of corruption.

Acquired by Hemisphere for International distribution, the film was dubbed into English (and severely cut) and released under the title *The Blood Drinkers* in 1966, and again in 1971 as *The Vampire People*, when it served as the bottom half of a double-bill with the atrocious American quickie *Brain of Blood*. Despite the careful staging of the photography, much of it making excellent use of misty settings and backlighting that call to mind the work

Top: Poe and Estrada mixing it up in *Ito ang Maynila* (*This Is Manila*; 1961/FPJ Productions). *Bottom: Brides of Blood* (1968/Hemisphere) featured an atomic mutation that required nude native girls to keep it satisfied.

Celia Rodriguez and Ronald Remy in Gerardo de Leon's *Kulay Dugo ang Gabi*. The film was acquired by Hemisphere Pictures, who dubbed it into English and released it internationally in 1966.

of directors like George Waggner and Mario Bava, Western critics were fairly dismissive of the work.

Fernando Poe, Jr. and Joseph Estrada were not the only ones starting their own production companies in the 1960s; actor Cesar Ramirez started CR Productions, actor Romeo Vasquez started RV Productions, and actor/director Efren Reyes became president of the Motion Picture Casting Corporation, while actor Ronald Remy became president of Medalyon Films. Among the other upstart production outfits, attorney Reynaldo Paulino started Pauline Productions, Joseph Albert presided over Tamaraw Pictures, Ramon Valenzuela ran Hollywood Far-East Productions, Nemesio Yabut ran Zultana International, Dominador Ad. Castillo ran AD Films International, Frisco N. Pascual, Jr. ran Ambassador Productions, Espiridion Laxa (later to become president of the Film Academy of the Philippines) ran Tagalog Ilang-Ilang Productions, and Antonio C. Montano ran Tagalog-Kislap Pictures. In 1963, Lou Salvador, Sr. turned his company, Golden Harvest Productions, over to his son, actor/director/writer/producer Leroy Salvador, who also started Jessica Films, which he had named after his daughter after her death at just six years of age. All of the smaller independent companies managed to keep the industry's output steady.

There were also Americans who continued to come to the islands to film pictures. One of those who became a regular in the 1960s was George Montgomery. A typically rugged Hollywood leading man of his era, Montgomery had first gone to the Philippines to star in the picture *Huk* in 1956. In 1961 he returned to produce, direct and star in a string of features, eventually under the banner of his own production company, Mont Productions. He and his partner, Ferde Grofe, Jr., focused primarily on WWII productions with titles like *The Steel Claw* (1961), *Guerrillas in Pink Lace* (1964) and *Warkill* (1965), but otherwise shot adventure pictures like the historical film *Samar* (1962) and the contemporary adventure story *From Hell to Borneo* (1964). They made use of many of the better character actors in the Philippines (Eddie Infante, Mario Barri, Vic Diaz, Bruno Punzalan, Joe Sison) and also acquired the services of cinematographer Emmanuel Rojas, who was also a respected director of Philippine films.

Montgomery's collaborator, Grofe is the son of a respected American composer, Ferdinand Rudolph von Grofe, a native New Yorker best known as the composer of the *Grand Canyon Suite*. Grofe, Jr. partnered with Montgomery on all of his Philippine productions as screenwriter and co-producer, even taking over as director for their final Philippine production, *Warkill*. Grofe must have found the working conditions agreeable in the Philippines, for he also worked independent of Montgomery in the islands, co-writing *Walls of Hell* with Eddie Romero, and producing, directing and writing his own 16mm short film, *Soul of a Fortress*, in the mid–1960s a largely silent meditation on Corregidor, and the fortress that housed MacArthur and Quezon during the war, which Grofe went on to expand into the ponderous and dour supernatural feature titled *Fortress of the Dead*. Although he went on to travel to such places as Africa and Mexico for his later films, Grofe periodically returned to the Philippines to make pictures like *Ethan* (1971), the story of a wayward Catholic missionary in a Muslim region of the Philippines, for which he served as associate producer, and the horror film *Judgement Day* (1988), which Grofe wrote, directed and produced, and which featured Cesar Romero in its cast.

Another American who proved useful to the local film community—even if he tended to gravitate toward the underground—was Michael J. Parsons: perhaps it was the dissipation of the old studio system that allowed for the emergence of talents outside the old constructs. Actually, Parsons is an American mestizo, an artist who tended to spend much of his time at the Café los Indios Bravos in Manila, a hangout for artists and poets. He helped Virginia Moreno—later the founder of the University of the Philippines Film Center—to import films from Hong Kong to be screened in the café, and Parsons began dabbling in 16mm short films himself. He also found his way into the mainstream of the Filipino film community as an actor, appearing in such films as the American production *Cry of Battle* (1963), which included Leopoldo Salcedo in its cast as well, the Eddie Romero films *Raiders of Leyte Gulf*, *Walls of Hell*, *The Ravagers*, *Moro Witch Doctor* and *The Passionate Strangers*, for which Romero won the FAMAS for Best Screenplay, and even Cornel Wilde's Philippine-lensed *Beach Red* in 1967. Although he began to drift more and more back into the fine arts, Parsons occasionally continued to keep a hand in the film business, appearing in the film *The Secret of the Sacred Forest* (1970), and serving as associate producer for *High Velocity* (1976), which boasted an international cast that included Ben Gazzara, Britt Ekland, Paul Winfield, Keenan Wynn and Alejandro Rey, as well as a fine cast of Filipino veterans like Joonee Gamboa, Rita Gomez and Bruno Punzalan.

More recently Parsons has constructed a paper mill and founded the Duntog Foundation in Baguio City, which experiments with making paper out of indigenous fibers.

While the heyday of the major studios had passed, some of them managed to carry on. In 1961 LVN reformed as Dalisay Pictures, but the company only lasted a few more years in its new incarnation. Sampaguita retained its place as one of the preeminent companies, although the studio became increasingly isolated during the 1960s, not for its position of prestige as one of the remaining big power players in the industry, but rather as the result of a scandal of sorts within the FAMAS Awards body.

Although the FAMAS had been founded by industry personnel, its original Academy membership included many from the local press. But after a few years, the press membership dwindled until the organization became the exclusive domain of movie industry insiders. Film studios would choose representatives to vote on nominees, and ultimately choose awardees, and being one of the larger studios, Sampaguita was permitted to send as many as twelve representatives. They were not the only studio sending that many representatives, but it was soon noted that, whereas representatives from other studios seemed to vote with a spirit of independence conducive to the competitive nature of the enterprise, the Sampaguita representatives consistently voted in harmony, effectively forming a voting bloc that ensured the studio a more-or-less favorable outcome. Smaller studios began to complain that they had little or no chance of winning awards. This continued over a five-year period, until 1960, when the consternation over the Sampaguita voting bloc was sufficient to prompt Sampaguita president Dr. Jose Perez to stop submitting entries or sending representatives to the event. More than that, in an apparent snit, he ordered all FAMAS Awards won by Sampaguita personnel to be returned, and he completely severed Sampaguita's relationship with the Academy, as well as with other studios, effectively isolating the company and its employees from all others.[19]

Perez was born in Bulacan, and after receiving his degree as a Doctor of Medicine from the University of Santo Tomas, he worked for the Bureau of Prisons. Although he intended to open his own medical practice some day, his marriage to Judge Vera's daughter Azucena more-or-less required his participation in the film business. Perez proved very helpful to Judge Vera in those dark days when fire razed the Sampaguita facilities in 1951, and his role in helping build the studio back up from the rubble impressed Judge Vera enough that he made Perez vice-president and general manager of the company. When Vera eventually became too ill to continue running the studio, he handed it down to Perez to run, although Mommy Vera maintained ownership. Perez eventually formed a subsidiary company, Vera-Perez Enterprises, in 1962, which was both a film production unit and advertising agency.[20]

Sampaguita's isolation from the filmmaking community after the 1960 FAMAS fracas was no real cause for concern. Traditionally, the larger studios had owned their own movie theaters, which were used exclusively for the showing of company product. Sampaguita owned Life Theater, which ensured a place to run the company's films in Manila, whereas the smaller studios had to fight for exhibition. Sampaguita could survive the scandal, but could the Academy?

The Sampaguita voting bloc was not the only untoward attention the Academy gathered unto itself in 1960. When Leroy Salvador won the Best Supporting Actor trophy for his performance in the film *Biyaya ng Lupa* (*Blessing of the Land*) at that year's Southeast Asian Film Festival, many in the local industry, as well as the local press, found it most curious that he was not even nominated for a FAMAS Award for the performance. How could the Academy fail to recognize a performance that foreign judges singled out from amid entries from ten nations? It only served to reinforce the perception of many that there was something seriously awry within the voting procedures of the Academy. At any rate, it was all enough to occasion FAMAS president Alfred Munoz to request the resignation of the Academy's original members, totaling more than a hundred. If the Academy was to regain the trust of the industry's workers, as well as the public, then it needed a new beginning—a fresh start. Although 33 of the original members who had resigned upon request would in time be asked to rejoin, the Academy reformed as an organization dominated by members of the press. Thus was the Academy able to put the scandals of 1960 behind and soldier on.

Ferdinand Marcos was born in Luzon, in the province of Ilocos Norte, on September 11, 1917. In his storied biography, it isn't always easy to discern the truth, cluttered as it is with myths of his own invention. As a young man, he had been an athlete, participating in boxing, wrestling and swimming, which he later enhanced into claims of having been an Olympian. He had always maintained that his father, Mariano, had been executed by the Japanese during the war, but subsequent investigation suggested that Mariano Marcos had been murdered by Filipino guerrillas who accused him of conspiring with the Japanese. Marcos himself had always traded heavily on his own boasts of having led an army of eight thousand guerrillas during the war, but the U.S. had concluded that Marcos' guerrilla movement was a fraud, and that they were no more than thugs that were trafficking with the enemy, and therefore refused his requests for supplies. He had also claimed to have received thirty medals during the war, which was, at best, a gross exaggeration: he was, however, known to have received a medal of valor after serving as a lieutenant in Bataan.

One thing that is known about Marcos is that he was a brilliant young man, excelling in law school, and scoring such high marks on the bar exam that some thought it impossible and accused him of cheating. He dispelled that notion by amazing his accusers with a verbatim recitation of certain legal texts. He was also apparently an extremely persuasive young man. Before graduating law school, Marcos was arrested in 1938 and tried for murdering a politician who had defeated his father in an election several years prior. He was convicted and sentenced to seventeen years in prison, but he appealed to the judge to allow him bail so that he might complete law school in order to better prepare his appeal. The teary-eyed judge granted the request. In October of 1940, Marcos got to argue his case before the Philippine Supreme Court, never claiming innocence, but instead wowing the court with Shakespearean quotes while arguing that the verdict should be overturned on technicalities. Noting that the country needed brilliant young men like him in the legal profession, Justice Jose Laurel ruled in Marcos' favor.

By the time Marcos was ready to make a run for the presidency in 1965 his largely fabricated war exploits were legendary, and he never missed an opportunity to play that angle. Marcos was looking to unseat incumbent Diosdado Macapagal, and the campaign turned very nasty, with Macapagal's camp even spreading rumors that Marcos' wife Imelda had appeared in pornographic films. As election day grew near, Marcos was anticipating a propagandistic gift by way of a biographical film, *Iginuhit ng Tadhana* (*The Mark of Destiny*), with popular leading man Luis Gonzales portraying Marcos. Even the title had a definite air of aggrandizement that must surely have appealed to Marcos' own exaggerated self-image. The Board of Censors had viewed the film on August 24th, and given it full approval, but just before the film was to have its premier on September 1st at the Rizal Theater in Makati, the Board suddenly requested to review the film again. The film's producers informed the Board that there were no available prints for review, as they had all been shipped to theaters, and the Board's Acting Chairperson, Rosalina Castro, promptly suspended the film's showing permit.

Popular actor Luis Gonzales portrayed Ferdinand Marcos in the 1965 biopic *Iginuhit ng Tadhana.*

The Manila press cried foul, many believing that someone had pressured the Board to suspend the film's permit. Whether or not Macapagal or anyone in his camp had a hand in it, it didn't cast his campaign in a positive light, and Marcos, of all people, wound up looking victimized. In his book *Film and Freedom: Movie Censorship in the Philippines*, Guillermo de Vega wrote, "It says a lot about the insanity of our pre-martial law politics in that this one movie should set the tone of a presidential campaign. Incredible as it may seem today, it was the suspension of this film which to a great extent decided the fate of that campaign in 1965, and made Ferdinand E. Marcos President. But so peculiar were campaign politics in those days that this one single movie made practically all the difference."[21]

The incident was scandalous enough that Board of Censors Chairman Jose L. Guevara resigned within days, perhaps seeking to salvage his own reputation, as he was himself in the news media business. De Vega wrote, "The Board of Censors, by a negative act, had sealed [Macapagal's] fate, and the atmosphere of campaign politics was so lunatic that ... one movie in effect was allowed to change the whole course of Philippine history."[22]

De Vega wrote that in 1975, and he had no way of knowing how portentous his words were. Being mindful of the times in which de Vega was writing, one should take his reference to "the insanity of our pre-martial law politics" with a grain of salt; after all, how could he have preferred the politics of the Philippines after Marcos had basically set himself up as dictator-for-life? Doubtless many writers during martial law were sure to alert the public to how greatly things had improved, when the opportunity arose. "Peculiar?" "In those days?" Indeed.

In 1967 Maggie dela Riva was, at the age of 25, one of the bright young stars of the Filipino film industry. She was making 8,000 pesos per film, a handsome sum for the time, as well as making 800 pesos a month in television and radio, plus various other fees for live promotional appearances. Not bad for a young lady who had graduated St. Theresa's College in 1960 with a career as a secretary in mind. But her fortunes were destined to take a tragic turn.

At 4:30 on the morning of June 26, 1967, dela Riva left the ABS television studio in Pasay with her maid and began the drive home to her house in Quezon City unaware that she was being followed. Jaime Jose, Basilio Pineda Jr., Edgardo Aquino and Rogelio Canal had spent the evening drinking at the Ulog Cocktail Lounge in Manila, beginning at 9:30 P.M. on the night of June 25th. They would stay until closing at 3:30 A.M. the 26th, at which time the four of them climbed into Jose's red convertible Plymouth with Pineda driving. They drove to the ABS studio on Roxas Blvd. and waited until they saw dela Riva depart, and after following her for a distance, Pineda tried to run dela Riva's car off the road. Dela Riva was able to avoid a collision and managed to make it to the front gate of her home, but Pineda caught up to her. Dela Riva lived in an affluent community where most of the homes had gated front drives, usually a worthy security measure, but in this case it worked against her as it necessitated that she exit her car and open the gate before she could enter the property. After pulling up alongside dela Riva's car, Pineda jumped from Jose's Plymouth and darted toward dela Riva's vehicle, prompting her to blow the horn in panic. But Pineda managed to reach the car and open the door before dela Riva thought to lock the door. Dela Riva clung desperately to the steering wheel, but, grabbing her by the left arm, Pineda was able to drag her from the car. After pulling dela Riva from the car, Pineda found himself in a tug of war with dela Riva's maid, Helen Calderon, who had jumped from the car and grabbed hold of dela Riva's right arm. Pineda's superior strength eventually won out and he was able to get dela Riva to the Plymouth, at which time his three accomplices pulled dela Riva into the backseat of the car and, with Pineda once more taking the wheel, they sped off, leaving Calderon behind.

As the car drove through the mostly empty streets, dela Riva pleaded with her captors to let her go, but she drew only lewd taunts in response. In time, as her abductors grew tired of her pleading, they threatened to either shoot her or disfigure her with acid. In the backseat, she was seated between Jose, who was forcibly kissing her, and Aquino, who was lifting up her skirt and feeling her up. Eventually, they blindfolded dela Riva and took her to the Swanky Hotel in Pasay City, where they led her up to a room on the second floor. Once inside the room, dela Riva was made to undress and perform a burlesque dance for her captors, who then took turns raping her. When dela Riva struggled, she was beaten; after the second rape, she went into shock, prompting the men to dump water on her face to bring her round again. After the third rape, she again went into shock, at which time her abusers, determined that she be cognizant of what was happening, again threw water on her.

After the abuse ended, the four men decided to drive her to a spot near a television station in order to make it appear that she had just left the studio. They told her that they were going to release her, but warned her that, should she report the incident to the police, they would post bond and return to disfigure her face. After the men dropped her off, dela Riva took a cab to her home. When she arrived home at 6:30 A.M., police and reporters were already gathered at her home, her abduction having been reported by Calderon. Dela Riva's abductors had instructed her to say that she had been mistaken for a nightclub hostess, and that once they had realized their mistake, her abductors had set her free. Upon her arriving home, dela Riva's family (she lived with her mother) requested that the police not question her for the moment. She would wait four days before reporting that she had been raped, perhaps partly due to fear of her assailants' promised reprisals, but probably more attributable to the accompanying shame and all of the loathsome publicity that it would bring, and the possibility of some corresponding effect on her career.

Upon her reporting of the assault, things happened rather quickly. The police arrested Jose that same day, and after obtaining a statement from him in which he admitted taking part in Miss dela Riva's abduction, but denied raping her, the other participants in the crime were identified and apprehended, Pineda and Canal in Lipa on July 1, and Aquino in Batangas on July 5. The ensuing trial became a major media event, and as it did, other women came forward to say that they too had been abducted and raped by the same men. It turned out that the men had made a habit of abducting women—usually cocktail waitresses—and raping them, but their threats of reprisal had managed to intimidate the women into keeping quiet in the past. Now, with dela Riva leading the way, some of them were willing to come forward. The trial culminated with dela Riva's own emotionally charged testimony, and the men were convicted and given the death penalty. Although the ruling would be appealed, eventually to the Philippine Supreme Court, the verdict would be upheld, and Jose, Pineda and Aquino would eventually be executed (Canal having died in prison in December of 1970). The executions themselves would become a media frenzy, reporters swarming the scene to try and get a last statement from dela Riva's attackers or their families. In time, dela Riva would resume her career as an actress.

6

1968–1973

During the 1960s the problems facing the Filipino film industry were manifold. There had always been the problem of foreign competition, but during the Golden Era, Filipino films had more than held their own. But now, with the days of the major studios passed, the smaller production outfits were finding the going tough. In the 1960s there were, on average, some 700 movie theaters in the Philippines, most of which showed foreign films. The larger studios, like Sampaguita, owned their own movie houses, and were therefore assured of exhibition, while others signed exclusive agreements with venues. Many foreign studios and distributors did the same. But for the small producers, which came to comprise a majority of the industry's output, bookings could be problematic. The Philippine Motion Pictures Producers Association sought to shield the industry from the deluge of foreign competition by encouraging protectionist legislation, toward which end PMPPA President Albert Joseph used the occasion of the 16th annual FAMAS Awards to get President Ferdinand Marcos to sign certification to congress to enact a bill that placed limitations on the importation of foreign films to 150. Under the bill, Filipino film producers and distributors could only import one foreign film for every three Filipino films that they distributed. Always eager to wow the people with his oratorical abilities, Marcos also gave a speech that night that was both humorous and scholarly in turns.

But there was more to the industry's troubles than a matter of foreign competition. It is also true that, although senators Rogelio dela Rosa and Roseller Lim were credited by some as having saved the film industry from what would have been a devastating tax levy in 1959, in the ensuing years, more and more taxes crept in to the point that the profit margin was increasingly choked. As much as they could, Filipino filmmakers tried to stem the tide of the increasing dominance of foreign imports, but the result was a creative drought that saw much of the industry's product being turned out as little more than pale imitations of popular international films. "Whenever a Pilipino movie imitates a Hollywood picture," wrote columnist Andy Salao in the May 1969 edition of *Movie Confidential*, "the result is usually very disappointing. You could not help feeling sorry for our producer or director when you see how inferior the movie is compared to the Hollywood original."[1]

One much imitated genre was the secret agent film, the result of the popularity of the James Bond films. The genre made a star of Tony Ferrer, who, as Tony Falcon, Agent X-44, made a series of popular secret agent knock-offs. Many of the Agent X-44 films were directed by actor Eddie Garcia, who was starting to make a name for himself as a director. The Garcia-directed X-44 film *Sabotage* was the big hit of the 1966 Manila Film Festival. More Asian in his appearance than many other leading men in the Filipino industry, Ferrer also started to

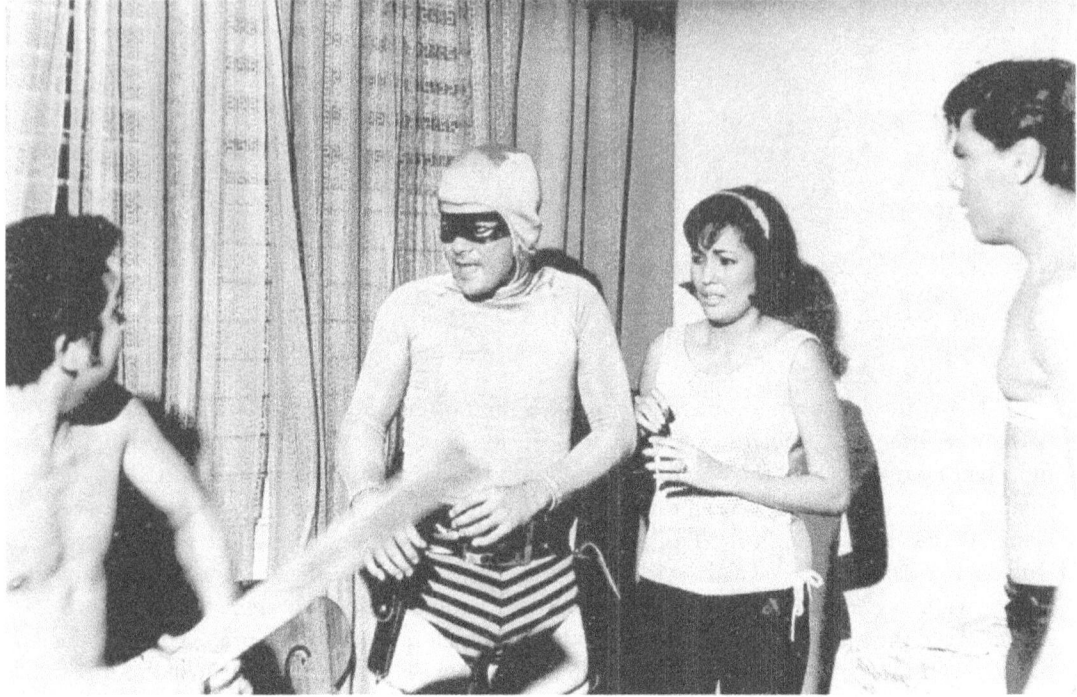

The 1960s film *Alias the Phantom* (D'Lanor) is a good example of how Philippine cinema emulated popular American culture.

make a showing in the martial arts genre with films like *Karate Fighters*, *The Blackbelter* and *Masters of Karate* (all in 1968), all of which pre-dated the wave of martial arts films spawned in the wake of Bruce Lee's success in the early 1970s, and he continued in the genre with later titles like *Blind Rage* in 1978 and *Deadly Fighters* in 1980. The Agent X-44 films also continued into the 1970s with titles like *Secret Witness* in 1972. Ferrer also saw a little global exposure, starring in Spanish director Jess Franco's international film *The Vengeance of Fu Manchu* in 1967 with Christopher Lee. In his later career he has transitioned into villainous roles.

One genre very prone to imitation was the comedy genre, which usually relied on spoofing popular international films, in particular those from Hollywood. In the world of comedy, Dolphy was King. Born Rodolfo Vera Quizon on July 25, 1928, he got his start as a comedian on the stage of the Orient Theater in Manila during the Japanese occupation. He was something of a vaudevillian at the time, going by the name Golay, but after the war he was given his first screen break by Fernando Poe, Sr., who renamed him Dolphy and cast him in the film *Dugo ng Bayan*. In 1953 he went on to work for Doc Perez at Sampaguita, initially in supporting roles as the ever-present bungling sidekick, a staple of even more dramatic fare in Philippine cinema, but he eventually got his chance at starring roles in 1954 with the film *Jack en Jill* (*Jack and Jill*), co-starring with Lolita Rodriguez. The film was a big success and it put Dolphy on the map as one of the premier comics of the 1950s; subsequent successes brought him the title "King of Comedy."

Jack en Jill was not only a commercial success, but quite a groundbreaker in Philippine cinema as well: it was the first film to be centered around an openly gay character, and with Dolphy playing the part, it led to more gay roles for the comedian, such as the very successful *Facifica Falayfay*. In fact, he became so identified with such roles that many assumed that

Tony Ferrer mixing it up with the bad guys as Tony Falcon, Agent X-44, in the 1960s. Ferrer portrayed the secret agent in a series of films from the late 1960s through the early '70s.

he *was* homosexual. The irony is that, as peculiar as he may have been in appearance—he grew into his looks with age—Dolphy was quite the ladies' man. Through the years he has had many well-publicized relationships with much younger actresses, such as Pilar Pilapil, Lotis Key and Alma Moreno; he has also fathered 18 children with 5 different women. Because many of his most well known roles tended to be homosexual, Dolphy periodically joked that his many love affairs may have been an attempt to shed his gay image. Nonetheless, he continued to accept such roles, including acclaimed portrayals in films like Lino Brocka's *Ang Tatay Kong Nanay* (*My Father, My Mother*) in 1978 (which, unlike his cross-dressing comedy roles, was a serious portrayal of a homosexual father, which won Dolphy a FAMAS Best Actor award), and more recently *Markova: Comfort Gay* (2000), the true story of a homosexual victimized by the Japanese during the war, which won Dolphy a Best Actor award at the Brussels International Film Festival, along with his sons Eric and Jeffrey Quizon, all of them portraying the title character at different stages of his life.

Dolphy also caused quite a stir in the late 1980s when he began a relationship with actress/singer Zsa Zsa Padilla, more than 30 years his junior. After starring with Dolphy in the film *Anak ni Facifica Falayfay* (*Child of Facifica Falayfay*) in 1988—a box office flop—Padilla left her dentist husband to be with Dolphy, and the scandal sheets had a field day with the romance: in fact the furor became so great that even priests were condemning the couple in sermons.

Comedians Chiquito (left) and Dolphy in the 1960s film *Doble Solo* (*Double Solo*; RR Productions).

Surprisingly, given his stature in the business, Dolphy found himself shunned by the entertainment industry, and with no movie offers coming, and even his long-running television sitcom *John en Marsha* (*John and Marsha*) being cancelled, the King of Comedy found himself out of work for three years and was forced to sell off various properties to survive. His career at a standstill, Dolphy considered immigrating to the U.S. (New York and Las Vegas being his favorite cities in the world), but better days lay ahead. The romance to Padilla survived it all—even the long wait for Padilla's annulment—and in time both the public and the industry were forgiving, allowing Dolphy to not only regain his stature as a giant in the industry, but to even grow in that respect. He returned to film, and even scored another long-running hit sitcom, *Home Along da Riles* (*Home Along the Rails*), in the 1990s. His popularity became so immense that it even reached the shores of the U.S. when Illinois Secretary of State Jesse White held a press conference on July 22, 2004, to officially declare July 25, 2004, "Dolphy Day" in the entire state.

But Dolphy's life has not been all romance and laughter: his son, Rodolfo Quizon, Jr., or Dolphy, Jr. as he became known in his own budding film career, was a drug addict who wound up being arrested for arson along with film comedian Jerry Pons in a case that resulted in the deaths of six people. Among the victims were the children of actress Mina Aragon. Rodolfo, Jr. wound up receiving a life sentence in 1980, but after serving 18 years, he was given a pardon by film actor-turned-president Joseph Estrada, a close friend of Dolphy's. Rodolfo Quizon, Jr. emerged from prison a changed man, having undergone a religious conversion during his incarceration.

There was also Dolphy's son, Wilfredo "Freddy" Quizon, who died in November of 2005 of internal hemorrhaging four days after taking a fall in his bathroom. Some of Dolphy's grandchildren have also given the comic reason to grieve. A 14-year-old grandson, Jelom Carlo Quizon, allegedly a member of a school fraternity gang, was shot to death in December of 2004 in what police surmised was a gang-related killing. A year later another grandson, 16-year-old Nico Quizon—son of Freddy Quizon, and allegedly another gang member—was the prime suspect in the stabbing death of a man in Quezon City.

As the 1960s wore on much of the world was undergoing a cultural revolution—the skirts got higher, the swimsuits got smaller, attitudes were changing. This was especially true of the Western world. As the Philippines always had at least one foot in the Western world, changing values in the West necessarily reverberated in the islands. It is also true that, through the growth of mass media, the world was getting smaller and cultural divides were evaporating to a degree. But no place in the world seemed to absorb American popular culture as readily as the Philippines; Filipinos soaked it up like a sponge.

A good example of just how much American films were changing is to note the introduction in the U.S. of the MPAA ratings system in the late 1960s. Suddenly, it seems, people needed to be warned that any given film was perhaps

Dolphy with Zsa Zsa Padilla in the 1990s. Some 30 years his junior, Padilla left her husband to be with the comedian after the two starred in a film together in 1988. Their relationship would cause an uproar that derailed Dolphy's career for several years.

not appropriate for certain age groups. In the Philippines no such system was adopted, but films were either approved or disapproved by a Board of Censors. With this system, Filipino films had remained fairly constant in their presentation, and the boundaries that filmmakers knew they could readily work within. That said, a Filipino film was as likely to attract the unwanted attentions of the censors over matters of ideology as much as taste. The repercussions on Filipino films were damaging. Certainly one can deal with distasteful themes or subjects tactfully, but as foreign films continued to push the boundaries of good taste further out, Filipino filmmakers found themselves losing their audience to imported films that operated under more liberal standards. And it wasn't just that they were operating under more liberal standards in their respective countries of origin: Filipino filmmakers had always maintained that foreign films were judged by far more lax standards than local films, and with international tastes becoming far more willing to pander to prurient interests, the problem was only worsening. In order to stay competitive, and lacking the money that the larger studios once had to spend on somewhat more elaborate productions, the small independent production companies had to find a selling point, and thus the bomba genre was born.

The term "bomba" would be similar to the English term "bombshell," and it was usually used as a form of political jargon; for instance, a revelation that might prove damaging to a politician's career would be considered a bomba. The term took on a different connotation in its application to film, where it was used to mean "bold" or "daring." The bombas were racier films, made cheaply, which used sex as their selling point. Though for the most part they were not pornographic by the current understanding of the term, they were much more frankly sexual than anything seen in Filipino films before.

In keeping with the times, there had occasionally been brief nudity in Filipino films. Charito Solis, for instance, had briefly bared her breasts in the 1968 film *Igorota*, a FAMAS Best Picture award winner. In fact, the film dominated the FAMAS Awards that year, winning the Best Actress award for Solis, Director (Luis Nepomuceno), Supporting Actor (Fred Galang), Color Cinematography (Loreto Isleta)*, Editing (Elsa Abutan), Filmscore (Tito Arevalo), and Sound (Juanito Clemente). With international distribution in mind, Nepomuceno had shot the film in English.

To see the film today, one could easily ask why it should have been so lauded. The film used a basic tragic love story to express what can only be seen as an extreme distaste for the Westernization of Philippine culture, in particular, Catholicism and its often hollow ritualism. The film starred Ric Rodrigo as a Catholic city dweller who goes off hunting and meets and falls in love with Solis, playing a princess of the Igorot tribe. After wedding in a tribal ceremony, Rodrigo takes Solis to his mansion in the city where she is given a frosty reception from Rodrigo's wealthy friends and family. Solis is very uncomfortable with her new surroundings and customs, be it the Catholic wedding ceremony the newlyweds are forced to undergo to make the union legally binding, or even the simple act of saying grace at the dinner table. The embarrassingly overstated premise upon which the narrative stakes itself is that the Igorots are noble savages, whereas the city dwelling Catholics are shallow, greedy, cruel and materialistic. In one scene, after Rodrigo and Solis' Christian wedding, Solis' new brother-in-law (Eddie Garcia) insults Solis' visiting family by encouraging the other guests to mimic an ancient Igorot dance, but Solis' father puts a stop to it by scattering gold nuggets all over the floor, causing a near riot as the greedy guests fight and scramble to gather them up. Apparently, the film would have one believe that, although they have a cavern spilling over with gold, the Igorots, being spiritual rather than materialistic people, have no use for the stuff, a view which is not altogether historically accurate. In another scene, Solis takes her young daughter to visit her Igorot family and the little girl exclaims, "I want to stay here! The people are all so friendly!"

Nepomuceno, who concocted the story upon which Amigo's screenplay was based, either has Igorot blood in his lineage, or is a Catholic with a hyper-sensitive guilt complex (which would hardly be a novelty), and while an honest examination of cultural biases should always be welcomed, Nepomuceno overcompensated to the point of obnoxious pandering. It would not be surprising in such a rigidly Catholic society to find any number of artists challenging the religious hierarchy, but the problem with *Igorota* is that the Christian characters are so cartoonish that it is impossible to take the film seriously. Without knowing Nepomuceno's faith, it is difficult to know whether this was merely a silly piece of anti–Catholic propaganda, or a ridiculously self-indulgent exercise in self-excoriation. Perhaps because the film was not a frivolous rip-off of some popular Western title, but presented itself—however clumsily—as a piece of social commentary, the censors were willing to allow Solis' brief topless moment in the film (which, incidentally, occurs when Solis is goaded by the evil Catholic city folk into

---

At the time, black and white was still so prevalent that the FAMAS awarded both black and white and color cinematography separately.

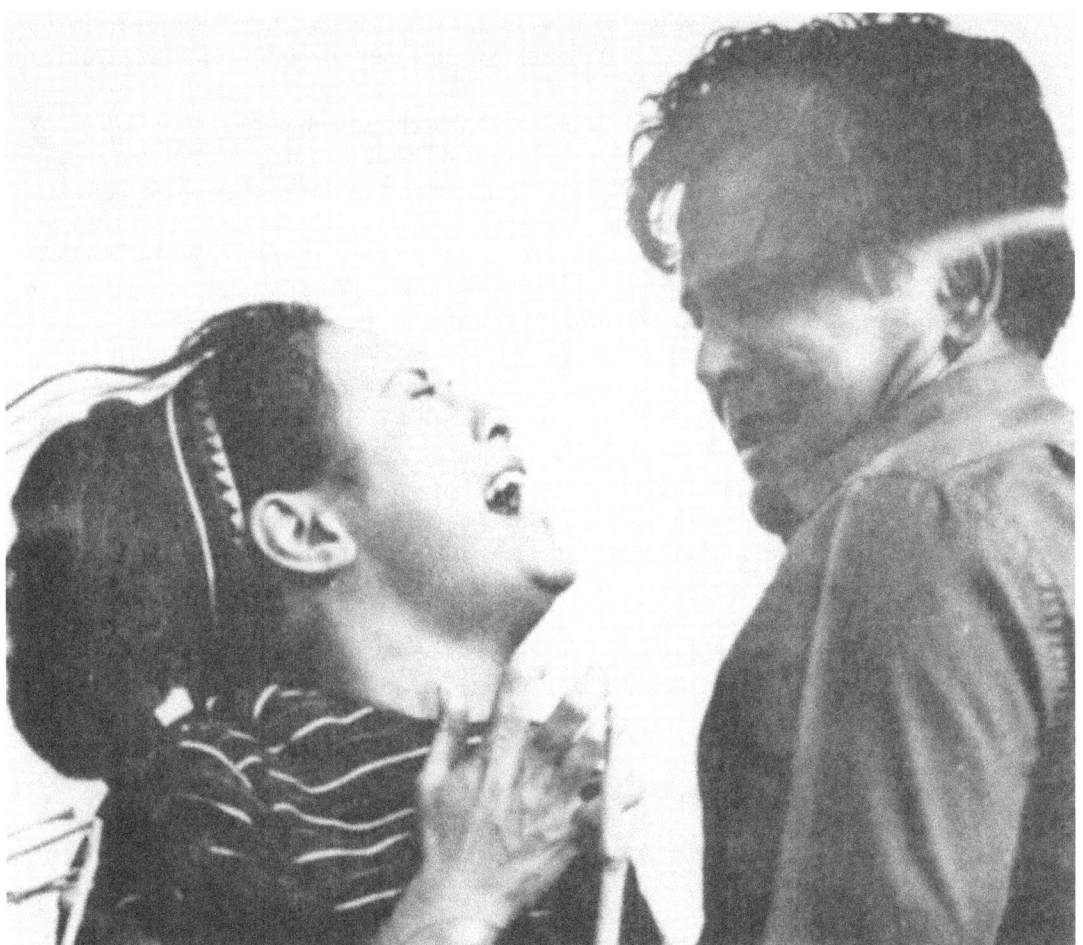

Charito Solis and Ric Rodrigo in *Igorota* (1968/Nepomuceno Productions). The film was shot in English in order to try and achieve global distribution, and it dominated the FAMAS Awards that year.

bearing her breasts like a savage). Nonetheless, it's hard to believe that it was truly the best Filipino film of its year.

Igorota pre-dated the bomba genre, but its topless scene was doubtless encouraging to producers who may have been inclined to explore the boundaries, particularly in that it involved such a popular and acclaimed actress. The bomba genre is considered to have begun in earnest with the 1970 film *Uhaw* (*Thirst*), directed by Ruben Abalos. The story concerned a woman (Merle Fernandez) and her two lovers (Tito Galla and Lito Legaspi), and the film was such a phenomenal success that it inspired independent producers to copy the formula. And why not? Focusing on eroticism, production costs could be kept low, and returns were guaranteed.

Fernandez, the lead actress in *Uhaw*, would quickly come to be regarded as the Queen of the Bombas, owing to the number of films she was featured in within the genre. No young filly, Fernandez's father was Gregorio Fernandez, and she had been appearing in Filipino films since the late 1940s. After some twenty-odd years in the business, she saw her career revived as a middle-aged sexpot. Her career would evaporate once censorship dealt the bomba genre a deathblow, but she continued to periodically make headlines, once as the victim in a highly publicized rape and robbery case, and again when she was named as the prime suspect in the murder of a Filipino basketball star, and she subsequently went underground—successfully, it would seem.

Another actress who began making a name for herself in the bomba genre was Rosanna Ortiz. Her real name was Violeta Orbeta, and she had begun her career in the late-1960s in teen-oriented fluff like *Drakulita* (1969), but with the advent of the bombas, she became better known for playing more risqué roles. She made a brief showing in the global market by appearing in international co-productions like Cirio Santiago's *Savage!* (1973) and Eddie Romero's *Savage Sisters* (1974), but once the government clamped down on the bombas, her career continued to flourish when she proved her acting mettle in acclaimed films like Celso Ad. Castillo's *Patayin Mo sa Sindak si Barbara* (*Kill Barbara with Panic*) in 1973, as well as starring in films alongside the biggest stars of the day, like Fernando Poe, Jr., Dolphy, Amalia Fuentes, Ramon Revilla and Zaldy Zshornack. But Ortiz left the film business at the height of her fame when she married a wealthy businessman.

In 1969 Ortiz figured prominently in a film industry murder scandal: she was appearing in the film *Ako ang Sasagupa* with Eddie Fernandez and Berting Labra when things went terribly awry during a location shoot. Fernandez was a popular action star of the latter-1960s who, like Tony Ferrer, had made a name for himself in secret agent knock-offs, in his case as Agent Lagalag. A screen tough guy, Fernandez became so identified with his screen persona that people sometimes referred to him by the nickname Lagalag, and his tough guy screen image seemed to carry over into real life, as he became known for being a hard drinking

Merle Fernandez and Bert Leroy, Jr., in the early '70s bomba film *Busog* (*Satiated*). Fernandez was quickly crowned Queen of the Bombas.

brawler who carried a gun. In September of '69, some of the cast and crew of *Ako ang Sasagupa* were at a house in Quezon City for a location shoot when a friend of Ortiz's arrived: Renato Pangilinan was the son of a wealthy family, and he arrived at the house sometime between 4 and 5 P.M. with his driver, Apolinario Lopez, and a gentleman named Hilario Sigua, apparently something of a bodyguard for Pangilinan. After greeting them, Ortiz introduced them to Fernandez and Labra, who were sitting in the house sharing a bottle of whiskey, before explaining that she had to return to shooting a scene elsewhere in the house. Pangilinan and Sigua joined Fernandez and Labra in having a few drinks, at which time Fernandez, fairly intoxicated from a day's drinking, began grousing about Ortiz having held up production—although she was supposed to arrive at the house for the filming in the A.M., Ortiz did not actually show up until 2:00 P.M., holding up production. Seeing that Sigua was carrying a gun, Fernandez told one of the crew members to phone the police and tell them that there were armed men in the residence, and the police arrived a short time later to inquire about the situation. Pangilinan and Sigua both admitted to being armed, but claimed that their guns were duly licensed, at which time the officers asked them to go with them to Precinct One of the Quezon City Police Department while the gun licenses were checked: Pangilinan and Sigua agreed to go without argument.

When Ortiz heard what was happening, she decided to go to the station to help clear things up, and she was accompanied by Fernandez, Labra, one Benjamin Barcelona, and Fernandez's driver, Antonio Antido. The licenses were verified soon enough and all were allowed to leave, but in returning, Ortiz chose to ride along with Pangilinan and his two companions. At around 7:00 P.M. Fernandez and company followed them back to the house, and when Fer-

Rosanna Ortiz with character actor Max Alvarado (wearing hat) in *Ang Kampana sa Santa Quiteria* (*The Bell in Santa Quiteria*; 1971/FPJ Productions). Ortiz was one bomba queen who had enough talent to break into mainstream films.

nandez saw that they were taking a wrong turn toward Manila, rather than follow the route back to the house, and he angrily ordered Antido to follow Pangilinan's car. They eventually caught up with them at a traffic jam near the Manila–Quezon City border, and the drunken and enraged Fernandez got out—gun in hand—and approached Pangilinan's car. The story became a little hazy from there. When Fernandez angrily accosted Pangilinan, and Pangilinan saw that he was armed, it didn't take long for the shooting to begin, although Ortiz had implored Fernandez to calm down. As firing commenced from both sides, Pangilinan was hit in the chest and slumped dead onto Ortiz's lap in the back seat. Lopez was also hit in the chest, while Sigua was hit in right hand. Fernandez was shot in the abdomen and fell to the side of the road, at which time someone helped him back into his vehicle and sped off for the hospital, Fernandez taking a parting shot at Pangilinan's car as they sped away.

Although there was no doubt in anyone's mind that Fernandez had been present—he had a gunshot wound to prove it—and all present remembered Antido being there, testimony differed as to the presence of Labra and Barcelona. Both Lopez and Sigua survived the incident and testified that Labra and Barcelona were among those who participated in the shooting, while Ortiz testified that she did not see either Barcelona or Labra present at the shooting, and even recalled that Labra had left the police precinct ahead of the rest with the film's director. Barcelona, on the other hand, stayed behind at the precinct when the rest left, and was in fact still there when the call came in that there had been a shooting near the Quezon-Manila border. Nonetheless, the police charged Labra and Barcelona as participants as well, largely on the testimony of Lopez and Sigua, but in Labra's case, also on the testimony of a teenage boy who had heard the gunshots, had witnessed Fernandez's departure, and identified Labra as the one he saw helping Fernandez back into his vehicle before departing. The boy could give no good details, however, as to how Labra was dressed—even being unable to say whether or not he wore a hat—and made no mention of Barcelona.

But it was more than enough to convince the judge, who was very obviously predisposed to condemn them all out of his distaste for their profession, or in the case of Barcelona, mere association with it. In rendering his decision, the judge went on a moralistic rant, condemning the entertainment profession in general for setting a poor example and gnawing away at the nation's moral fiber. "It is a sad commentary," he said in his decision, "but nonetheless a glaring truth that we have been witnesses to many incidents of the past where movie folks are in constant banner headline for their mischiefs [sic] in public, as well as private life. They seem to have that unsatiable [sic] quest of getting entangled in deadly brawls, acting as though they are those notorious bandits or rapacious pillagers ordinarily depicted on the screen. They lived as captives of their misguided illusions, exhibiting the stance of being untouchables, unconquerables, equal to none and afraid of no one."

More than that, the judge couldn't resist taking a potshot at Ortiz as well, without mentioning names: "With respect to women actresses and starlets," he said, "by their loose morals, conduct and behavior, they have gained that uncommon reputation as ruthless wreckers of decent homes and families, contributing to the already troubled society, in destroying the basic foundation of our democratic institution, the home. They defy even the basic element of decency inherent to Filipino womanhood, by parading themselves openly in public with nose high up and disgustedly with false pride for the whole world to know, in the company of men with burden of responsibilities."

Pretty strong words; one can only assume that Ortiz is fortunate that she herself was not on trial, though the presiding judge seems to have wanted to try her himself. Without dismissing the judge's viewpoints out of hand, it needs to be said that they do seem highly inappropriate and reveal a rather strong bias against the defendants. More than that, the judge went on to list the prior records of both Fernandez (including a murder indictment in Pasay, two for causing slight physical injury in Paranaque, and one for grave threats, also in Paranaque) and Antido (who had previously been convicted for concealment of a deadly weapon, as well as also being previously indicted for attempted murder, making grave threats, and illegal firearms possession). The prior records are telling of the character of both Fernandez and Antido, but had no bearing on the case itself, and even if they were bound to influence the judge in his decisions, it would have been more prudent for him not to trumpet the fact. It turned out to be lucky for all of the defendants that he did: although Fernandez, Labra, Antido and Barcelona would all be convicted and each received life sentences, they would eventually appeal the case to the Philippine Supreme Court, and while the original trial judge's comments were not the deciding factor, they did help paint a portrait of a judge who seemed to disregard crucial evidence, perhaps out of his own biases against the defendants.

Although they wound up serving 13 years in prison, the Supreme Court wound up setting all of them free in 1982, giving Labra and Barcelona full pardons (deciding in Labra's case that the evidence—including the testimony of Ortiz—proved that he was not present during the shooting, and in Barcelona's case finding that even the testimony of police officers proved that he was still at the police precinct when the shooting occurred), and deciding that while Fernandez's actions brought about the incident, it was difficult to say who fired first, and therefore whether or not he and Antido were firing in self-defense. Therefore, they were let out for having served sufficient incarceration.

Upon being released, both Fernandez and Labra resumed their respective film careers. Fernandez doesn't seem to have learned any lessons from the whole affair, however, as he died in a street shootout in 1993.

A large number of the bombas contented themselves with pushing the envelope with titillating scenes of nudity and seduction, but others crossed the line into pornography by any objective standards. Producers and distributors tried to finagle the censors by submitting edited prints to the censors and then distributing prints with pornographic inserts. A good case in point would be the 1970 film *Diabolika*. In a letter to Tower Productions General Manager Victoria Villanueva, Board of Censors Chairman Guillermo C. de Vega wrote:

> In view of repeated reports, the last one being from a Member of this Board who has verified them to be true, that in the exhibition of your motion picture entitled "DIABOLIKA" at the Pearl Theater objectionable scenes which had not been submitted to, nor passed upon by, the Board for approval, had been inserted therein, including the scene of a close full shot of the actress Merle Fernandez running in the nude with her pubic hair exposed, and the scene involving the same actress and Renato del Prado in various lewd sequences, please be informed that the permit for the further exhibition of your said film is hereby recalled, cancelled and revoked effecting as of the last screening hour of said picture tonight, November 6, 1970.
>
> In view hereof, the aforesaid motion picture "DIABOLIKA" shall not be exhibited any further in any theater in the Philippines as of the effective date of the cancellation of the permit thereof. In addition, you are hereby directed to surrender the print, together with all copies thereof, as well as the original permit issued to you, including copies thereof, to this office immediately but not later than 5 P.M.
>
> Strict compliance is desired.

The letter was entered into the public record on November 7, 1970, when Villanueva petitioned the Court of First Instance of Manila, Branch XXI to halt the Board's revocation of the showing permit; but rather than dispute the insertion of objectionable scenes that had not been passed by the Board, Villanueva chose the curious tactic of challenging the Board's authority to cancel permits, and posed the question "Has the Board of Censors for Motion Pictures or its Chairman the power and/or authority to recall, withdraw and/or cancel permits already issued after violations were found in the exhibition of the motion picture for which the said permit was granted?" It was a rather foolish maneuver since the law clearly bestowed such power on the Board, and indeed, the showing permit itself plainly stated: "This permit may be suspended or revoked any time without prior notice by the Board." Villanueva's challenge was in vain as Judge Juan O. Reyes issued a ruling in the Board's favor on December 9, 1970.

President Ferdinand Marcos appointed de Vega as Chairman of the Board of Censors for Motion Pictures in 1969, and he could hardly have chosen a more articulate advocate for his cause. A political scientist and historian with a Ph.D. in political history from the University of Sind in Hyderabad, India, de Vega wrote often and eloquently on the subject of censorship, citing its place in democratized countries throughout the world, and its legitimate function since Rome circa 433 B.C. Public outrage over the Board's permissiveness was not lost on de Vega. As early as September 15, 1967 *The Philippine Herald* had run an editorial critical of the Board, saying "The upsurge of crimes by minors and loose morality of youth are attributable to horrible examples drawn from unwholesome movies passed by the Board and exhibited in theaters and on television. If undesirable aspects of such kinds of movies were not eliminated or if the movies were not banned *in toto*, clearly the fault lies with the Board."[2]

The subsequent advent of the bombas could not have made the Board's job any easier, as it necessitated Board members to blaze trails through the provinces to follow up on reports of unapproved films, or films with unapproved inserts.

While de Vega clearly found the bomba films crude, inarticulate and worthy of the Board's efforts to eradicate, he allowed them credit for revitalizing the Filipino film industry. In his

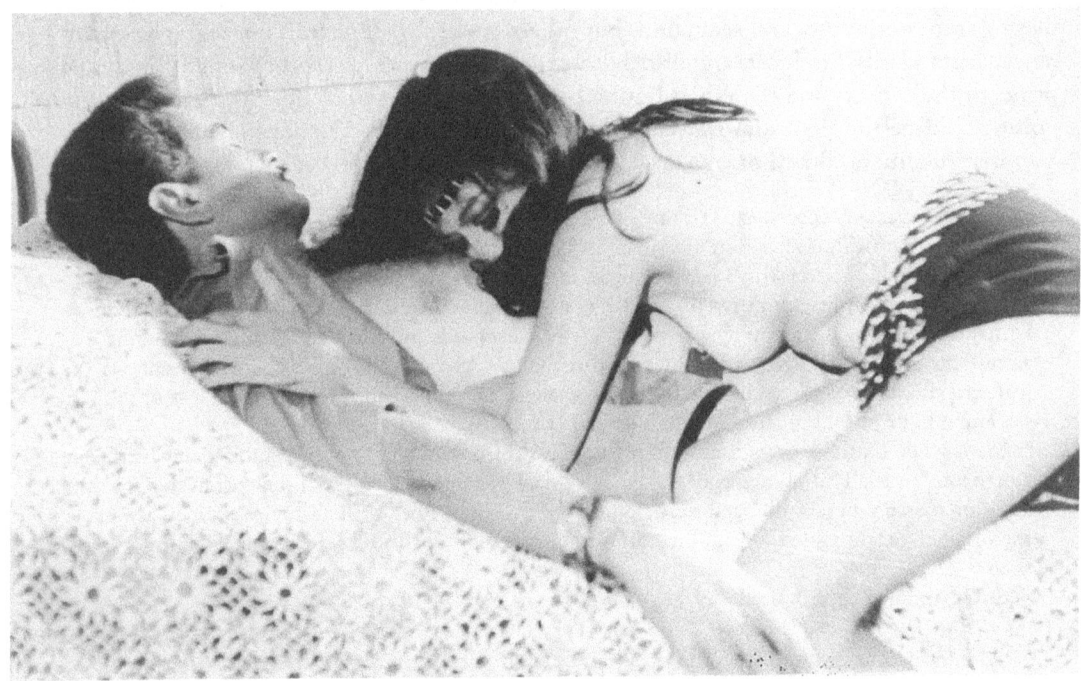

Eddie Garcia and Merle Fernandez in *Durando* (Estrella Pictures), one of the early '70s bomba films that began to flood the market.

1975 book *Film and Freedom: Movie Censorship in the Philippines*, de Vega wrote: "The 'bomba' film ... brought about a revitalization of the local film industry, which had settled into an artistic rut by the time the first local 'bomba' movies, like *Uhaw* and *Nympho* [sic] appeared in late 1970 and early 1971. Essentially the local 'bomba' was a defensive reaction to the foreign sex films that were preempting the audiences during the first 'bomba' years, but they also represented a new direction for the industry, which was wallowing in a deluge of puerile comedies, teenage musicals, and counterfeit secret agent movies. Unfortunately the new direction went wayward and floundered in a stream of gross sensationalism and bad taste. The local 'bomba' film was a promise that failed."[3]

The titles cited by de Vega were chosen with good reason: both were considered worthy artistic endeavors, in particular Celso Ad. Castillo's *Nympha*, and de Vega obviously meant to point out the Board's leniency toward controversial material were it deemed to have true artistic merit. Notwithstanding the low tolerance that free societies have for censorship, the truth is that the Board of Censors was reasonably understanding and accommodating toward the local film industry in its losing battle against the foreign films that were stealing audiences with their increasingly liberal standards. The Board realized that, in order to be competitive, the local industry had to be allowed certain liberties and an expanded parameter within which to operate. Like most of the world, Filipino culture was undergoing a transformation, and Filipino filmmakers needed to be allowed the liberty to keep abreast of such changes if they were going to stay relevant, as well as competitive. But the Board was also drawing heavy criticism from civic groups like the Citizens Council for Better Motion Pictures. This was not the Philippines that Ferdinand Marcos envisioned.

On September 22, 1972, President Marcos signed the decree declaring martial law in the Philippines.* Under Philippine law, Marcos was not permitted to seek a third term, but he was determined to stay in power. He used the threat of communist revolution as the flimsy pretext for the decree, although the U.S. Government did not take the communist threat seriously in the Philippines at that time. In fact, the CIA was aware that much of the violence blamed on

Rosanna Marquez and Eddie Garcia in the early '70s film *Querida* (*Mistress*).

The decree was backdated to the 21st, apparently to satisfy Marcos' superstitious nature since 21 is equally divisible by the dictator's favored number of 7.

communist rebels had actually been staged by Marcos and his cronies: an assassination attempt on Defense Minister Juan Ponce Enrile, for instance, was hoaxed. On September 22, Enrile was said to have been on the way home at the end of the day when gunmen from another car sprayed his Ford sedan with gunfire. Years later, Enrile would confess to writer Stanley Karnow that the attack was staged, and that he was not in the car at the time.[4] Enrile would eventually come clean publicly about the supposed assassination attempt amid the chaos of the People Power revolution that would topple Marcos in 1986, holding a press conference in which he would also confess to personally being involved in the faking of hundreds of thousands of votes.

With the U.S. fighting communism in Vietnam in the 1970s, Marcos probably felt that the best way to win U.S. approval for the decree was to use the communist threat but, seemingly, Marcos' only word on the move beforehand came from U.S. ambassador Henry Byroade, who had cautioned him against declaring martial law, telling Marcos that it would be unwise and could possibly create a backlash against him in the U.S. congress, effecting U.S. aid to the Philippines. Other than Byroade's advice, the U.S. had been fairly quiet on the subject, knowing that Marcos' communist woes were largely exaggerated and were being used as a ploy, and even Imelda Marcos could not elicit much of a response from President Nixon when she traveled to Washington to pay him a visit in October of 1971, testing the waters before Marcos put his plan into motion. The Philippine First Lady visited with the U.S. President for some twenty minutes, telling him that her husband was determined to stay in office until the communist threat was eradicated. Nixon, who had more urgent concerns at the time, like Vietnam, Watergate, and his reelection campaign, merely tolerated Imelda for the better part of a half-hour before bidding her farewell, but Imelda felt that his approval was implicit by his silence.

It isn't that Marcos didn't take Byroade's cautions to heart: as much as he wanted to stay in power, Marcos was weary of damaging his public image, perhaps in the U.S. as much as among his own people. He had spent years playing up his reputation as an ultra-patriot and war hero. With word getting around that martial law was in the offing, Marcos was very aware of public opinion and the growing student movement against him. But with his second term winding down, time was running out.

Rocco Montalban and Arlene Mesina in *Climax of Love* (AF Productions).

And so it was that Marcos took the reins of power in full: radio and television stations were closed, as well as newspapers. Those that were allowed to continue operations were under strict rules of censorship. Political prisoners were rounded up by the thousands, be they politicians, journalists, student activists or university professors—anyone that Marcos had reason to believe might conceivably stir up unrest.

Although political films—at least those that could in any way be construed as critical of the Marcos government—were ill-advised prior to September, with the decree of martial law, filmmakers were going to have to operate under stricter official guidelines. The ultimate irony in it all was that many felt that Marcos' ascendancy to the presidency was partially attributable to the fact that he was seen as being somewhat victimized by the censors when the showing permit for the film *Iginuhit ng Tadhana*, a film chronicling his largely embellished life story, was pulled by the censors in 1965. He had kept a valuable lesson from the experience, and if anyone had learned to respect the power of the medium, it was Marcos.

On September 27, 1972, five days after he declared martial law, Marcos issued Letter of Instructions No. 13, which proclaimed its purpose as being "to safeguard the morality of our society, particularly the youth, against the negative influence of certain motion pictures." The letter gave guidelines for the Board of Censors to follow in helping foster the proper environment for what Marcos termed the "New Society." The Board was instructed to ban films that fell into the following categories:

1) Films which tend to incite subversion, insurrection or rebellion against the state;
2) Films which tend to undermine the faith and confidence of the people in their government and/or duly constituted authorities;
3) Films which glorify criminals or condone crimes;
4) Films which serve no other purpose but to satisfy the market for violence and pornography;
5) Films which offend any race or religion;
6) Films which tend to abet the traffic in and use of prohibited drugs;
7) Films which are contrary to law, public order, morals, good customs, established policies, lawful orders, decrees or edicts.

The letter wound down with the terse directive:

"Any violation of this order shall mean the outright cancellation, withdrawal and revocation of the permits of the films, the closure of the theater or theaters involved, as well as the arrest and prosecution of any persons concerned. In the implementation hereof, you shall coordinate with the Department of National Defense and other agencies of the government."

Again it fell on de Vega to keep the filmmaking community in line. In his book de Vega wrote: "Accommodation had been read as weakness, liberalism misinterpreted as license. But now the Board was determined that film censorship should henceforth serve primarily the objectives of the New Society by helping create a better moral atmosphere through the careful and intelligent examination of films, eschewing in the process of censorship scenes that could create false or detrimental ethical values and banning altogether any film that could ideologically subvert the peace of the nation and the mind, aspirations and will of the people."[5]

Whatever de Vega's publicly stated views, it is certainly worth considering the fact that, not only was he appointed by Marcos, but he seems, at least at the time, to have been on friendly terms with the First Family—Imelda Marcos even wrote the introduction to his book. With the imposition of martial law, he doubtless felt obligated to toe the party line, and had he any reservations regarding his newly defined purpose as Chairman of the Board of Censors, Letter of Instructions No. 13 clearly left him precious little room for interpretation. Thus, in his book, de Vega would say that in order for film censorship to be useful as a positive tool to further the goals of the New Society, the Board would not merely exercise its right to order the removal of objectionable scenes from films, but would also use its rights "to encourage, to warn and to be consulted."[6]

For her part, First Lady Imelda Marcos spoke to many prominent members of the filmmaking community in November of 1972, and informed them that Filipino films would thereafter be expected to present a positive image of Filipino culture to the world, and she urged them to raise the artistic and technical standards of their craft. She further envisioned the industry going global by co-producing films with other Asian nations, seeing this as a possible solution to the problem of low budgets and production values. About this aim de Vega wrote that Filipino filmmakers should be cognizant of how the material related to and reflected the Philippine experience, and that they should seek to create works that accurately portrayed Filipino history and culture, hopes and dreams, as well as portraying the struggles of its people of all classes. He added that the Board would be paying heed to each work's relevance to the Philippine condition, and that they would be favorably inclined toward "vivid representations of traditional cultural values that would enrich the community, but more than all this, it respects and encourages flights of the intellect and imagination, and discard [sic] trivialities and gross imitation."[7]

The inherent dishonesty of this statement should be self-evident, since a primary struggle of the culture and people could be seen as being against the dictatorial rule of the Marcos regime. One also wonders how successfully "flights of the intellect and imagination" could truly flourish under the strict, watchful eye of the state. It is certainly true that in democratized societies the rights of the individual become idealized to the point that what often seems lost is the fact that societies must also be conceded certain rights. It must be weighed that a fundamental right of any civilized society is the right to guard against the pollution of its popular culture; some might even consider this an obligation. Certainly it is not beyond the reach of intelligent people to set reasonable guidelines. On this point, de Vega, writing in the *1974 Fookien Times Yearbook*, would say, "Under the circumstances, an authoritative, intelligent and rational body is called for to assume the responsibility of previewing, approving, classifying and, whenever necessary, of cutting or disapproving, motion pictures and similar mass media forms like television shows deemed incompatible with the valued moral and ethical judgements and traditions of the people."[8]

De Vega tried to paint a very rosy picture of the effects of the new more stringent censorship policies on the film industry, claiming that it led to higher quality productions, and more conscientious efforts by filmmakers. It can certainly be said to have brought more care and forethought to the scripting of films. Prior to the new policies, Filipino film scripts were often little more than story treatments, frequently ad-libbed as the filming progressed. Now, with all scripts requiring approval before shooting commenced, screenwriters had to be far more meticulous in their craft. But de Vega was right in another sense as well. Under martial law, the more rigid policies forced the younger breed of filmmakers to be more creative in airing their sociopolitical concerns so as not to attract too much attention from the censors. But in the *Fookien Times* piece, de Vega took on a regrettable tone, which could be construed as obnoxious condescension when he wrote: "Literature requires a sufficiently literate audience. On the other hand, movies, being audio-visual, can be understood even by the illiterate. If a literary product is as sophisticated and complex as, say, James Joyce's novel *Ulysses*, it will take some amount of intelligence to understand and appreciate it. But the cinema, being a mass art, demands of its audience nothing more than the faculties of hearing and seeing to draw pleasure and knowledge from it."[9]

It is not easy to discern whether or not de Vega's published views on censorship were sincere or merely an attempt to avoid invoking the wrath of Marcos. Were it the latter, de Vega then failed tragically as he was assassinated in Malacanang on October 27, 1975 in a hit that is widely accepted as having been ordered by Marcos. It seems a curious move even for a megalomaniac like Marcos, since de Vega was partly responsible for popularizing the Marcos mythology through his 1974 book *Ferdinand E. Marcos: An Epic*, a work which purported to chronicle the dictator's fabled life and career.

Many of the films that directors like Eddie Romero, Gerardo de Leon and Cirio Santiago were making for the international market, being exploitation features, could be considered as trans-continental kin to the bombas. Romero continued his association with Lynn and Hemisphere, and in 1968 he and de Leon co-directed *Mad Doctor of Blood Island*, which brought American actor John Ashley back to the islands. The project was actually initiated by Beverly Miller, a friend of Ashley's who owned a string of drive-in theaters in the American mid-west. When *Brides of Blood* played one of his theaters, Miller asked Ashley to make a personal appearance at the showing to help drum up business, and upon seeing the picture, Miller asked Ashley if he would be interested in going back to shoot another. With Miller's assurance to help put the deal together, Ashley agreed to sign on, and the deal was set.[10] Ashley returned to Blood Island in the person of Dr. Bill Foster, a pathologist dispatched from the mainland to investigate the discovery of a green-blooded corpse on the island. He eventually discovers that the bizarre cadaver is the result of experiments being conducted by the island's resident mad scientist, Dr. Lorca (Ronald Remy), who is conducting some rather advanced experiments involving chlorophyll. Remy attempts to cure a friend of leukemia, but somehow manages to turn him into a monster that runs around terrorizing the island. Beneath the typical horror genre trappings is a curious, layered, and sometimes convoluted melodrama in which the monster's former teen-aged mistress (Alicia Alonzo) also beds the beast's son (Ronaldo Valdez) while being allowed by the monster's wife (Tita Munoz) to occupy the family mansion. Meanwhile, Munoz and Remy have their own affair going, while Ashley gets busy

John Ashley taking on the chlorophyll monster in *Mad Doctor of Blood Island* (1968/Hemisphere Pictures). This was only a publicity photo; in actuality no such scene appears in the film.

with Angelique Pettyjohn, who has come to the island to look for her drunken, wayward father (Tony Edmunds). In Reuben Canoy's screenplay, the film's monster-on-the-loose scenario took a decided backseat to the family melodrama. Sam Sherman, who helped concoct another cheesy promotional campaign (this time involving an oath of green blood with packets of green liquid to be given out to patrons), has since said that he felt the film's story was a bit too complex for drive-in audiences,[11] and the film was routinely panned by critics in the U.S., but it did good business regardless. The rather involved melodrama within Mad Doctor of Blood Island may not have easily lent itself to the U.S. exploitation market, but the truth is that it is very representative of most types of Philippine cinema. In that respect, it is very typical of Filipino film. It was also liberally spiced with nudity and gore, a portent of things to come.

It was at Sherman's prodding that Hemisphere sought out Remy for the film. Sherman had been very impressed by Remy's performance in Kulay Dugo ang Gabi, which Hemisphere had acquired in 1966 and released internationally as The Blood Drinkers, and encouraged Lynn to use him again. Remy was a dominating screen presence whose sophisticated manner and excellent command of English made him ideal for American productions shot in the Philippines. He even played an American sailor in the 1962 film No Man Is an Island, which topbilled Jeffrey Hunter.

Born Ronald Kookoritchkin in 1936, Remy was descended from Russian ancestors, and as a young man in the 1950s he traveled to America to attend college in San Francisco. The highly intellectual Remy had planned on a career in engineering, and it was while attending college in the U.S. that his accent all but disappeared. It was also in America that he was bitten by the acting bug and began appearing on the stage. When he returned home to the Philippines he found that his cousin Zaldy Zshornack had become a matinee idol in local films, and while visiting him at the Premiere studios lot, Remy was approached by Gerardo de Leon about embarking on a film career of his own.[12] In 1959 he made his screen debut in de Leon's Aawitan Kita (I'll Sing to You), and otherwise had a busy year, co-starring with Zshornack in Ang Maton (The Bully) and with Fernando Poe, Jr. in the monster-runs-amok film Anak ng Bulkan (Child of the Volcano).

Mad Doctor of Blood Island was enough of a breadwinner for Hemisphere that Eddie Romero wrote and directed a sequel, Beast of Blood, in 1970. It was a deliriously cartoonish combination of mad science and jungle warfare that saw Ashley returning to Blood Island to once more battle the mad doctor (this time played by Eddie Garcia) and the now headless chlorophyll monster. Far more interesting was the film that wound up as the second feature on the double-bill. Hemisphere acquired a 1966 film titled Ibulong Mo sa Hangin (Whisper in the Wind), another vampire film directed by Gerardo de Leon, and after dubbing it into English, released it as Curse of the Vampires. If the familial circumstances in Mad Doctor of Blood Island seemed odd, they could scarcely compete with the weird family situation portrayed in Ibulong Mo sa Hangin, in which brother and sister Eddie Garcia and Amalia Fuentes are shocked to discover that their mother (Mary Walter), whom they thought dead, is not only alive (sort of), but is being kept chained in the basement by their father (Johnny Monteiro). Their shock is compounded when they discover that Walter is a vampire. Walter vampirizes Garcia, and he in turn seeks to vampirize Fuentes, but in order to accomplish this, must kill Fuentes' suitor (Romeo Vasquez). Though Garcia does eventually afflict Fuentes with the family curse, she is rescued by the prayers of Vasquez's ghost, who then proceeds to stake her. The film concludes with the disembodied spirits of Fuentes and Vasquez blissfully dancing off into the hereafter together.

Although there is considerable similarity to de Leon's Kulay Dugo ang Gabi in its familial approach to the subject of vampirism, there is a decided departure from much of that film's

Anak ng Bulkan (*Child of the Volcano*; 1959/Premiere Productions), one of Ronald Remy's earliest roles.

The chlorophyll monster was back in Eddie Romero's *Beast of Blood* (1970/Hemisphere Pictures/Sceptre Industries). Stuntman Johnny Long portrayed the beast.

romanticism. The most interesting—indeed disturbing—element of the film thematically is its depiction of the family unit as an incestuous, suffocatingly oppressive, and ultimately destructive entity. Coming from a Catholic society as it does, it is interesting to note that the film presents the physical manifestation of love in a thoroughly distasteful way, with Garcia mauling a young lady to satisfy himself, while lovers Fuentes and Vasquez are prevented from consummating their affections in the flesh, instead experiencing a spiritual union in the afterlife.

While the ghost of Spanish colonialism was represented by the aristocratic vampire Dr. Marco in *Kulay Dugo ang Gabi*, shown to still be parasitically preying on the populace, this time de Leon chose to depict the fading Spanish colonial aristocracy as maintaining its status through inbreeding. Some film commentators have more recently noted with dismay and perplexity the use of blackface on the actors portraying the household servants in the film. While it may be politically incorrect, even by Western standards of its own time some forty years ago, and it certainly does look ridiculous, the purpose behind it is only obscure to individuals ill-educated about the history of the Philippines and the prejudicial society in the Spanish colonial era that placed the darker-skinned Malays at the bottom of the social stratum. The rather extreme caricature here leaves little doubt that de Leon was commenting on the social structure in place during the era within which the film was set. With *Ibulong Mo sa Hangin*, de Leon offered one of the most fascinating and unnerving depictions of vampirism to date, rivaled only by the work of French director Jean Rollin.

Aside from their three Blood Island outings together, Romero and Ashley had worked together on *Manila: Open City*, an elaborate telling of the battle of Manila. Although Ashley

Amalia Fuentes and Eddie Garcia in Gerardo de Leon's *Ibulong Mo sa Hangin* (*You Whisper In the Wind*; 1966). The film was dubbed into English by Hemisphere Pictures, which released it internationally in 1970.

recalled first going to the Philippines for the film *Brides of Blood*, and he doesn't appear to have ever mentioned *Manila: Open City* in any interviews, Romero claimed that he first worked with Ashley on the war picture.[13] Ashley's part in the film is fairly minor, however (he received fourth billing), and it seems unlikely that he would have made the trip overseas just for that. It seems more likely that he may have appeared in the film after wrapping one of his horror pictures in the islands, possibly *Mad Doctor of Blood Island*. At any rate, Ashley and Romero had formed a friendship beyond their working relationship, and they decided to strike out on their own, forming their own production company, Four Associates, along with Beverly Miller and David Cohen. Their first picture for the new company was *Beast of the Yellow Night* in 1970. In it, Ashley portrayed a depraved U.S. Army deserter who strikes a deal with the devil (in the person of Vic Diaz) in order to escape justice, and must thereafter inhabit the bodies of various individuals in order to exploit their sinful nature. Eventually, when Ashley rebels, he is transformed into a raging beast. It was something of an interesting misfire, with a screenplay by Romero that was more intellectually ambitious than successful. Still, it showed that Romero had not lost his desire for serious filmmaking, even within a genre not often regarded for higher pursuits. The film was distributed stateside by Roger Corman's New World Pictures, and it was this association with Corman that would to a large degree sabotage any artistic aspirations that Romero may have entertained going into the arrangement. Thereafter, Corman and various American financers would saddle Romero with vapid, vulgar screenplays by no-account American screenwriters, resulting in a string of middling exploitation features dominated by the women-in-prison motif. But, above all, they were profitable. While Romero may

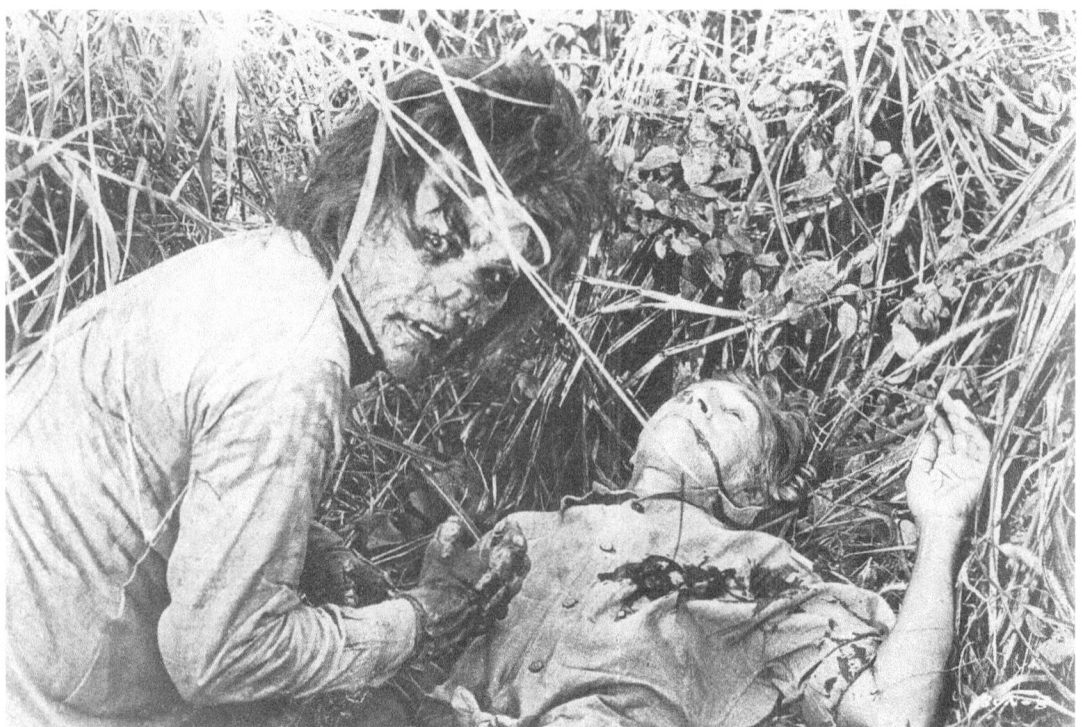

Character actor Andres Centenera with the *Beast of the Yellow Night* (1970/New World Pictures/Four Associates). That was stuntman Johnny Long under the makeup, not American star John Ashley.

have genuinely enjoyed working on these films, it may also be true that he was enjoying the international exposure, particularly during the period when the Filipino film industry was enduring its share of economic distress. It is worth noting that, after wrapping his string of co-productions with Ashley in the mid–1970s, Romero went back to work on serious films like *Ganito Kami Noon, Paano Kayo Ngayon?* (*This Is What We Were, How Are You Now?*) in 1976, a historical film that won Best Picture honors at the initial Gawad Urian (Urian Awards), as well as winning Romero trophies for Best Director and Best Screenplay. Interestingly enough, the film was made under the Hemisphere banner, as Romero had continued to keep his old Hemisphere offices on Aldecoa Street, Malate, Manila operating. Romero had obviously not abandoned his ambition for serious filmmaking, and yet he would continue to periodically return to frivolous international co-productions through the 1980s.

The chain of events set in motion by Kane Lynn's production deals in the Philippines would bring recognition to many within the Filipino filmmaking community, but would ultimately prove somewhat damaging to the image of Filipino cinema in general, fixing it with the perception of low-rent, tacky, vulgar drive-in productions. It was through Hemisphere that Ashley had initiated his own filmmaking odyssey in the country, and in turn, Ashley would convince Roger Corman to forsake Puerto Rico as the shooting location of Jack Hill's women-in-prison film *The Big Doll House* (1971) in favor of the Philippines. It was a nasty, sadistic little film, and Corman himself was appalled upon first viewing it, even to the point of telling his wife that if this is what it took to stay in the business anymore, then perhaps it was time to get out. Once the film was released and immediately saw remarkable returns, Corman

Pam Grier and Subas Herrero in *The Big Bird Cage* (1972/New World Pictures), one of the wave of women-in-prison films shot in the Philippines in the early 1970s.

quickly changed his mind and ordered a sequel. In fact, the film's enormous success brought a flood of women-in-prison and like-minded exploitation features, including de Leon's *Women in Cages* (1971), *The Big Bird Cage*, *The Hot Box*, *The Woman Hunt*, and *Black Mama, White Mama* (all in 1972), *Savage Sisters* (1974), *The Muthers* (1976), *Women of Hell's Island* (1978) and *Caged Fury* (1980). Suddenly the Philippines was beset by low budget American filmmakers cranking out drive-in titles like *Daughters of Satan*, *Night of the Cobra Woman*, and *Superbeast* (all in 1972), and *The Deathhead Virgin* (1973). With all of the quickie exploitation fare being shot there, the scum seemed to rise to the top, and Filipino directors like Bobby Suarez and, most prolific of them all, Cirio Santiago gained a degree of international exposure, though again, it was not to the benefit of the image of the local industry.

Although overtly political films were impossible to make under martial law, many of the international co-productions being shot in the Philippines were of a highly political nature, though always cautious to set the narrative in some fictitious banana republic. There was, for instance, the Eddie Romero film *Savage Sisters*, in which two female prison inmates and a female prison guard spearhead a revolution on a small island nation. Likewise, Romero's *Black Mama, White Mama* had a storyline that relied heavily on the subtext of a female prison inmate arrested for being involved in insurrectionist activities; when she escapes, she and her co-escapee flee to the hills where her rebel cohorts are hiding. The leniency toward films like these likely rested on two things: first, the films were being made primarily for the U.S. drive-

Cheri Caffaro and Rosanna Ortiz being led to their cell in *Savage Sisters* (1974/American International Pictures).

in market, as well as certain international markets, and exhibition in the Philippines was negligible, if it existed at all, and second, these films were bringing commerce to the islands. In fact, Imelda Marcos herself would honor John Ashley with a special award for the amount of film production and international recognition that he was bringing to the country. Ashley was by then producing films in the Philippines not only for his own company, Four Associates, but also for New World Pictures and American International Pictures. It is very interesting, and telling of Imelda Marcos' lack of taste, that she should have thought such types of films to be good for the local industry and the image of the country. She had, after all, requested that Filipino filmmakers present a positive image to the world of the nation's culture. But then, money does talk.

One thing that many of the above titles had in common was the presence of character actor Vic Diaz. So ubiquitous was Diaz that one could get the impression that American producers were under some mandate that required that Diaz be included in any film shoot in the Philippines. He almost seems to have made more films in English than Tagalog. A portly fellow with a mischievous grin and a naughty boy's gleam in his eye, Diaz was discovered in college by Gerardo de Leon, who saw him portraying the devil in a campus stage production.[14] But Diaz, whose father was a judge on the Philippine Court of Appeal, went on to complete his education, and even got a law degree himself. After becoming an actor, Diaz worked with many well known American actors, among them Jack Nicholson, Burt Reynolds, Tom Selleck, Cameron Mitchell, John Carradine, Robert Conrad, George Montgomery, Jock Mahoney, John Saxon, Dennis Weaver, Vera Miles, John Agar, Myron Healey, John Ashley, Pam Grier, Sid Haig,

Vic Diaz (left) with Sid Haig in *Savage Sisters* (1974/American International Pictures). Diaz became the most internationally known of Filipino character actors.

William Smith; the list goes on and on. Diaz became a favorite of directors like Romero and Santiago, which would account for a healthy share of his international films, but even without them he would not have been hurting for work. He would become the most internationally known of Filipino character actors. He was also a big help to many of his American co-stars, whether introducing them to Manila's trendier hotspots or, in the case of Jack Nicholson, watching his back while Nicholson carried on an affair with the wife of a Filipino actor.[15]

One of Diaz's sons, Teddy Diaz, was a highly regarded guitarist in a rock band called The Dawn. In the late 1980s the group had put out two albums, and in the eyes of many was about to emerge as more than a top act in Manila's music scene, with promoters from Hong Kong approaching the group about booking tours in Hong Kong and Malaysia, the band was about to make a bid for conquering southeast Asia. Unfortunately, Teddy Diaz was found stabbed to death outside his girlfriend's house in Tatalon late one night in 1988. His death somewhat ensured his stature as the Filipino Jimi Hendrix.

With his work in international co-productions, Vic Diaz would become something of a drive-in icon among aficionados of 1970s sleaze with titles like *The Big Bird Cage*, in which he portrayed a homosexual guard in a women's prison, *Vampire Hookers*, in which he played vampire John Carradine's flatulent hunchbacked servant, and *Raw Force*, in which he was cast as the leader of a group of cannibal monks who dined on the flesh of young women, but he also appeared in more reputable works, like Lino Brocka's sexy crime-noir film *Hot Property* in 1983. Although his once prolific schedule necessarily declined with age, he continued to work through the 1990s, and topped-off his career in 2000 with the acclaimed film *Yamashita*.

But like the industry as a whole, Diaz's most reputable works were not being seen by the world at large. What the world was seeing were low-grade martial arts and horror titles produced by foreigners for the international market, with titles like *The Thirsty Dead* and *Murder in the Orient*, which weren't showing the local talent in the best light. But a new breed of talented young directors was coming up within the industry, and they were determined to bring substance to the local industry. Through their works, Philippine cinema would grow some teeth as they sought for ways to call attention to the inequity running rampant under Marcos rule.

7

1974–1985

Before his murder in 1975, Board of Censors Chairman Guillermo de Vega had written in his book *Film and Freedom: Movie Censorship in the Philippines* that the new rules imposed on filmmakers under martial law had had a beneficial effect on the quality of work being done in the industry. He seems to have been mainly referencing the work of a handful of films by young filmmakers who, frankly, had an axe or two to grind, and many of whom had in reality been doing quality work prior to the decree of martial law. Still, de Vega's point was well taken: with filmmakers required to submit finished shooting scripts for official approval before filming could even begin, more care and forethought necessarily had to go into a film, and filmmakers had to forgo the loose, informal style that many of them had been accustomed to. In theory, this should have meant that the often-amateurish aspect that seemed to permeate so much of the industry's product should have been eradicated, but there was still a creativity drought to be dealt with. But de Vega was not alone in ceding certain positive aspects of martial law on the industry. More than twenty years later in a paper presented in September of 1999 at Ateneo de Manila University's "Conference on Memory, Truth-telling and the Pursuit of Justice: the Legacies of the Marcos Dictatorship," Bienvenido Lumbera explored the often contradictory ramifications that martial law brought. In his quest to tighten the grip of state control of the film industry, while also attempting to use it as a propagandistic tool, Marcos managed to stir the creativity of a generation of filmmakers whose discontent was let loose in various guises. Lumbera noted that the constraints on political debate through the media gave birth to genuine film criticism, where sociopolitical concerns were more tactfully dealt with by way of discussions centered on artistic endeavors. He further noted that certain other endeavors initiated by the regime—the creation of the Experimental Cinema of the Philippines and the Manila International Film Festival—schemes to show off the benevolence of the regime towards the arts, were in some respects beneficial to the industry. His reasoning may have differed somewhat from that of de Vega, but it is worth noting that, not only was de Vega Chairman of the Board of Censors, he was also a Presidential Advisor in Marcos' administration, and as such was guided by circumstance.

Whether or not there was a discernable increase in the quality of the work being done overall, one thing is beyond doubt: the Philippine film industry was shedding its woes and was entering into another period of prosperity; so much so that it would come to be known as the Second Golden Era. It is interesting to explore why this should have been so. To be sure, there were young filmmakers who were turning out films that would come to be regarded as some of the finest work the industry had ever produced, but these works comprised but a fraction of the industry's overall output; the resurgence of interest in Filipino films among the home crowd had to be attributable to something. Perhaps, circumstances being what they were at the time, and life being so turbulent with martial law having been declared and the future of the country uncertain, Filipinos needed to see something positive within their own culture—positive and cheering. Despite the young, serious-minded filmmakers who were beginning a new movement in Philippine cinema, for the most part Filipino films continued to rely on sappy melodrama and, following through from the latter '60s, frivolous juvenilia. Over-taxation had necessitated commerciality to dictate over the industry more than ever, and whereas the bombas had briefly usurped the old studio system, replacing star power with sex as a draw, once the censors had clamped down on the bombas, the independent production companies fell back again on old formulas, and a new studio system began to develop. Ever mindful of production costs, they needed new stars that were more affordable and would appeal to the youth market. It was the right environment for a couple of pretty, young performers to ascend the ladder to superstardom.

Vilma Santos was born on November 3, 1953, and she grew up in a middle-class family in Trozo. She began her film career by way of her uncle, Amaury Agra, who was a cinematographer employed by Sampaguita. As a child, Santos would entertain Agra whenever he came to the family home by singing him songs and doing impressions of Philippine stars of the day, like singer Pilita Corrales. One day Agra asked the young Santos if she would be interested in going into show business herself. The little girl told her uncle that she would love to be an actress, and soon enough she was being taken to the Sampaguita studios to audition. She had gone to try out for the part of Rita Gomez's daughter in the film *Anak, ang Iyong Ina* (*Child, I Am Your Mother*), and while she got the part, she also managed to catch the eye of Doc Perez,

Vilma Santos in the late 1960s or early 1970s.

who was auditioning little girls for the lead role in *Trudis Liit*, a Filipino komik adaptation. Santos got that part too, and she went on to win a FAMAS award for Best Child Actress in 1963. By her teens in the early 1970s she was starring in a seemingly endless stream of featherweight teenage musicals and syrupy love stories. The titles are illustrative of the type of fare that was selling: *Love Is for the Two of Us* (1970), *Young Love* (1970), *Aloha My Love* (1971), *My Pledge of Love* (1971), *Our Love Affair* (1971), *Teenage Senorita* (1971), *The Wonderful World of Music* (1971), *Don't Ever Say Goodbye* (1972), *Edgar Loves Vilma* (1972), *From the Bottom of My Heart* (1972), *I Do Love You* (1972), *Love at First Sight* (1972), *Love Letters* (1972), *My Little Darling* (1972), *Songs and Lovers* (1972), *Sweet Sixteen* (1972), *Sweet Sweet Love* (1972), *Sweetheart* (1972), *Teen-age Jamboree* (1972), *The Young Idol* (1972), *Because You're Mine* (1973), *Give Me Your Heart* (1973).... Well, you get the idea. In 1972 alone she made a jaw dropping 24 films. Working at such a pace—what amounts to two films per month—quality was not a major concern, but what was important was

Vilma Santos' famous improvised dance sequence in *Dama de Noche* (*Lady of the Night*; 1972/Tagalog Ilang-Ilang Productions). Santos won the FAMAS Best Actress award for her performance.

the public's hunger to see her as often as producers could churn the films out. This is not to say that Santos was confined exclusively to frivolous film work: in 1972 she also won a FAMAS Best Actress trophy for the film *Dama de Noche* (*Lady of the Night*), and during the era she otherwise busied herself with roles in various genres with titles like *Anak ng Aswang* (*Daughter of the Vampire*) and *Twin Fist for Justice* (both in 1973), and *Biktima* (*Victim*) and *Phantom Lady* (both in 1974), but the bulk of her prolific film work was in youth-oriented programmers. With the dawning of the Second Golden Era in 1974, however, she would soon begin to shed her saccharine image as she began to work with the industry's greatest young directors on some of their most impressive titles.

Although her own career in film started much the same as did Santos'—in teen-oriented fluff—Nora Aunor was somewhat against the grain in the Filipino film industry. Diminutive and petite, she was more dark-complected than the norm for lead actresses (in 1972 this was even highlighted by the title of one of her films, *My Little Brown Girl*). Born Norma Villamayor on May 21, 1953, Aunor was a child of poverty who began participating in local singing competitions as a teenager. After winning enough of those competitions, she left poverty-stricken Iriga City behind and went to live with her uncle in Manila, eventually adopted his surname. After winning a national talent show, *Tawag ng Tanghalan* (*Exhibition Call*)—something of a Filipino *Star Search* of its day—she began guesting on radio and television programs until scoring a major hit single with a cover of the song "The Music Played." That led to a job as co-host of her own television program, *The Nora and Eddie Show*, with singer Eddie Peregrina in the late 1960s. She also began appearing in films; inconsequential teen pictures like *Cinderella A-Go-Go* (1967), *Sitting in the Park* (1967), *9 Teeners* (1969), *Ye-Ye Generation* (1969), *D'Musical*

Teenage Idols (1969), *Teenage Escapades* (1969), *The Young at Heart* (1969), *Young Love* (1970), *Teenage Jamboree* (1970), *Tell Nora I Love Her* (1970), *Darling Nora* (1970), *Nora in Wonderland* (1970), *I Dream of Nora* (1970), *The Golden Voice of Nora* (1970)—has anyone ever had so many films named after them? She was even serenaded by Don Johnson, who crooned the Carpenters' hit "Close to You" while taking a boat ride with Aunor in the film *Lollipops and Roses* in 1974. Her most popular films were a string of features with her boyfriend, Tirso Cruz III, whose grandfather had been a very well known orchestra leader of the big band era. Aunor and Cruz would co-star in a steady stream of sentimental romance sagas like *Always in My Heart* (1971), *My Blue Hawaii* (1971), *A Gift of Love* (1972), *Nora, Mahal Kita* (*Nora, I Love You*; 1972), *Winter Holiday* (1972), and *Maalaala Mo Kaya* (*Do You Remember?*; 1973). Her singing career also flourished, eventually numbering some forty albums, but Aunor had her mind made up to be more than a teen sensation. She wanted to build a lasting career in film as a serious artist, and so formed her own production company, NV Productions, in the early 1970s. She would not only come to work with many of the brilliant young directors of the new generation, but would also begin in time to work with some of the great filmmakers of the generation that preceded them, including Gerardo de Leon and Lamberto Avellana.* Her work with de Leon in particular helped establish Aunor as a serious dramatic actress to be reckoned with. Both de Leon and Avellana had a hand in directing the anthology picture *Fe, Esperanza, Caridad* in 1974, which sought to showcase Aunor's talents as both a singer and an actress to the fullest advantage. While the film's first two stories were unspectacular—one pure soap, an obvious take on *A Star Is Born*, the other ending on an abysmally comedic note—the showpiece was the concluding story, directed by de Leon, in which Aunor portrayed a nun who falls in love with Ronaldo Valdez, the gardener who tends the convent grounds. That alone would have been scandalous enough, but imagine Aunor's horror upon discovering that Valdez is actually the devil himself. In a plot twist so characteristically de Leon in its conception, Valdez is not

Nora Aunor in the early 1970s.

---

* Vilma Santos also worked under Gerry de Leon's direction, though not in a film: de Leon directed Santos in a 1974 Filipino television commercial for Lux soap.

merely trying to steal Aunor away from a life of devotion to God, but is truly in love with her as well.

The following year, Aunor collaborated with de Leon again on the great director's final completed picture, *Banaue: Stairway to the Sky*, a brutal historical drama set in northern Luzon in 500 B.C. detailing tribal warfare. As with much of de Leon's work, the film contained some very disturbing and striking images, including the moment in which the decapitated, badly decomposing head of a slain warrior is returned to his wife, who tenderly embraces it.

Like Santos, Aunor would shine during the Second Golden Era, not just as one of the most popular box office draws, but also through starring roles in some of the most impressive films of the era. In fact, for a time she would outshine Santos. The rivalry between the two actresses was no publicity concoction or gossip columnist's contrivance. There was real resentment between the two. They were forever competing, even in the realm of teen love team pictures, Aunor and Cruz with their Guy and Pip

Nora Aunor and Eddie Peregrina in the late 1960s. The two were co-hosts of a musical/variety television program.

series, Santos and Edgar Mortiz with their Vi and Bot films. They were real-life sweethearts with Cruz and Mortiz as well, something that may be considered natural between two people working so closely together so often. But one can't help but wonder if *this* was a bit of publicity gimmickry, as the public's fascination with the young love teams seemed heightened by their real-life coupling.

Those close to Santos said that she was very envious of the reputation that Aunor was gaining as a superb dramatic actress, and that as Aunor began racking up acting trophies, one after another, Santos was determined to prove her mettle as a dramatic actress as well. Just as Aunor had started her own production company, NV productions, with the aim of producing quality dramatic features as starring vehicles for herself, Santos did the same with VS Productions, with much less success, however. After a handful of films, Santos found herself awash in debt, owing some 6-million pesos. Years later Santos admitted to the extent of competition between herself and Aunor, saying that the rivalry between the two actresses did bring out the best and worst in each other. On the one hand, they challenged each other to reach for new heights; on the other hand, the rivalry could be quite hostile. When they occasionally made films together, the two did not speak to one another when the cameras were not rolling: they went to separate sides of the set between takes. But it was not just their heated rivalry that was bringing out the best in them as actresses: the work being done by some of the day's directors demanded it.

Lino Brocka, Ishmael Bernal, Celso Ad. Castillo and Mike de Leon were making films that, unlike the co-productions of Cirio Santiago, Eddie Romero and company, were gaining the respect of international cineastes. They were directors eager to explore the social structure of the country, largely by combining the liberalized approach of the bombas with an aim at an honest examination of the nation's social stratum. Critical appraisals of the social and political infrastructure could hardly go unnoticed, and during the Marcos administration such issues had to be dealt with by filmmakers in a somewhat covert fashion, often making their point within the context of interpersonal relationships and how they are effected—even defined—by external societal factors. Censorship became a bigger problem after President Marcos declared martial law. Overtly political films became all but impossible, and even the title of Bernal's 1980 film *Manila by Night* had to be changed to *City After Dark* at the insistence of Imelda Marcos, who objected to the seamy portrayal of the nation's capitol city.

The Second Golden Era was initiated by Brocka. Born on April 3, 1939, in Nueva Ecija*, Brocka had an interesting family history. His father, Regino Brocka, was a carpenter, boat builder and salesman from the Bicol peninsula, who traveled throughout the neighboring islands. He married a schoolteacher and fathered six children, but when in Nueva Ecija on business, he abandoned his family after meeting a 15-year-old girl named Pilar Ortiz, whom he took to an island off the Bicol coast, where she gave birth to Lino, the couple's first child. In an attempt to get Regino to return to his family, his legal wife eventually reported him to the authorities as a bigamist, but as a result, Regino Brocka was arrested and sent to a Manila prison for two years. When he was released he returned to Pilar, Lino, and Lino's younger brother Danilo, who was born after Regino began serving his prison term.

Lino Brocka had fond memories of his father, who nurtured in him an inquisitive and independent spirit, but when Lino was only six years old, his father failed to return from one of his trips. After receiving word that an unidentified murder victim had been found and buried on a neighboring island, Lino accompanied his mother and brother to the island where the body was disinterred and positively identified as that of Regino Brocka. Life changed dramatically for Brocka's family after his father's death, and he was eventually sent

Nora Aunor and Tirso Cruz III in the early 1970s. The two became popular as a screen team through their series of Guy and Pip films, and were also a couple off-screen as well.

* *Sources vary as to the date of birth, many listing Brocka as having been born on April 7, 1939, which is apparently what his birth certificate states, but the date on the certificate is said to have been an error due to his birth being registered some days after the fact. Agustin V. Sotto lists the date as April 3 of 1940 in the book* Focus on Filipino Films, *but that seems to be an error. Sources also vary regarding Brocka's place of birth, many listing Pilar, Sorsogon, although that was where his father Regino had settled with his legal wife and family prior to Brocka's birth.*

to live with family members who did not appreciate the boy's precociousness, and he often felt stifled and endured ill treatment. His respite from troubles was the movies, mostly those from Hollywood. Through the magical world of film, Brocka took an idealized image of America, a place where it seemed to him the people were not only beautiful and free from want (obviously he missed *The Grapes of Wrath*), but where people had magical attributes. Esther Williams, for instance, could breathe under water. His own failed attempts to do so convinced young Lino that Americans were indeed special people.

After graduating from Nueva Ecija North High School in 1956, Brocka received a scholarship to attend the University of the Philippines where, at his mother's prodding, he studied pre-law. But his interest in the arts won out and he dropped pre-law in favor of courses that indulged his interests. His lack of interest in other subjects of academic consequence had a serious effect on his grades, and consequently his scholarship lapsed after his first year. But Brocka was resilient, and he continued his education by paying his way with a flurry of part-time jobs, a process that continued for the next nine years. He also joined the Drama Club, initially a disastrous experience, due to his thick provincial accent, so much out of place in Manila where proficiency in English seemed vital to success. But with hours of practice, and aided by viewing many more American films, Brocka's pronunciation improved.

Vilma Santos and boyfriend Edgar Mortiz in the early 1970s. They rivaled Aunor and Cruz's Guy and Pip films in popularity with their own film series, the Vi and Bot films.

He began his career in film as an assistant to Eddie Romero in the 1960s on films like *Flight to Fury* and *The Ravagers* and made his directorial debut in 1970 with the film *Wanted: Perfect Mother*, the story of a governess and a group of orphans that Brocka readily admitted drew heavily from *The Sound of Music*. The film was a box office hit in the Philippines, and the picture's production company, Lea Productions, was greatly impressed by Brocka's ability to shoot it on a three-week schedule. He otherwise impressed studio moguls and critics alike with films like *Santiago* and *Tubog sa Ginto* (literally *Dipped in Gold* or *Gold-plated*, a Filipino term denoting fakery) that same year.

Santiago was an especially impressive work, which starred Fernando Poe, Jr. as a guerrilla fighter during World War II who participates in an attack on the titular village, thinking that it is a Japanese stronghold. The guerrilla fighters are shocked to discover that their victims are all Filipinos, however, and Poe's conscience leads him to care for the attack's only survivor, Hilda

Koronel, who is left mute and blinded by the attack. After taking her to a neighboring village, Poe finds himself ostracized by the people once word spreads that he bore some responsibility for the massacre in Santiago. Poe, whose films had become very formulaic—Filipino variants on the western and brawling action pictures mostly—gave an excellent performance in a role that lent a new significance to his career.

Tubog sa Ginto was a complex melodrama that served as something of an assault on the ideal of the family unit, portraying it as some unrealistic and high-minded fraud, a theme that Brocka would periodically revisit. Eddie Garcia starred as a middle-aged family man who pursues a homosexual relationship with the family chauffeur (Mario O'Hara), devastating his son (Jay Ilagan), who is otherwise reeling from the discovery that his mother (Lolita Rodriguez) is also having an extra-marital affair. O'Hara turns out to be a conman who begins blackmailing Garcia in order to conceal his secret life, and the film ends with Garcia's suicide. Garcia's performance would win him a FAMAS Best Actor award. Brocka had adapted the screenplay from a komiks serial, and the jarringly frank depiction of the relationship between Garcia and O'Hara—admittedly very discomfiting to a Western viewer—could, perhaps, only have come during the permissive atmosphere of the bomba era.

But as impressive as his initial films were, Brocka also found himself bound by the dictates of commerce, and he was soon directing, however capably, komiks adaptations that were little more than glorified soap opera. The 1971 romance saga *Cadena de Amor* (*Chain of Love*) is representative of the genre, cluttered as it is with unlikely—sometimes even absurd—plot twists and dramatic clichés. Adapted from a Mars Ravelo serial, the film starred Rosemarie Sonora as a young woman abandoned at the altar on her wedding day by her fiancé (Mario O'Hara, who had also adapted the story into the film's screenplay), who flees down the aisle and jumps into the nearest car. Sonora falls into a deep depression, and when she is pursued by a new suitor (Dante Rivero), she tries to send him away. But Rivero won't take no for an answer, and he winds up raping Sonora. Afterward, he seems surprised that this hasn't won her over, and disappointed by Sonora's reaction to him, Rivero makes plans to leave for America. After a series of erotic dreams about Rivero, Sonora comes to the conclusion that she is in love with him after all, but when she rushes to the airport to try and see him before he departs for the United States, she is heartbroken again when she arrives just in time to see his plane leaving. Things worsen when she receives word that the plane has gone down in the ocean and Rivero's body has not been recovered. Though he is presumed to have perished, Rivero miraculously manages to survive the crash and washes ashore on the beach of one of the islands off the mainland, where he is found by a family that takes him in and hospitably nurses him back to health. The only problem is that Rivero has no memory of his past and no idea of where he belongs, so he stays with the family that rescued him and falls in love with the daughter of the house (Hilda Koronel), who is confined to a wheelchair. Koronel had lost the use of her legs after being struck by a car, though doctors can find no physical reason for the paralysis and therefore believe it to be psychosomatic. When Rivero falls out of a fishing boat one day and hits his head, Koronel instinctively jumps in to save him. Not thinking of her paralysis, Koronel manages to save Rivero, only realizing afterward that the dire circumstance has broken through the mental block that had deprived her of the use of her legs. But the knock on the head has also managed to jar Rivero's memory, and he begins experiencing flashbacks. Realizing that he needs to get in touch with his mother (Mary Walter) to let her know that he is alive, Rivero flies back to the mainland, where he is also warmly greeted by Sonora. However odd it may have been before, Rivero cannot help but to resume his relationship with Sonora, but Koronel flies to the mainland herself to see Rivero. Upon meeting Sonora, however, Koronel decides to do the honorable thing and stands aside. The film concludes with Rivero and Sonora happily exiting the church after being married, while a melancholy Koronel watches from across the street.

Despite being filled with clichés and melodrama to spare, the film is generally interesting and well directed by Brocka, who managed to cut through all of the soap opera with some interesting directorial touches. In one of the film's better moments, Rivero awakens after his fishing mishap to the sound of a haunting piano melody that was a favorite of Sonora's. He follows the melody to a room where he finds Koronel playing the piano, who he initially mistakes for Sonora. While the film's early depiction of romantic love is resoundingly negative, showing it as both paralyzingly obsessive and even violent, that pessimism is at least tempered at the film's denouement by Koronel's selflessness.

Much worse than his dabbling with soap opera was Brocka's screenplay for the 1971 Filipino western comedy *Arizona Kid*, which starred comedian Chiquito as a Filipino in the American west trying to find his way to Mexico to visit his uncle, but along the way he is roped into impersonating a famous gunslinger in order to help a town defeat a notorious outlaw. The film is notable only in that American blonde bombshell Mamie Van Doren was Chiquito's leading lady (an unlikely pairing if ever there was one), and it revealed that comedy was not Brocka's strongpoint.

Disillusioned with the commercial nature of the industry, Brocka left the film business for two years, beginning in 1972, the year that martial law was declared. He was apparently soured by the fact that he had to produce more commercially viable films in order to help broker deals to then produce the type of work that he preferred. He taught drama at two universities in Manila, and also worked in the theater with the Philippine Educational Theater Association (PETA). When he did return to film in 1974, it was on his terms: with friends and associates he formed a production company called Cinemanila, and sought to make socially relevant films that spoke to the downtrodden. The film that started it all off was *Tinimbang Ka Nguni't Kulang* (*You Have Been Weighed and Found Lacking*), the tragic story of a love affair between two of society's outcasts, a disturbed homeless woman (Lolita Rodriguez) and a leper (Mario O'Hara) living on the outskirts of town. What little acceptance Rodriguez is allotted by the people in town is merely the result of the cruel sport she provides to those who amuse themselves by tormenting her, and so she is taken in by O'Hara, who lives in a shack adjacent to the local cemetery. They are both befriended by Christopher de Leon, a high school student, who is the son of wealthy Lilia Dizon and ne'er-do-well rogue Eddie Garcia. De Leon is troubled not only by his parents' turbulent marriage, but also by his own relationship with his fickle, flirtatious girlfriend (Hilda Koronel), and he seems to take some comfort in the odd, but committed, relationship he sees between Rodriguez and O'Hara. When Rodriguez winds up pregnant, the shocked townspeople forcibly take her from O'Hara and place her in a home where she is to be cared for until she gives birth, after which a member of the local women's association is to adopt the child. But when she begins experiencing birth pangs, the very worried Rodriguez finds her way back to O'Hara, who rushes into town for a doctor. When the doctor (Ernie Zarate) refuses to come, O'Hara forces him at knifepoint, and a crowd is attracted by the cries of the doctor's wife. Soon a mob forms at the cemetery, and de Leon arrives just in time to witness O'Hara being gunned down by the police. As the crowd silently watches de Leon weeping over O'Hara's corpse, Rodriguez gives birth, and through a flashback it is revealed that her mental decline was the result of her own failed romance with Garcia, whom she never got over, and a traumatic abortion, performed by a haggard old woman, and forced on her by Garcia to hide his infidelity. After giving birth, Rodriguez entrusts her child to de Leon before she too dies, and the film concludes with the crowd solemnly watching de Leon as he somberly carries the child away.

An effectively compassionate statement on behalf of society's outcasts, and every bit as much an indictment of the judgmental proclivities of society at large, Brocka did an excellent job of turning two aesthetically unappealing characters—a leper and a filthy, mangy madwoman—into very sympathetic individuals. It is interesting that de Leon's fractured relationships (with his parents, with Koronel, and even with his friends, one of whom winds up marrying Koronel) leave him feeling disconnected also, and that he finds his ideal in the pure relationship between Rodriguez and O'Hara. O'Hara, who co-wrote the screenplay with Brocka, delivers some of the film's most poignant dialogue, at one point admonishing de Leon for ridiculing one of his teachers at school and lamenting the superficial criterion by which most people tend to judge. All the while, the film avoids the temptation to preach, rather allowing the circumstances naturally arising through the narrative to make its point. Brocka surely drew on his own life experiences, having served as a Mormon missionary in the Molokai leper colony before becoming a filmmaker.[1] He was also homosexual, and doubtless knew the sting of ostracism. *Tinimbang Ka Nguni't Kulang* was critically lauded and dominated the FAMAS Awards that year, winning Best Picture, as well as Best Director for Brocka, Best Actress for Rodriguez, Best Actor for the then fairly unknown de Leon, Best Filmscore for Lutgardo Labad, and Best Sound for Gregorio Ella. Brocka further dominated the FAMAS Awards that year with another of his titles, *Tatlo, Dalawa, Isa* (*Three, Two, One*) which won Best Supporting Actress for Anita Linda and Best Screenplay for Orlando Nadres.

Tatlo, Dalawa, Isa was an anthology picture that was written by three different screenwriters, each individually scripting the film's three tales, but apparently Nadres' penning of the film's concluding story was set apart as being FAMAS worthy. The film's opening segment, *Mga Hugis ng Pag-asa* (*Models of Hope*), was written by Tony Perez, and starred Jay Ilagan as a troubled teen committed by his mother (Perla Bautista) to a drug rehabilitation program, which at times has the feel of a boot camp, at others a prison work camp, and still at other times has the feel of a fraternity hazing. But Ilagan toughs it out and emerges successful. Ilagan gave a good performance, as did the rest of the cast, including Bembol Roco as another young man in the rehab program. Ilagan was at the height of his popularity in the 1970s, but his tendency to put on weight seems to have diminished his viability after a while as a leading actor.

The film's second segment, *Hellow, Soldier*, written by Mario O'Hara, is set in the 1960s and starred Hilda Koronel as a 17-year-old girl who was fathered by a U.S. soldier (Claude Wilson) in 1945. As Wilson had never been told that he had fathered a child during the war, Koronel writes to him, and Wilson and his wife (Barbara Browne) travel to the Philippines to meet her. The idea of seeing the man who fathered her child all those years ago is apparently a bit overwhelming for Koronel's mother (Anita Linda), and when Wilson and Browne arrive they find Linda stinking drunk. Wilson and Browne offer to take Koronel back to America with them, and although she desperately wants to go to the U.S., in the end Koronel finds that she is unable to leave her pathetic mother all alone.

While the two opening stories are interesting, it is easy to see why Nadres' work on the film's concluding segment, *Bukas, Madilim Bukas* (*Tomorrow, Dark Tomorrow*), was considered worthy of the FAMAS. The tale was a bit of Filipino gothic starring Lolita Rodriguez as a repressed, lonely middle-aged Catholic woman living in a mansion with her domineering, invalid mother (Mary Walter). At church one day Rodriguez meets Mario O'Hara, a younger man who takes an obvious interest in her, and flattered by the attention, Rodriguez quickly becomes infatuated with O'Hara. She hires him to work at the house as a gardener, and when they eventually wind up in bed together one night, Walter manages to get out of bed, and upon finding Rodriguez and O'Hara together, attempts to club O'Hara with her cane. But impossible to do so upon learning that he has been abruptly transferred and shipped out of the Philippines. In the end Aunor loses her desire to travel to America.

Screenwriter Marina Feleo-Gonzalez had gotten the original idea for the story ten years earlier when she witnessed a demonstration against the U.S. bases held outside the U.S. embassy. Like the record of the U.S. military stationed in other countries, its record in the Philippines is by no means spotless, but the outrageous and inexplicable behavior of the U.S. soldiers in the film—seemingly gunning down Filipinos out of sheer boredom—is really a bit much to take at face value. Presenting its case of the U.S. as an occupying bully, answerable to no one, and with this as its primary message, the crimes committed by the U.S. military in the film can be seen as a rather clumsy way of delivering the point. The film fares better in its less shrill moments; for instance, the news accounts viewed by Aunor's family on their small black and white television, in which they learn of President Nixon's resignation, as well as hearing about U.S. astronauts walking on the moon, seem to give a more level-headed portrait of the U.S. as a powerful, yet flawed nation.

Aquino-Kashiwahara won the FAMAS Best Director award for her work, as did screenwriter Feleo-Gonzalez, and editor Edgardo Vinarao. *Minsa'y Isang Gamu-gamo* also won the FAMAS for Best Picture. It wasn't, but it apparently struck a nerve at the time.

Nora Aunor won the FAMAS Best Actress award not for *Minsa'y Isang Gamu-gamo*, but for another of her films that same year instead: *Tatlong Taong Walang Diyos* (*Three Godless Years*) was produced by Aunor's own company NV Productions, and was written and directed by Mario O'Hara. Born in Zamboanga City in 1946, O'Hara had attended Adamson University where he majored in Chemical Engineering, but he did not complete his education, choosing instead to enter into the entertainment business in the early 1960s as actor, writer, and eventually director on radio station dzRH in Manila, and later station dzXL, owned by the Chronicle Broadcasting Network. Throughout the 1960s and into the 1970s he continued to work in radio, and eventually branched out into television. He would also become a respected thespian of the stage through his work with PETA, beginning in 1969, which began his fruitful association with Lino Brocka. For Brocka, O'Hara wrote *Isang Laro* (*One Event*), a one-act play that served as part of an omnibus directed by Brocka titled *Tatlo* (*Three*), in which O'Hara also performed. After working under Brocka as both an actor and screenwriter in film, O'Hara began to emerge as a formidable filmmaker himself, making his directorial debut in 1975 with the film *Mortal*, in which a mental patient gradually comes to terms with the fact that he murdered his wife. Aside from scripting Brocka's *Insiang* in 1976, O'Hara set out to make his own worthy contribution to the Second Golden Era's canon of cinematic showpieces.

Generally regarded as one of the most significant Filipino films of the 1970s, *Tatlong Taong Walang Diyos* was a tragic World War II melodrama which cast Nora Aunor as a young woman who is raped by a Japanese soldier (Christopher de Leon). It soon becomes obvious, however, that de Leon has more than a passing interest in Aunor, as he continues to visit her and shower her with gifts. Though Aunor steadfastly rejects him, her parents are won over by de Leon, who brings them food and other supplies scarce to the rest of the village during the Japanese occupation. This ostracizes the family from the rest of the community, and they become further social outcasts when Aunor turns out to be pregnant as the result of the rape. After giving birth, Aunor begins to let go of her hatred for de Leon and the two are married, which breaks the heart of Bembol Roco, a former beau of Aunor's who has returned from two years of service in the Philippine military. With the Japanese now firmly in control of the country, Roco no longer has a military to serve in, but upon finding Aunor married to a Japanese soldier (and her having given birth to his child as well), Roco goes off and joins the Philippine resistance. In time, Aunor's parents are accused of complicity with the rebels and are executed, but Aunor blames Roco and the resistance for making her life a hell. When the Americans return the Japanese flee the village, and Aunor and de Leon escape into the forest with their baby, where they are set upon by a band of Filipino rebels who kill de Leon. When Aunor returns to her village she is quickly chased by an angry mob of citizens who recognize her as the wife of a Japanese soldier, and she is turned over to a somber group of widows whose husbands had been killed by the Japanese. The women drive Aunor into the waiting grasp of resistance fighters, and the film concludes with Roco arriving in town and frantically searching for Aunor, who he finds lying dead in the street with a good many other corpses awaiting burial.

Initially, the film had been widely criticized as being overly sympathetic in its portrayal of the Japanese, a reaction only to be expected given the record of the Japanese during the occupation. In hindsight, however, this reaction does seem hypersensitive, since the only sympathetic Japanese character in the film is that portrayed by de Leon, who after all does begin the film as a rapist. Basically, the film is a tragic story in which Aunor is a victim of the circumstances of the war, having been victimized first by the Japanese, and then by her own people. It was an effectively thoughtful meditation on the delicacy of human emotions during the most trying of times. O'Hara's tendency to avoid easy classification in his characterizations made for compelling storytelling. The ambiguity prevalent in much of O'Hara's writing can be seen in de Leon's character in *Tatlong Taong*, a man that O'Hara refused to paint as evil merely for being a Japanese soldier (or even for being a rapist for that matter), endowing him instead with positive and negative attributes. This is apparent in O'Hara's screenwriting for Brocka as well, where good people are capable of bad acts (as in Koronel's manipulative scheme for retribution in *Insiang*), and even bad people are permitted positive aspects to their nature, otherwise fairly uncharacteristic of much of Brocka's work, Brocka's distinguishing between good and bad, right and wrong tending to be more distinct in the traditional manner of Philippine melodrama.

More than any of his contemporaries, Brocka seemed to bear the brunt of Marcos' wrath. An outspoken critic of Marcos' regime, Brocka participated in anti–Marcos rallies, was jailed a number of times, and was humiliated at having to be freed through the efforts of colleagues like Eddie Romero and Joseph Estrada, both of whom were on friendly terms with the Marcoses.[2] In 1983 Brocka had founded an organization called Concerned Artists of the Philippines (CAP), a group that had been present to greet Benigno Aquino, Jr. at the Manila International Airport upon his return from self-imposed exile in the U.S. After Aquino's assassination, CAP openly took part in organized protests against the regime. In January of 1985 Brocka was jailed for 16 days when he supported a strike by the Jeepney Drivers' Association, a favor returned for the support of some jeepney drivers when Brocka and other actors and filmmakers held an anti-censorship demonstration in December of 1984 directed at the Board of Review for Motion Pictures and Television. It was a somewhat odd alliance, which does rather highlight the Marcos government's ability to bring together disparate groups in concert against it. But after Cinemanila's early successes, Marcos saw Brocka's talent for making socially relevant films that could receive international attention, and appreciating the propaganda potential at play, sought to seduce Brocka into becoming an ally. The government offered him work directing government sanctioned films that could be entered in international festivals, thereby softening the regime's image globally, and even sweetened the deal by offering to pay off Brocka's mounting debts. Cinemanila's early success was fleeting, as Brocka, as its head, was less interested in commercialism and more with artistry. Brocka had personally guaranteed loans, and when subsequent films did not meet with appreciable success, he found himself some 800,000 pesos in debt. Even then Brocka refused to be a puppet for the regime: the snub would not be forgotten.

7. 1974–1985   143

In 1984, Brocka had perhaps his grandest showdown with the regime when he sought to release the film *Bayan Ko: Kapit sa Patalim* (*My Country: Gripping a Double-edged Knife*). The dual title was the result of Brocka's cobbling two separate stories together, both based on actual events and both scripts having been approved by the Board of Censors. The film starred Phillip Salvador as a factory worker who makes an agreement with his employer not to go on strike, although much of the plant is prepared to do so. Salvador's main concern is paying for medical care for his pregnant wife (Gina Alajar), and he is therefore reluctant to walk off his job. As a result, he is then shunned by his fellow workers, and his agreement with his employer notwithstanding, he soon loses his job. In order to pay his wife's medical bills, he is drawn into a robbery, which goes wrong and turns into a hostage situation.

Brocka had been able to get partial financing for the project from a French company called Stephan Films, and he was able to get further capital for the project from Malaya Films in the Philippines, a company said to be always sympathetic to anti–Marcos artists. The postproduction work was then to be done in France. With Brocka participating in anti-government protests and speaking at rallies during the day, much of the film had to be shot at night, helping that noir look that he was somewhat known for, and which has always appealed to the French. In fact, the film was given a very enthusiastic reception by critics at that year's Cannes Film Festival, and Brocka made a memorable appearance himself. He showed up in a Philippine shirt called a barong, with a blood red map of the Philippines emblazoned on

Gina Alajar and Phillip Salvador in Lino Brocka's *Bayan Ko: Kapit sa Patalim* (*My Country: Gripping a Double-edged Knife*; 1985/Malaya-Stephan). The film had censorship problems in the Philippines, initially being banned as "subversive," but after it was a hit at Cannes, the subversive charge was dropped. Philippine censors then charged the film with being obscene.

the front, beneath it the simple word "Justice." He laughed-off comments that his was a rather flamboyant and extremely theatrical method of gaining attention, noting that, as an artist, he was bound to call attention to a cause by theatrical methods.

None of this was well-received in Malacanang, and not only did the Board of Review for Motion Pictures and Television (BRMPT) deny the film a showing permit, calling it "subversive," but the government even refused to renew Brocka's passport and allow him to return to the Philippines. Again, the French proved useful; he was invited by the French Prime Minister to speak at a human rights conference, and ever mindful of his global reputation, Marcos decided to allow Brocka reentry into the country rather than have him carp about it before the world. More than that, the subversive charge against *Bayan Ko* was withdrawn, which should have cleared the way for the film to be exhibited in the Philippines—should have, but didn't. It was merely a ruse by the government, which then had the BRMPT refuse the film a showing permit on the grounds that portions of it were deemed to be obscene. Specifically, the Board cited scenes of nude female dancers in a nightclub scene and depictions of lesbians kissing and fondling one another. Malaya Films president Jose Antonio U. Gonzalez appealed the Board's decision to the Philippine Supreme Court, which many might have considered a waste of time during the trying martial law years. But Chief Justice Enrique M. Fernando, writing for the majority, showed that the Court was indeed independent of the regime and certainly no tool of Malacanang. Justice Fernando wrote that freedom from censorship was "beyond question, a well-settled principle in our jurisdiction," and went on to say that "to avoid an unconstitutional taint on its creation, the power of respondent Board is limited to the classification of films. It can, to safeguard other constitutional objections, determine what motion pictures are for general patronage and what may require either parental guidance or be limited to adults only. That is to abide by the principle that freedom of expression is the rule and restrictions the exemption." Fernando's levelheaded decision went on to note that censorship "is allowable only under the clearest proof of a clear and present danger of a substantive evil to public morals, public health or any other legitimate public interest." He also allowed that "There is, however, some difficulty in determining what is obscene."

Public morals? Public health? Public interest? Would the U.S. Supreme Court take such things into consideration or approach such a case with comparable sobriety? Likely, the rights of society at large would be of little consequence and would be, as always, unconditionally subservient to the rights of a particular individual's wish to express themselves, such is the current disposition of American jurisprudence. But Fernando's Court came to a well-reasoned decision, whereby the BRMPT could justifiably stamp the film with an "adults only" rating (which Gonzalez and Brocka were also objecting to), but could not order cuts to be made or prevent the film's exhibition; Fernando's court struck a sensible balance. Marcos had been thwarted in his attempt to prevent Brocka from presenting to the public—indeed the world— once again the conditions of the lower class in Philippine society. It was Fernando's final decision before retiring (he stepped down just four days later), and while the cynical might suggest that, under the circumstances, he could afford to throw caution to the wind, the truth is that he left with his integrity intact and the case was a fitting coda to his career.

Bayan Ko not only received gushing praise at Cannes, but also went on to win the Best Film of the Year Award from the British Film Institute, something that probably hung like a bad smell over Malacanang. The fact is that Ferdinand and (particularly) Imelda Marcos considered themselves champions of the arts and tried to cultivate them, provided artists show appropriate respect. Brocka didn't. Brocka was serious about his work, but paradoxically, the more seriously critics took him, the more aloof he seemed to become, even belittling as gullible those who praised his work. It played like a ridiculous game, since no one took Brocka more

Eddie Garcia and Dina Bonnevie in Lino Brocka's *Gumapang Ka sa Lusak* (*You Crawl in the Mud*; 1990/Viva Films), the story of a sleazy politician's abuse of power.

seriously than Brocka himself. A rebel always needs a nemesis, and when the Marcos regime did eventually fall, Brocka must have felt like Niagara without the Falls. When Marcos was overthrown and went into exile, Brocka did find himself able to make more openly political films, like *Gumapang Ka sa Lusak* (*You Crawl in the Mud*) in 1990, which portrayed the abuse of power by a sleazy politician, but Brocka also became an outspoken opponent of the Corazon Aquino administration. His opposition may have been genuine, but it is also worth considering that Brocka may have felt adrift in the post–Marcos years and was merely seeking to stay relevant in the way he had long been accustomed to. In 1991 Brocka died in a car accident in Quezon City.

Somewhat more commercial than Brocka, though no less capable of brilliant work, was Ishmael Bernal. Born in Manila on September 30, 1938, Bernal received his Bachelor of Arts degree in English from the University of the Philippines in 1962, and continued his education in France at the University of Aix-en-Provence, earning a Licentiate in French Literature and Philosophy, and the Film Institute of India, receiving a Diplomate in Film Directing in 1970. He worked briefly as a film critic for the *Manila Chronicle* before beginning his film career as an assistant to Lamberto Avellana, who had by then moved on to documentary filmmaking. Bernal began directing films in 1971, but it was not until the mid–1970s that he would begin creating his best works. *Ligaw na Bulaklak* (*Wild Flower*) and *Nunal sa Tubig* (*A Speck in the Water*), both in 1976, were two highly regarded films that helped establish Bernal as one of the preeminent film directors of the era. The former concerned a gardener (Vic Silayan) emasculated by the Japanese during the war who falls in love with a pretty high school girl (Alma Moreno). His frustration eventually erupts into murderous rage when he catches the girl with her boyfriend. The latter was a tragic love triangle set amid a poor fishing village devastated by pollution, which is killing the fish and robbing the people of their livelihood.

Bernal's tendency to split his time between the thought provoking and the formulaic may have made him more popular with film producers who were out to make a peso, but it also made his filmography considerably spottier than Brocka's. Amid Bernal's works are standard soapers like *Ikaw Ay Akin* (*You Are Mine*), a 1978 melodrama that brought together Vilma Santos, Nora Aunor and Christopher de Leon, all three of them superstars, for what was surely a studio mogul's dream love triangle. The film could hardly fail to make money, and Santos and de Leon became the era's most popular new screen love team. They would co-star together in one tearjerker after another, including films like Bernal's *Relasyon* (*The Affair*) in 1982, which saw Santos having an affair with the married de Leon, who eventually returns to his wife, but then suffers a brain aneurysm, a daring departure from the old standby of a brain tumor, which is always a popular plot contrivance in Filipino soap operas. (Not to worry, as de Leon eventually got to have his brain tumor in the 1985 film *God Save Me!*) Filipino films tend to ladle the melodrama on heavy until the story is awash in cliché; and yet they are still given no less serious consideration for it within the country's filmmaking and critical circles, particularly when in the hands of a highly regarded director.

It is interesting to read the words of writer Mario Hernando, who wrote the entry on Bernal in the book *Focus on Filipino Films* in 1983: while praising Bernal as "one of the most accomplished artists in terms of both quality and quantity of output,"[3] Hernando goes on to say, "Of the 39 films he has made, at least 20 are worthy of his name, out of which seven are quite good, [and] nine others are very good or outstanding."[4] In other words, roughly half of Bernal's considerable cinematic output was considered by Hernando to be worthwhile, which he seems to feel is a good percentage. That may not sound like much of a track record, but when Bernal was good, he was impressive. It also needs to be said that people in the Filipino film industry do not tend to make salaries comparable to those in Hollywood, even if one were to make the necessary currency adjustment, meaning that even a director the caliber of Bernal could really be referred to as a jobbing director—one who is not necessarily cherry-picking his assignments, but is accepting jobs as they come. Even those at the top in the industry tend to often work at a dizzying pace—a film can generally be shot in one week, and the post-production completed in another week—the result being that talented filmmakers might produce one or two good-to-brilliant works in a year mixed amid four-to-six middling-to-bad efforts. Bernal's tendency to make commercial allowances made him more prone to such an effect. He followed *Relasyon* by again teaming Santos and de Leon in *Broken Marriage* (1983), a film with a title descriptive enough to render any attempt at explanation unnecessary.

Bernal might have been willing to allow commercial considerations to lead him in his work with Santos and de Leon, but he put Aunor to better use, starring her in one of his more profound works, *Himala* (*Miracle*), in 1982. Aunor was cast as a 22-year-old girl in a small village who has a visitation from the Virgin Mary, and soon after begins to exhibit remarkable healing powers. When word of her abilities spreads, the sleepy little village in which she resides is transformed into a Mecca, and as people begin to flood the region for healings, opportunists of all kinds take advantage: saloons open, prostitution flourishes, and even t-shirts with Aunor's image are marketed. After Aunor is raped and winds up pregnant, the faithful begin spreading word of an immaculate conception. When Aunor reveals to one-and-all that the pregnancy was the result of rape rather than divine providence, a deranged follower guns her down.

City After Dark was perhaps Bernal's most notable work, a compelling and fascinating, if overlong, expose chronicling the Manila nightlife of a group of city residents whose lives are all linked in one way or another. Bernal depicted a mix of characters (some lonely, others simply obnoxious) who are searching for love and purpose (though they themselves may not be bothered to analyze their motivations), but whose lives seem to gravitate towards the opposite, as each one ultimately lives a shallow, deceptive and purposeless existence. Alma Moreno, for instance, works the nightshift as a nurse at the hospital. While she is at work, her husband carries on a homosexual affair, but much later in the film it is revealed that Moreno's job as a nurse is merely a cover for her real means of income, which is prostitution.

Bernal's direction occasionally lacked subtlety, as in the scene where Charito Solis discovers drugs in her son's room, and proceeds to then drive him from the house in a rage, battering him with anything and everything she can get her hands on, Bernal all the while intercutting the scene with various images of Christ displayed throughout the house (paintings, statuettes—even rugs). Still, in other moments his direction was inspired, at times adopting an almost surrealistic approach. The film's most interesting performance was delivered by Cherie Gil as a lesbian street tough.

The remainder of Bernal's career would fluctuate between impressive achievements—occasionally showing traces of cinematic brilliance, though, like *City After Dark*, sometimes marred by heavy-handed commentary—and more mundane works. Like Brocka, he would die prematurely, succumbing to a heart attack in 1996.

Somewhat more consistent in his cinematic vision was Celso Ad. Castillo. Born in Siniloan, Laguna on September 12, 1943, Castillo's approach was more balanced than many other filmmakers in that he gave equal consideration to both the visual and narrative aspects of film. This may be partially attributable to the fact that he had a background as a writer in Filipino komiks, long the reading material of choice with the Filipino public, and whereas many filmmakers tend to favor one approach over the other—perhaps not always consciously—Castillo understood that, like the illustrated medium, film was a combination of both visual and narrative. He began writing for film in the mid–1960s with a pair of James Bond parodies, which led to his own directorial assignments, but it was not until 1970 with the controversial black and white film *Nympha* that he really made a splash. Sometimes mingling religious and sexual imagery, the film was certain to cause a stir in a culture steeped in Catholicism, but the film was esteemed by critics both home and abroad, and it became the first Filipino film to play the Venice Film Festival since Manuel Conde's *Genghis Khan* in 1951. He used the notoriety as a springboard to vault his way into the mainstream, teaming with the King of Philippine Movies, Fernando Poe, Jr., for a string of features, beginning with *Asedillo* in 1971. Coming on the heels of Brocka's *Santiago*, the film helped place Poe at the vanguard of the new wave of Filipino film, and even won him another FAMAS Best Actor award. The film was the true story of a 1920s schoolteacher who became the leader of a rebel movement aimed at toppling the corrupt local bureaucracy. In the end he is ratted-out by one of his own, however, and the film ends with the distinctly Christ-like image of Poe, dead and put on display for all to see. It probably went a long way toward solidifying Poe's populist image.

In 1972, Castillo and Poe continued their collaboration with two films, *Santo Domingo* and *Ang Alamat* (*The Legend*), and finished in 1973 with the film *Esteban*, films which presented Poe as a quick-draw gunfighter who, after fighting the Huks, disavows his warring past, but then finds himself compelled to dust off his guns in order to defend the people of his province against a wealthy landowner laying claim to others' land.

Castillo gained international recognition with the 1977 film *Burlesk Queen*, which starred Vilma Santos as a burlesque dancer in the 1950s. If Bernal helped bring Nora Aunor acclaim as a serious actress, it was Castillo who brought the same acclaim to Santos, essentially making her career as a serious dramatic actress and launching her to superstardom. *Burlesk Queen* also prominently featured one of the old hands, Leopoldo Salcedo, who gave a moving performance as Santos' disabled father. In the film, Santos defies Salcedo's wishes by becoming a burlesque dancer in Joonee Gamboa's theater, taking the place of top draw Rosemarie Gil, who is off on an alcoholic bender pining for her ex-beau (Roldan Aquino). Having already lost the use of his legs, and then been humiliated when his wife left him for another man, Salcedo finds Santos' choice of profession more than he can bear, and he succumbs to a fatal heart attack. The heartbroken Santos retires from dancing and moves in with her boyfriend (Rolly Quizon), but when she gets pregnant, Quizon's parents convince him to leave Santos and go off to attend law school. Now pregnant and alone, Santos decides to return to dancing, but she finds Gamboa about to be put out of business by an ambitious politician who has vowed to clean up the city and rid it of such disreputable public displays. Nonetheless, Gamboa is determined to put on one last show—no less than the greatest burlesque show in history. It turns out to be quite a show indeed, climaxing with Santos doing a protracted bump and grind during which she begins to bleed and apparently induces a miscarriage of her pregnancy. Even so, the crowd cheered wildly on. Gamboa gave an excellent performance as the theater owner, for whom burlesque is more than a profession, but rather a life's passion. But amid the film's many impressive performances, none is better than Salcedo's brief appearance as Santos' tormented father.

Strangely, *Burlesk Queen* failed to win any FAMAS awards. Not so with Castillo's next effort, *Pagputi ng Uwak, Pag-itim ng Tagak* (*The Heron Turns White, the Seagull Turns Black*), which took the FAMAS Best Picture award for 1978, as well as netting Castillo the Best Director trophy. It was a strikingly bold political film for the martial law era, starring Vilma Santos as a classical violinist who returns to her small home village where she begins a romance with Bembol Roco, much to the dismay of her two aunts who consider the common Roco beneath them. Although Santos and Roco elope, Santos winds up leaving him when her aunts force her to choose between Roco and the family wealth. Humiliated, Roco runs off and joins the Huks, a communist movement whose members inhabit the nearby hills. While he is away, Santos gives birth to Roco's child, and the film reaches its climax when Roco sneaks into Santos' home to see his wife and child. As Santos and Roco make love, unseen government assassins open fire on the house, killing everyone inside save the infant, which is last seen crying in its crib. What may have made the film acceptable to censors at the time was the government's gunning down of Roco's character at the end of the film, perhaps viewed by the powers that be as a lesson of sorts, since the "good guys" could be said to have won in the end, but if that were the rationale, then they seemed to have missed the point. The truth is that Roco's character was more a protagonist within the narrative, a good man driven to extremes as a result of his disaffection brought about by the ruling class attitude that shunned him and his rejection by the bourgeois.

Castillo tried his hand at most every genre, from eroticism like *Nympha, Ang Pinakamagandang Hayop sa Balat ng Lupa* (*The Most Beautiful Creature on the Face of the Earth*; 1974), *Brown Emmanuelle* (1982) and *Virgin People* (twice, first in 1983, and again in 1996), to films with a political bent, like *Asedillo* and *Pagputi ng Uwak, Pag-itim ng Tagak*, to martial arts titles like *Return of the Dragon* (1974) and *Dragon's Quest* (1983), and horror films like *Patayin Mo sa Sindak si Barbara* (1974), *Kung Bakit Dugo ang Kulay ng Gabi* (*What If Blood Was the Color of Night*; 1974) and *Snake Sisters* (1984). And, of course, there were also the melodramas. While Castillo's dramas tended to be dark and brooding, he, like most every Filipino filmmaker, made time for twaddle. After not directing a film in four years, Castillo made his return in 1992 with the pathetic soap *Tag-Araw, Tag-Ulan* (*Stormy Summer*), and followed a year later with another turgid melodrama, *Kapag Iginuhit ang Hatol ng Puso* (*When the Line in the Heart*

Is Drawn). They were curiously mundane and mainstream for Castillo, but he was soon enough back into his stride with a series of impressive works, including three re-workings of his most impressive titles, *Ang Pinakamagandang Hayop sa Balat ng Lupa*, *Virgin People* and *Isla* (all in 1996) before moving on to the fascinating horror film *Lihim ni Madonna* (*Secret of Madonna*) and the sexy crime thriller *Mananayaw* (*The Dancer*) in 1997.

After the declaration of martial law and the crackdown on the bombas, Castillo found a way to titillate audiences nonetheless: he employed what came to be known as "the wet look," dressing actresses in skimpy clothing that could reveal much when wet. He seems to have started the trend off with *Pinakamagandang Hayop* in 1974, managing to find ways to get star Gloria Diaz wet enough that one could see just enough of what was beneath her garments. Diaz is an Ilocano who, at the age of 19, became the first Filipina to win the Miss Universe title when she was crowned in 1969. That already made her both a celebrity and something of a pioneer in the Philippines, but her role in popularizing the wet look made her a film celebrity and a pioneer of a different sort. She went on to enjoy a long and successful career as a film star, which continues at the time of this writing.

Gloria Diaz was the first Filipina to win the Miss Universe pageant when she was crowned in 1969. She naturally segued into a film career, popularizing the "wet look" in the mid–1970s after the banning of the bomba films.

If Castillo has shown a flaw as an artist, it has been his sometimes-deliberate tendency to court controversy through his work, and his presentation is occasionally tactless and self-conscious. Whereas it may have come naturally in his earlier works, enjoying his reputation as something of a button-pusher, his work began to give the impression of taking its motivation from this rather crude method of attention-getting.

The most consistently excellent filmmaker of the era, Mike de Leon was born in Manila on May 24, 1947, and came from one of the most prestigious show business families: his grandmother was Dona Narcisa Buencamino de Leon, longtime matriarch of LVN studios, and his father, Manuel de Leon, was an attorney who became a prominent film producer as well. With such a family history, it would seem only natural for Mike to have gone into the business, but his interest in film did not fully blossom until he attended the University of Heidelberg, and while in Germany he began attending screenings at a small German theater that ran classic films. After making a couple of short films in the early 1970s, de Leon founded the company

Cinema Artists, which produced Brocka's *Maynila, sa mga Kuko ng Liwanag* as its first film. De Leon served as cinematographer on the film, and his work would win him a FAMAS award.

His first directorial effort on a feature followed in 1976 with the ghost story *Itim* (*Black*). Tommy Abuel was cast as a photographer who becomes fascinated by Charo Santos, a beautiful, melancholy young woman he photographs by chance one day, and he begins to unravel the story behind the death of Santos' older sibling. The truth eventually leads to Abuel's disabled father (Mario Montenegro), a doctor who had an affair with Santos' sister and after getting her pregnant, performed an abortion on her, which resulted in her death. Montenegro then dumped the body in a nearby lake. De Leon's handling of the supernatural was quite measured; fans of modern horror may find his subtle approach to be too leisurely, but many fans of true horror, who recognize that the genre's greatest works are built on atmospherics, will likely appreciate de Leon's savoring the eerie aura of mystery. In particular, two scenes stand out, both involving Abuel's investigation of sounds within the old villa he shares with his father. In the first, he hears someone moving about at night and follows the sounds downstairs where he catches a glimpse of a figure crossing the hallway, but ultimately finds no one. Later in the film he is again drawn downstairs by noises in the night, which lead him to a room in which he finds a locked cabinet. Unable to open it, he is distracted by a flickering light, and after fidgeting with the bulb, he turns to find that the cabinet has mysteriously opened. Inside the cabinet he finds evidence of his father's affair with Santos' sister.

Catholic imagery and rituals may never have seemed as dark, eerie, or distressingly foreboding as they have often been presented in Filipino cinema. Even when depicted as counteracting the forces of evil, Catholicism seems to somehow encompass a discernable menace. In *Itim* Abuel happens upon a weird rural religious procession in which a group of masked men slowly make their way down a desolate road while flagellating themselves. In another sequence, Abuel has a dream in which he walks down the candlelit aisle of a small chapel, surrounded on either side by life-sized religious icons. He is quickly awakened when the icons startle him by suddenly springing to life and lurching toward him. De Leon's superbly understated approach to the supernatural is a refreshing change from the bombast of most work within the genre.

Perhaps because he tended to work much less than Brocka or Bernal, de Leon's filmography is uncluttered by the occasional dross that tends to mar the catalog of even great directors in the Philippines. In the early-to-mid 1980s, de Leon put together a string of excellent features, which included the entertaining comic rock opera *Kakabakaba Ka Ba?* (*Are You Nervous?*) in 1980, the disturbing and tragic incest-driven psychological drama *Kisapmata* (*In the Blink of an Eye*) in 1981, the scathing indictment of fraternity hazing in *Batch '81* (1982), which was rife with political metaphor, and *Sister Stella L* (1984), which starred Vilma Santos as a nun defending the rights of workers. De Leon had begun *Sister Stella L* under the banner of Cinema Artists, but when money ran short, he was only able to complete it with the assistance of Regal Films matriarch Lily Monteverde. Perhaps wary of ramifications from the Marcos regime, Monteverde's husband, Remy Monteverde, had warned de Leon that Regal Films was not in the business of political propaganda, but Mother Lily saw the project through nonetheless.[5]

Kakabakaba Ka Ba? was a madcap comedy, with a little rock opera thrown in, about four young adults who unwittingly become involved in a plot to take over the Philippines. It all begins when an inept Japanese smuggler gets cold feet and slips his contraband—a cassette tape—into the coat pocket of fellow airline passenger Christopher de Leon. Once he passes through customs with the tape, de Leon and his friends (Charo Santos, Jay Ilagan and Sandy Andolong) find themselves pursued by underworld figures, including the Chinese mob under the leadership of Armida Siguion-Reyna. The kids finally discover that it is the tape that everyone is after, and with some investigation they further discover that the tape is lined with a powerful opiate. The far-flung scheme is to control the populace by using the opium to create a super communion host, which would be taken by the people during mass. Infiltrating the enemy camp dressed as sisters and clergy, the foursome defeat main heavy Johnny Delgado during a bizarre musical number. While his work was usually much darker—certainly more serious—de Leon proved surprisingly adept at comedy.

Kisapmata was a tense melodrama, which cast Vic Silayan as a cruel and domineering patriarch who enjoys complete control over the lives of his wife (Charito Solis) and daughter (Charo Santos). Silayan has also forced Santos into an incestuous relationship (something de Leon tactfully insinuates without resorting to vulgar and sensationalized depictions), and he is not pleased when Santos accepts a marriage proposal from Jay Ilagan, a co-worker at the office where she is employed. Silayan immediately begins scheming to wreck the marriage, coaxing Solis to feign illness during the wedding reception, which sends her home early with Santos following closely to tend to her. Living in the same house with Santos' parents, Ilagan finds himself spending his wedding night alone in his bed, and he and Santos are only able to finally consummate their union on the sly, eventually managing to sneak off somewhere away from Silayan's manipulative presence. Ilagan eventually tires of Silayan's controlling manner, however, and he leaves, with Santos mustering the courage to follow soon after. The film concludes with Santos and Ilagan returning to the house to collect their belongings, and being confronted by Silayan, who proceeds to annihilate the family and then himself.

De Leon's direction could not be improved upon, allowing the tension to simmer quietly before erupting at the tragic denouement. His efforts were helped immeasurably by the strong principal cast, not the least of which would be Solis is the role of Silayan's long-suffering wife, having endured years of abuse and become timid to the point of becoming an almost invisible member of the household. The film was a veiled commentary on the brutality of the patriarchal system under martial law (although some would say the Imelda Marcos was pulling her share of the strings behind the walls of Malacanang).

Even more forthright as a political allegory was de Leon's *Batch '81*, an unflinching look at the inane and often cruel (actually, mostly cruel) process of fraternity initiations, which followed a group of pledges (Mark Gil, in particular) through their ordeals, which are at best humiliating, and at worst inhumane. The film takes a nasty turn when one pledge is beaten to death by members of another fraternity, touching off a war, which culminates in a violent brawl during which several students are brutally slain with a meat cleaver. While the film ends on a quasi-triumphant note, with Gil having survived his rite of passage and taken his place within the system that has emotionally brutalized him, the narrative cannot fail to leave the viewer in some confusion as to the point of such callous and barbaric behavior and the appeal of ritualized dehumanization. The rival fraternities can easily be interpreted to be representing nationalist fervor. For instance, in one particularly grim test, the pledges are all required to throw a switch sending an electrical current into a student strapped to a chair: they all reluctantly comply, but Gil requires a good deal of goading. Pushed to his limit, Gil proves his mettle by finally throwing the switch full-throttle and leaving it on until the student, screaming in agony, convulses and passes out. Of course, it is all a ruse, and the pledges are given the lesson to trust their fraternity brothers above all else, a blind form of patriotism that rings hollow at the film's conclusion.

Interestingly, it was after the demise of the Marcos regime that the film business really slowed and fell back on its reliance on tired formulas more than ever, and de Leon, soured by the contrite nature of the business, began to work sparsely. He became interested in computer graphics, and in 1988 established his own computer animation company, which specialized in television advertising (a curious pursuit for an artist disenchanted by commercialism). His eventual return to film in 1993 was facilitated by an invite from the Japan Foundation, which asked him to direct a segment of the anthology picture *Southern Winds*, which also included work by directors from Japan, Thailand and Indonesia.

De Leon was not the only one using allegory to mask disdain for the patriarchal system. One of the more significant filmmakers to emerge during the Second Golden Era was Marilou Diaz-Abaya. She had graduated from Assumption College in Manila, and later obtained a Master of Arts degree in Film and Television from Loyola Marymount University in Los Angeles, and did post-graduate studies at the London International Film School. She directed her first film, *Tanikala* (*The Chain*), in 1979, and though it tanked at the box office, she would come into her own in the 1980s with a string of critically acclaimed box office hits. Her films employed a harsh, gritty realism that starts critics fawning, though the predominant theme of her work—the brutalization of women and the patriarchal society that allows it—had her branded as an angry young woman.

In 1980 Diaz-Abaya directed *Brutal*, which starred Amy Austria as a traumatized young woman found at the scene of a triple homicide. As the film opens Austria is taken from her home by the police, who have found her husband (Jay Ilagan) and two of his friends dead, each having bled to death after having their wrists slashed. Austria is withdrawn and nonresponsive to police questioning, but reporter Charo Santos begins her own investigation, uncovering the details of Austria's tragic life. A shy, inexperienced young woman, Austria was raped by Ilagan and then forced by her enraged father into marrying him. Not surprisingly, the marriage turns out to be a big mistake, and Ilagan's cruelty reaches its height when he and his drunken friends take turns raping Austria. Eventually Austria snaps out of her withdrawn state and reveals to Santos how she served a pitcher of drugged beer to Ilagan and his friends and slashed their wrists after the drug had rendered them powerless. Austria won the FAMAS Best Actress award for her performance.

More complex, though still very discernible as a statement on patriarchal cruelty, was Diaz-Abaya's *Karnal* (1983), a dark and disturbing melodrama wherein top-billed Charito Solis appears sparingly as the film's narrator, relating a tale of woe from a generation prior. As the film opens, Phillip Salvador returns to the small rural village of his youth after several years away in Manila, bringing his young bride (Cecille Castillo) with him. But Salvador finds that his father (Vic Silayan) is still every bit the cruel and domineering patriarch that he ever was. It happens that Castillo is a dead ringer for Salvador's late mother, and Castillo is very distressed to learn the circumstances of her death. Salvador's sister (Grace Amilbangsa) tells Castillo the sordid story of how Silayan was very abusive towards his wife and how she in turn rebelled by becoming the town slut. When word of her wanton infidelity reached Silayan, he stripped his wife naked and dragged her through the streets for everybody to see, prompting her to commit suicide soon after. Castillo now being the perfect image of his late wife (with obvious oedipal ramifications for Salvador), Silayan takes an interest and tries to force himself on her. Though Castillo is able to escape being raped, she later winds up leading the family down a familiarly tragic path when she relieves her boredom with rural life by indulging in an affair with Joel Torre, a local deaf mute. Word of the affair soon makes the rounds in the small village, and Silayan becomes enraged and tries to impose the same punishment on Castillo that he had on his late wife, but he is prevented from doing so by Salvador. A violent confrontation ensues during which Silayan's attempted rape of Castillo is revealed, causing Salvador to lose all control. In a positively shocking moment, Salvador takes up an axe and beheads Silayan with one clean sweep. Salvador consequently winds up in jail, and the

Director Marilou Diaz-Abaya's *Baby Tsina* (*China Baby*; 1984/Viva Films), the true story of a prostitute who helped reform the prison system in the 1970s.

now-pregnant Castillo is left to fend for herself, having been thrown out of the family home by Amilbangsa. Through her pregnancy, Castillo's only source of comfort is Torre, who helps her in birthing the child. But the baby is hideous and, as Solis relates, the town legend is that the child was a demon baby, born with a complete set of teeth, facial hair, and even a set of horns. While the film does not show the baby, it is apparently monstrous enough to prompt Castillo to wander off alone somewhere and kill it. As for Salvador, having finally had enough, he commits a very messy suicide in prison, slitting his own throat.

Diaz-Abaya followed *Karnal* with *Baby Tsina* (*China Baby*), a true story which starred Vilma Santos as a prostitute who goes to prison for harboring her gangland fugitive boyfriend (played by Phillip Salvador), and winds up standing up to the brutal prison guards and leading the push for reforms in the prison system. Although grim in its realism, the film was hardly the compelling artistic work that *Karnal* had been.

Diaz-Abaya made the peculiar decision to leave film work for television in the late 1980s; maybe the work was steadier. The decision would have been strange enough, given the usually vapid nature of television in general, but Diaz-Abaya did not even go into the type of program that required much, if anything, in the area of artistic input. One might have thought that directing the public affairs program *Public Forum* would have been somewhat stifling for a creative individual, but Diaz-Abaya stayed with the program for the better part of a decade, and even counted the experience as valuable to her own growth artistically when she eventually did return to films in the late 1990s.

Meanwhile, after spending the better part of two decades in international co-productions, which at first tended toward noirish programmers and war pictures, but by the early 1970s had devolved into lewd and sophomoric exploitation, Eddie Romero was now taking note of the work being done by this new group of bright young filmmakers, and he decided to join the fold and return to Filipino films proper. Brocka may have begun his career as Romero's assistant, but Romero was now following Brocka's lead. But unlike many of the younger directors who were busying themselves with pointed political commentary, Romero was disinclined toward tossing brickbats at the regime, preferring instead to make historical pictures that meditated on the lingering ramifications of colonialism and the never-ending quest for answers regarding national identity. His preference may have had something to do with his friendship with the First Couple and his occasional dinner invites to Malacanang, something which confounded Brocka, but Romero maintained that he merely disliked message-oriented narratives, preferring instead to simply tell a good story, allowing the audience to draw from it what they would. In 1976 he produced, wrote and directed *Ganito Kami Noon, Paano Kayo Ngayon?*. The film starred Christopher de Leon as an amiable country bumpkin who bungles his way through the waning days of the Spanish colonial era and into the dawning of the American presence, constantly bewildered by the situations he finds himself in, understanding little of the fighting and strife he encounters, and for the most part, fairly impervious to their ramifications.

In 1980, Romero made *Aguila* (*The Eagle*), a three-hour epic examining Philippine history through the 20th century, again paying mind to the inherent question of national identity. Fernando Poe, Jr. starred as the title character, as the story details his life through a series of lengthy flashbacks depicting the end of the Spanish colonial era, the arrival of the U.S. presence, and then the Japanese occupation. It was quite far removed from the sort of tripe that Romero had been frittering away his time with through the first half of the 1970s with his American co-productions.

Despite the efforts of Brocka, Bernal, de Leon and Castillo, however, exploration of national identity and pensive introspection were not the norm, and Filipino films of that time remained, as they are today, highly formulaic, the melodramas tending toward soap opera, the comedies broadly farcical and unsophisticated, the action films ordinarily pitting the hero against a powerful and thoroughly evil organized crime boss. The end of the Marcos era would bring a freedom that permissively granted the interchangeability of the crime boss with corrupt politicians and law enforcement personnel, and action stars thereafter spent as much time toppling corruption within the system as without.

The horror genre tends to be somewhat more fascinating, mingling Catholicism with native pagan beliefs and customs. This is not surprising, or even unusual, since Catholicism itself began as a combination of Christian beliefs and Greek pagan customs. Seen in this context, the Catholicism of the Philippines is not out of line, as these things go. The ancient native superstitions are not normally juxtaposed against the predominant Catholic belief system, but are rather presented within the context of it.

In order to promote herself as the Grand Patroness of the Arts, Imelda Marcos, who had been appointed governor of Manila by her husband, had commissioned the building of the Cultural Arts Center of the Philippines, a complex that included the Manila Film Center. The ensuing disaster was to become more than an albatross for the Marcoses; it would become symbolic of the inhumanity of the regime. Reportedly modeled after the Greek Parthenon, the Film Center was to be both a theater and an archive in which to house Filipino films. The First Lady ordered that the building be completed in time to host another of her great arts endeavors, the 1982 Manila International Film Festival. Invited guests to the festival included filmmakers and celebrities from around the world—Jeremy Irons, Brooke Shields, Akira Kurosawa; it was a chance for Imelda to show off the nation's capital to the world—a grand propagandistic scheme to present the regime in a more favorable light to the rest of the world—as well as for her to bask in the limelight of celebrity, a place where she not only felt at home, but in which she felt she belonged: indeed, she seemed to regard it as her birthright.

But in order for the building to be completed on time, work was required to continue around the clock, and ultimately corners were cut. On November 17, 1981, tragedy struck when part of the building collapsed, burying some workers in the lower level. Insistent that the building be completed in time for the festival, Imelda Marcos ordered work to continue without retrieving the bodies of the workers who had been buried in the rubble: they were merely covered over with cement and became a permanent part of the foundation.

That much of the story seems certain, as does the rush to hush up the whole disaster. The government did what it could to quiet the tragedy, but inevitably, it became impossible to deny it, and with reliable details in short supply, rumor mingled with fact to the point that the real truth may never be known. Almost immediately, an urban legend was born, and the building was rumored to be haunted. Estimates on the number of workers killed vary wildly from several, to dozens, to thirty-six, and finally several hundred. A group of Filipino psychics known as the Spirit Questors set the number at 169 when they sought to appease the angry spirits of the dead workers with a séance in the late 1990s.

Ghost stories are the least of it: to accentuate Imelda's callous indifference, stories eventually made the rounds that some of the workers were still alive when the First Lady ordered more cement be poured in order to hurry the job along.* Of course, as there was no search and rescue to dig the bodies out, it is entirely possible that this was the case, but the stories were extremely gruesome and tailored to play to the regime's reputation for brutality. There

---

Imelda Marcos has always maintained that she was unaware of any workers, dead or alive, having been buried when she gave the order to continue work.

were rumors—now impossible to prove—of photographs confiscated by the government showing the faces of the perishing workers, frozen in time, fixed in concrete, tormented grimaces—hideous visages hauntingly peering through the surface of the quick-drying cement. And then there were much more fanciful stories, like the risible rumor that Imelda had sacrificed children and had their bodies entombed throughout the building as offerings to some non-descript deities.

In the end, the building was completed in time for the festival, though only just. The grass—still brown—had not yet taken root, and so Imelda ordered that it be spray-painted green, appearances being everything—*tubog sa ginto*, as they say.

Maintaining Imelda's prize edifice was another matter. One would think that with all of the money being pilfered from the government by the Marcoses, to say nothing of U.S. aid, that something could have been set aside to ensure the upkeep on one of Imelda's cultural trophies, but that money was disappearing into Swiss bank accounts—at least, what wasn't being spent on lavish parties in Malacanang. In order to pay for itself, the Manila Film Center became notorious as the nation's grandest—actually, only—porn palace, so curious in a country, and under a dictator, that had banned the bomba films a decade earlier. But, by the 1980s, the Filipino film industry, burdened by heavy taxation, foreign competition, and a grim national economy, was again traveling a rocky road. The Manila Film Center, it seemed, needed to pay its own way. Imelda was getting advice that—surprise!—sex sells, and that the Film Center could pay for itself by being the only place to go and see what other theaters dare not—in fact, legally could not—show.

The Manila Film Center was able to bypass any concerns in regards to censorship through Executive Order No. 770, issued on January 29, 1982, which created the Experimental Cinema of the Philippines (the ECP). The ECP was to function as a branch of the Ministry of Tourism, tipping its hand as a tool for disseminating global propaganda. Ferdinand and Imelda's daughter, Imee Marcos, was put in charge of the ECP. Although the ECP was responsible for funding some rather impressive works during the early-to-mid 1980s—like Bernal's *Himala*, for instance—Brocka himself ridiculed the enterprise for churning out cheap sensationalism and lewd works, even though some of his respected colleagues were reaping the benefits of the organization; aside from Bernal, Peque Gallaga, who had worked under Brocka in various capacities as a production coordinator and an actor, got his first big directorial break by way of funding from the ECP, and the work being done by him would place him on the shortlist of Filipino filmmakers to be reckoned with. Most likely Brocka was more put off by the fact that receiving funding from the ECP basically meant that artists were working for the corrupt, dictatorial regime than he was genuinely critical of the work itself. It's also possible that there was some professional jealousy, as he was an idealist and would not allow himself to stoop so low as to work for a government organization, while he likely felt that his friends and colleagues were selling out to a degree, yet receiving acclaim for it. Yet, Brocka was not the only one criticizing some of the work being done through the ECP. Many artists (some members of CAP—Concerned Artists of the Philippines) found themselves splitting their time between calling for an end to censorship and conversely criticizing the exploitation of women in much of the ECP-funded films. It made for an odd paradox—artists demanding their freedom, but criticizing other artists for exercising their freedom. One can't help but wonder if sex exploitation films would have been drawing as much criticism from the arts community were it not for the fact that they were being funded by a government entity.

One of the big attractions at the Manila Film Center in 1985 was Peque Gallaga's *Scorpio Nights*, the story of a peeping Tom who masturbates while watching through the floorboards of his ramshackle apartment as the couple below makes love. He eventually begins a sexual

Orestes Ojeda and Anna Marie Gutierrez in Peque Gallaga's *Scorpio Nights* (1985/Regal Films). The film was a phenomenal hit at the Manila Film Center, the only place in the country to go and see pornography, albeit arty porn.

fling with his sexy downstairs neighbor until her husband finds out, which brings about a thoroughly unpleasant climax—literally. Dark and nasty, the film was admittedly artistic.

Gallaga, who had worked as a production designer, art director and script consultant for filmmakers like Eddie Romero, Ishmael Bernal and even Brocka, as well as occasionally working as an actor, was just starting to make a name for himself as a film director. He had made quite an impression when he directed the WWII epic *Oro, Plata, Mata* (*Gold, Silver, Death*) in 1982 by way of the ECP, and the film was met with great praise; to this day it is regarded as one of the genuine masterpieces of Philippine cinema. Shot in black and white, the film followed the declining fortunes of two affluent families during the Japanese occupation as they are dispossessed of their land and are eventually forced to flee into the forest in an out of the way region.

Gallaga followed his triumph with another historical epic: in 1984 he directed *Virgin Forest*, a sexy period piece set against the backdrop of the early years of the American presence, and detailing the capture of Filipino rebel leader Emilio Aguinaldo. Setting the narrative in 1901, the film very obviously depicts Brigadier Frederick Funston's arduous journey to Palanan to capture Aguinaldo. The film does seem to take certain liberties, however, as Funston himself is seemingly not represented in the telling. Having intercepted a message from Aguinaldo to his men in Cavite in which the rebel leader professes a dire need of reinforcements, Funston hired some 80 men from the Macabebes tribe—loyal to the Americans—to pose as Aguinaldo's reinforcements while Funston and his men posed as captured American prisoners. Once inside Aguinaldo's camp, they then surprised the rebel army and captured Aguinaldo.

As the film unfolds, Miguel Rodriguez is in the city of San Mateo and overhears talk by the Americans of the proposed trek to Aguinaldo's camp in Palanan. After discovering that

Rodriguez understands English, the Americans order his arrest in order to prevent his revealing their plan to anyone. But Rodriguez escapes, and young lovers Sarsi Emmanuelle and Abel Jurado become unwilling accomplices in his flight when Rodriguez jumps into their fishing boat with them to flee. The trio are captured, however, and held prisoner by the Americans and the Macabebes, but they manage to get free and flee into the jungle during the night. Rodriguez does indeed plan to warn Aguinaldo, but as the three make their way through the jungle, a romantic rivalry develops between Rodriguez and Jurado after Rodriguez shares a night of passion with Emmanuelle. Despite this, the three of them must still rely on one another, and when Emmanuelle cannot choose between her two companions, she makes it plain that she wants them both; Rodriguez and Jurado comply, and they have a threesome in the jungle. The film concludes with the trio reaching Aguinaldo's camp only to find it abandoned, the Americans having already been there and captured the rebel leader.

The Americans do not come off too well in Gallaga's telling of events, which is only fair. While Funston does not figure in the film's reckoning, the truth is that he publicly boasted of all the Filipinos he had killed to compensate for his fallen American comrades. The film also includes a very questionable American-Macabebe massacre of a village while en route, supposedly to prevent word from spreading of their approach to Aguinaldo's camp. In reality, the Americans kept up the charade of their captivity at a nearby village, where they had word sent to Aguinaldo of their dire need for food. Their supplies depleted, and weary from the long and difficult journey, they stayed there until Aguinaldo had some rice sent to them. When they eventually did make it to Aguinaldo's camp, their surprise attack was so successful that Aguinaldo thought his capture was some sort of jest; it took some moments for him to realize that he really was being taken prisoner.

All quibbling about history aside, Gallaga's direction was impeccable, and both of the aforementioned massacres are among the film's most compelling moments, emotionally charged and superbly underscored by Jaime Fabregas' subtle musical score. Released by Regal Films, the specter of censorship arose due to some of the film's sexual content, including a scene in which Emmanuelle is gang-raped by the Macabebes while the Americans sing songs around a campfire. Though the rape occurs behind some bushes and out of sight of the Americans, the U.S. soldiers are depicted as being largely indifferent to the doings of the Macabebes. As for the Macabebes themselves, they are portrayed as treacherous savages who later turn on and slaughter their American allies. In reality, Funston did not die in the Philippines, but later returned to America as a hero, where he died in 1917.

The film, though not often mentioned in the same breath as the works of Brocka or Bernal—or even in the same breath as Gallaga's own *Oro, Plata, Mata*—must still surely be seriously considered as one of the great works in Filipino cinema.

When *Scorpio Nights* enjoyed its run at the Manila Film Center, the theater could not accommodate the throng of patrons clamoring to see this once-forbidden fruit. Even with 15 screening a day, hundreds of viewers were forced to sit in the aisles of the theater to watch the film. Customers waited outside for hours, often in torrential downpours, to get a seat for one of the showings, and when the gates were opened, the stampede to get in line was like festival seating at a Who concert. The building was often so packed that the air conditioning system would give out. And all just to watch people masturbate and dry-hump each other.

Thanks to Section 3 of Executive Order No. 770, the Board of Censors could simply ignore the content of the films playing the Manila Film Center in good conscience—in fact, they were obliged to do so—but not so shy were civic groups and Christian organizations that picketed the building, or church leaders who publicly decried the decadency of Imelda's porn palace. Cardinal Jaime Sin, who would eventually play his role in Marcos' fall and Cory

Aquino's ascendancy, would publicly label the Manila Film Center a "cesspool."⁶ The censors became somewhat expendable, as the industry sank deeper and deeper into financial collapse just like the rest of the country, and Marcos eventually allowed full-blown pornography to run in low grade movie theaters that were the equivalent of the New York 42nd Street grindhouses.

And so it was at the Manila Film Center, a place where Marcos hypocrisy found a comfortable home. In the post–Marcos years, the building, regarded as an embarrassment or abject lesson in dictatorial folly, fell into disrepair. Almost as if to live up to its reputation as a haunted landmark, it began to take on the appearance of a derelict eyesore. It eventually found purpose again as home to *The Amazing Philippine Show*, a gay cabaret act performed by what have been described as some of the most beautiful transvestites and transsexuals to be found anywhere in the world.

The generous sanction given the new wave of pornographic films spawned a new generation of bomba queens. Many of them were managed by an optometrist named Rey dela Cruz, who had a habit of renaming the girls he managed after soda brands—Coca Nicolas, Pepsi Paloma, Sarsi Emmanuel: they came to be known as the "soft drink beauties." Many of them also met an untimely demise: Claudia Zobel, star of the film *Shame* (1984), died in a car accident in Makati in 1984; Stella Strada hanged herself in 1984, as did Paloma in 1985. Shortly before committing suicide, Paloma had accused two members of the comedy trio Tito, Vic and Joey of raping her in a Quezon City hotel room. Tito, Vic and Joey consisted of Tito and Vic Sotto and Joey de Leon, three noontime television hosts on the program *Eat, Bulaga*. They became very popular, and in the mid-1980s they began starring in a torrent of ill-conceived,

(Left to right) Tito Sotto, Vic Sotto and Joey de Leon made up the comedy team of Tito, Vic and Joey. In the mid–1980s they became a box office sensation with a series of cheap quickie comedy films.

though apparently very popular, lowbrow comedy films. Paloma accused Vic Sotto and Joey de Leon of raping her, but after her death the case would eventually be dismissed.

Another of dela Cruz's discoveries was Myra Manibog. Born Geraldine Zervoulakous, dela Cruz had initially wanted to name her Mirinda Manibog, after another soft drink, but when the young Geraldine balked at the name, a compromise was made, and she agreed to "Myra." She was only 13 years old when her mother took her to see dela Cruz, who promptly hired her to replace Myrna Castillo, who had walked off the set of Celso Ad. Castillo's film *Snake Sisters*. Told that she was 17, both dela Cruz and Celso Ad. Castillo agreed to use Manibog as a stand-in for Myrna Castillo in her remaining scenes, which included one in which she was required to simulate masturbation. Years later, Manibog would reveal that she had been raped by a member of the production crew while filming *Snake Sisters*. She was only 13, but it wasn't the first time that she had been raped: at the age of 12 she was apparently well developed enough to pass herself off as being 16, and she got a job as a runway model. Doing a show at a hotel, she was lured to a room by the hotel owner, who locked her in the room for a week and eventually raped her before letting her go. Manibog's mother initially wanted to press charges, but wound up instead striking a deal with the man, who bought the family's silence with a home, a car, and other financial considerations.[7]

Manibog's career as a film star included titles like *Naked Island*, *Bomba Queen*, *Hindi Mapigil ang Init* (*No Holding Back the Heat*) and *Matukso Kaya ang Anghel* (*Seductive Angel*). The life of a bomba queen was hard on Manibog, and she eventually left Manila for Japan to work as a dancer, but she ended up in an abusive relationship in which she became addicted to drugs. Not having heard from her in years, Manibog's mother appealed to dela Cruz for help in tracking her down, but dela Cruz merely used the opportunity to drum-up publicity by spreading rumors that found their way into the tabloids: one such story purported to have Manibog murdered by the yakuza. Somewhat ironically, dela Cruz himself would be murdered shortly after Manibog returned to the Philippines, and circumstances would lead to Manibog being a person of interest in the investigation. Manibog had returned, and unable to locate her mother, she too turned to dela Cruz for help. She also wanted to quash all of the tabloid press that had been publishing false stories about her and worrying her family. Dela Cruz agreed to meet with Manibog at his office, but on the day that the meeting was to take place, Manibog heard the news that dela Cruz had been murdered. After seeing a news broadcast that mentioned her as a possible suspect, Manibog fled to Bulacan and went into hiding for a while. Eventually her life would turn around when she passed her time in Bulacan by reading a borrowed prayer book and she wound up joining a local congregation.

Given the preferential treatment being shown the porn industry through the safe haven of the Manila Film Center, it is somewhat odd that Marcos would go to the trouble of revamping the censorship system at all. But much of the dictator's concern had to do with appearances, as he still had delusions of presenting himself as a tolerant ruler, and he had the consternation of the Free the Artist Movement (FTA) and its later offshoot, Concerned Artists of the Philippines (CAP), and their very vocal protests to contend with. The BCMP (Board of Censors for Motion Pictures) created by RA 3060 had given way to the Board of Review for Motion Pictures and Television (BRMPT) created and continually redefined under a flurry of Executive Orders, the continual revisions alternately to broaden the Board's powers and to stave off criticism from the arts community. In February of 1983, the BRMPT saw its powers increased with Executive Order 868, which not only expanded the Board's domain to include live performances, but also necessitated the licensing of actors. By October of 1985, Marcos was again moved to reorganize the censorship board, issuing Presidential Decree 1986, which replaced the BRMPT with the Movie and Television Review and Classification Board

(MTRCB), which made allowances for the grievances of filmmakers by permitting personnel from the film industry to serve on the Board, as well as creating a film classification system, both seemingly to offer hope of future self-regulation within the industry. Otherwise, the new censorship body, was given much the same guidelines of previous boards, with a few notable exceptions. Like Article 1 of Letter of Instructions No. 13 in 1972, Article 1 of Presidential Decree No. 1986 forbade films "which tend to incite subversion, insurrection, rebellion or sedition against the State" ("sedition" being a somewhat redundant insertion), but went on to include films which "otherwise threaten the economic and/or political stability of the State."

Article 5 of Letter of Instructions No. 13, which prohibited "Films which offend any race or religion" was nixed, as was Article 7 banning "Films which are contrary to law, public order, morals, good customs, established policies, lawful orders, decrees or edicts." Article 7 of Presidential Decree No. 1986 banned instead films "which may constitute contempt of court or any quasi-judicial tribunal, or pertain to matter [sic] which are sub-judice in nature." The term "quasi-judicial" is interesting, to say the least.

Presidential Decree No. 1986, reshuffling a bit, included as Article 6 a ban on films "which are libelous or defamatory to the good name and reputation of any person, whether living or dead." Otherwise the prohibitions remained much the same. Article 4 remained intact in its prohibition against films "which serve no other purpose but to satisfy the market for violence and pornography."

Perhaps because the films packing the Manila Film Center could be deemed, to one degree or another, to be worthy artistic endeavors made by competent filmmakers, they were able to get around Article 4, but had they been otherwise, the results would likely have been much the same as long as they were keeping Imelda's precious white elephant afloat. In any event, they had already been given sanction.

The decree opened by acknowledging that the industry was "beset with manifold and multifarious problems," but rather than cede over-taxation as one of the problems, Marcos went on to note that the industry's woes were "accented by its nebulous stance towards the Board of Review for Motion Pictures and Television reorganized under Executive Order No. 876-A." But did the new decree really do anything to rectify this "nebulous stance?" In one rather obnoxious stroke of economic ignorance, the decree proposed that the new board should "cooperate with the industry to improve, upgrade and make viable the industry as one source of fueling the national economy." Tax incentives would have been more sensible, since diminishing returns were leading to reduced production values and shooting schedules.

The decree went on to adopt a ratings system not unlike that in the United States—"G" for "General Patronage," "P" for "Parental Guidance Suggested," "R" for "Restricted," in this case restricted to adults only. There was, however, a most curious departure: whereas an "X" rating in the U.S. restricted patronage to persons over the age of 18, in Marcos' new decree an "X" rating meant "Not for Public Viewing"—in other words, an outright ban, making the designation of an actual rating somewhat silly, since the purpose of a ratings system was to guide the public in its decisions. The MTRCB's very name designated it a ratings and classification board, yet it remained able to in effect censor films by imposing an X rating—a ban—which necessitated cuts to be made in order for public exhibition to be allowed at all; far from alleviating the "nebulous stance" toward the Board that Marcos had referred to, PD 1986 merely perpetuated the problem while trying to mask it in a new guise.

Marcos had already been meddling in the movie business by issuing Executive Order No. 640-A in 1982, which mandated the creation of the Film Academy of the Philippines. Although there had been a number of scandals that had periodically surfaced within the FAMAS and damaged its credibility, the creation of the Film Academy was merely another means of exercising control over the film industry. The order's preamble noted that film was both popular entertainment and art, and as such had a great degree of "influence in the life of a nation." Censorship-weary artists might react squeamishly to such a statement as they wait for the other shoe to drop, but the truth is that they are always quick to point out film's positive influence on culture. Common sense dictates that the door swings both ways. If films can have positive cultural benefits, they can also have negative. This is not to suggest censorship as the alternative, but merely to state the obvious, which filmmakers seem, for the most part, willfully ignorant of, lest they feel obligated to exercise restraint and refrain from indulging every base whim.

The other shoe may have dropped as the order's preamble continued. The Academy pledged to promote the "highest professional standards requisite to the enrichment and enhancement of the Filipino film and consequently our social and cultural values." The order went on to list a code of ethics aimed at fulfilling its goal of being "responsive and sensitive to the larger society," to wit:

1) The choice of subject matter shall be guided by the dictates of good taste, special restraint shall be exercised in portraying criminal or anti-social behavior in which minors participate or are involved.
2) Crime shall not be condoned nor criminal characters glorified on the screen.
3) Detailed and excessive acts of brutality, cruelty and physical violence shall be avoided.
4) Sex orgies, nudities and intimate scenes of passion which are not relevant to the story and cause, or tend to cause perversion shall not be allowed.
5) Excessive ridicule or mockery of physical and/or mental defects or people shall not be allowed.
6) Undue references or suggestions that tend to degrade or ridicule religions, the cultural communities, other races, the Philippine Flag and Flags of other Nations, shall not be allowed.
7) Indecent, suggestive, vulgar and profane speech, gestures or movements, shall be avoided unless necessary to the story.
8) Glorification or accentuation of bad habits, customs, attitudes, situations and practices, such as forms of gambling which are prohibited by law, disrespect towards duly constituted authorities and elders, which do not project a good image of our people, shall not be encouraged.
9) Cruelty to children and animals, unless absolutely essential to the story, shall not be allowed.
10) Stories and characters treated in a manner that works against the development of morals and the ideals of our society, especially in the light of national development, shall not be allowed.

Much of the order's dictates are fairly indistinct. Number 2, for instance, is more than a little subjective. As for number 10, well, that's martial law for you. Since Executive Order No. 640-A was merely establishing an awards giving body, one would have thought that the Academy was not in the official business of censorship, but the wording of the order was strong and was obviously meant to guide filmmakers as to what was considered acceptable. The truth is that the Academy had considerable power. The Academy was involved in no small part in handling the Metro Manila Film Festival, from which it took a healthy share of the profits. That money was in turn channeled into the various workers' guilds in the industry, which meant that virtually everyone in the industry was bound by the dictates of the Academy. Slick. Under the FAP umbrella were virtually all of the industry's workers' guilds: directors, screenwriters, editors, production designers, sound technicians, musical directors, producers, and even distributors. The FAMAS never wielded as much power. But as much as Marcos may have wanted to utilize the FAP as a means of reining in unruly filmmakers, the body proved difficult for the dictator to control, filled as it was with artistic temperaments.

The Second Golden Era could not truly match the Golden Era of the post-war years of 1946–1956 in terms of popularity. There were popular stars, to be sure, but what seems to have been primarily responsible for the designation was the quality of work being done by a select group of directors whose creativity was stirred by the political climate and the necessity to vent their concerns via allegory. It may have made for some of the most poignant work in Philippine cinema, but other than the occasional film festival, it didn't make the industry particularly viable as an export globally. Aside from dealing with wholly indigenous concerns, Philippine cinema was too stylistically set apart—much too leisurely in its pacing, often to the point of being prate—to appeal commercially to the more lucrative Western markets. There had always been the tendency in Philippine cinema to treat even the most routine of storylines as if they were grand epics, the result being longwinded melodramas that would drag on interminably.

One of the only directors to make a dent in the global market, if only just, was Kidlat Tahimik, although his work was destined to be no more than a fleeting art house sensation. Born Eric de Guia, he adopted the name Kidlat Tahimik (meaning "quiet lightning" in Tagalog), eventually making it his legal name, de Guia being too Spanish for his liking, Eric being too European. He seems to have stumbled into his film career by chance. In the 1970s he had traveled to Europe where he was going to try to make a living selling trinkets, but somehow along the way he managed to make contact with Werner Herzog, and using borrowed equipment, outdated film stock, and stock footage, he put together his first film, *Mababangong Bangungot* (*Perfumed Nightmare*) for a mere $10,000—a remarkably low cost even for its time in the 1970s. The film mirrored his own experience as Tahimik played the lead, a young man who dreams of escaping the stifling existence of his isolated rural community and seeing the modern world. Through an American acquaintance, he travels to Paris to run a gumball concession, and later ventures to Germany, ultimately concluding that the modern world may have much to offer, but has also sacrificed much of importance in the process of its development.

It took Tahimik years to complete the film, and being his first, it was a learning process. Consequently, it was technically primitive, which only heightened its appeal among many critics internationally, who read the narrative departure as a bold initiative. In fact, Tahimik's complete lack of know-how was considered to be one of the film's greatest assets. The film won the International Critics' Prize at the Berlin Film Festival in 1977, before having its premier in the Philippines in Balian in 1978. After meeting Tahimik in Cannes in 1979, Francis Ford Coppola acquired the U.S. distribution rights, and *Mababangong Bangungot* enjoyed a successful, if limited, run in America, playing for weeks at the Bleecker Street Cinema in New York. Coppola had just completed his own lengthy and rather trying experience with filmmaking in the Philippines, having finally completed his epic *Apocalypse Now*, which led to a succession of Vietnam War films being shot in the islands, many by international production units, and almost as many by producer/director Cirio Santiago, who sought to capitalize on the craze with a series of quickie Vietnam War films made for international distribution in cooperation with Roger Corman.

Although he managed to make an impression among critics at the *New York Times* and *The Village Voice*, Tahimik's unique approach proved too uncommercial for the Philippine market, which was still highly reliant upon convention to ensure saleability. Not that that was unique to the Filipino market; many Western markets are also largely reliant upon formulas, although deviations in Philippine cinema are much more scarce to come by.

Tahimik's other notable work, *Turumba*—named for an indigenous festival—found the filmmaker again pursuing his obsession with the destructive effects of free enterprise on the values of individuals. The story concerned a family who make papier mache animals for the Turumba festival, until a German entrepreneur arrives and buys them all, employing the family to make more for Germany's Oktoberfest. Soon the family's lifestyle and even their values are drastically altered by the work schedule.

Tahimik may have been working under primitive conditions, but it did rather tend to enhance his status among critics, most of whom waxed both poetic and philosophical about his meditating on the encroachment of the modern world on the innocence and serenity of native culture, and his work inspired high-minded appraisals that ranged from pedantic polemics on the destructive nature of American imperialism—in most cases viewed as a cultural imperialism somehow imposed on the world at large—to insidious Marxist ramblings about the negative effects of industrialization on the beauty and simplicity of traditional cultures. Amid all of the fawning, what no one seemed either willing or able to make note of was the fact that Tahimik was making these points in the most modern and technological of artistic mediums, however clumsily it may have been put to use. Although his work may have been quite deliberately uncommercial, it was nonetheless the product of the progress of invention, brought about largely through capitalism and its innate tendency to inspire human invention. If one were really going to take Tahimik *that* seriously, then one should be forced to contemplate why it was that he was not off in a hut somewhere making his point through the beauty and simplicity of wood carvings. In between promoting pagan deities, Tahimik publicly laments the cultural subversion polluting Philippine society via Hollywood, and yet his main artery of distribution for *Mababangong Bangungot* was Zoetrope, Coppola's company. Curious. None of which is to suggest that Tahimik's work is uninteresting or without points worth contemplating, but rather that it makes his career seem like a somewhat odd and droll assortment of contradictions.

There is also the interesting fact that Tahimik was born, raised, and apparently still lives in Baguio, a community in the province of Benguet, a mountainous region north of Manila. When serving as the first civilian governor of the Philippines under U.S. rule, William Howard Taft needed a place to escape the stifling summer heat of Manila, and hearing of the cool breezes that swept through the mountains of Benguet, he commissioned Baguio to be made into a summer retreat for Americans in the islands. It consequently became thoroughly American, with wealthy Americans building beautiful houses amid the groves of pine. Filmmakers like Cirio Santiago have since used the area in productions that needed to feign an American location, so convincing was the imitation. Perhaps growing up in such an environment made Tahimik lament all the more the Westernization of his native land.

In the end Tahimik has remained an obscure cult figure, well beneath the radar of even the Filipino film industry, within which he has always been a non-entity, which seems to suit him fine.

While people may have only been going to Bleecker Street in handfuls to see Tahimik's *Mababangong Bangungot*, they were going by carloads to see Cirio Santiago's films, which were less alienating to Western audiences, even if they did appeal to the trashier side of pop culture—or most probably *because* they appealed to it. They certainly could do no benefit to the reputation of Filipino cinema, but the truth is that Santiago's films were being made for the U.S. exploitation market, usually with at least partial, if not primary, backing from U.S. distributors. Santiago's technique left much to be desired, but he was efficient, and above all, cheap—Roger Corman could employ Santiago to direct a film for a mere $3,000.[8] At that meager sum—although it went much further in the Philippines—it's no wonder that Santiago cranked them out at such an exhausting pace.

He also had a tendency to jump on any passing bandwagon, which tended to make his films even easier to market. When the women-in-prison genre was profitable Santiago supplied *The Muthers* (1976), *Women of Hell's Island* (1978) and *Caged Fury* (1980). If martial arts films were big, he came out with *T.N.T. Jackson* and *Ebony, Ivory and Jade* (both in 1975), *Fighting Mad* (1977) and *Firecracker* (1981). When that genre resurged, Santiago brought out *Angelfist* (a re-working of *T.N.T. Jackson*) and *Live By the Fist* (both 1992), *One Man Army* (1993), and *Stranglehold* and *Angel of Destruction* (both 1994). With the success of Coppola's *Apocalypse Now*, Santiago got into the act with *Behind Enemy Lines* and *Eye of the Eagle* (both 1987), *The Expendables*, *Eye of the Eagle 2* and *Nam Angels* (all in 1988), *Eye of the Eagle 3*, *Beyond the Call of Duty* and *Field of Fire* (all in 1990), *Kill Zone* (1991), and *Firehawk* (1992). When *Mad Max* and its sequels were creating waves, Santiago rode along with a series of post-apocalypse titles like *Stryker* (1983), *Wheels of Fire* (1984), *Desert Warrior* (1985), *Equalizer 2000* (1986), *The Sisterhood* (1987), and *Raiders of the Sun* (1991). He even cashed-in on the popularity of the Rambo series with *Final Mission* (1984), and the video success of the revenge-for-rape sickie *I Spit on Your Grave* with the film *Naked Vengeance* (1985).

Unlike the overlong films shot for the home crowd, Santiago's international films usually ran for little more than an hour so as not to tax either the budget nor the attention span of drive-in and exploitation market patrons, who really wanted to see little more than some T & A, fisticuffs and cannon fire. An interesting case in point would be the 1994 film *Stranglehold*, which starred American martial arts champion Jerry Trimble and ran a mere 73 minutes. Santiago concurrently shot a Filipino version, which replaced Trimble with Filipino superstar Eddie Garcia: re-titled *Ultimatum*, the Filipino version clocked in at 102 minutes. Santiago also remade the 1959 child-meets-dinosaur film *Anak ng Bulkan* in 1997; while the Filipino version ran 116 minutes, the U.S. version, titled *Vulcan*, ran 81 minutes.

Through the 1970s, '80s and '90s, Santiago's films would undoubtedly be the most widely viewed works by any Filipino filmmaker in the industry's history, the unfortunate part of it being that they were seldom more than cinematic refuse. There were certainly films that would have better shown the local industry and its talents in a more favorable light, but dealing with more parochial concerns, these films were largely confined to the home crowd, while the world at large was seeing tawdry and repetitive women-in-prison yarns and loathsome softcore drivel like *Too Hot to Handle*, a sordid and thoroughly amoral piece of garbage released in 1976 about a female assassin who seduces her victims before killing them by such methods as asphyxiation and electrocution. Vic Diaz put in an appearance in the film, and while it wasn't uncommon to see him sinking to such depths, it was a bit more surprising to see an actor the likes of Vic Silayan also turning up for a small role.

The Second Golden Era drew to a close as the country erupted in turmoil. Economic mismanagement under Marcos had gutted the national economy, and whereas the Philippines had once been one of the most prosperous economies in the region, often second only to Japan, by the mid–1980s the country's economy was in dire straits. Marcos had come into office with a foreign debt of close to $600 million, a hefty enough sum for a nation that size, but through the 1970s and early '80s, that number was increasing by 27% per year. After twenty years of Marcos rule, the foreign debt had reached $28 billion.

It was in this climate that many Filipinos took to seeking jobs overseas and sending money back home to their families. This was encouraged by the regime, which considered it a temporary solution, but as time wore on, it came to comprise such a disproportionate percentage of the economy that it became a staple. But what really ignited the powder keg that would send Marcos packing was the assassination of Benigno Aquino, Jr., Marcos' most outspoken political opponent, in 1983. One might have thought that the end of the Marcos dictatorship would be as liberating for the film industry as for the country as a whole, but even darker days lay ahead for the business.

8

1986–1997

Under mounting international pressure, most especially from the United States, Ferdinand Marcos announced in November of 1985 that the Philippines would be holding presidential elections. His opponent was Corazon Aquino, widow of Benigno Aquino, Jr., Marcos' most tenacious opponent. Benigno Aquino, Jr. was a senator who had spent more than seven years in prison under Marcos. When he was released and allowed to leave the country, Aquino traveled to the United States where he spent three years, but still determined to bring about change in his country he decided to return to the Philippines in 1983. No sooner did he step off the plane at Manila International Airport, however, than he was shot and killed. Although it would take several years, it was Aquino's assassination that would set the wheels in motion in earnest to bring about Marcos' downfall.

The election was held on February 7, 1986, and although Marcos sought to convince the world of its legitimacy by tailoring the results so that he would emerge with a slim majority, nobody was fooled. The results were fraudulent and everybody knew it.

On February 22, 1986, 14 years after Marcos had declared martial law, his Defense Minister, Juan Ponce Enrile, and Deputy Chief of Staff, Fidel Ramos, defected from the government regime, eventually joining together in taking refuge with a small contingent of troops in Camp Crame. Enrile had held a televised news conference during which he confessed to personally being involved in the faking of hundreds of thousands of votes for Marcos, and he announced that he recognized Cory Aquino as the rightful victor in the election. As Marcos prepared to send the military to quash the rebellion, Cardinal Sin, through the Catholic Church's Radio Veritas, the only station outside of government control, called for the people of Manila to surround the Defense Ministry where the rebels had barricaded themselves. The response was extraordinary: hundreds of thousands of people packed Epifanio de los Santos Avenue—commonly called EDSA—preventing tanks from approaching Camp Crame. People parked buses at intersections, and even chopped down trees to block the streets.

As the standoff persisted, the citizens tried to win the government troops over by offering them cigarettes, and little girls handed out flowers. When the military threatened to open fire if the people did not disperse, priests and nuns knelt in prayer. Eventually, their bluff called, the military withdrew. The delusional Marcos thought that he would be able to wait the crowd out, but as the hours passed, the numbers only swelled. EDSA became something of a gargantuan festival, with people singing and dancing in the street, and as the hours turned into days, sleeping there as well. Souvenirs were sold, and the people continued to listen to Radio Veritas in order to keep informed. After two days, more government troops began to defect, and some of them seized control of one of the government-run television stations. As

Marcos' troops sought to take back the station they were again prevented by the people, who surrounded the military, offering them food from the local McDonald's restaurant. Again the troops withdrew.

On February 25th Corazon Aquino was sworn in as President of the Philippines by Senior Associate Justice Claudio Teehankee in a ceremony held near Camp Crame. Still defiant, Marcos held his own inauguration at the Presidential Palace a short time afterward. But for all of his maneuvering to remain in the country as "Honorary President," Marcos soon had to come to grips with reality, and by 9:00 P.M. that evening, he and his family were sneaking out of Malacanang. They were transported by U.S. helicopters to Clark Air Base, where they boarded a plane for Guam. Later they would be transported to Hawaii, where Marcos would live out his few remaining days in exile.

Is it any wonder that the ouster of Marcos would come to be called the "People Power Revolution?" It served as an inspiration to the world. The Philippines was beginning a fresh, exciting new chapter in its history—a new beginning.

But after years of mismanagement by Marcos, the economy was a shambles. Like every other business enterprise, the film industry was effected. Many of the independent producers and production outfits that had been responsible for some of the most interesting and daring works during the martial law years were folding, falling victim to the extremely trying economic circumstances in the post–Marcos years. One of the consequences of the devaluation of the peso that began in 1983 was that the cost of film stock increased dramatically, forcing many independents out of the business. As a result, a new studio system began to emerge. Moving to the head of the class were Viva, Regal and Seiko, but they brought with them the standard corporate mindset, profit being the bottom-line. These companies were far less willing to step out and take chances merely for art's sake. Therefore their films were built around formulaic constructs and the star system—bankable stars in worn concepts.

In 1986—the year that Marcos left office—there were 179 films produced for the domestic market, well below the all-time high of 280 in 1980, or even the 1971 total of 268, but a relatively healthy figure nonetheless. In fact, it made up a higher percentage of the overall Philippine market than either of those years (44.9% in 1986, as opposed to 32.7 in 1980 and 32.2 in 1971). But through the following years that market share would begin declining— 39.2% in 1987, 36.3 in 1988, 32.9 in 1989; numbers that were still higher than those in the 1970s when the annual average was 25.8%.

It isn't that the increasingly contrite nature of Filipino films could be entirely blamed on the safe practices of the big studios. While the end of the Marcos era promised a new beginning and the prospect of a brighter future for the country, a curious residual effect within the film industry was that it seemed to dry up the creativity that had made the Second Golden Era so replete with fascinating metaphorical morality plays. With the nation's bogeyman now officially gone, so too was the sense of urgency that seemed to inspire many filmmakers. The exception was Lino Brocka, who was still waving the banner. He had been chosen by the Aquino Administration to be a member of the Constitutional Commission in 1986, tasked with drafting a new charter, but Brocka would be among the commission members who would express grave doubts about the new charter, and he and some of the other members would eventually resign. Labelling the new charter both repressive and anti–Filipino, Brocka became disillusioned with the state of affairs in the post–Marcos era, and after a few years he set his sights on the Aquino administration, directing *Orapronobis*, considered by many to be his last truly substantive work (though there were those who conversely considered it a somewhat carelessly hurled brickbat), as well as one of the only truly substantive Filipino films of the post–Marcos '80s.

Orapronobis starred Phillip Salvador as a dissident priest jailed under Marcos and released with the advent of the Aquino administration. Upon his release, Salvador travels to a province that is being terrorized by the *Orapronobis*, a ruthless band of anti-communist vigilantes led by the sadistic Bembol Roco. Masking their atrocities behind religious and patriotic rhetoric, the vigilantes are apparently immune to the law, and Salvador decides that the only solution for the local residents is to evacuate them to Manila where they are given refugee status. Manila turns out to be no refuge, however, as many of them are accused of being involved with communist rebels and are detained. When Salvador tries to locate them, the local authorities deny any involvement in the detentions and the missing persons eventually turn up as corpses, all having been murdered by the *Orapronobis*. Afterward, the military holds a press conference to denounce the victims as communist rebels.

The film opened with a statement attesting to the authenticity of the events depicted, and what follows is a portrait of a country careening out of control. If the film's accounting is to be believed, then the Aquino administration was little improvement over Marcos, the difference being that the atrocities committed under Marcos were the actions of the government, while Aquino's administration allowed lawless bands of vigilantes to do the dirty work. Whether factual or not, the film is effectively disturbing. Getting part of its financing from French backers, *Orapronobis* received no commercial distribution in the Philippines. Although the Movie and Television Review and Classification Board had ordered certain cuts be made in the film before it would be cleared for exhibition, MTRCB Chairman Manuel Morato claimed that it was the theater owners' association itself that declined to give *Orapronobis* any commercial venue because of its portrayal of the new government, the military, and the Church. Morato's rationale was that theater owners feared retaliation from rightwing extremist groups. Assuming this to be true, it still does not explain why the film reportedly had to be smuggled out of the Philippines for its showing at Cannes in 1989. Under Morato, the MTRCB felt obligated to do its share to help protect the integrity of the new government, which some felt was understandable in light of the many coup attempts that the Aquino Administration continually had to deal with. In fairness to the Board, it certainly was a delicate period in the nation's political history.

Morato was a successful businessman before being appointed to the MTRCB, and he had a public reputation as a philanthropist. He also seems to be a man who draws attention to himself, probably never less so than when he became Chairman of the MTRCB. The son of Quezon City's first mayor, Tomas Morato, a former police chief who was appointed mayor by President Quezon in November of 1939, Manuel Morato attended college at Loyola University in Los Angeles, California, where he earned a Bachelor of Science in economics degree. He went on to serve as president of a succession of companies, including Philippine Plywood Corporation and Sta. Cecilia Sawmills. His service as chairman of the MTRCB from 1986–1992 made him the bane of the film and television industries. Outspoken and, apparently personable, Morato would go on to become a television celebrity himself, co-hosting the talk show *Dial-M* with film star Maggie dela Riva, originally a simple lotto drawing on the state-run National Broadcasting Network, that morphed into a talk show largely due to Morato's outspoken nature. Eventually the program came to include commentaries by Morato, and then viewer phone calls. He had higher aspirations, however, and made an unsuccessful run for the senate in 1992. Undaunted, he formed a new political party, *Partido Bansang Marangal* (National Dignity Party), and ran for the presidency in 1998, again without success. Still determined, he made yet another senatorial bid in 2001, but lost again. His only success in politics seems to have been by way of appointments: aside from being appointed chairman of the MTRCB under President Aquino, Morato was also appointed chairman of the Philippine

Charity Sweepstakes Office in 1995 by President Fidel Ramos. His life was considered colorful enough that it was made into a film in 1998, with Morato being portrayed by actor Joel Torre.

Brocka was not the only one experiencing censorship troubles under the newly "restored democracy." The Morato Board would be one of the most controversial in the industry's history, uniformly reviled by the artistic community. Under Morato's chairmanship, the MTRCB also banned the film *Dear Uncle Sam*, claiming that its obvious stand against U.S. military bases in the Philippines was inappropriate and disruptive at a time when negotiations between the two countries over the bases were still ongoing. Even foreign films, commonly given more favorable criteria when judged by past censorship boards, were not spared under Morato's board. Martin Scorsese's *The Last Temptation of Christ* (1988) was banned outright on the grounds that it was obscene, blasphemous, insulting, and antithetical to Catholic doctrine. Well, it was, and it might surprise no one that such a ruling would come about in a rigid Catholic society, even one entertaining notions of democratic restoration. Also under the gun of the Morato board were the erotic—even pornographic—films that had been allowed to flourish during the waning days of the Marcos regime. They did not vanish completely, but continued to survive as a form of illicit, underground entertainment, which is what pornography traditionally was throughout most of its history.

Hopes that things might change at the conclusion of the Aquino Administration were fleeting when, under President Fidel Ramos, Henrietta Mendez was appointed Chairperson of the MTRCB in 1992. Under Mendez's leadership, the Board not only continued the conservative policies of the Morato board, but in some respects intensified its grip on the arts community. Pornographic films—then referred to as "bold films"—were particular targets, as the Mendez Board seemed to make the eradication of smut a special priority. Even American films like *Groundhog Day* could not play without cuts, while movies like *The Bridges of Madison County* and *The Piano* were banned (decisions which were reversed upon appeal to the Appeals Committee, which had been set up in Presidential Decree 1986 by President Marcos). Under Morato's board, producers of erotica found that they could continue to ply their trade only so long as their product could be justified by virtue of having some redeeming social value and artistic merit. In other words, they had to be genuine films, not merely voyeuristic documents of fornication. For this reason, pornography in the Philippine industry differed substantially from Western pornography, which seems to need no justification other than individuals' right to "express themselves." The Morato board seemed more focused on protecting the Aquino Administration by curtailing political commentary, as well as shielding the Catholic belief system from assault. Under Mendez, however, the Board seemed more concerned about perceived moral decay in Philippine society, and was accused of going far astray in its attempts to protect the Filipino public. There was, for instance, the case of *Schindler's List*, a rare foray into serious filmmaking by Steven Spielberg, otherwise a specialist in callow blockbusters. The MTRCB would approve the film for showing only if certain cuts were made, specifically the removal of one simulated sex scene and two scenes that showed women's breasts. The ruling drew harsh criticism, not only from the film industry and from media pundits, but from politicians as well. But Mendez would not be moved, saying that the sex act was sacred and ought to be private. Spielberg refused to accommodate the MTRCB with the required cuts and instead withdrew the film from exhibition in the Philippines, something that may have made him a hero to the arts community around the world, but really seems more petty and ridiculous when you consider the insignificance of what he was being asked to remove. Was a brief moment of Liam Neeson humping his mistress really that crucial to the artistic integrity of the film? But Spielberg probably assumed that the decision would be reversed on appeal, which it was.

MTRCB Vice-Chairperson Edward Buenaflor noted that, under the terms outlined in Presidential Decree 1986, the MTRCB was indeed a morality board regardless of the wishes of individual board members, and that, although morality, obscenity and art were all subjective, and that trying to settle on a definition of contemporary Filipino values was a fruitless endeavor, the law mandated that someone had to do the job. And do it they did.

This may have been as stated in Presidential Decree 1986, but it also stood in contrast to the Philippine Supreme Court's ruling on the *Bayan Ko* case in 1985. The industry's "nebulous stance towards the Board of Review for Motion Pictures and Television" that Marcos spoke of in PD 1986 was obviously still at play in its relationship with the MTRCB. Despite the carping of civil libertarians about "morality police," Buenaflor was obviously fully cognizant of the complexities of the issue and was not one to take the matter lightly or suggest that the Board wield its power without due discretion.

As the film industry continued struggling into the 1990s, there were some who tried to blame the industry's economic woes on the overly-strict policies of the MTRCB, an argument that paled somewhat in light of the fact that the industry's reliance for survival increasingly rested on the drawing power of the bold genre. Still, it was a genre continually under siege, and needing to strike a delicate balance between the artistic and simple lewdness. The situation did not necessarily abate when Jesus Sison assumed chairmanship of the MTRCB in 1995, although the Sison board seemed more concentrated on television, in particular violent superhero cartoons watched by children. Under Sison, the MTRCB mandated that only television programs rated GP (General Patronage) could be aired between the hours of 6 A.M. and 7 P.M. and that only PG-rated (Parental Guidance) programs could run from 8 P.M. to 6 A.M. Films rated R-18 (those restricted to persons 18 years or older) could not play on television. But one hopeful sign from Sison was his stated objective that some sort of framework be established whereby the film industry could transition into self-regulation. Otherwise, Sison called on the film industry to produce more works that portrayed the heroism of the Filipino people, which Sison considered to be a natural character trait. Engendering national esteem has always seemed a preoccupation of the film industry.

For the most part, however, the film industry did not cause the censors too much consternation; the melodramas, for instance, remained as innocuous as ever, largely romantic soaps revolving around love and heartache. After the fall of the Marcos regime and the end of martial law, it was safe romantic melodramas which seemed to serve as a staple of the diet of the Filipino film going public, and with economic times being what they were, the studios seemed content to crank out more star-driven, non-offensive soapers. But there was far more interesting work being done during the period.

One genre that saw some benefit from Marcos' departure and the end of martial law was the action genre, which did gain certain liberties. Always popular with the masses, the action genre seemed to be creeping away from the tired formula that had bound it for years—the lone hero, usually a cop, locking horns with a powerful organized crime kingpin. In reality, the change was minor, merely supplanting the crime bosses with corrupt police commissioners, judges and politicians; one clichéd and worn concept was merely replaced by another, and the formula played and played and played again. More often than not, the corrupt politician was presented as being involved in organized crime, and while the films became as repetitive as their predecessors, they may have been performing a public service of sorts. Like the WWII pictures that flooded the market in the late 1940s, the action pictures of the post-martial law era were often a fount of emotional purging for audiences—a chance for patrons to nudge the person beside them and offer an "I *knew* it." It was a form of vindication for citizens who were frustrated by the rampant corruption, inequality and injustice that had become so all-encompassing within the political landscape. Not that it hadn't always been there, but somewhere along the way, it seems to have swallowed the system up entirely.

One of the action stars who made good in the crowded market was Lito Lapid. Born in Porac, Pampanga on October 25, 1955, Lapid is the nephew of 1960s action star Jess Lapid, whom he portrayed in a film version of the movie hero's life in *The Jess Lapid Story*. The film helped make him a star, but with the end of martial law, Lapid's films began to build-up his populist image as he began toppling corrupt local governments in a succession of titles. Even the titles themselves exhibited a definite attitude that revealed a wellspring of pent-up fury. *Kahit Singko Hindi Ko Babayaran ang Buhay Mo* (*I Wouldn't Pay Five Cents for Your Life*) in 1990 and *Dudurugin Kita ng Bala Ko* (*I Will Pulverize You with My Bullet*) in 1991 took the genre to rather extreme heights (or depths, depending on one's disposition). While the Filipino action genre had often bordered on the grotesque, *Kahit Singko*, directed by Jesus Jose, crossed the threshold, taking an outwardly standard tale of familial tragedy and retribution and

Action star Lito Lapid.

added in the popular new element of government corruption, and managed to set itself apart by virtue of a sadistic streak a mile long and every bit as deep. Former action hero Tony Ferrer was cast as a sleazy congressman whose son is killed in a shootout with the police, prompting Ferrer and his men to abduct the officer responsible (Robert Arevalo). They beat and torture Arevalo until Ferrer himself finally kills him by crushing his head in a vise, shown in excruciating detail as Arevalo's eyes pop out of his head. Arevalo's son (Lapid), also a police officer, seeks to bring his father's killers to justice, resulting in an ongoing war with Ferrer, who has one of his men rape and murder Lapid's sister. Lapid responds by nabbing the guilty party, tying him to the back of a motorcycle and leading him naked through the streets of the city. He also rigs a grenade to the man's genitalia, and when the pleading rapist/murderer tries to remove it ... well, you get the idea. Ferrer then orchestrates a drive-by shooting at the funeral of Lapid's sister, which kills Lapid's wife (Alma Moreno) and mother (Alicia Alonzo), and the story winds down with a showdown in a public park as Lapid does the expected (however improbably) by gunning down Ferrer's army of men before halting Ferrer's flight in an automobile by crushing his car with a steam shovel. The film closes with Lapid himself being arrested and led to jail, perhaps a reminder of sorts to the public that one shouldn't take the law into one's own hands, Lapid's character having grown frustrated by the limitations of working within the confines of the law and having resigned from the force before embarking on his quest for vengeance.

Obviously relishing its violence, and certainly too dyspeptic for mainstream Western audiences, this can all be seen as a form of national cleansing following the fall of the Marcos regime, and one can imagine the effect, both pleasing and purging, on the Filipino public upon seeing the portrayal of a brutally corrupt and abusive system brought down by equally brutal means. It was a highly symbolic moment in the film when Lapid resigned from the force before embarking on his savage retribution, an obvious show of contempt for a system that figuratively rapes the populace (or, in this case, literally), requiring justice to be obtained from without.

Perhaps what made films like *Kahit Singko* somewhat therapeutic was the fact that the EDSA "revolution" was basically a bloodless coup, and the villain, Marcos, was allowed to live out his days in balmy Hawaii, which more than likely deprived many of the feeling of true justice, or in the case of some, even left dangling some deep need for retribution of a sort. The show of gory retribution in such films may have fulfilled that longing for vengeance in the psyche of some, since Marcos had fled the country and had lived the good life, having salted his billions away in foreign bank accounts. The people needed to get some sense of satisfaction that the evil perpetrators of such abuses were dealt a fittingly nasty end, and it seems that the film industry was willing to give them this satisfaction.

Directed by Rogelio Salvador, *Dudurugin Kita* employed an approach every bit as sadistic—perhaps even more so—as that seen in *Kahit Singko*, casting Bernard Bonnin as a brutally ruthless provincial governor who will stop at nothing to get reelected. He has his squad of hitmen (in Filipino cinema, all bad guys have an army of thugs to do their bidding) murder his political rival (Ruben Rustia) in a hit that also kills Rustia's daughter-in-law, inviting Rustia's son (Lapid) to seek his own brand of justice. And so begins an escalating war between families, with Lapid eventually joining forces with a rebel army that has formed in the hills to combat Bonnin's unbearably corrupt and vicious local government. The film climaxes when Bonnin has Lapid's mother (Alonzo again) and his new girlfriend (rebel leader Maricel Laxa) kidnapped, setting up a climactic bloodbath in which Lapid attacks the governor's stronghold, killing all of Bonnin's formidable army of men, and finally Bonnin himself, while rescuing Laxa and Alonzo.

The story relied heavily on the already worn concepts that had become increasingly common to the action genre, with corrupt authoritarian figures and the expected violent retribution, but director Salvador seems to have been less interested in plotting, which served in this instance as a mere excuse for the increasingly brutal catalog of carnage. From beginning to end, the blood seldom ceased flowing, culminating in Lapid's final assault, during which he shoots off one man's arm, hangs another with a chain, and shoots off Bonnin lackey Robert Miller's leg, finishing him off while Miller is vainly trying to reattach his severed limb. The indignation that resulted in not only the longing for meaningful justice, but even for vengeance, surely made the savagery of Lapid's retribution appealing, even cathartic.

Even so, the censors were loath to allow such bloodletting to continue, and Lapid and other action stars had to temper their cruelty in future efforts. In 1993 Salvador and Lapid collaborated again, making the standard action film *Gascon: Bala ang Katapat Mo* (*Gascon: A Bullet Awaits You*), which saw Lapid back to the old grind, playing a cop trying to bring down a powerful crime boss. The violence was robust, but not as carnage-soaked as before, and the change was even more noticeable in 1994 when Lapid again collaborated with Jesus Jose on the film *Geron Olivar*, which starred Lapid as a policeman trying to bring down the criminal empire of drug dealer Edu Manzano. Whereas *Kahit Singko* was awash in blood and wanton cruelty, in *Geron Olivar*, the filmmakers chose spectacle in lieu of gore, with the shootings—although plentiful—being bloodless, and even a stabbing remaining basically unseen. To make up for this, the filmmakers sought to wow the audience with car chases and explosions. In one chase, Lapid is pursuing the criminals and has his car cut in half by a passing truck; undeterred, he continues the chase with only the front half of his car—and catches up! The film concludes with Lapid on a jet ski shooting Manzano's fleeing plane out of the sky with a grenade launcher.

Lapid's film heroics, toppling appallingly corrupt bureaucracies and bringing down crime kingpins, seems to have helped gain him a populist image and probably helped him immeasurably in his subsequent political career, first as vice governor of Pampanga in 1992, and later as that province's governor, and eventually senator.

The younger action stars were not the only ones displaying heroics in fighting the widespread corruption; old hands like Fernando Poe, Jr. found themselves mired in endless struggles with evil authoritarian figures. In 1988 Poe starred in *Agila ng Maynila* (*The Eagle of Manila*), playing an ex-cop-turned-taxi driver who can't get the cop out of his blood. Not only does he rid Manila of a homicidal sex maniac that has been terrorizing the city, but also goes to war with mob boss Vic Diaz and his cohort, dirty Manila police commander Charlie Davao. That same year, Poe also starred in *Kapag Puno na ang Salop* (*When the Package Is Full*), the first in a series of films in which he portrayed a cop who locks horns with evil judge Eddie Garcia, who has his hand in just about every imaginable criminal enterprise. Although Poe manages to have Garcia arrested at the conclusion of the film, Garcia is back out and at it again in the 1989 sequel *Ako ang Huhusga* (*I Am the Law*). Poe finally put an end to the judge's criminal ways in the 1990 climax to the series, *Hindi Ka na Sisikatan ng Araw* (*You Will Not See the Sunrise*), wherein Poe vanquished Garcia by nailing him point blank with a bazooka.

Poe may have still been "The King," but it was Garcia who was being proclaimed rather early in the 1990s as "Actor of the Decade." Garcia received the appellation rather early in the decade after a string of starring roles in highly successful action films. Born on May 2, 1921, in Sorsogon, Garcia is a World War II veteran who fought with the American troops as a member of the U.S. Army Philippine Scouts and initially planned on a career in the military. He made the switch to acting after the war, making his debut in the 1949 film *Siete Infantes de Lara*. In the 1950s Garcia came to be known as the "suave villain of Filipino films," and he gained recognition with an impressive three consecutive FAMAS Best Supporting Actor awards, for *Taga sa Bato* (*Carved in Stone*) in 1957, *Condenado* in 1958 and *Tanikalang Apoy* (*Chain of Fire*) in 1959. He would go on to win more FAMAS awards than anyone in the history of Filipino cinema, including awards for Best Actor and Best Director. In 1969 he won FAMAS awards for two separate films, one as Best Supporting Actor and one as Best Director.

Through the years, Garcia evolved into a formidable director, although his genre of choice in that capacity was often frothy melodrama. *Sinasamba Kita* (*I Worship You*), for instance, won Garcia the FAMAS Best Director award in 1983, despite being nothing more than an anguished and customarily overlong soaper. No doubt much of its appeal was due to its stellar cast, topbilled by Vilma Santos, who played a businesswoman who falls in love with business associate Christopher de Leon. But de Leon only has eyes for Santos' younger sister (Lorna Tolentino), whom he is discreet in pursuing, and who resists his advances out of loyalty to Santos, despite the fact that she has feelings of her own for de Leon. Soon Tolentino has her own suitor in Phillip Salvador, which infuriates de Leon. Well, there's your romantic conflict; now for the tragedy. Tolentino is in a car accident that leaves her in a vegetative state, although doctors can detect no actual brain damage. When de Leon tries to visit her, Salvador flies into a rage and takes Tolentino away to an isolated country house. While Santos searches high and low for Tolentino, de Leon slips into an alcoholic haze, spending his nights in cheap bars with cheaper women. When Tolentino does regain her senses, she enrages Salvador by calling out for de Leon and, out of his mind with jealousy, Salvador rapes her and holds her captive. Eventually Santos finds Tolentino, and Salvador regains his composure long enough to allow

Eddie Garcia in *Ako ang Batas* (*I Am the Law*; 1990/Viva Films). Garcia had been playing the villain in Filipino films for more than 30 years until becoming an action hero himself in the 1990s.

them both to return home, where Tolentino and de Leon are finally united, Santos having been big enough to put her own feelings aside.

The film was representative not only of the soap opera genre, but of Garcia's apparent preference as a director. He otherwise directed films like *P.S. I Love You* (1981), *Cross My Heart* (1982), *Forgive and Forget* (1982), *My Only Love* (1982), *Friends in Love* (1983), and *Paano Ba ang Mangarap* (*How Do You Dream?*; 1983), the last being another overwrought love story for Santos and de Leon, which was adapted from a komiks serial. Many of Garcia's romance films starred a popular young actress named Sharon Cuneta.

Born on January 6, 1966, Cuneta is the daughter of Pablo Cuneta, who had served for over four decades as Pasay City Mayor, and actress Elaine Gamboa, whose sister Helen Gamboa was a more well-known film star. Cuneta had begun her career in the entertainment business as a singer. In 1978, at just 12 years of age, she had scored a major hit with the song "Mister DJ," and her album that year, *DJ's Pet*, was a top seller. By the early 1980s she had embarked on her own film career in teen love pictures; aside from the above-mentioned titles, she also appeared in films like *Dear Heart* (1981), but like others before her who had started in teen-oriented pictures, Cuneta soon enough transitioned into more adult-oriented films. In particular, films in which she co-starred with her then-husband, actor Gabby Concepcion, proved popular with the public. In her career as an actress anyway, Cuneta seems to owe a debt to Garcia, who used her frequently in films that helped popularize her with the movie going public.

As an actor, Garcia had played the villain opposite most of the action heroes of more than one generation, including Poe and Joseph Estrada from the old guard, and newcomers like Rudy Fernandez (son of director Gregorio Fernandez), Phillip Salvador and Ronnie Ricketts. But entering the 1990s, Garcia began to star in one action film after another, many of them true accounts of national heroes, in which he now always had the lead. It seemed unlikely that Garcia would become an action hero at such an advanced stage in both his career and his life (he had, after all, been in the business some 40 years), but that is what happened as he became the superstar of choice for many of the more impressive action films of the 1990s, typically cast as a lovable, roguish cop. Perhaps due to the increasingly repetitive nature of the flurry of films he had been making, Garcia sought a change in the mid-'90s and signed on for a three-year run on a television sitcom. It was a decision that he would later claim to regret, saying that it prevented him from doing more film work. Still, his film career remained healthy enough by most standards, and he was as popular as ever. His 1997 film *Padre Kalibre* was the top draw at that year's Metro Manila Film Festival.

And then there were the bad boys. Although Letter of Instructions No. 13, issued by President Marcos in September of 1972, had forbidden "Films which glorify criminals or condone crimes," filmmakers took advantage of Marcos' departure and presumed a new liberalism within their craft. Young, punk anti-heroes became increasingly popular with audiences, none more so than Robin Padilla.

Padilla was one of eight children of actor/director/producer Roy Padilla and actress Eva Carino, whose career serves as a good example of how inbred the Filipino film industry can be. LVN soundman July Hidalgo was the stepfather of Carino's sister, and through him Carino met Juan Silos on the studio lot one day in the mid-1950s. He was taken by her charm and beauty, and it wasn't long before Carino was signed to a contract. Her career got off to something of a false start, however, as she experienced some health problems and dropped out of the business for a time. But she returned in 1958 when director Consuelo Osorio, who was the neighbor of Carino's sister, brought her to the attention of her brother, filmmaker Roy Padilla. As there was another film star by the name of Aida Carino (who coincidentally took Eva Carino's place as the female lead of Manuel Conde's *Krus na Kawayan* in 1956 when Eva's health problems prevented her from playing the part), Osorio renamed her, and Eva Carino became Eva Rivera.

She began working with Padilla as her producer and director, but it was a sometimes volatile working relationship, as Carino years later recalled, recounting how Padilla had cursed her for blowing a dramatic scene. Co-starring in a film with Padilla's brother, Amado Cortez, Carino recalled that she was weeping profusely in the scene when Cortez suddenly cracked her up by passing gas. As Carino laughed, Padilla went into a tirade against her to the point that Carino walked off and refused to return unless Osorio stepped in as director, which she did.[1] However difficult Padilla may have been to work with, a personal relationship blossomed and Padilla and Carino married. Years later, Padilla entered politics, being elected governor of Camarines Sur, but he was assassinated on Election Day in 1988 as he was seeking re-election.

As a youth, Robin Padilla already had dreams of being a star. Well, why not? Coming from a show business background, it seemed only natural. He was apparently not the least bit interested in his studies at school, preferring to spend his days break dancing with friends behind a local Cathedral. When Carino confronted her son about his truancy, he shrugged it all of by telling her that he'd rather be an actor anyway. Padilla's lack of interest in his schooling eventually got him kicked out of Saint Louis University, but after meeting filmmaker Deo Fajardo, Padilla's film career got off the ground. He began appearing in films in the mid-1980s, and by the end of the decade he was top-billing youth-oriented action pictures. He quickly earned the tag "Bad Boy of Philippine Cinema," partly due to the types of roles that he was playing, portraying various hoods, hooligans, street punks and gang members in films like *Carnap Gang* (1989), *Bad Boy* (1990) and *Bad Boy 2* (1992), *Grease Gun Gang* (1991), and *Ang Utol Kong Hoodlum* (*My Hoodlum Brother*) in 1991 and its inevitable sequel, *Ang Utol Kong Hoodlum 2* in 1992. His films were box office gold, and he became so popular that for a time he was considered to be surpassing Fernando Poe, Jr., as the reigning box office king.

Perhaps it was already a part of his personal make-up (although simple truancy a hooligan doesn't necessarily make), or maybe he began to take his "Bad Boy" screen image too seriously, but whatever the reason, Padilla came to be as famous for his off-screen exploits as for his rough and tumble screen persona. Tabloids readily printed every tidbit they could get on him, including his notorious womanizing (by which he frequently humiliated his longtime girlfriend, Liezl Sycangco, the mother of his three daughters), or slugging fellow actor Richard Gomez in the presence of President Corazon Aquino while also making advances toward Aquino's daughter Kris Aquino, also a film star. Not to worry, the Madam President took care to scold both Padilla and Gomez for their unseemly behavior. There was even a case wherein Sycangco was taken to the hospital with a bullet wound to her hand, and the press eagerly speculated that Padilla had shot her during an argument. Sycangco refused to testify against Padilla, however, saying that she had merely injured herself when Padilla's gun went off as she was cleaning it.

Padilla's days of fast living came to a head on October 26, 1992: driving excessively fast through Angeles City at approximately 8 P.M. during a rainstorm, Padilla ended up running down a balut vendor.* Rather than help the poor fellow out, or even see if he was all right, Padilla sped away, but a witness followed on motorcycle and reported his license plate number and the make of the car—a Mitsubishi Pajero—to the Angeles City branch of the Philippine National Police. A short time later, a patrol car stopped Padilla and ordered him to get out of his car. When he complied, they noticed a gun—a Smith and Wesson .357 caliber revolver—tucked into the waist of his pants. After confiscating the gun, they found it to be loaded with six live rounds; they further found a long magazine for an Armalite rifle in Padilla's back pocket. Padilla angrily denied being involved in any hit and run accident, and when he tried to get back in his car one of the officers stopped him. With the car door open, the police officers could see an M-16 baby Armalite rifle lying horizontally by the driver's seat. They checked it and found it to be loaded in semi-automatic mode with a long magazine filled with live bullets. Padilla claimed that the guns were registered, but police informed him that he was being arrested for hit and run, and that the permits for his guns would have to be checked at the station. Once he had been taken to the station Padilla voluntarily surrendered a black bag containing still more weapons and ammunition—a .380 Pietro Barretta with a single round in its chamber, and various other long and short magazines. He could produce neither carrying permits nor receipts for any of the weapons, claiming that they were at his home, and he was consequently charged with illegal weapons possession.

Let out on 200,000 pesos bail, Padilla appeared in court on January 20, 1993, but refused to enter a plea, at which time a not guilty plea was entered on his behalf. The wheels of justice turn slowly, especially if the accused is a famous celebrity with the money to hire lawyers sharp enough to contrive motion after motion to try and get the case dismissed. In Padilla's case, it wasn't easy, caught red-handed as he was. Although the case dragged on for years, Padilla was eventually convicted in the Angeles City Regional Trial Court for illegal weapons possession on April 25, 1994 (the hit and run charge apparently fell by the wayside in light of the

---

*A balut is a boiled duck's egg with a partially developed embryo, a favorite native delicacy.

weapons charges: perhaps the balut vendor was not seriously injured), and was given a harsh sentence indeed—a minimum of 17 years, 4 months and one day to 21 years maximum. His lawyers immediately filed a petition for review of the decision along with another application for bail, and various excuses were put up in his defense, to wit: 1) that his arrest was illegal and therefore the weapons confiscated were inadmissible as evidence; 2) the severe penalty for illegal possession of fire arms amounted to excessive and cruel punishment, and, most interesting of all, 3) that he was in actuality a confidential civilian agent authorized by a Mission Order and Memorandum Receipt to carry the firearms.

But as his appeals wore on, Padilla was required to begin serving his sentence, and on August 29, 1995, he was incarcerated in the Bilibid Prison in Muntinglupa. Padilla himself seemed stunned that he was actually going to jail. "I don't believe it," he said. "I haven't killed anyone. The only thing I like to do is help my fellow men. Is this the reward I get?"[2] Interesting that he didn't think to help the balut vendor after running him down.

Being in prison may have severely hampered his career, but it didn't end it completely. After being incarcerated, Padilla wrote a biographical film which was shot in prison in which he portrayed himself; he even wrote and sang the film's theme song. Actually, the film, *Anak, Pagsubok Lamang ng Diyos* (*Son, You're Only Testing God*), was the idea of Padilla's mother, Eva Carino, who could not bear the press painting her son as a hooligan and a jailbird, and so sought to soften his public image with a more sympathetic portrayal of the poor, misunderstood Padilla. To bankroll the film, Carino approached FLT Films matriarch Mommy Rose Flaminiano, and the offer was readily accepted. The only problem was that Padilla was still under contract to Viva Films, which sought to block the release of the film after its completion, and also threatened to sue Padilla for breach of contract. By the time the film finally did come out, Padilla was some time into serving his sentence and was already beginning to fade from the public's thoughts. Consequently, the film did not come near doing the business that Padilla's previous offerings customarily did.

But something more significant happened to Padilla while he was in prison: he experienced a religious awakening. Raised a Jehovah's Witness, Padilla had occasion to meet someone whom he later described as a Muslim terrorist from Africa convicted for being involved in the plot to assassinate Pope John Paul II during his visit to Manila in 1995. Although Padilla said that he was initially afraid of the man, he was also impressed by his devotion to his faith, and Padilla began to study the Islamic religion, eventually deciding to become a convert. It was a decision that didn't sit well with Padilla's mother, who was not only a devout Jehovah's Witness, but even went on to preach her faith in the most impoverished areas. Although Carino was very displeased by her son's decision to convert, she later admitted that she did see a positive change in his character afterwards. Padilla even finally married his longtime girlfriend, Liezl Sycangco, is a Muslim ceremony held in the Bilibid prison. He also became a model prisoner, and started an anti-drug program in the prison in order to try and stop the widespread use of drugs among the prisoners.

As far as his prospects of getting out of jail before serving his minimum of 17 years, Padilla was fortunate to have some heavy hitters going to bat for him within the government: Senator Gloria Macapagal-Arroyo proposed a bill in the senate to reduce the penalties for cases like Padilla's. And then there was former-actor-turned-senator Ramon Revilla, who had himself enjoyed a successful run as an action star in the 1970s, and who seemed moved to try and get Padilla released. Eventually, the laws were changed, and the new laws were made retroactive, meaning that Padilla's sentence could be lessened. Padilla had appealed his case to the Supreme Court, and although the Court made rather short work of the actor's various excuses and contrivances for why his conviction should be overturned, they did allow that, with the law having since been changed, Padilla's sentence should be accordingly altered: Padilla's sentence was modified, and he was then required to serve from 10 years minimum to 18 years maximum, still a long enough stretch, but there was good news on the horizon. He would be eligible for parole after serving one-third of his sentence, which would be just slightly over three years. That would have been good enough news, but it just got better from there: President Fidel Ramos decided to grant Padilla a conditional pardon, and he was released from prison on April 17, 1998, less than three years after he had begun serving his sentence. And why would President Ramos consider Padilla's case worthy of such consideration? Would an ordinary, average citizen be granted such pardon after such a short time? One could cynically suggest that Padilla's celebrity figured heavily in the decision, but another consideration that should be weighed is the fact that Padilla had campaigned for Ramos in 1992 when Ramos was first seeking the presidency. And then there is the question of the exceedingly withering Filipino film industry: there were some who thought—perhaps hoped—that Padilla's release and return to the film business would help revive interest in local films, which were frequently considered all but invisible in a market crowded by Hollywood blockbusters.

Many may have looked to Padilla as a potential savior for the local industry's economic woes, hoping that his release and return to films would revive interest in local movies, but it didn't exactly turn out that way. Padilla resumed his career, and while he had occasional hit films, he had as many or more that were not so enthusiastically received. His status as box office gold was gone, and he eventually felt compelled to accept an offer to do a television series to pick up the slack. He needed the money, not merely to pick up the slack in light of his hit and miss film career, but also to help fund his private ventures. Stepping up as a public leader of his adopted faith, Padilla decided to open a school for Muslim children in his home. There was, however, a matter of building an addition to his house in order to accommodate not only the school itself, but also lodging for the children: as they were being given free room and board to go with their free education, the money for it all had to come from somewhere. The television series—an action/drama show—provided a steadier income than his wavering film career, but Padilla still found himself dogged by the tabloids, which began printing stories of an affair between Padilla and his series co-star, Ara Mina. It was likely no more than the expected tabloid gossip, but after Padilla's womanizing past, it apparently was the last straw for Sycangco, who left Padilla. She relocated with her children (which by then came to include a young son) in Australia as Padilla traveled back and forth in his attempts to keep working and reconcile with his wife.

Whatever disarray his personal life and career may have been going through, he nonetheless remained a leader among the nation's Muslim minority. He would, for instance, agree to be paid in paint after signing on to endorse Dutch Boy Nalcrete in the Philippines, saying that the free paint would be used to repaint all mosques in the Philippines. Gestures like that would indeed endear him to the nation's Muslim community. Whatever problems there were in his film career, he was, after all, still a celebrity and the nation's most high-profile member of the faith. Such being the case, he became the first person to come to mind among Muslim terrorists in a bind. On March 20, 2000, the Muslim terrorist organization Abu Sayyaf attacked a Philippine Army outpost in Basilan. Unable to take the outpost, they retreated and wound up finding a target that they were more capable of taking: they marched into two different Basilan schools and took more than 50 hostages, most of them little school children. Such machismo may have made them heroes to the Islamic terrorist world, but the group feared reprisals and soon found themselves bartering off hostages for food. Eventually down to just 29 hostages, they began to dread a rescue mission staged by the Philippine military, and they first threatened to begin killing the hostages should any such rescue attempt occur. But they were still looking for a way out, and a spokesman for the group appeared on a local radio station to announce that the group would only negotiate with movie star Robin Padilla ... or a member of the Vatican.

Padilla agreed to meet with them, and although the government's decision to endorse the meeting struck many as a foolish concession, Philippine movie star-turned-president Joseph Estrada tried to wriggle out of the controversy with his customary good humor. "There is nothing wrong in their demand for Padilla's personal appearance," Estrada was quoted as saying, adding "Padilla is not even asking for a talent fee."[3] Truth is Estrada's willingness to allow Padilla to step in and handle the situation probably had much to do with the fact that his own presidency was facing serious problems, and the hostage situation was just one more headache that Estrada didn't need. There was little he could do anyway, and being a popular Muslim convert, maybe Padilla really could help. It was a nice thought, but it didn't turn out that way.

When Padilla was taken to the Abu Sayyaf's secret camp, the star struck terrorists lined up to get his autograph before eventually getting down to telling Padilla their demands. The demands were ridiculous, as they seem to have been dreamed up to appeal to hardcore Islamic groups and make the group into greater heroes to the Islamic terrorist world, basically insisting on things that were completely beyond the control of the Philippine Government: they demanded the release of three convicted Islamic terrorists incarcerated in the United States, including Ramzi Yousef, convicted of the 1993 World Trade Center bombing. Obviously the Philippine Government had no means of accomplishing this, and really had no leverage with the U.S. Government to even suggest such a thing. The demand was foolish on its face, and even Padilla must have known it. Not surprisingly, the negotiations really didn't accomplish much, and the Abu Sayyaf continued with taking more hostages from Christian villages, beheading some of them, prompting Padilla to become rather quiet about the whole thing. Padilla's involvement did rather work in the terrorists' favor, however, as the group got the publicity it so badly craved, as well as getting a movie star's autograph. Even so, Padilla continued to try and show how much his faith had changed his character, and further demonstrated his benevolence by offering to take the place of a Philippine hostage being held by terrorists in Iraq, who said that the hostage would only be released if the Philippine military left Iraq and withdrew its support for the U.S. in the war in Iraq. President Gloria Macapagal-Arroyo complied, while claiming that the Filipino withdrawal had nothing whatever to do with the terrorists' demands.

Padilla's Muslim affiliations continued to be somewhat dicey: despite nothing constructive coming of his attempts at negotiations in Basilan, he remained the Muslim celebrity of choice in a pinch. In March of 2005, Abu Sayyaf members being held at Camp Bagong Diwa managed to overtake their guards and seize control of the facility; among their demands—to speak with Robin Padilla. Otherwise, Padilla's faith had been kept in the public eye by the arrest of a man said to be Padilla's bodyguard in 2004 on charges of being an Abu Sayyaf member involved in a plan to bomb targets in Metro Manila, and the arrest of Padilla's uncle, Virgilio Carino, in 2005 for involvement in yet another Muslim terrorist organization, the Rajah Soliman Revolutionary Movement.

While it all may have tested Padilla's patience with his Muslim brothers, it was really no reflection on him or his newfound change of character. He continued to try and remold his public image, even asking film producers to keep his "bad boy" screen antics to a minimum, so as not to give the wrong impression.

Although he was not quite as popular with audiences as Padilla, Ace Vergel was nicknamed "Bad Boy" before Robin Padilla even began his film career, and like Padilla his on-screen antics seemed to facilitate his off screen persona. Born Ace York Aguilar in 1952, Vergel was the son of Golden Era screen icons Cesar Ramirez and Alicia Vergel. He began his screen career in the late 1950s as a child star, going by the name Ace York. By the time he had come of age, he was renamed Ace Vergel and was starring in action films that cast him as the protagonist even though he was often portraying street thugs and drug dealers. There was, for instance, the 1983 Carlo Caparas film *Pieta*, which Caparas adapted from his own komiks serial, and which cast Vergel as the title character, a drug gang member, who rapes his boss's daughter and gets her pregnant. The boss sends a hit man gunning for him, but Vergel manages to kill the hit man, as well as his erstwhile boss, and after finding that he has become a father, he seeks out the boss's daughter again, chasing her through the jungle, where he meets his end at the hands of the pursuing police.

In the 1990s Vergel's personal life took a nasty turn with a series of arrests, some for drugs, others for rape. The rape allegations were dropped or dismissed, including one made by a 16-year-old girl in 1998, who claimed that Vergel had raped her three times after her neighbor had pimped her out to him. Vergel had also been accused of rape in 1995 by a former maid in his employ, who claimed that the actor had forced her to use methamphetamine hydrochloride (referred to in the Philippines as "shabu") and then raped her. The maid's statement prompted police to raid Vergel's home, and although the rape charges would later be dropped, the drugs seized during the raid would lead to Vergel's eventual conviction in October of 1998, which was affirmed on appeal by the Court of Appeals in March of 2004. He had been successful in having previous drug charges thrown out by claiming that he had been setup, and that arresting officers had tried to shake him down for one million pesos after taking him to a lodge in Pasig City rather than to the Narcotics Command headquarters. Vergel had maintained that some narcotics agents held a grudge against him after the actor had filed unlawful arrest charges against them a number of times in the past. It worked for a time, but eventually Vergel's drug problems caught up with him, and he found himself sentenced to six years in prison, four for illegal possession of 39.49 grams of shabu, and two for illegal possession of marijuana.

In 1992, Vergel had also been convicted by the Makati City Regional Trial Court along with actress Alona Alegre for stealing a rental car from a Philippine agency in 1991. Vergel maintained that

Troubled action star Ace Vergel, the bad boy of Filipino films, had a reputation as a bad boy off screen as well.

the car had been stolen, but his appeal to the Supreme Court was met with a 17–20 year sentence. He then set about appealing to the Chief Justice of the Supreme Court to grant him new trials in all his various convictions. Somehow, through all of his seemingly endless legal battles, his career managed to limp along, each new film branded a comeback.

A much more reputable role model among the younger generation of action stars was Ronnie Ricketts, who doesn't seem to have had the same kind of problems in his personal life. Although he began his career being cast as communist insurgents in films like *Sparrow Unit: The Termination Squad* (1987) and *Urban Terrorist* (1988), his parts were secondary supporting roles; by the time he graduated to playing leads he was often cast as an avenger, righting wrongs done to his family, or as cops tackling the ever-present local crime kingpin. He did sometimes play street toughs, but they were most often amiable lugs inadvertently sucked into conflicts by circumstance. The worst of his characters were his occasional turns as bank robbers, which in Philippine culture were more along the lines of populist folk heroes, much like Jesse James was in his day.

The action genre was crowded, due to its popularity with audiences, but it began to thin out somewhat as audiences for local films once more began to dwindle. Sonny Parsons, a Muslim actor who had a tendency to portray characters of his own faith—sometimes imaginary, sometimes true life accounts—left the film business for a while to pursue his singing career. He had moderate success there and periodically returned for a film here and there. One problem with the action genre was that, despite its popularity, the returns were often not as lucrative since the costs were higher, what with all the special effects, pyrotechnics, blowing up cars and planes and boats and such.

But one genre that seemed to spark with the public was the true crime genre—the "massacre films"—that capitalized on the public's morbid curiosity for horrendous crimes by dramatizing them on screen. Within the genre, no one was quicker at the draw to jump on a gut-wrenching tragedy than Carlo Caparas, who quickly became the king of the massacre films. Caparas was a fourth grade dropout who had spent his youth listening to the folk tales of farmers in the mountainous region in which he lived, and it fed his love of storytelling. As an adult Caparas worked as a security guard before becoming a writer for Filipino komiks in the 1970s, when komiks were in their heyday. Throughout Manila people could be found by the hundreds, occupying benches reading komiks serials. The popularity of komiks in the 1970s is said

Action hero Ronnie Ricketts.

to have even eclipsed that of television. Among the biggest names in the profession were Pablo Gomez and Mars Ravelo, whose stories and characters were frequently made the subject of film adaptations. And then there was Caparas.

Caparas was a very prolific writer, at one point penning the stories of 40 serials at the same time. His characters would also make it to the movie screen, in particular Ang Panday (the Blacksmith), a man who fashions a magic sword and fights the forces of darkness. He was first played on screen in 1979 by the King himself, Fernando Poe, Jr., after Poe's wife Susan Roces read the komik and brought it to her husband's attention as good fodder for the big screen. Poe went on to portray the character four times, and other actors inherited it later. Although Caparas had many of his komiks stories adapted to the screen—some in films that he himself produced and directed—Panday was his greatest source of fame: that is until he latched on to the massacre film.

What seemed to kick start it all was *The Vizconde Massacre: God Help Us!* in 1993. The Vizconde Massacre was one of the most horrific and highly-publicized crimes in Philippine history. On either the night of June 29, 1991, or the early morning hours of June 30, Estrellita Vizconde and her daughters, Carmela, age 18, and Jennifer, 7, were brutally stabbed to death, and Carmela raped; husband and father Lauro Vizconde was out of the country, working in the United States, at the time of the crime. He was called home by relatives with the story that his father had suffered a serious heart attack, but upon arriving in the Philippines he learned the awful truth, and passed out after receiving the news. The crime shocked the nation, with bloody crime scene photos being printed in full color on the front pages of newspapers, and it remained front page news for quite some time as the police struggled to solve the case, eventually arresting a set of suspects only to have them acquitted after it was revealed that they were tortured into confessing.

At the time that Caparas made his film of the crime, the case was still unsolved and public fascination still being high, it was assured of good box office returns. The film managed to include the expected scenes depicting the murders, though it could do no more than speculate as to what really happened. Otherwise, Caparas could do little else but show the grief-stricken Lauro Vizconde (portrayed by Romeo Vasquez) agonizing over his loss and becoming embittered over the lack of resolution.

The enormous box office success of *Vizconde Massacre* touched off a wave of true crime films, and Caparas threw himself back into the genre right away with *The Myrna Diones Story: Lord, Have Mercy!* that same year. It was the story of a teenage girl (portrayed by Kris Aquino, who had also starred in *Vizconde Massacre*) who travels to the city of La Union to enroll in high school. Accompanied by her elder sister and two female cousins, all four are arrested by two policemen who accuse them of shoplifting. They are taken to a small jail cell, and are removed late that night by six police officers who drive them out into the wilderness, brutally rape and murder them, and then toss the bodies down a hillside. The bodies are discovered the next day, but after they are taken to the morgue something miraculous happens: an autopsy is about to be performed on Aquino when she suddenly revives. After being rushed to the hospital, Aquino is interviewed by newspaper editor Boots Anson-Roa, and after Aquino reveals that it was the police who assaulted her and murdered her companions, Anson-Roa calls all of her connections at newspapers across the mainland and makes a national cause out of the case. Aquino identifies her attackers, and the officers are put on trial; but although Anson-Roa champions Aquino's case in the press and convinces attorney Eddie Rodriguez to

Opposite: The Vizconde Massacre (1993/Golden Lions Films) started off the trend in gruesome true crime films.

prosecute, the case is not easy. The six officers obviously have friends in high places as the families of two of the murder victims are paid off to sign statements accepting the ridiculous assertion that the women were struck by a car and knocked down the hill. Other witnesses are also paid off (one woman, for instance, is paid to testify to confirm the shoplifting charge), and there are concerns for Aquino's own safety, prompting policeman Joel Torre to place her under police protection and take her to a safe house. Anson-Roa and her family also find it necessary to go into hiding, but in the end it is all worth it when five of the six officers are convicted. The real Myrna Diones went into the witness protection program, since her testimony mentioned the participation of a mysterious seventh individual who was not a member of the police force, but seemed to be the one in charge: this individual was never brought to trial. Having arrived at the jail late that night and accompanied the police when the women were taken out into the wilderness, this person participated in the crimes. It was strongly intimated that this individual was the son of a very prominent citizen. The film ended with an ominous postscript which revealed that, soon after the trial, the attorney portrayed by Rodriguez discovered a bloody corpse dumped in front of his home, presumably as a warning not to pursue the case any further.

In 1993 Caparas also produced, wrote and directed *Humanda Ka Mayor! Bahala na ang Diyos* (*Beware Mayor! God Will Judge You*), a film that was not specifically a dramatization of a crime, but was rather loosely based on a case involving former Calauan mayor Antonio Sanchez, who was charged with the rape and murder of a young woman and the murder of her boyfriend. The cast again included Kris Aquino, this time portraying a reporter who helps the murder victim's brother uncover the truth, which leads to maniacal mayor Dick Israel. The daughter of former president Corazon Aquino and Benigno Aquino, Jr., the bane of the latter chapter of Ferdinand Marcos' dictatorship, Kris Aquino was born on February 14, 1971, and she began her acting career on television in various comedies and drama series as a teen. Her film career began in 1990 with a series of comedies with actor Rene Requiestas, but her later work for Caparas quickly earned her the title "Massacre Queen." She later became a TV talk show hostess.

The enormous success of *Vizconde Massacre* and the true crime films that it spawned seemed to keep Caparas busy for some time; he certainly knew which side his bread was buttered on. He also couldn't refrain from returning to the case that started it all off: although the case was still unsolved in 1994, that did not prevent Caparas from making *Vizconde Massacre 2*, which presented still more speculation on what really happened that fateful night, and in 1996 went to the well once more with *The Untold Story of Carmela Vizconde*, which sought to document the ill-fated teen's life prior to her murder. Otherwise, Caparas was busy making *Annabelle Huggins Story: Ruben Ablaza Tragedy*, *Antipolo Massacre: Jesus Save Us!*, and *Lipa Massacre: Lord, Deliver Us from Evil* (all in 1994), and *Marita Gonzaga Rape-Slay: In God We Trust*, *Victim No. 1: Delia Maga (Jesus, Pray for Us!)* and *The Lilian Velez Story* (all in 1995). Although public fascination for the genre eventually waned, Caparas' own passion for it persisted, and he occasionally returned to the genre with films like *The Cory Quirino Kidnap: NBI Files* in 2003.

As a filmmaker, Caparas' work lacks polish, but his films within the true crime genre admittedly pack a punch by virtue of the appalling nature of the events depicted. On the other hand, it is sometimes difficult to know exactly how to react to much of his work because so much of it seems merely crass and exploitative, prompting many to dismiss him as a hack and something of a cheap shot artist. There is, for instance, his tendency to utilize the actual crime scenes in some of his films, which he did by filming in the actual house where the murders occurred in *Vizconde Massacre*, and using the actual ramshackle shed where the titular character was brutally raped and murdered in *Marita Gonzaga Rape-Slay*, revealing either a morbid fascination on his own part, or a rather tasteless willingness to capitalize on the public's own morbid curiosity. Marita Gonzaga was a young woman who was gang-raped and then bludgeoned to death with a brick by three psychotic drug addicts. There is a moment in Caparas' film on the murder when actress Sunshine Cruz (in the role of Gonzaga) walks past the shed, and after she has walked out of the shot, Caparas freezes on the shed itself as the screen reads "The actual place where Marita Gonzaga was brutally raped and murdered." It is moments like this that tend to force Caparas' work firmly into the category of cheap sensationalism. But the film otherwise has very effective moments, in particular an event that the film assures the viewer truly happened just ten days before Gonzaga's murder, when her mother awakens to find Marita standing in the bedroom doorway looking dazed and somewhat spectral in her white nightgown. When her mother asks what is wrong Marita relates a dream that had awoken her in which a man clad in a white robe sat in her room and silently beckoned to her.

At other times Caparas' films included disclaimers admitting to fictionalizing certain aspects of the narrative. In the case of *The Myrna Diones Story*, this can be presumed to be the supernatural elements wherein Diones hears the voices of her murdered family members calling out to her. Caparas was somewhat prone to inserting the supernatural into his true crime narratives, but they sometimes proved to be some of the more interesting moments. *Lipa Massacre*, for instance, is the story of a mother (Vilma Santos) who is murdered along with her two young daughters, again while the father (Joel Torre) is out of the country working, on this occasion in Saudi Arabia. In a particularly striking moment in the film, Santos takes her two daughters out shopping, and while riding up an escalator, she sees a beautiful blonde woman—an obviously angelic figure—staring at her from a distance. She glimpses this mysterious angelic figure again while driving home, seeing her standing alone on the sidewalk while driving across a bridge. The strange music—lifted from a brief musical passage in Coppola's *Apocalypse Now*—lends an eerie touch to the two encounters, and gives the unmistakable impression that this is intended to be an otherworldly figure.

There were far more supernatural implications in *Antipolo Massacre*, which was promoted with the tag line "The night even hell fell silent." The film starred Cesar Montano as a discontented rural laborer who begins to come unglued after his brother is murdered by the village drunk (Celso Ad. Castillo). After purchasing a bolo knife from the widow of a murdered man, Montano's personality changes drastically as he seems to almost become possessed by the bolo, sharpening it incessantly. He finally goes off the deep end one night, murdering five members of a neighboring family with the bolo before chasing his own wife and children into the forest. More than any of Caparas' previous true crime films, *Antipolo Massacre* seemed centered on spooky atmospherics, which increased the sense of foreboding.

Caparas would also occasionally throw cinematic logic out the window, as in the moment in *Lipa Massacre* when Joel Torre, in the role of Ronald Arandia, leaves for Saudi Arabia and, walking away with his rucksack over his shoulder, stops in parting to take one last look at his wife and daughters, at which time Caparas replaces Torre with the real Arandia. This interchanging of Torre with the real person that he is portraying—something that Caparas repeats toward the end of the film—should logically hinder the continuity of the narrative; instead, in some way, it heightens the reality of the drama being portrayed. It is odd that a filmmaker would even try this, but stranger still that he would be able to pull it off. Caparas also chose to open the film with actual audio recordings of the victims, which were recorded letters sent to Arandia while he was in Saudi Arabia. In some way this seems somehow cruel, and yet there is no denying the power it had in personalizing the tragedy. He had used this method of personalizing events from the start when, in *Vizconde Massacre*, he closed the film with video clips from the 18th birthday party of Carmela Vizconde, powerful and haunting images that accentuated the horror of the story that had preceded it. On the downside, Caparas was sometimes not averse to using distressingly graphic crime scene photos of the victims in his films, which smacks of the lowest form of sensationalism.

Caparas was not the only one tapping the Vizconde massacre for profit. Investigators finally got a break in the case in April of 1995 when a woman named Jessica Alfaro came forward to the NBI with the tale that she was the lookout for the killers of the Vizcondes. She named eight men as being involved in the killings, among them Hubert Webb, the son of former Philippine basketball star and then senator Freddie Webb, and Antonio Lejano II, the son of actress Pinky de Leon and nephew of actor Christopher de Leon. Claiming to be coming forward because she had been plagued by recurring nightmares of the murders, Alfaro's two statements (first on April 28, 1995, then on May 22, 1995), however contradictory to one another, led to the arrest and eventual conviction in 2000 of six of the eight men she named, the other two remaining at large. Though her story was riddled with inconsistencies and certainly left at least a reasonable doubt, it was enough to convince Judge Amelita Tolentino of the guilt of the accused (there are no jury trials in the Philippines), and on January 6, 2000, she gave all six men life sentences. Although it seemed to be welcome news to most, finally giving the nation some sense of closure in the case after almost a decade, in the years since the convictions many, particularly newspaper editorialists, have expressed grave doubts as to the wisdom of Judge Tolentino's decision. In particular, Webb has been seen as having been victimized by the authorities', Judge Tolentino's, and indeed the country's thirst for justice at all costs. Webb presented quite a mountain of evidence that he was not even in the Philippines at the time of the murders, but rather in the United States, something testified to not only by friends, relatives, and Philippine singing star Gary Valenciano, who met Webb in Florida sometime between October and November of 1991, but also by certified documents provided by the U.S. Immigration and Naturalization Service showing that Webb entered the United States on March 9, 1991, and did not depart until October 26, 1992, a California driver's license issued to Webb on June 14, 1991, employment records for Webb's part-time job with a California pest control company in June of 1991, and even a receipt for a bicycle that Webb purchased in California on the very day of the murders. Among those who testified to being with Webb in the U.S. on June 28th and 29th was Honesto Aragon, the nephew of former NBI Director Antonio Aragon, who had been director of the NBI at the time of the murders, and died of a heart attack the day before the Vizconde murder trial began. Apparently bound and determined for a conviction, Judge Tolentino disallowed 132 of the 142 pieces of evidence that the defense tried to admit into evidence. Even officials of the U.S. embassy, who had worked with Philippine authorities in gathering evidence to confirm Webb's presence in the U.S. during the time in question, going so far as to get assistance from the FBI, were aghast at Judge Tolentino's surreptitious rulings. The FBI had painstakingly reconstructed a paper trail showing Webb's whereabouts during the time in question, yet Judge Tolentino chose to take the word of a woman who was an admitted drug addict and a former NBI informant.

When the verdict was read in the Vizconde trial—a 186-page document that took five hours and two court clerks to get through—defense attorney Vitaliano Aguirre stormed out of the courtroom while the marathon reading was still underway, denouncing the decision as "unjust, unjustified and biased."[4] All true, perhaps, but the guilty verdict brought a moment of applause in the courtroom, and the nation, which had been watching the five-hour reading on live national television, seemed pleased that the whole thing was finally over and done with. Perhaps it was the national mood—the very palpable yearning for closure—that made Tolentino so biased against the defendants—and make no mistake, she was biased against them from the very beginning—and made her so reluctant to give the defendants a fair chance. They had, after all, been vilified in the press before the trial even began, the media loving the new turn the case had taken; among the accused, the son of a former basketball superstar and sitting senator, and the son of a movie star—what could be better in attention-grabbing headlines? But it wasn't just the press that were painting very unflattering portraits of the accused: even before the trial had begun—in fact, while Alfaro's story was still being investigated by authorities—Alfaro signed a contract with Viva Films in 1995 giving them the film rights to her life story, the only aspect of which was of any interest to anyone being her claim to have been present at the Vizconde home on the night of the murders. Webb succeeded in getting an injunction to stop the planned September 1995 exhibition of the film, as he had not yet even had his day in court and the film was already portraying him as guilty. Viva Films appealed the decision, and after two years was able to obtain permission to release it. But by then the public seems to have lost interest in Jessica Alfaro, notwithstanding the ongoing interest in the court case, and the film tanked at the box office. Actress Alice Dixson, who portrayed Alfaro in the film, declined to promote the movie once it finally saw release, but chose to blame its failure at the box office on the two-year delay in releasing it. As for Alfaro, Dixson defended the prosecution's star witness, saying "The movie was based on her testimony, her own story, and she was honest in telling it."[5]

Not everyone shared Dixson's faith in Alfaro; in the years since the conviction of Webb and his co-accused, Robert Heafner, who had been the FBI's legal attaché in the U.S. embassy in Manila, and who had worked closely with Philippine authorities on the case, providing them with all of the necessary documentation to prove Webb's presence in the U.S. during the time in question, has come forward to offer his own thoughts on the case. "I believe it is my moral obligation to tell the truth about what I know," he said. "I have told the truth since day one, when the National Bureau of Investigation asked me to get involved in securing documents and evidence that would prove Hubert was in the States when the Vizconde massacre took place.... In our initial finding, we were able to get Webb's immigration and customs records. We were able to verify his flight number and seat assignment. We also subsequently obtained his visa application from the embassy."[6] Due to his diplomatic status, however, Heafner had been prohibited from testifying in the trial; not that it would probably have made a difference to Judge Tolentino, who disregarded the testimony of virtually everyone the defense brought in anyway, including Philippine Supreme Court Justice Antonio Carpio, who was called as a defense witness to testify that he had spoken to Senator Freddie Webb on the phone on June 29, 1991, and confirmed that on that date the Senator was in America visiting his son Hubert Webb.

After the convictions in the case, defense attorney Aquirre told the press, "We are glad that this case is finally out of Judge Tolentino's hands, and will be reviewed by an intelligent, impartial, collegiate and more competent tribunal."[7] But that was all wishful thinking: in September of 2004 the Supreme Court refused to review the decision, instead handing it off to the Court of Appeals for review. In December of 2005 the Court of Appeals refused to overturn Judge Tolentino's decision: incidentally, Judge Tolentino had by then been appointed an Associate Justice of the Court of Appeals by President Gloria Macapagal-Arroyo. At the time of this writing, Hubert Webb is still in Bilibid Prison in Muntinglupa, and has been in prison for more than ten years now.

Caparas' reputation as king of the massacre films may not have really been to his advantage, but his work was often compelling simply by virtue of the fact that the horrendous crimes being portrayed were real events. His best work in the true crime genre, however, was not a massacre film, but rather a telling of the abduction and gang-rape of actress Maggie dela Riva in 1967. In 1994 Caparas made *The Maggie dela Riva Story: God.... Why Me?*, which was aided tremendously by a strong performance from Dawn Zulueta in the role of dela Riva. While not being overly-graphic in its depiction of the crime, Caparas did not skimp in portraying dela Riva's harrowing ordeal, spending a half-hour of the film's running time depicting how dela Riva was repeatedly raped, beaten, burned with cigarettes and degraded in various ways. The film retained its dramatic power right through to the end, as Caparas took the viewer through the trial, and finally the executions of the perpetrators. The film also included an appearance by the real dela Riva in the film's final moments, portraying herself years after the crime, greeting her daughter, who has come home from school in tears and asking her mother if what the children in school are telling her about what happened to her years before is the truth. The film concludes with dela Riva walking with her daughter and telling her the story of the horrific assault she survived all those years before.

Caparas was by no means the only filmmaker making capital off of horrible crimes: in 1993 Joey Romero, the son of Eddie Romero, made *Maricris Sioson: Japayuki*, the story of a young woman who travels to Japan to work as a dancer and winds up being shipped home in a crate. Janice de Belen played an activist who, troubled by the number of young Philippine women who have likewise returned from Japan in boxes, travels to Japan with government investigator Joel Torre to uncover the truth. In the end, although they suspect nightclub owner Monsour del Rosario of being responsible for Sioson's death, they are unable to prove anything against him, or prove their suspicions that Filipino women are being drugged and forced into prostitution. Despite the fact that Sioson's body was covered with bruises, gashes, cigarette burns and grievous injuries that include a cracked skull and genital mutilation, the Japanese government maintains that she died of hepatitis, and the Philippine government placidly accepts the explanation.

Probably the most respected filmmaker to dabble in the genre was Laurice Guillen. She had begun her career as an actress in the early 1970s, having worked under some of the best. In the late–1960s she was studying at Ateneo de Manila where she became acquainted with Rolando Tinio, a theatrical director and advocate of dramatic naturalism, certainly a departure from the norm in Filipino film and theater. She went on to work under some of the best directors in Philippine cinema, including Lino Brocka, Mike de Leon and Marilou Diaz-Abaya. Her own directorial career had begun in 1980, her initial efforts being met with some skepticism and middling enthusiasm, but her 1981 film *Salome* proved something of a breakthrough; the story of three people giving alternate versions of the same murder, it was obviously inspired by Akira Kurosawa's *Rashomon* (1950), and enjoyed both commercial and critical success. While her films have often received critical praise, she never did quite make her way to the frontlines of Filipino filmmakers, but remains highly-respected in the industry.

In 1994 Guillen directed *Elsa Castillo Story ... Ang Katotohanan* (*Elsa Castillo Story ... The Truth*), which starred "massacre queen" Kris Aquino as the title character, who had been dubbed "the Chop-Chop Lady" by the press due to the circumstances of her demise. In the film, Aquino marries Eric Quizon, but quickly becomes dissatisfied with the marriage, and she begins spending a lot of time with her boss (Miguel Rodriguez) after receiving a promotion at work. Their relationship soon progresses to romance, and Aquino leaves Quizon to move in with Rodriguez, but upon learning that Rodriguez is also married, and that his wife is merely away tending to her ailing father, Aquino becomes disenchanted with her new relationship as well. When she tries to leave Rodriguez, however, he becomes enraged and brutally murders her, cuts her body in pieces, and then enlists the aid of his driver (Johnny Delgado) in placing the pieces of the corpse in plastic garbage bags and discarding them in a field of weeds along a desolate stretch of road. But the horrified Delgado turns Rodriguez in and shows the police where the body parts were discarded.

The Elsa Castillo Story (1994/Octoarts Films) was directed by Laurice Guillen. It is an example of how even esteemed filmmakers were drawn into the popular true crime genre.

Given the grisly nature of the crime, the film would have had to go to great lengths to avoid being gruesome, but nonetheless, Guillen did not go overboard in depicting the morbid details of the crime (though body parts are glimpsed, in particular the head as Delgado picks it up and places it in a garbage bag). Otherwise, the bulk of the running time leading up to the crime—undeniably the showpiece—played much like any other love triangle melodrama. Less reluctant to show the gory details of the crime was *The Elsa Santos Castillo Story: The Chop Chop Lady*, released that same year.

The true crime genre was lucrative for a time in the early 1990s, but soon ran out of steam; perhaps Filipino murderers could not keep pace with the need for gruesome killings. Whatever the reason, the public lost its fascination with the genre. But true stories have always been of great interest within the culture, and one that really struck a chord with audiences was the story of Flor Contemplacion. Employed as a domestic worker in Singapore, Contemplacion was arrested for the murder of a fellow Filipina domestic, 34-year-old Delia Maga, and her ward, a 4-year-old boy, on May 4, 1991. Maga had been strangled while the boy had been drowned. Contemplacion had come to the attention of Singaporean officials by way of entries in Maga's diary, and after being arrested she confessed to the murders. Contemplacion (38 years old at the time of the murders) was a wife and mother of four who had been working in Singapore since 1988 in order to send money back home to her family. In her confession, Contemplacion had told authorities that she had visited Maga that day in order to ask her to take some items back to the Philippines with her, but when Maga refused, saying that the package was too heavy, Contemplacion snapped. The Singaporean authorities had maintained that Contemplacion's work schedule (18 hour days, beginning at 6:00 A.M. and ending at midnight) had caused her a great deal of mental strain, and that when Maga had refused to take her package back to the Philippines, she became enraged and attacked Maga. Perhaps, but that doesn't explain the drowning of the child.

In the Philippines, very few were buying the story, and word was quickly being circulated that Contemplacion had been stripped naked and tortured into confessing, something that is certainly within the realm of possibility, but not provable without one of the Singaporean interrogators coming forward. Still, Contemplacion's case—she received the death penalty— became something of a national cause, and as her date of execution drew near in 1995, even Philippine President Fidel Ramos felt moved (under considerable political pressure in an election year) to implore the Singaporean government to stop the execution and further investigate the case. Just prior to the date of execution, a Filipina accused of prostitution who had briefly shared a prison cell with Contemplacion came forward to tell a different story, in which the father of the drowned boy had come home to find his child drowned in the bathtub—the result of an epileptic seizure, as the story went—and in a fit of rage strangled Maga and framed Contemplacion. As the story went, Contemplacion had been visiting Maga when the two women discovered that the child had drowned in the bathtub. Maga phoned the child's father, who then rushed home, but in the story, Contemplacion was no longer at the residence when the father arrived. Therefore, how could she know that it was the father who had strangled Maga?

In the Philippines protests were being held, which could do little to sway the Singaporean government, but were more to prompt the Philippine government to somehow try and intervene. Desperate to do anything to stop the execution, witnesses, including a doctor, came forward to say that Contemplacion had since childhood suffered from periodic bouts of insanity, and one even claimed that she was possessed by the devil, all of which was denied by Contemplacion's mother. People in the Philippines seemed desperate to not only stop the execution, but in some way understand the crime in order to come to terms with it. In the end, nothing could be done, and Contemplacion was hanged on March 17, 1995. The execution itself was carried out under greater-than-usual security, as Singapore officials were concerned about the possibility of violent protests by the country's estimated 60,000–75,000 Filipino workers.

Contemplacion's execution caused a furor in the Philippines, but the reasons behind the anger are probably more complex than simply being a matter of a belief in Contemplacion's innocence: she had, after all, never recanted her confession, and had in fact made public statements to the effect that she was resigned to it and ready to die, while thanking the people of the Philippines for their support. Contemplacion became something of a symbol of the desperation of the Philippine underclass, driven to leaving their families and traveling to foreign lands just to earn money to send back home. Her execution did rather put a strain on relations between the Philippines and Singapore, President Ramos recalling the Philippines' Singapore ambassador, and otherwise cancelled various other pending exchanges with the country. When Contemplacion's body was flown home to the Philippines, Ramos' wife was there at the airport to receive it, and thousands of mourners lined the streets.

Contemplacion's case revealed certain contradictory traits in the culture, on the one hand inspiring emotional protests against Singapore's legal system and its use of the death penalty, at a time when, as a result of the Vizconde massacre, many in the Philippines were also calling for the country's return to the death penalty, an equally emotional reaction to the Vizconde tragedy.

With Contemplacion's execution being such a hot button subject, work was immediately undertaken to bring the story to the movie screen. Viva films hired director Joel Lamangan to film *The Flor Contemplacion Story*, which starred superstar Nora Aunor (ironically, said to be Contemplacion's favorite actress) in the lead. Helping the public to both vent their frustrations and, by virtue of its take on events, to feel vindicated in their righteous indignation, the film was a great box office success. Less successful, though more articulate in its presentation, was director Tikoy Aguiluz's *Bagong Bayani* (*Modern Hero*), which starred Helen Gamboa as Contemplacion. While Lamangan's film basically seemed to stake itself on Aunor and was basically a showcase for her abilities as a thespian, and a chance for her to reap more acclaim unto herself by-way-of yet another powerful dramatic performance, Aguiluz's film was not personality-driven, and was a far more understated telling of the story, though it too seemed to take Contemplacion's innocence for granted (the title alone would suggest that). Aguiluz seemed to desire to draw attention to the conditions of Filipino OCWs (overseas contract workers), showing Contemplacion's cramped quarters in the home where she worked, a tiny room with a cot to sleep on, one folding chair, and a television set, which for reasons of space must sit atop the chair, rather giving the impression that Contemplacion was already inhabiting

Director Joel Lamangan. He touched a national nerve with *The Flor Contemplacion Story* in 1995, the true account of a Filipina maid hanged for murder in Singapore.

a kind of prison cell before her arrest. Adopting an approach similar in some respects to that of Carlo Caparas—though certainly more articulate and without the vulgarity of Caparas' sensationalism—*Bagong Bayani* interspersed real interviews within its narrative, and Aguiluz felt moved to include real footage of the outside of the prison in which Contemplacion was held, something that he could only accomplish covertly, dressing in a turban and filming the prison with a hidden camera as he passed by. Aguiluz sought to avoid the traditional trappings of Philippine melodrama, and consequently his film was far less showy than Lamangan's, earning praise from some by virtue of its measured performances (not only Gamboa's portrayal of Contemplacion, but also Chanda Romero's performance as Delia Maga) and somewhat pensive presentation. It stood as quite a contrast to Lamangan's film, which opted for hysterics and grand melodrama in the more traditional style of Filipino film.

Bagong Bayani may have gathered more critical praise, but it was not the enormous box office attraction that *The Flor Contemplacion Story* turned out to be, partly due to its lack of a superstar lead like Aunor, but mostly due to its trouble in finding a venue. The small independent production was shunned by distributors and exhibitors alike, which some attributed to pressure from Viva Films, by then one of the industry giants, which did not want to see any competition for what was predicted to be one of its main moneymakers that year. *Flor Contemplacion* may have won out in box office returns, but there were those who were unable to choose between the two versions, as the Gawad Urian, for instance, gave the Best Actress trophy that year to both Aunor and Gamboa for their respective portrayals. It was, however, *Bagong Bayani*'s only recognition, whereas Viva's film went on to win a slew of awards, including Lamangan winning the Golden Pyramid award at the 1995 Cairo International Film Festival, as well as the film being very well represented in all of the various local awards ceremonies.

Of course Carlo Caparas couldn't help but to weigh in with his own version of the Contemplacion story, but as he had a tendency to focus his attention on the victims in his films, he chose to make Delia Maga the main character. *Victim No. 1: Delia Maga (Jesus, Pray for Us!)*, also released in 1995, was easily the weakest of Caparas' true crime films, and far and away the weakest of the trio of films to deal with the case. As was his wont, Caparas included real footage of the bereaved family, in this case Maga's husband as he watched the exhumation of his wife's body several years after her murder, which was an attempt to discern if her injuries were too great to have been caused by another woman. But the findings were that, although the corpse was obviously in an advanced state of decay, examination of the bones revealed that Maga's injuries could have been caused by someone of lesser strength, therefore making it entirely possible that Contemplacion's confession was, in fact, true. Caparas could also not resist showing gruesome crime scene photos of Maga's corpse lying on the bathroom floor.

Although his work in the genre was frequently tasteless, it was also often capable of conjuring strong emotions; not so with *Delia Maga*, which proved surprisingly monotonous. Often seeming like no more than marathon weeping (when Maga leaves for Singapore, when she comes home for a visit, when she leaves again, when she is killed, weeping at the funeral, weeping, weeping, weeping), the film revealed Caparas at his sloppiest and most excessive, letting scene after scene run on and on to no good end. Even his strong cast (Gina Alajar, Joel Torre, Elizabeth Oropesa, and even director Celso Ad. Castillo) could do nothing to liven the presentation. Ultimately, the film revealed that Caparas may have gone to the well once too often, but then, how could he resist trying to capitalize on such a famous tragedy?

Having scored a hit in telling Contemplacion's story, Lamangan may have taken a page out of Caparas' book, and he decided to follow it up with a similar story. *The Sarah Balabagan Story* (1997) was a true account of a teenaged Filipina maid in the United Arab Emirates who was given the death penalty in 1995 for stabbing her employer to death after he raped her. Originally, in an odd quirk of justice, Balabagan had been awarded $27,000 in damages for the rape, but had been ordered to pay her employer's family $40,000 in damages (referred to as blood money), and she had been given a seven-year prison sentence for manslaughter. With the case so close on the heels of Contemplacion's execution, the Philippine government sought a retrial, which was granted—unfortunately, it seemed. In the retrial, Balabagan's claim to have been raped was disputed and she then received the death penalty. The outrage reached well beyond the Philippines, and international human rights organizations became involved. She was quickly given yet another trial, the result of which was the overturning of the death sentence: she was then given one year in prison and 100 lashes with a cane. Although she had by then spent 15 months in jail, that was not counted toward her sentence, and her year in prison was to begin upon completion of the trial. It wasn't the absolution that had been hoped for, but Balabagan and her family were happy that she had avoided a death sentence.

In 1996 Balabagan returned to the Philippines to a heroine's welcome, and Lamangan even asked her to portray herself in his upcoming film of her life. But Balabagan declined: a Muslim from Mindanao, she said that it was against Islamic beliefs for women to appear in films. This did not stop her from embarking on a singing career in 1999, however, when she signed with Sony Music Philippines, nor from making television appearances.

Lamangan's film was a cause of some concern for the Philippine government: President Fidel Ramos personally asked the MTRCB in a letter in March of 1997 to "Take all necessary action to defer public showing of said movie due to anticipated extremely negative impact on Philippine–U.A.E. relations and risk of failure in negotiations to save John Aquino."[8] Aquino was another Filipino national who had been given the death penalty in the U.A.E. after being convicted of killing an Indian in 1990. The Philippine government was also concerned about repercussions against the estimated 80,000 Filipinos in the U.A.E. should the film be released.

The MTRCB complied with President Ramos' wishes and postponed the release of the film; it was not the first postponement that Viva Films, the film's production company, had encountered. In February 1997, Viva Films had complied with a request from the Department of Foreign Affairs to delay release of the film after the U.A.E. government had voiced displeasure over the release of the film. Even so, Viva had only agreed to withhold its release for several weeks, but again ran into problems when the Muslim Screenwriters' Club began to complain that the film would send a negative image of the Islamic faith, its culture and traditions. It was all enough to give Lamangan fits, as he told the *Philippine Free Press* "I am very secure in the way ... I portrayed the Middle East, in the way I portrayed Islam. It is unfortunate that our Muslim brothers are fighting a movie they have not seen."[9] Eventually, the film was released, but despite the public's affection for Balabagan, it did not meet with the same success as *The Flor Contemplacion Story*.

The enormous success of *The Flor Contemplacion Story* seemed to give hope to many in the industry that the flagging local film business would be turning around, but the hope was not based on particularly sound reasoning, as the film was merely capitalizing on a subject that had great, though perhaps only momentary, emotional pull with the masses. Perhaps what made the film so encouraging from the perspective of filmmakers was that once again someone had made a film that seemed important, was using the medium for something more meaningful than simple entertainment. After the ouster of Marcos and the end of martial law, the film industry had retreated to its previous terrain of cloying romance sagas, action genre fisticuffs and insipid, unsophisticated comedies. But *Flor Contemplacion* and *Bagong Bayani* were films that mattered, films that had a purpose—not unlike the works of Brocka and Bernal, both by then deceased, during the Second Golden Era. It had revived the hope in some that, not only would the Filipino film industry regain its relevance, but that it might even become viable as an export, as *Flor Contemplacion* had received some attention in international film festivals. But if the industry was truly going to reverse its waning fortunes, it could hardly hope to do so by virtue of one film centered on a fleeting issue. As the 1990s wore on, what seemed more and more to be keeping the industry afloat was its increasing reliance on bold films, the most recent variant on the bombas, and the new generation of sex stars that were emerging.

From the mid–1970s through the 1980s, the Filipino film industry had remained fairly strong and very active, and the Philippines remained one of very few countries with a national film industry that had continued to thrive against the Hollywood juggernaut and its stream of blockbuster imports. But moving into the 1990s, the industry increasingly showed signs of slipping, and would eventually fall into a slump that would come to be considered critical as Hollywood product consistently outdrew Filipino films at the box office. With the Hong Kong film industry disintegrating in the 1990s, many personnel from that industry sought work elsewhere, and while such luminaries as Jackie Chan, Sammo Hung and John Woo made their way to the U.S. and found success in Hollywood, others, like Philip Ko, preferred the shorter trip to the Philippines and began working in the very crowded Filipino action genre. But no sooner did they arrive than the Filipino industry's troubles began to truly sink in. Critics complained of a lack of creativity in Filipino films, citing both a proliferation of rip-offs of Hollywood films and the generally clichéd nature of Filipino films. Some even took to blaming the slump on Chinese producers who, frankly, did overload the already crowded action genre with a plethora of repetitive films. Films like *Flor Contemplacion Story* could offer no more than a brief reprieve, and the optimism that sprang from its success proved short-lived as the industry continued to spiral downward, and stars whose names once guaranteed box office returns began appearing in films that tanked at the tills. Such high profile flops only served to heighten anxiety.

It was here that Filipino studios showed both ingenuity and resilience, many diversifying, forming production alliances and sharing production costs, while also cutting deals with the growing number of video and cable TV markets. Viva Films signed a lucrative deal with Paramount Pictures to handle distribution in the Philippines of blockbuster films like *Independence Day*.

Just as the collapse of the studio system in the 1960s had given rise to the bomba genre, it didn't take long for most of the money men to realize that sex sells, and softcore pornography emerged, not merely as one of the most lucrative propositions, but more pointedly, as the best means of survival. Seiko Films, who were quick to adopt the sex film formula when troubling economic indicators arose, was the only company to consistently turn a profit through the decade of the '90s.

The steamy sexual melodramas guaranteed a return to the producers, not only by virtue of their enticingly permissive presentation, but also because production costs could be kept low. With a minimum of cast, crew and sets, not much money was needed, and the dominance of more erotic films in the market created new stars. The subsistence of the Filipino film industry was seemingly at the possible expense of whatever integrity it was holding on to.

Among the top stars to emerge during the new wave of bold films was Rita Magdalena. Although most of her work was in rather undistinguished softcore trash, Magdalena graduated to working for some acclaimed directors in more serious efforts. Celso Ad. Castillo, for instance, began using her, as he had used bold stars in the 1980s, casting Magdalena in his 1997 film *Mananayaw*, and again in 1998 for *Droga: Pagtatapat ng Isang Babaing Addict*. But although she was not completely without talent as an actress, Magdalena's continued popularity hinged on her willingness to disrobe on camera.

More successful in the bold genre was Rosanna Roces, whose films were better by-and-large, and who also went on to act as producer on some of her films. In 1997 she appeared as the title character in Carlos Siguion-Reyna's *Ligaya ang Itawag Mo sa Akin* (*You Call Me Joy*), which, beyond all the trimmings, was the standard tale of a prostitute trying to go straight, casting Roces as the Ligaya of the title, a hooker who marries a farmer with the hope of escaping her unfortunate lot, only to find herself victimized all over again in her new surroundings. The film became quite a sensation when it was initially banned by the MTRCB, a decision which was reversed when the film's producers took the matter to the Presidential Appeals Board. In the interim, all of the publicity helped the film considerably, and when it was finally granted a showing permit it was met by a most eager public. It also went on to play the 1997 Toronto Film Festival.

Roces teamed up with Siguion-Reyna again on another somewhat controversial feature, *Ang Lalake sa Buhay ni Selya* (*The Man in Selya's Life*), wherein she marries the only man she can find who is interested in her for something other than

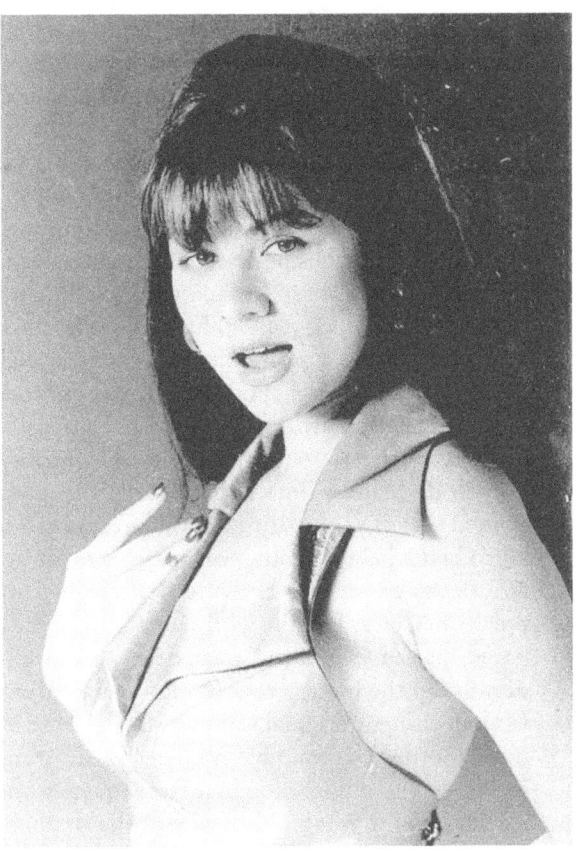

Bold genre star Rosanna Roces. She used her talent to work her way into more mainstream film roles.

sex—unfortunately that man is a homosexual. But unlike some of the characters that she portrayed in films, who were trying to find a way to survive beyond the marketability of their physique, Roces was relying on hers to make her career. She kept secret the fact that she was not only married, but was also a mother, two things that would probably hold her back as a star in the bold genre; calculated, certainly, but with the aim of obtaining security for herself and her family. More than the help that Magdalena's career seemed to get from her brief collaborations with Castillo, Roces was aided by working with directors like Siguion-Reyna, Mel Chionglo, Romy Suzara and Chito S. Rono on a series of impressive features, but like Magdalena, her career seemed to flag once the film industry sank deeper and deeper into malaise, and she wound up as hostess of the television program *Star Talk*.

But there was hope on the horizon for the future, coming from the emergence of new filmmakers, and even some who had been around for some time, but were only then coming into their own and moving to the forefront with the deaths of top directors like Brocka and Bernal. There was also the impending Philippine Centennial celebration coming up, and it promised some impressive works to commemorate the occasion.

One of the more curious aspects to emerge in Philippine cinema was the increasingly pervasive use of the English language. Although Philippine cinema's introduction to sound,

1933's *Ang Aswang*, had been shot in a combination of English and Spanish, with President Manuel Quezon's 1937 declaration that Tagalog be made the basis for the national dialect, Tagalog quickly became the norm in the film industry (except in the Visayas), and films from then on were almost entirely in Tagalog. Although Filipino filmmakers occasionally shot dual versions of films (in Tagalog and English), this was most often with an eye toward some degree of international distribution. But for the home crowd, Tagalog was the norm from the 1940s through the 1970s. But in the metropolitan areas, the heavy reliance on English as the primary language of business seemed to keep the English language very much in use. This was the case for years, so it's not certain how this would have come to increase its usage in film, but somewhere along the way, English use reached the point where it often became interchangeable with Tagalog, a phenomenon known as Taglish.

The late playwright and screenwriter Rolando Tinio had claimed credit, with some regret, for having personally instigated the use of Taglish in the arts. A somewhat unpopular figure within the arts community, Tinio got his start in theater, staging classical Greek plays, first at Ateneo de Manila University. He went on to help establish Teatro Pilipino, for which he worked tirelessly translating many literary classics, including Shaw and Shakespeare, into Tagalog to better help his countrymen aspire to greater literary works. Derided by some in the theatrical community for not directing original works by Filipino playwrights, Tinio bluntly proclaimed most Filipino works unworthy of the effort required to stage a production. He preferred instead to produce great works of world literature, hoping to light the fire of inspiration under the literary community, and he denounced in no uncertain terms the prevalent wisdom that any original work was laudable merely due to its ethnicity. However, Tinio's own translations were somewhat hindered by his own lack of familiarity with Tagalog, and he consequently found himself unable to adequately find a way to express certain passages in the vernacular. Not wanting to lose any of the dramatic force or artistic intentions of the original source, he chose to simply leave certain passages in English, the result being a constant flip-flopping between languages. It is this decision, Tinio maintained, that spawned the use of Taglish, and he would spend the latter years of his life disparaging the move.

Whether or not this can be accepted as the true genesis of Taglish is certainly debatable. The widespread use of both Tagalog and English in common areas would seem to make such a phenomenon almost inevitable, and one can certainly trace the roots of English incorporation into the Tagalog dialect back further, though admittedly to a lesser degree. But as to its increasing use in films, perhaps Tinio has a point. In any event, whatever the reason, Taglish began to increase in Filipino films during the 1980s and '90s. Entering the 21st century, however, there seemed to be something of a backlash against it as more filmmakers seemed to make it a point to curtail English use and stick with Tagalog.

9

1998–2005

Although the U.S. did not grant the Philippines sovereignty until after the war in 1946, Filipinos themselves considered 1898, the year that the U.S. took control of the Philippine Islands from the Spanish, to be the year of their independence. Thus, the nation was set to celebrate the centennial of its independence in 1998. The centennial of Rizal's execution by the Spanish was 1896, and as Rizal was widely regarded as the father of the Philippine nationalist movement, that was also a very significant year for the country. With two very significant dates so close together, it was natural that the film industry should seek to commemorate the events with appropriate film offerings.

Amable "Tikoy" Aguiluz seemed to get the ball rolling in 1997 with his own version of the life of Rizal. A graduate of the University of the Philippines, Aguiluz had also studied at New York University on a John D. Rockefeller III Grant and the British Film Institute on a British Council Grant. He had started his own filmmaking career with short documentaries, one of which, *Mount Banahaw, Holy Mountain*, was awarded the Silver Trophy at Iran's Young Filmmakers of Asia Festival. He was co-founder of the University of the Philippines' Film Center, serving as its Assistant Director until 1990. Aguiluz entered feature filmmaking with a bang in 1984, the waning days of the Second Golden Era, with the film *Boatman*, an outwardly standard tale of the usual provincial hayseed who travels to Manila to seek his fortune. Portrayed by Ronnie Lazaro, the film's protagonist, Felipe, finds himself working as a "torero," a live sex performer (nice work if you can get it), and he winds up in a relationship with his female stage counterpart, torera Sarsi Emmanuelle, while also servicing wealthy older woman Suzanne Love, an American. The story may not have been terribly inventive, but it was sexy enough to get attention, and Aguiluz's presentation gritty enough to grab critics where they live. It also seemed to appeal to the industry's infatuation with "Manila noir," portraying the misguided and naïve people who flock to Manila to seek their pot of gold, only to find themselves drawn into its seamy underbelly. It was a hit at the 1985 London Film Festival, and played festivals throughout the world. It was also likely the inspiration for the efforts of other filmmakers in their similar meditations on the subject of sex performers, such as Chito Rono's 1985 film *Private Show*, and Jose Javier Reyes' much later work *Toro*. Even Brocka himself must have been impressed by it, as he offered a gay version of the Torero profession with *Macho Dancer* in 1988.

Aguiluz's tribute to the nation's greatest hero was *Rizal sa Dapitan* (*Rizal in Dapitan*), which chronicled the four years that Rizal spent in exile just prior to his execution. With Albert Martinez in the lead, the film opened with his arrival in Dapitan, to which he had been banished by the Spanish authorities for his involvement in the *Liga Filipina*, a Filipino think tank which promoted reforms in the colonial system, and went on to show how Rizal occupied his time, setting up a school for the children in the region and opening a medical clinic. He soon becomes renowned as an oculist, and is visited by a blind American (Paul Holmes), who had once been a neighbor of Rizal's when he was residing in Hong Kong. He takes a liking to Holmes' adopted daughter Josephine Bracken (Amanda Page) and proposes marriage, but the Church refuses to grant them a proper ceremony for purely political reasons; still determined to be together, Rizal and Bracken enter into a common-law marriage, which effectively ostracizes both of them from the Church, and makes Rizal something of a pariah. The marriage certainly has its problems, with Rizal accusing his wife of being a spy sent to watch him. His suspicious nature springs from Bracken's having visited the friars in an attempt to be granted a proper marriage. Rizal and Bracken also suffer the misfortune of a stillborn child.

The film ends on a somber note (given history, it could not have ended otherwise), with Rizal's departure for Cuba in 1896 to help combat an outbreak of Yellow Fever. As he leaves the island, a village band is portrayed as having played a funeral dirge. Aguiluz makes an attempt to document Rizal's quite varied interests and enterprises, with token depictions of his dabbling in sculpture, collecting insect specimens to send to European naturalists, teaching the locals better farming and fishing techniques, and so on. The film's principal strength was the beautiful cinematography of Nap Jamir and Romy Vitug, and it went on to become the hit of the Manila Film Festival that year. It was also entered in the 1998 Brussels International Film Festival, where it was awarded the Grand Jury Prize.

As beautiful-looking a work as *Rizal sa Dapitan* was, it had nothing on *Jose Rizal* (1998), Marilou Diaz-Abaya's epic film tribute to the national martyr. In all fairness to Aguiluz, he could not have hoped to compete with Diaz-Abaya's film in a straight-up historical recounting of Rizal's life, as Aguiluz was not given the budget that Diaz-Abaya enjoyed. Primarily financed by GMA Films, owner of one of the Philippines' major television networks, *Jose Rizal* was a sprawling, nearly 3-hour epic, costing an estimated 80 million pesos, or the equivalent of $2 million U.S. That made it far and away the highest budgeted Filipino film of all time, and it was generally believed that the film would be unable to recoup its production costs at the box office. It was indeed a huge undertaking.

The film opens with Rizal (Cesar Montano) in prison awaiting trial for involvement in an uprising against the Spanish. The film then relates Rizal's life through flashbacks as he reminisces in his cell, beginning with his childhood memories of his family and the injustices suffered by Filipinos at the hands of the Spanish, and more particularly the Catholic Church. Of special importance was the execution of priest Jose Burgos, considered a dissident by the Spanish clergy for advocating equality for Filipinos. Foreshadowing Rizal's own fate, Burgos was accused of complicity in an uprising in Cavite in 1872 and cruelly executed by garrote. Though Rizal was only eleven years old at the time, his older brother Paciano (Pen Medina) was a student in Manila, and was considered as being friendly with the dissident clergy. The young Rizal was greatly influenced by his older brother's anguish over the execution of Burgos. The film follows Rizal through early adulthood and his education, first in Manila, and later Madrid, where his sense of Spanish injustice grows as he notes the freedom allowed in Spain and questions why Filipinos are not granted the same rights in their own land. After writing and publishing his two novels in Europe, which expose the shame and iniquity of Spanish colonial rule, he is denounced by the Church for portraying the Spanish friars as cruel and libidinous, and upon his return to Manila, Rizal founds the Liga Filipina. For this he is banished to Dapitan on Mindanao, where he spends the next four years. While there, he is contacted by an emissary of revolutionary Andres Bonifacio about fleeing Dapitan and helping to organize an uprising on the mainland, but Rizal declines the request. Nonetheless, when the revolt fails, Rizal is arrested and accused of being its mastermind. Though he is given an eloquent defense by the Spanish officer (Jaime Fabregas) assigned to be his counsel, Rizal is found guilty and executed by firing squad.

Lavish in its production values and superbly directed by Diaz-Abaya, the film also contained an interesting performance by Joel Torre as Crisostomo Ibarra, the fictitious protagonist of Rizal's literary works. Appearing periodically throughout the film in black and white scenes portraying passages from Rizal's fiction, the character finally appears to Rizal in person in his prison cell on the eve of his execution and castigates the author for having him shot dead in the streets by Spanish guards at the conclusion of a novel, thus not allowing him to successfully complete his mission to overthrow the Spanish. The conventional wisdom has always been that the protagonist of Rizal's fiction was his own alter-ego, perhaps Rizal imagining himself as a revolutionary hero rather than the intellectual he was, limited to merely making vain attempts to rectify the Filipinos' lot through more pragmatic methods. This view has more recently fallen with disfavor among revisionists who seek to break with convention, but the truth is that, given the parallels that Rizal's background shares with his fictitious counterpart, the conventional wisdom still stands as a reasonable and most likely accurate assessment. In that context, it is interesting to see Rizal basically berated as a coward by his own conscience in Diaz-Abaya's film.

GMA's gamble paid off: while there were those who predicted that the film could not possibly recoup its investment owing to the state of the Philippine industry at the time, the lack of commercial viability of Filipino films abroad, and the generally poor performance of historical films, not to mention the familiarity of the story—including its less-than-happy ending—to virtually all Filipinos, the film went on to surpass everyone's expectations. Released on Christmas Day 1998 during the Metro Manila Film Festival—a prudent decision, since by presidential decree only Filipino films may be screened in the nation's capital during the 10-day festival, held during the very important holiday season—*Jose Rizal* proved to be the festival's top draw, and dominated the awards, taking 16 of the festival's 17 awards. But its success was not limited to the festival season, as it went on to pack movie theaters in the Philippines, making millions of pesos in the first few weeks of its release. It even did good business outside the Philippines: in a single week alone, playing just one theater in Tokyo, the film made an estimated $1.5 million during a ten-week run, more than half its original budget. The film's theme seemed to appeal to the sense of Asian nationalism that the Japanese had sought to promote during its brief rule of the Philippines during the war.

The film went on to play festivals throughout the world and won 11 FAMAS awards (Best Picture, Best Director, Best Actor for Montano, Best Supporting Actor for Fabregas, Best Cinematography for Rody Lacap, Best Editing for Jess Navarro and Manet Dayrit, Best Musical Direction and Best Theme Song for Nonong Buencamino, Best Production Design for Leo Abaya, Best Special Effects for Rolando Santo Domingo, and finally Best Screenplay for Ricardo Lee, Jun Lana and Peter Ong Lim), as well as 6 awards from the Gawad Urian and 8 from the Star Awards, held by the Philippine Movie Press Club. Strangely, the film was snubbed by the FAP, and although it was reaping more than its fair share of awards and acclaim, it also had its detractors. There were those who felt that Diaz-Abaya's film took too much of the historical account for granted, in particular the question of whether or not Rizal truly did sign a statement retracting his previous views that had been deemed both anti-clerical as well as anti-colonial in its message, and were expressed through his literary works. Had Rizal renounced his previously stated views—those which got him into trouble in the first place—one could make a reasonable case for his being no genuine hero at all; a reasonable case, perhaps, but by no means definitive. After all, who can say what any of us would do when facing death?

Whatever take one had on the film, Diaz-Abaya seemed gratified by the fact that it had gotten people talking once more, not only about its subject, but about the implications of colonialism in general.

But whatever complaints some may have had over questions of historical reckoning, they all paled in the light of the film's enormous success. It was enough to give renewed hope to the industry that Filipino films could compete at home again, and even make further inroads in the international market. Some were even speculating on whether or not it was signaling the beginning of a new Golden Era in Philippine cinema. Financially, only time could tell, but artistically, there were indeed some impressive works being done. Although for a new Golden Era to be initiated, one would expect a new generation of filmmakers to serve as its impetus, it seemed that the old cannons were still firing the loudest, and the best works were coming from some of the workhorses of the Second Golden Era. While Diaz-Abaya and Aguiluz may have offered up eloquent and visually stirring takes on Rizal, there were more interesting meditations on the national hero coming from two of the greatest contributors to the Second Golden Era's list of classics.

Brocka protégé Mario O'Hara wrote and directed *Sisa* (1998), not a remake of Gerry de Leon's 1951 film, but rather a bizarre and surrealistic delving into Rizal's state of mind in the final days leading up to his execution. The film speculated on the reality of Sisa, one of the characters from Rizal's fiction, and envisioned her as a person from Rizal's past, a lost love in the fashion of Edgar Allan Poe's Lenore. In O'Hara's film, Rizal (played by Gardo Versoza, who had portrayed revolutionary Andres Bonifacio's emissary in Diaz-Abaya's film) is haunted while in his cell by taunting phantasms, but is also periodically comforted by Sisa's occasional appearances to calm him as he awaits execution. O'Hara chose to break from the claustrophobic environment of Rizal's prison cell with periodic flashbacks which, as in Diaz-Abaya's film, reflected on Rizal's youth, including meeting Sisa, a beautiful girl who liked to entertain people with her singing (though she was apparently tone deaf), and Rizal's fighting with another young man over Sisa's affections. The film also portrayed abuses Rizal both witnessed and personally felt as a youth under Spanish rule. On the lighter side, he is also visited in his cell by the apparition of a portly magician (Master Dem), whom he apprenticed under as a young man.

O'Hara set his film apart from the rest by being less interested in documenting history, and more in speculating about its hero, his possible state of mind in his final hours, and the mysteries surrounding his life. There was also the film's surrealism, often incorporating a narrative flow akin to that of a fever dream, which eventually begins to meld with reality to the point that it becomes increasingly difficult to differentiate between reality and fantasy. This would seem to be an attempt to explore Rizal's troubled psyche while awaiting the inevitable end, though again, this is speculative.

Less delirious and manic than O'Hara's offering in the Rizal mania derby was Mike de Leon's *Bayaning Third World* (*Third World Hero*), which took an altogether different approach to exploring its subject. De Leon's approach was more cerebral than that of Aguiluz and Diaz-Abaya, giving more thoughtful meditation as to the accuracy of the historical record, and while its premise was certainly surreal, neither was it as outwardly bizarre as O'Hara's film. De Leon had, in fact, been the original director assigned to helm *Jose Rizal*, but he left the project shortly after shooting commenced, some say out of exasperation over production delays. But given his unique approach to the subject in his own subsequent film, one might reasonably speculate that de Leon found the film's straightforward take on history not to his own liking, and perhaps even a bit stifling. Rather than take history at face value, as Diaz-Abaya's film had done, de Leon's film forced its audience to question whether or not Rizal had in fact renounced his life's work prior to his execution, and wondered how it is that, if he did, he is then considered a national hero nonetheless.

De Leon funded the film himself, shooting in black and white—an aesthetic rather than financial consideration—and it would be somewhat late in arriving for the Philippine Centennial, making its debut in Manila in the year 2000 before a crowd of art house patrons. In *Bayaning Third World*, the premise is the impending centennial and the efforts of two filmmakers—a director and a screenwriter—to come up with an appropriate offering, toward which end they set off on a surreal journey to interview the people in Rizal's life (his lover Josephine Bracken, his mother and siblings, even the priest who claimed to have taken his confession and given him communion just hours before his execution) in an attempt to discover the real Rizal. But they find the truth elusive, as their subject's loved ones all give conflicting opinions, his mother and brother doubtful of his execution eve recantation, his lover declaring that she and Rizal had indeed been wed in a proper Catholic ceremony, his sisters noncommittal. They also interview Padre Balaguer, who claimed to have received Rizal's confession, a curious impressionistic moment wherein the film director interviews the priest in his office, a coffin-shaped room with neither windows nor even a door. All along, the two filmmakers debate the subject of Rizal's alleged retraction and its ramifications to his standing in history. Eventually they confront their subject in person, but are confounded by his elusive nature, and ultimately come away as bewildered by their subject as they were from the start.

De Leon did rather seem to be taking Diaz-Abaya's portrayal to task, as in her film Diaz-Abaya chose to end where official history declared the end, with Rizal tearfully confessing to Padre Balaguer and being marched to his execution while clutching his rosary beads, perhaps the most acceptable coda in such a predominantly Catholic culture.

The hope that the popularity of *Jose Rizal* might spur a new Golden Era was not altogether unrealistic. Although the industry was in sore shape—seemingly more than ever—*Rizal*'s financial success was certainly encouraging, although it came on a wave of nationalist sentiment. But there were other very interesting works being released in 1998.

There were, for instance, some interesting offerings by Chito Rono. Among the first crop of students to have trained at the University of the Philippines' Film Center, Rono had also studied at New York's Grey Film Atelier and had studied cinematography at the Centro Statale di Cinematografia e Film in Rome. His debut film, the sexual drama *Private Show* (1985), was chosen to be the Philippine entry at the 1986 Chicago International Film Festival, and he followed it with *Itanong Mo sa Buwan* (*Ask the Moon*) in 1987, which won him Best Director awards from both the Gawad Urian and the Star Awards. He tried his hand at various genres, like the brutal crime drama *Alyas Stella Magtanggol* (*Alias Stella Magtanggol*) in 1992, and like most Filipino filmmakers, he dabbled in high melodrama, as in the locally acclaimed, but thoroughly overwrought *Nasaan ang Puso* (*Where the Heart Is*) in 1997, which was awarded the Best Film prize at the 1997 Manila Film Festival, as well as winning FAMAS and FAP Best Actress awards for lead actress Maricel Soriano, and a FAP Best Supporting Actor award for Ronaldo Valdez.

In 1998 Rono made *Curacha: Ang Babaeng Walang Pahinga* (*Curacha: The Woman Without Rest*), a film set against the backdrop of the turbulent mid-1980s and the coup attempt that came early in Corazon Aquino's administration. Bold genre star Rosanna Roces starred as the title character, a prostitute who, in between servicing clients like military colonel Lito Legaspi during the day, works by night at Dick Israel's nightclub as a torera, having sex on stage before a paying audience. Roces is at the hospital one night to buy drugs from an orderly when she spots Jaclyn Jose, a friend and former torera who is recovering from a suicide attempt. Roces helps Jose make her way to a boat so that she can leave the mainland, and the following morning, after taking an overdose of drugs, Roces gives all of her money—a fair-sized wad of cash—to a young girl in the street, and then collapses after watching a group of people salute the Filipino flag and sing the national anthem. Roces lies dying in the street as the crowd, for the most part, wanders off.

Roces gave a good performance as the disillusioned Curacha, a young woman whose only hope seems to be in the continuing marketability of her remarkable physique, which she uses not merely to earn a living, but also to navigate her way through the city by night, trading sex with a checkpoint guard for the right to pass through, and convincing a cabbie on his way to a fare to take her instead by agreeing to bare her breasts.

One of the film's most interesting moments comes early on when Roces, having just finished an appointment with Legaspi, tries to assuage her guilt by going to church to pray, where she daydreams of the Virgin Mary appearing in a shaft of light and joyfully greeting the crowd gathering around her. But Roces' guilt wins out, and when she approaches the Blessed Virgin, Mary's serene countenance turns to a scowl and she slaps Roces.

Rono also used Roces to good advantage in *Babae sa Bintana* (*Woman in the Window*), an excellent film noir also released in 1998. Richard Gomez portrayed a young man who attempts suicide after his wife walks out on him. He is saved by the intervention of friends, and when he returns to his apartment to recuperate, he becomes intrigued by Roces, the new tenant in the apartment across the street. Watching her daily through the window, Gomez's interest turns to obsession as he observes her relationship with her abusive policeman boyfriend (John Estrada). Eventually Gomez and Roces meet and begin an affair, and Roces entrusts a handbag full of cash to Gomez. Though the cash is the ill-gotten gains of Estrada's ties to organized crime, Roces intends to use the money to leave the mainland and begin anew elsewhere, and she asks Gomez to accompany her. But Estrada discovers the affair and comes looking for the money.

It's a good thing for Roces that she began to work in more mainstream fare, as the specter of censorship was once more looming. The industry had been steadily declining in the years since 1995 after the Asian economic crisis had caused a serious devaluation in currency, making film production costs that much greater a burden. With the added burden of the Philippine government's 30% amusement tax, the returns that studios saw on their investment, up against production costs and taxation, were dwindling fast. The safest investment had been the bold genre, and what came to be known as the pito-pito, or "seven-seven," films that could be shot in seven days, with post-production taking just another seven days. The pito-pito formula dated back earlier, some say to the 1980s when Regal Films began to churn out formulaic quickies. Truth is, it was a chance for younger filmmakers to break into the business and earn their stripes, and some of the filmmakers who came to notice in the later 1990s cut their teeth in the pito-pito system, bringing some in the industry to see the pito-pitos as a means of salvation for the ailing industry. Some, but by no means all; Marilou Diaz-Abaya was among those who lamented the pito-pito system as just another sign of the industry's troubles. "The idea that the pito-pito is a source of promise for Philippine cinema is a myth," she said. "The pito-pito is hell, from checks postdated to six months after the film shoot, to the lack of decent wages for the film crew—100 to 150 pesos a day!* It's very exploitative. Sometimes the shoot goes on for 24 hours straight, with no sleep. People collapse from exhaustion. Far from keeping Philippine cinema afloat, the pito-pitos will make our industry sink to the very bottom. There is no redemption to be found in pito-pitos."[1]

The pito-pitos were said to have originated when the film industry felt the crunch after

---

* About equivalent to $3 a day.

the end of the Marcos regime, a curious turn of events that was likely the result of the country's coming to terms with the massive debt and horrible shape that Marcos left the economy in. There was also the demise of the ECP, which had funded some of the greatest Filipino films of the Second Golden Era. But, truthfully, the system must have dated back further; if Vilma Santos was making the equivalent of two films per month in the early 1970s, then the pito-pito system must already have been an industry staple.

Well, in the latter 1990s it was still around and thriving, giving voice to young directors like Lav Diaz and Jeffrey Jeturian. But if the bold genre was what was primarily keeping the industry afloat, how long could it do so, especially as the MTRCB now seemed to be focusing its attention yet again on erotic films? Rono's works had sometimes fallen in the bold category, and he felt obliged to offer his thoughts on the encroachment of censorship, giving a curiously tolerant opinion: "With freedom of expression being threatened," he said, "you just have to temper your work with a sense of responsibility. You should be responsible enough not to offend if there is no reason to be offensive. I only deliberately 'offend' for a special reason: if you want to unveil the truth and they don't want to accept it."[2]

The irony was that the film industry had every reason to be optimistic about more lax standards from the MTRCB: not only was famous movie icon Joseph Estrada now President of the Philippines, but the MTRCB was finally being chaired by one of their own, as actress/producer Armida Siguion-Reyna assumed the job of Chairperson on July 1, 1998. She was not the only film industry insider on the Board, as other actors and actresses were assigned to view and rate films. It wasn't new for there to be film industry personnel serving on the Board (Siguion-Reyna had previously been appointed to serve on the Board by President Marcos, and then was later the MTRCB's Officer-in-Charge during the Aquino administration), but now more than half of the Board was comprised of entertainment industry people. But although Estrada had reaped his fame and fortune from the film industry, he publicly took the industry to task for the wave of smut that he saw proliferating, and instructed the MTRCB in October of 1999 to be "more sensitive to public sensibilities,"[3] and he informed the Board that he expected them to be more vigilant in their efforts to stem the tide of pornography. Siguion-Reyna countered that under her chairpersonship, the MTRCB had already closed more theaters for violations than any other post-martial law board, something that didn't sit well with some in the film industry. Manuel Morato's Board had not closed down a single theater between June of 1986 and 1992*, while Henrietta Mendez's Board had closed 28 theaters between July of 1992 and 1995, and Jesus Sison's Board had closed 45 theaters between September of 1995 and June of 1998. Sigioun-Reyna's Board had already topped that number by closing down 52 theaters in just the time from July of '98 to October of '99. It should be noted that theater closings were not usually due to film distributors and theater owners trying to get around censorship by inserting scenes that had not been approved by the Board, but rather were usually a matter of theaters being caught allowing underage patrons in to see R-rated, or adults-only, films. But in his October '99 meeting with Siguion-Reyna, Estrada instructed her to not stop at merely closing theaters down and revoking showing permits, but to even pursue legal action against film producers and theater owners who distribute and exhibit films with any footage that had not been reviewed and passed by the Board. There was, however, a little problem of funding, which Siguion-Reyna claimed was inadequate to really accomplish the task at hand; after all, it wasn't just movie theaters that the MTRCB had

---

* *Siguion-Reyna had claimed the zero closing figure for Morato's board, but her co-board member, Jose F. Lacaba, claimed in the December 8, 1999, edition of* Forum, *the official publication of the University of the Philippines, that records were simply unavailable.*

to watch over, but television stations as well. "[I]t takes money to monitor everything," she said in July of 1999. "There are 900 cable operators throughout the Philippines, each one with the capability of operating 45 channels. There are about 400 provincial TV stations. There are five major networks in Metro Manila, exhibiting at an average of 15 hours a day. And then 800 theaters all over the Philippines. How can 41 members of the review board of (the) MTRCB and 65 employees on the board possibly monitor all of this?"[4] But Siguion-Reyna did not seem altogether comfortable in her role as MTRCB Chairperson, always having to walk a very thin line, pleasing to both her entertainment industry colleagues, and the politicians, religious and civic groups. She pointed out that, under Presidential Decree 1986, issued by President Marcos quite some years before, the MTRCB was meant to be a temporary entity which would segue into self-regulation by the industry. She seemed to see one of her board's principal purposes as being to lead the industry by the hand into more responsible practices that would mature it enough that it would be considered worthy of being entitled to police itself. But she allowed that such a lofty goal might not see fruition in her lifetime, and in the meantime she had President Estrada to placate. In order to put the industry on notice, Siguion-Reyna scheduled a November meeting with film producers, and otherwise informed Estrada that the Board would indeed be pursuing violators and filing criminal charges against both film producers and theater owners.

Siguion-Reyna was indeed between a rock and a hard place: even the film industry was divided into opposing camps, some supporting the MTRCB under Siguion-Reyna, seeing it as their best hope to transition into self-regulation, while others, interestingly enough, were calling for her resignation for allowing the proliferation of pornography. "Do they know what pornography is?" asked Siguion-Reyna, adding, "I can honestly say that in my last 20 years in the industry, I have never actually (seen) real pornography."[5] Obviously, pornography was in the eye of the beholder, and while Siguion-Reyna was most probably talking about hardcore pornography, many of her detractors were referring to what they felt was excessive nudity and perhaps simulated sex scenes. The film industry broke up into separate camps, one side planning a protest before the senate on November 8th against the MTRCB and its perceived passivity toward the film industry's descent into sex-dominated product, while the other side proposed staging a rally in support of Siguion-Reyna and the MTRCB.

The demonstrators against the MTRCB came out by the thousands (police officials estimated the number to be 5,000, while the demonstration's organizers predictably doubled that estimate), many calling in no uncertain terms for Siguion-Reyna's resignation, or better still, for Estrada to fire her. Aside from including prominent Catholic priests and protestant ministers, representatives from the National Council of Churches in the Philippines, and Islamic religious leaders, the demonstration was also attended by former MTRCB Chairman Manuel Morato, and prominent actresses like Carmi Martin, Alice Dixson, Maritoni Fernandez and Princess Punzalan. Martin, ironically enough, had come to prominence in the 1980s with somewhat risqué, though admittedly artistic, titles like Lino Brocka's *Hot Property* (1983), a film in which she portrayed a stripper—billed as "the cleanest woman in Manila," as her act consisted of stripping on stage and bathing herself while standing in a wash basin—and the Ishmael Bernal comedy *Working Girls* (1984). Such being the case, MTRCB board member Jose F. Lacaba was inclined to dismiss the actresses as "guilt-ridden starlets,"[6] which doesn't seem entirely fair, since the actresses were likely put off by the fact that the proliferation of erotic films meant that, in order to keep working, they would be required to disrobe more often than not anymore.

But while the actresses were appealing to their film business colleagues to avoid falling into the sex film trap, some of the more scathing and bizarre comments came from Morato, who accused Siguion-Reyna of publicly berating him, and said that her comments had made him so angry that "If not for the prayers of Brother Eddie Villanueva, I would have wanted to rape all of them at the MTRCB."[7] The comment met with approving cheers from the crowd, although it was a most curious statement coming as it did at an anti-porn rally. Not that Morato could not be an artistic spokesperson for the anti-porn movement when he wanted to be: in January 2000, the *Philippine Inquirer* published two editorials by Angela Stuart-Santiago, who berated Morato, among others in the anti-porn movement, for being draconian moralists who were woefully behind the times, while also repeating filmmaker Carlitos Siguion-Reyna's popular phrase in labeling them "moral terrorists." Stuart-Santiago trotted out the old standbys, hailing Denmark as a model of sexual liberation and harmony, accusing the "moral terrorists" of condescending toward the Filipino public by presuming to guard consenting adults against what they should not see, while she herself condescendingly allowed that Morato was himself perhaps ill-informed, or that maybe he was simply not one to pay heed to facts, allowing politics and religion to guide him instead. The paper printed Morato's rebuttal—a simple letter to the editor—wherein Morato effectively put Stuart-Santiago in short pants, trotting out a list of facts and studies—much having to do with Denmark—that Stuart-Santiago was either unimpressed by herself, or simply ignorant of.

The Eddie Villanueva of whom Morato spoke was the head of the Jesus Is Lord Movement, and his comments at the rally were just as provocative, though less bizarre, than Morato's. Villanueva led a ten minute prayer to rid the nation of what his followers termed the "board of demons," and he went on to label the exhibition of obscene movies a "heinous crime," and called it a conspiracy by film producers in cahoots with the MTRCB.

The rally was also attended by a number of senators, including Robert Jaworski, perhaps the most famous Filipino basketball star of all time. Jaworski gained legendary status in the PBA (Philippine Basketball Association), continuing to play after becoming a coach, and even into his 50s. He had also tried his hand at acting, starring in a number of films in the 1970s. Jaworski suggested that the Board should exercise its authority more often, but proposed slashing the Board's budget should it continue to allow the proliferation of smut, a peculiar suggestion that somewhat played into Siguion-Reyna's argument that the Board was too woefully under-funded to do its job properly. Senator Raul Roco was a bit more dour in his assessment, calling the MTRCB "hopeless," and suggesting that the consumers should assert themselves as they were the ultimate authority to which the MTRCB had to answer. He otherwise presented himself as an advocate for the abolition of the MTRCB.

It was certainly a fine line that Siguion-Reyna had to walk, trying to accommodate the film industry personnel upset by censorship on the one hand, and those upset by the lax attitude that they perceived within the MTRCB toward the sex films on the other. But as the pro-censorship camp was, for the moment, screaming the loudest, Siguion-Reyna felt obliged to point out her board's hard line on, of all things, film titles, noting that the board refused to allow titles that were obscene, or otherwise suggestive of sex acts or bodily functions. The film *Monay* (*Bun*) was given an X rating when initially screened by members of the Board, who found it contrary to Presidential Decree 1986's prohibition against films that merely appeal to prurient interests without any redeeming artistic merit. The film's producers quickly re-titled it *Masarap Habang Mainit* (*Good While It's Hot*), which really wasn't much of an improvement, and didn't seem to impress a different panel of board members who reviewed it three days later and still found it simply vulgar, once more giving it an X rating.

There were plenty more examples of the Siguion-Reyna board's hard stand on lewd titles and content. The film *69* (1999) was disapproved upon two screenings, and after being edited by the filmmakers and resubmitted under the title *Batch 69*, was still rejected. Eventually, the film had to be substantially re-shot and resubmitted as *Aliw, Masarap na Lason* (*Pleasure, Delicious Poison*) before it was given an R rating, clearing it for exhibition. There was also the film *Bayagra Brothers* (1999), a comedy with a title obviously referring to Viagra, but which was disapproved by the Board because the title was a double entendre that included the Tagalog word "bayag," which means "testicle." The film was able to receive approval by being re-tagged *Bayadra Brothers*. The film *Shame* (2000) was only able to get approval from the board after all of its sexual scenes were excised, which critics noted made the film entirely purposeless, as it had staked itself entirely on the physical attributes of star Ina Raymundo. The film *Senswal* (*Sensual*) met a similar fate that same year.

Far more controversial than the Board's disapproval of lewd sex films and cheaply sensationalistic comedies was the X rating it gave to Jose Javier Reyes' *Toro*, which actually received its X rating based on its title alone when Reyes admitted to the Board that the title was not a reference to a bull, but rather to the sex act and that it was a reference to toreros. The film was yet another meditation on slum dwellers drawn into a life of selling their bodies in the sex business just to make a living. The MTRCB had disapproved the film before even having seen it. That didn't stop the film's producers from submitting it for screening at the 2000 Berlin International Film Festival, for which it was accepted. The film went on to play a good many festivals throughout the world, always receiving acclaim to one degree or another, but was only able to get approval from the MTRCB after changing its title to *Live Show*: but the story was far from over. The controversy was only just beginning: fortunately for Siguion-Reyna, she would not be bothered with dealing with the whole affair as her term as MTRCB chairperson had ended before the real brouhaha commenced: more on that in a bit.

But Siguion-Reyna's departure from the MTRCB was a minor change in power compared to what was about to occur in the nation's political arena. Joseph Estrada was about to be drummed out of office. And how was it that Estrada came to be president in the first place? He did not run for the presidency on a lark; the truth is that his political career had been almost as long as his acting career, dating back to the late 1960s. Although he had begun his film career playing thugs and hooligans, by the later 1960s his screen persona was increasingly that of a working class hero, or defender of society's less fortunate, and this populist image was no doubt a great springboard for his political aspirations. At the height of his film stardom in 1968 Estrada decided to run for mayor of San Juan del Monte, a small suburb of Manila. Although his opponent, Dr. Braulio Sto. Domingo, was initially declared the winner, the election results were disputed; after all the dust had settled, Estrada was later declared the winner, and he took office in 1969. Perhaps his municipality being small, the job of mayor was not terribly taxing for Estrada, and he continued his film career as both an actor and producer, without slowing his pace a bit. Likewise, his show business career does not seem to have stood in the way of his mayoral duties, and he was noted for turning his town into a model community. By 1972 he was receiving accolades for his performance as mayor, being named Most Outstanding Metro Manila Mayor, as well as making the list of the Ten Outstanding Young Men in Public Administration. Throughout the 1970s, Estrada's film career and political career both thrived, but his political career was derailed briefly with the end of the Marcos regime. When Corazon Aquino assumed the presidency, she felt the need to purge the government of anyone with close ties to the Marcos regime, under the pretext of suspected malfeasance, and so, after 16 years of service as San Juan Mayor, Estrada was removed from office and replaced by an appointed officer.

Estrada had indeed been a friend of Ferdinand Marcos, but that fact did not diminish his popularity among the people, however they may have felt about Marcos, and his unceremonious removal from office only seemed to heighten his political ambitions. He ran for the

Joseph Estrada as the title character in *Padre Pugante* (1970/FPJ Productions).

senate in 1987 and had no problem winning, and continued to set his sights higher still. He most likely already had his eye on the presidency at the time that he made his last film, *Sa Kuko ng Agila* (*In the Claw of the Eagle*) in 1989. The film was not only an opportunity to shore up Estrada's populist image, but also to put him on what was weighed to be the right side of one of the hot-button issues of the day, that being the continued U.S. military presence in the Philippines through the Clark and Subic bases. Marcos had always been a strong advocate of keeping the U.S. bases, for reasons of his own that probably had more to do with self-interest, as so much of his career did, but in setting himself up against the U.S. military bases, Estrada could not only distance himself from Marcos, but could also align himself with a growing movement with a decidedly nationalist flavor—he could play the super patriot.

The eagle of the title being the bald eagle, the symbol of the United States, the very title *Sa Kuko ng Agila* was a very obvious political statement in itself, and the film played like a very blatantly nationalistic piece of tripe, casting Estrada as a bus driver who finds a local girl lying in an alley. He takes her to a hospital, and upon receiving treatment, the girl reveals that she was raped by an American soldier (Nick Nicholson). The enraged Estrada then involves himself in seeking justice for the crime (are all Filipino bus drivers this civic?), but Nicholson is not charged, and it seems to Estrada that wealthy businessman Subas Herrero has pulled some strings within the system. Herrero likes the local economy created by the U.S. bases, which seems to be the status quo, something Estrada discovers when he tries to organize a demonstration against the bases only to find himself outdone by the large crowd who turn up in favor of keeping the bases. Targeted by Herrero and his expected assortment of goons, Estrada manages to survive various attempts on his life, but is dismayed when charges brought against Herrero don't stick. The film manages to end with Estrada triumphant, after a fashion, as a crowd gathers outside the courthouse to shout Herrero down and march behind Estrada.

Considering that Estrada was a crony of Ferdinand Marcos, and that Marcos not only considered his relationship with the U.S. to be a major asset, but saw America's continued habitation of the Clark and Subic bases as being vital to both Philippine security and economy, Estrada's starring in a film of this type wound up playing like a hypocritical act by a shameless political opportunist. It is also interesting to see Estrada portrayed as being bested by a corrupt political system wherein the wealthy are able to buy the results they seek; in fact it is wholly ironic. How fitting that Estrada's own presidency a decade later would be a complete disaster, filled with the type of cronyism that *Sa Kuko ng Agila* set him up in opposition to, and would be considered as having rivaled Marcos' administration for unbridled corruption. It is also ironic, given the premise of the film, that the provocative presence of Chinese Navy ships in the South China Sea in the late 1990s, along with China's claim of ownership of everything in the South China Sea, including some small Philippine islands, had then–President Estrada scrambling to negotiate a return of the U.S. Military to Clark and Subic (it didn't happen).

As for the film itself, aside from the bovine posturing, it strained credulity watching Estrada, middle-age spread and all, running around getting into one brawl after another, and never taking so much as a single punch—not even Fernando Poe, Jr., was that much of an egotist. But Estrada most probably imagined that it would help his image with the public to have him portrayed as an almost mythic force for justice; it probably also sprang from Estrada's own self-image as being untouchable, something that would manifest itself in full when he was driven from office and put on trial, still defiant and believing that no one could get to him.

Most probably Estrada already had his eye on the presidency when he made his final film, but for whatever reason, he put his presidential ambitions on hold and, in 1992, ran for vice president instead. Although his running mate, Eduardo Cojuangco, Jr., lost the election for the presidency, Estrada won the vice presidential election (in the Philippine system, presidential and vice presidential candidates are not listed together on a ballot, but are voted for separately), and so Estrada became Vice President to the nation's President-elect, Fidel Ramos. It's possible that Estrada had opted to run for vice president because he was unsure of his chances against Ramos in a presidential election, and if that were the case, his strategy paid off. Whatever the reason, he was now just one step away from his goal. As vice president, Estrada was appointed to head the Presidential Anti-Crime Commission, something that fit his tough guy screen image. That was all fine for marking time while awaiting his chance to run for the presidency, but when that time came in 1998, it was the other facet of his screen image that his campaign handlers chose to highlight—his image as defender of the proletariat. Those in charge of running Estrada's campaign were not fools, and they knew that the nation's considerable underclass was feeling very disaffected from their rulers, so they sought to play up Estrada's image as champion to the poor. There was precious little of substance in the campaign, merely slogans, but they seemed to go over well, and so, as with politics everywhere, if simple phrases would do the trick, then why bother with details? While his opponents were busying themselves trying to trumpet Estrada's reputation as a gambler, a drinker and a womanizer, and intellectuals were belittling him and perpetuating the image of him as a half-wit, Estrada was busy telling everyone that he would look after the little people. Well, it worked: he won a landslide victory come May 11—one of the largest victory margins in the nation's

Opposite: Sa Kuko ng Agila (*In the Claw of the Eagle*; 1989/Richfilm, Inc.) was Joseph Estrada's final film. The film stood in opposition to the U.S. military presence in the Philippines, which Estrada hoped would bolster his populist image and help his political career along.

history—in an election that was also noted for being relatively free of violence (only slightly more than 40 people were killed, a fairly low number for Filipino elections), and his inauguration at the Barasoain Church—the place where the first Philippine constitution was drafted a century earlier—was the highlight of the centennial. Ironically, aside from his pledge to focus on helping the Filipino underclass, Estrada also vowed to try and end corruption among government officials. Such lofty goals.

Despite his overwhelming victory in the elections, Estrada started his presidency on the wrong foot by giving permission for Ferdinand Marcos to be buried in the Libingan ng mga Bayani (the cemetery for heroes). As more than a decade had passed since Marcos had fled the country and subsequently died, perhaps Estrada felt that few would take the bother to object, but if that was his reasoning, he missed his guess. He also somewhat tipped his hand as a Marcos crony, something that, while hardly a secret, was a portent of things to come. Estrada's presidency would be short and not-so-sweet. Although his approval rating was consistently high early in his administration, often topping 80%, before long his numbers began dropping, dipping down to 44% according to a September 1999 poll. The reasons for his declining popularity were varied: there seemed to be little progress on his war on poverty, although that is something that would not necessarily hurt his poll numbers since much of the polling would have been done via telephone, and very few shantytown squatters would have been involved in such polls.

Estrada was also believed to have been behind an advertising boycott of the *Philippine Daily Inquirer*, the most widely read paper in the country, and perhaps the most critical of the administration. In 1999 government organizations withdrew advertising from the *Inquirer*, as did some film production companies and various other businesses known to be Estrada-friendly. Estrada drew heavy criticism as many firmly believed that he had orchestrated the boycott. Even international free-speech groups took note of what was believed to be an attempt to control the voice of the media.

Perhaps most damaging to his popularity was his support of a constitutional amendment that would permit foreigners complete and total ownership of land that had been zoned for industrial and commercial purposes. Because the nation was not only small, but also had spent so much of its history as a possession of foreigners, the idea of allowing non–Filipinos complete ownership of Philippine land was prohibited, the fear seemingly being that the nation could eventually fall into the control of outsiders again by way of controlling economic interests. Foreign ownership of land had been limited to 40% and many seemed dead set against changing that, but economic realities being what they were, the proposal to allow complete foreign ownership of land in industrial zones made perfect economic sense; still, it was an affront to the fragile nationalist ego, and Estrada's support of the idea did not sit well with the image many had of him as a super-patriot, rather than an economic realist. Although all of these factors effected his popularity in the polls, they were trifles compared to what was to come.

In October 2000, less than halfway into his 6-year term, Estrada was accused of corruption when Ilocos Sur governor Luis "Chavit" Singson admitted to giving Estrada 400 million pesos (about $8 million) in payoffs from an illegal gambling operation, as well as 180 million pesos (close to $4 million) in tobacco excise taxes. Known to be a gambling racketeer, Singson's testimony confirmed what many had already suspected about Estrada; the shady characters that he associated with, and indeed, that his own aides admitted he spent late nights drinking with, had given Estrada's administration something of a Mafioso air about it. There were also Estrada's alleged mistresses, by most accounts numbered at six, who were living well in rather fancy digs, and the question of where that money was coming from. One such mistress, former actress Laarni Enriquez, was residing in a mansion worth close to $2 million.

Singson's revelations stoked the fires and helped Estrada's opponents gather the ammunition that they needed to proceed to remove him from office. But Estrada's popularity remained strong among the common people; in early November 2000 Estrada's opponents, with Corazon Aquino to lead them, as well as top members of Manila's business community, and Cardinal Sin, always one for a cause, rallied some 80,000 people in the streets of Manila to call for Estrada's resignation. That number would have been more impressive if Estrada's supporters had not come out that same month with over one million strong.

But in reality, the power of the people was always subordinate to other powers that be. In November the House of Representatives impeached Estrada on charges of accepting bribes, graft, betrayal of public trust, and culpable violation of the constitution. Meanwhile Estrada was busy playing up to his public, visiting impoverished squatters in shantytowns, and drawing cheers from crowds in the slums by telling them that he was their only true friend in government. About his accusers, Estrada told the crowd, "These people never thought of anybody but their businesses, their own interests. They don't care about you."[8]

The House did not vote on the impeachment, Speaker Manuel Villar reasoning that there were enough signatures (more than one-third) on a petition of impeachment to make an actual vote unnecessary. Paying no mind to the protests of some members of the House, Villar read the articles of impeachment, announced that the House was indicting the President, and that the matter was then to go before the Senate. He banged his gavel and it was done—all in less than ten minutes: Joseph Estrada had become the first President in Philippine history to be impeached.

Estrada's trial before the Senate came to an abrupt end on January 16, 2001, when the impeachment court by a slim majority voted not to open an envelope allegedly containing incriminating evidence against Estrada, prompting the prosecution panel to walk out in protest. The vote should have been good news for Estrada, but that isn't quite how it played out. Things happened pretty fast from there: those who doubt the nature of the uprising against Estrada should take note of the fact that the rapid mobilization against Estrada was the result of text messaging, a means of communication among the upper and upper-middle class in Philippine society. They began to make their way to EDSA, of course, in a giddy attempt to rediscover the spirit of '86 and feel empowered.

The name "People Power II" notwithstanding, Estrada's ouster was really not an act of democracy and a show of the genuine will of the people. It was instead quite the opposite— an affirmation of the power of big business and the ruling class. Had the economy been solid, Estrada could most probably have weathered the storm and stayed in office: people can forgive greed in politicians, which is, after all, generally expected. They can also forgive a man his appetites, and the need to keep his mistresses in comfort, as long as the people themselves are not perceptibly inconvenienced. But Estrada's problems were not so much with the people at large as they were with the business community. The economy was at its lowest point since the Marcos regime, and Estrada's vows to fight on were only driving the market down further, the Philippine peso reaching new depths, unemployment figures threatening, at 14%, to scale new heights.

The protestors that began gathering at EDSA on the night of January 16 continued to grow until they numbered in the hundreds of thousands, including a student population too young to have participated in the ouster of President Marcos, but stumbling all over themselves to be a part of it all this time. The truth is that it set an unfortunate precedent in Philippine politics. The ouster of Marcos was many years in the making, the result of years of martial law, and a dictator who had decided that he would stay in power until he died. The ouster of President Estrada, on the other hand, came after little more than two years, and was a result of a segment of the populace deciding that it did not like the outcome of a senate proceeding. In a real democracy, the offending senators would be voted out of office when they came up for re-election, but the machinery would continue to function; in the Philippines, the entire country closed down as people left home and job to flood the streets. By January 19, with the people still flooding the streets, the military became nervous and decided to withdraw its support for Estrada, giving its allegiance instead to Vice President Gloria Macapagal-Arroyo. Without the support of the military, Estrada knew he was fighting a lost cause, and he and his family were evacuated from Malacanang on January 20th. That same day, the Supreme Court declared the presidency vacant and swore Arroyo in as president.

By April the new government was ready to charge Estrada with the crime of plunder—a capital offense—and Arroyo ordered his arrest. But Estrada still had his supporters, and his arrest sparked protests from mostly poor supporters, who marched on Malacanang. Arroyo was forced to declare a State of Rebellion—just a little shy of martial law—when violence erupted and the military had to quell the rebellion. Initially held at a military hospital, Estrada was eventually allowed to be kept under house arrest as his pending case wore on year after year after year.

Estrada's son, Jinggoy Estrada—also an actor—had followed his father into politics as well, first becoming mayor of San Juan like his father, and then later a senator, also like his father. Estrada's wife also became a senator after the deposed president's arrest. If everyone from the entertainment community seemed eager to enter politics, those from political families seemed eager to enter the entertainment business. Aside from former president Corazon Aquino's daughter Kris Aquino becoming an actress, President Arroyo's son Mikey became a film actor, which then meant he would eventually have to do the reverse and run for public office, which he did by winning election to the House of Representatives; Jinggoy Estrada swore never to appear in a film with him.

Perhaps it was the film industry's waning fortunes, but whatever the reason, there was certainly no shortage of film personalities entering politics. It may not be fair to everyone who was making the transition, but the trend was so prevalent and the celebrity campaigns so generally devoid of even much of an attempt to articulate a message that one could really do little else but to conclude that, with their careers being threatened by the tottering of their industry, celebrities were merely trying to maintain their station as cultural elites. Estrada's pledge to help the poor may have been exceedingly non-specific, but compared to some of his colleagues, it was a real roadmap. Many celebrities figured it was enough to sing a song for the crowd or, as in the case of Nora Aunor in her bid to become governor of Carmines Sur, to tell the crowd yet again her rags to riches story. Aunor, incidentally, had been a former mistress of Estrada's, but wound up a staunch supporter of Gloria Macapagal-Arroyo. During his low ebb as he faced trial for plunder, Aunor felt moved to publicly proclaim that during her relationship with him, Estrada used to beat her black and blue. Although name recognition seemed to be the number one asset for any political candidate in the Philippines, and few names were bigger than Aunor's, she lost the election: karma.

Although there were plenty of celebrities entering politics in the 1990s, there were a few who got an early start on the trend. Ramon Revilla was elected to the senate in 1992, but prior to that he had put his acting career on hold in the 1960s to work as an intelligence officer at the Customs Bureau from 1965 to 1972. Not that he was giving up much at the time, as his film career was stalled. Born on March 8, 1927, in Cavite, Revilla's real name is Jose Bautista, and he began his film career in the mid-1950s when film producer Cortes Quilatan discovered him pumping gas one day. After offering him a film contract, Quilatan renamed him Acuna Gallardo. He had little success with Quilatan, and moved on to LVN Studios, where he was confined to minor supporting roles. Eventually he moved on to Sampaguita, where Doc Perez decided to rename him Ramon Revilla and cast him in *Ulila ng Bataan* alongside child sensa-

Hitman (1987/Viva Films) was one of the latter film appearances of action star Ramon Revilla before he became a senator in the early 1990s.

tion Tessie Agana. But although he was getting fairly good roles at Sampaguita, and then afterward with Larry Santiago Productions, Revilla's status as a star didn't really seem to take off. In 1965 he left film for more than seven years to work as an agent with the Customs Bureau. He returned to the film business in 1972 with the film *Nardong Putik* (*Dirty Nardong*), a film about a street thug that Revilla wrote, produced, directed and starred in himself. The film played Manila for a month, shattering box office records at the time, and making Revilla an overnight superstar in his second go round as an actor. He established his own production company, Imus Productions, named for his place of birth in Cavite, and wrote and directed his own starring vehicles, which tended to be fantasy stories which cast him as something of a superhero. They were also very amateurish, as Revilla's directing style was entirely uninventive, and wholly mundane. But somehow, despite the exceedingly plain presentation, third rate production values, as well as Revilla's lack of any talent as an actor, writer or director, the films became popular, and Revilla became one of the top action stars of the 1970s.

In 1987 he decided to run for the senate, and would likely have won but for a miscalculation on his part. He decided to run under his real name, Jose Bautista, although the people knew him as Ramon Revilla. While many people cast their votes for Jose Bautista, many others wrote in the name Ramon Revilla. The Commission on Elections refused to allow him to receive votes under two separate names, and as he had registered under his real name, the votes for Ramon Revilla were thrown out. But he would eventually take another shot, and won election to the senate (as Ramon Revilla) in 1992, and was re-elected to a second term in 1998. Aside from serving as an advocate in the senate for the film industry, making it a priority to get the amusement tax lowered, as Chairman of the Labor and Human resources Committee, Revilla helped pass a child labor law that closely followed the recommendations of the International Labor Organization, which won the praises of the international community as it made the Philippines the first Asian nation to adopt such a law.

One of the last pieces of legislation to be passed by Revilla as his second term in the senate was winding down in 2004 was a law allowing illegitimate children to use their father's surname. Claiming that children should not be made to bear the stigma of illegitimacy, Revilla wanted to change the law that forced illegitimate children to use their mother's surname. Revilla had plenty reason to feel an interest toward illegitimate children, as he is said himself to have fathered his share—by some counts, as high as 80, by others, as low as ... 70. Revilla himself has claimed to officially recognize only 41, and said that one of his daughters keeps a record of all of his children. Such a wonderful role model.

Among Revilla's legitimate, recognized offspring is Ramon "Bong" Revilla, Jr. (real name: Jose Bautista, Jr.), who turned out to be a real chip off the old block. Like Jinggoy Estrada had with his father, Bong Revilla had also followed in his father's footsteps by becoming a film star. Born on September 25, 1966, in Manila, Bong Revilla began his acting career in the 1980s, often being cast to play a younger portrayal of his father's characters in either flashbacks or prologue segments of his father's films. He went on in the 1990s to become an action hero himself, and then followed his father into politics as well, first as Vice Governor of his father's old province of Cavite from 1995 to 1998, and then as its Provincial Governor from 1998 to 2001. After serving a term as Cavite Governor, Bong Revilla won election to the senate. Bong Revilla seems to have only 6 children, all of them by his wife, actress Lani Mercado, so he is obviously not inclined to aspire to his father's caddish persona.

But aside from the likes of Jinggoy Estrada and Bong Revilla—those who were following their fathers' paths—there were plenty of celebrities running for public office. Tito Sotto, whose real name was Vicente Sotto III, had for years been a member of the popular comedy trio Tito, Vic and Joey (which included his brother Vic Sotto and Joey de Leon), as well as being a musical artist and music executive, when he became Vice Mayor of Quezon City in 1988; in 1992 he moved on to become a senator. Maybe he wasn't following in his father's footsteps, but Sotto did have pols in his family line: his grandfather and one of his uncles were both senators. Sotto went on to serve two terms in the senate from 1992 to 2004, and was so popular that his name was being thrown around as a possible presidential contender; that is, until a minor scandal seemed to make him a less viable candidate. Sotto was accused of having ties to a known drug lord, who was rumored to have financed his 1992 senatorial campaign. The rumor was all the more embarrassing in that Sotto was Chairman of the Senate Committee on Illegal Drugs, and had rather made a reputation for himself as an anti-drug crusader. Sotto was one of four senators named by one of the drug lord's top men—a dirty former police officer—as being the drug lord's go-to people when in trouble. One of the other senators named, incidentally, was Gloria Macapagal-Arroyo. President Fidel Ramos dismissed the idea that Arroyo had any such links to the underworld: he did not do Sotto the same courtesy. Ironically, Sotto had also been high on the list of potential running mates for Arroyo as she considered her own presidential bid.

Just as Joseph Estrada had parlayed his populist screen image into political currency, other action stars were likewise to use their tough guy, working class hero persona to good advantage in the pursuit of their political ambitions. In 1992 Lito Lapid was elected vice governor of Pampanga, and whereas bad boy wannabes like Robin Padilla and Ace Vergel seemed determined to live up to their hooligan screen images with outrageous behavior and arrests for drug and weapons charges, Lapid had a more noble and heroic screen image to live up to. Lapid was surely an anachronism in Pampangan politics, which tend to gravitate toward wealthy families, which dominate the political landscape election after election. Being an uneducated film star from a humble background, Lapid would certainly be something other than business as usual when he took office. He came into office in the aftermath of the eruption of Mount Pinatubo, and he quickly earned the admiration of the people for his relief efforts, as well as personally helping in the evacuation of villages experiencing flash flooding and continuing lahar flows. His off-screen heroics impressed the public indeed, and in 1995 he was elected governor of Pampanga with better than 80% of the vote. The confidence was apparently well-placed as, unlike President Estrada, who merely paid lip service to the poor, Lapid considered industrial development key to the economic growth required to raise the average standard of living. As he focused on promoting investment in the region, entrepreneurship grew and Lapid was re-elected—twice. He also found himself on President Estrada's unfavorable list after the 1998 elections, when Estrada was soundly beaten in the region, which Estrada and his people attributed to Lapid's lack of support. Originally members of the same party, Estrada had been something of a mentor to Lapid, in both his film career and politics. Since they were now members of opposing political parties, one would have thought that Estrada would have expected Lapid to campaign against him, but perhaps owing to the fact that they were more than both just actors, that they had a relationship that ran somewhat deeper than being simple colleagues, the sense of rivalry within Estrada was doubtless more sensitive toward Lapid. During Estrada's presidency Lapid became a target for attack as *someone* would have liked to have seen him driven from office—or worse. The Ombudsman during Estrada's brief administration filed graft charges against Lapid three times, one—involving alleged illegal taxes collected from lahar quarrying—resulting in a one-year suspension. In an almost endearing display of naiveté, Lapid seemed taken aback by the rough and tumble world he had jumped into, offering little more than the simplest of observations on the cruelty of politics. Of course Lapid appealed the decision of the Ombudsman, and of course the case went on for years, long after Estrada was driven from office and arrested and Lapid had been re-elected twice: karma. It all played like something out of one of Lapid's films, with Lapid being victimized by more powerful figures pulling the strings behind the scenes to try and bring him down. Lapid's former allies in local politics began to slink away and keep their distance, fearing that the same fate might befall them, but just like in the movies, Lapid would remain defiant. A later Deputy Ombudsman recommended the dismissal of the graft case against Lapid in 2004, which had previously been the recommendation of a special prosecuting officer in 2002 after reviewing the case. Lapid eventually went public with his belief that the entire case had been politically driven and was no more than simple harassment orchestrated by Estrada and his cronies in Pampanga.

On the other hand, Lapid was on good terms with the new president, Gloria Macapagal-Arroyo; he even put her son Mikey Arroyo in a couple of his films, one of which, *Tapatan ng Tapang (Shortcut of the Courageous)* in 1997 was directed by Augusto Buenaventura, who interestingly enough had been one of Estrada's most favored directors, even directing his final films, *Order to Kill* (1985) and *Sa Kuko ng Agila* (1989). But since Mikey had become an actor, he now, naturally, had to enter politics as well—perhaps the expectation for him to do so was even stronger since, not only was he an actor, but also came from a political family—and so he decided to run for congress. Problem was, as a candidate from the 2nd District in Pampanga, he would be running against his aunt, Cielo Macapagal, a former vice governor of Pampanga herself, who had lost her own gubernatorial bid to Lapid. Cielo Macapagal is the half-sister of President Gloria Macapagal-Arroyo, both of them being the daughters of former President Diosdado Macapagal; Cielo's mother, Purita dela Rosa, was the sister of one-time matinee idol-turned-senator Rogelio dela Rosa. Gloria Macapagal-Arroyo discreetly asked her half-sister to drop out of the Pampangan congressional race so as not to hurt her son Mikey's chances, which half-sister Cielo did. In return Cielo Macapagal got to watch Lapid, not only the one who defeated her for the governorship, but someone whom she resented serving under when she was herself vice governor, considering him an inarticulate, uneducated performer who needed to be told what to say, where to go, etc., being hand-picked by sister Gloria for her own senate ticket in the upcoming elections.

After three terms as governor Lapid had decided to move up and he won a seat in the senate in 2004. And then there was action film star Rey Malonzo (a step down from Lapid in terms of celebrity, to be sure, so therefore the lesser office), who became mayor of Caloocan in 1995, like Lapid, going against longstanding tradition, charging in like a real life action hero and challenging the incumbent mayor, Boy Asistio, whose wealthy family had controlled local politics in the area for decades. In fact, it was considered pointless to even challenge them anymore, but then along came a movie star. Asistio was more than a little reluctant to accept the results, not wanting to be the one to bring disgrace on his family, and so asked for a recall: small matter, as Malonzo won again. Had they been Democrats they would have tried to litigate the matter rather than just accept the plain truth. Malonzo won re-election in 1998, the year that Estrada became President, and being that Estrada was tight with the Asistio clan, it wasn't long before Malonzo had troubles similar to Lapid's. In March of 1999 President Estrada ordered Malonzo's suspension for 20 days after he was charged with—you guessed it—graft. Even after Estrada would himself be charged with graft and was safely out of the way, Malonzo's opponents continued to try their best to bring him down. The Asistio clan, for instance, continued to make graft charges against Malonzo: in three terms covering 9 years, Malonzo was accused of graft 30 times by his rivals and enemies. Each case was dismissed. In his last bid for re-election, Malonzo beat Luis "Baby" Asistio, who promptly filed a protest against Malonzo for jumping the gun in declaring victory. It seems that the Commission on Elections had not declared Malonzo the winner yet, and "Baby" Asistio found it thoroughly distasteful that Malonzo should proclaim himself winner without any official word. Well, the situation required investigating, and as a result, Malonzo was made to wait four months before he could resume his duties as mayor. "Baby" indeed.

After serving three terms, Malonzo was obliged to step down, and decided to run for the

Joseph Estrada starred in *Order to Kill* (1985/Amazaldy), a film directed by Augusto Buenaventura, who went on to direct one of Estrada's political rivals, Lito Lapid, in films.

congress, while his wife Gigi would run for Caloocan Mayor, perhaps with an eye toward starting a dynasty of their own in the region. But, alas, it was not to be; Malonzo and his wife both lost their respective elections in 2004.

The same fate befell comedic actor Joey Marquez, a former PBA basketball player who became a television and film star ("star" perhaps, but a middling one at that), and then later a three-term mayor of Paranaque. His father was film director Artemio Marquez, while his mother was actress Melanie Marquez. Like Malonzo, he was required to relinquish his office after three terms, and like Malonzo he made a run for a congressional seat, and like Malonzo, he lost. The similarities do not end there: like Malonzo, Marquez came into office in 1995, and by 1997 the Ombudsman was filing charges against him for letting the organizers of a Michael Jackson concert in Paranaque get away with paying taxes on only 2% of the gross receipts, although the internal revenue required a 30% tax. A few years hence, the Ombudsman was recommending charges of graft. On this latter occasion it had something to do with the misappropriation of some 600 million pesos of city funds. Otherwise, Marquez was busy that year trying to get his marriage to actress Alma Moreno annulled as he carried on an affair with Kris Aquino. There were those who surmised that his affair with Aquino was an attempt to help his political career, what with her being the daughter of a former president and one of the nation's most famous martyred politicians as well (the late Benigno Aquino, Jr. being her father). It didn't work.

There were plenty others: action star Rudy Fernandez ran for mayor of Quezon City in 2001 (he lost), while his running mate, comedic actor Herbert Bautista, ran for vice mayor (he won). Bautista had originally run for mayor himself in 1998 but lost to incumbent Ismael Mathay. Mark Lapid (son of Lito and also an actor, of course) succeeded his father as governor of Pampanga, actor George Estregan, Jr. (Joseph Estrada's nephew) became mayor of Pagsanjan, actress Aiko Melendez won a council seat in Quezon City, as did actor Dennis Padilla in Caloocan. But while many actors were winning elections, many others were losing: actresses Boots Anson-Roa and Pilar Pilapil lost senate races, actor Dan Fernandez lost a gubernatorial race in Laguna, Gary Estrada lost the mayoral race in San Antonio. But one of the biggest news stories in celebrity politics was the election of superstar Vilma Santos in 1998 as mayor of Lipa City. She was not a native of Lipa, but she had, after all, starred in the film *Lipa Massacre*, so who better to run the city? True, her husband was from Lipa, which brings up her other qualification for holding public office—her husband is Senator Ralph Recto.

Both the Filipino film industry and Filipino politics have always been exceedingly inbred: now they were interbreeding with each other. The line between the entertainment industry and politics was becoming so blurred as to be nonexistent. Former President Corazon Aquino's daughter Kris was the Queen of Massacre Films, Ferdinand and Imelda Marcos' daughter Imee was a film producer-turned-senator-turned film producer again, the President's son was an actor-turned congressman, who had to get mommy to talk auntie out of running against him for congress, and the deposed president was an aging action film hero skulking in detention in a military hospital. How to top it all off? Perhaps the King of Philippine Cinema, Fernando Poe, Jr., could run for president, and that would make him and his wife King and Queen of not only the film industry, but indeed the entire country. After all, was there really a difference any more? What a droll idea.

Joseph Estrada's story would likely make for a good movie in itself (and no doubt one will be forthcoming), but as interesting and sometimes strange as it was, it had nothing at all on the story of Dennis Roldan when it came to the bizarre. His real name is Mitchell Gumabao, and like Robert Jaworski and Joey Marquez, Roldan was a former PBA basketball player who then transitioned into acting, and again like both of them, from acting into politics.

Roldan had appeared in Laurice Guillen's *Salome* in 1981, in which he was cast as the rapist/murder victim of the story, and went on to play mostly villainous roles through the 1990s. In 1992 Roldan won a congressional seat as representative for the third district of Quezon City; he only served one term. As film work began drying up in the late 1990s, Roldan, like many other Philippine actors, went into television work, appearing in two different series between 1999 and 2001. With the money from his PBA days and acting career, as well as his term in congress, Roldan was able to pursue various financial interests, owning a farm with hundreds of mango trees, a piggery, a Zambales beach resort, and a Quezon City restaurant. But he also had a very expensive habit: Roldan was a compulsive gambler. By one report, he lost hundreds of thousands of dollars in one trip to Las Vegas with his girlfriend, Suzette See Huang. Incidentally, Roldan was a family man, with a wife and five children.

When his gambling debts began mounting beyond his ability to keep up, authorities theorized that Roldan, in his desperation, hatched a plot to lay hands on a substantial amount of money quickly—he was the alleged mastermind of the kidnapping of the 3-year-old son of a wealthy Chinese-Filipino businessman. The child was abducted on February 9, 2005, while his nanny was walking him to daycare. After he had been taken to a safe house, the child's parents received a ransom call demanding 270 million pesos, but over the next 11 days during subsequent contacts between the parents and the kidnappers, that figure was whittled down to 3 million pesos. All along, the parents were in touch with the authorities, and on February 19th, acting on a tip from a concerned neighbor who reported suspicious activities going on at a house on Harvard Street in Cubao, the police raided the house and rescued the boy. They also arrested three of Roldan's alleged gang, and through them, were able to arrest Roldan later that day. With Roldan, the police wound up arresting seven suspects in all, including Octavio Garces, a 50-year-old barangay chairman in Quezon City, and presented them to the media the following day. Although he was not allowed to address the media himself, those in attendance noted that Roldan seemed agitated, particularly when Philippine National Police Chief Edgar Aglipay repeatedly referred to him as a former congressman.

While authorities claimed that Roldan admitted to taking part in the kidnapping during his interrogation, and even of being its mastermind, his attorney, Salvador Panelo, was quick to dismiss such claims by authorities, telling reporters that his client had signed no confession, and had been tortured into making certain statements. "If I had a plastic bag covering my face," Panelo said, "I would have admitted (to it) myself." [9] He certainly started earning his fees in a hurry.

But all indications were that Roldan was talking; in fact, although some of the other members of the gang fingered Roldan as the mastermind, according to authorities, Roldan himself said that it was his girlfriend, Suzette See Huang, who came up with the idea. Apparently, the child they abducted was the son of a good friend of Huang's—an old schoolmate, no less—and knowing that they were wealthy, she seems to have seen it as a way for Roldan to escape his financial troubles: such a helpful person, Miss Huang. When police decided to interview Miss Huang, they were initially unable to find her until receiving a call that there was a woman seemingly about to jump from the terrace of her 9th floor condominium in Greenhills, San Juan. When police arrived, they talked the woman out of jumping, but she promptly went back inside and tried to slash her wrists with a kitchen knife. She was taken to the hospital and released after only a day, her injuries being fairly insignificant. According to police, Huang, who must have feared her arrest was imminent, had sent surrender feelers to police in the hope of receiving a lighter sentence, but her offers were rejected. Authorities didn't feel they needed her testimony, as their case against Roldan and the rest was fairly strong already, and besides, if what they were learning was true, then Huang was more responsible than anyone for the targeting of that particular family. She was a lifelong friend of the child's mother, who seems to have been willing to betray that friendship in order to help her married boyfriend pay off his gambling debts. Unfortunately, the police did not issue a warrant for her arrest while she was in the hospital, and she soon disappeared after being released.

As these things tend to do, the case dragged on and on, suspects' stories changing all the while. While one suspect claimed to have been driving the car that Roldan was in when he made the ransom call, two of the co-accused claimed to have no knowledge at all of any involvement by Roldan, one of which claimed that prosecutor Mario Ongkiko had tried to convince him to finger Roldan as the mastermind. Although kidnapping, as a capital crime, is a non-bailable offense in the Philippines, Judge Agnes Reyes Carpio confounded everyone from prosecutors to the victimized family, and left victim's rights advocates like the organization Citizens Against Crime aghast by granting Roldan's bail request. Judge Carpio reasoned that the evidence against Roldan was not strong enough to deny him bail, and so, after more than a year in jail, Roldan was allowed out on July 27, 2006, even if only temporarily. Beaming as he left the prison, Roldan said that he was grateful for the opportunity to spend time with his family again. He also announced that he had spent time in jail ruminating over the direction his life had taken, and wondering what path to take next. He came to an important—if predictable—decision: he announced his desire to become a pastor.

There were those who speculated that Malacanang may have brought pressure on the judge to release Roldan; he was, after all, a friend of Congressman Mikey Arroyo, the son of the President. In reality, the statement made by Mikey Arroyo had been very innocent, merely saying upon getting the news of Roldan's arrest on kidnapping charges that he found it unbelievable that Roldan would be involved in such a thing. "I consider him as my friend," the congressman said. "I was disturbed when I heard the news. I doubt very much if his character is capable of doing kidnapping."[10] Arroyo went on to say that he was certain that Roldan was innocent. But the press jumped all over it at the time, and Malacanang felt the need to issue a statement through Presidential Spokesman Ignacio Bunye, who pointed out that Congressman Mikey's opinions were his own and not necessarily those of the President herself. Many months later, the Movement for the Restoration of Peace and Order, seemingly at a loss to explain Judge Carpio's inexplicable ruling, seized upon Mikey Arroyo's defense of Roldan as if it were proof of powerful people greasing the machinery for Roldan. How else to explain someone being granted bail for a non-bailable offense?

Meanwhile, Roldan's last film, *Terrorist Hunter*, which was shot in 2002 and shelved for some reason, was finally released in 2005. Roldan's new notoriety may have helped the producers along in their decision to release the film at last; although they had claimed to have wanted to make some changes to improve the film—hence the delay in its release—and for some reason the film's main star, Eddie Garcia, denied that it was an old film, and in fact got annoyed with journalists who called it such, it was probably Roldan's kidnapping case that prompted studio executives to scramble to release the film: in the film, Roldan played the leader of a gang of kidnappers. Go figure.

At approximately 7:30 A.M. on November 7, 2001, a security guard was making his rounds through the parking garage of the Atlanta Center building on Annapolis Street, Greenhills, in San Juan. While walking through the sixth floor of the garage he spotted what looked like blood on the garage floor, and he followed the trail to a green Nissan Sentra. The car was locked, but peering into the window, he could see a woman slumped over in the backseat. When the police arrived they confirmed that the woman was dead, and they established her identity: it was Nida Blanca, one of the greatest icons in the history of the Filipino film industry. She was 65. She had been stabbed 13 times, with wounds to the neck, left ear and jaw, and left armpit. The fatal wound was one that hit the jugular vein. Blanca had apparently been beaten as well, as she had broken ribs and a blackened right eye. After examining the wounds, Chief Medical Officer Edgardo Guico surmised that two weapons were used in the attack. He further noted that Blanca seemed to have been killed in a rage. Rigor mortis had not yet set in by the time the police arrived, so the murder was estimated to have occurred sometime between 4 and 5 A.M. on the morning of the 7th.

Blanca had been serving as a member of the Movie and Television Review and Classification Board, which kept its offices on the 33rd floor of the Atlanta Center building. She had left her office shortly after 5 P.M. on the 6th.

News of Blanca's murder sent shockwaves throughout the country. "It seems to me nobody is safe around here anymore," said Joseph Estrada.[11] The grief and outrage from the public was so immense that President Gloria Macapagal-Arroyo felt the need to order the Philippine National Police and the National Bureau of Investigation to solve the murder "quickly," a rather superfluous command, but, under the circumstances, a president is expected to say something. Arroyo also felt moved to tell the people that Blanca was her favorite actress; in fact, it was Arroyo who had appointed her to the MTRCB. Ex-president Joseph Estrada, though under arrest, was permitted to attend the wake. An estimated 20,000 people showed up at the cemetery for Blanca's funeral.

The PNP went to work by forming "Task Force Marsha," named for the character that Blanca had portrayed for 16 years in the popular television sitcom *John en Marsha* (*John and Marsha*), in which she was cast as the spouse of the constantly bungling comedian Dolphy.

Police speculated that Blanca's killers were either drunk or on drugs, a curious conclusion under the circumstances: her belongings seemed to be intact, her car had not been broken into, and the killers even took care to lock it up after depositing her body in the backseat. They were also careful to leave no fingerprints. In fact, all indications were that Blanca had been killed somewhere else and then brought back to the Atlanta Center parking garage and placed in her car. Drug addicts would not likely have gone to so much trouble. The police were not the only ones speculating: fans and amateur sleuths around the country were concocting scenarios, which covered the turf from organized crime to disgruntled film financers angry over strict MTRCB policies.

The first order of business in such a case would be to investigate those close to the victim, in particular a

Screen icon Nida Blanca was murdered in 2001.

spouse. In this case, the spouse was Rod Lawrence Strunk, Blanca's American husband. Strunk was a California native, born in Fresno in March of 1940. He was himself a former actor, having appeared in films and television programs in the U.S. during the 1960s under the name Rod Lauren. He is best remembered by cult film enthusiasts for a string of B-grade horror films in which he appeared in 1963, including *The Black Zoo*, *Terrified* and, most memorably, *The Crawling Hand*. He also had a brief career as a singer and recording artist for RCA Victor, for whom he recorded a couple of albums. He even scored a minor hit in 1959 with the song "If I Had a Girl."

Strunk and Blanca first met in 1964 when Strunk traveled to the Philippines to star alongside Ursula Andress in John Derek's WWII film *Once Before I Die*. Although there was mutual interest, Blanca would later say that she decided not to pursue a relationship with Strunk at the time because she knew that he would be returning to America. Strunk must have enjoyed his time in the Philippines, however, as he made periodic return trips to the country for singing engagements, and to make appearances on Philippine television variety programs.

By 1979, both Blanca and Strunk were divorced from their respective spouses, and while vacationing in the U.S. Blanca decided to look Strunk up and give him a call. The two would eventually marry in Las Vegas in 1981.

Although the police admitted to looking into an insurance policy on Blanca and investigating the beneficiaries, within days of the murder they publicly announced that Strunk had been ruled out as a suspect. They said that they had other leads, and made vague references to looking into somebody who had a grudge against Blanca. News reports referred to an employee of Blanca's, known to be a drug user, who had a habit of asking Blanca for money. Nestorio Gaulberto, head of the Criminal Investigation and Detection Group, publicly announced that the case was nearing resolution. But was it? Pressure to solve the case was enormous, with everybody pitching in: Blanca's show business colleagues had raised more than one million pesos (roughly the equivalent of $20,000) as a reward for information leading to an arrest; Joseph Estrada's son, San Juan Mayor JV Ejercito, was offering a 300,000 peso reward (about $6,000) after his father, apparently under the illusion that he was still president, had "ordered" a speedy resolution to the case. Meanwhile, the real president, Gloria Macapagal-Arroyo, was still trying to reassure the shocked and grieving public with thoroughly useless announcements. "I told the police chief to get to the bottom of this, and that the offenders should be punished to the full extent of the law," she said. She also urged citizens "to unite against all forms of criminality in our midst."[12]

Whatever leads the police were pretending would bring the case to a close (or perhaps truly believing would do so), things were about to take a drastic turn. On November 18, 2001, Philip Medel, Jr. turned himself in to police and confessed to killing Blanca. In a 10-page handwritten confession, done in the presence of his attorney, Medel claimed to have been hired by Strunk to murder the actress. "I am now turning myself [in] as a voluntary witness against the evil design of Mr. Strunk and his evil cahoots," Medel said.[13] In theory, such a confession should have just about wrapped up the case. In reality, it went a long way toward muddying the case and taking it down a long, winding and ever more convoluted path.

Claiming that his conscience would not abate, Medel approached a man named Romulo Kintanar, a security consultant for the Bureau of Immigration and Deportation (BID) with surrender feelers. How he came to choose Kintanar would be just one of the curious aspects of the new turn the case was taking. Kintanar had been one of the leaders of the New People's Army (NPA), a communist revolutionary movement, but after his expulsion from the NPA for alleged criminal activities, he became a government intelligence agent undercover of his position in the BID. On November 11, 2001, Kintanar informed BID Commissioner Andrea

Domingo of Medel's desire to surrender and she referred the matter to the PNP. The day after Medel's surrender, the government announced Medel as their prime suspect. The Department of Justice began preparing parricide charges against Strunk, and the police surrounded his house in White Plains, Quezon City, where Strunk remained cloistered away with his lawyers. All ports and airports were alerted of the possibility that Strunk might try to flee the country.

Friends of Strunk and Blanca expressed dismay that Strunk would be implicated in the murder. Actor Eddie Gutierrez said that he was unconvinced that Strunk was involved, and actress Caridad Sanchez said that Strunk was a good person and she didn't seem sure of what to think. The staff at the MTRCB where Blanca had been working also seemed doubtful. MTRCB Executive Director Racquel Rey said she found Medel's story unbelievable, and that Blanca often spoke of her husband with the staff members at the MTRCB offices and described their relationship as loving and committed. Likewise, the household help in Strunk and Blanca's home expressed extreme doubt about the accusations against Strunk. Strunk's lawyers issued a public statement in December of 2001 condemning the NBI for attempting to try their case in the court of public opinion by using the media to portray their client as the mastermind behind Blanca's murder. NBI Director Reynaldo Wycoco responded by threatening to force Strunk's attorneys to undergo polygraph tests if they continued interfering in police attempts to interview their client.

If Strunk did hire Medel, he didn't do himself any favors: Medel turned out to be a criminologist's dream, very eager to talk about the case, and seemingly craving the fame or notoriety, probably both. Apparently enjoying his newfound celebrity, Medel began granting jailhouse interviews to the media in which he recounted details of the murder. All along, he maintained that he did not know that the woman he had killed was Blanca until he began seeing news reports about the killing. Thereafter, he said, his conscience gave him no rest. This was contradicted by Medel's landlady, who would later tell police that Medel had told her about Blanca's murder even before it was being broadcast in the news media.

Medel claimed to have been hired for the killing through a third party, a man named Mike Martinez, but police were unable to locate Martinez, whose brother told them that he hadn't been seen since the day of Blanca's murder, and his family feared that he had been kidnapped or murdered. Still, Medel's confession was damning evidence against Strunk.

In Medel's telling of events, he was hired through Martinez with the understanding that Strunk was to pay him 50,000 pesos (about $1,000). Medel waited for Martinez at a spot on EDSA on November 6, 2001, but Martinez failed to show up: instead it was Strunk himself who met Medel at around 5:30 P.M. The two dined at a restaurant on EDSA and were then picked up by a group of men who took Medel to the 6th floor of the Atlanta Center parking garage at about 10:00 P.M. Strunk used a spare key to let Medel into Blanca's Nissan, and then left. Strunk returned hours later with Blanca and another woman, and after an argument, variously described as being over financial documents, inheritance documents, and an attempt to get Blanca to sign a new will, Strunk ordered Medel to kill Blanca. Medel said he killed Blanca sometime between 1:00 and 2:30 A.M. on the morning of the 7th, which CIDG head Nestorio Gaulberto said was consistent with police estimates (actually, the medical examiner had placed it at 4:00 to 5:00 A.M.). Police had been able to obtain a receipt for a Swiss army knife that they said Strunk had purchased in a Mandaluyong City mall two days before the murder, and which they maintained was used by Medel in the killing. If Strunk did hire Medel, he doesn't seem to have been very cautious, as he seems to have let quite a few people in on the plan. The police were filing murder charges against Medel and five unnamed "John Does," while informing Strunk that he should begin preparing his defense with his attorneys. They seemed to have a pretty good case. Then the other shoe dropped.

During a televised pre-trial hearing on November 24, 2001, Medel turned the proceedings into grand theater, flying into hysterics, tearing up his confession and screaming to the press that he had been tortured by the police into confessing to the murder. He specifically singled out Task Force Marsha spokesman Senior Superintendent Leonardo Espina in the torture allegation. Holding out his arms for all to see, Medel drew attention to bruises on his arms, and further shouted that he had never met Strunk and wanted no part in convicting an innocent man. In Medel's new story, he was walking along a street in Quezon City shortly past noon on November 16, 2001 when he was abducted by members of the CIDG, blindfolded and driven to a house where he was beaten and tortured until he agreed to confess to Blanca's murder. The police dismissed the claim to the press; after all, it was Medel who had first approached authorities on the 11th with surrender feelers. But under the circumstances, the Department of Justice was forced to send the case back to the NBI for reinvestigation. One of the lingering hangovers of the Marcos era was a pronounced willingness—eagerness in some—to believe the worst of the authorities, and so such matters had to be dealt with.

Parricide charges against Strunk would then have to wait. Although Strunk had been put on a hold-departure list, that order was only good for five days while parricide charges against him were being prepared and an arrest warrant could be issued. With Medel now undergoing a psychiatric evaluation and the case being reinvestigated, Strunk had more breathing room. He applied for permission to return to the United States to see his ailing mother in California, and after signing a letter of undertaking to return to the Philippines, he was allowed to leave the country. Strunk left the Philippines in January of 2002.

While he was away, authorities continued to build a case against him. One person who did not seem surprised by news of Strunk's involvement in the murder was Blanca's daughter by her first marriage, Katherine "Kaye" Torres. The sole beneficiary of Blanca's will, Torres told police that her mother's marriage to Strunk was on the rocks, and that Strunk was a drug addict. She related to authorities that her mother had come home one night in 1998 and caught Strunk with friends using methamphetamine hydrochloride, commonly referred to in the Philippines as "shabu." She said that her mother had considered having Strunk involuntarily committed to a drug rehabilitation clinic, but that Strunk had dissuaded her from doing so through pleas and promises to kick his habit. Actor-turned-senator Vicente Sotto, who was at that time Vice Mayor of Quezon City and chairman of the city's Anti-Drug Abuse Council, confirmed Torres' accounts by saying that Blanca had come to him for help regarding Strunk's drug use.

Meanwhile, Wycoco said that they had been compiling evidence that Strunk had mounting debts, was using up large sums of Blanca's money, and was upset at having been disinherited by Blanca. Household servants, who at first seemed reluctant to believe that Strunk could have been involved in his wife's murder, now came forward with new information, saying that everyone in the house knew that Strunk was using drugs and that his behavior had changed considerably. Wycoco also pointed out that, as Medel's public retraction of his confession was not done under oath, his original statement could still be used as evidence. A new witness, one Alfredo Rodriguez, claimed to have taken part in surveillance of Blanca during the weeks leading up to her murder. There were also new witnesses who said that they saw Medel in the 6th floor parking garage of the Atlanta Center shortly after Blanca's body had been discovered: again, a criminologist's dream.

By July of 2002, authorities were ready to make their case, and the NBI filed parricide charges against Strunk and murder charges against Medel, two John Does and one Jane Doe. They also filed obstruction charges against three Atlanta Center security guards for allegedly withholding evidence. Torres tried to get the charges against Strunk changed from parricide to murder, claiming that her mother's marriage to her father, Dr. Arturo Torres, had not yet been annulled when she married Strunk. A charge of murder would carry a heavier sentence than one of parricide. It is a peculiar quirk of the Philippine justice system that killing one's spouse is apparently viewed as somehow being a lesser offense than killing anybody else. Philippine authorities would weigh changing the charges against Strunk, but actually that might only weaken their case. Under Philippine law, if a person dies before their marriage is annulled, then the spouse is automatically entitled to a part of the estate, irrespective of the deceased's will. This would have given Strunk plenty of motive to have Blanca killed before she could annul the marriage. But the truth is that Philippine law does not recognize divorce; being Catholic to the core, the system does not allow for divorce, unless it is in the form of an annulment: in other words, you can get out of a 30-year marriage by getting the Church to say that the marriage never happened. The problem in using this as a motive in building a case against Strunk is that, being twice divorced in the U.S., his Las Vegas marriage to Blanca was never legally recognized in the Philippines. That being the case, he had no real legal claim to Blanca's estate. In the end, owing to the marriage's non-legal status in the Philippines, the charges against Strunk would have to be changed from parricide to murder.

Though parricide charges had been filed against Strunk, he was still in the U.S., and his letter of undertaking notwithstanding, he was not returning to the Philippines. Instead, his lawyers in Manila filed a motion to have the charges against him dismissed, which was quickly quashed by the DOJ. CIDG Chief Gaulberto said that authorities were compelling Strunk to return to the country and face charges, a singular waste of time. The terms were not encouraging. "Mr. Strunk will be forced to return to the Philippines and personally take oath before prosecutors who are conducting the preliminary investigation," Gaulberto said, "At this stage, he cannot be represented here by his lawyers or anybody else."[14] It was not a statement likely to persuade any defendant, and it couldn't possibly help the government in its inevitable attempt to extradite.

With the case dragging on and on, and the public's patience wearing thin, NBI Director Wycoco said that prosecutors might be prepared to file the case in court by February of 2003. That would give them more time to build a stronger case. But along the way, investigators were losing bits here and there. Romulo Kintanar, for instance, suddenly became unavailable to testify when his former cronies in the NPA had him murdered. The NPA had been seeking to mete out their brand of justice on Kintanar for years, and finally succeeded in doing so when they caught up with him in a Quezon City restaurant where he was dining with film director Willy Milan and gunned him down on January 23, 2003. Still, state prosecutors were able to use Kintanar's prior testimony in filing charges against Medel.

On February 14, 2003, the DOJ recommended filing murder charges against Strunk and Medel. The NBI was expecting that an arrest warrant would be issued for Strunk within the month, and so began coordinating with the FBI through the U.S. embassy. Charges were filed in the Pasig Regional Trial Court, and Judge Alex Quiroz issued arrest warrants on February 21, 2003. While Medel would be arraigned in April 2003, Strunk's arraignment was held up by the fact that the DOJ had still not filed an extradition request with the U.S. government. On behalf of the DOJ, Undersecretary Merceditas Gutierrez finally sent a request to the U.S. Justice Department requesting Strunk's provisional arrest on April 10th.

It took a month to go through, but on May 13, 2003, U.S. marshals arrived at Strunk's house in Tracy, California to place him under arrest. They found him sitting on the front porch, by all appearances not surprised that they had come. Perhaps he had been in contact with his attorney; maybe he had been following the case on the internet. He was taken to the Sacramento County Jail. The following day, U.S. marshals informed Philippine authorities that Strunk was in custody. In order to get a jumpstart on extradition and sweeten their chances, the DOJ publicly announced on May 15th that, owing to the U.S.–Philippine extradition treaty, Strunk would certainly be spared the death penalty. Ultimately, however, that decision would be up to the president. In response, the Presidential Palace quickly gave a sovereign guarantee to spare Strunk's life.

Strunk's bail hearing on May 30 was disappointing for the defendant, as U.S. Federal Magistrate Gregory Hollows denied bail for Strunk, stating that he was a flight risk. He would have to remain in jail pending the extradition hearing, which Hollows set for July 28, 2003; Hollows himself would preside over the hearing. But Hollows did give Strunk reason for optimism: in his decision, Hollows noted that he had serious doubt about some of the Philippine government's evidence against him. Hollows said that any further contradictory evidence would likely put the "competency of the government's evidence ... beyond rescue."[15] Conversely, Hollows' comments did not go over well with Philippine authorities.

The DOJ had until July 11, 2003, to supply the necessary evidence against Strunk to the U.S. Justice Department, but one very key document was missing: the NBI had apparently misplaced Strunk's letter of undertaking in which he had promised to return to the Philippines after visiting his sick mother (Strunk's mother had since died). A defendant's signed declaration to return would have been useful. As the case wore on, Strunk continued to sit in the Sacramento County Jail, with a brief temporary leave granted to visit his dying sister in Tracy, until Judge Hollows finally rendered his decision on November 12, 2003. Hollows denied the Philippine government's request to extradite Strunk.

The decision set off a firestorm in the Philippines. Blanca's daughter, Kaye Torres, was calling for the resignation of NBI Director Reynaldo Wycoco for mishandling the extradition procedure. Philippine politicians were asking for a review of the Philippine–U.S. extradition treaty, calling it one-sided. After all, the Philippines had just complied with a U.S. extradition request for Manila congressman Mark Jimenez, who was subsequently convicted in a Miami court of making illegal campaign contributions to President Bill Clinton. If the Philippines could grant extradition of a sitting Philippine congressman to the U.S., surely the U.S. could send back a murder suspect. Media editorialists waxed exceedingly wroth about the condescending attitude of not just Judge Hollows, but of the U.S. in general, evoking a bygone era when U.S. politicians referred to Filipinos as "our little brown brothers." Some saw the U.S.–Philippine relationship as one of mere convenience to America, not just in the matter of extradition treaties, but military alliances as well, whether it be past use of military bases at Clark and Subic, or the presence of the U.S. military in the Philippines to train Philippine troops to combat Muslim rebels in the southern Philippines as part of the war on terror, a most curious point of reference for those seeking to paint the U.S. as all take and no give.

The truth is that Judge Hollows' concerns were legitimate. Among the evidence that the government claimed to have was the murder weapon, a knife that was said to still have blood on it, but later tests revealed that it was not human blood. Of course, there was also Medel's retraction to contend with, and his allegations of torture. That might have seemed somewhat less significant if not for the fact that the Philippine government had paid Medel's family 30,000 pesos (about $600) upon his confession, a fact that Hollows termed "bizarre." And then there was the fact that all of the talk of money as a motive, with Strunk upset at being disinherited by Blanca, paled somewhat under Philippine law, which did not recognize the Strunk-Blanca marriage as legally legitimate. The truth is that, as enticing as much of the testimony of various witnesses was, in the end it became a jumble of contradictory timelines and events, all pointing toward Strunk, yet each contending against the next to do so. It just wasn't enough to convince Hollows, who was not unaware of the intense media coverage that the case was generating in the Philippines and the need of authorities there to bring quick closure, perhaps at any costs.

Everybody seemed anxious to dole out blame: Torres met the press in front of her mother's tomb, saying that she hoped to wake the country up to the corruption within the government. She also mentioned that President Arroyo had personally guaranteed her that the case would be solved during her term in office. Arroyo responded with some vague threat to impose sanctions of some sort against DOJ and NBI officials who had been derelict in their duties. Torres' attorney, Harriet Demetriou, brought out the time-honored hobgoblin of racism to try and explain Hollows' decision, while also repeating the call for NBI Director Wycoco's resignation and added Justice Undersecretary Gutierrez to the list. Gutierrez took her turn by announcing that she would talk to prosecutors to find out if Strunk's Manila attorney could be held liable for the fact that Strunk did not live up to his sworn undertaking to return to the Philippines. Even if she could sail that boat on principle, with the document lost, that ship had already sailed. Justice Secretary Simeon Datumanong ordered Gutierrez instead to look into whether or not Judge Hollows' decision could be appealed. It couldn't. The government could, however, file another extradition request should new evidence surface. If Philippine authorities were ever going to get their hands on Strunk, it would have to wait for them to build a stronger case.

As the weeks passed into months, the case continued its roller coaster run: the Court of Appeals denied a motion by Strunk's Manila attorneys to have the murder charge against him dismissed. One new witness—a relative of Blanca's—came forward to say that Strunk had been calling Blanca to check on her whereabouts more than usual in the weeks before the murder. That was hardly enough to raise realistic hopes of a successful second attempt at extradition. And then there was a witness who claimed to have seen Strunk get into a car at Blanca's wake that fit the description of a vehicle said to have been used in surveillance of Blanca prior to the murder. Unfortunately, the most useful witness vanished. Alfredo "Aldo" Rodriguez claimed to have been one of the people tasked to do surveillance of Blanca, but after coming forward, he was beaten and left for dead by unidentified individuals in Tarlac province. Rodriguez had said that, with Medel and another individual, he had followed Blanca for a week prior to the killing. Another interesting thing about Rodriguez was that he knew retired General Galileo Kintanar, the former chief of the Intelligence Service of the Armed Forces of the Philippines, and the uncle of Romulo Kintanar, the former NPA chief who had been assassinated by his former communist cohorts in January of 2003. Galileo Kintanar's name began to come up again and again in the investigation. Police were interested in the fact that Kintanar owned the Quezon City apartment that Medel was staying in prior to the murder. Another witness, a security guard named Rogelio Salutin, had claimed that he had seen Strunk and Medel together in the Kintanar apartment. Salutin said that he had gone into hiding himself in August of 2002 when two armed men, allegedly associates of Kintanar's, came to his apartment looking for him. Two other witnesses claimed to have been in Kintanar's home where they heard a Colonel Benny Letrondo speak about methods of keeping Kintanar's name out of the Blanca murder case after Medel's surrender, using terms like "damage control." Blanca's murder was beginning to sound like a covert and rather serpentine military operation. At the time of this writing it was still hanging in limbo.

Just as he had been in the fall of dictator Ferdinand Marcos in 1986, Jaime Cardinal Sin was also very instrumental in the ouster of President Joseph Estrada and the ascension of Gloria Macapagal-Arroyo to the presidency. Just how much power the Church had (or has) within the government of the Philippines is something that obviously makes many uneasy, but seems to be a matter of convenience for others. It is not easy to downplay the Church's importance to the overthrow of Marcos (Radio Veritas was truly the lifeline of the People Power Revolution), which made the power of the Church in matters of State a big help as it turned out, and while its importance to EDSA II was not as great, text messaging seeming to be the lifeline of that uprising, the Church did play its role in promoting Arroyo to the presidency. Opinion seems divided on whether it was Arroyo's own devout Catholicism or simply the time-honored Philippine tradition of *utang na loob* (a kind of debt of gratitude) that prompted her to more or less do the Church's bidding, but just two months into her presidency she created quite a furor when she used the powers of her office—powers bestowed on the office by Presidential Decree 1986, Ferdinand Marcos' doing—to ban the film *Live Show*.

Live Show was, of course, Jose Javier Reyes' film *Toro*, disapproved by the MTRCB because of its title, no less, but being granted approval by the Board upon the title change. The film had been reaping international acclaim through film festivals through the year 2000, and now the Filipino public was finally able to see it, although it was restricted to adults only, a well-reasoned decision. But after the film was approved by the MTRCB under Armida Siguion-Reyna's chairpersonship, the change of power came, and Cardinal Sin suggested Nicanor Tiongson for the position of chairman of the MTRCB. The president accepted the Cardinal's suggestion and appointed Tiongson.

A respected film critic and university professor, Tiongson has a Ph. D in Philippine Studies from the University of the Philippines and a Bachelor of Humanities degree from Ateneo de Manila. He was one of the founding members of the Manunuri ng Pelikulang Pilipino (Critics of Filipino Film), which vote on and give out the annual Star Awards. Under the Aquino administration he had been appointed as artistic director of the Cultural Center of the Philippines in 1986, serving as such until 1994. His background made him seem like a good choice for the role of MTRCB Chairman, although the fact that he was a known liberal also made him seem an odd choice coming as he did on the recommendation of the extremely conservative Cardinal Sin. Perhaps it was his having been a seminarian that made Tiongson appeal to Cardinal Sin as an appropriate choice, but whatever the reason, Sin suggested him and President Arroyo acceded to the request: it didn't take long for that one to blow up in everyone's face.

Just over a month into his chairmanship, Tiongson granted a meeting with Cardinal Sin, who was disturbed by the public showing of *Live Show*, and suggested that Tiongson withdraw its permit. Tiongson politely informed the Archbishop that the film's permit had been granted by the previous Board, and that he did not have the authority to rescind permits granted by the prior Board. This was not what Cardinal Sin wanted to hear, and he became irate; Tiongson would later describe the meeting as a traumatizing experience. "He tried to get me to ban the film," Tiongson said. "He berated me in the harshest language. He said that I was clearly ineffective and had no backbone."[16]

Many feared that President Arroyo was a puppet doing the Church's bidding, and they openly decried the incursion of the Church in matters of State. Perhaps it was merely to deflect such criticisms, but according to Cardinal Sin's spokesman, Monsignor Socrates Villegas, it was the President who got in touch with the Archbishop and asked him if he could somehow convince Tiongson to resign. Arroyo had let it be known to Tiongson that she wanted *Live Show* banned (probably due to pressure from various Christian organizations, not necessarily the Catholic Church itself, but groups like the God's People Coalition for Righteousness, Couples for Christ, and the Jesus Is Lord Movement), but she found Tiongson more than a little resistant to the idea. After he refused to grant the request, the President let Cardinal Sin know that she had problems with Tiongson and asked if he could help. She may have turned to

Cardinal Sin simply because he was a person of authority and persuasion, but he was also the one who recommended Tiongson for the job, and so Arroyo may have hoped to use that as leverage in asking Sin to handle the situation. Cardinal Sin's meeting with Tiongson went nowhere, despite the Archbishop's continually inserting the word "resign" into the conversation at every opportunity, and in a meeting with the President, Tiongson tried to explain to her that, under the law, he did not have the authority as Chairman of the MTRCB to withdraw a permit that had been issued by a previous Board. The President kindly offered to rewrite the laws in order to give him the authority to facilitate her wishes, but Tiongson refused. Gloria Macapagal-Arroyo was then forced into doing her own dirty work. And do it she did, announcing that she was using her authority under PD 1986 to ban the film; the ensuing firestorm, while wholly predictable, was certainly not the kind of thing the President wanted, particularly in the first weeks of her term, but she should have seen it coming. Immediately after Arroyo announced the ban, Tiongson resigned as Chairman of the MTRCB, having only served five weeks. "I refuse to be an instrument for the repression of freedom of expression," he said.[17]

The outcry from the film industry was immediate and effusive. Filmmaker Gil Portes read a statement on behalf of the Coalition of Filipino Film and Television Workers, saying "We are disturbed by the fact that these ultraconservative attacks have prompted the newly installed government to short-circuit due process by banning *Live Show*, a critically acclaimed film that has been exhibited in various international film festivals and has even been praised by the head of the prestigious Organisation Catholique Internationale du Cinema, or OCIC, for its very strong social concerns."[18] The film's director, Jose Javier Reyes, was more demonstrative in his outrage, saying "Anyone who says *Live Show* is pornographic is sick in the head. The toro, or sex scenes, are to dramatize the dehumanization of the toreros. No obscene interest could be aroused except if they are sick in the head."[19]

Tiongson expressed the same sentiment, saying "If anyone gets titillation by this film, he must be sick."[20] He also noted the irony that the freedom of expression that had been so crucial to bringing down Estrada and lifting up Arroyo should then be the first casualty of the new administration. Tiongson's points were well articulated, but those of others tended to be more blunt in their attacks on the President. The Concerned Artists of the Philippines (CAP) issued a statement accusing the President of "stooping to the whims of some Catholic ultraconservatives," and saying that she "exposed herself as a president without a backbone."[21] If Monsignor Villegas was telling the truth, then it was the President who was proving to be the ultimate Catholic ultraconservative. Ironically, CAP was, along with the Directors Guild of the Philippines, very active in turning the entertainment industry against one of its own, Joseph Estrada, and promoting the presidency of Gloria Macapagal-Arroyo.

Others, like screenwriter Pete Lacaba, went overboard in their condemnation almost to the point of hysteria. Lacaba said that *nothing* could be as immoral as the suppression of artists' freedom to express themselves, certainly a self-serving statement coming from a writer, and one that could be called silly if not for its callous disregard for far more grievous human rights violations.

And then there was Jean Enriquez, the Deputy Director of the Coalition Against Trafficking of Women-Asia Pacific," who took the occasion to attack the Church on other issues like its opposition to abortion. "There is something sinister," she said, "about a Church that claims to protect and defend women, but limits their choices and then labels them when they are driven to work in dehumanizing jobs just so they can feed their families.... Now that's something pornographic, when others, and not the person herself, have the say on matters pertaining to her own body."[22] Some people can't miss an opportunity to make an obtuse point.

Well, what was it all about anyway? *Live Show* was really nothing new, depicting the lives of destitute and impoverished young people and how they are driven to desperate measures to try and survive and supply a means of support for their families and loved ones, making spectacles of themselves for the amusement and pleasure of perverts and voyeurs, stripping all meaning from the deepest and most intimate form of human contact. It had certainly been done before, by Tikoy Aguiluz with *Boatman* (1984), Chito Rono with *Private Show* (1985), and Lino Brocka with *Macho Dancer* (1988). Had any of them captured the desperation and despair more accurately? Perhaps not, but that's a matter of individual perception. While Aguiluz's film was well-received in 1984, some have in recent years looked back on it and dismissed it as cheap sensationalism.

In any event, Arroyo had further opened herself up to criticism for being a puppet of the Church by admitting that she hadn't even seen the film when she ordered it banned. She rectified that by ordering a private showing in the Malacanang screening room. After watching the film alone, she emerged from the screening room feeling vindicated in her decision, telling an aide that there was "something really lewd about" the film.[23] But offering up that opinion was not going to be enough to calm the members of the entertainment industry, who had turned out by the hundreds on the streets of Manila on March 26th along with free speech advocates, carrying signs and protesting the administration's assault on free expression. Unfortunately, the demonstrators chose to make their point by mooning police officers, which was not only embarrassingly childish—reinforcing the image of the entertainment industry as one populated by spoiled, infantile and overpaid brats—but was a thoroughly obnoxious way of promoting self expression.

Although the President was loathe to alienate the nation's celebrity population, what else could she do? It was them or the Church: who was more responsible for getting her where she was? Close call, perhaps, but movie stars couldn't excommunicate her or intimidate her with talk of hellfire and damnation for presiding over the decline of the nation's moral character. The Church may not have started the whole brouhaha, but Arroyo had, after all, dragged the Church into it, and should she turn back now the Church might look ineffectual. But, knowing that she was suddenly being portrayed as the bane of the film industry, and eager to get back on the entertainment industry's good side, Arroyo held a press conference on March 27th with the intent of softening her image. She took some time to explain her reasoning for the ban, saying that the issue was bigger than the mere banning of one film, and that the right to expression was not absolute, but should conform to the culture's values. But didn't *Live Show* do just that, since it was merely depicting a facet of contemporary society, albeit of Manila's underground? To drive her point home all the more, Arroyo quoted the film's own director from a paper he had written in 1999, in which he said that Filipino films were an economic, social and cultural force, and she took some delight in quoting Reyes again where he had written "The film industry realizes and accepts that accountability and responsibility on the part of the artist must accompany freedom of expression."[24]

But one could reason that many of the President's reasons could just as easily serve to illustrate the opposing viewpoint. For instance, she remarked that Philippine films were not only for the entertainment of the audience, but should also be for their enlightenment. Well, didn't *Live Show* serve to enlighten its audience to the degradation that poverty was bringing on the society?

After doing what little she could to try and explain the ban, Arroyo, desperate to win the industry over, made certain pledges to help the ailing industry overcome all its problems, and even mentioned, as so many before her had done, the subject of finding ways to make the Filipino film industry more globally competitive. In order to win the industry over, she mentioned the longstanding problem of over taxation, thanked the municipal mayors of Metro Manila for lowering the amusement tax—which she described as "onerous"—from 30% to 15%. She had mentioned that the exorbitant tax was partially responsible for the proliferation of pornographic films, since the decreasing profit margin made smut the safest economic bet. She also mentioned the problem of video piracy, something that had been eating away at the industry for many years and was, with the advent of digital technology, looking like the last nail in the industry's coffin. Film production had fallen off to a distressingly high degree; in 1999 there were 118 films produced for the domestic market, a considerable drop from the 1998 total of 147, but the number would drop all the way down to 86 films in 2000, the first time that the annual number had dipped below the 100-count in over 30 years: it would remain under 100 per annum thereafter.

With Tiongson gone, Arroyo appointed 76-year-old writer Alejandro Roces to be the new MTRCB Chairman. Roces had served as Education Secretary from 1961–65 during the administration of Arroyo's father, President Diosdado Macapagal, and his outlook would seem to have been in line with what the administration and the Church were looking for in a censor. After being sworn-in as Chairman, Roces informed the press of his intention to lobby congress in order to have the laws changed to make pornography a criminal offence. He also proposed the licensing of film directors, whose licenses could be revoked for making porn films. He was certainly making the entertainment industry jittery, all the more so when he told a reporter after his appointment that the last worthwhile film he had seen was *Gandhi* in 1982. He also made known his partiality to pre-war films. Roces did, however, have one curious characteristic for someone being pegged to head up a presumably puritanical group of scissor-happy thought police: an essayist and humorist, Roces was known to have a particular fondness for telling smutty jokes.

Roces didn't really have time to be too upsetting to the film industry, serving for little more than a year. The reason for his departure was never really made clear; some say he merely got bored and requested to be replaced, or was perhaps not thrilled by the job's lack of remuneration—he did, after all, move on to a cushy banking position. Others seem to feel that Malacanang asked him to step down, perhaps out of disenchantment over his inability to do much about the film industry's continued reliance on erotica. Whatever the reason for his departure, he was given some reward for his service shortly afterward when, in June of 2003, President Arroyo bestowed upon him the honor of naming him a National Artist for Literature. Eddie Romero was announced as a National Artist for Film, making him one of very few in that category (His mentor Gerry de Leon had previously been given the honor, as had the late Lamberto Avellana). Although Roces was an awarded short story writer, essayist and journalist, some seemed to think that he was undeserving of National Artist honors. Poet Virgilio Almario, for instance, was also named a National Artist for Literature that same year, and had the extreme poor taste to make his acceptance speech an occasion to belittle Roces' inclusion by criticizing President Arroyo and whoever else bore responsibility for placing Roces on the list.

It seemed to be a revolving door at the MTRCB after that: Roces was replaced by MariLen Dinglasan, whose problems were not so much with the film industry as they were with the Board itself, its members and employees turning on her to the point of holding daily protests outside the Quezon City building where the Board kept its offices. It got to be enough of a nuisance that Dinglasan either left, or was asked to leave, and although her absence was officially listed as being a simple leave, it was a leave that lasted until everyone forgot that it was technically just a leave. In the meantime she was replaced by Dennis Manicad, a lawyer who had been serving on the Board since 1998. Although many thought that he was well-suited for the job,

Manicad was never officially named Chairman, but was instead listed as Officer in Charge, until the President named economist Consoliza Laguardia as the new Chair in 2003. Laguardia, a long-time employee of the Philippine National Bank, is said to be a distant relative of Arroyo's. Her tenure has not given the entertainment industry much reason to rejoice, television shows seeming to be a particular obsession of the Board under her watch. The MTRCB under Laguardia has suspended many television programs for various reasons, even including news programs. In May 2005 Laguardia issued a memo in which she required that all public affairs programs, news documentaries, and even socio-political editorials were listed as requiring MTRCB approval before airing, a policy which rather remarkably was to include live talk shows. Shortly thereafter, one of Laguardia's harshest critics, MTRCB member Monsignor Nico Bautista, began to speak out publicly against Laguardia, saying that she was unqualified to serve as Chairperson, and supporting Senate Minority Leader Aquilino Pimentel, Jr.'s call for her to resign. Laguardia tried to gloss over the stupidity of her memo by saying that producers of live television programs could submit their programs for what she called a "post-review," whereby the Board could then determine if there was anything inappropriate within the program.

The question is, are filmmakers deliberately testing the boundaries with the MTRCB or are they just generally obsessed with sex as their primary source of material? Are they really and genuinely incapable of making an interesting film without skirting the limits? The moneymen are, of course, obsessed with profits, which would explain their predilection for more provocative material to try and maximize potential financial gain, but how is it that even the most respected of directors often seem incapable of avoiding run-ins with the MTRCB? Are they perhaps merely infatuated with the publicity and notoriety they can milk from inviting controversy, or is it that the MTRCB really has, under Arroyo and her appointees, become the puppet of the Church?

Among those who have had a run-in with the Laguardia Board is Tikoy Aguiluz, whose film *pinaysex.com* (2003) ran into trouble basically over its title. The MTRCB refused to grant the film approval owing to its title, Laguardia reasoning that the film's title might give foreigners the impression that most Filipino women are involved in some kind of internet sex trade, be it pornography, prostitution or even mail-order brides. For the record, the film is about a Filipina who returns to Manila from the United States and finds work in the internet pornography business. Feeling that the image of Filipino women had been maligned enough and that mail-order bride websites had already given the impression of Filipinas as either gold-diggers or sexually promiscuous, Laguardia felt that the film's title would only reinforce that misapprehension. Aguiluz scheduled a meeting with Laguardia and felt certain that he could convince her to reconsider the decision and allow him to keep the title. No such luck: the film's title was changed to *www.XXX.com*, but, hey, at least it wasn't banned.

The film industry was doing more than merely tempting the Church, Arroyo, Laguardia and the MTRCB: some of the nation's largest theater chains announced a ban on R-18—adults only, but MTRCB approved—films from exhibition in their theaters. Many thought that the decision was at least in part a backlash against a scandal involving bold genre actresses and congressmen. In 2004, a high-priced escort girl came forward with the information that some of her clients were congressmen, who also liked hiring bold film actresses moonlighting as escorts for out of town trips. It somehow seemed to some that the film industry was dragging the whole culture down, and there were those who had had enough. In August of 2004 Chinese-Filipino tycoon Henry Sy, Sr., the nation's Retail King, and the owner of SM Malls, the country's largest chain of shopping malls, let it be known that R-18 films would no longer be playing in SM theaters. It was quite a blow to the film industry: there are 25 SM Malls in the Philippines, each with 6–10 theaters.

The SM stands for Shoe Mart. Sy began his business empire very modestly in 1946 with a single shoe store in Quezon City. In 1958 he opened the first Shoe Mart in Manila, and by the 1970s the stores had morphed into full department stores. In 1985 the company opened the nation's first super mall with SM City in Metro Manila, and with the addition of seven more SM super malls in the 1990s, the mall-going experience became a staple of Filipino culture, particularly for weekend family outings. The company has added 17 more SM Malls since 2000, and has 8 more on the drawing boards from late 2006 to 2008.

The loss of that many exhibition venues was upsetting news for the film industry, although many politicians and clergy praised the decision. It should be remembered, however, that not all R-18 films are sex films. Many action films, due to their violent content, also get stamped with R-18 ratings, which made at least one politician recoil at the announcement. While most politicians were praising the move, some no doubt in order to try and distance themselves from the escort scandal, Senator Ramon "Bong" Revilla, Jr., who still found time to star in an action film here and there despite his schedule as a legislator, was quick to inform the SM management that the R-18 ban in SM theaters could truly be the last nail in the Filipino film industry's coffin; it was that bad. But the appeal fell on deaf ears, as the SM R-18 ban had already started a chain reaction. The Alturas Group of Companies (ASG), owner of Island City Malls on the island of Bohol announced in October of 2004 that the company would be permanently banning R-18 films from its theaters. The company's public relations manager, Loy Palapos, explained that the earlier SM ban was not the reason for the decision, but rather the desire of the ASG company to remain faithful to Bohol culture, which tends to be conservative and religiously observant. Still, it came so fast on the heels of the SM announcement that one can't help but feel that ASG took its inspiration from Henry Sy, Sr. Again it was to Bong Revilla's great consternation. He reiterated the impending collapse of the Filipino film industry, and said that such bans would only facilitate the industry's demise. But the company, like Sy, would not be moved. "I disagree with Bong's stand," said Palapos. "It is the Filipino sexy films that had given the industry a bad name."[25]

Everyone seemed to have their own idea as to what was killing the industry. Revilla saw the R-18 bans as the potential end, Palapos saw the industry's reliance as cheap sensationalism as its downfall, conversely, others saw censorship as killing the industry; then there was filmmaker Carlo Caparas, who blamed the industry's freefall on overly-harsh critics, saying that their savaging of Filipino films in their reviews were discouraging people from wanting to go see the films. He had a rather odd solution to the problem: he asked film critics to hold off on reviewing films until *after* the films had completed their run, which basically makes the purpose of a film review irrelevant. But by and large, the reasons for the industry's troubles were accepted as being a combination of longstanding problems: foreign competition, over-taxation and video piracy. It certainly was taxed in every way possible; President Arroyo had made gestures to reduce the amusement tax, but that was the one tax that she was most powerless to change. The amusement tax was not a federal tax, therefore all she could do was to ask municipal mayors and lawmakers at the city level to lower the amusement tax. Some agreed to cut it in half, lowering it from 30% to 15%: saying it and doing it were two different things, and some time after making the suggestion and getting word from some Metro Manila mayors that they would indeed be lowering the tax, Arroyo found herself obliged to remind some of them of their commitment.

Aside from the 30% amusement tax, there is also the 32% corporate income tax, which would be levied after the deduction of the costs of production, advertising and promotion, a 10% value-added tax, 5% withholding tax, and various other payments, including tariff and customs duty to be paid on unexposed film stock, license and permit fees, and of course the

8,500-peso fee collected by the MTRCB for screening the film. When all is tallied up, better than half of a film's gross receipts are eaten away by taxes; if a film should fail to do well at the box office, then that 52–55% in taxes could make all the difference. Simply lowering tax rates—and eliminating the amusement tax entirely—would make a big difference, but that would make too much sense. Instead, the Arroyo administration brainstormed to find ways, other than sensible federal fiscal policy, to help the film industry. Some of the ideas were actually quite good: others were simply awful.

One idea to better help the administration understand the problems of the film industry and find solutions to those problems was the creation of the Film Development Council of the Philippines (FDCP) in June 2002. Headed by filmmaker Laurice Guillen, the FDCP included the Cinema Evaluation Board (CEB), a body that would review films and grade them. It was a good way to encourage filmmakers to produce quality work, as films were given the opportunity to earn tax rebates based on their ratings. Films that received the highest rating, an A, were entitled to 100% of the amusement tax collected from the film's gross, while B-graded films entitled the producer to 65% of the amusement tax collected. It was a creative way of inspiring the film industry to aim higher than cheap erotica, short of actually *eliminating* the burdensome amusement tax. In this way, only the most ordinary or awful of films had to pay the full tax.

Otherwise, the FDCP's ideas tended to lean heavily on protectionism, suggesting the government enact a law similar to Korea's quota system, which requires Korean theaters to screen Korean films 40% of the time. The FDCP members were not the only ones proposing protectionism; for years it had been brought up from time to time that the Philippines was one of the only nations in the region that did not place a quota on foreign films, and indeed, attempts to do so through the years had always failed. But when it came to shortsighted and ill-advised protectionist ideas, none came close to the nonsensical policy enacted by the Bureau of Immigration in alliance with FAP. In August of 2004, the Bureau of Immigration announced that foreign film producers seeking to shoot in the Philippines had to go through a screening process by way of FAP, and that they would also have to make "equity payments" to the Actors' Guild before they could begin work. This so-called equity payment would be the equivalent of the Filipino actors and technicians who would be displaced by foreigners coming into the country to shoot a film. It was a bewildering concept, since the number of Filipino actors and crew members who were being displaced by foreign film crews could be easily estimated as being ... zero. Foreign film crews were not robbing Filipinos of their jobs; if anything, foreign productions often brought more work to Filipino film industry personnel since they frequently employed Filipinos on their staff in various capacities, from caterers to film crew personnel to supporting actors. The new policy was so mind-numbingly stupid that it was hard to believe that anybody could possibly defend it. But the Bureau issued a statement saying that the equity payment would be "equivalent to the performance rates of the total number of local film artists and workers to be displaced from work as a result of the film shooting."[26] In other words, if Chuck Norris were to return to the Philippines to shoot another of his *Missing in Action* films, he would have to pay for displacing a Filipino actor who would not be getting his role: how stupid is that? It just got dumber from there.

FAP would also require the foreign film's producers to pay not only for filming permits, licenses, and city and municipal taxes, but also entertainment taxes to the local governments involved. Basically, the new policy told foreign film producers thinking about filming in the Philippines that they would be a lot smarter to go film their movie somewhere else. Gone were the days when the likes of Roger Corman and Antonio Margheriti shot films in the Philippines by the dozen. Corman had passed on shooting *The Big Doll House* in Puerto Rico in 1971 because the Philippines offered such a wonderfully exotic location at such reasonable rates. If he were filming it today, he'd take Puerto Rico over the Philippines in a heartbeat.

There were problems more dire than the tax situation, which had after all been around almost as long as the industry itself. The more modern and very vexing problem of video piracy was robbing the industry of billions of pesos a year. It was estimated that as many as nine out of every ten videos, VCDs or DVDs sold in the Philippines were bootlegs. The piracy rate in the Philippines in 2003 was estimated by the Optical Media Board to be 89%, a stunning figure that put the country fourth in the region. And that was an increase from the 2002 piracy rate of 80%, a high enough figure as it was. It wasn't just the film industry losing out; the Philippine government was missing out on all of those taxes as well, to the tune of some 800 million pesos annually (yes, there is an amusement tax on DVDs and CDs as well). Senator Bong Revilla, Jr. was appointed head of the Videogram Regulatory Board, and being a film star himself, he was keenly aware of the devastating effect of piracy on not just the film industry, but the entire entertainment industry; recording and releasing a music CD in the Philippines became a most un-worthwhile financial venture as pirated copies could be had openly through sidewalk vendors for a fraction of the price. The same was happening with pirated VCDs and DVDs of films, some of which could be bought in retail outlets in shopping malls even before the films premiered theatrically. The problem had reared its head in the 1980s during the dawning of the video age, but with the expansion of digital technology the problem reached critical mass. Whereas pirated video tapes often displayed a very discernible inferiority in quality, digital technology made it possible to duplicate copyrighted materials without losing a generation.

Stepping up the fight against piracy, Bong Revilla presided over the destruction by steamroller of millions of illegal CDs and DVDs in February of 2003, just as he had in July of 2002, hoping that the seizures and destruction would not only show the pirates that the Videogram Regulatory Board was serious, but show the world as well. The London-based International Federation of the Phonographic Industry had ranked the Philippines as the third worst country in Southeast Asia for intellectual piracy, and U.S. officials were openly criticizing the Philippine government for not doing enough the eradicate or curtail the piracy situation in the country. Revilla found reason to boast somehow in announcing that the government's efforts had managed to cut the number of pirated discs in the market to ... 60%. That's not saying they cut the number *by* 60%, but rather, pirated discs made up 60% of the market in the Philippines. And this was an improvement!

It seemed like a hopeless battle for authorities; the truth is that the ever-advancing digital technology was making piracy easier and easier all the time. The only advantage that digital technology was bringing to the Filipino film industry—and it was hardly amounting to a trade-off—was that it was making it easier for young filmmakers to break into the business. Also for filmmakers like Lav Diaz to indulge themselves; Diaz had made the 5-hour film *Batang West Side* (*West Side Boy*) in 2002, a film which was shot in the U.S. and explored the Filipino-American experience in a roundabout way, following a Filipino detective through his investigation into the death of a Filipino youth in New Jersey. Diaz seemed to bristle at the suggestion that the movie was too long and that it was a bit much to expect people to sit and watch a movie for 5 hours, and critics defended the film, some hailing it a masterpiece. When he ran out of money, Diaz completed his next film, *Ebolusyon ng Isang Pamilyang Pilipino* (*Evolution of a Filipino Family*) by way of digital video, which made it affordable to pursue his vision. No, it wasn't another 5-hour film: this time Diaz outdid himself with a 10-hour epic. He should probably consider television work, as he can't reasonably expect people to want to sit in a movie theater for half their day. While there were those who praised Diaz for challenging the status quo in Philippine cinema and how it is perceived, the truth is that Diaz's work is artistic self-indulgence taken to extremes that could pass as a caricature of Filipino cinema's tendency toward long-windedness. It may be laudable to a handful of critics, but one wonders if those same critics form enough of an audience to support Diaz in his endeavors. The truth is that very few Filipinos have seen his films, and even fewer non–Filipinos. And this is the future, some insist, of Philippine cinema.

By all accounts, Fernando Poe, Jr., was a reluctant candidate for the presidency in 2004. He had been asked before to go into politics, especially as it was becoming more and more fashionable for celebrities to run for office in the country: what better candidate than the King of Philippine Movies? He had declined before, seemingly disinterested in the idea. What made 2004 different? Well, what else was there for him to do? He had been the King of Philippine Movies for some 40 years; perhaps there was a yearning to finally move on and conquer new ground. Besides, the film industry was dying—some say dead in the water already—and what satisfaction in being proclaimed ruler of a razed kingdom. Or maybe he really did feel that he could do something meaningful for the country. But there was also his friend of 40 years to consider. Poe was, by the account of all who knew him, a fiercely loyal individual. Could he allow his old buddy Joseph Estrada to continue to suffer the indignity and humiliation of his ongoing detention and perpetually impending trial for plunder? Before Poe made his decision he visited Estrada at the Greenhills home where the disgraced ex-president was allowed to stay under house arrest. "Ikaw na pare," Estrada told him—"My friend, it's your turn."[27]

It isn't likely that helping Estrada out of his situation would have compelled Poe to do something so drastic as run for president. Those who knew him personally say that Poe was not dissimilar to the characters he played on screen; he really did have a deep and abiding compassion for the people, and a keen sense of injustice. While he had professed no desire to run for office in the past, he may have been feeling a sense of destiny, a beckoning call that was being helped along by all of the speculation in the media and among political parties, many of which were eager to court him. And if he should become president and should find himself able to help his old friend Joseph Estrada out, so much the better. Poe was always quick to help a friend, even if he was slow to ask for help himself. "Even when I was mayor, senator, vice president and president," said Estrada, "he never asked me any favor."[28]

As Poe traveled to Pampanga, Davao City and Cebu City in early 2003 to promote his film *Ang Alamat ng Lawin* (*The Legend of the Hawk*), many could not help but notice that his appearances had all the pomp and circumstance of a political rally, Poe being paraded through the streets and waving to the crowds. The political parties trying to seduce him eventually agreed to merge into one new party, the Koalisyon ng Nagkakaisang Pilipino (Coalition of United Filipinos), or KNP. Polls were encouraging too: most showed Poe as the leading candidate, ahead of incumbent Gloria Macapagal-Arroyo. Finally, in late November 2003, Poe announced his intention to run. "In the life of a person," he said, "the day will come when he has to face the toughest decision of his life, and that day for me has come."[29] Accompanying him during the announcement was Senator Vicente "Tito" Sotto III, a longtime friend and former show business colleague.

Claiming that he could not turn his back on the people clamoring for him to run, Poe deflected criticisms about his lack of qualifications and his being a high school dropout, saying "I would like to be given a chance. I'm sincere, dedicated, and I love my country."[30] He also dodged questions about what he would do with Estrada by saying that the former president had not yet been convicted and that the trial was still ongoing, a shrewd way of saying that it was too early to be thinking of pardons.

It was films like *Matimbang ang Dugo sa Tubig* (*Blood Is Thicker Than Water*/FPJ Productions) that established Fernando Poe, Jr., as the King of Philippine Cinema in the early 1960s. He would remain so for 40 years until his death in 2004.

Poe's announcement that he would be seeking the presidency must have sent titanic shockwaves through Malacanang. President Arroyo was not especially popular, and the idea that the country's most popular cultural hero would be running against her seemed to give Arroyo a panic attack. More a political opportunist than an actual competitor, Arroyo is a product of the political system, and she must have known that it would take everything in her political bag of tricks to derail a Poe presidency. One ploy that Arroyo used prior to Poe's candidacy was to announce in December 2002 that she would not be seeking election in 2004, claiming that this would free her administration up to spend its last year-and-a-half focusing on solving the nation's problems rather than campaigning. What it really did was to take media scrutiny off of her and lessen political attacks from her adversaries, who would have considered such attacks pointless when aimed at an outgoing president. It would not be until October of 2003 that Arroyo would announce her change of heart, letting it be known that she was willing to put her own needs and wishes aside for the good of the country, which so clearly needed her leadership.

But the fear of a Poe candidacy was enough to cause some to seek to disqualify him by any means possible; although it was a private citizen who filed the case against Poe's candidacy on the grounds that he was not a natural born Filipino and therefore not eligible to run for the nation's highest office, there's no telling who put him up to it. Poe's father was Spanish, his mother American. Truth is, Fernando Poe, Jr., had no actual Filipino blood. The complaint was dismissed by the Commission on Elections, prompting the civic-minded citizen to appeal his case to the Supreme Court. But the Court ruled in Poe's favor, reasoning that the Philippine Bill of 1902 stated that "all inhabitants of the Philippine Islands who were Spanish subjects on the eleventh day of April, eighteen hundred and ninety-nine, and then resided in said Islands, and their children born subsequently thereto, shall be deemed and held to be citizens of the Philippine Islands." That said, Poe was cleared to run for President.

His popularity among his show business colleagues had always been extremely high, with few exceptions; those who were not fond of Estrada, like Nora Aunor for instance, were giving their support to Arroyo, as was Carlo Caparas, the man who created the komiks character Panday, whom Poe himself popularized in films. And then there was Lipa City Mayor Vilma Santos, who had co-starred with Poe in a number of films. Santos was busy running for reelection in Lipa, and as Poe was supporting her opponent, Santos refused to grant Poe's party a permit to hold a political rally in Lipa. It was the only city in Batangas that denied the KNP a permit. Such a political move might have hurt most candidates, but aside from being an exceedingly popular film star, Santos was also a popular incumbent, and she went on to win reelection. Many pundits were not altogether enthusiastic about the prospect of a Poe presidency, some fearing another debacle like Estrada's truncated term, others put off by Poe's reluctance to articulate a plan of action should he be elected. In fact, he wasn't debating anyone either. His campaign eventually settled on the simple slogan "breakfast, lunch and dinner" as its simple promise to provide for all Filipinos. His handlers obviously felt that it was enough for him to greet the masses with a wave; after all, they knew him well enough. He was the strong, silent defender of the people from countless movies for over a generation. What more did the people need to know? Former MTRCB Chairman Nicanor Tiongson, who had moved on to become a film professor and dean of the University of the Philippines' College of Mass Communication, said that a Poe presidency might be even worse than Estrada's. "I'm not looking down on him," Tiongson said, "but having gone to school is equated with having developed certain skills of analysis. It's equated with having accumulated enough knowledge in your mind to be able to make correct judgments on relationships, on policies."[31] So, Tiongson claimed not to be looking down on Poe, while very visibly looking down on him.

Polls were mixed, and even come election day on May 10th exit polls were confusing, one polling organization, Social Weather Stations, initially announcing that Arroyo took 34% of the Metro Manila vote to Poe's 25%, then saying that a rather huge mistake had been made in its calculations, and that Poe had actually had 37% to Arroyo's 26%. Another research group had Poe winning 38% to 34%. But whatever the exit polls were showing, in the final vote tally, Arroyo was declared the winner on June 20th by more than one million votes. It seemed impossible, but in a country enamored with celebrity politics, the most popular film star in the nation's history had lost to an incumbent whose popularity was middling. It was enough to cause some to quickly cry election fraud, accusing Arroyo and her camp of switching ballots and manufacturing votes; Poe himself contested the election results and in July 2004 he asked the Supreme Court to annul Arroyo's victory. Others speculated that Poe had run too soon on the heels of the disastrous Estrada presidency, and that the country was in no mood for another action hero/movie star administration so soon. The truth is, Poe had squandered his early lead in the polls, and by election day, he was actually trailing in most polls. Many thought his lack of any coherent roadmap for his proposed presidency had finally caught up to him.

As the Supreme Court weighed the issue, Poe receded from public life, making few public appearances in the months following the election. But unlike the movies, Poe would not be able to defeat the system; not this time, for he was running out of time. On a Saturday night, December 11, 2004, Poe was holding a Christmas party at the Quezon City offices of his film production company in San Francisco del Monte. Among the guests were Congressman Francis Escudero of Sorsogon, the spokesman of the KNP, and his longtime acting pals Eddie Garcia and Jaime Fabregas. As the night wore on Poe began complaining of dizziness, nausea and a pain in the back of his neck. Days earlier he had complained of blurred vision, but put it down to his need for a new prescription for his eyeglasses. But as he sat with his guests at the dinner table on the night of the 11th, Poe suddenly slumped forward in his chair. He was immediately taken to St. Luke's Medical Center in Quezon City. Doctors determined that Poe, who slipped into a coma upon arriving at the hospital, had suffered a stroke.

News spread quickly of Poe's admittance to the hospital, and the Philippine National Police had to help the hospital's security team control the crowd gathering outside. From his confinement, Joseph Estrada heard that his best friend of 40 years was in the hospital, and he immediately called Poe's wife, Susan Roces, on her cell phone. After she told him the situation, Estrada tried to encourage Roces with talk of divine providence. He then made a request: he wanted to talk to Poe. Although he was in a coma, Estrada had things to say to his old friend, and he hoped that Poe would hear. Fighting back tears, Roces held the phone to her husband's ear as Estrada said what was on his mind; perhaps words of encouragement, perhaps a farewell. The following day Estrada was granted an hour to go and visit Poe in the hospital, which was especially comforting to Roces, as she recalled the 40 years of friendship the two had shared.

An entire floor of the hospital had been cordoned off for security purposes, not only for the family, but for the many prominent visitors coming to offer encouragement to Roces. Imelda Marcos, who, with her husband Ferdinand, had attended the wedding of Poe and Roces in 1968, came to leave some rosary beads that she claimed had healing powers. Another visitor was Corazon Aquino, the woman who had helped unseat Ferdinand Marcos and drive him and Imelda from the country. Poe's charismatic personality obviously transcended such differences. Poe died on December 14, 2004, without regaining consciousness.

In the week between Poe's death and funeral, for some the grief began to mix with rage as supporters came to feel increasingly convinced that they had been cheated, and that Arroyo had stolen the election. It was cause for concern for the government, as Poe's funeral promised to bring out mourners by the tens of thousands. Susan Roces asked the mourners not to turn her husband's funeral into a political event, and Poe's half-brother, actor Conrad Poe, announced, "We want a solemn burial," and asked the people to "Please avoid painting any political color."[32]

But despite the family's wishes, the government was getting information that the opposition could use the occasion as the impetus for another populist uprising, like the one that brought Arroyo to power. President Arroyo felt compelled to speak to the military the day before the funeral at an awards ceremony in which she told the soldiers that she expected the military to remain faithful to her. There was enough reason to be concerned; the funeral itself would be held at Santo Domingo Church in Quezon City, the very same place where Benigno Aquino, Jr. had lain in state. For Arroyo the parallel was a bit unnerving. To hear the funeral itself, one could understand her concern. One after another, film stars got up to say their piece in bidding farewell to the King of Philippine Films, and many of them took the occasion to denounce the Arroyo administration with impassioned and melodramatic speeches worthy of their calling. Joseph Estrada, allowed to attend the services and deliver the eulogy, could not resist; he remarked that both he and his departed best friend had each been robbed of the presidency, and he offered an ominous warning: he told the government to prepare for trouble. There was more than the threat of an opposition uprising to worry about. Military intelligence had been notified of possible attacks by communist rebels and Islamic terrorists;

with such an enormous crowd, the opportunity for mischief was tremendous. Security would be necessarily tight.

Mourners waited for as long as 12 hours—longer than it takes to watch a Lav Diaz movie—to file past Poe's coffin and get one last glimpse of their idol. Hundreds of thousands lined the streets to watch the horse drawn carriage carrying Poe's casket make its way to the cemetery, a process that took hours as the crowd pressed in on the procession from both sides. The carriage was pulled by Poe's favorite horse, which had appeared with him in some of his films. But, despite all of the concern, in the end the funeral went off without any trouble. Other than occasional chanting, the crowd remained respectful of the family's wishes. And then, the King was gone, having made his last curtain call.

Perhaps, given the dire situation that the Philippine film industry found itself in through the first five years of the 21st century, nothing could have been quite so symbolic as the death of Fernando Poe, Jr. He had ridden atop the industry for 40 years, its constant box office champion and most cherished hero to the masses. Poe's death seemed somehow larger than the loss of a popular film star; it had a definite finality about it beyond his own mortality, and it seemed to create a gaping chasm that was widening enough when he was alive, but now seemed almost unbridgeable. Following Poe's death there were other smaller, but still telling signs that not only was an era gone, but that time itself seemed to be leaving the Filipino film industry behind. Although LVN Studios had long since ceased as a film production company, its color processing lab—the very lab set up by William P. Smith in 1951—had remained open and functioning, still esteemed as the best color lab facility not only in the country, but perhaps in the entire Fareast. The lab closed down in 2005, the latest symbol of the industry's death throes. Truth is, there just wasn't enough business anymore to keep the lab operating. In 1998, the year that gave the industry so much hope that a new renaissance in Philippine cinema was dawning, there were 147 films produced by the local industry. In 2004, the year that Poe died, the Filipino film industry only produced 52 films, down from the already low number of 82 in 2003. By October of 2005, that number stood at 37. The end is indeed in sight.

In September 2005 President Arroyo again promised that the policies of her administration would be beneficial to the growth of the industry. She further spoke of her dream to make the Philippines into the entertainment center of Asia. That has a familiar ring to it. Ah, yes; it harkens back to those two trailblazing Americans, George F. Harris and Edward Tait, who had started Filippine Films in 1932. In a lot of ways it was the beginning of it all—the solidifying of the studio system that came to dominate the industry for so many years. And when they started Filippine Films, Harris and Tait also had a dream: they dreamed of making Manila into the filmmaking capital of Asia. With Arroyo's statement it would be tempting to say that things have come full circle, but the sad truth is that things simply never changed. The industry dreamed big dreams that never came true, and more than 70 years later, not only was that dream unfulfilled, but seemed farther away than ever.

On March 27, 2001, as President Arroyo was trying to make nice with the film industry as it continued to savage her over the banning of *Live Show*, she made reference to the hopes and aspirations of the great directors in Philippine cinema, saying: "Legendary directors Gerry de Leon, Manuel Conde, Bert Avellana, Lino Brocka and Ishmael Bernal had dreams for the Filipino film industry. They dreamt of the day when Filipino films would blossom into a major force in world cinema. They dreamt of foreign audiences which are aware of the identity of filmmaking in the Philippines. The legendary directors dreamt of the day when the perception that Filipino films are immoral and inferior to foreign movies would disappear."[33]

Filmography

The following filmography lists the titles alphabetically. For those unfamiliar with Tagalog some clarifications are necessary. For instance, the Tagalog word "ang" is a topic marker for non-personal nouns, thereby often fulfilling the same basic function as the English word "the." Therefore, just as the title *The Brown Ninja* will be alphabetized under B for *Brown Ninja*, the Tagalog title *Ang Dalubhasa* will be alphabetized under D for *Dalubhasa*. The reader should note also that in Tagalog "mga" is not actually a word, but is merely a plural marker (i.e. "agila" means "eagle"; "mga agila" means "eagles"). Titles that begin with "mga" will be alphabetized by the word being pluralized. For instance, the title *Mga Agila sa Gubat* would be alphabetized under A for "Agila."

Adultery: Aida Macaraeg, Case No. 7892

1984 Regal Films; 110 minutes/color
Director: Lino Brocka; Screenwriter: Jose Javier Reyes; Cinematographer: Conrado Baltazar; Editor: Rogelio Salvador; Filmscore: Lutgardo Labad; Cast: Vilma Santos, Phillip Salvador, Mario Montenegro, Deborah Sun, Anita Linda, Tita de Villa, Alvin Enriquez, Menggie Cobarrubias, Diddo dela Paz, Aida Carmona, Benjie Ledesma, Tessie Padua, Ricky Gonzales, Rene Hawkins, Nonoy de Guzman, Jimmy Reyes, Fred Capulong, Rene Romero, Roger Moring

In this melodrama based on a true story, Vilma Santos portrays a young woman whose boyfriend (Phillip Salvador) becomes involved in a drug trafficking gang. Salvador is arrested in a police sting operation and is sentenced to seven years in prison. After he begins serving his sentence, Santos agrees to marry him, and as they are allowed conjugal visits, Santos soon becomes pregnant. But feeling unable to support the child on her own, Santos seeks out an abortion, and it is about this time that Salvador ceases to hear from her. When Salvador is released from prison, he sets out looking for Santos, and he is enraged to discover her living in a plush home with an older man (Mario Montenegro) and a young son. Adultery being a criminal offense in the Philippines, punishable by prison, Salvador presses charges and the case goes to court, and things get worse for Santos when it is revealed in court that she aborted Salvador's baby (abortion also being illegal in the Philippines), and so Santos goes to Salvador and on her knees pleads for mercy and forgiveness. The following day in court Santos' attorney is not optimistic, but Salvador gets up and announces that he is dropping all charges. Santos is then reunited with her son, and she and Salvador say a sad farewell. (In Tagalog with some English)

Agila ng Maynila
(The Eagle of Manila)

1988 FPJ Productions; 111 minutes/color
Director: Pablo Santiago; Screenwriter: Pablo S. Gomez; Cinematographer: Ver Reyes; Editor: Augusto Salvador; Filmscore: Jaime Fabregas; Cast: Fernando Poe Jr., Vic Vargas, Paquito Diaz, Charlie Davao, Vic Diaz, Raoul Aragon, Dencio Padilla, Lito Anzures, Mario Escudero, Lucita Soriano, Nello Nayo, Max Alvarado, Encar Benedicto, RR Herrera, Aida Pedido, Alma Lerma, Louella de Cordova, Gwen Avila, Rene Hawkins, Nonoy de Guzman, Bello Borja, Eddie Tuazon, Ernie David

When Manila police are unable to catch a homicidal sex maniac who is terrorizing the city, they get a helping hand from Fernando Poe, Jr., a former cop currently working as a taxi driver. Poe uses his cabby's street savvy to uncover the killer's identity, and guns the killer down himself. But he doesn't stop there: determined to clean up the streets—something the police seem disinclined to do—Poe invokes the wrath of crime boss Vic Diaz by knocking off some of Diaz's top men. One might expect the police to be grateful for Poe's help, but with police commander Charlie Davao on Diaz's payroll, Poe becomes Manila's most hunted man. After killing Diaz, Poe is cornered in a massive dragnet, but although wounded, he manages to slip through and get away. (In Tagalog with some English)

Aguila (The Eagle)

1980 Bancom Audiovision Corporation; 200 minutes/color
Director/screenwriter: Eddie Romero; Cinematographer: Mike de Leon; Editor: Ben Barcelon; Filmscore: Ryan Cayabyab; Cast: Fernando Poe Jr., Amalia Fuentes, Christopher de Leon, Elizabeth Oropesa, Jay Ilagan, Charo Santos, Chanda Romero, Daria Ramirez, Eddie Garcia, Celia Rodriguez, Orestes Ojeda, Susan Valdez, Johnny Delgado, Andrea Andolong, Conrad Poe, Ruben Rustia, Lito Anzures, Ricky Sandico, Joonee Gamboa, Yvette Christine, Roderick Paulate, Odette Khan, Ariel Muhlach, Behn Cervantes, Dave Brodett

Christopher de Leon portrays a wealthy, middle-aged politician who gets word of the whereabouts of his long-lost father (Fernando Poe, Jr.). After hearing that his father was in Mindanao fairly recently, de Leon catches a plane and begins his search, always arriving in some barrio one step behind Poe. As he journeys, the film reveals Poe's life in a series of lengthy flashbacks, which date back to his childhood during the waning days of Spanish colonialism at the turn of the century, when Poe's father died while fighting the Spanish as a member of a Filipino nationalist group. As a young man, Poe serves in the military under U.S. command, where he battles Moro rebels, and later, during WWII, he leads a resistance army against the Japanese, in which he is joined by his then-teen-aged son de Leon. Years later de Leon develops political aspirations, and it is not long afterward that Poe, who has gone on to become a very successful businessman, dropped out of sight. The film concludes when de Leon finally finds the 88-year-old Poe living in the jungle with a primitive tribe, and the two experience a poignant and wonderfully understated reunion. (In Tagalog with some English)

Alfredo Lim: Batas ng Maynila
(Alfredo Lim: Law of Manila)

1994 Golden Kay International/Harvest International; 120 minutes/color

Director: Ramje; Screenwriters: Ramon Jesus Capinpin, Bomboy Cruz, Erwin Llanado, Johnny Wood; Cinematographer: Johnny Araojo; Editor: Jess Navarro; Filmscore: Marita Manuel; Cast: Eddie Garcia, Dang Cecilio, Timmy Cruz, Gabriel Romulo, Rod Navarro, Charlie Davao, Dick Israel, Dan Fernandez, Rando Almanzor, Alicia Alonzo, Luz Valdez, Lovely Rivero, Conrad Poe, Ruel Vernal, Romy Diaz, Augusto Victa, Jigo Garcia, Jojo Alejar, Danny Labra, Beverly Salviejo, Joey Romero, Ernie Zarate, Rey Ventura, Archie Adamos, Pocholo Montes, Robert Talby

Eddie Garcia has the lead in this true account of the life of Manila mayor Alfredo Lim. The film recounts a number of high-profile busts spanning Lim's 30-year career in law enforcement and his appointment to Director of the National Bureau of Investigation, where his popularity leads to public calls for him to run for mayor of Manila. Lim runs, and wins, and the film covers his attempts to clean up the city by closing down the many dens of iniquity. This is Garcia's show all the way, and he gives an outstanding performance, particularly in the person of the aging Lim, reflecting back on the events in his life. (In Tagalog with some English)

Aliw (Pleasure)

1979 Seven Stars Productions; 115 minutes/color

Director: Ishmael Bernal; Screenwriters: Ishmael Bernal, Franklin Cabaluna; Cinematographer: Sergio Lobo; Editor: Ike Jarlego, Jr; Filmscore: George Canseco; Cast: Lorna Tolentino, Amy Austria, Suzette Ranillo, Dick Israel, Laura Danao, Jojo Santiago, Ruthie Roces, Juan Rodrigo, Ramon Recto, Ruby Regala, Butz Aquino, George Estregan, Antoinette Bass, Manny Castaneda, Ronnie Quesada

This interesting, if meandering, effort by Ishmael Bernal follows the lives of a group of prostitutes lodging together and plying their trade in a Manila discotheque. The young and ridiculously girlish Lorna Tolentino uses her earnings to help support her family, giving her money to her poverty-stricken mother. Suzette Ranillo does the same, supporting her mother and a younger brother. Amy Austria tries to better herself, enrolling in secretarial school where a classmate—a naïve young man who seems oblivious to what she does for a living—pursues her romantically. Bernal's technique was still lacking polish at this point, seeming more documentarian in nature than thoughtfully artistic in its approach; whether this is deliberate or merely down to inexperience is debatable, but Bernal had been directing for some seven years by then. Particularly interesting is the fact that, despite its subject matter, the film is less preoccupied with the tawdry, and more with the mundane aspects of the day-to-day lives of its characters. Bernal gets good performances from Austria and Dick Israel (as a guitarist in the disco's house band), but the film does take a shot in the foot by way of an annoying and unconvincing performance by Tolentino. (In Tagalog)

Alyas Batman en Robin
(Alias Batman and Robin)

1991 Regal Films; 102 minutes/color

Director: Tony Y. Reyes; Screenwriters: Joey de Leon, Tony Y. Reyes; Cinematographer: Oscar Querijero; Editor: Eduardo Jarlego; Filmscore: Mon del Rosario; Cast: Joey de Leon, Rene Requiestas, Dawn Zulueta, Vina Morales, Keempee de Leon, Panchito (Alba), Almira Muhlach, Chinkee Tan, Cathy Mora, Ruben Rustia, Mon Alvir, Bomber Moran, Joaquin Fajardo, Rene Hawkins, Danny Rojo

Panchito Alba and Rene Requiestas go on a bank-robbing spree disguised as the Penguin and the Joker, respectively, and in order to thwart them, Joey de Leon and his son Keempee become Batman and Robin. There are comedic musical numbers (all take-offs on classic American songs by the likes of Little Richard and the Beach Boys), and the film ends with Alba and Requiestas making nice with the de Leons and performing a musical number in which they are all joined by a variety of comic book characters, including the Hulk and a midget Spiderman. (In Tagalog and English)

Ama Namin (Our Father)

1997 Premiere Entertainment; 121 minutes/color

Director: Ben G. Yalung; Screenwriter: Senen Dimaguila; Cast: Christopher de Leon, Sunshine Cruz, Mat Ranillo III, Tonton Gutierrez, Chin Chin Gutierrez, Daniel Fernando, Rez Cortez, Rey Ventura, Patrick dela Rosa, Mandy Ochoa, Pocholo Montes, Marita Zobel, Suzette Ranillo, Amado Cortez, Edgar Mande, Joane Salazar, Marithez Samson, Robert Ortega, Tom Olivar, Vince Borromeo

Set in the 1970s amid the brutal inhumanity of the Marcos regime, this film stars Christopher de Leon as a Catholic priest who takes a trip to see his family in Mindanao. But while he is there his family is murdered by the military, who accuse them of giving aid to communist rebels in the area. As for de Leon, though injured, he manages to escape into the jungle, where he is rescued by those same communist rebels, who nurse him back to health. De Leon falls in love with rebel girl Sunshine Cruz, who dies giving birth to his son. By now very embittered, de Leon forsakes his priestly calling, receives an education in guerrilla warfare, and joins the rebel cause. He is wounded during a shootout with government troops, and after staggering into the jungle and dropping to his knees, he is visited by a glowing apparition of Jesus Himself (in the person of Vince Borromeo). After begging for forgiveness and direction, de Leon passes out, but survives to rejoin the priesthood. Years later, after the fall of Marcos, de Leon is gunned down in church by government soldier Tonton Gutierrez, who had fought the communist rebels and is enraged to learn that de Leon was once a member of the rebel faction.

Purportedly based on a true story, the film is carried along nicely by a strong performance from de Leon and Ben Yalung's direction. It's a pretty straightforward indictment of Ferdinand Marcos' legacy of shame. One scene particularly worth noting comes when de Leon, having turned his back on his Christian faith, fights alongside the rebels against government troops in a small village. After entering the local church, de Leon proceeds to shoot the place up in a fit of rage, and is stunned when the life-sized icon of Jesus begins to bleed from the bullet holes he has filled it with. (In Tagalog with occasional English)

Anak Dalita (Child of Sorrow)

1956 LVN Pictures; 117 minutes/black & white
Director: Lamberto Avellana; Screenwriter: Rolf Bayer; Cinematographer: Mike Accion; Editor: Enrique Jarlego; Filmscore: Francisco Buencamino; Cast: Tony Santos, Rosa Rosal, Joseph de Cordova, Vic Silayan, Leroy Salvador, Oscar Keesee, Rosa Aguirre, Alfonso Carvajal, Johnny Reyes, Eddie Rodriguez, Arturo Moran, Vic Bacani

Tony Santos stars as a Filipino soldier who returns home from service in Korea just in time to say goodbye to his dying mother. Having been wounded and lost the use of his left arm, Santos finds the added burden of his mother's death to be one load too many and he goes on a bender. Sympathetic prostitute Rosa Rosal takes Santos in and the two begin a love affair. Knowing that Santos needs work, priest Vic Silayan offers him a job repairing the many religious icons that were damaged when the church took heavy shelling during WWII, but Santos soon becomes frustrated by the limitations of having only one good arm to work with, and when he is approached by underworld figure Joseph de Cordova he accepts an offer to make some quick cash by helping smuggle stolen currency out of the country to Hong Kong by hiding it inside one of the hollow religious icons that he is restoring. When customs agent Alfonso Carvajal insists on looking inside the icon, he finds it empty, and surmising that Rosal has removed it, de Cordova tries to retrieve it from her. Santos rushes to Rosal's aid, and during a fight atop the ruins, de Cordova falls to his death.

The film manages to remain fairly absorbing throughout its considerable running time, and, unlike many of his contemporaries in Philippine cinema, director Lamberto Avellana clearly had a sophisticated sense of cinematic composition. (In Tagalog)

Anak ng Bulkan (Child of the Volcano)

1997 Premiere Entertainment; 116 minutes/color
Director: Cirio H. Santiago; Screenwriter: Jose Mari Avellana; Cinematographers: Ricardo Remias, Leodigario Dalawis, Jr.; Editor: Joseph Zucchero; Filmscore: Ryan Cayabyab; Cast: Tom Taus Jr., Beth Tamayo, Bembol Roco, Amy Austria, Lloyd Samartino, Denise Joaquin, Bella Flores, Lou Veloso, Joey Galvez, Bon Vibar, Joseph Reyes, Gary Lim, Joe Towers, Ramon Recto, Boots Anson-Roa, Cris Daluz, Bobby Greenwood, Manny Samson, Paul Holme, Thelma Crisologo, Cherry Manila, Nato delos Reyes, Giselle Sanchez, Ernie Baron

Unlike the rush jobs that director Cirio Santiago churned out for American producers, a little money seems to have been spent here. The eruption of Mount Pinatubo brings forth a dinosaur egg, which is discovered by young lad Tom Taus, Jr., who watches it hatch a baby pterodactyl. Taus takes the beast home to care for it, but it grows up in a hurry and soon becomes impossible to hide. Once word gets around, the pterodactyl is captured, and Taus has to free it from the clutches of greedy entrepreneurs, who naturally want it for commercial reasons. The special effects are adequate, even occasionally impressive. This was a remake of a 1959 film by the same name, which was directed by Emmanuel Rojas. Santiago simultaneously shot an English version titled *Vulcan*, which featured Robert Vaughn in its cast. (In Tagalog with some English)

Anak ng Dagat (Son of the Sea)

1991 Pacwood Films International/Silver Screen; 116 minutes/color

Director: Francis "Jun" Posadas; Screenwriter: Ricardo Lee; Cinematographer: Ver Dauz; Editor: Nap Montebon; Filmscore: Marita Manuel; Cast: Ronnie Ricketts, Eddie Gutierrez, Maritoni Fernandez, Donita Rose, Bing Davao, Conrad Poe, Fred Moro, Lora Luna, John Steele, J.J. Sunico, Mario Escudero, Jobelle Salvador, Robert Miller, Renato del Prado, Ernie Forte

Ronnie Ricketts returns to the island of his youth intending to make a living as a pearl diver, but upon arriving he finds the island controlled by sadistic Eddie Gutierrez, who uses his thugs to intimidate the local residents into selling him their pearls for a fraction of their worth. Island girl Donita Rose finds a large black pearl, and when she refuses to hand it over to Gutierrez, he has her kidnapped, prompting Ricketts to do his hero routine. The film climaxes with an excellent showdown, culminating in Ricketts' shooting Gutierrez's fleeing helicopter out of the sky with a bazooka. (In Tagalog with some English)

Anak ng Dilim (Daughter of Darkness)

1997 Regal Entertainment; 93 minutes/color

Director: Nick Lizaso; Screenwriter: Bong Ramos; Cinematographers: Charlie Peralta, Sergio Lobo, Ely Cruz; Editor: Randy Brien; Filmscore: Jessie Lasaten; Cast: Gladys Reyes, Amy Austria, Gina Pareno, Christopher Roxas, Jericcson Matias, Boxer Flores, Alyssa Joy Reyes, Jo-Ann Rosales, Melanie Lazaro, Michael Pascual, Marcus Ramilo, Jefferson Masaangkay

When a mother dies giving birth to her daughter, a tremor convulses the house and a hoary old midwife flies into hysterics, rushing into town and spreading stories of a demon baby. In no time at all a mob of locals gathers outside the house calling for the child. While the baby is hidden by its older sister, the baby's father is killed trying to keep the mob out, but unable to find the child, the mob disperses. In order to keep the mob from returning, the child's grandmother (Gina Pareno) keeps the baby hidden in her house, and 16 years later the child (Gladys Reyes) and her older sister (Amy Austria) are basically prisoners in their grandmother's mansion. Pareno is a cruel and domineering matriarch, and Austria takes the drastic step of chaining her grandmother up in a remote part of the house. Telling Reyes that their grandmother has gone away, Austria enrolls Reyes in high school, and although she has never attended a day of school, Reyes proves to be a genius. She is not accepted by her peers, however, who treat her cruelly, with the exception of Christopher Roxas, who has fallen in love with her. But back home, Austria proves no better than her grandmother, not allowing Reyes any visitors and making one wonder why she introduced Reyes to the outside world at all. The film climaxes with an unconscionable cribbing of *Carrie* (1976), as Reyes is elected Homecoming Queen, is doused in pig's blood, and unleashes a telekinetic fury on her classmates. She then returns home to find Austria with the corpse of Pareno, who has died in her captivity, and the now deranged Austria attacks her, trying to strangle Reyes with Pareno's confining chain. Reyes uses her powers to reanimate Pareno's corpse, which attacks Austria. A blaze erupts and swallows up both Austria and Pareno, and a happy ending is provided by the arrival of Roxas, who takes Reyes away from it all.

While the filmmakers certainly show no shame in ripping off Brian De Palma's *Carrie*, the reanimation of Pareno's dead body is a definite improvement over the pretentious demise of Piper Laurie in De Palma's film. (In Tagalog)

Andres Manambit: Angkan ng Matatapang (Andres Manambit: Tribe of the Brave)

1992 Viva Films; 94 minutes/color

Director: Ike Jarlego, Jr.; Screenwriter: Humilde "Meek" Roxas; Cinematographer: Joe Batac, Jr.; Editor: Ike Jarlego, Jr.; Filmscore: Jaime Fabregas; Cast: Eddie Garcia, Eddie Gutierrez, Pinky de Leon, Kier Legaspi, Joko Diaz, Jaime Garchitorena, Ramon Christopher, Mia Pratts, Subas herrero, Dick Israel, Berting Labra, Atong Redillas, Michelle Ann Lopez, Michelle Bautista, Ruth Tuazon, Johnny Vicar, Telly Babasa

Winner of top honors at the 1993 Manila Film Festival, director Ike Jarlego Jr.'s involving, if familiar, tale of corrupt politics stars Eddie Garcia as the title character, a small town police officer who refuses to look the other way after finding out that Subas Herrero's saw mill is a front for a smuggling operation. Unaware that his good friend Eddie Gutierrez is in cahoots with Herrero, Garcia goes after the criminal operation. Meanwhile, Gutierrez runs for mayor (his campaign being funded by Herrero) and wins. When Garcia goes to congratulate his old friend, he is given a very frosty reception. The real kicker is when Garcia returns to the police station and finds that Gutierrez has fired the police captain and replaced him with sleazy Dick Israel. Garcia resigns, but the murder of friend and fellow officer Johnny Vicar by one of Israel's men prompts Garcia to fight back against the new corrupt regime. The film climaxes with an exciting shootout at a county fair, which begins when Garcia's wife and daughter are killed by a car bomb. As the crowd erupts in pandemonium, the panic-stricken people fleeing in every direction, Garcia finishes off Israel and Gutierrez before being gunned down himself by one of Gutierrez's sons.

Although the storyline is certainly a familiar one, what makes the film work so well is the splendid performance of Garcia, who makes his character so likable (despite his shameless philandering) that watching the destruction of his friends and family is difficult. In terms of execution, the work here is far superior to other such tales of one man's war with a corrupt power structure (which would be a significant percentage of the Filipino action genre), and the film scores high marks in every department. (In Tagalog with some English)

Angela Markado

1980 Four Seasons Films; 100 minutes/color
Director: Lino Brocka; Screenwriter: Jose F. Lacaba; Cinematographer: Conrado Baltazar; Editor: Augusto Salvador; Filmscore: Jeric Soriano; Cast: Hilda Koronel, Johnny Delgado, Celia Rodriguez, Rez Cortez, Ruel Vernal, Tonio Gutierrez, Dave Brodett, Raul Aragon, Archie Adamos, Menggie Cobarrubias, Ely Roque

In this dark melodrama, Hilda Koronel portrays a young cocktail waitress who is abducted by five men who take their turns raping her. They conclude their fun by tattooing their names on her back, and then try to sell her into prostitution, but when the brothel is raided, Koronel manages to escape in the pandemonium. Some time later she takes up a switchblade and goes after her tormentors, knocking them off one by one until the remaining pair (Johnny Delgado and Ruel Vernal) find her out. After catching up with her, the pair pursue Koronel into a junkyard where Delgado accidentally shoots Vernal before he himself is killed by Koronel. Director Lino Brocka spares little in the protracted depiction of Koronel's gang rape, but her retribution is surprisingly perfunctory by comparison. Aside from the strong performance from Koronel, the major attribute here is an interesting filmscore by Jeric Soriano. (In Tagalog)

Antipolo Massacre: Jesus Save Us!

1994 Golden Lions Films/Viva Films; 111 minutes/color
Director/screenwriter: Carlo J. Caparas; Cinematographer: Ernesto Dominguez; Editor: Abelardo Hulleza; Filmscore: Demet Velasquez; Cast: Cesar Montano, Dawn Zulueta, Romeo Vasquez, Robert Arevalo, Boots Anson-Roa, Joel Torre, Celso Ad. Castillo, Richard Bonnin, Liezl Martinez, Jojo Acuin, Perla Bautista, Lito Legaspi, Juan Rodrigo, Fred Moro, Susan Africa, Danny Riel, Danny Labra, Benjie Felipe, Ernie David

Promoted with the tag line "The night even hell fell silent," this true crime film stars Cesar Montano as a discontented rural laborer who begins to come unglued after his older brother is murdered by the village drunk (Celso Ad. Castillo). After purchasing a bolo (a large knife) from the widow of a murdered man, Montano's personality changes drastically, as he becomes increasingly withdrawn and obsessed with the bolo, sharpening it incessantly, until he finally goes off the deep end one night, using the bolo to hack to death five members of a neighboring family. The film portrays Montano's character (whose real name was Winifredo Masagca) as having committed suicide, though an epilogue mentions speculation among locals that he was involved with a group of criminals who may not only have killed him, but may have been behind the titular massacre. In the end, however, the film rests its case on the testimony of the only eyewitness, Masagca's widow, who both witnessed the massacre and survived her deranged husband's pursuing her through the forest afterward. Then again, she also claims that her husband's spirit continues to haunt her and her children.

The true crime films of Carlo Caparas are always harrowing by their nature, but here he improves somewhat on the formula with a fair amount of spooky atmospherics that increases the sense of foreboding. While the reenactment of the massacre itself is not terribly gory, the film's epilogue contains distressingly graphic crime scene photos of the victims. (In Tagalog with some English)

Aristokrata (Aristocratic Woman)

1954 Sampaguita Pictures; 95 minutes/black & white

Director: Olive la Torre; Screenwriters: Conrado Conde, Willie P. Orfinada; Cinematographer: Higino Fallorina; Editor: Domingo Botes; Filmscore: Nestor Robles; Cast: Rogelio dela Rosa, Alicia Vergel, Aruray, Panchito Alba, Eddie Garcia, Etang Discher, Bert Olivar, Totoy Torrente, Tony Dungan, Pepe Salameda, Pablo Guevarra, Felicito Espiritu, Francisco Espiritu, Sabas San Juan

In this Golden Era melodrama, Rogelio dela Rosa leads a group of locals against greedy aristocrat Panchito Alba, who has laid claim to more land than he has a right to. One day while riding her horse in the hills, Alba's daughter (Alicia Vergel) has her own encounter with dela Rosa, and so begins a love/hate relationship. Alba brings in shady Eddie Garcia to coordinate a plan to be rid of the pesky dela Rosa, but dela Rosa consistently proves too cunning a foe. Eventually Garcia stages a raid of dela Rosa's camp, with Alba along for the ride, but during the chaotic struggle the power-hungry Garcia takes the opportunity to kill Alba, hoping that he can then take Alba's land and assume his position. But Alba's men are defeated and Garcia is captured by dela Rosa, who then unites with Vergel. (In Tagalog)

Arizona Kid

1971 Premiere Productions; 111 minutes/color

Director: Luciano B. Carlos; Screenwriter: Lino Brocka; Cinematographer: Felipe Sacdalan; Editor: Ben Barcelon; Filmscore: Restie Umali; Cast: Chiquito, Mamie Van Doren, Gordon Mitchell, Mariela Branger, Bernard Bonnin, Dan Van Heusen, Victor Israel, Ralphy Arando, John Mark, Felipe Solano, Gene Reyes, Tony Brandt, Vicente Roja, Pilar Vela, Ramon Serrano, Zaldo Moreno, Manolito Revilla

Set in the early 1900s, the story here finds Filipino comic actor Chiquito traveling to America to find his uncle. Receiving word that his uncle is in Mexico, Chiquito sets off in that direction, but along the way he gets roped into impersonating the Arizona Kid, a revered gunslinger (now deceased), and tries to save a town from a notorious outlaw called Coyote. The bungling Chiquito manages to kill Coyote (albeit by accident) during a climactic showdown and wins the affections of bimbo Mamie Van Doren (dubbed with a ridiculously girlish voice). Chiquito and Van Doren then set off for Mexico together. Given the cast (which includes a brief appearance by Spanish character actor Victor Israel as a bandit), and the fact that the screenplay was written by Lino Brocka (!), this must surely rank as one of the all-time cinematic curios. Which is good, since the odd assortment of talents is the only real point of interest here. Otherwise, there is only Chiquito's painfully unsubtle comedic approach, and the focus of the humor (Chiquito's poor English and his inability to either communicate or fully comprehend) wears very thin very early on. Chiquito and Mamie Van Doren? Not likely. (In English with Tagalog and some Spanish)

Asedillo

1971 FPJ Productions; 120 minutes/color

Director/screenwriter: Celso Ad. Castillo; Cinematographer: Sergio Lobo; Editor: Augusto Salvador; Filmscore: Restie Umali; Cast: Fernando Poe Jr., Barbara Perez, Rebecca, Paquito Diaz, Imelda Ilanan, Carlos Padilla Jr., Lito Anzures, Angelo Ventura, Ruel Vernal

Fernando Poe, Jr. plays the title character in this true-life story of a 1920s schoolteacher who became a rebel leader. Tired of the injustice he both witnesses and personally experiences under the local bureaucracy, Poe gathers other discontented citizens together into an opposition force. Though the local populace is skeptical at first, he eventually wins them over. But in the end he is ratted-out by one of his own, Paquito Diaz, who, after challenging Poe's authority and losing, discloses Poe's location to the local constabulary. The film concludes with the distinctly Christ-like image of Poe, killed and put on display for all the people to see. Poe won the FAMAS Best Actor award for his performance. (In Tagalog)

Aswang (Vampire)

1992 Regal Films; 119 minutes/color

Directors: Peque Gallaga, Lorenzo Reyes; Screenwriters: Pen P. Medina, Jerry Lopez Sineneng; Cinematographer: Joe Tutanes; Editor: Danny Gloria; Filmscore: Jong M. Cuenco; Cast: Alma Moreno, Manilyn Reynes, Aiza Seguerra, Aljon Jimenez, John Estrada, Berting Labra, Dick Israel, Janice de Belen, Leo Martinez, Mary Walter, Orestes Ojeda, Romy Romulo, Eva Ramos, Rey Solo, Pen P. Medina, Gigette Reyes, Joey Marquez, Lilia Cuntapay

Cute little Aiza Seguerra arrives home one night with her nanny (Manilyn Reynes) and driver (Berting Labra) only to find that a vicious gang of thieves led by Dick Israel has slaughtered her entire family. The murderous robbers are still in the house, but Seguerra, Reynes and Labra manage to escape and flee to the country where they go into hiding. But they find that things aren't any better in the tiny village they decide to hide out in, since it is currently being victimized by an aswang, a malevolent spirit that sometimes appears as the beautiful Alma Moreno, and at others as a ravenous, flesh-eating, wild pig monster. Israel and his gang eventually find the trio, but they are duly slaughtered by the aswang before they can harm Seguerra and her companions. The film has some very effective moments, like the scene wherein Reynes encounters old witch Lilia Cuntapay in the forest, who frightens her into fleeing across a stream. Reynes is seemingly rescued by the placidly beckoning Moreno, who pulls her from the stream and then proceeds to savagely bight her. There is also the spectacle of Joey Marquez torn in half by a wild pig after being lured into the forest by Moreno, his upper torso crawling across the ground, entrails dragging behind. On the downside, the running time is excessive and the film would have benefited from the trimming of some unfortunate comic relief. (In Tagalog)

Atrocities of the Orient

1959 Film Import Company/Social Services Pictures; 78 minutes/black & white

Director: Eduardo de Castro; Cinematographer: William H. Jansen; Filmscore: Julio Esteban Anguita; Cast: Linda Estrella, Fernando Royo, Mona Lisa, Teddy Benavides, Rosa Aguirre, Bimbo Danao, Andres Centenera

This 1959 Social Services Pictures release is actually comprised of two earlier Filipino films, *Outrages of the Orient* (1948) and *Beasts of the East* (1950), both of which saw U.S. release through distributor Lloyd Friedgen. Both were films dealing with the Japanese occupation. Early in the film, two brothers, both officers in the Philippine military, are in love with the same woman, but the brother (Fernando Royo) who marries her also winds up killing her, shooting her to prevent her from falling into the hands of the Japanese. When American forces withdraw and the Japanese overrun the islands, Filipino forces are instructed by the Americans to surrender. But the Filipinos refuse to give in and continue to valiantly resist the Japanese. Royo leads his troops into the jungle where they hook up with a band of guerrillas led by the beautiful but ruthless Mona Lisa. Lisa is shot during a fight with the Japanese and dies in Royo's arms, which is where the film abruptly ends. (In English)

Babae sa Bintana
(The Woman in the Window)

1998 Regal Entertainment; 102 minutes/color

Director: Chito S. Rono; Screenwriter: Roy Iglesias; Cinematographers: Ely Cruz, Charlie Peralta; Editor: Jaime Davilla; Filmscore: Jessie Lasaten; Cast: Richard Gomez, Rosanna Roces, John Estrada, Johnny Manahan, Efren Reyes Jr., Raymond Keannu, Mon Confiado, Menard Marcellano, Jhong Hilario, Cris Cruz, Cloyd Robinson, Janice Jurado, Eula Valdez, Lucita Soriano, Ihman Esturco, Adriana Agcaoili, Lui Manansala, Benett Ignacio, Resty Vergara, Renato Morado, Chris Aguilar

In this well executed noir melodrama by director Chito Rono, Richard Gomez plays a man who becomes intrigued by Rosanna Roces, the new tenant in the apartment across the street. Watching her daily through the window, Gomez's interest turns to obsession as he observes her relationship with her abusive policeman boyfriend (John Estrada). Eventually Gomez and Roces meet and begin an affair, and Roces entrusts a handbag full of cash to Gomez. Though the cash is the ill-gotten gains of Estrada's ties to organized crime, Roces intends to use the money to leave the mainland and begin anew elsewhere, and she wants Gomez to accompany her. But Estrada discovers the affair, and when he bursts into Gomez's apartment, he also finds the money. Gomez and Roces attempt to flee, but Gomez is shot and wounded by Estrada. Roces then shoots and kills Estrada, and at the insistence of Gomez, she flees as the police arrive. Estrada was brought into his underworld dealings by Johnny Manahan, his commanding officer in the department, and Manahan brutally beats Gomez to try and get him to divulge the location of the money, but when he cannot get Gomez to talk, Manahan douses him with gasoline and takes out a lighter. Gomez manages to grab the lighter, embraces Manahan, and they both go up in flames. The film concludes with the melancholy Roces aboard a boat setting off to begin her new life. In 1998 Rono also directed Roces in the even more impressive *Curacha: Ang Babaeng Walang Pahinga*. (In Tagalog)

Babayaran Mo ng Dugo
(You Will Be Paid in Blood)

1989 Seiko Films; 115 minutes/color
Director: Francis "Jun" Posadas; Screenwriter: Humilde Roxas; Cinematographer: Ver Dauz; Editor: Augusto Salvador; Filmscore: Benny Medina; Cast: Jestoni Alarcon, Rita Avila, John Regala, Robert Arevalo, Michael de Mesa, Subas Herrero, Dick Israel, Maita Soriano, Jovit Moya, Rachel Lobangco, Baby O'Brien, Precious Hipolito, Dan Fernandez, Fred Moro, Rusty Santos, Usman Hassim, Turko (Cervantes), Ernie David, Chris Daluz, Naty Santiago, Ernie Zarate, Big Boy Gomez, Feling Cudia, Telly Babasa, Ben Romano, Max Buwaya, Danny Labra, Eddie Tuazon, Rocky Ramos, Dave Moreno, Teddy Perez

When exotic dancer Rita Avila is abducted by psychotic Michael de Mesa, who gets his thrills by watching three of his cronies take turns raping her, she gets a helping hand from reporter Robert Arevalo, who champions her case in the press and helps her to press charges. After being convicted, de Mesa is killed in prison, which guarantees retaliation of some sort against some one by de Mesa's father (Subas Herrero), who is a prominent and not too reputable businessman. Herrero targets Arevalo and his family, abducting them (wife Maita Soriano, son Jestoni Alarcon, and a teenage daughter) and taking them to a small island where they are set loose in the jungle to be hunted like game by Herrero and his men. After Arevalo and his family are killed, Herrero has them hastily buried in a mass grave, but Alarcon survives, and after Herrero and his men depart, he manages to crawl from his premature grave. Naturally, Alarcon goes on a quest for revenge, prompting Herrero to return to the island and dig up the grave, which he finds to be one body short. Meanwhile, Alarcon has a chance meeting with Avila and the two become intimate, which only makes Alarcon easier to find since Herrero has his eye on Avila. Herrero has both of them abducted and taken to his favorite island, where he proposes to end things once and for all. But the police arrive and defeat Herrero's men in a shootout, while Alarcon impales Herrero himself with a tree branch.

The film is moderately entertaining despite an extremely sloppy screenplay by Humilde Roxas, which director Francis "Jun" Posadas would have been smart to tighten up by excising the more extraneous story elements. For instance, Alarcon's chance meeting with Avila occurs when he is stabbed during an altercation in a restaurant where Avila is working as a waitress, which is an awfully contrived method of getting Avila back in the story (and throwing in some brawling as well). After becoming intimate with Avila, Alarcon also begins a sexual relationship with another woman, allowing the film to fit in a few more sex scenes (all while showing no nudity) into a story that is already having a hard time staying focused. Still, given the rather undisciplined nature of the screenplay, Posadas manages to turn in a fair piece of work with what could easily have become a disaster. (In Tagalog)

Baby Tsina (China Baby)

1984 Viva Films; 121 minutes/color
Director: Marilou Diaz-Abaya; Screenwriter: Ricardo Lee; Cinematographer: Manolo Abaya; Editor: Ike Jarlego, Jr.; Filmscore: Willie Cruz; Cast: Vilma Santos, Phillip Salvador, Dindo Fernando, Caridad Sanchez, Chanda Romero, Johnny Delgado, Zeny Zabala, Deborah Sun, Manny Luna, Cecille Castillo, Romeo Rivero, Susan Bautista, Grace Amilbangsa, Vangie Labalan, Jocelyn Cruz, Len Santos, Augusto Victa, Malu de Guzman, Raquel Villavicencio, Manjo del Mundo, Mary Walter, Rez Cortez, Dexter Doria

Set in 1969, this true story stars Vilma Santos as the title character, a prostitute who begins a relationship with Manila gang leader Phillip Salvador. She is abducted and gang-raped by some of Salvador's underworld rivals, and Salvador retaliates by gunning down the men responsible, a mass killing that has the police searching Manila for him. Santos seeks the help of friend Dindo Fernando, an attorney who allows her and Salvador to stay with him for a time, but when the police spot them one day, Salvador dies in the ensuing shootout and Santos is arrested. Despite the efforts of Fernando, Santos is sent to prison where she gives birth to Salvador's child, a girl which is promptly taken from her and given to Santos' mother to raise. Santos endures the brutality of prison life but manages to escape with a number of other inmates during a prison riot. She is quickly recaptured, however, when she shows up at her mother's house to retrieve her baby. Upon her return to prison she helps the inmates to stand up to the brutality of the prison system, and the film ends with her triumphant upon her release in 1978 after being acquitted in a retrial. (In Tagalog with some English)

Back Door to Hell

1964 Lippert Inc./Medallion Films/20th Century–Fox; 69 minutes/black & white

Director: Monte Hellman; Screenwriters: Richard A. Guttman, John Hackett; Cinematographer: Mars Rasca; Editors: Fely Crisostomo, Monte Hellman; Filmscore: Mike Velarde; Cast: Jimmie Rodgers, Jack Nicholson, John Hackett, Annabelle Huggins, Conrad Maga (Conrad Parham), Johnny Monteiro, Joe Sison, Henry Duval, Ben Perez, Vic Uematsu

This is a fairly slight WWII melodrama wherein a five-man U.S. reconnaissance team slips into the Philippines to radio back information about the Japanese to help pave the way for MacArthur's return. It turns out that the group's leader (Jimmie Rodgers) is gun-shy, and his inability to fire on a Japanese soldier costs the lives of two of his men. Rodgers and his remaining men (John Hackett and Jack Nicholson) meet up with a group of Filipino resistance fighters led by the cruel and embittered Conrad Maga. When a Filipino bandit leader destroys their radio, Rodgers and his men are forced to infiltrate a Japanese camp so that Nicholson can send a radio message back to the American fleet. They succeed in sending their message, but they do not go undetected, and the Filipino resistance fighters are forced to open fire on the Japanese in order for the Americans to flee the camp. Nicholson is killed, and the film ends rather abruptly with Rodgers and Hackett meeting up with the Filipinos in the jungle and being told that Maga has also perished in the conflict.

Co-produced by America's Lippert and the Philippines' Medallion Films (with actor Ronald Remy acting as associate producer), the film does have its moments of tension, but seems generally to have been conceived in haste. Director Monte Hellman followed up by shooting *Flight to Fury*, which was co-produced with Filipinas Productions, and again featured Nicholson and Hackett. (In English with some Tagalog and Japanese)

Bad Girl

1991 Regal Films; 103 minutes/color
Director/screenwriter: Mauro Gia Samonte; Cinematographer: Ricardo Jacinto; Editor: Edgardo Vinarao; Filmscore: Demet Velasquez; Cast: Cristina Gonzales, Zoren Legaspi, Ricky Belmonte, Jean Saburit, Bong Regala, Bernard Banares, Dexter Doria, Dante Castro, Gigette Reyes, Christopher Paloma, Manilyn Viray, Julie Ann Arpon

Ditsy Cristina Gonzales has the hots for Zoren Legaspi, but he seems very reluctant to become intimate with her (hmmm). He eventually surrenders to temptation, however, and Gonzales gets pregnant. By the time she realizes that she is with child, Legaspi has left the island and gone to the mainland with a wealthy woman who had come to the island to buy-up all the coconuts. In time Legaspi becomes disillusioned with being a kept boy in the big city and he returns to the island, where he finds Gonzales waiting with their baby boy. For the most part, the film does not live up to either its title, or the scene early on when Gonzales masturbates on the beach, rather curiously while covering her body in sand. (In Tagalog)

Bakit May Kahapon Pa? (Why Is There a Yesterday?)

1996 Viva Films/IAM Productions; 109 minutes/color
Director: Joel Lamangan; Screenwriters: Roy Iglesias, Julius Alfonso; Cinematographer: Romeo V. Vitug; Editor: Jess Navarro; Filmscore: Jessie Lasaten; Cast: Eddie Garcia, Nora Aunor, Dawn Zulueta, Mellise Santiago, Daniel Fernando, Alain Sia, Sarah Jane Abad, Tony Mabesa, Rolando Tinio, Elmer Jamias, Jim Pebanco, Ernie Zarate, Rey Ventura, Raul Dimaano, Angel Baldomar, Richard Quan, Irma Adlawan, Lucy Quinto, Josie Galvez, Mads Nicolas, Tess Dumpit, Gammy Viray

Retired military general Eddie Garcia is shocked by the murder of his son, a young military man gunned down in an ambush believed to have been carried out by a group of anti-government rebels. After the funeral, Garcia and his daughter (Dawn Zulueta) meet Nora Aunor, who was a friend to Garcia's late son. Zulueta's young daughter (Melisse Santiago) takes to Aunor immediately, and so Garcia and Zulueta invite Aunor to stay in their guesthouse and work as nanny to the girl. Aunor and Santiago quickly form a close bond, but Zulueta begins to resent what she sees as interference in the raising of her daughter on the part of Aunor; Santiago becomes increasingly disobedient toward Zulueta, and downright hateful toward Garcia as a result of Aunor's influence. Though Garcia and Zulueta are unaware of it, the viewer has already been tipped off to the fact that Aunor is crazy, troubled by recurring nightmares in which she relives the memory of the killing of her parents when she was a little girl. What eventually comes to light is a dark secret in Garcia's past; as a young officer in the military in 1971, Garcia had sought to eradicate a band of rebels in a place called San Marco, and to be sure that he had gotten them all, ordered an outright massacre of the village. Aunor's parents were among those killed, and she had been tormented by the memory ever since. As an adult, Aunor became a member of a terrorist group herself, but her ultimate goal was to avenge the death of her parents. Now, as a member of Garcia's own household, that day has come. Sneaking into his bedroom one night, Aunor awakens Garcia by shooting him in the leg (that'll do it), and reveals her true identity to him. While Zulueta and Santiago manage to escape the insane Aunor, Garcia dies with her upon the detonation of a bomb that Aunor has planted in the house.

This is a very solid piece of work with outstanding performances by the principals. Aunor plays crazy well: maybe too well since, despite her unfortunate past, it is very difficult to sympathize with her. (In Tagalog and English)

Bamboo Gods and Iron Men

1974 Premiere Productions/American International Pictures; 91 minutes/color

Director: Cesar Gallardo; Screenwriters: Ken Metcalfe, Joseph Zucchero; Cinematographer: Felipe Sacdalan; Editor: Gervasio Santos; Filmscore: Tito Solo; Cast: James Iglehart, Shirley Washington, Chiquito, Marissa Delgado, Eddie Garcia, Ken Metcalfe, Joe Zucchero, Michael Boyet, Robert Rivera, Subas Herrero, Leo Martinez, Benny Pestano, Steve Alcarado, Robert Picate, Boy Picate, Tony Uy, Vic Diaz, Joonee Gamboa, Mary Walter

Ken Metcalfe hires Joe Zucchero to dig up the grave of a 10th century Chinaman who wrote in his diaries of making a discovery so powerful that whoever possesses it could rule the world. From that grave Zucchero retrieves a leather pouch, which he hides inside a Buddha statuette that is subsequently purchased in a Hong Kong shop by American boxer James Iglehart and his wife Shirley Washington. When Iglehart and Washington arrive in Manila, Metcalfe sets out to steal the statuette, and he hires hitman Eddie Garcia and beautiful Marissa Delgado to shadow Iglehart and his mute Chinese buddy Chiquito. This results in a rowdy martial arts punch-up, and Metcalfe resorts to kidnapping Washington in order to arrange a trade with Iglehart. Chiquito goes to the police and they follow Iglehart to Metcalfe's digs, where the film climaxes with a wild donnybrook in which Iglehart kills Garcia, Washington and Delgado have an excellent catfight, and policeman Subas Herrero arrests Metcalfe. The pouch is then opened and it is discovered that it contains nothing more than gunpowder. Even Metcalfe can't help but laugh at the irony. The film earns points for not taking itself too seriously, and Herrero and Leo Martinez are amusing as the inept police officers. (In English)

Banaue: Stairway to the Sky

1975 N.V. Productions; 122 minutes/color

Director: Gerardo de Leon; Screenwriters: Gerardo de Leon, Toto Belano; Cinematographer: Fermin Passisihan; Editor: Ben Barcelon; Filmscore: Tito Arevalo; Cast: Nora Aunor, Christopher de Leon, Ronaldo Valdez, Gloria Sevilla, Johnny Delgado, Ben Perez, Andres Centenera, Precy Marquez, Eddie Villamayor, Mercy Bartolome, Ben Velasco, Lope Policarpio, Ben Romano, Sim Pajarillo, Linda Castro, Francisco Cruz, Max Rojo

In this brutally savage melodrama set in northern Luzon in 500 B.C., tribal chief Andres Centenera finds his people at war with a ruthless tribe of headhunters ruled by Ronaldo Valdez. After a conflict in which Valdez and his warriors decapitate many of Centenera's men and take the heads home as trophies, the widowed women in Centenera's tribe take up spears and decide to retrieve the heads of their slain mates to rejoin them with the bodies for proper burial. They sneak into the rival tribe's camp but are quickly captured, prompting Centenera to send his remaining warriors in to rescue them. The rescue succeeds, and some of the slain warriors' heads are even retrieved. The two tribes then meet, not in battle, but in a staged duel wherein the best warriors from each tribe square off. Only Johnny Delgado (from Centenera's tribe) survives the showdown, and though severely wounded, he shows his contempt for Valdez by taking the head of Valdez's slain brother as a trophy. This can only mean all-out war, which Nora Aunor tries to avert by taking the head of Valdez's brother back to Valdez. Though Aunor succeeds in averting a major bloodbath, Valdez has her take back a message that he will personally fight to the death with any warrior of Centenera's choosing. Christopher de Leon readily volunteers to fight Valdez, though he was badly wounded in the leg by Valdez in a previous conflict and is unable to walk without a pronounced limp. The following morning they meet, and de Leon does indeed defeat Valdez, but when he refuses to finish him off, Valdez takes the opportunity to retrieve his dagger from the ground and is poised to kill de Leon when Aunor again intervenes, pleading for an end to all the bloodshed. Surprisingly, Valdez relents and the two tribes are reconciled.

There are probably more beheadings here than in any film in history. As with much of director Gerry de Leon's work, there are some very striking (and disturbingly so) images, including the moment when the decapitated, badly decomposing head of a slain warrior is returned to his wife, who tenderly embraces it. But more than ever, the film also reveals the director's enthusiasm for experimentation (some would consider it mere quirkiness), which manifests itself here in the form of a strange halo around the outer frame, more prominent in some scenes than others. The effect given is not unlike the yellowing, frayed edges of a weathered old photograph, its purpose possibly being to give the impression of antiquity. But as it is present throughout the film, it will no doubt annoy many viewers, similar to the garish red tint meant to announce the arrival of an evil presence in de Leon's *Kulay Dugo ang Gabi* (1964), or even the over-exertive zoom lens in *Mad Doctor of Blood Island* (1968). (In Tagalog)

Bangis (Ferocious)

1995 Regal Films; 102 minutes/color

Directors: Rogelio Salvador, Philip Ko; Screenwriter: Humilde "Meek" Roxas; Cinematographer: Eduardo "Baby" Cabrales; Editors: Rogelio Salvador, Philip Ko; Filmscore: Jimmy Fabregas; Cast: Monsour del Rosario, Jasmine Reyes, Orestes Ojeda, Ruel Vernal, Dindo Arroyo, Philip Ko, Mike Gayoso, Alex David, Rando Almanzor, Luoie Katana, Raymond Tan, Ernie David, Froilan Nebre, Dante Castro, Danny Riel, Raymond Keannu, Robert Talby, Jess Santos

Monsour del Rosario and his troops, being experts in jungle warfare, are sent down to Mindanao to root out rebel forces. Coming across a rebel base camp, they are engaged in battle, but the conflict stops abruptly when a glowing orb passes overhead. When the orb moves on the battle resumes, with del Rosario's troops emerging victorious. Moving on, they come to a village littered with bloody, dismembered corpses, and they discover a lone survivor (Jasmine Reyes) hiding in a barrel. As she is in shock and unable to tell them what happened, a Muslim soldier places his hand on her head and is thereby able to envision her memories of the sudden traumatic demise of the village (Is there something in the Koran about this?). Through this mystic mumbo-jumbo it is discovered that the source of the massacre was a carnivorous space monster that arrived in the glowing orb encountered by the soldiers earlier. The government troops soon come face-to-face with the beast, and after much hardship and many lost lives, prevail against it.

The film reaches its crescendo in absurdity when one soldier has his arm ripped off by the monster and continues fighting, prompting the monster to rip the soldier's other arm off. Then, in a moment right out of *Monty Python and the Holy Grail* (1974), the soldier, sans arms, proceeds with high-kicking the beast. (In Tagalog)

Batang Quiapo (Quiapo Boy)

1986 Regal Films; 123 minutes/color

Director: Pablo Santiago; Screenwriter: Joe Carreon; Cinematographer: Ver P. Reyes; Editor: Augusto Salvador; Filmscore: Jaime Fabregas; Cast: Fernando Poe Jr., Maricel Soriano, Sheryl Cruz, Manilyn Reynes, Kristina Paner, Chuckie Dreyfus, Christopher Paloma, Mel Martinez, Anita Linda, Rez Cortez, Dencio Padilla, Paquito Diaz, Bomber Moran, Bayani Casimiro, Bella Flores, Augusto Victa, Tony Carreon, Tina Loy, Jose Romulo, Karim Kiram, Rudy Meyer, Abbo dela Cruz, Geena Zablan, Bello Borja, Dedes Whitaker, David Anderson, Nonoy de Guzman, Rene Hawkins, Rey Tomenes, Bert Garon

In this lightweight action/romantic comedy, Maricel Soriano plays a crook teamed up with pickpocket Rez Cortez. But she meets and falls in love with Fernando Poe, Jr., who is working with a policewoman to bring down a local drug gang headed by Tony Carreon. Naturally he succeeds, and he and Soriano stop bickering long enough to hook up. Poe gives his usual tough guy performance, and even sings a song with Soriano (who sings two numbers). As for Soriano, well, she gives her usual bratty performance, which, frankly, wears very thin. (In Tagalog)

Batang X (X Boy)

1995 Regal Films; 94 minutes/color

Directors/screenwriters: Peque Gallaga, Lorenzo Reyes; Cinematographer: Joe Tutanes; Editor: Danny Gloria; Filmscore: Archie Castillo; Cast: Aiko Melendez, Michael de Mesa, Janus del Prado, John Prats, Anna Larrucea, J.C. Tizon, John Ace Zabarte, Chuck Perez, Al Tantay, Jimmy Fabregas, Jon Achaval, Troy Martino, Theresa Loyzaga, Amy Perez, Orestes Ojeda, Tess Michelena, Mel Kimura, Jinky Laurel, Michelle Rufo, Jeofrey Eigenmann, Ricky Santos, Derick Carmona, Froilan Sales, Boy Fabregas, Dolly Espinosa, Junell Hernando

In this rather lame "kids" science fiction fantasy, five children are kidnapped by alien Dr. Axis (Aiko Melendez), who is stranded on earth in her spaceship, which is disguised as a highrise office building. She has nutty professor Michael de Mesa fit the children with mechanical devices, basically turning them into a squadron of bionic super kids. The plan is to send the children into a government test and development facility to steal some energy source needed by Melendez to fuel her spaceship. The kids end up doing battle with another alien, Zygrax (Chuck Perez), a big, ugly guy with a costume that calls to mind *Robocop*.

With a cast of children as its stars, and being adapted from a komiks series, one might assume that this little fantasy is aimed at a fairly young audience, but there is a pronounced cruel edge to it all. After their abduction, the children go through a rather lengthy orientation in which one of their weapons is demonstrated by blowing a man's head off (rather graphically), which sends the children all into a screaming fit. They are also given a weapon that can alternately make people believe that they are sheep, chickens, dogs (all supposedly funny), or turn them into ballerinas (funny), or kill them by disintegration (not so funny). The kids don't seem to use any particular criterion when choosing which firing mode to use on whom. Aside from the rather cavalier cruelty, the film is definitely sunk by the extremely witless slapstick. (In Tagalog)

Batang Z (Z Boy)

1996 MAQ Productions; 96 minutes/color
Director: Bey Vito; Screenwriter: Rolf Mahilom; Cinematographer: Ding Austria; Editor: Edmund "Bot" Jarlego; Filmscore: Jessie Lasaten; Cast: Tom Taus Jr., Jorge Estregan (George Estregan, Jr.), Melissa Mendez, Berting Labra, Dan Pacia, Marco Ballesteros, Marivic Duenas, Charles Jordan Sabalboro, Karel Santos, Dwight Gaston, Flora Gasser, Boy Gomez, Sammy "Ewok" Vencio, Nonong de Andres, Panyang, Bert Mansueto, Pong Mercado, Jun Garcia, Perry Jose, Resty Herrera, Ed Francisco, Linda Aspiras, Dantley Reyes, Oscar Moran

This is another juvenile superhero fantasy. Aging Berting Labra imparts to young Tom Taus, Jr. a blue mask and relates an incredible tale of how, when he was a boy, he hooked the mask while fishing in the ocean. He found that putting the mask on transformed him into a superhero with extraordinary powers. Labra goes on to tell of how he battled the bizarre, mohawked, bat-eared Jorge Estregan, and thwarted his evil plans by vaporizing him and trapping him in a bottle. With Labra's death, Taus (who has been raised by Labra) finds himself out on the street where he befriends a group of street urchins. Finding that the mask has the same remarkable effect on him that it had on Labra, Taus transforms into a superhero and runs around thwarting various criminals. Some children rummaging through a landfill come across the jar in which Estregan is imprisoned, and when the jar is smashed Estregan is loosed. He then goes about using his magical powers to transform various thugs into an army, and also looses a hulking reptilian beast, which he sends out to terrorize the populace. In order to combat these menacing forces, Taus likewise uses his powers to transform his little band of street urchin friends into a squad of superhero children, who succeed in defeating the weird Estregan and his boys, and the monster too.

It's all pretty silly, but then, it's for the kids. It's also an improvement over *Batang X* (1995), a like-minded effort by Peque Gallaga and Lorenzo Reyes, and while Estregan over-exerts himself as usual, at least it's more suitable to the outrageous material served up here. (In Tagalog)

Batas ng .45 (Law of the .45)

1991; 121 minutes/color
Director: Ronwaldo Reyes (Fernando Poe, Jr.); Screenwriters: Pablo S. Gomez, Erwin Castillo, Chris Michelena; Cinematoghrapher: Ver P. Reyes; Editor: Augusto Salvador; Filmscore: Jaime Fabregas; Cast: Fernando Poe Jr., Timmy Cruz, Paquito Diaz, Charlie Davao, R.R. Herrera, Tito Arevalo, Bert Olivar, Kevin Delgado, Romeo Rivera, Berting Labra, Renato del Prado, Danny Riel, Vic Varrion, Rene Hawkins, Rolly Lapid, Jimmy Reyes, Buddy Salvador, Robert Miller, Jess Vargas, Boy Mediavillo

In this charged Fernando Poe, Jr. action film, Poe is a narcotics officer who makes a big bust, making him a priority target for the syndicate, who sets him up. They plant a stash of heroin in his car, and when the police get an anonymous tip and find it, Poe is suspended pending an investigation. But commanding officer Charlie Davao, noting that it was an obvious setup, vows to stand behind Poe. In the meantime, Poe conducts his own unofficial investigation, prompting the syndicate to abduct him, hold him prisoner, and feed him a steady diet of heroin (Why not just kill him?). Once he is sufficiently hooked, they turn him loose, dumping him on the street a full-fledged junkie. Even then Poe manages to continue his investigation while fighting the monkey on his back, and he eventually uncovers widespread corruption, with the drug operation including every one from police chief Davao to a local Catholic priest. Poe's young son is kidnapped in a last effort by the syndicate to dissuade him in his pursuit of the truth, but Poe charges in and guns down a good-sized army of syndicate thugs, while also getting his boy back. Davao shows up and the remaining syndicate men join him in chasing Poe into an old, derelict building for one more showdown, in which both Poe and his son are wounded before Poe guns down Davao, who is by then the last bad guy left.

Fighting clichés at every turn, Poe (who directed under the pseudonym Ronwaldo Reyes) manages to turn in a pretty tight action film here, though largely indistinguishable from much of the genre. There is, however, a very good performance by Tito Arevalo as Poe's father. (In Tagalog with some English)

Batch '81

1982 MVP Pictures; 103 minutes/color
Director: Mike de Leon; Screenwriters: Mike de Leon, Clodualdo del Mundo Jr., Raquel Villavicencio; Cinematographer: Rody Lacap; Editor: Jess Navarro; Filmscore: Lorrie Ilustre; Cast: Mark Gil, Sandy Andolong, Ward Luarca, Noel Trinidad, Ricky Sandico, Jimmy Javier, Charito Solis, Chanda Romero, Johnny Delgado, Rod Leido, Bing Pimentel, Criselda Cecilio, Mike Arvisu, Vic Lima, Dodo Cabasal, Edwin Reyes, Nanette Inventor, Joe Jardi, Ed Trinidad, Joseph Olfindo, Raquel Villavicencio

Director Mike de Leon's look at the inane and cruel process of fraternity hazing stars Mark Gil as one of a group of pledges who must prove himself to his would-be fraternity brothers. The film takes the fraternity hazing process to extremes and turns it into a psychological and physical endurance test which culminates in a brutal war between two fraternities that ends in murder. Still, Gil passes his rite of passage and earns his place with his brothers. The film won Best Picture and Best Director awards at the first annual Film Academy of the Philippines Awards in 1983, and had been shown at the Directors' Fortnight at Cannes in 1982. (In Tagalog and English)

Beast of Blood

1970 Hemisphere Pictures/Sceptre; 90 minutes/color
Director/screenwriter: Eddie Romero; Cinematographer: Justo Paulino; Editor: Ben Barcelon; Filmscore: Tito Arevalo; Cast: John Ashley, Celeste Yarnall, Eddie Garcia, Liza Belmonte, Bruno Punzalan, Beverly Miller, Angel Buenaventura (Angelo Ventura), Alfonso Carvajal, Johnny Long

Picking up where its predecessor, *Mad Doctor of Blood Island* (1968), left off, John Ashley's third and final trip to Blood Island begins as he departs the island thinking that Dr. Lorca and his monster are dead. But the monster pops out of a lifeboat and proceeds to go on a massacre of the ship's crew with an axe. During the melee a fire starts and the ship explodes, leaving Ashley and the monster as the only survivors. Some time later Ashley returns to the island on the suspicion that Lorca (Eddie Garcia this time, taking over the role originally played by Ronald Remy) is still alive and up to no good. Accompanying Ashley to the island is reporter Celeste Yarnall, who is abducted by Garcia's men and held captive in Garcia's jungle fortress. Ashley comes looking for her, as Garcia knew he would, and the good doctor is only too anxious to show Ashley the progress he has made in his experiments. And what progress it is! He has managed to recapture the monster, remove its head, and keep both the head and body alive independent of one another. What Garcia doesn't realize is that the monster's head has mustered the mental abilities to control the headless body from a distance. As the local villagers raid the fortress, Garcia is killed by the headless beast, which rises from the operating table and attacks him, as the disembodied head chortles maniacally from across the room. The whole thing ends with the mandatory conflagration, and Ashley, having saved the girl yet again, departs satisfied that this time the mad doctor really has perished. Apparently he was correct.

His first solo Blood Island picture without co-director Gerardo de Leon and the infusion of complex and interesting sexual and familial subtexts that filled much of his work, director/screenwriter Eddie Romero opts for a more straightforward approach, offering an excellent and kitschy mix of jungle adventure and mad science. Stripping everything down to the bare bones, Romero delivers straight-up drive-in entertainment without any pretense. The opening credit sequence in which the monster goes on its murderous rampage aboard the departing ship, hacking away at the crew with an axe, is one of Romero's most inspired moments as a filmmaker, as is the climactic moment when the monster's head gleefully laughs at the sight of its own body savagely murdering Garcia. Maybe Romero would prefer not to hear that, but it's true. Make-up man Tony Arteida also does an excellent job, creating one of the most sublimely grotesque monsters in horror movie history. It's all like an absurd comic book come to life. (In English with some Tagalog)

Beast of the Yellow Night

1970 Four Associates/New World Pictures; 83 minutes/color
Director/screenwriter: Eddie Romero; Cinematographer: Justo Paulino; Editor: Ben Barcelon; Filmscore: Nestor Robles; Cast: John Ashley, Mary

Wilcox, Vic Diaz, Ken Metcalfe, Eddie Garcia, Leopoldo Salcedo, Andres Centenera, Ruben Rustia, Joonee Gamboa, Don Lipman, Jose Garcia, James Spencer, Carpi Asturias, Jose Roy Jr., Peter Magurean, Nora Nunez, Johnny Long

John Ashley plays a U.S. Army deserter, traitor, rapist and murderer who sells his soul to the devil (Vic Diaz), who then sends Ashley's soul to inhabit the bodies of a succession of individuals in order to exploit the evil potential in each person's psyche. A problem arises when Ashley inhabits the body of an American businessman in the Philippines (and Ashley's spitting image by the way). A growing affection for the businessman's wife (Mary Wilcox), and a sense of restlessness and discontent with his purpose in the devil's scheme causes Ashley to rebel. Diaz responds by turning Ashley into a hideous beast whenever he feels compelled toward disobedience, and Ashley runs around killing people and feeding on them. Ashley meets his end when the military and policemen Eddie Garcia and Leopoldo Salcedo hunt him down.

Director Eddie Romero's screenplay contains some fairly thoughtful exchanges between Ashley and Diaz in which Romero is obviously trying to address some theological issues. Unfortunately, he is either unsure of how to express his thoughts on such concepts, or is simply incapable of tackling them, the result being some occasionally awkward dialogue. The best example of this is the character portrayed by Andres Centenera, an old blind man who helps Ashley in his flight from the authorities. The character fluctuates between some of the most poignant dialogue in the film and some of the most peculiar. Still, the film shows Romero to be not only competent as a director, but further reveals his ambition for a serious approach as a screenwriter and a desire to forgo the weightlessness of most horror and exploitation fare in favor of more inquisitive material. Unfortunately, this film also marked the beginning of Romero and Ashley's association with Roger Corman's New World Pictures. As a result, Romero was drawn into directing a string of films written by no-account American screenwriters for the increasingly vulgar and distasteful U.S. market. (In English with some Tagalog)

Berdugo ng Escalante (Executioner of Escalante)

1989 El Nino Films; 96 minutes/color
Director: Cesar Sb. Abella; Screenwriter: Humilde "Meek" Roxas; Cinematographer: Rey de Leon; Editor: Tony Sy; Filmscore: Rey Ramos; Cast: Baldo Marro, Dick Israel, Ruben Rustia, Philip Gamboa, Renato Robles, Edgar Mande, Mario Escudero, Rocco Montalban, Mayleen Gonzales, Nonong de Andres, Ernie Forte, Boy Ranay, Mark Tiongson, Jordan Castillo, Eruel Tongco, Billy Vina, Bobby Lopez, Pepsi Paloma II, Eric Borbon, Rey Alonza, Dave Guanzon, Peter Menen, Mon Recto, Jing Caparas, Bebeng Amora

One of the earlier and more impressive collaborations between actor Baldo Marro and director Cesar Sb. Abella, this film casts Marro as an ex-police officer living in the small town of Escalante. A new mayor is elected, and soon afterward the mayor's lawless sons throw the townsfolk into the grip of terror. The people appeal to Marro for help, but as he is no longer a police officer, he declines to get involved. Marro's daughter is raped and his son is shot to death after he angrily confronts the mayor's sons, and the film builds to an excellent climax as the mayor's sons abduct Marro's daughter, and Marro is forced to engage them in a shootout. Marro receives help at the last moment from his good friend, police officer Dick Israel, but upon seeing Israel Marro's daughter, who had been extremely withdrawn and unable to identify her attacker, becomes hysterical and accuses Israel. The enraged Marro charges Israel with a knife, and although he empties his gun into him, Israel is unable to stop Marro and is forced to spear him through the gut with a long bamboo pole. Desperately swinging his knife, Marro is unable to reach Israel until he pulls himself forward on the impaling bamboo pole, running it further and further through himself until he is close enough to stab Israel.

The identification of Israel as the rapist does come as quite a surprise, and the film certainly livens up in the final twenty minutes, with director Abella showing a good deal of enthusiasm for the impressive and extremely gory climax, but the bulk of the running time seems more-or-less standard with its familiar mix of political corruption, familial tragedy and the need for vengeance. Both Marro and Israel give very good performances. (In Tagalog)

Beyond Atlantis

1973 Dimension Pictures; 91 minutes/color
Director: Eddie Romero; Screenwriter: Charles Johnson; Cinematographer: Justo Paulino; Editor: Andrew Herbert; Filmscore: Ed Norton; Cast: Patrick Wayne, John Ashley, Leigh Christian, Sid Haig, Lenore Stevens, George Nader, Vic Diaz, Eddie Gar-

cia, Kim Ramos, Angelo Ventura, Ken Warren, Andres Centenera, Gil Arceo

Pimp Sid Haig and two-bit hustler John Ashley find out about an island with a fortune in pearls and hire Patrick Wayne to take them there on his boat. Lenore Stevens talks them into taking her along by threatening to spread word around about the pearls. Upon arriving, the group finds the island inhabited by a bizarre tribe of aquatic, fish-eyed people, supposedly the descendants of the people of the city of Atlantis; hence the title. The only normal-appearing members of the tribe are ruler George Nader and his daughter Leigh Christian. It is unclear why they appear different from the rest of the tribe, and equally unclear why Christian must mate with an outsider in order to perpetuate the race, but be that as it may, she is smitten by Wayne and chooses to mate with him. Wayne, on the other hand, has fallen in love with Stevens and declines Christian's sexual offer. The tribe then tries to prevent the group from leaving, and Haig devises a plan to distract the Atlanteans by dynamiting their sacred temple, thereby giving the fortune seekers an opportunity to abscond with the pearls to their boat. The plan results in an all-out battle in which Christian is killed, after which the now doomed tribe allows the outsiders to leave. But after leaving, Haig, Ashley and Wayne are waylaid by Vic Diaz and his men, who try to take the pearls. In the end everybody loses as the chest full of pearls falls overboard and sinks into the sea.

Forgoing his usual stoic lead (which here goes to Wayne), Ashley is far more animated here as the greedy, obsessed fortune seeker, and consequently gives his best performance in years. Nonetheless, this is perhaps the weakest of his collaborations with co-producer/director Eddie Romero, and it was their only joint effort to lose money. Despite its failure at the box office, their next collaboration, *Savage Sisters* (1974), would be an even bigger-budgeted work. (In English)

The Big Bird Cage

1972 New World Pictures; 95 minutes/color
Director/screenwriter: Jack Hill; Cinematographer: Felipe Sacdalan; Editors: Jere Huggins, James Mitchell; Filmscore: William A. Castleman, William Loose; Cast: Pam Grier, Anitra Ford, Candice Roman, Teda Bracci, Carol Speed, Karen McKevic, Sid Haig, Marissa Delgado, Vic Diaz, Rizza Fabian, Andres Centenera, Wendy Green, Subas Herrero, Roldan Aquino

Anitra Ford stars as a slutty socialite who is wrongly accused of involvement with rebels Sid Haig and Pam Grier, and without benefit of trial, she is sent to a jungle prison camp where the women are worked tirelessly as laborers on warden Andres Centenera's sugar mill. In the meantime, Haig's men, longing for the recreational pleasures that Haig enjoys with Grier, speculate on what a wonderful revolution they could have if they only had more such women. They hatch a plot to free the women from the jungle camp, in the name of the revolution of course. The plan calls for Grier to infiltrate the camp as an inmate, which she does by intentionally botching the assassination of a political figure, and Haig to infiltrate the camp as a guard, which he accomplishes by posing as a flaming queen, thus appealing to gay guards Vic Diaz and Subas Herrero. Once inside, the prison break is on, and the film climaxes with a chaotic escape in which most every one dies (including Grier and Haig), and the sugar mill is burned to the ground, crashing down atop Centenera. Only Ford and fellow inmate Marissa Delgado seem to survive the escape. Though the film has its share of torture, death and destruction, it is played largely for laughs, Diaz and Herrero being particularly amusing as the bitchy prison guards. It's especially nice seeing the beautiful Delgado in her prime as a traumatized inmate, one of the film's only straight dramatic roles. Otherwise, most of the actors have fun hamming it up, particularly Teda Bracci as an obnoxious inmate, and the always irrepressible Haig. (In English)

The Big Doll House

1971 New World Pictures; 94 minutes/color
Director: Jack Hill; Screenwriter: Don Spencer; Cinematographer: Fred Conde; Editor: Cliff Fenneman; Filmscore: Hall Daniels; Cast: Judy Brown, Roberta Collins, Pam Grier, Brooke Mills, Pat Woodell, Sid Haig, Christiane Schmidtmer, Kathryn Loder, Jerry Franks, Gina Stuart, Jack Davis, Letty Mirasol, Shirley de las Alas, Myrna de Vera, Siony Cardona, Kathy McDaniel

This drive-in blockbuster kick-started the revival in the women-in-prison genre. Judy Brown stars as a young woman sent to prison for killing her unfaithful lover. Sharing a cell with a group of inmates consisting mostly of Americans (all young and attractive, of course), the film chronicles catfights between cellmates Roberta Collins and Pam Grier, Brooke Mills' heroin addiction, and the torture of most of them at the hands of head matron Kathryn Loder. Not surprisingly, the story builds to a prison break by the group, who are aided by outsiders Sid Haig and Jerry Franks. Taking warden Christiane Schmidtmer and prison doctor Jack Davis as hostages, they are hunted through the jungle, and when the prison guards find them everyone dies in the ensuing conflict except for Brown, who makes her way to a country road and accepts a ride from a passing motorist (director Jack Hill in a cameo), who tells her that he has come to take her back to prison.

Although New World Pictures president Roger Corman was, by his own admission, very put-off by the film's violence, it proved to be such a big moneymaker that Corman sent Hill back to the Philippines to shoot a sequel, *The Big Bird Cage* (1972), which was considerably less brutal, and consequently less lucrative. Despite Corman's personal distaste for the genre's violence, in 1971 he also released director Gerry de Leon's *Women in Cages*, which was even more violent, though more stylized in its presentation. (In English)

Biktima (Victim)

1990 Viva Films; 113 minutes/color

Director: Lino Brocka; Screenwriters: Jose Dalisay Jr., Roy Iglesias; Cinematographers: Pedro Manding Jr., Clodualdo Austria; Editor: George Jarlego; Filmscore: Jaime Fabregas; Cast: Christopher de Leon, Sharon Cuneta, Gina Alajar, Rowell Santiago, Nanette Medved, William Lorenzo, Lucita Soriano, Johnny Wilson, Lollie Mara, Jess Ramos, Nanding Fernandez, Lulu Arrieta, Joji Isla, Robert Talabis, Dodie Lacuna, Millet Advincula, Ben Rivera, Carmi Matic, Susing Yazon, Tom Alvarez

In one of his last films before his death, director Lino Brocka turns in a fairly effective thriller, which serves as an unusual pairing for superstars Christopher de Leon and Sharon Cuneta. De Leon plays a wealthy, successful photographer who also happens to be a sadistic serial killer who periodically abducts, rapes and murders women. But one of his victims (Gina Alajar) survives and hires attorney Cuneta to help her press charges. De Leon uses his wealth to hire a group of brutes to intimidate Alajar, and she winds up taking a payoff to drop the case. Afterwards, de Leon surprisingly pursues a relationship with Cuneta, and even more surprisingly, Cuneta relents and has dinner with him. It doesn't take long for de Leon to become a fixture in Cuneta's home, charming both her and her young daughter, all of which infuriates de Leon's fiancé (Nanette Medved), who tries to persuade Cuneta that de Leon is dangerous after all. It's to no avail, as Cuneta dismisses it all as the ranting of a jealous woman. But de Leon can only suppress his homicidal tendencies for so long, and he winds up abducting Cuneta and her daughter and driving them to his house in the country. Cuneta and her daughter manage to get free, but de Leon catches up with them and is on the verge of killing Cuneta when he is shot and killed by Medved, arriving just in time.

Though Brocka made his reputation in the mid–1970s with gritty and poignant films like *Tinimbang Ka Nguni't Kulang* (1974) and *Maynila, sa mga Kuko ng Liwanag* (1975), his latter efforts seem to have fallen more within the mainstream, which is not to be dismissive. De Leon gives a very effective performance here, and Jaime Fabregas supplies a good score. (In Tagalog with some English)

Black Mama, White Mama

1972 Four Associates/American International; 86 minutes/color

Director: Eddie Romero; Screenwriter: H.R. Christian; Cinematographer: Justo Paulino; Filmscore: Harry Betts; Cast: Pam Grier, Margaret Markov, Sid Haig, Lynn Borden, Zaldy Zshornack, Laurie Burton, Eddie Garcia, Alona Alegre, Dindo Fernando, Vic Diaz, Wendy Green, Lotis Key, Alfonso Carvajal, Bruno Punzalan, Ricardo (Subas) Herrero, Jess Ramos, Carpi Asturias, Andres Centenera

This thoroughly obnoxious women-in-prison film is likely the most embarrassing title on director Eddie Romero's resume. Pam Grier and Margaret Markov star as a prostitute and revolutionary respectively, who are sent to a jungle prison in the usual fictitious Third World republic. They manage to escape, but being shackled together, they run into problems since they each have different destinations in mind. Markov wants to hurry back to Zaldy Zshornack and his revolutionary buddies, while Grier wants to seek out Andres Centenera, who can get her off the island in his boat. Policeman Eddie Garcia pays Sid Haig and his bandits to hunt the girls down, but the women are also being sought by mobster Vic Diaz, who wants Grier for some kind of double-cross she pulled on him. It all comes down to a shootout at the dock in which most everyone perishes (including Markov), while Grier manages to make her getaway with a briefcase of Diaz's money aboard Centenera's boat.

While only the first third of the film takes place in prison, it manages to meet its quota of genre clichés (shower scenes, catfights), including a sadistic lesbian guard, portrayed by Lynn Borden (a veteran of the final season of the wholesome American television sitcom *Hazel*), who masturbates while watching the inmates bathe. Self-consciously vulgar, the film is interesting only as a kind of who's who of Filipino cinema of the era. Unfortunately, many of them—talented and distinguished performers—are left humiliated by H.R. Christian's abysmal screenplay, aimed at the thoroughly tacky U.S. market. (In English)

Black Mamba

1975 Filmmakers Organization; 92 minutes/color

Director: George Rowe; Screenwriter: Carl Kuntze; Cinematographer: Justo Paulino; Editor: Rudy O. Montecajon; Filmscore: Lamberto Avellana, Jr.; Cast: John Ashley, Marlene Clark, Pilar Pilapil, Eddie Garcia, Rosemarie Gil, Laurice Guillen, Alfonso Carvajal, Andres Centenera, Vivian Velez, Willie Nepomuceno, Stevie Maniquiz, Angelo Ventura, Subas Herrero, Jimmy Fabregas, Antonio Carrion, Dick Adair, Mary Walter

American actor John Ashley's only Filipino film without partner Eddie Romero, this is also one of the more interesting of his films in the country. Beautiful Pilar Pilapil stars as a widow with a young son who goes to live with her sister and brother-in-law (Rosemarie Gil and Eddie Garcia) after the death of her husband. One day in church she sees her late husband's ring on the finger of witch Marlene Clark, and when she confronts Clark outside the church an angry exchange ensures. Clark puts a curse on Pilapil, and after Pilapil suffers a series of fainting spells, nasty spills and hospitalizations, doctor Ashley is frustrated by his inability to help her. All of his medical knowledge exhausted, Ashley is forced to try reversing the evil spell, and after going to Clark's home, he recites a rite related to him by librarian Jimmy Fabregas, and turns Clark into a blackbird.

The film is fairly unsophisticated in its presentation, which is actually part of its charm, and is helped considerably by a superbly eerie score composed by Lamberto Avellana, Jr. There are also a number of creepy moments that utilize traditional horror genre imagery, including the opening sequence, in which a hunchbacked graverobber opens the coffin of Pilapil's husband and steals the ring. He sells it to shopkeeper Alfonso Carvajal, who in turn sells it to Clark. Afterward, Carvajal is haunted by the image of death beckoning for him (Willie Nepomuceno with the traditional black robe and scythe, wearing white greasepaint fashioned in the manner of a skull), and after a number of these disturbing visitations, he drops dead of a heart attack. As for the hunchback, he too drops dead of fright after robbing another grave and having the rotting corpse of a woman sit up and glare at him. There is also an interesting passage where Clark takes a moonlight boat ride with two hooded figures to a nearby island where she takes part in a black mass in which she dances with the Devil himself. (In English)

Blind Rage

1977 Trans World Films; 81 minutes/color

Director: Efren C. Pinon; Screenwriters: Jerry O. Tirazona, Leo Fong; Cinematographer: Ben Lobo; Editor: Edgardo Vinarao; Filmscore: Tito Sotto; Cast: Tony Ferrer, Leila Hermosa, Leo Fong, Charlie Davao, Fred Williamson, Carlos Padilla Jr., D'Urville Martin, Dick Adair, Darnell Garcia, Golay, B.T. Anderson, Jose Garcia, Fred Param, Ben Datu, Bello Borja, Rocco Montalban, Carlos Diaz, Mandy Bustamante, Telly Babasa, Val Iglesias, Romy Nario, Rey Sagum, Subas Herrero, Max Alvarado

In this international caper film, Manila banker Charlie Davao becomes involved in a plot to rob his own bank. It is a rather unique plot, as the idea is to rob the bank using a team of blind men specially trained in the bank's layout so that they will not appear to be blind. The idea is that the police will not come looking for blind men afterward, but in fact they do. After a period of intense training using a mock-up of the bank's interior, the five blind men (D'Urville Martin, Leo Fong, Darnell Garcia, Dick Adair and Tony Ferrer) are ready to go, and while the other four go into the bank to pull the robbery itself, Ferrer goes to the electrical room to disarm the security alarm. His job being the only one that does not require feigning sight, Ferrer uses his white cane to find his way. They pull off the robbery and make good their escape, but Ferrer is forced to engage two security officers, and while he does manage to get away, he leaves his cane behind. The cane becomes the only piece of evidence that the police have, and things begin to unravel pretty quickly from there. The cane is traced to Ferrer, and he wastes no time in cutting a deal and leading the police to his accomplices. The rest of the robbers perish when the truck they are being transported in crashes and bursts into flames. Meanwhile, Davao has fled to Los Angeles with half the money, where he is nabbed by policeman Fred Williamson.

There is no actual "star" here, but in true ensemble fashion, any number of players are prominent at different points during the narrative. Davao figures heavily during the beginning and ending of the film, Leila Hermosa (as a woman hired to train the blind men regarding the bank's layout) and the five bank robbers in the mid-section, and Williamson takes over for the finale. In an apparent attempt to impress as an international production, the film was shot in Los Angeles and Long Beach, California, as well as in Mexico, Tokyo, Hong Kong and Manila (though the footage in Mexico, Tokyo and Hong Kong is so brief that it seems pointless and not worth the expense). The most interesting thing that the film has to offer is the climactic fight between Davao and Williamson. While it's not exactly a stirring climax, just the sight of the two of them mixing it up—a once in a lifetime event—is interesting. Otherwise, there is an interesting score by Tito Sotto. (In English)

The Blood Drinkers

1964 Hemisphere Pictures; 83 minutes/color and Black & white

Director: Gerardo de Leon; Screenwriter: Cesar Amigo; Cinematographer: Felipe Sacdalan; Editor: Atilano Salvador; Filmscore: Tito Arevalo; Cast: Amalia Fuentes, Ronald Remy, Eddie Fernandez, Eva Montez, Celia Rodriguez, Renato Robles, Mary Walter, Paquito Salcedo, Felisa Salcedo, Andres Benitez, Fred Param, Eddie Arce, Conchita Cruz, Vicky Velasquez, Cesar Aguilar, Frank Saavedra, Evelyn Shreve, Mona del Cielo, Tiva Lava, Jess Buenaflor

This is the U.S. release of Gerry de Leon's *Kulay Dugo ang Gabi*, which was released in severely truncated form in the international market by Hemisphere in 1966. Adapted from a popular komiks serial, the film stars Ronald Remy as the vampire Dr. Marco, whose lover Katarina (Amalia Fuentes) has apparently died. But Remy—something of a mad scientist in addition to being a vampire—is able to revive her by way of a strange gizmo of his own making. He is barely able to sustain her, however, and as she wastes away, Remy decides that a heart transplant is needed. The logical choice of a donor is Katarina's twin sister Charito (Fuentes again), separated at birth when mother Mary Walter gave her up to be raised by Paquito and Felisa Salcedo. Unable to resist Remy's persuasion, Walter is drawn into a scheme to bring Charito back home, offering her a place to stay after Remy has killed and vampirized her adoptive parents. Charito's beau (Eddie Fernandez) is powerless to stop Remy, but after one too many victims turn up, the locals storm Walter's home and save Charito just as Remy is preparing to transplant her heart. Remy carries Katarina off into the forest, but with the mob closing in, he is forced to leave her behind and he merely vanishes into thin air.

Charmingly gothic, and refreshingly unambiguous regarding its Christian faith, Cesar Amigo's screenplay is not in the least self-conscious regarding the religious struggle at the core of most horror films, and virtually all vampire films. But whereas Christianity is most often a mere prop in Western horror cinema, Amigo brings it to the forefront, most noticeably in the running narration by Andres Benitez, portraying a Catholic priest, who at one point informs a roomful of concerned cast members, "We have one weapon against the Devil, and that is Jesus Christ." Within the film, it is not a unique statement.

Aside from the religious imagery prominent throughout the film, de Leon employs some traditional oddities (Hunchbacks, dwarfs) often associated with the genre, and a skillful use of misty settings and eerie backlighting that calls to mind the work of Italian director Mario Bava, which was itself inspired by the work of American director George Waggner. While some of the film was shot in color, much of it was shot in black and white and tinted in garish tones of red and blue. This may well annoy many viewers, but it does somehow succeed in giving the feel of an otherworldly, nightmarish fairytale.

Also worth noting is the then uncommonly romantic approach to the subject of vampirism. While much has been said about the subjective sex appeal of screen vampires like Bela Lugosi and Christopher Lee, there is no comparison at all to the tormented, romantic figure portrayed here by Remy. An interesting amalgamation of suavity, menace, cruelty, and romantic yearning, Remy's characterization was ahead of its time, and while similar portrayals of Dracula would follow years later (notably, Paul Naschy in Spanish director Javier Aguirre's *Dracula's Great Love* in 1972, and Frank Langella's portrayal in 1979), they are not nearly as fascinating as the work offered here.

This is a very interesting work by de Leon, and he would return to the subject of vampirism in 1966 with the far more disturbing *Ibulong Mo sa Hangin* (*Whisper in the Wind*), which saw international release—again through Hemisphere—in 1970, retitled *Curse of the Vampires*. (Dubbed into English)

Blood Thirst

1965 Journey Productions; 73 minutes/black & white

Director: Newt Arnold; Screenwriter: N.I.P. Dennis; Cinematographer: Hermo Santos; Editor: Tony DiMarco; Cast: Robert Winston, Katherine Henryk, Yvonne Nielson, Vic Diaz, Vic Silayan, Eddie Infante, Bruno Punzalan, Judy Dennis, Max Rojo, Ching Tello, Minda Morena, Isidoro Francisco, Felix Martil

Baffled by a series of vampiric murders, Manila policeman Vic Diaz sends for American sex crime expert and personal friend Robert Winston to help him solve the case. The victims are all attractive young women employed as dancers at the Barrio nightclub, so Winston sets his sights on club owner Vic Silayan. It is eventually revealed that Silayan and club dancer Katherine Henryk are members of an ancient pagan cult who use the blood of young women to stay eternally young. Though no explanation is given as to why, Silayan transforms into a hideous monster whenever he goes on the prowl for fresh blood. Of course, Winston discovers the truth and puts a stop to it.

While the plot is not exactly original, the horror genre does tend to thrive on familiarity, and the transformation that Silayan undergoes is merely a contrivance meant to liven things up a bit, which it does. Once you get past the condescending premise of needing to bring an American all the way across the Pacific to solve what seems to be a fairly simple case (in premise, if not in its ultimate revelation), the film is entertaining, playing much like the American International films of a few years prior. (In English)

Boy Ahas (Snake Boy)

1990 Super 9 Films; 95 minutes/color

Director/screenwriter: Jerry O. Tirazona; Cinematographer: Apolinar Cuenco; Editor: Rodel Capule; Filmscore: Rey Valera; Cast: Sonny Parsons, Charlie Davao, Nick Romano, Marithez Samson, Dick Israel, Leo Lazaro, Robert Talby, Robert Miller, Rey Sagum, Joe Baltazar, Myleen Nokom, Allan Gilbert, Martin Parsons, Vilma Venus, Mike Vergel, Nonong de Andres, Joey Galvez, Ramon Laxa, Gerry Roman, Jeric Vasquez, Ariel Araullo

Set up by one of his own men in an ambush, crime boss Charlie Davao avenges himself by hunting down his Judas and killing him. Davao kills the man's wife as well, and then has Robert Talby tattoo a King Cobra on the chest of the couple's young son. The boy manages to escape, but grows up with the tattoo as a constant reminder of the murder of his parents. Played in adulthood by Sonny Parsons, he leaves his rural home behind and finds work in the city as a bartender, but his tattoo soon begins to work against him. Mistaken by the police for a gang member during a shootout, Parsons is arrested and brutally tortured during an interrogation by sadistic cop Dick Israel. He manages to escape, only to be arrested again after a street brawl with three would-be muggers. During his night in lock-up, one of Parsons' cellmates offers to get him a job in the criminal organization for which he works, but the next day when they go to see the big boss man, Parsons discovers that his new buddy works for Davao. Parsons joins up with Davao's gang, and even participates in some of the dirty work to earn his stripes, but of course his ultimate aim is to be avenged on Davao for the murder of his parents. The film concludes with Parsons storming Davao's house, tossing grenades everywhere and blowing away Davao's men with a shotgun before finally killing Davao himself in a brutal fistfight.

Directorially, Jerry Tirazona shows very little of the flair for the genre that he would exhibit in 1991 with *Sgt. Patalinghug: CIS–Special Operations Group*, a far superior effort. (In Tagalog)

Boy Condenado

1982 Seiko Films; 86 minutes/color

Director: Efren C. Pinon; Screenwriter: Mauro Gia Samonte; Cinematographer: Jun Rasca; Editor: Edgardo Vinarao; Cast: Rudy Fernandez, Laarni Enriquez, Charlie Davao, Mario Montenegro, Dexter Doria, Greggy Liwag, Val Iglesia, Rusty Santos, Perry Baltazar, Gil de Leon, Tony Carreon, Bomber Moran, Baldo Marro, Danny Riel, Big Boy Gomez, Alex Donna, Rey Santos, Pons de Guzman

In this interesting action film from director Efren Pinon, Rudy Fernandez becomes enraged when he returns home from a date one night and finds his mother in bed with mobster Charlie Davao. When Fernandez bursts into the room, Davao goes for his gun, which goes off during the ensuing struggle, killing Fernandez's mother. Davao flees through the window and Fernandez is arrested and tried for killing his own mother, all of which causes a good deal of humiliation for Fernandez's father (Mario Montenegro), who is a police officer. Not only is his son on trial for the murder of Montenegro's wife, but Montenegro has the added humiliation of the revelation of his wife's affair with a prominent crime figure. Fernandez manages to escape from jail and seeks to settle accounts with Davao, pursuing him to an island where Davao and his gang are hiding out. But the police, led by Montenegro, follow Fernandez there, and when a shootout ensues, Fernandez is wounded. It is revealed that Davao is Fernandez's real father, yet when Davao tries to shoot Montenegro, Fernandez takes a bullet to save the man that he always thought was his father. Montenegro then shoots and kills Davao as Fernandez lay dying. (In Tagalog)

Boy Recto

1992 Moviestars Productions; 112 minutes/color

Director: Jett C. Espiritu; Screenwriters: Jun Lawas, Jett C. Espiritu; Cinematographer: Baltazar Dauz; Editor: Renato de Leon; Filmscore: Jaime Fabregas; Cast: Ronnie Ricketts, Aiko Melendez, Bembol Rocco, Michael de Mesa, Fortunato "Atoy" Co, Jess Lapid Jr., Kimberly Diaz, Marita Zobel, Zandro Zamora, Fred Moro, Philip Gamboa, Ramil Rodriguez, Renato del Prado, Gilda Aragon, Jeena Alvarez, Rowel Mariano, Mely Tagasa, Ben Datu, Alex David, Ross Rival, Rey Sagum, Conrad Poe, Monching Reyes, Nanding Fernandez, Roland Montes, Mike Magat, Ronnie Madrigal, Mike Vergel, Jojo de Leon

Street tough Ronnie Ricketts and drug dealer Michael de Mesa are both interested in Aiko Melendez, and they wind up brawling over her. Ricketts gives de Mesa a sound beating, which naturally starts a process of escalating retaliation. Ricketts' sister is raped and murdered, and his mother is killed too, and when Ricketts enlists the aid of friend Jess Lapid, Jr., Lapid's girlfriend is murdered as well. Eventually, Lapid is added to the fatality list, but Ricketts is finally able to kill de Mesa, and he and Melendez go on to have a child together. Despite the extremely formulaic pattern of tragedy and retribution, this is a fairly engrossing and well-played film, though it is predictably overlong. (In Tagalog)

Brides of Blood

1967 Hemisphere Pictures; 92 minutes/color

Directors: Gerardo de Leon, Eddie Romero; Cast: John Ashley, Kent Taylor, Mario Montenegro, Beverly Hills, Eva Darren, Oscar Keesee, Ely Ramos Jr., Bruno Punzalan, Andres Centenera, Pedro Navarro, Carmelita Estrella, Quiel Mendoza, Willie Tomada, Ben Sanchez, Angelita Alba

Peace Corps worker John Ashley arrives on Blood Island with scientist Kent Taylor and Taylor's wife (Beverly Hills) just in time to witness a funeral procession for some dismembered native girls. They eventually discover that the girls were sacrificed to a monster that had only recently begun to terrorize the island. They are further shocked to find the island populated by carnivorous plants. All are thought by Taylor to be the result of atomic mutation caused by nuclear testing, possibly from the tests on Bikini, with contaminated sea life migrating and contaminating the island in turn. Eventually it is revealed that the fearsome beast terrorizing the natives is wealthy recluse Mario Montenegro, who himself undergoes periods of radical mutation. After Ashley shames the natives into standing up to the monster, it is finally killed in the usual climactic conflagration.

There is an overt sexuality to this film which in unmatched by either of the two Blood Island movies that followed (*Mad Doctor of Blood Island* in 1968 and *Beast of Blood* in 1970). To start with, there is the frustrated nymphomaniac portrayed by Hills, who is apparently ready to have sex with any available male, married to the much older, disinterested, and possibly impotent scientist portrayed by Taylor. There is also the obvious sexual implication of the beast's craving only young, nude, virgin native girls, the carnal nature of which is confirmed (if, indeed, it needed any further confirmation) when native girl Eva Darren explains to Ashley that the beast only wants women, and satisfies himself by tearing them to pieces.

With all of the aberrational sex, the film seems to be making some sort of comment on the corrosive effect of carnal desires (a very Catholic notion in a very Catholic culture), particularly when the sexually savage beast meets up with the over-sexed Hills, presumably the culmination of both their desires, she being ravished unto death while he overpowers and destroys the sexually promiscuous female. It would be easy—in fact, too easy—to dismiss all of this deviant and bestial sex as just so much exploitation fodder, but such points of view do not simply emerge out of a vacuum, and the fact remains that the film rather brazenly lays bare a conundrum within the male psyche as regards female sexuality.

Gerardo de Leon and Eddie Romero would only direct one more film together—*Mad Doctor of Blood Island*—and while that film would not match their work here as regards deviant sexual motifs, screenwriter Rueben Canoy would fill it with his own layered, involved and somewhat odd familial dynamics. (In English)

The Brown Ninja

1987 Bathala Film Productions; 100 minutes/color

Director: Leonardo "Ding" Pascual; Screenwriter: Mar Santana; Cinematographer: Danny Bustos; Editor: Ruben Pantua; Filmscore: Willy Yusi; Cast: Dante Varona, Tanya Gomez, Ramal Rodriguez, Michael Chan, Janet Price, Frank Juhaez, Mario Escudero, Tom Alindogan, Boy Fernandez, Noel Aguilar, Renato Robles, Sheila Kingscote, Ed Garlan, Tony Agunsaya, Tanya Faye Almanza, Farah Floro, Manny Tibayan, Naty Santiago, Joseph de Cordova, Rocco Montalban, Fred Moro, Eric Robles

When his mother's birthday party is disrupted by a drive-by shooting, Dante Varona jumps in his car and gives chase. The hit men shoot up Varona's car, wounding him in the shoulder and causing him to crash, but he manages to escape before the car explodes. After wandering into the forest and passing out, Varona is discovered the following day by a blind old hermit, who takes him back to his cave dwelling and nurses him back to health. It should come as no surprise that the blind old woodsman is a martial arts expert (aren't they all?), and before he dies, he manages to train Varona in the ways of the ninja. After burying his teacher, Varona returns to civilization ready to be a full-fledged crime fighter. He proves to be a formidable foe for the crime syndicates, and he avenges himself on the gunmen responsible for the deaths of his family members in the drive-by shooting, but his adversaries eventually capture him. The crime boss who is holding him is very impressed by Varona's martial arts skills, and as he and a rival crime boss enjoy staging competitions in which their best men fight to the death, he forces Varona to participate. Varona defeats his opponent (a black man with a mace), and is then aided in his escape by the syndicate chief's girlfriend (Tanya Gomez), who is fed up with her mob boss boyfriend's sexual sadism (something she recounts in a flashback sequence). During the climactic fight, Varona exhibits all of those curious ninja abilities, such as being able to jump twenty feet in the air and, with sword in hand, he slashes up all his opponents. (In Tagalog with some English)

Brutal

1980; 105 minutes/color
Director: Marilou Diaz-Abaya; Screenwriter: Ricardo Lee; Cinematographer: Manolo Abaya; Editors: Manolo Abaya, Mark Tarnate; Filmscore: George Canseco; Cast: Amy Austria, Gina Alajar, Charo Santos, Jay Ilagan, Joonee Gamboa, Ogie Martinez, Jun Villena, Perla Bautista, Johnny Delgado, Nello Nayo, Robert Tongko, Boy Sabiniano, Luis Benedicto, Ric Celis, Clemente Vergara Jr., Carlo Kimpo, Pinky Sabinosa, Peachy Mercado

Amy Austria won the FAMAS Best Actress award for her performance here as a traumatized young woman found at the scene of a triple homicide. As the film opens, Austria is taken from her home by the police, who have found her husband (Jay Ilagan) and two of his friends dead, each having bled to death after having their wrists slashed. Austria is withdrawn and nonresponsive to police questioning, but reporter Charo Santos begins her own investigation, uncovering the details of Austria's tragic life. A shy, inexperienced young woman, Austria was raped by Ilagan, and then forced into marrying him by her enraged father. Not surprisingly, the marriage turns out to be a big mistake, and Ilagan's cruelty reaches its height when he and his drunken friends take turns raping Austria. Eventually Austria snaps out of her withdrawn state and reveals to Santos how she served a pitcher of drugged beer to Ilagan and his pals and then slashed their wrists after the drug had rendered them powerless. Austria does give an excellent performance, and Marilou Diaz-Abaya's direction is inventive. (In Tagalog with some English)

Bulaklak sa City Jail
(The Flower in City Jail)

1984; 100 minutes/color
Director: Mario O'Hara; Screenwriter: Lualhati Bautista; Cinematographer: Johnny Araojo; Editor: Efren Jarlego; Filmscore: Tony Aguilar; Cast: Nora Aunor, Gina Alajar, Celia Rodriguez, Perla Bautista, Maya Valdez, Zenaida Amador, Maritess Gutierrez, Gloria Romero, Ricky Davao, Shyr Valdez, Bella Flores, German Moreno, Augusto Victa, Alvin Enriquez, Toby Alejar, Mandy Bustamante, Carmen Enriquez, Gidgette Reyes, Aida Arellano, Rod Francisco, Tom Olivar, Renato Morado, Edwin O'Hara, Josie Galvez, Tony Aguilar, Estrella Antonio, Cris Daluz, Gil Arceo, Greg Rocero

Superstar Nora Aunor won the FAMAS Best Actress award for her performance in this bleak melodrama in which she portrays a lounge singer who is arrested for murder after stabbing a woman in self-defense during a fight. Pregnant at the time of her arrest, she is sent to a holding wing of a penitentiary and finds herself trapped in a living hell of sexual abuse (perpetrated by guards and inmates alike), brutality and deplorably filthy living conditions. The wheels of justice turn slowly, and Aunor progresses in her pregnancy to the point that she requests to be taken to the hospital, claiming to be experiencing contractions. But it is only a ruse, and after being taken to the hospital, Aunor manages to escape while waiting to be seen by a doctor. The following day, the police spot her wandering the streets, but she evades them by disappearing into a crowd entering a zoo. The police close the zoo, but after observing everyone exiting the grounds, they still fail to spot Aunor and continue searching the zoo into the night. Though she continues to elude the police, Aunor goes into labor and, after giving birth, she is given away by the crying of her newborn child. She is re-arrested, but the film ends happily as she is acquitted at trial and walks out a free woman with her child.

Director Mario O'Hara takes the high road, and despite the exploitable potential of the setting and material, refuses to go the route of directors like Eddie Romero and Cirio Santiago, turning in a legitimate work rather than merely another sleazy women-in-prison cliché piece. (In Tagalog with occasional English)

Burlesk Queen
(Burlesque Queen)

1977 Ian Film Productions; 113 minutes/color
Director: Celso Ad. Castillo; Screenwriters: Celso Ad. Castillo, Mauro Gia Samonte; Cinematographer: Ben Lobo; Editor: Abelardo Hulleza; Filmscore: George Canseco; Cast: Vilma Santos, Rosemarie Gil, Rolly Quizon, Leopoldo Salcedo, Roldan Aquino, Joonee Gamboa, Chito Ponce-Enrile, Dexter Doria, Yolanda Luna, Celso Ad. Castillo, Pat Ilano, Grace Zaldivar, G.V. Misa, Estrella Kuenzler, Mervyn Samson, Rio Locsin, Bino Garcia, Jr.

Filmmaker Celso Ad. Castillo achieved a degree of international recognition with this melodrama, which also catapulted Vilma Santos' career in the Philippines into the superstar stratum. Santos portrays a young woman who defies the wishes of her crippled father (Leopoldo Salcedo) and takes a job in Joonee Gamboa's burlesque theater in the 1950s. Salcedo suffers a fatal coronary, and for a time Santos leaves the burlesque profession and moves in with her boyfriend (Rolly Quizon), but when she gets pregnant, Santos is abandoned by Quizon, who leaves to attend law school. With no means of support, Santos decides to return to burlesque, but upon visiting Gamboa, she finds that he is about to be put out of business by an ambitious politician determined to clean up the city. Gamboa decides to put on one last amazing show, and Santos closes the show by shaking it up until she manages to abort her child. (In Tagalog with some English)

Cadena de Amor (Chain of Love)

1971 Lea Productions; 121 minutes/color
Director: Lino Brocka; Screenwriter: Mario O'Hara; Cinematographer: Loreto U. Isleta; Editor: Felizardo V. Santos; Filmscore: Jose Mari Chan; Cast: Rosemarie (Sonora), Dante Rivero, Hilda Koronel, Mary Walter, Patricia Mijares, Nello Nayo, Arnold Gamboa, Raul Aragon, Joe Gruta, Ursula Carlos, Luis Benedicto, Alfredo Alferez, Inday dela Cruz, Mario O'Hara, Eddie Garcia

This bittersweet love story is very representative of the soap opera genre, which tends to draw heavily from Filipino komiks serials, and is generally replete with unlikely and absurd plot twists. Rosemarie Sonora plays a young woman who falls in love with Dante Rivero, her rapist—yes, that's right, her rapist. But Rivero boards a jet that goes down in the ocean, and he is thought to have perished like everyone else on board. Not so, as Rivero washes ashore on an island and is rescued by a kindly family that takes him in. Suffering from amnesia, Rivero knows not where to go, but he soon falls in love with daughter of the house Hilda Koronel, a paraplegic since being struck by a car. Apparently the problem was psychosomatic, as Koronel regains the use of her legs under duress when she is required to jump in the ocean to save Rivero after he falls out of a boat and hits his head. Rivero eventually regains his memory, courtesy of the knock on the head, and he rushes back home to see his mother (Mary Walter) and Sonora, leaving Koronel heartbroken. (In Tagalog)

Caged Fury

1980 Lea Productions; 84 minutes/color
Director: Cirio H. Santiago; Cinematographer: Romulo Araojo; Filmscore: Ernani Cuenco; Cast: Bernadette Williams, Jennifer Lane, Taaffe O'Connell, Catherine March, Margaret Magick, Gina Alajar, Elizabeth Oropesa, Efren Reyes Jr., Jose Mari Avellana, Leo Martinez, Ken Metcalfe, Bobby Greenwood, Ernie Zarate, Mike Cohen, Nello Nayo, Eddie Villamor, Dave Martin, Bill Scott, Bello Borja

Bernadette Williams stars as a Canadian reporter abducted and taken to a Vietnamese prison camp where commander Jose Mari Avellana and doctor Leo Martinez brainwash their female captives into becoming suicidal assassins, willing to blow themselves and their respective targets to pieces. U.S. government man Ken Metcalfe negotiates with Vietnamese Elizabeth Oropesa for the release of the women in exchange for Vietnamese general Ernie Zarate, who had defected to the West. While being transported by train to the designated exchange spot, the women discover that their captors do not truly intend to let them go, and they manage to overtake their captors and take over the train. When the train fails to stop at the station, Vietnamese soldiers, led by Oropesa, give chase, but the girls are rescued by Metcalfe, who shows up with two helicopters to airlift them to safety.

Efren Reyes, Jr., has a good role as a Vietnamese camp guard who falls in love with Williams and helps her try to escape, but winds up being killed when she is recaptured, and Gina Alajar is featured as a Vietnamese plant, who poses as a captive in order to keep Avellana apprised of any escape plans being formed among the women. Alajar is killed when her cover is blown and the girls throw her from the train.

Ever so slightly more competent than director Cirio Santiago's other works from the same period, the film is generally more watchable than most of his work, managing to be somewhat entertaining in an admittedly trashy way. (In English)

Cavalry Command

1959; 77 minutes/color

Director/screenwriter: Eddie Romero; Cinematographer: Felipe Sacdalan; Editors: Gervasio Santos, L.S. Ted Smith; Filmscore: Tito Arevalo, Ariston Avelino; Cast: John Agar, Richard Arlen, Pancho Magalona, Alicia Vergel, Bill Phipps, Myron Healey, Cielito Legaspi, Eddie Infante, Boy Planas, Vic Diaz, Jennings Sturgeon, Max Alvarado, Paquito Salcedo

Director/screenwriter Eddie Romero's accounting of America's imperial presence in the Philippines finds U.S. Cavalry moving into Northern Luzon in 1902 to restore peace and order after the departure of the Spanish. After three centuries of brutal Spanish rule, the Americans have a hard time getting the local residents to trust their good intentions. There is also a lawless tribe of Igorots to contend with, and Pancho Magalona, a rebel army of one intent on driving the Americans out. Magalona is captured and thrown in jail, even as the villagers begin to warm up to the American presence. The Cavalry is given orders to pull out, and commanding officer Myron Healey leaves behind three men (John Agar, Richard Arlen and Bill Phipps) to maintain things. Agar lets Magalona go free, and the proud and embittered Magalona convinces a handful of the locals to stage an overthrow of the Americans. After taking the three Cavalrymen prisoner, Magalona tries to get the locals to show their contempt for the Americans by burning their new schoolhouse down, but when he finds no willing participants, he leaves in disgrace. Still nursing his wounded pride, Magalona plans one final attack, and learning that the three remaining Americans are pulling out, he plans to intercept them. But Magalona is there to witness an ambush on the Americans by the Igorots, and when the Igorots set fire to the bridge which is vital to the village, Magalona swallows his pride and helps the Americans put out the fire.

Co-produced by Cirio Santiago and American Harry Smith, the film was made largely with the U.S. market in mind, which may account for the rosy depiction of the Americans. While America's only imperialist experiment was, by all accounts, far preferable to the Filipinos than was the Spanish presence, the U.S. record was by no means spotless. On the other hand, having lived through WWII, Romero may be expressing a genuine affection for America (which he does seem always to have had) and the joint history shared by the two nations. (In English with some Tagalog)

Combat Killers

1968 Cinema East Productions; 95 minutes/color

Director/screenwriter: Ken Loring; Cinematographer: Mars Rasca; Editor: Joseph Zucchero; Filmscore: Pepe Merto; Cast: Paul Edwards, Marlene Dauden, Leopoldo Salcedo, Claude Wilson, Ken Metcalfe, Vic Silayan, Kim Ramos, Chuck Jamison, Von Serna, Eddie Arenas, Fred Galang, Ernie Holt, Luis Florentino, Ding Tello, Ching Tello, Bruno Punzalan, Paquito Fajardo, Jerry Bailey

In this more or less standard WWII combat film, U.S. lieutenant Paul Edwards uncovers a plot by the Japanese to blow up a hydroelectric dam in Santa Maria. Against Edwards' strongly worded advice, captain Claude Wilson orders his troops in and walks right into an ambush laid by Japanese general Leopoldo Salcedo. With his men dying all around him, Edwards relieves Wilson of command and radios for air support. With the arrival of U.S. bombers the U.S. and Filipino troops are finally able to overcome the Japanese forces. This seems to be among the last of the old-school WWII films, but aside from an excellent cast of Filipino character actors, the film is unexceptional. (In English)

Comfort Women: A Cry for Justice

1993 Alyssa Films; 88 minutes/color
Director: Celso Ad. Castillo; Screenwriter: Alice "Lissa" Poltan; Cinematographer: Isagani Sioson; Editor: Abelardo Hulleza; Filmscore: Tats Luna; Cast: Joel Torre, Ricardo Cepeda, Sharmaine Arnaiz, Shirley Tesoro, Jiryuro Arashi, Tony Mabesa, Roldan Aquino, Jessica Rodriguez, Karen Salas, Mariel Salvador, Glenda Garcia, Lora Luna, Ana Maceda, Kristine Zablan, Elli Rose Apple, Hideo Nishizawa, Donna Luoise, Alicia "Lissa" Poltan, Rodelo Poltan

Detailing the plight of the residents—the women in particular—of the small town of Santa Monica under the Japanese occupation during WWII, Ricardo Cepeda here portrays a Japanese lieutenant who becomes frustrated by the resilience of the Filipino resistance. After the killing of two Japanese soldiers, Cepeda orders the execution of ten Filipinos for every one Japanese soldier killed. He is then convinced by underling Jiryuro Arashi to boost the morale of his troops by allowing them to round up the young women in town for use as "comfort women," that basically being sexual slaves. Kept in a kind of stockade prison camp, the women are subjected to repeated rape until they rebel, jumping the guards and seizing some weapons. A shootout ensues in which the women are aided by the conveniently timed arrival of rebels, but the film ends without showing the final outcome of the conflict.

Though the film sets itself up as noble-minded in its intentions, it plays not unlike the women-in-prison films and related genres, but in all fairness it would be difficult, if not impossible, to deal substantively with such a topic without being accused of exploitation to one degree or another. The film's best performance is delivered by Joel Torre in the role of a traitorous villager who first works for the Japanese as an informer, then crosses over to the rebel camp after being tortured by the Japanese, who accuse him of holding out. (In Tagalog and English)

Cover Girl Models

1975 Filmgroup International; 73 minutes/color
Director: Cirio Santiago; Screenwriter: Howard Cohen; Cinematographer: Felipe Sacdalan; Editor: Gervasio Santos; Filmscore: D'Amarillo; Cast: Pat Anderson, Lindsay Bloom, Tara Strohmeier, John Kramer, Rhonda Leigh Hopkins, Zeneida Amador, Vic Diaz, Joe Zucchero, Mary Woronov, Nory Wright, Tony Ferrer, Howard Shaw, Ken Metcalfe, Leo Martinez, Victor Ordonez, Paquito Salcedo, Joonee Gamboa, Joe Mari Avellana, Mark Lebeuse, Jordan Rosengarten, Barbara Perez

Here we have yet another piece of 1970s exploitation from director/producer Cirio Santiago. The story concerns three fashion models (Pat Anderson, Lindsay Bloom and Tara Strohmeier) sent to Hong Kong on a photo shoot with photographer John Kramer. Upon Arriving they are unwittingly drawn into a struggle between U.S. intelligence agents and Chinese spies when wardrobe mistress Zeneida Amador sews some microfilm into the seam of one of Anderson's dresses. While being pursued by spies, Anderson falls in love with undercover agent Tony Ferrer, and after the three models are kidnapped, the film climaxes with a shootout in which they are rescued by Ferrer and Kramer (!).

Howard Cohen's screenplay is extremely unfocused, and aside from much of the running time being devoted to Kramer's trying his luck with the models, the narrative meanders aimlessly as one of the models tries to impress a movie producer by impersonating a U.S. ambassador's daughter, precipitating her abduction by a terrorist group who quickly release her upon learning that she is an imposter. There is an impressive cast of Filipino actors here, all wasted, as they usually are in Santiago's films. It's not a complete and total loss, but in general the film is entertaining for all the wrong reasons. (In English)

Curacha: Ang Babaeng Walang Pahinga (Curacha: The Woman Without Rest)

1998 Regal Films; 99 minutes/color
Director: Chito S. Rono; Screenwriter: Ricky Lee; Cinematographer: Charlie Peralta; Editor: Jaime Davila; Filmscore: Jaime Fabregas; Cast: Rosanna Roces, Jaclyn Jose, Ara Mina, Ruby Moreno, Mike Magat, Lito Legaspi, Richard Bonnin, Lucita Soriano, Maureen Maurencio, Dick Israel, Tito Arevalo, Roy Alvarez, Richard Quan, Tom Olivar, Bea Lopez, Alex Cortez, Tony Mabesa, Richard Pinlac, Vangie Labalan, Frencesca Torres

Set against the backdrop of the turbulent mid–1980s and the coup attempt that came early in Corazon Aquino's administration, this film stars Rosanna Roces as Curacha, a prostitute who, in between servicing clients like military colonel Lito Legaspi during the day, works by night at Dick Israel's nightclub as a torera, that being a woman who has sex live on stage for a paying audience, her male counterpart being the torero. Roces is good as the disillusioned Curacha, a young woman whose only hope seems to be in the continuing marketability of her remarkable physique, which she uses not merely to earn a living, but also to navigate her way through the city by night, trading sex with a checkpoint guard for the right to pass through, and convincing a cabbie on his way to a fare to take her instead by agreeing to bare her breasts. Obviously Roces flaunts her considerable charms a good deal during the film, which could be considered crassly exploitative, but can be reasonably argued to be a plus.

One of the film's most interesting moments comes early on when Roces, having just finished an appointment with Legaspi, tries to assuage her guilt by going to church to pray, where she daydreams of the Virgin Mary appearing in a shaft of light and joyfully greeting the crowd gathering around her. But Roces' guilt wins out, and when she approaches the Blessed Virgin, Mary's serene countenance turns to a scowl and she slaps Roces. This is a very interesting film. (In Tagalog)

Curse of the Vampires

1966 Sceptre/Hemisphere; 82 minutes/color
Director: Gerardo de Leon; Screenwriters: Ben Feleo, Pierre L. Salas; Cinematographer: Mike Accion; Editor: Ben Barcelon; Filmscore: Tito Arevalo; Cast: Amalia Fuentes, Romeo Vasquez, Eddie Garcia, Johnny Monteiro, Rosario del Pilar, Mary Walter, Francisco Cruz, Paquito Salcedo, Quiel Mendoza, Andres Benitez, Luz Angeles, Tessie Hernandez, Linda Rivera

This is the English-dubbed international release of Gerardo de Leon's *Ibulong Mo sa Hangin*, in which brother and sister Eddie Garcia and Amalia Fuentes are shocked to learn that their family has a dark secret: they have a history of vampirism, and the mother (Mary Walter), whom they thought dead is actually alive and being kept chained in the basement by family patriarch Johnny Monteiro. This shameful secret causes Fuentes to refuse a proposal of marriage from suitor Romeo Vasquez, but Vasquez is persistent. As the family disintegrates under the weight of its secret, each becoming victim to its incestuous nature, Garcia kills Vasquez. But that proves Garcia's undoing, as he is then bedeviled by Vasquez's ghost, which kills Fuentes and releases her from the nightmarish existence in the fleshly world.

Unlike most vampire films of its era, the subject here is given a very earthly spin, presented as a human affliction, decidedly sexual in nature, with vampire Garcia even being extremely unnerved by the appearance of Vasquez's spirit. Released in the West in 1970, it was one of the last chances for Western audiences to see de Leon's work, the very last chance being the crude exploitation feature *Women in Cages* (1971), which was severely hamstrung by an exceedingly pedestrian screenplay. (Dubbed into English)

Dahil Mahal Kita: The Dolzura Cortez Story
(Because I Love You: The Dolzura Cortez Story)

1993 Octo Arts Films; 112 minutes/color
Director: Laurice Guillen; Screenwriter: Ricardo Lee; Cinematographer: Eduardo Jacinto; Editor: Efren Jarlego; Filmscore: Nonong Buencamino; Cast: Vilma Santos, Christopher de Leon, Charito Solis, Eula Valdez, Maila Gumila, Jackie Aquino, Mia Gutierrez, Mikee Villanueva, Nonie Buencamino, Jaime Blanch, John Gaddi, Tessie Dumpit, Cris Michelena, Shamaine Centenera, Ernie Zarate, Pocholo Montes, Gil Portes, Richard Chaney

It's hard to believe that ten years after the onset of the AIDS epidemic, it was still an anonymous, faceless disease in the Philippines. Dolzura Cortez was the first AIDS victim in the Philippines to forsake her anonymity and publicly proclaim her condition in the press. Portrayed by superstar Vilma Santos, the film follows her through a marriage to a man who, it turns out, already has a wife, but sees nothing wrong with keeping two. After six years and three children, Santos leaves him, moving on to a brief affair with Christopher de Leon, and then on to a second marriage that turns sour when an Arab businessman takes advantage of her. She goes on to have a good many lovers afterward. Aware of AIDS, she becomes emboldened with each negative test result, but when she falls ill and has to be hospitalized, she is stunned to find out that she is not merely HIV-positive, but has full-blown AIDS. During her hospitalization, Santos has an unexpected reunion with de Leon, whom she hasn't seen in ten years, when he shows up working as an AIDS counselor. Despite de Leon's shock, and their ensuing rocky reunion, de Leon returns and the two become close. De Leon sees Santos through her illness, and it is he who convinces her to go public with her story. Despite the inevitable conclusion, the film tries to put a positive spin on things, with Santos lecturing and being told by young people that her story has convinced them to stop playing Russian roulette with their lives. The life she had notwithstanding, the filmmakers seem to go to great lengths to avoid being judgmental about their subject, leaving that to the discretion of the viewer. Aside from Santos and de Leon, Charito Solis is very good as Cortez's mother. (In Tagalog with some English)

Ang Dalubhasa (The Specialist)

2000 Millennium Cinema; 112 minutes/color
Director: Ronwaldo Reyes (Fernando Poe, Jr.); Screenwriters: Pablo S. Gomez, Manny Buising; Cinematographer: Ver P. Reyes; Editor: Augusto Salvador; Filmscore: Jaime Fabregas; Cast: Fernando Poe Jr., Nanette Medved, Maritoni Fernandez, Cris Villonco, Paquito Diaz, Ricardo Cepeda, Berting Labra, Bob Soler, Romy Diaz, Zandro Zamora, Johnny Vicar, Marco Polo Garcia, Dindo Arroyo, Manjo del Mundo, Nonoy de Guzman, Gerald Ejercito, R.G. Gutierrez, Bong Francisco, Tony Carreon, Mark Angelo Francisco, Nanding Fernandez, Bert Olivar, Bon Vibar, Vic Varrion, Eddie Tuazon, Marita Zobel, Dante Castro, Dedes Whitaker, Maita Sanchez, Jesette Prospero, Naty Santiago, Robert Miller

Fernando Poe, Jr. gathers together his usual group of collaborators for this effective, if routine, action film. Poe plays an army surgeon whose wife is killed when a group of assassins come gunning for her father, a prominent judge. Poe spends the next few years hunting down and killing the gunmen responsible for his wife's death, until he's gotten them all save the leader (Johnny Vicar). He all but forgets his quest for vengeance when he meets Maritoni Fernandez, and is on the verge of marrying her and settling down in Cebu, but things again take a tragic turn when Fernandez's niece is diagnosed with a brain tumor, and Poe, whose specialty is neurosurgery, is unable to save her. Tormented by guilt, Poe leaves Cebu and winds up in an alcoholic haze in the slums of Manila, where he is befriended by Nanette Medved, a nurse in a small health clinic. Poe soon finds himself lending his services to the clinic, and one night he is taken at gunpoint by members of a criminal gang who want him to tend their wounded leader, who has been shot by police. Poe is shocked to discover that the gang's leader is Vicar, but he does a good job of patching him up nonetheless. Soon after, Poe gets a tip that Vicar's gang is planning to rob a cargo ship, and Poe arrives in time to help thwart the gang and finally gets to kill Vicar. This is certainly nothing out of the ordinary, as Poe action films go, but it is well done for what it is. (In Tagalog with some English)

Dama de Noche (Lady of the Night)

1998 Neo Films/Tikbalang; 98 minutes/color
Director: Lorenzo Reyes; Screenwriter: Elsie Martinez Coscolluelo; Cinematographer: Richard Padernal; Cast: Ynez Veneracion, Jaclyn Jose, Mark Gil, Anita Linda, Junell Hernando, Richard Merck, Maureen Mauricio, Aiza Marquez, Lara Fabregas, Sherilyn Reyes, Mel Kimura, Michelle Rufo, Maricor Fortun, Simon Ibarra, Cedric Incarnacion, Boy Salvador, Josie Galvez, Checcs Osmefia, Marilu Santamaria, Beng Marquez, Arthur Cervantes

After years of co-directing pictures with Peque Gallaga, Lorenzo Reyes steps out on his own with this stylish sexual melodrama (Gallaga serves as producer). Ynez Veneracion stars as an emotionally troubled young woman married to a very successful businessman (Mark Gil) and haunted by traumatic memories of sexual abuse at the hands of her stepfather (Richard Merck). Though Gil is a loving husband, he is also away from home a good deal on business, and left on her own, Veneracion begins to exorcise her sexual demons. Dressing as a common streetwalker, she has a succession of tawdry back alley sexual dalliances with anonymous partners (at one point with a group of men who take their turns with her). Things eventually come crashing down around her when one of her sexual partners discovers her identity, shows up at her house and rapes her. Gil returns home that night to find Veneracion an emotional wreck, and when she tells him of her double-life, they both agree that she needs time to work through her problems. She travels to the country to stay with her mother (Jaclyn Jose), who had given her over to a Catholic orphanage as a child in order to stop the sexual abuse that she was suffering at the hands of Merck.

Aside from the fairly impressive job by Reyes as director, the film also features some very good cinematography by Richard Padernal. Cashing in on the trend toward more erotic fare, the film features a good amount of nudity and softcore sex, though to his credit, Reyes tries to turn in a legitimate artistic work. Despite the increasingly frivolous nature of much of his work with Gallaga, Reyes seems to have wanted a more serious work with which to form his own directorial identity, with positive results. (In Tagalog)

Darna

1991 Viva Films; 108 minutes/color
Director: Joel Lamangan; Screenwriter: Frank

G. Rivera; Cinematographer: Ramon Marcelino; Editor: Ike Jarlego, Jr.; Filmscore: Willy Cruz; Cast: Nanette Medved, Edu Manzano, Pilar Pilapil, Tonton Gutierrez, Nida Blanca, Bing Loyzaga, Dennis Padilla, Atong Redillas, Donna Cruz, Tony Lambino, Dencio Padilla, Errol Dionisio, Archie Adamos, Ray Ventura, Boy Roque, Jun Hidalgo, Jim Pebanco, Carmi Matic, Guila Alvarez, Roland Montes, Rachel Alejandro, Herbert Bautista, Manny Castaneda, Joko Diaz, IC Mendoza, Keempee de Leon, Vina Morales, Sylvia Sanchez, Mary Walter, Raymart Santiago, Jinky Oda, Oscar Peralta

Superheroine Darna, originally introduced in Filipino komiks, has been an enduring character in films as well, played by various actresses through the years since the 1950s. This '90s update stars Nanette Medved in the role. The film opens in South America in 1900, as evil Edu Manzano discovers an amulet that bestows him with extraordinary powers. Quickly jumping ahead to the Philippines in the 1970s, a young girl named Narda is visited by an angelic figure who gives her a magic pearl. When she pops the pearl in her mouth and utters the word "Darna," she is immediately transformed into a superheroine with powers not unlike Superman. Regurgitating the pearl and likewise uttering the name Narda reverses the process.

Jumping ahead yet again, the grown-up Narda/Darna is portrayed by Nanette Medved. Working as a reporter, she has feelings for fellow reporter Tonton Gutierrez, but he only has eyes for Darna. The fact that Gutierrez (or anyone for that matter) can't tell that Narda and Darna are one-and-the-same is about as ridiculous as Lois Lane not seeing that Clark Kent is Superman. Not Even Medved's mother (Nida Blanca) knows that Medved is Darna.

Manzano shows up on the scene impressing everyone as a philanthropist, but he actually has a plan to take over the country. Toward that end, he teams up with Medusa lady Pilar Pilapil and turns poor Bing Loyzaga into an aswang (a bat-winged vampire creature). When Darna threatens to mess up his plans, Manzano abducts Blanca, but of course Darna flies to the rescue. She winds up thwarting Manzano by snatching the magic amulet from around his neck during a fight to the death, causing Manzano to go up in smoke.

The film is played largely for laughs, and there are some fairly amusing moments, including a romantic liaison between Manzano and Pilapil in which he changes the aging supermodel into a gorgon, thereby bestowing eternal youth on her. Of the highlights, there is a wonderful scene where Pilapil comes down the runway at a fashion show and strips off her headdress, revealing her serpentine hair, at which time a horde of snakes descends on the audience. Darna's midair fight with the aswang is also a high point.

On the downside, there is a thoroughly annoying talking serpent puppet (voiced by Ruby Rodriguez), which tries one's patience with its incessant smart-alecky jabbering. There is also the fact that, as important as the magic pearl is, Medved seems pretty cavalier about it, losing it a number of times. As for the special effects, by-and-large they don't come off very impressively, particularly when Darna is flying through the air, but in this type of childish fantasy, that's not a huge drawback. The film also features a brief and very irrelevant cameo by young action star Raymart Santiago. (In Tagalog with some English)

Darna! Ang Pagbabalik
(Darna! The Return)

1994 Viva Family Entertainment; 104 minutes/color

Directors: Peque Gallaga, Lorenzo Reyes; Screenwriter: Floy Quintos; Cinematographer: Marissa Floirendo; Editor: Danny Gloria: Filmscore: Archie Castillo; Cast: Anjanette Abayari, Edu Manzano, Rustom Padilla, Bong Alvarez, Pilita Corales, Cherie Gil, Lester Llansang, Ai-Ai de las Alas, Eva Ramos, Pen Medina, Jemanine Campanilla, Romy Romulo, Jun Achaval, Dwight Gaston, Jinky Laurel, Bong Regala, Noel Carpio, Mel Kimura, Justine Dee, Elsa de Venecia, Marissa de Guzman

Darna is back, sexier than ever in the person of busty Anjanette Abayari (meaning no disrespect to all previous Darnas, each lovely as well). As the film begins, Abayari is knocked cold and her necklace stolen. The necklace contains the magic stone which, when swallowed, transforms Abayari into Darna. When Abayari awakens, she is little more than a babbling fool with the mind of a toddler, but she is assisted in getting around by her younger brother (Lester Llansang) and a friend (Rustom Padilla). By chance Llansang discovers that the necklace was swiped by Medusa lady Cherie Gil, who herself works for queen Medusa Pilita Corales. Llansang manages to retrieve the pearl, and Abayari is back on track, thwarting crime and making headlines. Padilla falls in love with Abayari, but she is crushing on police lieutenant Edu Manzano, who unfortunately turns out to be one of the bad guys. Manzano abducts Abayari, dragging her down to Corales' subterranean lair, where she *again* loses her magic stone. But as Manzano and Gil transform into hideous, fanged beasts, Llansang again saves the day, retrieving the stone and getting it to Abayari in time for her to transform into Darna and vanquish the powers of evil. She then, presumably, ends up with Padilla, who loved her even before he knew that she was Darna.

The effects, as Darna flies through the air, are pretty awful, but otherwise, the special effects are fairly well done. As Darna films tend to be, this is kids' stuff all the way, with Abayari's six-year-old brother Llansang continually pulling her bacon out of the fire and practically upstaging her as the film's hero. Director Peque Gallaga once had an interesting career, but in his work with co-director Lorenzo Reyes his work has become increasingly childish, as in films like *Batang X* (1995) and *Magic Kingdom* (1996), in which children are the heroic saviors of the world. (In Tagalog)

Darna, Kuno ...?
(Are We Darna?)

1979 Regal Films; 125 minutes/color
Director: Luciano B. Carlos; Screenwriters: Toto Belano, Luciano B. Carlos; Cinematographers: Claro Gonzales, Ricardo Jacinto; Editor: Rogelio Salvador; Filmscore: Ernani Cuenco; Cast: Dolphy, Lotis Key, Marissa Delgado, Tita de Villa, Romy Nario, Tonio Gutierrez, Dray Dadivas, Karlo Vero, Brenda del Rio, German Moreno, Sandy Garcia, Christopher de Leon, Bella Flores, Celia Rodriguez, Charo Valdez, Rio Locsin, Lily Miraflor, Ruel Vernal

In this comic fantasy, a very pregnant Darna is needing to take a leave of absence to have her baby, and for some reason trusts the hapless Dolphy to fill in for her. Upon popping that pearl in his mouth, Dolphy is blessed with super powers, as well as being decked out in Darna's skimpy outfit. He saves Lotis Key from a group of horse-headed demons in the forest, and afterward, when Key's sister (Marissa Delgado) literally vanishes into thin air on her wedding day, Dolphy resolves to get to the bottom of things. Posing as a bride (with a very reluctant Christopher de Leon acting as the groom), Dolphy too vanishes, and he finds himself in a netherworld where he battles some sort of weird demonic queen and her henchmen. Dolphy defeats them and frees a whole host of captive brides who had vanished on their respective wedding days. Finally, when a UFO abducts Key and some local women, it's Dolphy to the rescue again, but even with his super powers he finds that the leader of the aliens (Ruel Vernal) is too much for him. Fortunately, Dolphy is finally able to vanquish the aliens, not with his super powers, but with his smelly feet, which sends them packing. The real Darna then returns with her newborn baby and retrieves the pearl.

The main gag here, such as it is, is in having Dolphy running around in Darna's tiny outfit, but for those of us who prefer the more curvaceous, feminine Darna, the film takes a slight detour when the lovely Key takes the pearl, transforms into Darna and rescues a group of children being held captive in a cave by a hoary old witch, who plans to cook and eat them. Key is lovely enough to have made a suitable successor to the Darna role, but, regrettably, this was not to be. (In Tagalog)

Diligin Man ng Dugo ... !
(Even When Drenched in Blood!)

1992 ATB-4 Films; 88 minutes/color
Director/screenwriter: Jose "Kaka" Balagtas; Cinematographer: Amado de Guzman; Editor: Nap Montebon; Filmscore: Boy Alcaide; Cast: Anthony Alonzo, Melanie Marquez, Ilonah Jean, Bobby Benitez, Job Gavino, Eric Esguerra, Freddie Ondra, Jeric Vasquez, Allan Laceda, Ariel Reyes, Erwin Montebon, Warren Escudero, Jon-Jon Gonzales

Military commander Anthony Alonzo is dispatched with government troops to Mindanao to deal with Muslim rebels calling for an independent Republic of Mindanao. The rebels are led by Melanie Marquez, and through a series of meetings with her, Alonzo comes to a better understanding of the grievances of the people of the region. During an impassioned exchange with Marquez, Alonzo is able to sway a fair amount of public opinion more toward amicably working with the government to iron out their differences. After a time, Marquez too finds this to be the best solution, but her views split the rebel camp, and in the concluding battle she winds up fighting alongside the government forces. When Alonzo falls wounded, Marquez rushes to his aid and is shot and killed: after the rebels are defeated, the film ends with Alonzo mournfully carrying Marquez's body from the battlefield.

While there is no shortage in Filipino cinema of films dealing with the problem of anti-government rebels in Mindanao, this film is a cut above the norm. Director/screenwriter Jose Balagtas seems more concerned with showing the cultural differences between regions, juxtaposing Alonzo's nationalism with Marquez's more parochial patriotism, and also being mindful of the religious differences without condescension. (In Tagalog)

Dirty Games

1979 Cinex Films/F. Puzon Film Enterprises/Movieworld International; 89 minutes/color

Director: Leonardo Velasco Uy; Screenwriter: Jose Mari Avellana; Cast: Eddie Rodriguez, Christopher de Leon, Ace Vergel, Amalia Fuentes, Eddie Garcia, Lorna Tolentino, Dranreb, Angelo Buenaventura (Ventura), Tino de Lara, Orly Onza, Tirso Mediavilla, Jesse Sapitan

This crime drama stars Eddie Rodriguez as a successful businessman who suspects that his wife (Amalia Fuentes) has been having an affair with one of his business partners (Eddie Garcia). More than that, Rodriguez is convinced that his 10-year-old son (Dranreb) is a byproduct of said affair. In order to somehow confirm his suspicions, Rodriguez hatches a bizarre plot, hiring sleazy ex-con Ace Vergel to kidnap Dranreb and demand a $1 million ransom. Apparently the idea is that Rodriguez will be able to discern the truth of his suspicions by gauging Garcia's reaction to the crisis. While Garcia is quite concerned, Rodriguez turns out to be wrong nonetheless, but his efforts to call everything off are futile since Vergel has already used the situation for a little plot of his own. While Vergel was in prison, petty crook Christopher de Leon managed to steal his wife (Lorna Tolentino), and knowing that de Leon will not miss a chance to make a dishonest buck, Vergel puts in a ransom call to de Leon, pretending not to know that he is calling the wrong party. Sure enough, de Leon takes the bait and calls Rodriguez, demanding a $2 million ransom, his plan being to pocket $1 million off the top and use the remaining million to pay the ransom, get the boy back and return him to his family. With so many people playing, uh, dirty games with one another, tragic consequences were always on the horizon. Vergel is shot and killed by Rodriguez, and while de Leon is able to free Dranreb to collect the ransom, he arranges for Rodriguez to pay Tolentino, who promptly double-crosses de Leon and tries to catch the first boat off the mainland. Rodriguez is shot and killed by police as he is in the process of shooting and wounding de Leon, who survives and is able to give the police enough information to nab Tolentino before she can make her getaway. Angelo Ventura is the cop who has to sort the whole mess out. All in all, a fairly entertaining caper film. (Dubbed into English)

Disco Fever

1978 Lea Productions; 110 minutes/color

Director: Al Quinn; Screenwriter: Maryo delos Reyes; Cinematographer: Joe Batac; Editor: Nonoy Santillan; Cast: Vilma Santos, Christopher de Leon, Victor Laurel, Rio Locsin, Romeo Enriquez, Ernie Zarate, Freddie Aguilar, Sandy Garcia, Geleen Eugenio, Allan Quinn

Vilma Santos has a problem with her boyfriend, whom she considers prudish. He, on the other hand, doesn't like her spending so much time at the local discotheque, which he considers nothing more than a pick-up joint (well, aren't they?). Santos dumps her boyfriend and begins a relationship with college student Christopher de Leon. Complications arise when de Leon's roommate (Victor Laurel), the DJ at the local disco, also falls for Santos. With everyone falling head-over-heals for Santos, there was bound to be tension. The roommates fight over Santos, and in a teary climactic anti-climax, the three of them meet at the disco where Santos expresses her preference for de Leon. They all dry their eyes, make nice, and then trot down to the dance floor to kick up their heels. It's all too overly dramatic for such a slight concept. (In Tagalog and English)

Dito sa Pitong Gatang
(Here in Pitong Gatang)

1992 FPJ Productions; 105 minutes/color

Director: Pablo Santiago; Screenwriters: Pablo S. Gomez, Jose Bartolome, Manny Buising; Cinematographer: Ver P. Reyes; Editors: Augusto Salvador, Rene Tala; Filmscore: Jaime Fabregas; Cast: Fernando Poe Jr., Nanette Medved, Harlene Bautista, Dencio Padilla, Max Alvarado, Jose Romulo, Ruel Vernal, Larry Silva, Dindo Arroyo, Chinggay Riego, Robert Ortega Jr., Paquito Diaz, Vic Varrion, Rene Hawkins, Nonoy de Guzman, Jimmy Reyes, Naty Santiago, Carmen Enriquez, Renato del Prado

Widower Fernando Poe, Jr., is chairman of the city council and he organizes a neighborhood watch team, putting him at odds with new councilwoman Nanette Medved, who feels that the local watch team is frequently impinging on her jurisdiction. Mischievous councilmen Paquito Diaz and Max Alvarado, who both want more prominent positions on the council, encourage Medved's ill will. Of course, Medved's distaste for Poe begins to soften in time, and by the time Poe beats up local thug Ruel Vernal in a knock-down, all-out brawl worthy of an American 1940s B-western, Medved is totally smitten. Later, a teenage girl—a classmate of Poe's daughter—kills herself by jumping from atop a building while in a drug-induced euphoria, and Poe feels moved to go after the drug pushers, gunning them all down in a shootout. Poe then surrenders to the police, but the kindhearted police commander turns him loose, dropping all charges, to the dismay of Diaz and Alvarado, who were poised to take over the council.

The first two-thirds of the film basically play like a romantic comedy, with some over-the-top, and frankly annoying, comedic performances from Diaz, Alvarado, and Larry Silva (as Medved's brother). This type of material isn't necessarily Poe's strength, but he does handle himself credibly through it. (In Tagalog with occasional English)

Divine Mercy sa Buhay ni Sister Faustina (Divine Mercy in the Life of Sister Faustina)

1993 Cinesuerte/Divine Mercy; 112 minutes/color

Director: Ben G. Yalung; Screenwriter: Emmanuel H. Borlaza; Cinematographer: Joe Tutanes; Editor: Joe Solo; Filmscore: Marita Manuel; Cast: Donita Rose, Christopher de Leon, Maila Gumila, Paquito Diaz, Liza Lorena, Alicia Alonzo, Dexter Doria, Romy Rivera, Eddie Infante, Emil Malvar, Ruby Regala, Ding Salvador, Lorrie Mara, Noel Colet, Anna Marie Falcon, Edgar Mande, Robert Talby, Bert Olivar, Philip Gordon, Wendy San Juan, Rosa Morato

Based on the diaries of Polish nun Sister Faustina, Donita Rose has the lead here as the film recounts how Faustina made the decision to become a nun after claiming to hear the voice of Christ directing her. As a nun, she continues to hear Christ's voice, and even experiences physical manifestations of his presence. Her story causes quite a stir within the Church, and her claims are investigated, forcing her to recount her story to a rather stoic gathering of priests, who rather surprisingly (given their demeanor) rule in her favor, believing the sincerity of her claims of miraculous visitations. Afterward, the sickly Faustina's health continues to deteriorate and she is hospitalized, where she dies. The film ends with something that obviously could not have been taken from Faustina's diaries; a trip to Heaven after her death, where she is greeted by Christ and led up a winding white stairway through the clouds to the pearly gates, where angels shower her with rose pedals as she is ushered in. While interesting in its contrast of the natural and the supernatural, the frankly hokey ending tends to spoil the mystique. Top-billed Christopher de Leon has a very minor role as the heartbroken suitor Faustina leaves behind when she decides to devote her life to the Church. (In Tagalog)

Doring Dorobo: Hagupit ng Batas (Doring Dorobo: Lash of the Law)

1994 Lea Productions; 118 minutes/color

Director: Augusto Salvador; Screenwriter: Antonio Pascua; Cinematographer: Johnny Araojo; Editors: Augusto Salvador, Danny Gloria; Filmscore: Jaime Fabregas; Cast: Eddie Garcia, Eddie Gutierrez, Boots Anson-Roa, Paquito Diaz, Dick Israel, Rey (PJ) Abellana, Vivian Foz, Ali Sotto, Sharmaine Arnaiz, Mia Gutierrez, Robert Miller, Ernie Zarate, Eric Francisco, Ernie David, Vic Varrion, Joey Padilla, Eddie Tuazon, Danny Labra, Miko Manzo, Mike Castillo, Romy Romulo, Edward Salvador, Don Umali, Bobby Henson, Bert Cayanan

Eddie Garcia portrays the chief of the narcotics division of the NBI (National Bureau of Investigation). Along with fellow NBI agent Dick Israel, he goes after a gang of drug smugglers led by Eddie Gutierrez. The problem is that Gutierrez is himself a high-ranking police official in the province. There is plenty of action, melodrama, and even a touch of humor. All in all, it's a very solid entry in the line of Garcia action films, and it's interesting to see Israel playing it straight as one of the good guys for a change. (In Tagalog with some English)

Droga: Pagtatapat ng Isang Babaing Addict (Drugs: Confession of a Woman Addict)

1998 EDL Productions/Gloanna Films; 99 minutes/color

Director/screenwriter: Celso Ad. Castillo; Cast: Rita Magdalena, Emilio Garcia, Aya Medel, Roy Rodrigo, Ramona Revilla, Leo Rabago, Ria Alonzo, Roldan Aquino, Boy Roque, Jojo de Leon, Romy Romulo, Trovador Ramos Jr., Vic Gaza, Rommel Padilla, Conrad Poe, Bino Garcia Jr., Tony Martinez, Stephen Fisher

Celso Ad. Castillo's look at the pervasiveness of the drug problem stars Rita Magdalena as a narcotics officer who is addicted to drugs herself. Even while going undercover to bring down Roldan Aquino's international drug cartel, Magdalena is fighting her own addiction. In the end, she and fellow officer Emilio Garcia raid Snake Island, Aquino's hideaway, and destroy the cartel. The film ends triumphantly with Magdalena recounting, via voiceover, how she entered a drug treatment program and beat her addiction. Magdalena's voiceover, which opens the film and continues throughout, grows somewhat tiresome, and even intrusive, rambling on even through the softcore sex scenes.

Castillo seems to be aiming for a more commercial work here, with all of the firefights between police and drug dealers, an extremely common sight in Filipino cinema, and there is a much higher than average amount of nudity here (Magdalena bares her breasts and flabby midriff incessantly). Watching Magdalena running around in her bikini blowing away drug dealers during the climactic shootout is a bit of a hoot, and the opening credit sequence with her shaking it up to a song on the radio while brushing her teeth is so silly that it threatens to make a joke of the film before it's really gotten underway. Ultimately, this can be seen as a bit of a misfire by Castillo. (In Tagalog and English)

Dudurugin Kita ng Bala Ko
(I'm Going to Pulverize You with My Bullet)

1991 Regal Films; 107 minutes/color
Director: Rogelio Salvador; Screenwriters: Rod Santiago, Joji Vitug; Cinematographer: Vic Anao; Editor: Rogelio Salvador; Filmscore: Nonoy Rodriguez; Cast: Lito Lapid, Maricel Laxa, Ramon Zamora, Roi Vinzon, Bernard Bonnin, Conrad Poe, Ruel Vernal, Ali Sotto, Alicia Alonzo, Rosemarie Gil, Roldan Aquino, Ruben Rustia, Johnny Vicar, King Gutierrez, Philip Henson, Usman Hassim, Robert Miller, Rex Lapid, Edward Salvador

When ruthless provincial governor Bernard Bonnin has Ruben Rustia, his opponent in the upcoming election, killed it causes Rustia's son (Lito Lapid) to go on a quest for vengeance, touching off an all-out war between the two families. Lapid joins up with a rebel army that has formed as a result of Bonnin's tyrannical rule, but eventually it is he himself who must bring down Bonnin on his own.

Director Rogelio Salvador is an editor by trade, who still seems to find more work in that capacity, but he shows considerable enthusiasm for the visceral depiction of the brutality from both sides, jumping in with something more than mere gusto. He and Lapid would reunite in 1993 for *Gascon: Bala ang Katapat Mo*, but little that the director has done since has come close to his work here, as he has taken to wasting his time with frivolous work like *Super Ranger Kids* (1997). (In Tagalog with some English)

Dugo ng Panday
(Blood of the Blacksmith)

1993 Regal Films; 120 minutes/color
Directors: Peque Gallaga, Lorenzo Reyes; Screenwriter: Jerry Lopez Sineneng; Cinematographer: Joe Tutanes; Editor: Danny Gloria; Filmscore: Archie L. Castillo; Cast: Ramon "Bong" Revilla Jr., Edu Manzano, Leo Martinez, Max Alvarado, IC Mendoza, Aiko Melendez, Jaime Fabregas, Max Laurel, Ram Mojica, King Gutierrez, Edwin Reyes, Rey Solo, Romy Romulo, Bien Garcia, Ramon Confiado, Edison Magno, Toto Perez, Jinky Laurel, Fame de los Santos, Bella Flores, Koko Trinidad, Peque Gallaga, Don Escudero

In this fantasy adapted from a komik serial by Carlo Caparas, directors Peque Gallaga and Lorenzo Reyes pull out all the stops. Ramon "Bong" Revilla, Jr. has the lead as a poor young man who turns out to be the chosen one; the only person capable of retrieving a magic sword from a subterranean crypt. Once he's done this, Revilla sets out to rescue Aiko Melendez, and a good many others being kept captive by a brotherhood of sorcerers ruled by the disembodied head of Max Alvarado, kept alive in a tank of fluid from which it barks orders. Along the way, Revilla battles a horde of flesh-eating zombies before facing off with an army of masked swordsmen (looking not unlike ninjas), led by evil cyborg Edu Manzano. When Manzano is the only one left, Revilla takes him on, one-on-one, and finds him a seemingly indestructible foe, until realizing that Manzano is controlled by the head of Alvarado. Revilla smashes the glass tank containing Alvarado's head, and Manzano goes up in smoke.

There are plenty of weird fantasy elements here, though the special effects are sometimes on the dicey side. Still, it's the kind of feature that could have found a Western audience if Regal Films could have been bothered to have it dubbed. (In Tagalog)

Durugin ng Bala si Peter Torres (Spray Peter Torres with Bullets)

1989 Regal Films; 97 minutes/color
Director: Toto Natividad; Screenwriter: Tony Pascua; Cinematographer: Boy Dominguez; Editor:

Toto Natividad; Filmscore: Demet Velasquez; Cast: Jess Lapid Jr., Melissa Mendez, Lucita Soriano, Mario Escudero, Fernando Fernandez, Dick Israel, Romy Diaz, Rodolfo "Boy" Garcia Jr., Turko, Cris Castillo, Rey Alfon, Lucy Quinto, Jose Romulo, Veronica Valerio, Grace Alano, Jimmy Reyes, Robert Miller, Rene Hawkins, Rolando Falcis, Eddie Samonte, Efren Belardo, Boy Santa Maria, Boy Ranay, Joe Baltazar, Rene Tupaz, Conrad Poe

Jess Lapid, Jr., plays the title character in this violent true story. He takes the rap for his older brother for a stabbing committed during a street brawl, and after being sent to prison he is raped by Romy Diaz. Lapid gets even by sodomizing Diaz with a broom handle, but thereafter settles down to become a model prisoner. After being paroled, Lapid joins a gang with a friend of his and winds up killing a police officer during a hold-up. It isn't long before he is apprehended and sent back to prison. Sentenced to hard labor, he becomes friends with inmate Dick Israel after saving Israel's life in a fight, and the two of them are joined by several other inmates in a successful escape. Once outside, they look up Lapid's old gang members and form a formidable hold-up gang. Diaz has since been released from prison, and he brutally beats Lapid's brother, so of course retribution is in order. Lapid and his gang don their olive green raincoats and solemnly march through a driving rainstorm to a garage where Diaz and his gang are, and opening fire from outside, massacre the whole bunch. Now the most wanted man in the country, Lapid and his boys meet their fate when Israel is arrested in a whorehouse and agrees to cooperate with the police. He tells them the location of the gang's hideout, and Lapid and company die in a shootout with the police.

True story or not, the film is the standard violent gangland story, though director Toto Natividad does deserve credit for some of the more striking moments, in particular the slaughter of Diaz's gang, with Lapid and his men marching through the rain to the musical bombast of Led Zeppelin, the ominous sound of the approaching music tipping Diaz off just a little too late to avoid the slaughter. (In Tagalog)

Duwelo (Duel)

1996 Regal Films; 95 minutes/color

Directors: Philip Ko, Teddy Gomez; Screenwriter: Al Marcelo; Cinematographer: Eduardo Cabrales; Editor: Joe Solo; Filmscore: Mon del Rosario; Cast: Eddie Garcia, Zoren Legaspi, Bernard Bonnin, Luis Gonzales, Johnny Vicar, Allyson Lualhati, Mike Gayoso, Alex David, Rando Almanzor, Raymond Tan, Jimmy Ko, Pocholo Montes, Dante Castro, Enrico Salcedo

Unable to get over his daughter's drug-induced suicide, wealthy Luis Gonzales hires renowned hit man Eddie Garcia to do away with the city's top drug kingpins. Garcia begins by assassinating mayoral candidate Johnny Vicar, who has close ties with mobster Bernard Bonnin. Though Bonnin knows who Garcia is, he is unable to discover who has hired him, and so hires his own hit man (Zoren Legaspi) to take out Garcia. As things escalate, Garcia arms himself to the teeth and goes crashing onto Bonnin's property, conducting a seminar in annihilation, killing Bonnin and all of his men. Unfortunately, Legaspi is not on the property, but is giving his own demonstration back at Gonzales' house, killing Gonzales and his guards. Garcia returns to find the aftermath of Legaspi's visit and finds a note. Knowing that Garcia has a fondness for Gonzales' young granddaughter (Allyson Lualhati), Legaspi abducts her, setting up a final showdown. Legaspi is well aware of Garcia's reputation as the number one hit man around, and it is an appellation Legaspi covets, but during their climactic, fiery face-off, Garcia bests him and saves Lualhati. Though Legaspi appears to perish, the film concludes with Garcia and Lualhati visiting the graveside of Gonzales where Garcia is shot and killed by an unseen sniper, proving that even good assassins meet a bad end.

Old hands Garcia and (especially) Gonzales give excellent performances, and Legaspi is effective in what basically amounts to a one-note performance. The action is boisterous and tightly directed in Philip Ko's usual way, and it's interesting to see him direct something outside of the martial arts genre. This is a fine film. (In Tagalog with some English)

Dyesebel (Jezebel)

1973 Tagalog Ilang-Ilang Productions; 112 minutes/color

Director/screenwriter: Emmanuel H. Borlaza; Cinematographer: Ben Lobo; Editor: Gervasio Santos; Filmscore: Tito Arevalo; Cast: Vilma Santos, Romeo Miranda, Divina Valencia, Mina Aragon, Rosanna Marquez, Ike Lozada, German Moreno, Christina Reyes, Eva Linda, Janet Clemente, Mildred Ortega, Desiree Destreza, Chanda Romero, Joseph Sytangco, Geena Zablan, Patria Plata, Ricky Valencia, Cris Santos, Greg Lozano, Doming Viray, Romy Luartes, Oscar Zaldivar, Hermie Esguerra, Burke Perdez, Lito Calzado

The character of Dyesebel is a mermaid created by Mars Ravelo for Filipino komiks. Played here by Vilma Santos, Dyesebel is drawn inland by a love song sung by Romeo Miranda. When Miranda discovers the beautiful mermaid in his swimming pool he decides to keep her, and the two fall in love. But Dyesebel is kidnapped by a group of men hired by Miranda's jealous ex-girlfriend and then put on display in a carnival sideshow. Miranda manages to rescue Dyesebel, but fearing for her safety, he decides to return her to the sea. When she returns to her mermaid clan, however, Dyesebel's living amonst humans is considered an act of treachery by the mermaid queen, who has her thrown to a giant octopus. With the help of a colony of electric eels, Dyesebel manages to escape the clutches of the ravenous octopus, and using a magic sea shell to transform her aquatic lower torso into human form, she returns to Miranda, who she finds sitting forlornly on the beach. The film is passably entertaining, though the special effects are very primitive. (In Tagalog)

Dyesebel (Jezebel)

1978 Sampaguita Pictures; 116 minutes/color

Director: Anthony Taylor; Screenwriter: Orlando Nadres; Cinematographer: Gener Buenaseda; Editor: Jose H. Tarnate; Filmscore: George Canseco; Cast: Alma Moreno, Mat Ranillo III, Gloria Sevilla, Nova Villa, Ruby Anna, Raquel Montessa, Chona Castillo, Bella Flores, Carissa, German Moreno, Lily Miraflor, Tony Carreon, Sharon dela Merced, Carol Bernardo, Ann Villegas, Zeny Bernardo, Cecile Castillo, Rey Tomenes

Mars Ravelo's popular mermaid character has had a long screen life, having first been brought to the screen in 1953 by director Gerardo de Leon. In the 1978 version Dyesebel is raised from infancy by a human couple who find her on the beach. But by the time she grows into a beautiful young woman (played by Alma Moreno), Dyesebel longs to be like everyone else. Forced to use a wheelchair to get around on land, and always kept indoors and away from people in general, she is one unhappy mermaid. But her world is turned around when she falls in love with Mat Ranillo III, a young handyman who has been hired to tend the family grounds. Ranillo also falls for Dyesebel, but since she always keeps her lower torso covered by a blanket, Ranillo has no idea that he has fallen for a mermaid. Not that it matters, since Ranillo is so in love that even when Dyesebel does reveal herself to him he is fairly unfazed. They marry and seem to be happy together, but their idyllic life is disturbed when Dyesebel is lured back into the ocean by a group of comely mermaids. After spending some time with her own species in the sea, where she is assured that she will better fit in and therefore be happier, the melancholy Dyesebel finally returns to Ranillo after obtaining a magic stone that transforms her lower torso into human legs. As silly as the premise is, the story is played remarkably straightforward, like any other romantic melodrama, which is somehow admirable: weird, but admirable.

The character would return in the 1990s, being played by Alice Dixson in 1990, and by Charlene Gonzales in 1996. (In Tagalog)

Ebony, Ivory and Jade

1976 Cosa Nueva/Capricorn Films; 79 minutes/color

Director: Cirio H. Santiago; Screenwriter: Henry Barnes; Cinematographer: Ricardo Remias; Editor: Gervasio Santos; Filmscore: Eddie Nova; Cast: Rosanne Katon, Colleen Camp, Sylvia Anderson, Ken Washington, Jun Aristorenas, Leo Martinez, Butz Aquino, Christie Mayuga, Dick Piper, Dick Adair, Ken Metcalfe, Max Alvarado, Mike Murray, Rocco Montalban, Dan Francisco, Percy Ordonez

In this bit of high camp from director/producer Cirio Santiago, a Chinese terrorist group kidnaps a team of American female athletes in Hong Kong. The terrorists demand a $5 million ransom for the women, but much to the consternation of U.S. ambassador Ken Metcalfe, the U.S. government refuses the deal. The next best hope is that, since one of the women (Colleen Camp) is the daughter of an American supermarket tycoon, that her father will put up the money. Afraid that Camp's father will cut a deal for his daughter only, Ken Washington, whose girlfriend (Rosanne Katon) is one of the hostages, seeks the help of Jun Aristorenas in getting the girls back. Aristorenas seems to have the right connections to locate the girls, and as he and Washington roam around the city asking questions and getting into fistfights and shootouts, the hostage women make periodic escape attempts which allow them (or their obvious male doubles) to show off their kung fu skills. They finally manage to escape, with the help of terrorist turncoat Leo Martinez.

Intended primarily for the U.S. exploitation market, the film plays up to the black audience by making privileged white heiress Camp an object of derision among her black teammates/co-captives, and in the spirit of political correctness, it is white males who prove to be the arrogant, greedy enemies of the world, including Camp's father, who is involved in the whole kidnapping plot in some inane, inexplicable way, as is the white male coach of the athletic team.

Though this film was made after *TNT Jackson* (1974), Santiago manages to be even more incompetent here, and the saving grace of camp value, which has made some of his films salvageable, is just not strong enough to turn the trick this time. (In English)

Elsa Castillo Story ... Ang Katotohanan
(Elsa Castillo Story ... The Truth)

1994 OctoArts Films; 94 minutes/color and Black & white

Director: Laurice Guillen; Screenwriter: Ricardo Lee; Cinematographer: Eduardo Jacinto; Editor: Efren Jarlego; Filmscore: Nonong Buencamino; Cast: Kris Aquino, Eric Quezon, Miguel Rodriguez, Johnny Delgado, Perla Bautista, Ann Villegas, Jenette Fernando, Lucy Quinto, Ernie Zarate, Carmen Enriquez, Angie Castrence, Carmela Millado, Polly Cadsawan, Vic Belaro, Bobby Henson, Joe Jardi

In this true crime film, Kris Aquino portrays the title character, dubbed "The Chop Chop Lady" by the press due to the circumstances of her demise. She leaves husband Eric Quizon and moves in with her boss (Miguel Rodriguez), but tries to end the relationship after learning that he too is married and that his wife is merely away tending to a sick relative. The enraged Rodriguez murders Aquino and then chops the body into pieces, enlisting the aid of his driver (Johnny Delgado) in disposing of it, but the horrified Delgado ends up going to the police. Despite the grisly nature of the crime, the film is far less gruesome than it could easily have been (or would have been had it been directed by the likes of Carlo Caparas, the busiest of the true crime genre filmmakers), and director Laurice Guillen does not go overboard in depicting the morbid details of the crime (though body parts are glimpsed, in particular the head as Delgado picks it up and places it in a garbage bag). Guillen does make the curious stylistic decision of depicting the murder itself in a grainy monochrome, which, while interesting, may have robbed the moment of some of its impact, denying the power of the crimson flow. Otherwise, the bulk of the running time leading up to the gory crime—without question the showpiece—plays much like any other standard love triangle melodrama. The shocking case had also been filmed as *The Elsa Santos Castillo Story: The Chop Chop Lady* (1994). (In Tagalog with some English)

Elvis & James: The Living Legends!

1989 Filmstar; 103 minutes/color

Director: Tony Y. Reyes; Screenwriters: Joey de Leon, Tony Y. Reyes; Cinematographer: Oscar Querijero; Editor: Efren Jarlego; Filmscore: Mon del Rosario; Cast: Joey de Leon, Rene Requiestas, Maricel Laxa, Panchito (Alba), Gigi Posadas, Beverly Salviejo, Vangie Labalan, Jon Achaval, Ruben Rustia, Michelle Bautista, Magenda, Richie Gallego, Ricky Fernando, Cutie del Mar, Badette Balingit

In this comedy, Joey de Leon and Rene Requiestas play two guys perpetually trapped in the 1950s. They have even named themselves after their favorite '50s icons, de Leon going by the name of Elvis Presto, and Requiestas under the name James Dean. They also never got through high school, and so they decide to go back and finish their education. Naturally they take a lot of ribbing from their classmates because of both their age and their 1950s attire. Nonetheless, they make friends easily, and their childish nature helps them fit in (or perhaps stand out). The screenplay by de Leon and director Tony Reyes sees the boys getting into mischief in various familiar situations (beach parties, dance contests) while pursuing romance (with high school girls!), as de Leon falls for Maricel Laxa in the role of Marilyn Monroy. There are plenty of musical numbers (as usual, mostly takes on old American hits of the '50s and '60s, with new lyrics written by de Leon), and Panchito Alba as a very gay music teacher. It's pretty innocuous, as de Leon again has fun spoofing American popular culture. (In Tagalog and English)

Emong Salvacion: Humanda Ka, Oras Mo Na!
(Emong Salvacion: Beware, Your Time Has Come!)

1996 Regal Films; 111 minutes/color

Director: Francis "Jun" Posadas; Screenwriter: Humilde "Meek" Roxas; Cinematographer: Ely Cruz; Editor: Danny Gloria; Filmscore: Nonong Buencamino; Cast: Eddie Garcia, Gardo Versoza, Raymond Keannu, Beth Tamayo, Giorgio Ortega, Ara Mina, Dennis Roldan, Ruel Vernal, Rez Cortez, Manjo del Mundo, Luis Gonzales, Tony Carreon, Ernie Zarate, Pocholo Montes, Ramil Rodriguez,

Gammy Viray, Gloria Sevilla, Lucita Soriano, Mon Confiado, Michelle Krizia Alba, Charles Sabalboro, Francis Benton, Robert Miller, Robert Talby, Max Laurel

Eddie Garcia, Gardo Versoza and Raymond Keannu portray three escaped convicts on the run. While making their way through the jungle they come across several children who have escaped from a gang of kidnappers who planned on selling them into slavery to a group of foreigners in exchange for a large arms shipment. Hearing that a good many more children are also being held by the same gang, Garcia is determined to free them, but Versoza and Keannu bow out. Garcia goes it alone and is quickly captured by the criminal gang, but Versoza and Keannu show up at the climax to help Garcia get free and defeat the kidnappers. After freeing the children, the three escaped convicts are apprehended by police, but after the story of their heroism becomes known, the three of them are lauded as heroes and set free. The film is fairly entertaining, though Humilde Roxas' screenplay tends to meander from time to time. Garcia gives his usual excellent performance, both humorous and moving in the right doses. (In Tagalog with some English)

Enforcer from Death Row

1975 Koinonia PSI West; 87 minutes/color
Directors: Efren C. Pinon, Marshall M. Borden; Screenwriters: Jerry O. Tirazona, Leo Fong; Cast: Leo Fong, Darnell Garcia, Cameron Mitchell, Lotis Key, George Estregan, Ann Farber, B.T. Anderson, Charlie Davao, Johnny Hammond, Michael Sullivan, Leroy Fong, Gene Weisner, Jeff Lynn, Marwin Roberts, Perry Baltazar, Dick Adair, Jonathan Beg, Candice Thayer, Hal Bokar

When a criminal organization headed by Charlie Davao threatens to unleash a deadly chemical weapon around the world, a secret world police organization proposes to stop it. They know that there is only one man for the job, and of course that man is Leo Fong. The problem is that Fong is on death row and scheduled to be executed soon for a murder that he did not commit. They manage to fake Fong's death and then brief him, and off he goes to Manila. Once there, Fong is aided by Lotis Key, who has infiltrated Davao's organization as a lab technician, and her brother (George Estregan). Fong and Estregan roam around fending off attacks from ninjas before busting into Davao's digs and burning his laboratory.

Fong had disparaged over the quality of his first film in the Philippines, *Murder in the Orient* (1973), but this is hardly an improvement. The screenplay (by Fong and Jerry Tirazona) is more than a little confusing, the martial arts scenes are very lackluster, including a climactic showdown between Fong and disfigured assassin Darnell Garcia (actually, especially the face-off with Garcia), and most of the performances (aside from Davao and Estregan) are very sub-par. All of which helps score points for camp value, so it is somewhat salvageable in that respect. It is interesting to see the rather slight Estregan in a tough guy role, engaging in his fair share of fighting, and there is a very brief appearance by Cameron Mitchell, which lends the film *some* credibility, even if he does seem ill-prepared. Mitchell and Fong would return to the Philippines for *The Last Reunion* (1978), in which Mitchell's role would be far more substantial. (In English)

Enteng Manok: Tari ng Quiapo (Enteng Manok: Gaff of Quiapo)

1993 Magdalena Films; 112 minutes/color
Director: Francis "Jun" Posadas; Screenwriter: Leleng Ubaldo; Cinematographer: Johnny Araojo; Editor: Edgardo Vinarao; Filmscore: Nonong Buencamino; Cast: Eddie Garcia, Paquito Diaz, Bob Soler, Dick Israel, Rez Cortez, Tetchie Agbayani, Rio Diaz, Berting Labra, Ruel Vernal, Philip Gamboa, Eric Borbon, Prospero Luna, Patrick dela Rosa, Edgar Mande, Rommel Valdez, Danny Labra, Bernie Fineza, Panfilo Lacson Jr., Danny Riel, Robert Miller, Art Veloso, Ernie Forte, Robert Talby, Rene Hawkins, Renato del Prado, Edward Salvador, Tony Bernal, Rey Roldan, Vic Belaro, Joe Andrade, Leo Lazaro, Edgar Santiago, Bebeng Amora, Pons de Guzman, James Gaines

In this film set in Manila in the early 1950s, Eddie Garcia portrays the title character, a devout Catholic, even more devout philanderer, and above all, a cockfight enthusiast. Though married to Rio Diaz, Garcia carries on an affair with Tetchie Agbayani, but gives up the affair when he learns that his wife is pregnant. He also runs afoul of a powerful criminal organization, and after a few run-ins with them, he is rushed to the hospital with a stab wound to the stomach. While he is in the hospital, some hitmen come calling, but Garcia is spirited away by his brother (Dick Israel) and some friends just in time. Taken to a remote rural area to recover, Garcia's spirits are lifted when his wife gives birth to a son, and they are able to enjoy a peaceful life together in the country until someone arrives to tell Garcia that one of his friends in Manila has been murdered. Knowing that the murder is an act of retaliation against him, Garcia returns to Manila to settle accounts, and though he does gun down gang leader Bob Soler, both Garcia and Israel perish in the end.

The scene of the wounded Garcia being smuggled out of the hospital to avoid a group of assassins is, of course, lifted from *The Godfather* (1972), and has been used repeatedly in Filipino crime films, including *Padre Amante Guerrero* (1992), in which Garcia hurries his wounded brother Dennis Roldan out of the hospital for the same reason. As the lead in *Enteng Manok*, Garcia gives a splendid performance, and Dick Israel is also very good as Garcia's loyal brother. The production values are high, and Francis Posadas does a splendid job at the helm of it all. In short, this is top shelf. (In Tagalog)

Ethan

1971 Nemours Productions; 83 minutes/color
Director: Michael DuPont; Cinematographer: Emmanuel Rojas; Editor: George Reys; Filmscore: Paul Glass; Cast: Robert Sampson, Eddie Infante, Joseph de Cordova, Rosa Rosal, Jennings Sturgeon, Vicente Liwanag, Rod Navarro, Bruno Punzalan, Henry Duval, J.C. Sturgeon, Yvonne Nielson, George Torres

In this ponderous, tragic melodrama, Robert Sampson portrays the title character, a Catholic missionary sent to a small, mostly Muslim community in the Philippines. He is seduced by Rosa Rosal, and their passionate moment having been observed by voyeur Joseph de Cordova, word spreads quickly through town, effectively making Sampson an outcast. Deeply stung by the local gossip, Rosal's father (Bruno Punzalan) sets out to kill Sampson, and when the town drunk (Jennings Sturgeon) intervenes, he is stabbed and killed. The police then arrive and shoot and kill Punzalan before he can assault Sampson. The traumatized Sampson sees the deaths of both men as the result of his own failure to keep the vows of the Church, but he quickly turns his guilt into anger directed at God. He leaves the Church and goes on a binge, boozing it up in the local dive, and he winds up getting mugged and dumped in the ocean. Fortunately, he is found and taken in by a fisherman and his family, and after a period of soul searching, Sampson returns to the Church ready to rededicate himself, but he is shot and killed by de Cordova, who has become enraged that he himself is now ostracized by the community for spreading the gossip that has led to so much grief.

Punzalan gives a good performance as Rosal's tormented father, a dedicated Muslim who is enraged that his daughter has been compromised by a Christian, whom Punzalan considers to be perverting the local children by teaching them about the Christian faith. (In English)

The Fastest Gun Alive

1988 Kelly Ellis Films; 101 minutes/color
Director: Ronnie San Juan; Screenwriters: Bonnie Paredes, Mariano Ninonuevo; Cinematographer: Carlos Salcedo; Editor: Edgardo Vinarao; Filmscore: Ramon del Rosario; Cast: Sonny Parsons, Marianne dela Riva, Eddie Garcia, Bella Flores, Paquito Diaz, Raoul Aragonn, Rez Cortez, Max Alvarado, Romy Diaz, Larry Silva, Bomber Moran, Renato del Prado, King Gutierrez, Ann Villegas, Telly Babasa, Jimmy Reyes, Tony Tacorda, Nonoy de Guzman, Buddy Salvador, Pons de Guzman, Bert Cayanan, Robert Talby, Ernie David, Robert Miller, Bernard Atienza, Buddy Dator, Roland Falcis

Sonny Parson portrays Sgt. Ninonuevo of the Western Police District in this true account of the career of the celebrated law enforcement officer. The film somewhat haphazardly runs through a series of busts (purse snatchers, drunks and various thugs) as Ninonuevo works his way up the ladder. After he receives a promotion, the film chronicles a number of shootouts with hold-up artists and gangs. Through it all, there seems to be no narrative cohesion until our hero goes up against drug kingpin Eddie Garcia, an ongoing struggle that offers the first sign of any structured storyline. Ninonuevo's persistence results in a single-minded determination on the part of Garcia to eliminate the sergeant, and he stages a raid on Ninonuevo's home. Though wounded, Ninonuevo manages to gun down all of Garcia's men, and finally Garcia himself.

While the film gets a shot of prestige from Garcia's appearance (as well as that of Paquito Diaz and Rez Cortez), it comes too late to turn the trick since by then the film has meandered away the bulk of its running time. It doesn't help matters that director Ronnie San Juan doesn't bring any particular creativity to his presentation. Aside from playing the lead, Parsons also wrote and sings the theme song. In the early 1990s he would put his film career on hold to pursue his musical aspirations. (In Tagalog with some English)

Fatima Buen Story

1994 Regal Films; 107 minutes/color and black & white

Director: Mario O'Hara; Screenwriter: Frank Rivera; Cinematographer: Romulo Araojo; Editor: George Jarlego; Filmscore: Nonong Buencamino; Cast: Kris Aquino, Zoren Legaspi, John Regala, Gina Pareno, Janice de Belen, Perla Bautista, Bob Soler, Leni Santos, Shintaro Valdez, Noni Mauricio, Carmen Enriquez, Brando Legaspi, Naty Mallares, Dante Balois, Josie Galvez, Nonong de Andres, William Thayer Jr., Judy W. Teodoro, Gil Arceo, Frank Rivera

Purportedly based on a true story, this film could just as easily have been merely another run-of-the-mill recounting of the antics of the dregs of society if not for the unique approach of director Mario O'Hara and screenwriter Frank Rivera. Kris Aquino portrays the title character, an ambitious, though thoroughly unpleasant young woman who runs a talent agency. Arrested for "illegal recruitment" in her business, she is sent to jail pending trial, and during her hearing she falls in love with Zoren Legaspi, a prison guard assigned to watch her. Another guard (John Regala) falls for Aquino, but one day during a delay in the court hearings, Regala is knocked cold by Legaspi, who helps Aquino escape with fellow inmate Janice de Belen. Feeling betrayed, not only by Legaspi, but by Aquino as well, who treated him kindly while in prison, Regala pursues them, catching up and capturing them after de Belen has already parted company. Legaspi loses his job, but manages to weasel out of real trouble, while Aquino is sent back to prison. After a brutal beating from some bulldyke inmates, Aquino winds up in the infirmary, where she once more manages to escape. She finds Legaspi, but he gives her the cold shoulder, and Aquino winds up with de Belen, who is a lesbian. But after seeing de Belen commit a murder, Aquino tries to break free of her, and the possessive de Belen chases her to the bell tower of a church and shoots her. De Belen is then electrocuted by a severed electrical cable: Aquino manages to survive.

Although supposedly based on a true story, much of the film is hard to swallow (de Belen's demise, for instance, seems very improbable), but the liberties taken by the filmmakers are actually what lift it above average. There are, for example, Aquino's nightmares, which are inhabited by an ominous figure (Nonong de Andres) who begins to appear to her outside of her dreams as well. The film features some excellent cinematography by Romulo Araojo, and an interesting score by Nonong Buencamino. Regala won the Urian Best Supporting Actor award for his performance. (In Tagalog with some English)

Fe, Esperanza, Caridad

1974 Premiere Productions; 128 minutes/color

Directors: Gerardo de Leon, Lamberto V. Avellana; Screenwriters: Ka Ikong, Jojo M. Lapus, Gerardo de Leon; Cinematographer: Ricardo David; Editor: Ben Barcelon; Filmscore: Tito Arevalo; Cast: Nora Aunor, Ronaldo Valdez, Dindo Fernando, Jay Ilagan, Ruben Rustia, Laurice Guillen, Andres Centenera, Ramon D'Salva

When Nora Aunor emerged as one of the major Filipino film stars of the 1970s, this anthology film probably seemed like the perfect showcase for her talents as both an actress and a singer. In the opening story Aunor portrays Fe Amor, a singer who marries her manager (Dindo Fernando). But as Aunor's career progresses to superstardom, Fernando begins to feel more insignificant by the minute, and he slips into vice, becoming an alcoholic and gambling his money away. The alcohol takes its toll on his health and he is hospitalized, but on the night of a big concert to be performed by Aunor, Fernando feels compelled to attend. Unfortunately, he staggers out of the hospital only to be struck and killed by a car. Aunor receives the news just before going on stage, but being a trooper, she goes on with the show. The segment is pure soap opera, and is unexceptional in every way.

As Esperanza in the second story, Aunor portrays a barrio girl who marries her sweetheart (Jay Ilagan). The newlyweds live in a slum, but Aunor is approached by a former suitor who offers her a way out of poverty: all Aunor has to do is accept packages at her home and hold them until the addressee arrives to claim them. Sounds simple enough, but when Ilagan finds out he blows his stack since he realizes that his naïve wife has actually been acting as a go-between for drug transactions. Aunor tries to back out of the arrangement, which leads to a big brawl when the pushers get angry and Ilagan tries to send them packing. The tale ends happily when the police arrive and haul the drug gang off to prison. Like the first segment, there is nothing particularly noteworthy here.

Unfortunately, available prints of the film are skimpy on credits, but Lamberto Avellana directed either one or both of the film's first two stories. What is more certain is that the film's third and concluding segment was written and directed by Gerardo de Leon. It is also the film's most substantial segment by far, both artistically and thematically. Portraying a nun named Caridad, Aunor falls in love with gardener Ronaldo Valdez, who invites her back to his home. After being whisked away to Valdez's abode, Aunor finds it populated by strange, cabalistic people who worship Valdez, and it is then that Valdez comes clean regarding his true identity: it turns out that Valdez is Satan himself. After recovering from the shock, Aunor tries to convert Valdez to Christianity (!), and his love for her apparently being deep and genuine, he gives it a try (!!). Grasping a crucifix, Valdez refuses to let go, even as it sears his hand. The two lovers share a brief moment of bliss, but Valdez's conversion seems to make him a mere mortal, and when he tries to save Aunor from falling off the edge of a cliff, Valdez is killed when he ends up falling himself. A simple analysis would have de Leon romanticizing evil, but like much of his previous work (i.e. 1964's *Kulay Dugo ang Gabi*), the point is more obviously love's redemptive power (Valdez does, after all, try to change, rather than trying to corrupt Aunor). In Valdez, the portrayal of Satan avoids caricature, presenting instead of pure evil an interesting mix ranging from pride, bitterness and defiance, to regret, melancholy and deep longing. Unfortunately, the rest of the film cannot match the closing segment's artistic focus, the first segment being overblown fluff, while the second is frequently rudderless. (In Tagalog with some English)

Firecracker

1981 New World Pictures; 77 minutes/color
Director: Cirio H. Santiago; Screenwriters: Ken Metcalfe, Cirio H. Santaigo; Cinematographers: Ben Lobo, Ricardo Remias; Editor: Gervasio Santos; Filmscore: Nonong Buencamino; Cast: Jillian Kessner, Darby Hinton, Reymond King, Ken Metcalfe, Peter Cooper, Don Bell, Carolyn Smith, Chanda Romero, Tony Ferrer, Vic Diaz, Omar Camar, Ramon D'Salva, Tony Carreon, Paquito Salcedo

Having scored their biggest success in 1974 with the cheesy martial arts exploiter *TNT Jackson*, director Cirio Santiago and screenwriter Ken Metcalfe hoped lightning would strike twice with this remake. This time it is Jillian Kessner who flies to Manila to find her missing sister, and all clues quickly lead her to crime boss Metcalfe who, aside from dealing heroin, also runs a martial arts death match for high-stakes gamblers. Seeing a demonstration of Kessner's martial arts skills, Metcalfe is eager to get her to participate in one of his death matches, knowing that a female competitor will create a lot of interest, but Kessner is reluctant. She begins a romance with one of Metcalfe's men (Darby Hinton), but after learning from Metcalfe's girlfriend, undercover cop Chanda Romero, that Hinton was actually the one who killed her sister, Kessner agrees to a death match—but only if Hinton is her opponent. Though he doesn't want to fight her, Kessner doesn't leave Hinton any choice, and she kills him in the end, as policeman Tony Ferrer and his men move in to arrest Metcalfe and his cronies.

While the film follows the story from *TNT Jackson* almost page-for-page, and as uproariously campy as that film was, this may even out-do that effort as regards high camp. Both films use male doubles in wigs for the more acrobatic maneuvers, but Kessner is definitely an improvement over Jeanne Bell when it comes to martial arts. Among the film's more outrageous highlights is a scene wherein Kessner is chased by a trio of thugs who only get close enough to grab at her clothing, most of which is torn off during the chase. Running into a building, Kessner finally turns to face her pursuers, and in no more than bra and panties, strikes a classic martial arts pose. It is among the more sublime moments in exploitation film history. Better still, she winds up losing her bra as well, and has to finish the fight topless.

Santiago and Metcalfe would go to the well again in 1992, remaking the story yet again as *Angelfist*. While in the Philippines, Kessner also appeared in the martial arts/horror film *Raw Force* (1981). (In English)

Fist of Glory

1991 Davian International; 89 minutes/color
Director/screenwriter: Jose Mari Avellana; Cinematographer: Ricardo Remias; Filmscore: Hector Pedero; Cast: Dale "Apollo" Cook, Maurice Smith, Robert Marius, Eric Hahn, Bob Larson, Jim Moss, Chris Aguilar, James Gaines, Geno Bolda, Engel Wilson, Philip Gordon, Charlie Vincent Ike, Tonichi Fructuoso, Tony Cooper, Ernie Santana, Joe Fischer, Ernie David, Caloy David

Director/screenwriter Jose Mari Avellana enters the American low budget market with this martial arts film set against the backdrop of the Vietnam War. When his buddy Maurice Smith goes A.W.O.L., U.S. G.I. Dale "Apollo" Cook begins a tireless search for him through Saigon, which eventually takes him into the shady world of the Death Match. Cook discovers that Smith is the prizefighter of an ex-patriot

American entrepreneur who rewards Smith's victories in the ring by feeding his ever-growing heroin addiction. Cook enters the Death Match in order to free Smith, but finding Smith too doped-up to even recognize him, Cook has to resort to force. He defeats Smith in the ring, but rather than do the expected and kill him, Cook hustles him out to safety. After helping Smith beat his drug habit, Cook finds that Smith's erstwhile employer is not too pleased about losing his top fighter, and so Cook and Smith have one last battle to fight before returning home to America.

Avellana proves to be competent, if not too inventive, as a director. After years of working in various capacities (actor, screenwriter, assistant director, art director), Avellana certainly had time to learn his craft. Serving here as both director and screenwriter, he seems to have been eager to enter the American market as a filmmaker, and in that sense, his years of working under Cirio Santiago would have served him well. On the other hand, the work offered here is almost indistinguishable from Santiago's work in co-productions during the same period. (In English)

Flight to Fury

1964 Lippert, Inc./Filipinas Productions; 72 minutes/black & white
Director: Monte Hellman; Screenwriter: Jack Nicholson; Cinematographer: Mike Accion; Cast: Dewey Martin, Fay Spain, Jack Nicholson, Joseph Estrada, Vic Diaz, Jaclyn Hellman, John Hackett, Lucien Pan, Serafin Sacat, Robert Arevalo, Juliet Pardo, Vic Uematsu, Henry Duval, Joe Dagumboy, Jennings Sturgeon

When a small charter flight with a half dozen passengers goes down in the jungle, it is discovered that passenger John Hackett was carrying a pouch full of diamonds. When Hackett dies the rest of the group begin fighting over the diamonds before being taken captive by a group of bandits led by Joseph Estrada. The group manages to free themselves from their captors, but continue to fight among themselves over the diamonds, until the wounded Jack Nicholson casts them in a river before killing himself.

The film is largely routine, but it is interesting to see Estrada, who became a Filipino superstar that year and won his first FAMAS Best Actor trophy in 1964, getting his only shot at international exposure in a co-production. Though not released until 1966, director Monte Hellman shot the film on the heels of *Back Door to Hell* in 1964, which also featured Nicholson and Hackett. (In English)

For Y'ur Height Only

1979 Liliw Productions; 91 minutes/color
Director: Eddie Nicart; Screenwriter: Cora Ridon Caballes; Cast: Weng Weng, Anna Marie Gutierrez, Beth Sandoval, Yehlen Catral, Tony Ferrer, Carmi Martin, Max Alvarado, Nonong de Andres

In this secret agent parody, midget Weng Weng portrays Agent 00, who is called on to defeat the crime syndicate of the reclusive and mysterious Mr. Giant. The syndicate has abducted a visiting scientist to try and get information from him to help them in building a neutron bomb. Weng is assigned the task of freeing the scientist and bringing down Mr. Giant, and is aided in his assignment by a beautiful female agent named Irma, who infiltrates the syndicate and feeds Weng information as to its activities. Eventually Irma's cover is blown and she is taken captive. After discovering that she is being held on Hidden Island, Mr. Giant's secret hideout, Weng dons a jetpack and flies to the island, finally meeting Mr. Giant (who turns out to be a dwarf, of course), and after a martial arts duel, Weng shoots and kills him. He then frees Irma, and the two of them retrieve the captive scientist and make a run for the beach. Irma is shot and killed as government forces arrive, and the film ends on a surprisingly somber note as Weng lays flowers on her grave.

One would expect the novelty of watching a tiny, diminutive midget knocking full grown men around to wear thin after a while, but the film is so deliriously ridiculous that it never quite loses its appeal. Weng is a surprisingly nimble and acrobatic guy, though honestly, he's no actor. Carmi Martin makes a brief appearance as a reporter who helps Weng. (Dubbed into English)

Forbidden Women

1948; 62 minutes/black & white
Director: Eduardo de Castro; Filmscore: Josefino Cenizal; Cast: Fernando Poe (Sr.), Berting Labra, Mona Lisa, Fernando Royo, Luningning, Bimbo Danao

In one of very few Fernando Poe, Sr. films to have survived the years, Poe plays the sultan of what the film describes as "an unknown island in the south Pacific." He plans on turning his kingdom over to his son (Berting Labra), which infuriates Poe's widowed sister-in-law

(Mona Lisa), who somehow feels entitled to the throne. Lisa conspires with her lover to have Labra murdered, and she herself begins poisoning Poe. Labra escapes his assassins and seeks refuge on a small nearby island, but he eventually returns in time to save his father, who has abdicated his throne to Lisa's lover due to declining health, being slowly poisoned by Lisa as he was. After revealing Lisa's evil plot, Labra then assumes the throne.

Poe died of rabies several years after making this film. Other than the rare chance to see Poe, Sr., it is also interesting to see Lisa in her prime, and a then-teenaged Labra as well. In 1969 Labra began serving a life sentence in prison for a killing committed by actor Eddie Fernandez. After 13 years in prison, Labra was exonerated by the Philippine Supreme Court and let free with a full pardon.

The forbidden women of the title are a harem kept in a temple which no man is allowed to enter, but Labra finagles his way in anyhow. There is a brief shot of a topless woman that seems to have been inserted by U.S. distributor Lloyd Friedgen, who brought the film to America as an exploitation attraction. (In English)

Fortress in the Sun

1978 Jowell Film Productions; 89 minutes/color
Director: George Rowe; Screenwriter: Humilde Roxas; Cinematographer: Armando Dulag; Editor: Josepino Marcos; Filmscore: Emy Munji; Cast: Nancy Kwan, Tony Ferrer, Eddie Garcia, Fred Galang, Chanda Romero, Logan Clarke, Ruel Vernal, Mel Francisco, Dave Raymundo, Johnny Vicar, Paquito Salcedo

While Nancy Kwan appeared in a number of films in the Philippines during the 1970s, she was cast mostly in fairly minor supporting roles. She has a more substantial role here as the daughter of sugar plantation owner Eddie Garcia. After six years overseas, Kwan returns with the hope that things on the plantation have improved in her absence, but upon arriving she soon realizes that her father is as ruthless as ever, being brutally indifferent to the plight of the sakadas (sugar cane workers). The leader of a local army of bandits regards Garcia as a robber baron, but after a number of battles, Garcia triumphs over them. He is not as successful with his own work force, however, as the sakadas eventually rise up against him with the help of undercover government man Tony Ferrer, who kills Garcia in a climactic shootout and then runs off with Kwan, who has discovered that Garcia was not her true father.

That's the basic storyline, but as is common in Filipino films, the plot is considerably more involved, with various revelations (for instance, Garcia's own bodyguard, Ruel Vernal, turns out to be the son of a man Garcia murdered many years prior in order to acquire his land). The main highlight of the film is Garcia's terse delivery of his steady stream of vulgarities, but there is also the young and beautiful Chanda Romero as a sakada girl, and while Ferrer's personal appearance doesn't particularly seem suited to tough guy roles (that's what he got most of the time anyway), he proves fast and nimble as a martial artist. George Rowe's direction is passable. (In English)

Fortress of the Dead

1965; 73 minutes/black & white
Director/screenwriter: Ferde Grofe, Jr.; Cinematographer: Remigio Young; Editor: Stanford Tischler; Filmscore: Gene Kauer, Douglas Lackey; Cast: John Hackett, Conrad Parham, Eddie Infante, Jennings Sturgeon, Ana Corita

In this extremely low-key supernatural melodrama, John Hackett plays the only American survivor of a battle on Corregidor with the Japanese during WWII. He returns 20 years later to see friend Conrad Parham, and Parham convinces him that the only way to be free of the guilt that has haunted him—guilt over being the only one spared while his comrades died horribly, trapped in a tunnel that caved in—is to take a boat back to Corregidor and exorcise his demons. Hackett agrees, but upon revisiting the ruins he is made uneasy by sounds that only he hears, and a general sense of some force that has called him back. Staying on the island overnight at the home of Eddie Infante, Hackett returns to the ruins late at night and is shocked upon hearing the sounds of battle, and thinking that he still must save his comrades, he rushes to a jeep and speeds off to get help. But he turns to find his deceased c.o. (Jennings Sturgeon) sitting in the passenger seat and loses control of the jeep, dying when it plunges over a cliff.

Originally shot as a 16mm short film title *Soul of a Fortress*, it was a mostly silent and somewhat expressionistic piece, but filmmaker Ferde Grofe, Jr. expanded it to barely feature-length by adding some very wordy passages. The results are interesting, but the film does tend to move slowly, its brief running time notwithstanding. (In English)

From Hell to Borneo

1964 Mont Productions; 87 minutes/color
Director: George Montgomery; Screenwriter:

Ferde Grofe, Jr.; Cinematographer: Emmanuel Rojas; Editor: Kenneth Crane; Filmscore: Gene Kauer; Cast: George Montgomery, Julie Gregg, Torin Thatcher, Liza Moreno, Vic Diaz, Joe Sison, Carol Varga, Vicente Liwanag, Diki Lerner, Michael DuPont, Pedro Faustino, Henry Duval, Max Rojo, Armando Crisola, Pamboy, Achmad Sulaiman, Danny Jurado, George Cramer, Albert Jurado, Don McLaughlin, Jim Montgomery

Ne'er-do-well George Montgomery is eking out a living as a smuggler in the Philippines, though he is part owner of a small south Pacific island inherited from his father, when wealthy entrepreneur Torin Thatcher makes him an offer for the property. Located just outside Philippine jurisdiction, the island is apparently outside the governing laws of any nation, which is one of the things that Thatcher finds so appealing about it, along with the money to be made from its natural resources. Montgomery promises to consider Thatcher's offer, but immediately thereafter gets word that his brother, who has been living on the island and overseeing operation of the family plantation, has been murdered. Montgomery rushes back to the island, followed by Thatcher and his business partner, foreign dignitary Vic Diaz. Thatcher also brings along his daughter (Julie Gregg) to help sweeten the deal, but no sooner do they arrive than Montgomery and his plantation workers are forced into battle against an army of hooligans led by Montgomery's half-brother (Joe Sison), the bastard son of Montgomery's father. It comes as no surprise that Sison has been hired by Thatcher and Diaz to make life miserable enough for Montgomery that he will be only too happy to sell the island. In the climactic showdown, Montgomery's men intercept an arms shipment to Sison's men on the island, leading to a shootout on the beach in which Diaz is killed and Sison's men are overpowered, while Montgomery throws Sison from a boat to the sharks before shooting Thatcher's plane from the sky. As for Gregg, who knew nothing of her father's evil scheme, she regretfully departs, leaving Montgomery to pursue happiness with pretty island girl Liza Moreno.

Perhaps not as ambitious as previous efforts in the Philippines by star/director/producer Montgomery and screenwriter Ferde Grofe, Jr., the story is still fairly entertaining, though some of the secondary characters are a bit taxing in their pursuit of comic relief. (In English)

Galvez: Hanggang sa Dulo ng Mundo Hahanapin Kita (Galvez: I Will Search for You to the End of the Earth)

1993 Regal Films; 103 minutes/color
Director: Manuel "Fyke" Cinco; Screenwriters: Henry Nadong, Lavindico Diaz; Cinematographer: Edmund Cupcupin; Editor: Edmund "Bot" Jarlego; Filmscore: Nonong Buencamino; Cast: Eddie Garcia, Edu Manzano, Pilar Pilapil, Sunshine Cruz, Cristina Gonzales, Jaime Fabregas, Berting Labra, Dick Israel, Jess Ramos, Marithez Samson, Delia Razon, Ernie Zarate, Nanding Fernandez, Joseph Serra, Christopher Rojas

In one of the more effective action vehicles for actor Eddie Garcia, he is cast here as a prosecutor who succeeds in convicting suave millionaire drug lord Edu Manzano of a series of rape/murders. But Garcia finds that prison hardly diminishes Manzano's power. Manzano's men abduct Garcia's son and send his head back in a box, and then force Garcia's daughter (Sunshine Cruz) out of a hospital window and she falls to her death. Garcia and his wife (Pilar Pilapil) go into hiding, and Garcia then turns the tables on Manzano. Discovering that Manzano's men have succeeded in smuggling Manzano out of prison, Garcia becomes the hunter in order to enact his revenge, which he accomplishes.

Garcia gives another strong performance, but what constantly surprises is how effective a villain Manzano makes. Sometimes cast as an action hero himself, and with the looks of a natural leading man, Manzano is frequently called on to play villainous roles nonetheless, and he has become very popular in that capacity. The film also offers another of Dick Israel's by then patented turns as a psychotic, drugged-out gang member, which he always does well. Manuel Cinco's direction is taut, not allowing the running time to get away from him (a problem that the action genre, among others, frequently succumbs to). This is a superb film. (In Tagalog)

Ganito Kami Noon, Paano Kayo Ngayon? (This Is What We Were, How Are You Now?)

1976 Hemisphere Pictures; 125 minutes/color
Director: Eddie Romero; Screenwriters: Eddie Romero, Roy Iglesias; Cinematographer: Justo Paulino; Editor: Ben Barcelon; Filmscore: Lutgardo Labad; Cast: Christopher de Leon, Gloria Diaz, Eddie Garcia, Leopoldo Salcedo, Rosemarie Gil,

Dranreb, E.A. Rocha, Johnny Vicar, Tsing Tong Tsai, Ken Metcalfe, Alona Alegre, Jaime Fabregas

After years of producing and directing exploitation films for the international market, Eddie Romero began to take note of the new breed of young Filipino filmmakers leaving their mark and altering the direction of the local industry. Inspired by what he was seeing, Romero returned to Filipino films proper, producing, writing and directing this ambitious historical drama starring Christopher de Leon as an amiable country bumpkin who bungles his way through the waning days of the Spanish colonial era and into the dawning of the American presence. He hooks up with Leopoldo Salcedo's traveling road show and falls in love with Gloria Diaz, a singer (and a rather bad one) is Salcedo's troupe. But he eventually loses her to aristocratic Eddie Garcia, who at first plays Pygmalian with de Leon, teaching him some refinement and introducing him to high society. De Leon wins Diaz back, but finally walks away from everything, unsure of where he fits in as the American era commences. The film concludes by giving the impression that de Leon is contented to go through life as the happy-go-lucky hayseed he started out as caring nothing about the Spanish aristocracy or the world of changes signaled by the arrival of the Americans.

De Leon gives an excellent performance as a simpleton bewildered by the situations he finds himself in, understanding little of the fighting and strife he encounters, and for the most part, fairly impervious to their ramifications. The film also features a fiery performance by Johnny Vicar as a citizen very discontented with Spanish rule. Salcedo won the FAMAS Best Supporting Actor award for his colorful characterization, and the film was picked Best Film by the Gawad Urian. In fact, the film dominated the Urian awards, also winning Best Picture, Director, Actor (de Leon), Screenplay, and Production Design (Laida Lim-Perez and Peque Gallaga). (In Tagalog)

Gascon: Bala ang Katapat Mo (Gascon: A Bullet Awaits You)

1993 Regal Films; 119 minutes/color
Director: Rogelio Salvador; Screenwriter: Amado Ansuara; Cinematographer: Vic Anao; Editor: Rogelio Salvador; Filmscore: Willie Yusi; Cast: Lito Lapid, Ruffa Gutierrez, Tirso Cruz III, Jess Lapid Jr., Bob Soler, Janine Barredo, Isabel Granada, Dave Brodett, Max Laurel, Conrad Poe, Jose Romulo, Mario Escudero, Ric Avellano, Vic Varrion, Robert Miller, Ernie David, Nonoy de Guzman, Allan Rogelio, Robert Talby, Bomber Moran, Frank Lapid, Johnny Vicar

Lito Lapid is a police officer determined to bring down the criminal empire of Bob Soler, who sends some of his men (led by sadistic Jess Lapid, Jr.) to try and buy Lito off with a briefcase full of money and a beautiful woman. But when their offer is refused and Lito sends them away, Soler resorts to drastic means: confronting Lito in a restaurant, Soler turns Jess, Jr. loose on him, and in a lively, old-school slugfest, Jess soundly pummels Lito. In a separate storyline, which does merge with the main conflict at the film's conclusion, Lito oversees a truce between two violent, warring street gangs. In the end the two gangs get word of Lito's staging of a raid on Soler's warehouse, and they rush to the scene to assist Lito in defeating Soler's men. The gang members kill Soler, and Lito chases after Jess, Jr., who appropriates a tour bus. Lito does likewise in order to give chase, eventually catching up after a lively pursuit, after which he shoots and kills Jess, Jr.

While not quite as carnage soaked as *Dudurugin Kita ng Bala Ko* (1991), the prior collaboration between Lapid and director Rogelio Salvador, the violence is certainly robust. In an interesting bit of casting, Tirso Cruz III plays the leader of one of the street gangs, and does a good job of it. There is also a good, albeit brief, performance by Johnny Vicar as the father of a boy accidentally killed during a rumble between two rival gangs. (In Tagalog)

Gen. Tapia: Sa Nagbabagang Lupa (Gen. Tapia: In the Burning Land)

1995 Sunlight Films; 95 minutes/color
Director: Roland S. Ledesma; Screenwriters: Bert Duenas, Eddie Joson, Roland S. Ledesma; Cast: Ronnie Ricketts, Ronald Gan, Daniel Fernando, Rhey Roldan, Rachel Lobangco, Rez Cortez, Rex Lapid, Lovely Rivero, Bobby Benitez, Boy Fernandez, Jing Abalos, Robert Miller, Usman Hassim, Rudy Dominguez, Tony Ferrer, Jose Romulo, Lucita Soriano, Sheila Ysrael, Conrad Poe, Nick Romano, Philip Gamboa, Rommel Valdez, Ernie David, Rolly Lapid, Ernie Zarate, Renato Robles, Carol Dauden

In yet another true account of strife with Muslim rebels on Mindanao, Ronnie Ricketts portrays General Cesar Tapia (actually, still a lieutenant colonel at the time that the story is set, in the 1970s). He is sent by general Ernie Zarate to the province of Jolo to combat Ronald Gan's rebel forces. There isn't much to tell here, since the film is basically a string of battles (some quite effectively shot), and Ricketts periodic attempts to negotiate a peace with the stubborn rebels. The filmmakers do not seem particularly interested in portraying the rebels as necessarily being bad guys, but seem to stress the need for unity and keeping Mindanao a part of the Republic. In fact, long stretches of the film are given over to the rebels in their camp venting their frustrations. Nontheless, Ricketts is clearly the hero here, and the film concludes with the defeat of the rebels, though as the rebel leader dies he extends a bloody hand to Ricketts. The film then recounts Tapia's military achievements, culminating in his being made commander of all troops in the southern Philippines. (In Tagalog with some English)

Geron Olivar

1994 Regal Films; 103 minutes/color
Director: Jesus Jose; Screenwriters: Jun Lawas, Henry Nadong, Joji Vitug; Cinematographer: Rey de Leon; Editor: Rogelio Salvador; Filmscore: Nonong Buencamino; Cast: Lito Lapid, Edu Manzano, Zoren Legaspi, Kris Aquino, Nida Blanca, Tony Ferrer, Efren Reyes Jr., Jess Lapid Jr., Edgar Mortiz, Edgar Mande, Jackie Forster, Ruel Vernal, Rez Cortez, Rando Almanzor, King Gutierrez, Manjo del Mundo, Robert Talby, Rey Roldan, Frank Lapid, Edwin Reyes, Rex Lapid, Jordan Castillo, Rolly Lapid, Ernie Zarate

In this showy, but relatively insubstantial action film, policeman Lito Lapid seeks to bring down Edu Manzano's drug empire. Manzano is a pretty shrewd guy, so it isn't easy to pin anything on him, but Lapid's brother, an up and coming reporter, is out to get the story that will make his career, and he manages to get his publisher to run a story that strongly implicates Manzano in various criminal activities. Manzano retaliates by more-or-less declaring war: Lapid's brother is abducted and his severed hand is mailed to Lapid. Of course, this only strengthens Lapid's resolve, spelling Manzano's doom.

Director Jesus Jose pulls out all the stops, going for spectacle. There are car chases, chases on foot, plenty of shooting (of course)—you name it. The film concludes with Lapid on a jet ski shooting Manzano's plane out of the sky. Except for the afore mentioned severed hand, there is little gore to speak of, not even in any of the shootings. This is quite a contrast from Jose and Lapid's previous collaboration, *Kahit Singko Hindi Ko Babayaran ang Buhay Mo* (1990), which was replete with gore. Manzano performs well as the heavy, and is surrounded by the usual complement of familiar faces playing his goons, including Rez Cortez, Ruel Vernal and Jess Lapid, Jr. (In Tagalog with some English)

Get: Commander Jack Moro (Bangsamoro Army)

1989 Airoh Media Services; 85 minutes/color
Director: Eddie N. Nicart; Screenwriters: Bonnie Paredes, Rollie Arceo; Cinematographer: Bhal Dauz; Editor: Francis Vinarao; Filmscore: Ernani Cuenco; Cast: Sonny Parsons, Marianne dela Riva, Raoul Aragonn, Romy Diaz, Rommel Valdez, Marithez Samson, Jay Mendez, Usman Hassim, Romy Nario, Avel Morado, Romeo Barromeo, Jose Romulo, Ernie Ortega, Avon Cortez, Winnie Cendana

In this true account of the life of Jack Moro, a Muslim rebel on Mindanao, Sonny Parsons has the lead as the film recounts Moro's battles with other rebel factions, as well as with the government. Parsons and his army battle Romy Diaz and his rebels before government troops are dispatched to Mindanao to stop the fighting by eradicating both factions. The government soldiers succeed in eliminating Diaz and his forces, but find Parsons' army more formidable. After a number of battles, Parsons negotiates a settlement with the government, by which he and his men would surrender and then would be reincorporated into the national armed forces. The film opens with an on-camera announcement by the real Jack Moro, who expresses his hope that the film would encourage his Muslim brothers to work out their grievances within the system. (In Tagalog with some English)

Goat Buster: Sa Templo ni Dune (Goat Buster: In the Temple of Dune)

1982 Lea Productions; 118 minutes/color
Director/screenwriter: Ben Feleo; Cinematographer: Ricardo Herrera; Filmscore: Dominic; Cast: Dolphy, Gloria Diaz, Panchito Alba, Gretchen Baretto, Nanette Inventor, Rolly Quizon, Rodolfo "Boy" Garcia, Tatlong Itlog, Conde Ubaldo, Naty Mallares, Robert Miller, Edgar Garcia, Rago Apollo, ER Canton Salazar, Ben Johnson, Paquito Bautista, Rod Francisco, Ramon R. Vera, Fred Esplana, Jay Grama, Tibo Legazpi, Ramon D'Salva, Rocco Montalban

Dolphy, the elder statesman of Filipino comedy, takes dual roles in this farce. Playing the usual country bumpkin, he travels to the city to sell a baby goat (presumably this is how "goat" found its way into the title), and is promptly arrested after being mistaken for a gangster named Bogart (also played by Dolphy). Quickly realizing that a mistake has been made, police captain Panchito Alba releases Dolphy. Bogart's rival, crime boss Ramon D'Salva, dies and is replaced by an ambitious young hood who immediately seeks to eliminate any competition. He orders a hit on Bogart, which only succeeds in putting him in the hospital, but Alba hatches a plan to collar both of the rival crime gangs. He convinces Dolphy to impersonate Bogart, and when Dolphy agrees he is put through a rigorous training and orientation program in order to pull it off. Well, it works, and on Alba's orders Dolphy forms an alliance with Bogart's rivals, merging the two gangs into one. Eventually Dolphy's cover is blown, but he is helped in his escape by Bogart's girlfriend (Gloria Diaz), who is relieved to discover that the man she has fallen in love with is not the nasty gangster Bogart after all, but the kindly Dolphy. Meanwhile, Dolphy's wife (heavyset Nanette Inventor)—yes, he has a wife back home—and Alba have fallen in love, which is fine with Dolphy, since he naturally prefers the beautiful Diaz. Bogart manages to recover from the hit attempt and escapes from the hospital, and during a wacky climactic chase, culminating in a big fight between the police and the gang members, it's Dolphy vs. Dolphy as Bogart confronts his imposter. The face-off is resolved when Diaz shoots Bogart to save Dolphy's life. Interestingly, Dolphy tearfully embraces his criminal look-alike as Bogart lay dying. The film then ends with Dolphy and Diaz in the country happily raising goats together. As Filipino comedies go, this is reasonably amusing, though as usual, overlong. (In Tagalog with some English)

Gobernador (Governor)

1992 Filmstar Productions/Stellar Films; 103 minutes/color

Director: Romy Suzara; Screenwriter: Tony Pascua; Cinematographer: Johnny Araojo; Editor: Edgardo Vinarao; Filmscore: Jaime Fabregas; Cast: Eddie Garcia, Pinky de Leon, Dante Rivero, Rez Cortez, Lito Legaspi, Berting Labra, Patrick dela Rosa, Bomber Moran, Charlie Davao, Romeo Rivera, Ernie Zarate, Lucita Soriano, Beverly Vergel, Bing-Bing Prieto, Joey Padilla, Polly Cadsawan, Jim Morales

Governor Eddie Garcia survives an assassination attempt by sniper Rez Cortez, but unfortunately his wife is hit and thereafter confined to a wheelchair. Garcia's troubles are coming from ex-governor Dante Rivero, who wants his old job back, and to that end has formed an alliance with a powerful crime syndicate, who would like to have things nice and easy again, since Garcia has been cracking down on everything from prostitution to smuggling. Rivero brings some powerful players into the alliance, including corrupt local mayor Charlie Davao and police major Lito Legaspi. With muscle like that, Garcia has a sizeable number of the police force actually working against him. It all builds up to what amounts to a coup, with Rivero, Legaspi and a lot of their cronies launching an attack on the regional capitol building. Garcia and some loyalists try to stave off the assault, but while they put up a valiant fight, they are overrun, and Rivero celebrates the victory. But back home later that same night, Rivero enters his house and is confronted by a bloody but unbowed Garcia, who proceeds to gun him down.

The film is helped by its cast of veteran players, and finishes strongly with the impressive battle at the capitol building, which includes some excellent stunt work and pyrotechnics, followed quickly by Garcia's confronting Rivero, which, although predictable, has just the right punch to it. (In Tagalog)

God Save Me!

1985 Seiko Films; 116 minutes/color

Director: Carlo J. Caparas; Screenwriters: Orlando Nadres; Cinematographer: Sergio Lobo; Editor: Edgardo Vinarao; Filmscore: Snafu Rigor; Cast: Christopher de Leon, Rio Locsin, Cherie Gil, Charito Solis, Tommy Abuel, Juan Rodrigo, Rose Ann Gonzales, Rosemarie Gil, Jaime Fabregas, Naty Santiago, Lucy Quinto, Ross Olgado, Greggy Liwag, Joonee Gamboa, Joey Sanchez, Odette Khan, Jimmy Reyes, Alex Toledo

Husband and wife Christopher de Leon and Cherie Gil have a baby girl, but while de Leon is a proud and doting father, Gil shows an immediate disinterest in the child. As the girl grows into an adorable seven-year-old (played by Rose Ann Gonzales) she has a deep love for her father, while her mother, who is too busy partying and carrying on, is little more than a stranger to her. Tired of Gil's running around, de Leon leaves, but finds himself in a fierce custody battle for his daughter, waged largely by his in-laws (Jaime Fabregas and Rosemarie Gil). Though he is not nearly as well off, de Leon manages to get custody of his child, and father and daughter are quite happy together. Of course, things could never be that simple, and trouble comes when de Leon begins to experience violent headaches, and then convulsions. He is diagnosed with a malignant brain tumor, which is inoperable. In the meantime, Gil's parents have also grown weary of their daughter's lack of maturity, and so they discontinue her stipend, leaving her to fend for herself. She goes to see de Leon and is shocked to learn of his condition and to find him wasting away. She again becomes a presence in de Leon's home, helping to nurse her ex-husband in his dying days, after which she has presumably matured enough to become a proper, loving mother to her daughter.

This basically plays like an ABC TV movie from the 1970s, only longer—much longer. While the performances are all good, on the whole this is little more than a two-hour cliché. (In Tagalog with some English)

Goosebuster

1992 Regal Films; 93 minutes/color
Director: Tony Y. Reyes; Screenwriters: Tony Y. Reyes, Joey de Leon; Cinematographer: Oscar Querijero; Editor: Renato de Leon; Filmscore: Demet Velasquez; Cast: Joey de Leon, Aiza Seguerra, Racel Tuazon, Panchito Alba, Ruby Rodriguez, Lady Lee, Kathleen Quieng, Noel "Ungga" Ayala, Sammy Lagmay, Bert Olivar, Gigi Posadas, Bomber Moran, Danny Rojo, Nonong de Andres, Pong Pong, Don Pepot, Nemie Gutierrez, Felia Cudia

When Joey de Leon and two of his buddies eat a goose owned by a rather sinister old hobo, it leads to big trouble. During a séance de Leon's girlfriend is possessed by the spirit of the goose, and poor Joey is faced with the prospect of spending his life with a woman who squawks and struts around like a bird. Things are eventually resolved when the spirit of the goose leaves her and takes possession of the old hobo who was once its owner. The title is drawn from a dream sequence in which three little girls and dwarf Noel Ayala, decked out in Ghostbuster-like attire, do battle with evil spirits and the skeleton of a giant goose. Even measured by the standards of previous collaborations between de Leon and director Tony Y. Reyes, this is very silly. (In Tagalog with some English)

Grease Gun Gang

1991 Viva Films; 110 minutes/color
Director: Eddie Rodriguez; Screenwriter: Humilde "Meek" Roxas; Cinematographer: Sergio Lobo; Editor: Ike Jarlego, Jr.; Filmscore: Jaime Fabregas, Nonong Buencamino; Cast: Robin Padilla, Michael de Mesa, Daniel Fernando, Roi Vinzon, Bing Loyzaga, Dennis Padilla, Alou Gonzales, William Lorenzo, Rommel Padilla, Jun Hidalgo, Ruben Rustia, Ruel Vernal, Berting Labra, Dexter Doria, Val Iglesias, Jess Ramos, Koko Trinidad, Michelle Ann Lopez, Romeo Enriquez, Rosauro "Boy" Roque, Mike Castillo, Nonoy de Guzman, Gia Santos, Rico Orbita, Kim Tumibay

Popular "bad boy" Robin Padilla stars in this stylish gangland offering from director Eddie Rodriguez, which often takes on the feeling of an homage to the classic American gangster films of the 1930s and '40s. As the film opens Padilla has just been released from prison and hooks up with his old motley crew. He also comes to the rescue of wealthy Ruben Rustia and his wife Dexter Doria, saving them from a hold-up man in the streets. Padilla and his men are then drawn into Rustia's struggle with Chinatown mob boss Michael de Mesa, while also having to deal with old rival Roi Vinzon and his gang. Padilla and his boys wipe out Vinzon's gang, and when Rustia is killed, they have a showdown with de Mesa and his gang in which Padilla is left the only one standing.

The film seems to be striving to evoke a bygone era with a musical score that leans heavily on big band music, and there are an uncommonly high number of 1950s cars. Not surprisingly, the violence is robust; Padilla's friend Berting Labra has his arm hacked off by Vinzon's gang, and even a funeral procession turns into a gang war shootout. One surprise is Padilla's lack of a leading lady. Though he takes an interest in Vinzon's sister—and she in him—she is accidentally killed after getting caught in the crossfire during a shootout between the two gangs. With no time for the romance to progress, the film manages to avoid the standard softcore love scenes, which usually fail to deliver much anyway.

Padilla apparently began to take his bad boy image too seriously, and in 1995 he began serving a three-year prison sentence after being arrested and convicted on illegal weapons charges. Upon his release in 1998 he successfully resumed his film career. (In Tagalog)

The Grepor Butch Belgica Story

1995 Viva Films; 110 minutes/color
Director: Toto Natividad; Screenwriters: Butch Belgica, Ferdinand Galang; Cast: Joko Diaz, Ronaldo

Valdez, Boots Anson-Roa, Albert Martinez, Cristina Gonzales, Gary Estrada, Isabel Granada, Kier Legaspi, Bembol Roco, Daniel Fernando, Richard Bonnin, Vina Morales, Ferdie Galang, Shintaro Valdez, Rez Cortez, Rommel Montano, Roldan Aquino, Romeo Enriquez, Rommel Valdez, Boy Roque, Rex Lapid, Danny Labra, Johnny Vicar

Joko Diaz has the title role in this true story of the life of Butch Belgica, who has been in and out of jail from an early age for various gang-related crimes, including murder. During his time in prison, Belgica became a crusader for prison reform, and the personal change in him did not go unnoticed. In 1976 he was released and granted a full presidential pardon. The film ends with Belgica's release from prison, and does not portray his becoming a preacher a year later. Belgica's pardon is more than a little startling given the unblinking portrayal of some of his crimes, including a brutal murder committed in prison. Belgica himself co-wrote the screenplay; the film is well directed and played, but somehow seems to fall short of its lofty ambitions. (In Tagalog with some English)

Gumapang Ka sa Lusak
(You Crawl in the Mud)

1990 Viva Films; 115 minutes/color
Director: Lino Brocka; Screenwriter: Ricardo Lee; Cinematographer: Pedro Manding, Jr.; Editor: George Jarlego; Filmscore: Nonong Buencamino; Cast: Dina Bonnevie, Christopher de Leon, Eddie Garcia, Charo Santos, Bembol Roco, Allan Paule, Francis Magalona, William Lorenzo, Perla Bautista, Anita Linda, Lucita Soriano, Timmy Diwa, Maureen Mauricio, Ernie Zarate, Ray Ventura, Tess Dumpit, Fred Capulong, Jimmy Reyes, Archie Adamos, Rey Malte-Cruz, Rikki Jimenez, Benjie Ledesma

Actress Dina Bonnevie is in love with Christopher de Leon, who is serving a stretch in prison, when she begins an affair with wealthy and ambitious politician Eddie Garcia. In return for her sexual favors, Garcia helps look after Bonnevie's parents and is pulling some strings to get de Leon released from prison. But Garcia has an alterior motive: when de Leon gets out of prison, Garcia hires him to assassinate his opponent in the upcoming senatorial elections, which de Leon succeeds in doing. Garcia repays de Leon by sending Bembol Roco and a compliment of goons to kill him. The only loose end now is Bonnevie, who is threatening to expose Garcia, and so Roco and company kidnap her parents in order to lure her into a trap. But things go wrong, and while Bonnevie manages to escape the trap, her parents are killed. In a dramatic finale, Bonnevie disrupts Garcia's speech at a political rally, grabbing a live microphone and telling everyone the type of guy Garcia really is. Friends of Bonnevie's then take over the control booth and play an incriminating tape over the P.A. system—a phone conversation recorded by Bonnevie in which Garcia implicates himself in the assassination of his rival. An enraged Roco pulls out a gun and shoots Bonnevie before being gunned down himself by the police. As Bonnevie lay dying, Garcia is left to face a room full of anxious reporters and stunned voters.

Made only four years after the end of the Marcos dictatorship, the concept of political corruption was not only appealing conceptually, but was finally more permissible as a topic without as much fear of censorship, or even legal reprisals. The performances here are all good, as is Brocka's direction, but Ricardo Lee's screenplay is, aside from the conclusion, a bit on the average side. (In Tagalog with some English)

Gumising Ka ... Maruja
(Awaken ... Maruja)

1978 FPJ Productions; 117 minutes/color
Director: Lino Brocka; Screenwriter: Tony Perez; Cinematographer: Conrado Baltazar; Editor: Augusto Salvador; Filmscore: Ernani Cuenco; Cast: Susuan Roces, Phillip Salvador, Mario O'Hara, Laurice Guillen, Mary Walter, Many Ojeda, Fritz Ynfante, Peque Gallaga, George Atutubo, Aida Carmona, Estrella Antonio, Cora Magno, Joel Torre

This is a superb ghost story of the old-school variety, and appears to be director Lino Brocka's only excursion into the supernatural. Susan Roces portrays an actress whose next film is planned to be a true story based on the life of a woman named Maruja (Laurice Guillen), and the tragic love affair that drove her to her death in the 19th century. Intending to shoot the film in the now-abandoned gothic mansion where Maruja lived and died, Roces rents the mansion and decides to move in for a week to get a feel for the place where the film's story will unfold. Accompanying her are her director (Mario O'Hara), leading man (Phillip Salvador), and a small company of personal assistants and Roces' household servants. It turns out to be a bad idea: Roces sees mysterious figures on the grounds, O'Hara suffers a series of disturbing nightmares, and Salvador struggles through periods during which he is possessed by Maruja's angry lover. With Roces' servants turning up dead, the group find themselves trapped in the isolated mansion as the ghost of Maruja's lover guards the bridge that is the only means of returning to civilization, sitting astride his horse and wielding a sword, slashing to death anyone who tries to cross. Eventually Salvador is completely controlled by the spirit, who sees Roces as being Maruja, and he goes on a violent rampage trying to get to her, pummeling two of her male employees with a shovel before O'Hara knocks him cold. The next day, an ambulance takes Salvador away, and Roces and O'Hara leave the mansion dazed and bewildered.

Not surprisingly within its genre, the most impressive moments are those that are understated. Early in the film, for instance, Roces throws a party in the mansion, which also serves as something of a press conference to announce her new project. The houseful of guests are too preoccupied to notice the somber group of women dressed in mourning who slowly make their way throughy the house, and when party guest Joel Torre goes looking for a bathroom, he opens the wrong door and inadvertently walks in on a spectral gathering. Not realizing that he has interrupted a group of phantoms, Torre merely excuses himself. There is also an effective moment when Salvador, looking out an upstairs window during a thunderstorm, observes a phantom funeral procession making its way across the grounds.

If the film does have a drawback, it would be the inclusion of several melodramatically wordy passages in which Salvador professes his love for Roces, but she is reluctant to surrender to any romantic feelings that she may have for him. Still, Brocka, whose specialty was noirish melodrama, shows a firm understanding of the supernatural genre, which makes one wish that, in a genre littered with hacks, he would have ventured into such territory more often, or at least again. (In Tagalog with some English)

Hagedorn

1996 Merdeka Film Productions; 113 minutes/color

Director: Ronwaldo Reyes (Fernando Poe, Jr.); Screenwriters: Manuel Buising, Senen Dimaguila, Henry Nadong; Cinematographer: Ver Reyes; Editors: Augusto Salvador, Rene Tala; Filmscore: Jaime Fabregas; Cast: Fernando Poe Jr., Sharmaine Arnaiz, Bob Soler, Jun Aristorenas, Dante Rivero, Rosemarie Gil, Eddie Arenas, Zandro Zamora, Maita Sanchez, Paquito Diaz, Delia Razon, Romeo Rivera, Dick Israel, Rez Cortez, Dedes Whitaker, Robert Ortega, Jigo Garcia, Dawnlyn Piette, Marjorie Inumorable, Jameson Lozada, Elmer Banaag, Marco Salvador, Ernie Zarate, Dindo Arroyo, George Estregan Jr., Ruel Vernal, Teresa Loyzaga, Renato del Prado, Suzette Ranillo, Johnny Vicar, Ernie Ortega, Rudy Meyer, Tony Mabesa, Marco Polo Garcia

Fernando Poe, Jr., stars in and directs this account of the life of Puerto Princesa Vice Mayor Edward Hagedorn, detailing his family's struggles with regional smugglers and corrupt police and officials, through to his rise to the top. There is also a protracted flashback sequence midway through the film detailing Hagedorn's turbulent teenage years. Despite a plethora of cameos by familiar faces, and the obvious aim at grand epic, this is fairly uncaptivating stuff, and it never really achieves the status that it is aiming for. (In Tagalog)

Halik ng Vampira
(Kiss of the Vampire Woman)

1997 Octoarts/Cinemax Studios; 93 minutes/color

Directors: Peque Gallaga, Lorenzo Reyes; Screenwriter: Henry Lopez; Cinematographer: Richard Padernal: Editor: Danny Gloria; Filmscore: Tony Cortez; Cast: Anjanette Abayari, Raymond Bagatsing, Beth Tamayo, Patrick Guzman, Mark Solis, Jason Salcedo, Jaime Fabregas, Michael V., Romy Romulo, Nathan Forest, Ian Veneracion, Celina Cortez, Aileen Angeles, Patrick Perez

Though a flawed film, this interesting—even occasionally inspired—offering from the directing team of Peque Gallaga and Lorenzo Reyes is probably the most interesting vampire film since the 1970s, when vampires were in their cinematic heyday. Michael V. plays Deadhour Dave, a late night radio DJ who regularly receives calls on the air from a woman calling herself "Midnight Solitaire." Solitaire says she is a vampire, which V. doesn't take seriously, of course. Many male listeners of the program tune in specifically to hear Solitaire's calls, and they regularly leave phone numbers to be forwarded in hopes of a rendezvous with the mysterious woman. V. happily forwards the numbers, thinking that he is doing no more than setting up sexual encounters between consenting adults, but of course Solitaire really is a vampire, and V. is actually supplying her with victims. It turns out that the mysterious Solitaire is nurse Anjanette Abayari, who works the night shift at a hospital. She is attracted to young doctor Raymond Bagatsing, but whenever she becomes sexually aroused in his presence, her vampiric tendencies surface, and she feels compelled to run off. Eventually V. helps Bagatsing cure Abayari of her vampirism; using a book that V. obtains from a bizarre, grotesque doctor (Jaime Fabregas), Bagatsing tries an experiment and drains Abayari's blood, replacing it with some of his own. For the first time in years (maybe ever) Abayari sees the sunlight as she and Bagatsing walk off arm-in-arm.

Vampirism has forever been used as a sexual metaphor—seldom as obviously as here—so in that sense the concept here should be easily read; Abayari's victims being random, meaningless sexual dalliances, while she continues to fear true intimacy, fleeing whenever she becomes aroused by the man she truly desires. Through the gift of Bagatsing's blood—a selfless and loving gesture by the man who knows her sins and forgives her—Abayari is freed.

No doubt there are those who will be disappointed that the film splits its time between horror and satire, but the sardonic humor seldom strays far enough to disrupt the mood. When it does, however, it is quite damaging. There are, for instance, two teenage boys who are forever spying on the beautiful Abayari: when they come to realize that she is a vampire they turn up at her house armed with squirt guns filled with holy water. That's actually one of their better moments. In one of the film's potentially devastating mood wreckers, the two boys show up at the home of a girl that they have likewise been peeping at, and she sends her dog after them. In a moment straight out of Benny Hill, the boys beat a bumbling retreat in fast motion, scrambling to their moped. Other than that, the humor provided by V. is in keeping with his character, and there is also the thoroughly weird doctor played by Fabregas, who is a nightmarish mess of scars and stitches, but is also the highlight of the film's comic bent.

Gallaga and Reyes do earn bonus points for keeping the running time down to a manageable 93 minutes. Some of their other genre films, like *Tiyanak* (1988) and *Aswang* (1992), run for a good two hours, which tends to make one impatient for the climax. (In Tagalog and English)

Hamog (Dew)

1976 Regal Films; 121 minutes/color
Director: Romy Suzara; Screenwriter: Pierre Salas; Cinematographer: Ernesto dela Paz; Editor: Ben Barcelon; Filmscore: Ernani Cuenco; Cast: Alma Moreno, Rafael (Bembol) Roco, Raul Aragon, Ellen Esguerra, Lucita Soriano, Lito Anzures, Mary Walter, Jojo Santiago, J. Antonio Carrion, Freddie Yance, Buddy Salvador, George Azner

This dour melodrama casts Bembol Roco as a biology student who falls in love with pretty pearl diver Alma Moreno. Moreno, however, is more than a little reluctant, and through his persistence Roco finally gets the story as to why. Moreno relates a tragic story of her having been raped, her mother leaving her father, her father's subsequent suicide, and how Moreno eventually ended up in an abusive relationship with her rapist (Raul Aragon). One night Moreno returned home to find her mother (Lucita Soriano) in an intimate moment with Aragon, and when Soriano tried to make a quick exit, Aragon became enraged and strangled her. Frantic, Moreno grabbed a machete and, after hacking off Aragon's ear, proceeded to plunge the weapon into his groin. With Aragon apparently dead, Moreno and Soriano fled and spent the night on the beach, but Moreno awoke the following day to find that her mother had drowned.

Obviously Moreno comes with a lot of emotional baggage, but Roco is too in love to care, and before long the two of them are making wedding plans, but things take a nasty turn when Moreno has a surprise encounter in the marketplace with Aragon, who is very much alive. Though Moreno manages to elude him in the market, Aragon is somehow able to track her down, and he kills her in the dorm room she shares with the other women pearl divers. The film climaxes as Roco finds Aragon, chases him onto a boat and kills him.

The script by Pierre Salas is engrossing, though there are some extraneous moments, including a mass catfight in the dormitory that is entertaining (aren't they all?), but in no way necessary. It would have behooved the filmmakers to tighten the narrative up a bit. (In Tagalog with some English)

Hanggang Kailan Kita Mamahalin? (How Long Will I Love You?)

1997 Star Cinema; 130 minutes/color
Director: Olivia M. Lamasan; Screenwriters: Ricky Lee, Olivia M. Lamasan; Cast: Lorna Tolentino, Richard Gomez, Ronaldo Valdez, Gina Pareno, Chanda Romero, Angelica Panganiban, Eula Valdez, Cherry Pie Picache, Sylvia Sanchez, Mandy Ochoa, Toby Alejar, Dwight Gaston, Farrah Flores, Jericho Rosales, Julia Clarete, Ronalisa Cheng, Bong Regala, Nante Montreal, Cris Daluz

Lorna Tolentino and Richard Gomez portray a happily married young couple who both work at the same marketing firm. When Tolentino receives the promotion that Gomez was hoping for himself the results are predictable; further bruising his pride is his own transfer to another department, which he sees as a demotion. But more than Gomez's wounded ego, the marriage is strained by the new and considerable demands on Tolentino's time. With his wife too busy to return his phone calls, the enraged Gomez feels the greatest blow to his dignity when his wife turns down his funding requests at a budget meeting in favor of more prominent accounts. As time passes, Gomez leaves his job, becoming a house husband to the couple's two young daughters and infant son, much to the dismay of his father, successful Ronaldo Valdez, who berates his son as a nobody. The very strained marriage continues to limp along until Gomez shows up unexpectedly at a company party and a heated argument ensues in which he winds up dragging Tolentino off, and during the drive home, with the argument still raging, the couple gets into an accident. While Gomez is unhurt, Tolentino suffers a fractured skull; by the time she recovers the couple realize that they cannot do without each other and patch things up.

While certainly within the ordinary bounds of Filipino high melodrama, the film is a cut above, though it could have stood to stray from the norm as regards running time, since it lingers too long before reaching its resolution (in Philippine films, you basically just have to get used to that). (In Tagalog with some English)

Haunted House!

1985 Bukang Liwayway Films; 120 minutes/color

Director/screenwriter: Ramje; Cinematographer: Ver Reyes; Editor: Pepe Marcos; Filmscore: Jun Latonio; Cast: William Martinez, Janice de Belen, J.C. Bonnin, Lito Patrana, Yani de Veyra, E.R. Ejercito, Marivee Santos, Ernie Forte, Heidi Alemania, Jopet de Guzman, Carlos de Leon, Tina Godinez, Gia Guison, Bubbles Lee, Michael Pigar, Raquel Rodriguez, Ampy Salonga, Ruben Rustia, Rosemarie Gil, Tony Carreon, Luis Benedicto, Jimmy Fabregas, Flora Gasser, Fred Navarro, Joseph de Cordova

In this old dark house comedy, a group of high school kids sitting around a bonfire on the beach at night start discussing ghosts and are persuaded by one member of the group to spend the night in a haunted house. One of the boys knows the caretakers of a supposedly haunted mansion, and so arrangements are made for the kids to spend the night. They arrive at the house the following day and are startled by the caretakers (a husband and wife, both hunchbacked, with the man bearing more than a passing resemblance to Quasimodo), and after spending the early part of the evening playing with the Ouija (as well as playing various pranks on one another), they retire for the night. Things turn very serious during the night when they are haunted by the traditional lady in white, and still more serious when one of the girls (Janice de Belen) is possessed by a demonic entity, which transforms her into a werewolf. Priest Ruben Rustia shows up with all of the priestly trappings to exorcise the evil spirit and save the kids.

Though the early part of the film plays like an unexceptional youth-oriented comedy, chronicling the hijinx of the high school kids (cheating on exams, holding drag races, getting into fist fights, having beach parties), the comedy becomes less frequent once inside the titular house, and by the final half hour, director/screenwriter Ramje decides to play it like a straight horror film (which is also unexceptional). The make-up for de Belen's transformation (accomplished by Maurice Carvajal) is quite good, though Ramje appears to have been negligent in giving her any instruction as to how to *act* like a monster. As it is she strolls through the house as if she were on her way to the kitchen for a late night snack. (In Tagalog with some English)

Hayop sa Hayop (Beast to Beast)

1978 Showbiz, Inc.; 102 minutes/color

Director: Lino Brocka; Screenwriter: Jose Y. Dalisay, Jr.; Cinematographer: Conrado Baltazar; Editor: Augusto Salvador; Filmscore: Ernani Cuenco; Cast: Hilda Koronel, Bembol Roco, Phillip Salvador, Paquito Diaz, Mario Escudero, Rene Hawkins, Bello Borja, Carpi Asturias, Domingo Landicho, George Atutubo, Josie Shoemaker, Edna May Landicho, Joe Jardi, Jimmy Calaguas

When a Manila bank robbery goes awry, a shootout ensues in which a number of people are killed. Bank robbers Bembol Rocco and Phillip Salvador succeed in escaping the scene with the money, and after picking up Salvador's girlfriend (Hilda Koronel), they flee to the country. But policeman Paquito Diaz is ever on their trail, and as the trio make their way through the forest, a romantic rivalry develops between Roco and Salvador over Koronel. Inevitably, Diaz and his posse catch up with them and Roco is wounded in a shootout. Salvador and Koronel again manage to escape, dragging the badly wounded Roco with them, but while Salvador lay sleeping that night, Koronel, fearful that Roco is dying, slips away, finds Diaz and leads him back to their camp. Salvador and Roco are awakened by Diaz's demands of surrender, and when Koronel tries to convince them that it is their only option, she expresses her fear that Roco will die without medical treatment. She also professes her love for Roco, which infuriates Salvador, who turns his weapon on Koronel. But before he can fire, Salvador is shot and killed by Roco, who is then shot and killed himself by the police. (In Tagalog)

The Headhunters

1973 Roda Film Productions; 88 minutes/color
Director: Pablo Santiago; Screenwriter: Armando de Guzman; Cinematographers: Jose Batac Jr., Fermin Pagsisihan; Editor: Ben Barcelon; Filmscore: Tito Arevalo; Cast: Zaldy Zshornack, Vic Vargas, Eva Reyes, Eddie Garcia, Paquito Diaz, Van de Leon, Scarlett Revilla, Ben Perez, Lito Anzures, Ding Salvador, Rocco Montalban, Joaquin Fajardo, Ruben Ramos, ER Salazar, Elizabeth Oropesa, Lydia Galvez, Lilian Madrigal, Angel Confiado, Ben Dato, Alex Flores, Ben Sanchez, Alfonso Adriano, Nestor Brillantes, Josie Shoemaker, Turing Cleofas

One doesn't have to look hard to find the classic American western motif of cavalry vs. Indians in this offering from director Pablo Santiago. Set in 1930, the story concerns a tribe of headhunters in the hills of Nueva Vizcaya who have the unfortunate habit of appeasing their god by offering the heads of Christians (while also taking offense to the notion that they are cannibals—go figure). After tribesman Vic Vargas decapitates two locals to impress his bride-to-be (Elizabeth Oropesa), the cavalry are sent in to deal with the lawless tribe. Captain Eddie Garcia plans to beat the headhunters into submission, while peace loving lieutenant Zaldy Zshornack would prefer to negotiate a peace, and after building their fort near the hill where the headhunters reside, the cavalry manage to capture tribal princess Eva Reyes. Zshornack convinces Garcia to allow him to negotiate with the tribal chief, and Reyes leads him to her village, but Zshornack is taken prisoner upon arriving. He does make an impression on the chief, however, and during his stay with the headhunters he earns the chief's respect. When Garcia tries to rescue Zshornack, he too is captured, but together he and Zshornack manage to broker a peace with the tribal chief and convince him to travel into town and meet with the provincial mayor. This causes a major schism within the tribe, and a renegade faction breaks off which tries to thwart the peace process by attacking the remnant of Garcia's troops (now commanded by sergeant Paquito Diaz). The film concludes with a battle in which Garcia and Zshornack join with the chief and his tribe in putting down the renegade tribal faction, and peace is then established.

The film opens with two brutal beheadings as Vargas seeks to win over his bride-to-be Oropesa by bringing back the heads of Christians to offer to their god. He succeeds, as Oropesa is spilling over with pride upon seeing Vargas returning home with two heads in tow. The heads are then placed on poles and the tribe dances around them in a circle. All of this notwithstanding, the film goes to great lengths and through all sorts of contortions of logic to portray the tribe in a positive light, depicting them as reasonable people who genuinely seek peace—interesting, since their running around beheading Christians in order to please their god is the whole problem to begin with. And will their god be happy if they stop hacking off the heads of Christians? In fact, the cavalry come off in a less positive light, with Garcia initially prepared to kill the entire tribe, berating them as animals. Well ....

Zshornack was a matinee idol in the 1950s and '60s, and he managed to maintain his career since, though frankly he seems somewhat limited in his abilities as an actor. He basically gives a one-note performance. (In English)

Himala (Miracle)

1982 Lea Productions; 105 minutes/color
Director: Ishmael Bernal; Screenwriter: Ricardo Lee; Cinematographer: Sergio Lobo; Editor: Ike Jarlego, Jr.; Filmscore: Winston Raval; Cast: Nora Aunor, Veronica Palileo, Spanky Manikan, Gigi Duenas, Vangie Labalan, Ben Almeda, Laura Centeno, Pen Medina, Amable Quiambao, Cris Daluz, Aura Mijares, Joel Lamangan, Ray Ventura, Tony Angeles, Joe Gruta, Estela de Leon, Lem Garcellano, Cesar Dimaculangan, Vicky Castillo

In this thought provoking melodrama, Nora Aunor plays a young woman who has a divine visitation during a solar eclipse. She hears a voice calling to her (presumably the Madonna), and feeling that the voice is coming from a dead tree nearby, she drops to her knees at the root of the tree and goes into a trance. Afterward, she exhibits healing powers, and word of her abilities quickly spreads, bringing a deluge of visitors to the tiny country village from far and wide. It turns out to be quite an economic boon for the village; a ramshackle tavern opens with a well-stocked bar and compliment of hookers, roadside bandits find easy prey in the parade of pilgrims from all over, and people even sell T-shirts with Aunor's image. But after being raped, Aunor abruptly loses her healing powers and the village becomes a ghost town as the people become disillusioned. As a result of the rape, Aunor is soon revealed to be pregnant, and with the rape not being common knowledge, rumors quickly spread of an immaculate conception. Once more the village is besieged by thousands of people all clamoring to see Aunor. But when she addresses the crowd, she tells them the truth about her pregnancy, causing a crazed member of the crowd to shoot her. Aunor appears to die as the scene becomes chaotic, cripples being trampled by the panicked crowd. As Aunor's body is put in an ambulance and rushed to the hospital, a weeping remnant of true believers is left behind, and one can see the seeds of a religious movement taking root.

Director Ishmael Bernal delivers an impressive work here, and while he has at times used film to comment on hypocrisy within organized religion, he this time exhibits a disdain for the commercialization of religious faith and the fickle nature of the faithful. (In Tagalog)

Hindi Ka na Sisikatan ng Araw (You Will Never See the Sunrise)

1990 FPJ Productions; 118 minutes/color
Director: Pablo Santiago; Screenwriters: Pablo S. Gomez, Jose Bartolome; Cinematographer: Ver P. Reyes; Editor: Augusto Salvador; Filmscore: Jaime Fabregas, Nonong Buencamino; Cast: Fernando Poe Jr., Eddie Garcia, Monica Herrera, Romy Diaz, Cathy Mora, Janno Gibbs, R.R. Herrera, Mely Tagasa, Rudy Meyer, Danny Riel, Gamaliel Viray, Nanding Fernandez, Marvin Rafael, Angelo Vergel, Jess Vargas, Jimmy Reyes, Ernie David, Turko, Buddy Dator, Efren Belardo, Eddie Tuazon, Telly Babasa, Steve Alcarado, Bert Garon, Boy Santa Maria, Bebeng Amora, Nato Tanchingco, Pons de Guzman

In the third—and apparently final—meeting of Lt. Guerrero (Fernando Poe, jr.) and corrupt Judge Valderama (Eddie Garcia), Garcia is loosed from the premature grave he was placed in by Poe at the conclusion of Ako ang Huhusga (1989) when a couple of hapless grave robbers hear his cries for help. Once freed, Garcia resumes running his criminal empire without missing a beat, and has his men abduct Poe so that he can repay him in kind by burying him alive. Poe is rescued from his earthy grave by a troop of boy scouts who observe his burial from behind some bushes, and once he gathers himself, Poe once again single-handedly defeats Garcia's army of thugs before definitively putting an end to the evil judge by firing at him from a distance of a few yards with a bazooka.

The series had begun with Kapag Puno na ang Salop (1987), and picked up again with Ako ang Huhusga before climaxing here. This seems also to have been the final teaming of Poe and Garcia to date. Not long afterward, Garcia would become an enormously popular action hero himself with a constant string of action features. (In Tagalog with some English)

Hindi Laruan ang Puso (The Heart Is Not a Plaything)

1990 Seiko Films; 103 minutes/color
Director: Leroy Salvador; Screenwriter: Ricky Lee; Cinematographer: Clodualdo Austria; Editor: Ferren Salumbides; Filmscore: Benny Medina; Cast: Gretchen Barretto, Rita Avila, Cesar Montano, Raul Zaragoza, Marita Zobel, Romeo Rivera, Ramon D'Salva, Malu de Guzman, Dan Fernandez, Ramil Tolentino, Alma Lerma, Ann-Marie Falcon, Julie Ann Arpon

This fairly weightless romantic melodrama stars Gretchen Barretto and Rita Avila as cousins who become romantic rivals. Barretto is the good girl, sweet and lovely and from a humble background, while Avila is the bad girl, rich and spoiled, who enjoys the empowerment that her good looks bring. Avila has a tendency to spread herself around and hops from one boyfriend to the next. When Barretto arrives at Avila's birthday party, Avila immediately sets her sights on Raul Zaragoza, Barretto's date. It doesn't take Avila too long to get Zaragoza into bed, and she leaves her own beau (Cesar Montano) behind. The brokenhearted Montano is consoled by Barretto, and before long they begin a relationship of their own. When Avila finds that one of her cast-offs has wound up with Barretto, she becomes furious and begins an intense campaign to win Montano back. But despite Avila's best efforts, Barretto and Montano eventually marry. Aside from the trite concept, the film suffers from the cartoonish and clichéd nature of Avila's character. (In Tagalog with some English)

Hot Property

1983 Golden Dragons Films; 112 minutes/color Director: Lino Brocka; Screenwriter: Jose N. Carreon; Cinematographer: Conrado Baltazar; Editor: Efren Jarlego; Filmscore: Willie Yusi; Cast: Phillip Salvador, Carmi Martin, Dennis Roldan, Tony Santos Jr., Vic Diaz, Johnny Wilson, Rosanna Jover, Fred Param, Telly Babasa, Greg Santa Inez, Susan Africa

Opening with an assassination attempt on crime boss Vic Diaz, this sultry crime melodrama from director Lino Brocka largely revolves around a love triangle within Diaz's organization. Though he is married and has a child, Dennis Roldan is carrying on an affair with stripper Carmi Martin, who is herself involved in Diaz's diamond smuggling operation. Roldan is one of Diaz's most trusted men (although he was secretly Diaz's would-be assassin in the film's opening scene). Diaz recovers, and naturally suspects a rival crime organization of trying to muscle in on his various criminal enterprises (gambling, prostitution, smuggling). New man Phillip Salvador begins his own fling with Martin, and the two of them decide to get out of the crime business by ripping off one of Diaz's diamond transactions. But Diaz abducts Martin's younger sister and arranges an exchange of the girl for the diamonds. In an effective climax, the two parties meet in a dilapidated old mansion where a shootout ensues in which Diaz and Roldan are killed, and Martin is wounded. It is not clear whether or not Martin survives, since the film ends on a freeze-frame of Salvador hurriedly carrying her body from the building.

Brocka spices the narrative with plenty of softcore sex (Martin with Roldan and Salvador, alternately) and plenty of scenes of Martin on the job, including the opening sequence in which Martin, introduced as "the cleanest girl in town," comes on stage clad in only a towel. After stripping off the towel, she stands over a wash basin and proceeds to lather up and rinse off, after which male audience members are invited to come up on stage in turns, pick up the bar of soap and wash Martin over again (perhaps showing her spots she may have missed). Brocka's direction is solid, and the film is also helped by an interesting filmscore by Willie Yusi. (In Tagalog with some English)

Humanda Ka Mayor! Bahala na ang Diyos (Beware, Mayor! God Will Judge You)

1993 Regal Films/Golden Lions Productions; 112 minutes/color Director: Carlo J. Caparas; Screenwriters: Carlo J. Caparas, Gigi Javier Alfonso, Efren Montano; Filmscore: Rey Ramos: Cast: Kris Aquino, Aga Muhlach, Nida Blanca, Luis Gonzales, Dick Israel, Tommy Abuel, Robert Arevalo, Luz Valdez, Jeffrey Santos, Sunshine Cruz, Romy Diaz, Bomber Moran, Ramil Rodriguez, Ali Sotto, Gigi Javier Alfonso, Ernie Forte, Ernie David, Nonoy de Guzman, Eddie Tuazon, Boy Antiporda, Manny Rodriguez, Ronnie Francisco, Rey Fabian, Tony Tacorda

When Sunshine Cruz is murdered, her brother (Aga Muhlach) attempts to find out who is responsible. He is aided by reporter Kris Aquino, and they find out that all roads lead to maniacal provincial mayor Dick Israel and his band of well-armed goons. Aquino's boss (Robert Arevalo) tries to get her to back off the story, feeling that it is getting too dangerous, but when Luis Gonzales tells Aquino and Muhlach that he witnessed the abduction of Cruz and her boyfriend by Israel's men, Aquino confronts Israel during a live television interview. Shortly thereafter, Israel's men attempt to hijack Aquino's car, but she flees into the forest, and after being pursued for a day, she finds refuge at the home of Gonzales' family. But in the dead of night Israel's men show up, unaware that Muhlach has been following them. In a superb and atmospheric jungle shootout, Muhlach manages to gun down a number of Israel's top men (including Romy Diaz and Ernie David), but Aquino is captured nonetheless. Back at Israel's lavish home, Aquino is held hostage by the thoroughly insane mayor as federal law enforcement officers move in and surround the place. As Israel's men engage in a shootout with the feds, Muhlach manages to shoot his way into the house and capture Israel, and he is prepared to kill him. But Aquino and the police prevail over him to allow Israel to live and face justice. The film ends with a curious and wholly unnecessary postscript that informs the viewer that Israel managed to escape and went into hiding, living in disguise.

Directed by Carlo J. Caparas, the king of the true crime genre, this film is loosely based on the case of Calauan Mayor Antonio Sanchez, who was charged with the rape and murder of a young woman and her boyfriend. This is not, however, an actual accounting of the case, which makes the postscript fairly pointless. Thereafter, Caparas would begin focusing heavily on true crime docu-dramas, beginning with *The Vizconde Massacre: God Help Us!* (1993). *Humanda Ka Mayor!* is probably one of Caparas' better works overall, and is greatly aided by a good score by Rey Ramos. (In Tagalog with some English)

Hustler Squad

1976 Crown International; 97 minutes/color
Director: Cesar Gallardo; Cast: John Ericson, Karen Ericson, Lynda Sinclaire, Nory Wright, Liza Lorena, Johanna Raunio, Ramon Revilla, Ken Metcalfe, Vic Silayan, Vic Diaz, Leo Martinez, Joe Zucchero, Ramon D'Salva, Bruno Punzalan

Set in WWII, the story here concerns a plot by U.S. Army Sergeant John Ericson and Filipino guerrilla leader Ramon Revilla to assassinate four Japanese commanders on a small island in the Philippines. They recruit four women (Lynda Sinclaire, Nory Wright, Liza Lorena, and Johanna Raunio) and have them infiltrate a group of prostitutes sent to entertain at a party held in honor of the Japanese officers. The women first bed, then kill their targets and attempt to make their escape amid the chaos of an attack on the Japanese, headed by Revilla. Only Raunio survives and makes it to the boat offshore where Ericson is waiting to pick them up, which is somewhat ironic since she only accepted the dangerous assignment because she was already dying of some nondescript ailment.

Despite the obvious budgetary constrictions, director Cesar Gallardo makes the most of what he has to work with, and the film's title and concept notwithstanding, he gives the subject more serious treatment than most coproductions aimed at the exploitation market. The concluding battle is well done, and amid the many uncredited performances is character actor Vic Silayan, impressive as a more sympathetic Japanese officer. Surprisingly, even Revilla is unbilled, though he appears to have more screen time than American lead Ericson. (In English)

Ibulong Mo sa Diyos (Your Whisper to God)

1987 Regal Films; 126 minutes/color
Director: Elwood Perez; Screenwriter: Orlando Nadres; Cinematographer: Ricardo Jacinto; Editor: George Jarlego; Filmscore: Jaime Fabregas; Cast: Vilma Santos, Gary Valenciano, Miguel Rodriguez, Eric Quezon, Eddie Garcia, Barbara Perez, Nadia Montenegro, Nida Blanca, Armida Siguion-Reyna, Perla Bautista, Rachel Ann Wolfe, Deborah Sun, Ruben Rustia, Vangie Labalan, Sandy Garcia, Flora Gasser, Tony Mabesa, Joseph de Cordova, Subas Herrero, Romeo Rivera, Tony Carrion, Mia Gutierrez, Ernie Zarate

There may be no better example of the Filipino soap opera genre than this tragic, lengthy tearjerker that somehow manages to slowly snake its way to a happy ending. Vilma Santos plays a dancer who is in love with singer Gary Valenciano, but she is heartbroken when she leaves for an extended engagement in Japan. Her boss, choreographer Miguel Rodriguez, rapes her, and not wanting to lose her job, Santos allows herself to be bullied into a relationship with him. Valenciano returns, and he and Santos briefly enjoy a reunion until he discovers her relationship with Rodriguez and leaves in a huff. The distraught Santos then wanders the streets in a daze and is hit by a car driven by wealthy businessman Eddie Garcia, who drives her to the hospital, pretending to be only a concerned passerby who found her lying in the street. Santos is left blinded by the accident, and the guilt-stricken Garcia takes her home to his mansion where he falls in love with her. As a result of her brief reunion with Valenciano, Santos winds up pregnant and gives birth to a son. Discovering Santos' whereabouts, Rodriguez shows up, and belligerent as ever, tries to force himself on her again, but seeing the baby and assuming it to be his, he settles for taking the child. Santos' good friend Eric Quizon, who is himself secretly in love with Santos (well, now, join the club), confronts Rodriguez and tries to take the baby back (no need to get the police involved now), but winds up stabbing and killing Rodriguez in the process. Quizon is sent to prison, but it happens that he is dying of an inoperable brain tumor (Oh no! Not that!). Before dying, Quizon agrees to donate his eyes to be used in an operation that will restore Santos' sight, and after the operation proves successful, Santos rejects Valenciano's attempts at reconciliation, agreeing instead to marry Garcia. The heartbroken Valenciano is invited to sing at the wedding, which he does—but wait! We're not finished yet! After exchanging vows, Garcia is shot and killed by his jilted ex-lover (Barbara Perez), and during the ensuing struggle the gun goes off again, injuring Santos' baby. The baby is saved by a blood transfusion from Valenciano, and Santos then finally reveals to him that he is actually the baby's father. The film then ends happily with Santos, Valenciano and their baby strolling through the park together. Presumably, they live happily ever after on Garcia's fortune. You see, it all did work out in the end.

Wow. How many tragic and unlikely circumstances can you squeeze into a paltry ... two-plus hours? Though the performances are mostly good, and Elwood Perez at least shows an interesting sense of composition, the film is so weighed down in clichés that it goes well beyond parody and winds up playing like one long superfluous joke. There are also some rather cartoonishly villainous characters; not only the thoroughly despicable Rodriguez, but also Armida Siguion-Reyna, typecast again as the most hateful woman in the world, here playing a wealthy sadist who employs Santos' mother (Nida Blanca) as a maid and enjoys terrorizing her by taking potshots at her with a revolver.

The episodic nature of the narrative would lead one to think that, like many such soaps, the film may have been adapted from a komiks novella, but the credits don't say specifically, so more than likely the filmmakers merely aped the tried and true formula. The running time could only have been supported by a more inventive story. (In Tagalog with some English)

Igorota

1968 Nepomuceno Productions; 85 minutes/color

Director: Luis Nepomuceno; Screenwriter: Cesar J. Amigo; Cinematographer: Loreto Isleta; Editor: Elsa Abutan; Filmscore: Tito Arevalo; Cast: Charito Solis, Ric Rodrigo, Mario Monte (Montenegro), Eddie Garcia, Fred Galang, Eva Darren, Ben Perez, Cachupoy, Tita de Villa, Ernesto la Guardia, Lanie Gentica, Stella Mapua

Ric Rodrigo is hunting in the hills when he comes across a tribe of Igorots, and while staying with them he falls in love with tribal princess Charito Solis. She likewise falls for him, and though she is told that the "spirits" do not look kindly on the union, she professes her undying love for Rodrigo, and they are wed in a tribal ceremony. Rodrigo then takes Solis back to his mansion in the city, and while she is warmly greeted by Rodrigo's father, the rest of the family belittle her as a primitive savage. Solis is very visibly uncomfortable with the family's Catholic customs, including everything from the official wedding ceremony she and Rodrigo undergo in the Church to the simple act of saying grace at the dinner table. As time passes, Solis and Rodrigo have a baby girl, and when the child is old enough to attend school, she is cruelly taunted by the other children, who mockingly chant "Igorota." Solis herself is enduring another round of taunts from her sister-in-law and all of her society friends, who goad Solis into baring her breasts like a primitive savage. Solis then grabs a spear from the wall and threatens the roomful of women, forcing them to kneel before her, and when her brother-in-law (Eddie Garcia) enter the room and snatches the spear away from her, a struggle ensues between them. Hearing the commotion, Solis' daughter races from her room and tumbles down the stairs to her death. After this awful tragedy, Solis leaves the city and returns to her people, followed soon afterward by Rodrigo. Upon arriving in Solis' village, however, Rodrigo is challenged to a duel to the death by Solis' brother (Mario Montenegro), who claims that Rodrigo's family has dishonored Solis. Rodrigo reluctantly complies, and as they struggle, Montenegro slips and falls from a cliff to his death. Rodrigo is then killed by a hatchet to the head, courtesy of the jilted Igorot suitor that Solis left behind (Gee, you mean the noble Igorots are not above such things as petty jealousy?), and Solis then spears Rodrigo's killer through the gut. The film then ends with Solis stripping naked and jumping from the mountain to her death, after which her birth tree (planted by her father when she was born) is struck by lightning, catches fire, and collapses to the ground.

The embarrassingly over-stated premise of the narrative is, simply, Christian bad, pagan good. Aside from the character of Rodrigo's father, the Christian characters are so cartoonish that it is impossible to take the film seriously (Rodrigo's character is presumably Catholic, though he never expresses religious faith of any sort). The film goes to risible and all-too-obvious lengths to paint the Igorots as wise and noble, while the city-dwelling Catholics are condescending, cruel and greedy. Igorot—good; Catholic—bad. Got it?

Despite the film's hamfisted commentary, it went on to dominate the FAMAS Awards that year, winning Best Picture, Best Director, Best Actress (Solis), Supporting Actor (Fred Galang), Best Cinematography, Editing, Filmscore, and Sound (Juanito Clemente). Oh, well. The film was shot in English in an attempt for some significant international distribution. (In English)

Ikaw! (You!)

1968 Virgo Film Productions; 105 minutes/color

Director: Luis Enriquez (Eddie Rodriguez); Screenwriters: Luis Enriquez (Eddie Rodriguez), Dianing Rivera; Cinematographer: Ricardo Remias; Editor: Fely Crisostomo; Filmscore: Tony Maiquez; Cast: Eddie Rodriguez, Lolita Rodriguez, Marlene Dauden, Renato Robles, Alfonso Carvajal, Patricia Mijares, Lauro Delgado, Joe Sison, Rebecca Gonzales, Maritess Quintana, Annabelle Reyes

In this standard soaper, Eddie Rodriguez plays a married congressman who begins an affair with a nurse who tends to him during a brief illness. Unable to hide the affair, Rodriguez separates from his wife, but this only makes things worse since he misses his two young daughters. Eventually, guilt gets the better of Rodriguez's mistress, and she leaves him. Rodriguez tries to reconcile with his wife, but finds her unreceptive as she leaves, taking the children with her. The running time consists largely of anguished conversations between the principals, and the only noteworthy aspect of the film is the thoroughly unhappy ending with Rodriguez sitting miserably alone. (In Tagalog)

Ikaw Ay Akin (You Are Mine)

1978 Tagalog Ilang-Ilang Productions; 116 minutes/color

Director: Ishmael Bernal; Screenwriter: Jose Carreon; Cinematographer: Sergio Lobo; Editor: Augusto Salvador; Filmscore: The Vanishing Tribe; Cast: Nora Aunor, Vilma Santos, Christopher de Leon, Nick Romano, Andrea Andolong, Nick Romano, Ellen Esguerra, Odette Khan, Zandro Zamora, Ven Medina, Angel Confiado, Renato Requiestas, Ernie Zarate, Ricky Rivero, Ogie Sanchez, Eddie Recto, Rose Gacula, Joey Sison, Cris Vertido

In this superstar roundup, Christopher de Leon plays a young businessman in a relationship with Nora Aunor. But after meeting kooky Vilma Santos, de Leon is pursued by her and soon succumbs to her charms. Feeling very conflicted, de Leon continues relationships with both women, but that is only fermenting trouble, and the jealous Santos begins to come unhinged, almost running de Leon down with her car one night when she catches him leaving Aunor's apartment. Eventually, de Leon comes clean with both women and apologizes for his caddish behavior. So whom does he end up with? Who cares? The film closes with a hysterical moment where Santos goes to see Aunor, apparently to apologize and make peace. Unable to find the right words to express herself, Santos merely stares at Aunor, who stares back quizzically—for three full minutes! Awful!

When one considers some of the impressive work done by director Ishmael Bernal, as well as the film's three stars, it's hard to believe that, for their only gathering as a group, the best that they could do was to offer this exceedingly ordinary overdose of tree sap. Still, love sagas like this one are so popular in the Philippines that this is likely to have been exactly what the audience wanted to see these three actors in. Certainly, this was familiar territory for each of the film's three stars, but one would have hoped for something more interesting from Bernal. (In Tagalog with some English)

Ikaw Lang (Only You)

1993 Movie Stars Productions/Silver Screen/Cinestars; 114 minutes/color

Director: Chito S. Rono; Screenwriters: Chito S. Rono, Humilde "Meek" Roxas, Gina Tagasa-Gil, Tom Adrales; Cinematographer: Jun Dalawis; Editor: Renato de Leon; Filmscore: Mon del Rosario; Cast: Vilma Santos, Ronnie Ricketts, Cesar Montano, Zeny Zabala, Dencio Padilla, Janine Barredo, Roldan Aquino, Vangie Labalan, Cris Daluz, Feling Cudia, Aurora Yumul

Librarian Vilma Santos thinks she's found her Prince Charming in Cesar Montano, and when she gets pregnant, she and Montano marry in a hasty civil ceremony. They go to live in the gothic home of Montano's mother, but Santos is given a very frosty reception by her new mother-in-law. It quickly becomes obvious that Montano's mother is not merely verbally abusive, but is also mentally disturbed, if not outright insane: her dogs lounge around atop the dinner table during meals, and Santos witnesses her force-feeding dog food to one of the maids. Montano begins to show signs of mental instability himself; one night Santos awakens to find the drunken Montano standing over the bed urinating on her before he passes out. Not surprisingly, Santos decides to leave, and knowing that she will need money to take care of her newborn baby, she tries to steal some from the family safe. But Montano catches her, and begins beating her in a rage: so badly, in fact, that he thinks he's killed her. He puts the body in a sack and tries to get rid of it by throwing it over the side of a bridge, unaware that a small fishing boat is underneath the bridge, whose occupants are sheltering themselves from the rain. The occupants of the boat fish Santos out of the water and take her home to nurse her (why is it that none of these people ever contact the authorities or take them to the hospital?).

When Santos recovers, she wants desperately to get her child back, but still needing money, she acquires a gun and robs a bank. Coincidentally, she robs a bank which has already been marked for robbery by Ronnie Ricketts and Dencio Padilla. No sooner does Ricketts enter the bank than Santos runs out and the tellers are screaming for the police. Ricketts and Padilla give chase and manage to get Santos into a Mexican standoff, but with the police closing in, the three of them escape together. Later, at the abode of Ricketts and Padilla, the three of them form a partnership, robbing banks and supermarkets together. In time, Santos returns to Montano's house for her son, bringing Ricketts and Padilla as back-up—and she needs it. During her time away, Montano and his mother have curiously hired an army of armed guards, and Ricketts and Padilla are forced to engage them in a firefight. With all of the gunfire, someone actually calls for the police, and when they show up, Santos attempts to leave with her son, at which point Montano grabs a gun and rushes outside to stop her and is promptly gunned down by the police. The film ends happily with Ricketts and Santos marrying, and apparently owing no debt to society for their Bonnie and Clyde exploits.

This is really like two separate films; the first half—which is far more interesting—dealing with Santos unsettling experiences within her insane mother-in-law's house has an appealing gothic flavor, and makes one wish that the film had stayed along that tack. The second half, while still unsettling, covers much more familiar territory, liberally spiced with humor. Regarding the sudden appearance of armed guards at the climax, this would seem to be in consideration of Ricketts' fans, who expect to see him do a fair amount of shooting in his films. (In Tagalog with some English)

Impaktita (Demon Woman)

1989 Regal Films; 114 minutes/color
Director: Teddy Chiu; Screenwriter: Bugsy Dabao; Cinematographer: Vic Anao; Editor: Edgardo Vinarao; Filmscore: Demet Velasquez; Cast: Jean Garcia, Richard Gomez, Aga Muhlach, Nida Blanca, Gloria Romero, Rez Cortez, Ruel Vernal, Romeo Rivera, Mario Escudero, Ruben Rustia, Toby Alejar, R.R. Herrera, Judy Ann Santos, Richard King, Lucy Quinto, Pons de Guzman, Harvey Vizcarra, Ruther Batuigas, Dexter Doria, Vic Belaro, Dante Castro, Dante Belen, Mel Arca

Jean Garcia stars as a young woman whose adoptive parents found her abandoned as an infant and took her home to raise as their own. Garcia grows up not knowing that her mother (Gloria Romero) was an aswang, a kind of winged vampire beast, and although she seems to be a perfectly normal young lady, Garcia's gang rape at the hands of a local group of thugs causes a startling transformation. She sprouts wings, fangs and claws, seeks out her attackers and exacts a bloody revenge. Unfortunately, the film digresses for some youthful romance when Garcia meets reporter Aga Muhlach and must choose between her feelings for him and those that she has for her hometown sweetheart (Richard Gomez). The film then begins to lose its bearings as Muhlach uses his connections to get Garcia a job as a fashion model. Basically, the film becomes a cliché-ridden mess about another small town girl gone to the big city to find fame and fortune. But Garcia again experiences a transformation and flies back to her village to kill the rest of the gang that raped her. Muhlach comes to realize that Garcia is an Aswang, and he and Gomez put aside their rivalry long enough to bring in priest Ruben Rustia to exorcise the evil from Garcia.

To be fair to director Teddy Chiu and screenwriter Bugsy Dabao, the film was adapted from a komiks serial, which accounts for the runaway plot, but they would have been wise to excise some of the plot elements. What starts out as an interesting story steeped in rural superstitions almost disintegrates amid all of the youthful love triangle trappings and poor-girl-makes-good drivel. The film is overlong anyway, and freeing it of such baggage would certainly have given it an easier flow. As it is, the last half of the film is very tedious. (In Tagalog)

Impakto (Demon)

1995 Regal Filmsl; 100 minutes/color
Director: Don Escudero; Screenwriter: Wali Ching; Cinematographer: Ely Cruz; Editor: Danny Gloria; Filmscore: Jaime Fabregas; Cast: Gelli de Belen, Antonio Aquitania, Daria Ramirez, Ernie Zarate, Cherry Pie Picache, Rochelle Barrameda, Candy Pangilinan, Mon Confiado, Ama Quiambao, Mike Austria

This superior horror effort by director Don Escudero is a stark anti-abortion statement wherein Gelli de Belen accepts an appointment as nanny for the infant son of doctor Ernie Zarate. Upon arriving at Zarate's home, de Belen finds the surroundings gloomy, the family even more so, with Zarate being rather abrupt and his wife (Daria Ramirez) positively morose. Puzzled by how the constantly wailing baby is always kept in a dark room with the curtains drawn, de Belen begins to experience disturbing nightmares, and is stunned one day while holding the baby when it bites her on the neck. De Belen finally learns the truth after seeing the bloodied household maid knocked down a flight of stairs by the now monstrous baby, and while Zarate takes the maid's body out to dispose of it, Ramirez tells de Belen the sordid family secret: a large part of Zarate's income has been from performing abortions (which are illegal in the Philippines), and when their teenage son had gotten his girlfriend pregnant, Zarate convinced the two of them that abortion was the answer. The experience proved traumatic for the patient, who died, and for Zarate's son as well, who committed suicide, and when Ramirez tried to dispose of the fetus, she was shocked to find that it was still alive. As a result of the shock, Ramirez fainted, and the fetus managed to find its way inside of her and she carried it to term. This pleased Zarate, who believed that the child was his and could serve as a replacement for the son that they had lost. The film climaxes with the monstrous child going on a bloody rampage through the house, during which it kills Zarate before dissolving into a puddle of water when de Belen opens the curtains and lets the sunlight in.

Fiercely unapologetic regarding its point of view, the film reaches the height of its commentary when Zarate dumps the dead body of the maid in the forest behind the house, where he has for years disposed of aborted fetuses, and is then attacked by a swarm of said fetuses, which emerge from the ground. Escudero does an excellent job directing, and unlike his *Multo In the City* (1993), he manages here to avoid the use of comedic characters that destroy the atmosphere. Escudero had previously served as screenwriter on the horror anthology film *Shake Rattle and Roll 2* (1990), in which the first story, "Multo," was a gruesome anti-abortion commentary. (In Tagalog)

Ina, Kasusuklaman Ba Kita? (Mother, Should I Despise You?)

1984 Seiko Films; 118 minutes/color

Director: Pio de Castro III; Screenwriter: Raquel Villavicencio; Cinematographer: Clodualdo Austria; Editor: Edgardo Vinarao; Filmscore: Willy Cruz; Cast: Rita Gomez, Dante Rivero, Liza Lorena, Mark Gil, Michael de Mesa, Lorna Tolentino, Carol Dauden, Charlie Davao, Jaime Fabregas, Moody Diaz, Madie Gallaga, Lollie Mara, Linda Montenegro, Madeleine Nicolas, Ernie Forte, Cris Daluz, Fred Capulong, Aurora Yumul, Len Ag. Santos

Successful businesswoman Rita Gomez does not believe in marriage, and so has three children out of wedlock by three different men. The children grow up resenting their mother and the way in which she prevents them each from having relationships with their respective fathers. The son (Michael de Mesa) grows up very emotionally troubled, and when he and one of his two sisters (Carol Dauden in her debut) are killed in a car accident, their remaining sibling (Lorna Tolentino) seeks a relationship with her father (Dante Rivero), whom she has not seen since she was a child. She finds that Rivero is in prison, but is scheduled to be released soon, and when he gets out Tolentino uses her mother's money to set Rivero up in an apartment with his wife (Liza Lorena), and even helps them start their own business. When Gomez discovers all of this, it causes a major rift between mother and daughter, and Tolentino leaves home to move in with her father. Things begin to crumble for Gomez, who loses her business and is forced to sell her mansion and move into an apartment. In time, Tolentino is convinced by her father and her boyfriend (Mark Gil) to make amends with Gomez, and the film ends with mother and daughter embracing.

The performances are all good, and the direction by Pio de Castro III is also well handled, none of which negates the fact that this is nothing more than glorified soap opera. The screenplay by Raquel Villavicencio was adapted from a komik serial. (In Tagalog and English)

Inay (Mother)

1977 Lotus Films, Inc.; 108 minutes/color

Director: Lino Brocka; Screenwriter: Jose Dalisay; Cinematographer: Jose Batac, Jr.; Editor: Augusto Salvador; Filmscore: Ernani Cuenco; Cast: Alicia Vergel, Dindo Fernando, Chanda Romero, Orestes Ojeda, Laurice Guillen, Dexter Doria, Ace Vergel, Hilda Koronel, Fred Montilla, Maea Atger, Mely Mallari, Aida Carmona, Peachy Atutubo, Doming Landicho

This uncharacteristically bland offering from director Lino Brocka stars Alicia Vergel as a middle-aged woman who has a knack for alienating her adult children. As the film opens, Vergel is living in the home of her eldest son (Dindo Fernando) and his wife (Laurice Guillen), but decides to leave when her crass, obnoxious and overbearing behavior frequently reduces Guillen to tears. Vergel moves on to the luxurious home of her middle son (Orestes Ojeda) and his wife (Dexter Doria), but she feels out of place among Doria and her snobbish friends, a feeling encouraged by Doria in order to more quickly drive Vergel away. It works, and Vergel moves on to the home of her daughter (Chanda Romero). Trying to make a peso holding meditation classes in her home, Romero tolerates Vergel's disruptions, but when Vergel drives away Romero's much older boyfriend, that seems to be the last straw. Vergel moves on to the apartment of Ace Vergel, the baby of the family, but she proves to be a major obstacle to the young man's lifestyle. Still, the film manages to end happily, with Vergel returning to Fernando's home and being overjoyed to see her new grandchild. Anyone who recalls Vergel from her glory days in the 1950s will likely be disheartened to see her here: she makes Rosanne Barr look demure. As for Brocka, he's definitely marking time here. (In Tagalog)

Init sa Tag-Ulan
(Heat in the Rainy Season)

1996 Good Harvest/Regal Films; 113 minutes/color

Director/screenwriter: Ramje; Cinematographer: Eduardo Cabrales; Editor: Rogelio Salvador; Filmscore: Marita Manuel; Cast: Ara Mina, Raymond Keannu, Jorge Estregan (George Estregan, Jr.), Dan Fernandez, Ramon Recto, Daniel Pasia, Berting Labra, Tony Mabesa, Rando Almansor, Bobby Benitez, Dante Castro, Lou Veloso, Panyang, Melissa Buencamino, Rowena Deyto

In this erotic ghost story, Ara Mina plays a virginal young woman living in a gothic house in the year 1896. She falls in love with the painting of a deceased young man, and after taking it home and hanging it in her bedroom, she is visited nightly by a spectral lover. The film then jumps forward 100 years to reveal that Mina is still living in the house, and strangely enough, is still a young woman. She is also still having a love affair with the ghost of the man in the painting. Two escaped convicts (Raymond Keannu and Jorge Estregan) seek refuge in Mina's house, and after getting over the shock of finding them in her home, Mina allows them to stay. The boys begin to feel at home, but when Estregan attempts to rape Mina, he is killed by her phantom lover. Though he doesn't fully understand what has happened, Keannu helps Mina dispose of Estregan's body, which they haul to a nearby cemetery. But while burying him, they are observed by drunken hunchback Berting Labra, who runs to the police. While the police are busy recovering Estregan's body and searching the area for Keannu, Mina and Keannu are back at the house succumbing to their mutual attraction. Once they consummate their relationship, Mina's ghostly lover returns to the painting, and after Mina tells her incredible tale to Keannu, they decide to bury the painting as well. But the man in the painting won't stay buried, and after the painting shoots up out of the ground, Mina's century-old lover steps out of the picture and appears in the flesh. He tries to drag Mina away, but is vanquished once and for all when Keannu sets fire to the painting. Mina and Keannu then embrace, but Mina deteriorates into an old crone.

The special effects are primitive and tend to detract from the film, but director Ramje (who also wrote the screenplay) still manages to deliver an intriguing, claustrphobic narrative with a nice gothic flavor. Even Estregan's usual over-playing doesn't get in the way, and there is an effectively atmospheric score by Marita Manuel. Dan Fernandez has a fair amount of screen time in what amounts to a throwaway role as a policeman tracking Keannu and Estregan. (In Tagalog)

Insiang

1976 Cinemanila Corporation; 93 minutes/color

Director: Lino Brocka; Screenwriters: Mario O'Hara, Lamberto E. Antonio; Cinematographer: Conrado Baltazar; Editor: Augusto Salvador; Filmscore: Minda Azarcon; Cast: Hilda Koronel, Mona Lisa, Ruel Vernal, Rez Cortez, Marlon Ramirez, Nina Lorenzo, Mely Mallari, Carpi Asturias, George Atutubo, Eddie Pagayon, Joe Jardi, Danny Posadas, Estrella Antonio, Jimmy Calaguas, Belen Chicote, Tommy Yap

As the title character, Hilda Koronel stars as a young woman living with her mother (Mona Lisa) in the slums of Manila. She is raped by Lisa's lover (Ruel Vernal), and then begins to concoct a plan of vengeance by manipulating Vernal by leading him into an affair, which drives Lisa into a jealous rage that causes her to murder Vernal. The film is considered by many to be director Lino Brocka's best work—it isn't, but it is a very impressive film. (In Tagalog)

Isang Araw Walang Diyos
(One Day Without God)

1989 Regal Films; 126 minutes/color

Directors: Peque Gallaga, Lorenzo Reyes; Screenwriters: Peque Gallaga, Don Escudero, Lorenzo Reyes; Cinematographer: Eduardo F. Jacinto; Editor: Augusto Salvador; Filmscore: Dionisio Buencamino, Jr.; Cast: Richard Gomez, Janice de Belen, Edu Manzano, Alice Dixson, Eric Quizon, Joey Marquez, Manilyn Reynes, Aiko Melendez, Chuckie Dreyfus, Smokey Manaloto, Isabel Granada, Carmina Villaroel, Romy Romulo, Tito Arevalo, Rey Solo, Crispin Medina, Sammy Brillantes, Ray Ventura, Ronnie Quizon, Mary Walter, Raquel Villavicencio, Lucy Quinto, Susan Quinto, Rudy Castillo, Mae Ann Adonis

This is a very effective combat story wherein army lieutenant Richard Gomez leads a squadron into Mindanao to deal with a bizarre religious cult that has been terrorizing the people of a small village. The cultists, led by Tito Arevalo, enter the local church and brutally massacre a group of nuns, but nun Janice de Belen, seeing the attack coming, is able to escape into a hidden basement chamber with a group of orphans. They are found there by Gomez, and the government soldiers soon find themselves barricaded in the small church with de Belen, the orphans, and television reporter Edu Manzano and his crew. The church is eventually overrun by the cultists, but Gomez and de Belen manage to escape with a number of the children and a handful of soldiers. Manzano also survives the ordeal.

This is an excellent work by the filmmaking team of Peque Gallaga and Lorenzo Reyes, which makes the frivolous nature of much of their work all the more exasperating. The film's climactic battle scene is very gripping, but as is so often the case in film, the best moments are not the showiest. There is, for instance, a moment early in the film when de Belen sees the approach of the cultists, somehow made more ominous by the slow-motion photography, and hurriedly gathers the children together to hide them. There is also the tense moment when soldier Eric Quizon accompanies Manzano on a reconnaissance mission. While driving along a narrow dirt road, they run right into the cultists, and after Quizon falls from the jeep, Manzano quickly backs the jeep back down the road and is forced to leave Quizon behind. After being captured, Quizon is bound and dragged to the church where Gomez is unable to negotiate his freedom, but he leads Quizon in a defiant recitation of the oath of the Filipino soldier as the cultists drag Quizon back into the jungle.

The film also contains a very effective performance by comedian Joey Marquez as a government soldier who is given a lookout position in a pigeon coop. There may be no more strikingly grim moment than the sight of Marquez covered in pigeon droppings and going mad from listening all night to the agonizing screams of Quizon being tortured in the distance.

For his performance here, Tito Arevalo won the Best Supporting Actor trophy at the 1990 Film Academy of the Philippines awards, while Eduardo Jacinto won for Best Cinematography. (In Tagalog with some English)

Iskalawag: Ang Batas ay Batas (Scalawag: The Law Is the Law)

1997 Star Cinema; 104 minutes/color
Director: Francis "Jun" Posadas; Screenwriters: Jose Carreon, Francis "Jun" Posadas, Sonny Saret Abelardo; Cinematographer: Joe Batac, Jr.; Editor: Danilo Gloria; Filmscore: Nonong Buencamino; Cast: Raymart Santiago, Gelli de Belen, Victor Neri, Ronaldo Valdez, Daria Ramirez, Bembol Roco, Dennis Roldan, Dick Israel, Bob Soler, Manjo del Mundo, Jim Rosales, Polly Cadsawan, Leo Lazaro, Vic Belaro, Edgar Santiago, Ernie David, Lora Luna, King Gutierrez, Roldan Aquino, Bon Vibar, Chrisma Tigman, Cris Daluz, Ira Garcia, Ramil Rodriguez, Lucita Soriano, Banjo Romero, Mike Castillo

In this absorbing action/melodrama, young police academy graduate Raymart Santiago is quickly disillusioned by his experiences on active duty. His partner, veteran officer Roldan Aquino, routinely abuses his authority, taking bribes for parking tickets and muscling free lunches from local eateries. After some high-profile busts, Santiago is moved to the vice squad under sergeant Bembol Roco, where he finds that things are not so nickel and dime. Roco and his boys have a close affiliation with a criminal organization involved in any number of robberies and kidnappings. Santiago finds that his father, police major Ronaldo Valdez, is no help since he too is involved on the fringes of the illegal organization. Santiago increasingly finds himself in collusion with Roco and his men, causing a personality change that puts a strain on his marriage to Gelli de Belen, who takes their child and leaves. One day on the job as Santiago is riding with Roco, they witness a kidnapping, and against Roco's orders, Santiago attempts to thwart it. Chasing one of the suspects down, Santiago is shocked to find that it is his best friend (Victor Neri). When Santiago is caught in the crossfire of the ensuing shootout, he is wounded, and knowing that Roco and his men would just as soon see him dead, Neri pulls Santiago into the getaway van and drives off with him. Neri and his gang doctor Santiago up and let him know that the police will be coming, not for them, but for him. Neri and his boys are part of a group of criminals that are not only under Roco's protection, but also that of congressman Bob Soler. When the police do arrive, Neri takes a round of bullets to save Santiago's life, and Santiago is forced to kill cop Dick Israel. Meanwhile, Valdez has attempted to bow out of his alliance with Soler, and narrowly survives a group of hit men who come gunning for him. In the end, father and son join forces to defeat Soler's gang (including Roco), and Valdez then surrenders to his son and faces charges of graft.

While police corruption and dirty politicians are by now very well established stock concepts in Filipino films, what stands out here is the more detailed and realistic characterization of Santiago's naïve young rookie. He is terrified during his first shootout, amusing his fellow officers by vomiting after his first shooting. The father and son conflict also provides an interesting situation, and both Santiago and Valdez give very strong performances. (In Tagalog with some English)

Isla: The Young Version

1996 Four Aces Entertainment; 102 minutes/color

Director/screenwriter: Celso Ad. Castillo; Cinematographer: Isagani F. Sioson; Editor: Ruben Pantua; Filmscore: Nonong Buencamino; Cast: Via Veloso, Ronaldo Valdez, Jean Saburit, Tonton Gutierrez, Anthony Cortez, Rachel Lobangco, Anna Capri, Dick Israel, Raquel Romero, Roldan Aquino, Larry Silva, Wilfredo Milan, Sylvia Sanchez, Johnny Vicar, Allan Paule, Alma Antonio, Prospero Luna, Ernie Zarate

One of the most consistently interesting Filipino filmmakers over the past 30 years, Celso Ad. Castillo chose here to remake his 1983 film *Isla* (which is the name of the lead character). Newcomer Via Veloso plays a teenage girl caught in an incestuous relationship with her abusive alcoholic father (Ronaldo Valdez). Veloso is forced into sex by Dick Israel as well, but when Israel returns home to find his wife in a compromising moment with Tonton Gutierrez, he goes beserk. While battering Gutierrez, Israel is stabbed by his wife, and taking the knife, Gutierrez finishes the job. Policeman Roldan Aquino arrives, and quickly suspects Veloso of Israel's murder after learning of her having had sex with him, which was incidentally witnessed by a young woman. But before long, Aquino hits on the truth and arrests Gutierrez. Veloso continues to suffer at the hands of her father, and while the whole town is excitedly watching the construction of the Ferris wheel of a visiting carnival to the island, Valdez again rapes Veloso while in a drunken state. The following day, Valdez suffers a fatal heart attack while riding the Ferris wheel, and the stunned Veloso wanders down the beach where feelings of liberation set in and she joyously strips off her clothes and runs into the ocean.

Castillo's execution is first rate, but the whole enterprise seems too deliberate in its pursuit of controversy—incest, the rape of a teenage girl—and while those are, after all, central to the drama, there are gratuitous elements that seem to be no more than an excuse for Castillo to indulge in his favorite pastime of pushing the envelope, such as the thoroughly obnoxious moment when Veloso amuses herself by watching the blind village idiot (Larry Silva) masturbating on the beach.

Veloso gives a very good performance in her debut, and the cast all impress, including the expected strong performance from Valdez. All in all, it's a mixed bag, though. In 1996 Castillo also remade another of his older works, 1983's *Virgin People*, with much more impressive results. (In Tagalog)

Itim (Black)

1976 Cinema Artists; 105 minutes/color

Director: Mike de Leon; Screenwriters: Clodualdo del Mundo, Gil Quito; Cinematographers: Ely Cruz, Rody Lacap; Editor: Ike Jarlego, Jr.; Filmscore: Max Jocson; Cast: Tommy Abuel, Charo Santos, Mario Montenegro, Mona Lisa, Sarah Joaquin, Susan Valdez, Moody Diaz

Mike de Leon made his feature directorial debut with this impressive, haunting ghost story starring Tommy Abuel as a photographer who becomes infatuated with Charo Santos, a melancholy young woman he snaps a photo of during a wake. After meeting her, Abuel is drawn into unraveling the mystery regarding the disappearance years earlier of Santos' older sister, and eventually finds that his disabled father (Mario Montenegro) is a key player in the answer to the mystery. The film is atmospheric, in the best tradition of the genre, and de Leon proves a remarkably sure and mature artist for someone making his debut. He also has a sophisticated understanding of the genre and takes a subtle approach. (In Tagalog)

Jaguar

1979 Bancom Audiovision Corp.; 123 minutes/color

Director: Lino Brocka; Screenwriters: Jose F. Lacaba, Ricardo Lee; Cinematographer: Conrado Baltazar; Editor: Rene Tala; Filmscore: The Vanishing Tribe; Cast: Phillip Salvador, Amy Austria, Johnny Delgado, Anita Linda, Menggie Cobarrubias, Sonny Gaston, Mario Escudero, Jimmy Santos, Joe Cunanan, Fred Param, Nonoy de Guzman, Eddie Gicoso, Nando Tiongson, Rey Tomenes, Eddie

Iaburiante, Aida Carmona, Domingo Landicho, Estrella Antonio, Joy Luna, Dexter Doria, Gigi Salvador, A.C. de Guia, Lando Jacob, Joe Viterbo, Cloyd Robinson

Phillip Salvador plays a security guard who accepts a job as bodyguard to magazine publisher Menggie Cobarrubias. When Cobarrubias steals Amy Austria away from Johnny Delgado, a fued erupts between the two men. Cobarrubias turns Austria into a super model, and although Salvador had always been loyal to his employer, he allows himself to be seduced by Austria, and the two of them fall in love. At a nightclub one night, a brawl breaks out between Cobarrubias, Delgado and their respective entourages, and Salvador pulls a gun and kills a man. Forced to flee and go into hiding, Salvador is aided by Austria, but eventually the police catch up and apprehend him. The film ends with Salvador sitting despondently in his prison cell. (In Tagalog)

Jesus Calderon: Maton (Jesus Calderon: Bully)

1993 Moviestars productions; 94 minutes/color
Director: Leonardo L. Garcia; Screenwriter: Humilde Roxas; Cinematographer: Jun Dalawis; Editor: Ruben Natividad; Filmscore: Mon del Rosario; Cast: Ronnie Ricketts, Isabel Granada, Miguel Rodriguez, Rina Reyes, Edgar Mande, Dencio Padilla, Nick Romano, Dinky Doo Jr., Mariel Salvador, Rudy Distrito, Onchie dela Cruz, Sonny Cabatu, Rommel Valdez, Usman Hassim, Dong Serrano

After putting up a valiant fight, snobby rich girl Isabel Granada falls in love with working class jeepney driver Ronnie Ricketts. This infuriates Granada's discarded suitor, wealthy gangster Miguel Rodriguez, who tries to do away with Ricketts. It all comes down to the usual climactic shootout in which both Ricketts and Granada are injured, while the police show up and apprehend Rodriguez. The body count is customarily high at the climax, as Ricketts guns down most of Rodriguez's men (the police get a few too), but what is not in keeping with the formula is the fact that Ricketts does not finish off his nemesis, but merely helps the police to arrest main heavy Rodriguez. This could indicate that the filmmakers may have had a sequel in mind, but if this were the case, it doesn't seem to have materialized. The first half of the film, which devotes itself to the developing romance between Ricketts and Granada, is surprisingly tender, but the latter half is typical action genre fodder. (In Tagalog)

Jose Rizal

1998 GMA Films; 175 minutes/color and black & white
Director: Marilou Diaz-Abaya; Screenwriters: Ricardo Lee, Jun Lana, Peter Ong Lim; Cinematographers: Manolo Abaya, Rody Lacap; Editors: Manet A. Dayrit, Jess Navarro; Filmscore: Nonong Buencamino; Cast: Cesar Montano, Joel Torre, Jaime Fabregas, Gloria Diaz, Gardo Versoza, Monique Wilson, Chin Chin Gutierrez, Pen Medina, Peque Gallaga, Bon Vibar, Subas Herrero, Tony Mabesa, Chiqui Xerex Burgos, Archie Adamos, Fritz Infante, Jhong Hilario, Gina Alajar, Tanya Gomez, Tess Dumpit, Crispin Medina, Mon Confiado, Gregg de Guzman, Eddie Aquino, Manolo Barrientos, Dennis Marasigan, Gilbert Onida, Troy Martino, Richard Merck, Tony Carreon, Nonie Buencamino, Cloyd Robinson, Kidlat Tahimik, Toto Natividad

This epic dramatization of the life of Philippine national hero Jose Rizal wound up being the most expensive Filipino film ever made, costing the equivalent of 2 million U.S. dollars; it was also proclaimed by some as the greatest Filipino film ever made, though that may have had more to do with its significance as a historical account of the most prominent and revered of all of the nation's historical figures rather with any artistic considerations. Which is not to suggest that the film was not well made; it is a lavishly produced and excellently photographed account of Rizal's life, with some very good performances, not the least of which would be Cesar Montano in the role of Rizal. The film went on to become the biggest box office grosser in the history of Philippine cinema. (In Tagalog with some Spanish and German)

Judge Max Asuncion: Hukom Bitay (Judge Max Asuncion: Hanging Judge)

1995 Viva Films; 118 minutes/color
Director: Francis "Jun" Posadas; Screenwriters: Amado Lacuesta, Francis "Jun" Posadas; Cinematographer: Johnny Araojo; Editor: Danilo Gloria; Filmscore: Nonong Buencamino; Cast: Eddie Garcia, Evangeline Pascual, Mat Ranillo III, Efren Reyes Jr., Rod Navarro, Luis Gonzales, Dick Israel, Perla Bautista, Roy Alvarez, Manjo del Mundo, Lovely Rivero, Pocholo Montes, Danny Labra, Jim Rosales, Shintaro Valdez, Michelle Parton, Berting Labra, Lennon Serrano, Dexter Doria, Dan Fernandez, Cloyd Robinson, Tony Mabesa, Rey Serrano, Lito Legaspi, Johnny Vicar, Robert Miller, Romy Romulo, Rolan Montes, Polly Cadsawan

In this true story, Eddie Garcia portrays Judge Asuncion as the film recounts some of his more high-profile cases, some of which lead to attempts on his life. For instance, one criminal conviction leads to a drive-by shooting in which the courthouse entrance is sprayed with gunfire. Though Garcia escapes without injury, fellow judge Luis Gonzales is fatally wounded. In another case, Garcia presides over the trial of Dan Fernandez, son of sleazy mayor Rod Navarro, who is convicted of rape and murder, prompting retaliation in the form of a hit squad headed by Dick Israel. In another drive-by shooting, Garcia again survives, and although his son is wounded, he manages to recover. The film winds down with the judge's elevation during the Aquino Administration, and his presiding over the trial of a military colonel accused of illegal arms possession. As he was caught with a rather large stash of weapons, a number of suspicions arise, including trafficking, and possible involvement with Marcos loyalists plotting a coup attempt. On the day of the colonel's trial, a coup attempt does indeed occur, delaying Garcia's arrival at the courthouse. In a rather remarkable display of devotion to duty (which some might say borders on insanity), Garcia drives through the streets, dodging gunfire and mortar shells, racing to the courthouse, only to wind up dismissing the case.

The film certainly paints an unsettling picture of the perils of the Philippine justice system, particularly for a judge as principled as Asuncion. Garcia shows himself to be an actor's actor, not only in the quality of his performance, but also by allowing himself to be given an unflattering make-up job in order to better resemble Asuncion. The film's principal drawback is the generic score by Nonong Buencamino. (In Tagalog with some English)

Kahit Singko Hindi Ko Babayaran ang Buhay Mo
(I Wouldn't Pay Five Cents for Your Life)

1990 Regal Films; 115 minutes/color
Director: Jesus Jose; Screenwriter: Joji Vitug; Cinematographer: Vic Anao; Editor: Rogelio Salvador; Filmscore: Jaime Fabregas; Cast: Lito Lapid, Alma Moreno, Tony Ferrer, Raoul Aragon, Robert Arevalo, Melissa Mendez, Dick Israel, Robert Talabis, Alicia Alonzo, Robert Talby, Rex Lapid, Ernie Zarate, Alex de Leon, Jim Rosales, Robert Miller, Usman Hassim, Amanda Amores, Apple Bautista, Amy Siotico, Boy Bagatsing, Philip Henson, Gerber Morado, Allan Garcia, Frank Lapid, Max Buaya, Avel Morado, Dante Belen

In this violent action film, Tony Ferrer portrays a corrupt congressman who seeks revenge against the police officer who killed his son in a shootout. After killing the officer responsible, Ferrer finds himself in a war with the officer's son (Lito Lapid), culminating in Lapid's killing of Ferrer's army of armed thugs before he does away with Ferrer by crushing him with a steam shovel. (In Tagalog with some English)

Kakabakaba Ka Ba?
(Are You Nervous?)

1980 D'Wonder Films; 103 minutes/color
Director: Mike de Leon; Screenwriters: Clodualdo "Doy" del Mundo, Raquel N. Villavicencio, Mike de Leon; Cinematographer: Rody Lacap; Editor: Ike Jarlego, Jr.; Filmscore: Jim Paredes; Cast: Christopher de Leon, Charo Santos, Jay Ilagan, Sandy Andolong, Boboy Garrovillo, Johnny Delgado, Armida Siguion-Reyna, Leo Martinez, Moody Diaz, Joe Jardi, Danny Javier, George Javier, Nanette Inventor, Bert Miranda, Tommy Yap, Ella Reyes, Marietta Santa Juana, Roger Vivero, Manny Tibayan, Lily Miraflor, Ike Jarlego Jr., Danny Rojo

Given the rather dour nature of most of his work, director Mike de Leon proves surprisingly adept at comedy in this lighthearted effort about a group of young adults who unwittingly become involved in a plot to take over the Philippines. The scheme by a group of underworld figures is to control the population by using opium to create a super communion host that will be taken during mass (in a heavily Catholic nation, this would, presumably, affect the majority of the population). The kids wind up defeating the bad guys during a climactic rock opera sequence. De Leon seems to have a natural feel for comedy; even better, in fact, than most of the Filipino directors who have devoted their careers to it. (In Tagalog with some English and Japanese)

Kakambal Ko sa Tapang
(My Twin in Courage)

1993 Harvest International; 109 minutes/color
Directors: Philip Ko, Johnny Wood; Screenwriter: Johnny Wood; Cinematographer: Baby Cabrales; Editors: Rudy Tabotabo, Philip Ko; Filmscore: Mon del Rosario; Cast: Ricky Davao, Cynthia Luster (Yukari Oshima), Monsour del Rosario, Charlie Davao, Philip Ko, Subas Herrero, Patrick dela Rosa, Franco Guerrero, Robin Shaw, Rachel Lobangco, Bunny Paras, Sopia Crawford, Gabriel Romulo, Rez Cortez, Ruel Vernal, Boy Fernandez, Rey Roldan, Johnny Vicar, Telly Babasa, Fredmore delos Santos, Ace Espinosa, Jimmy Ko, Kristine Zablan, Larisa Ledesma

Director Philip Ko gathers together many

of the personnel from *Magkasangga 2000* (1993), with much better results this time. Manila police officer Ricky Davao barely escapes with his life after videotaping a meeting between crime bosses Franco Guerrero and Subas Herrero, but when he and partner Monsour del Rosario turn the tape over to police chief Charlie Davao, they are perplexed by the lack of police action. It turns out that the chief is in cahoots with Herrero, and he erases part of the tape to protect him. Interpol agents from Hong Kong arrive in Manila (including perpetual Interpol agent Yukari Oshima) to nab yet another crime boss who hits town to cut a counterfeiting deal with Guerrero. Chief Charlie Davao finds out that del Rosario has gotten hold of the video shot by his partner, and worried that del Rosario will put things together after viewing the tape and finding footage with Herrero missing, he has del Rosario killed. The Interpol agents become suspicious and enlist Ricky Davao's help in solving the case. Herrero and Chief Charlie Davao have a falling out and kill each other during a police raid on Herrero's home, and the film concludes with two boisterous showdowns, first at Guerrero's mansion, and then at the ever-popular burned-out ruin for a climactic shootout/punch-up in which Ricky Davao and Yukari Oshima seem to be the only survivors.

As with all of Ko's films, there is a prominent amount of humor, though it is blended more easily into the action here than in *Magkasangga 2000*, which was sunk by the weight of its own witlessness. As usual, Oshima does her riotous gravity-defying tricks, but Ko does not restrict the gymnastics to the martial arts scenes, as people are constantly flying through the air, shooting while jumping out of windows, swinging on cables, sliding down banisters, and so on. Ko's films tend to be very lively—even ridiculous—in the outrageous nature of their action sequences, and are therefore impossible to take seriously, but they are usually entertaining, and isn't that what it's all about? (In Tagalog and English)

Kapag Iginuhit ang Hatol ng Puso (When the Line in the Heart Is Drawn)

1993 Viva Films; 123 minutes/color
Director: Celso Ad. Castillo; Screenwriters: Raquel Villavicencio, Sam Murillo; Cinematographer: Loreto U. Isleta; Editor: Edgardo Vinarao; Filmscore: Nonong Buencamino; Cast: Dina Bonnevie, Gary Estrada, Rustom Padilla, Bing Loyzaga, Monique Wilson, Alicia Alonzo, Johnny Vicar, Pocholo Montes, Rio de Guzman, Michelle Ann Lopez, Michelle Bautista, Grace Figuez, Isla Castillo, Mel Kimura, Marissa de Guzman, Angie Cantero, Lulu Arietta, Jon Achaval, Amir Castillo, Derek Carmona, Rosemarie Gil, Lucita Soriano, Lorli Villanueva, Dexter Doria

When successful businesswoman Dina Bonnevie is stood up at the altar by fiancé Rustom Padilla, she goes on an alcoholic binge culminating in a suicide attempt. She is rushed to the hospital on the same night that lounge singer Monique Wilson is brought in with a gash on her forehead resulting from a brawl with the jealous girlfriend of one of the patrons she gets fresh with in the nightclub where she is singing. Wilson befriends Bonnevie, and in time Bonnevie is able to recover. She is still reluctant, however, to seek out another relationship, though she very much wants a child. Wilson convinces her to "hire" a man to father her child, and shows her pictures of Gary Estrada, whom she suggests as a suitable candidate: Bonnevie agrees and Wilson sets it up. What Bonnevie doesn't know is that Estrada is Wilson's boyfriend, and the sizeable stud fee she is paying will actually go toward plastic surgery for Wilson to repair the scar left by the gash on her forehead, as well as giving her a stake to go to Japan and try her luck as a singer there. Bonnevie and Estrada meet at a hotel, and after they spend the night together, Estrada awakens alone to find an envelope full of cash on the bed. He takes the money back home to Wilson and indignantly refuses his share. But despite Estrada's protests, Wilson takes the money and leaves for Japan. When Bonnevie gets word that she is pregnant, she goes to tell Wilson the news, but is surprised to find Estrada living in Wilson's apartment. Estrada pursues a relationship with Bonnevie, as does Bonnevie's ex-fiancé Padilla, whom she rejects. Though she initially avoids becoming involved with Estrada, Bonnevie eventually relents, and Estrada is with her through her pregnancy. They plan to marry after the child is born, but Wilson returns from Japan and is upset to find out about the engagement. Bonnevie naively invites Wilson to stay with her and Estrada, and Wilson immediately begins conspiring to break up the engagement. She brings Padilla in on the scheme, having him call Bonnevie at work to tell her that while she is working all day, Estrada and Wilson are back at the house indulging themselves. Bonnevie rushes home and—sure enough—catches Estrada in a somewhat compromising position, set up by Wilson, naturally. Bonnevie orders Wilson out of the house and, in a bizarre and unexpected plot turn, while Bonnevie and Estrada are having it out, Wilson sneaks out with their baby, whom she and Padilla hold for ransom. The film climaxes with a meeting to exchange the ransom for the baby, which is attended by the police. Both Wilson and Padilla are shot and killed, and Bonnevie and Estrada get their child back.

The ending is completely out of place, and seems contrived merely to supply an exciting climax to the story. As for the rest of the story, the screenplay by Raquel Villavicencio and Sam Murillo is the standard soaper, throwing in just about everything, including a fatal car accident that claims the life of Bing Loyzaga, the woman that Padilla had left Bonnevie for. Bonnevie and Estrada give good performances, but there is a fairly annoying performance from Wilson to contend with. As for director Celso Ad. Castillo, well, he has definitely done better work. (In Tagalog with some English)

Kapag Puno na ang Salop (When the Package Is Full)

1987 FPJ Productions; 118 minutes/color
Director: Arturo San Agustin; Screenwriters: Pablo Gomez, Fred Navarro; Cinematographer: Ver P. Reyes; Editor: Augusto Salvador; Filmscore: Ernani Cuenco; Cast: Fernando Poe Jr., Eddie Garcia, Paquito Diaz, Jose Romulo, Dencio Padilla, Roy Alvarez, Rowena Moran, Lito Anzures, Jimmy Fabregas, Augusto Victa, Ernie Zarate, Nanding Fernandez, Delia Razon, Rudy Meyer, Rene Hawkins, Luis Benedicto, Eddie Tuazon, Jimmy Reyes, Buddy Salvador, Mel Arca

As police Sergeant Ernie Sarrento, Fernando Poe, Jr. is really up against it: not only is psycho-killer Roy Alvarez running around Manila murdering policemen, but Poe also has to contend with wealthy, prominent, and extremely corrupt judge Eddie Garcia, who seems to have his hand in most every type of illegal activity. Poe manages to gun down Alvarez in an old-fashioned western-style draw on a desolate stretch of road, but upon returning to the city, Poe is shot by Garcia's goons. Knowing enough to bring him down, it seems that Poe is a threat to Garcia, and so Garcia resolves to be rid of him. But Poe survives the hit attempt, and the enraged Garcia next sends his hit men to the hospital where Poe is recovering from his wounds. Poe manages to escape again when his girlfriend (Rowena Moran) helps to smuggle him out of the hospital just in time to elude the would-be assassins. Though not fully recovered, Poe stages a one man raid on a warehouse where most of Garcia's men can be found, and after wiping them all out, he confronts Garcia in his home. Although Garcia is defiant, he is arrested on the testimony of his own wife, who corroborates Poe's story.

It's Poe at his populist best, portraying an almost mythical hero fighting corruption and injustice in high places. The real highlight, however, is the teaming of Poe and Garcia in adversarial roles. It is no surprise that Garcia acquits himself nicely in the role of the heavy. Poe and Garcia would reprise their respective roles and lock horns in two sequels, *Ako ang Huhusga* (1989) and *Hindi Ka na Sisikatan ng Araw* (1990). (In Tagalog with some English)

Karnal (Carnal)

1983 Cine Suerte; 110 minutes/color
Director: Marilou Diaz-Abaya; Screenwriter: Ricky Lee; Cinematographer: Manolo R. Abaya; Editor: Marc Tarnate; Filmscore: Ryan Cayabyab; Cast: Charito Solis, Phillip Salvador, Vic Silayan, Joel Torre, Cecille Castillo, Grace Amilbangsa, Joonee Gamboa, Vangie Labalan, Crispin Medina, Rolando Tinio, Ella Luansing, Gil de Leon, Rustica Carpio

In this effectively disturbing melodrama, Phillip Salvador brings his new bride (Cecille Castillo) back to the rural home of his youth, but finds that he has to contend all over again with his cruel and domineering father (Vic Silayan). Years before, Silayan had been abusive toward his wife, who had rebelled by becoming the town slut. Silayan meted out punishment by stripping her naked and dragging her through the streets, after which she committed suicide. It happens that Castillo is a dead ringer for Salvador's mother, and that being the case, Silayan feels compelled to make strong advances toward her. She is able to fend him off, but otherwise relieves her boredom by beginning an affair with Joel Torre, a local deaf mute. When Silayan hears of it, he again becomes enraged and tries to impose the same punishment that he had years earlier on his own wife. When Salvador discovers this, a violent confrontation ensues in which Salvador winds up beheading Silayan with an axe. Salvador is sent to prison, where he commits suicide, and Castillo ends up giving birth to what the locals describe as a demonic child.

Top-billed Charito Solis appears intermittently as the film's narrator. Silayan won the FAMAS Best Supporting Actor trophy for his performance. (In Tagalog)

Katawan (The Body)

1999 Neo Films; 103 minutes/color
Director: Abbo Q. dela Cruz; Screenwriter: Uro Q. dela Cruz; Cast: Christopher de Leon, Rosanna Roces, Bobby Andrews, Leandro Baldemor, Dindi Gallardo, Daniella, Alicia Alonzo, Tony Mabesa, Alicia Lane, Amah Quiambao, Lora Luna, Dante Castro, Jessel Jimenez, Merdilou Abcede, Archie Ventosa, Chad Danielle Feliciano, Abbo Q. dela Cruz, Jun Cudia

Basically a sentimental and melodramatic love story set in the realm of the supernatural, this film stars Christopher de Leon as a building contractor who suffers a severe attack of vertigo on the day that his wife (Dindi Gallardo) gets word that she is pregnant. With the test results all coming back negative, de Leon's doctor advises him to take a rest, putting it all down to overwork. Deciding to follow his doctor's advice, de Leon drives to the now dilapidated mansion of his deceased grandfather, a house long rumored by the locals to be haunted. He snaps some photos of the house, with a mind toward renovating it, and when he has the photos developed, he is struck by one shot in which a beautiful young woman (Rosanna Roces) can be seen on the grounds, though de Leon had no memory of seeing her at the time that he took the picture. While staying at the house, de Leon begins to have increasingly erotic dreams of Roces, and when he returns to his wife he is shocked by a vision in a mirror, shown to him by the spectral Roces, in which his wife is making love to another man. He confronts Gallardo about her infidelity, and leaves in a rage after she admits to it. Upon returning to the mansion he sees Roces, who appears to him in the flesh after taking possession of a young witch who belongs to a local coven. Roces then tells de Leon her sad story, relating how, in the early part of the century, she was drugged and taken advantage of by Bobby Andrews, one of de Leon's wealthy ancestors. She wound up pregnant and died during childbirth, but took her revenge by taking possession of another woman who was likewise in the process of being raped by Andrews, and stabbing Andrews to death. Roces departs after telling her story, but de Leon seeks her out by visiting the coven, and the witches perform a ceremony, which enables him to reunite with Roces in the spiritual plane, where they make love. De Leon is pulled violently back into the physical world, however, at the exact moment that Gallardo gives birth to their son. Gallardo dies in childbirth, and the film ends with de Leon raising the boy in the now-restored family mansion, with Roces still appearing on the grounds.

There are some effectively eerie moments early in the film, as when de Leon takes Gallardo to see the old mansion and she is disturbed by a glimpse of someone moving about inside the house, and a scene in which de Leon dreams of making love to Roces and awakens to catch a fleeting glimpse of her leaving the room. Unfortunately, such atmospherics take a backseat to the rather mundane romance saga. There is also a fair amount of nudity, particularly (though hardly surprisingly) by the top-heavy Roces, who helped concoct the film's story, as well as being credited as line producer. (In Tagalog)

Katayan (Slaughterhouse)

2000 Regal Entertainment, Inc.; 107 minutes/color
Director: Uro Q. dela Cruz; Filmscore: Herminio Augusto, Toto dela Cruz; Cast: Jomari Yllana, Maricar de Mesa, Orestes Ojeda, Ryan Ignacio, Rex Arce, Patricia Dans, Lindsay Kennedy, Kyle Mondejar, Jay Bermudo

In this dark melodrama, Jomari Yllana plays a slaughterhouse worker who falls in love with Maricar de Mesa, a young woman who lives with her uncle (Orestes Ojeda). Ojeda runs a popular eatery, but what helps to make it so popular is the fact that his sexy young wife is rather free and easy in giving out sexual favors to some of the patrons, and when Ojeda discovers this, he sends her packing. Once alone, Ojeda begins to rely on de Mesa, and becomes very possessive of her. While drinking with Yllana one night, Ojeda becomes aware of the romance between Yllana and de Mesa, and he becomes insanely jealous. Yllana passes out during a struggle with Ojeda, and he awakens to find Ojeda stabbed to death and de Mesa unconscious and bleeding from a gash to her wrist. The police arrest Yllana after he admits to having no memory of what happened, but once de Mesa recovers sufficiently, she clears Yllana, claiming that she stabbed Ojeda after he raped her, and then slit her own wrist. The police free Yllana, and under the circumstances, decline to press charges against de Mesa. But de Mesa has kept the real story to herself, as a flashback reveals in closing.

Uro dela Cruz, who both wrote and directed, seems to be bidding fair to lead the pack of serious Filipino filmmakers of the new millennium. His work is edgy, and is accentuated nicely here by an appropriately moody score by

Herminio Augusto and Toto dela Cruz. There is also a surprising amount of nudity, including full frontal nudity by Patricia Dans as Ojeda's promiscuous wife. (In Tagalog)

The Killing of Satan

1975 Cinex Films/F. Puzon Film Enterprises; 92 minutes/color

Director: Efren C. Pinon; Screenwriter: Jose Mari Avellana; Cinematographer: Ricardo Herrera; Editor: Boy Vinarao; Filmscore: Ernani Cuenco; Cast: Ramon Revilla, Elizabeth Oropesa, George Estregan, Paquito Diaz, Cecille Castillo, Erlyn Umali, Charlie Davao

After nearly dying of a gunshot wound, Ramon Revilla has a compelling urge to visit his uncle. When he is well and able he travels to the village where his uncle is some kind of shaman protecting the local villagers from a disciple of Satan's named the Prince of Magic (Paquito Diaz). Revilla (who has also brought his wife and daughter with him) discovers that his uncle has died after a recent magic duel with Diaz, and that he has now inherited his uncle's special powers and must assume the responsibility of protecting the locals. When his daughter is kidnapped, Revilla travels to Diaz's cavernous lair to retrieve her. Along the way, he meets God, battles a serpent that transforms into a bizarre demon, and frees a cage full of naked young women. Eventually, he finds his daughter and has a magic duel with Satan himself (in the person of Charlie Davao), which Revilla wins with God's help.

This is one of very few Filipino films of its era to be dubbed into English. While the story may be too outrageous for some tastes, the comic book approach will likely appeal to others. Director Efren Pinon, whose execution is a bit lacking, plays the narrative straight without regard for its potential camp value, which is still there just the same. Revilla proves a somewhat wooden lead, but the film benefits from the performance of Elizabeth Oropesa in the role of Revilla's wife. (Dubbed into English)

Kisapmata
(In the Blink of an Eye)

1981; 95 minutes/color

Director: Mike de Leon; Screenwriters: Clodualdo del Mundo Jr., Raquel N. Villavicencio, Mike de Leon; Cinematographer: Rody Lacap; Editor: Jess Navarro; Filmscore: Lorrie Ilustre; Cast: Vic Silayan, Charo Santos, Jay Ilagan, Charito Solis, Ruben Rustia, Juan Rodrigo, Aida Carmona, Cora Alforia, Dindo Angeles, Mely Mallari, Edwin O'Hara, Mandy Bustamante, Monette Alfon, Teresita Sanchez

Vic Silayan portrays a domineering patriarch who enjoys complete control over the lives of his wife (Charito Solis) and daughter (Charo Santos); he also has forced Santos into an incestuous relationship. When Santos decides to marry co-worker Jay Ilagan, Silayan begins conspiring to wreck the marriage, even manipulating Santos in order to prevent her from consummating her marriage after the ceremony. Eventually, Santos and Ilagan attempt to leave, sending Silayan into a homicidal rage.

Considering the consistently high caliber of work done by director Mike de Leon, it would indeed be saying something to state that this is his greatest work, which it may well be. De Leon allows the tension to simmer quietly before erupting at the tragic conclusion. He also has an excellent cast to work with here, all of whom turn in splendid performances. (In Tagalog)

Kulayan Natin ang Bukas
(Let Us Give Color to
Our Tomorrow)

1997 Regal Entertainment; 102 minutes/color

Director: Boots Plata; Screenwriter: Irma Dimaranan; Cinematographer: Johnny Araojo; Editor: Rene Tala; Filmscore: Marita Manuel; Cast: Judy Ann Santos, Ronaldo Valdez, Eric Fructuoso, Cherrie Pie Picache, Sylvia Sanchez, Mylene Dizon, Lito Pimentel, Anita Linda, Dino Guevarra, Andrea Blasey, Nikka Ruiz, Adana Villa, Joana Paula Plata, Pocholo Montes, Francis Ong, Arthur Solinap, Sherwin Ordonez, Dexter Doria

In this emotionally charged tearjerker Judy Ann Santos is a teenage girl who adores her father (Ronaldo Valdez). But when the truth comes to light about Valdez's sixteen-year affair with a woman, and the twelve-year-old daughter that is its byproduct, the family begins to unravel. Though her older sister, who prides herself on being open-minded, accepts her father's mistress and her new half-sister, Santos is not nearly so forgiving. She begins to resent the time that Valdez spends with his other family, and there follows a number of emotional confrontations, the last of which sees Valdez suffer a fatal coronary. Santos is eventually able to accept her half-sister when she goes to visit her father's grave and sees her newfound sibling already there and equally as forlorn.

Obviously designed as a showpiece for the

dramatic talents of the young Santos (for which she takes advantage of the opportunity), the film features uniformly fine performances all around, not the least of which is a fiery turn from Valdez. (In Tagalog with some English)

Kumander Kalbo
(Commander Kalbo)

1993 Emperor Films/Roda Films International; 97 minutes/color

Director: Segundo Ramos; Screenwriter: Tony Pascua; Cinematographer: Roger Estrada; Editor: Segundo Ramos; Filmscore: Boy Alcaide; Cast: Eddie Garcia, Gloria Diaz, Efren Reyes Jr., Conrad Poe, Aurora Sevilla, George Estregan Jr., Carol Dauden, Johnny Vicar, Rommel Valdez, Eric Francisco, Jim Rosales, Marvee "Bamba" Leelin, Eddie Fernandez, Lito Legaspi, Ernie David, Danny Riel, Robert Miller, Rodolfo "Boy" Garcia, Gari "Boy" Garcia, Steve Alcarado, Ver Sagum, Johnny Ramirez, Efren Belardo, Bert Garon, Richard Duran, Bert Cayanan, Tony Pascua, Greg Moreno, Butch Bautista, Pong Pong, Maita Sanchez, Joe Watts, Andy Calma

This is the true-life story of police officer Napoleon Velasco, chronicling his rise through the ranks, fighting crime in Quezon and battling rebels in the hills. Portrayed by Eddie Garcia, Velasco comes across as something of a saint, which is hardly surprising since Velasco himself is given story credit on the film. Otherwise, we get comic relief from Velasco's tempestuous relationship with his frequently jealous and perpetually pregnant wife (Gloria Diaz). Given Garcia's popularity, and the Filipino zeal for national heroes, this would seem to be a surefire hit. While the film plays easily enough, it would have benefited from a more focused presentation, preferably centralizing one of Velasco's more significant struggles. As things are, the film seems to be marking time much of the way; amid the flurry of action films starring Garcia through the 1990s, it doesn't quite measure up. At the time the film was made Velasco was still active as Police Chief of Matingalupa. (In Tagalog with some English)

Kumukulong Dugo
(Boiling Blood)

1991 Viva Films; 96 minutes/color

Director: Augusto Salvador; Screenwriter: Humilde "Meek" Roxas; Cinematographer: Val Dauz; Editors: Augusto Salvador, Danny Gloria; Filmscore: Mon del Rosario; Cast: Ronnie Ricketts, Edu Manzano, Eddie Gutierrez, Amy Perez, Cherrie Pie Picache, Malu Barry, Alicia Alonzo, Bembol Roco, Dick Israel, Val Iglesia, Dencio Padilla, Orestes Ojeda, Cristina Crisol, Michelle Ann Lopez, Jose Romulo, Jeffrey Veloso, Zandro Zamora, Robert Talabis, Ernie David, Freddie Ondra, Rene Hawkins, Vic Varrion

Car thief Ronnie Ricketts and hold-up man Edu Manzano are half-brothers who are brought together for the first time when Ricketts and buddy Dick Israel try to steal Manzano's getaway car while Manzano is busy pulling a heist. After becoming fast friends, the two brothers fall in with Bembol Roco, who enlists their aid in ripping off a heroin shipment from crime boss Eddie Gutierrez. While Gutierrez avenges himself on Roco, he is unable to prevail in his attempts to kill Ricketts and Manzano, who wipe out Gutierrez and his gang. However, the brothers do wind up in prison, proving in the end that crime does not pay. (In Tagalog)

Kurdapya

1954 Sampaguita Pictures; 157 minutes/black & white

Director: Tony Cayado; Screenwriter: Luciano B. Carlos; Cinematographers: Higino Fallorina, Amaury Agra; Editor: Jose H. Tarnate; Filmscore: Pastor de Jesus; Cast: Gloria Romero, Ramon Revilla, Ric Rodrigo, Eddie Garcia, Dolphy, Aruray, Rebecca del Ria, Etang Discher, Herminia Carranza, Aring Bautista, Ric Gutierrez, Vitang Ortega, Jaime Javier, Vic Guevarra

In this Golden Era musical/comedy/melodrama Gloria Romero has dual roles: first she is the title character, a rather weird and homely girl; second, she is Joana, a beautiful college student who gets pregnant by boyfriend Ric Rodrigo. In order to hide her pregnancy from Grandma Etang Discher, a plot is hatched: after getting an extreme makeover courtesy of goofy friend Dolphy, Kurdapya winds up looking remarkably like Joana, and so she takes her place. It leads to some zany situations, of course, but not to worry: when Discher discovers the truth, she is very understanding and loves her great grandchild. Given the running time, one might have expected *Gone with the Wind*, but it's just another example of how even very ordinary fare is treated like grand epic in Filipino cinema. (In Tagalog with some English)

Lacson: Batas ng Navotas
(Lacson: Law of Navotas)

1992 Regal Films; 119 minutes/color

Director/screenwriter: Leonardo "Ding" Pascual; Cinematographer: Vic Anao; Editor: Rogelio

Salvador; Filmscore: Jaime Fabregas; Cast: Lito Lapid, Snooky Serna, Miguel Rodriguez, Cristina Gonzales, Patrick dela Rosa, Rachel Lobangco, Jeffrey Santos, Max Laurel, Charlie Davao, Orestes Ojeda, Dick Israel, Rez Cortez, Conrad Poe, Renato del Prado, Danny Riel, King Gutierrez, Don Pepot, Tony Bernal, Rey Sagum, Usman Hassim, Robert Miller, Mar Lopez, Ben Sagmit

In this by-the-numbers action film, police officer Lito Lapid takes on the local mob with very predictable results. His free-wheeling style, and some unfortunate civilian casualties, has Lapid branded as a "killer cop" by some of the local residents, upsetting Lapid's wife (Snooky Serna). Lapid seems to defeat his foes in a warehouse shootout, but in a closing seemingly lifted from a Sonny Parsons film, he is ambushed by a carload of assassins and the film ends on a freeze-frame of Lapid, badly wounded, but still firing back. With nothing to tell otherwise, one can assume he perishes.

There are some very good action sequences (boisterous shootouts, car chases, explosions), and a very visceral violent edge (there are a number of gunshots to the head that are not for the squeamish), but the film is sorely hampered by the extremely formulaic screenplay. It's also a little surprising how inconsequential Serna's role is, and there is a very strange moment when nightclub singer Cristina Gonzalez serenades Lapid with a love ballad, then hands him the microphone to take over for a verse. Gonzalez is definitely not a singer, and while Lapid is only slightly better, he's a terrible lip syncher. (In Tagalog)

The Last Reunion

1978 Ian-Koinonia-Pelifilm; 99 minutes/color
Director: Jerry Wertz; Screenwriter: Donald G. Thompson; Cinematographer: Frank Johnson; Editor: Jay Wertz; Filmscore: William Loose; Cast: Cameron Mitchell, Leo Fong, Vic Silayan, Chanda Romero, Hal Bokar, Philip Baker Hall, Charlie Davao, Stack Pierce, Hope Holiday, Paul LeClair, Mariwin Roberts, Butz Aquino, Jose Mari Avellana, Minnie Badong, Paul Bailey, James Gaines, Kim Ramos

During the Japanese occupation of the Philippines in WWII, a young Japanese boy witnesses his father, a general in the Japanese Army, shot dead by American soldiers; one of the soldiers then proceeds to rape and murder the boy's mother. The boy resolves to avenge the indignity suffered by his mother, and thirty years later when the American soldiers stage a reunion in the Philippines, the now-grown Japanese boy is a samurai (Leo Fong), who flies to Manila and begins knocking off the soldiers responsible for the death of his parents, culminating in the killing of Hal Bokar, the man who raped Fong's mother. As an action picture, the film is fairly insubstantial and would probably disappoint fans of the genre, with most of the running time being spent on the squabbles and revelries among the reunited soldiers. Still, it is the best of Fong's Filipino films, though this has nothing to do with Fong himself, since he has little screen time, his character showing up only for hit-and-run killings. The main point of interest is the teaming of veteran actors Cameron Mitchell and Vic Silayan as two old comrades in arms with a lot of catching up to do. (In English)

Legacy

1998 ABS-CBN Entertainment/Quantum Entertainment; 106 minutes/color
Director: TJ Scott; Screenwriters: Kevin Lund, TJ Scott, James Grady; Cinematographer: Sharone Meir; Editor: Bert Kish; Filmscore: Ennio Di Berardo; Cast: David Hasselhoff, Rod Steiger, Donita Rose, Corin Nemec, Douglas O'Keeffe, Chin Chin Gutierrez, Victoria Pratt, Junix Inocian, Benzon Ventura, Naess Verano, Gary Lim, Richard Joson, Mon Confiado, Pen Medina

Produced by ABS-CBN, the Philippines' largest satellite company, this action tale stars David Hasselhoff as a photo journalist who arrives in Manila and quickly gets drawn into helping beautiful Donita Rose find her long lost father, a Vietnam veteran who went AWOL in 1969. Rose had come to Manila after getting a letter from her father, whom she thought dead, asking her to meet him there. Hasselhoff and Rose need only turn over one rock in going to visit Chin Chin Gutierrez in order to attract the attention of international crime potentate Rod Steiger and his entourage. Hasselhoff dodges attempts on his life while unraveling the truth, and eventually discovers that Rose's father was a crony of Ferdinand Marcos, as was Steiger. For some twenty years Steiger has been searching for Rose's father in order to recoup some ill-gotten gains appropriated by him. Not to worry: Hasselhoff will sort it all out.

The film is interesting, featuring some good performances and a generally sharp look, but is somewhat marred by TJ Scott's kinetic direction, which would be better suited to music videos. (In English)

The Lethal Hunt

1988 Cine Suerte/Davian International; 88 minutes/color

Director: Ben Yalung; Screenwriters: Ben Yalung, Tony Blacksmith; Cinematographer: Sergio Antonyo; Editor: Stephen Soul; Cast: Fernando Poe Jr., Michael St. James, Armida Siguion-Reyna, Miguel Rodriguez, Paquito Diaz, Romy Diaz, George Estregan, Greggy Liwag, Eddie Arenas, Bomber Moran, Bing Davao, King Gutierrez, Shalimar Alcantara, Candy Crisostomo, Alex Leviste, Alan Bautista, Fred Moro, Elsa Acana, Steve Alcarado, Rene Hawkins, Rey Tomenez, Ernie Zarate

In this clichéd Fernando Poe, Jr. action yarn, insufferably tyrannical millionaire Armida Siguion-Reyna orders her driver to run a red light, resulting in a collision with policeman Poe, who is pursuing a carload of bank robbers. Siguion-Reyna's daughter is killed in the crash, and Siguion-Reyna unleashes her vengeance on Poe, having charges brought against him. She also has her son (Miguel Rodriguez) bribe a police officer to get rid of anything in the police record to show that Poe was in pursuit of robbery suspects. With nothing to confirm his account, Poe is convicted of negligent homicide and sent to prison. As he begins serving his sentence, Poe's pregnant wife dies giving birth to a son. Poe is released after five years, and he takes his son and moves to a small town where his brother is running for mayor against sleazy incumbent George Estregan. Poe quickly becomes involved in his brother's struggle, mixing it up with Estregan's goons, but Estregan acquires a powerful ally when Siguion-Reyna learns of Poe's whereabouts. Still nursing a serious grudge, Siguion-Reyna succeeds in having both Poe and his son abducted and plans to kill them the following day. But Poe escapes during the night and flees with his son into the jungle. Pursued by an army of thugs, Poe manages to kill every last one of them before shooting Siguion-Reyna's helicopter out of the sky.

Filled with the expected exuberant violence, which is handled enthusiastically by director Ben Yalung, the film plays like most any other Poe action film, but holds up well enough. In particular, the jungle shootout that climaxes the film is well done, and although Siguion-Reyna is a risible caricature, she is despicable enough to have the viewer panting for her demise. (Dubbed into English)

Life Begins at 40

1984 Regal Films; 119 minutes/color
Director/screenwriter: Mike Relon Makiling; Cast: Eddie Rodriguez, Eddie Garcia, Rod Navarro, Janice de Belen, Gretchen Barreto, Nadia Montenegro, Benedict Aquino, Albert Anido, Mon Alvir, Liza Lorena, Marissa Delgado, Rosemarie de Vera, Rod Navarro Jr., Pia Moran, Melinda Mendez, Vilma Vitug, Charlie Davao, Matutina, Soxy Topacio, Butch Bautista, Bella Flores, Lucita Soriano, Poleng, Don Pepot, Joaquin Fajardo, Balot, Matimtiman Cruz, Mario Escudero, Danny Riel, Joe Baltazar, Augusto Victa, Jojo Lapuz, Evelyn Vargas

In this slight but appealing comedy, Eddie Rodriguez, Eddie Garcia and Rod Navarro all experience a collective mid-life crisis. Feeling neglected by their wives, and generally underappreciated, they all three start chasing after younger women and hanging out in discos. Eventually, they come to their senses and return to their wives, leaving their much younger girlfriends to beaus their own age. Seeing Rodriguez, Garcia and Navarro dancing to Chaka Khan by itself makes the film worth seeing. There is also an unexpected performance by Charlie Davao as a flamboyantly gay hairdresser, which is also quite something to see. (In Tagalog and English)

Ligaw na Bulaklak
(Wild Flower)

1975 Crown Seven; 116 minutes/color
Director: Ishmael Bernal; Cinematographer: Arnold Alvaro; Editor: Edgardo Vinarao; Filmscore: Ernani Cuenco; Cast: Alma Moreno, Vic Silayan, Marissa Delgado, Yvonne, Anita Linda, Charina Alonzo, Jun Mariano, Elvie Escarro, Edgar Garcia, Jesse Lee

This superior melodrama by director Ishmael Bernal stars Alma Moreno as a teenaged schoolgirl whose mother (Marissa Delgado) runs a sleazy dance hall/whorehouse. Moreno befriends the school gardener (Vic Silayan), a shell-shocked combat veteran who lives in a modest shack on the school grounds. Silayan has recurring nightmares of being wounded in battle, which is especially understandable since the wounds left him emasculated. Tired of the cruel treatment from her mother, Moreno leaves home and seeks refuge with Silayan, moving in and setting up house with him. Silayan is happy for the company, though it is necessarily platonic, but in time Moreno attracts a local boy and begins secretly seeing him during the day while Silayan is off tending the school grounds. Eventually, Silayan realizes what is going on and, returning home to find Moreno and her boyfriend together, proceeds to hack the boy to death. The film ends abruptly there, with a freeze-frame of Moreno cowering in the corner, screaming and spattered with blood.

Silayan gives an excellent performance in its quiet understatement, particularly in the moment when he silently creeps over to the sleeping Moreno's bedside and watches her longingly. In the end, his growing frustration erupts in fury over a girl he has come to feel possessive of, though he can never truly possess her. Moreno is also very good as the naïve girl whose youth is basically stolen by the sordid surroundings that her insidious mother brings her up in. Bernal's direction is flawless, but he followed it up with the overly-ponderous, hopelessly self-indulgent drama *Nunal sa Tubig* (1976). (In Tagalog)

Lihim ni Madonna
(The Mystery of Madonna)

1996 Four Aces; 118 minutes/color
Director: Celso Ad. Castillo; Screenwriter: Lualhati Bautista; Cinematographer: Isagani F. Sioson; Editor: Ruben Pantua; Filmscore: Willy F. Cruz; Cast: Sunshine Cruz, Celia Rodriguez, Tonton Gutierrez, Anthony Cortez, Dick Israel, Paquito Diaz, Roldan Aquino, Alexandra Gerhards, Flora Gasser, Jenny Smith, Dana Revilla, Criselda Volks, Lucas Valdez, Paolo Ramirez, Pat Salem Jr., Romeo Revilla, Danny Labra, Joe Baltazar, Raymond Vargas, Manny Tibayan

In this fascinating and creepy work from director Celso Ad. Castillo, Sunshine Cruz portrays Madonna, an emotionally disturbed young woman in Baguio with an infant son. Forsaken by the man who fathered her child (policeman Anthony Cortez), Cruz lives alone in her family's dilapidated ancestral mansion where she is haunted by nightmarish memories from her childhood, like having seen her mother (Celia Rodriguez) hack up a drunken neighbor (Paquito Diaz) with an axe. She is also haunted by her cruel mother's apparition. With no means of support, Cruz takes to begging in the streets, but without enough money to feed her child, the boy sickens and dies. Thereafter, Cruz slips deeper and deeper into a homicidal lunacy, with her mother's ghost to goad her on, eventually hacking retarded cemetery caretaker Dick Israel to pieces and scattering his body parts throughout the graveyard. Eventually Cortez pays her a call, suspecting her of Israel's killing, and she stabs him with some scissors before he shoots her and wounds her. Cruz makes her way to the chapel where her mother had perished after being pushed into a row of candles and catching fire, and lays down to die, now being comforted by her mother's spirit. The church then spontaneously catches fire.

The film is typically ambiguous about the nature of the haunting of Cruz by Rodriguez's ghost, not committing to whether it is a genuine spiritual apparition or the fantasies of a disturbed psyche, but given Cruz's mental instability from the get-go, some will no doubt be inclined toward the latter. That assessment loses its persuasiveness at the film's climax, however, when the mortally wounded Cruz literally floats through the air while approaching the church, a curious touch, to say the least. And then there is the church itself, igniting without any apparent agent.

The story was concocted by Castillo and adapted into a screenplay by Lualhati Bautista. Castillo is at his best here as a filmmaker, presenting an excellent and troubling portrait of a headlong descent into madness. That same year Castillo would again use Cruz in the equally impressive *Virgin People*, a remake of one of his earlier works. (In Tagalog)

Lipa Massacre:
Lord, Deliver Us from Evil

1994 Golden Lions Films/Viva Films; 124 minutes/color
Director/screenwriter: Carlo J. Caparas; Cast: Vilma Santos, Joel Torre, John Regala, Perla Bautista, Robert Arevalo, Philip Gamboa, Charina Scott, Angelica Panganiban, Liezl Martinez, Ronnie Lazaro, Mia Gutierrez, Ana Rivera, Soraya, Marie Rowe, Tony Mabesa, Paolo Martin, Fred Moro, Ernie Forte, Benjie Felipe, Smith Caparas, Boy Caparas, Congressman Ralph Recto, Mayor Robert Umali, Rod Navarro

Another of filmmaker Carlo Caparas' true crime stories, this one stars Joel Torre as a man who has to leave his wife (Vilma Santos) and two young daughters behind for a time and earn a living in Saudi Arabia. While he is away, his family is brutally murdered by psychotic John Regala, who inflicts a total of 91 stab wounds on the three victims. While Torre's co-workers see the news on television, they seek to shield him from it; knowing that he has been called home, they buy up all the Filipino newspapers in town to try and prevent Torre from seeing them, but on the flight home he catches a glimpse of a fellow passenger's paper bearing the headline "Lipa Massacre," and after borrowing the paper, he learns the truth. Unlike Caparas' film *The Vizconde Massacre: God Help Us!* (1993), at least this case had a resolution at the time that it was made. (In Tagalog)

Little and Big Weapon

1990 Regal Films; 113 minutes/color

Director: Tony Y. Reyes; Screenwriters: Joey de Leon, Tony Y. Reyes; Cinematographer: Oscar Querijero; Editor: Rene Tala; Filmscore: Mon del Rosario; Cast: Joey de Leon, Rene Requiestas, Tetchie Agbayani, Rez Cortez, Lola Rodriguez, Noel "Ungga" Ayala, Robert Talby, Jack Fajardo, Tsing Tong Tsai, Amay Bisaya, Berting Labra, Danny Labra, Sylvia Sanchez, Manila Munoz, Mini Aguilar, Evelyn Vargas, Emylou Lunar, Jimmy Fabregas, Cris Aguilar, Yoyong Martirez, Mel Feliciano, Pong Pong, Torling, Martin Peters

In this crime genre spoof, police officers Joey de Leon and Rene Requiestas team up to bring down a gang of narcotics traffickers straight out of a comic book. Led by the evil Madame Butterfly (Tetchie Agbayani), the gang also includes characters named Mr. Rambo, Dick Tracy, Berting Labra as a little fellow named "Spider," and Robert Talby as the outrageous Fred Chicken, who is put to death in a giant microwave oven. Of course, our heroes eventually succeed in bringing down the syndicate. As always, the humor is anything but subtle, but de Leon and Requiestas work well together, and the film is generally entertaining. Talby's musical number is a highlight. (In Tagalog with some English)

Live by the Fist

1992 Concorde/New Horizons; 77 minutes/color

Director: Cirio H. Santiago; Screenwriter: Charles Philip Moore; Cinematographer: Joe Batac, Jr.; Editor: Edgardo Vinarao; Filmscore: Nicolas Rivera; Cast: Jerry Trimble, George Takei, Ted Markland, Laura Albert, Vic Diaz, Romy Diaz, Roland Dantes, Nick Nicholson, Steve Rogers, Berting Labra, John Crank, Ramon D'Salva, Zernan Manahan, Jim Moss, Ned Hourani, Ronald Asinas, Jet Sahara, Dardo de Oro, Greg Rocero, Ray Ventura, Koko Trinidad, Cris Aguilar, Eddie Gaerlan, Henry Strzalkowski, Joe Zucchero

In this surprisingly absorbing prison film from director Cirio Santiago, Jerry Trimble is at a port in the orient where he tries to save a young woman from a group of assailants. The leader of the would-be rapists slits the woman's throat, but then falls on his own knife while mixing it up with Trimble. Unfortunately, Trimble is knocked unconscious and awakens to find himself accused of the woman's murder, and is sent to an island penal colony. He quickly makes enemies in the institution, where the Asians and Caucasians are split into separate feuding groups. Trimble fits in with neither, refusing to join sides for mere racial considerations, and he is frequently forced to defend himself against both sides, the Caucasians being led by Ted Markland, and the Asians by Romy Diaz. Trimble's cellmate (George Takei) has been smuggling letters out to a world human rights organization with the help of prison doctor Koko Trinidad, and human rights activist Laura Albert arrives to investigate the institution. She arrives just in time to witness a violent prison uprising instigated by the murder of Takei by Markland and Diaz, who did so under the orders of sleazy warden Vic Diaz, who has discovered one of Takei's correspondences. Trimble and Albert manage to flee the island on the warden's boat as the prisoner's overrun the place.

This is one of Santiago's better works, and it shows his directorial skills to be maturing considerably. The martial arts are well done, and World Kickboxing Champion Trimble has plenty of opportunity to show off his skills. Aside from Santiago regulars among the American actors, there is also a very impressive cast of Filipino veterans, including stickfighting pro Roland Dantes as the brutal captain of the prison guards, and veteran character actor Berting Labra in a significant supporting role as an inmate. It is also rare to see old hand Trinidad in an international co-production. (In English)

Long Ranger & Ton Ton (Shooting Stars of the West)

1989 Regal Films; 107 minutes/color

Director: Tony Y. Reyes; Screenwriters: Joey de Leon, Tony Y. Reyes; Cinematographer: Oca Querijero; Editor: Efren Jarlego; Filmscore: Mon del Rosario; Cast: Joey de Leon, Rene Requiestas, Panchito Alba, Maricel Laxa, Lorna Glavez, Vangie Labalan, Bing Angeles, Celeste Bueno, Joaquin Fajardo, Tsing Tong Tsai, Bomber Moran, Rommel Valdez, Ruel Vernal, Romy Nario, Teroy de Guzman, Danny Labra, Rey Solo, Minnie Aguilar, Joey Galvez, Ernie Forte, Ding Salvador, Kris Aguilar, Sonny Valencia, Eddie Samonte

In this western parody, Joey de Leon and Rene Requiestas escape from a brutal Mexican prison camp and are pursued by Army General Panchito Alba. In order to hide his identity as a fugitive, de Leon dons a mask and becomes the Long Ranger. The film has fun spoofing many western genre conventions, including the crooked saloon card game and the classic shootout. There is also the fairly amusing moment when a rather effete gunman challenges de

Leon to a draw, and identifies himself thusly: "They call me Trinity. Trinity Lopez: Trini Lopez for short." As usual, the humor may be too broadly farcical for some, but the film definitely has its moments. Maricel Laxa made her film debut here, playing an Indian girl—de Leon's love interest. (In Tagalog with some English)

Lost Battalion

1961 COM/American International; 82 minutes/black & white

Director: Eddie Romero; Screenwriters: Eddie Romero, Cesar Amigo; Cinematographer: Felipe Sacdalan; Editor: Jovan Calub; Filmscore: Les Baxter, Ronald Stein; Cast: Leopoldo Salcedo, Diane Jergens, Johnny Monteiro, Jennings Sturgeon, Joe Dennis, Joe Sison, Bruce Baxter, Renato Robles, Rosie Acosta, Arsenio Alonso

Set during the Japanese occupation in WWII, this film stars Leopoldo Salcedo as an emotionally hardened resistance fighter who escorts American civilians Jennings Sturgeon and his daughter Diane Jergens through the jungle to make their rendezvous with a boat that will take them out of the country. Trying to stay one step ahead of the advancing Japanese, and forced into a number of gunfights with them along the way, Salcedo must also rescue Sturgeon and Jergens from the clutches of bandit leader Johnny Monteiro. Although Salcedo succeeds in all of this, he is unable to overcome the bite of a cobra, and Jergens, who has fallen in love with Salcedo, is forced to leave him behind and catch her boat. This is a pretty standard WWII melodrama, but it is made more interesting by the fact that it features a rare lead for Salcedo in an international film; he gives a good performance. (In English with some Tagalog)

Maalaala Mo Kaya?
(Will You Remember?)

1954 Sampaguita Pictures; 114 minutes/black & white

Director: Mar S. Torres; Screenwriters: Conrado Conde, Luciano B. Carlos, Mar S. Torres; Cinematographer: Cesar Silos; Editor: Jose H. Tarnate; Filmscore: Ariston Avelino; Cast: Carmen Rosales, Rogelio dela Rosa, Patria Plata, Rosa Mia, Dolphy, Aruray, Precy Ortega, Tony Cayado, Jose de Villa, Horacio Morelos, Marcela Garcia, Jose Salameda, Leleng Isla, Herminia Carranza

This is a sentimental melodrama from the Golden Era casting Rogelio dela Rosa as a songwriter who pens a tune for sweetheart Carmen Rosales. But when he travels to the city to try and sell the song, he is pursued by a beautiful music publisher, who likes his song, and likes him even more. Dela Rosa falls in love with her and they marry, and years later they have a young daughter but a declining marriage. Dela Rosa again encounters Rosales when she turns up as a music teacher at the school that dela Rosa's daughter attends. After he has a few chance encounters with Rosales, dela Rosa's wife becomes insanely jealous, and she pulls a gun on him as they are arguing one evening. They begin to struggle, and of course the gun goes off, killing dela Rosa's wife. He stands trial for killing his wife, but is acquitted after his daughter, who witnessed the incident, testifies on his behalf. The film ends with dela Rosa's daughter playing the piano at a school recital in which she plays the song that dela Rosa had written for Rosales all those years ago, which has the effect of bringing the two back together again. (In Tagalog)

Mabuting Kaibigan, Masamang Kaaway
(Good Friend, Bad Enemy)

1992 Tagalog Ilang-Ilang Productions; 110 minutes/color

Director: Augusto Salvador; Screenwriters: Tony Mortel, Jose Bartolome, Manny Buising, Laurente Diaz; Cinematographer: Ver P. Reyes; Editors: Augusto Salvador, Rene Tala, Danny Gloria; Filmscore: Jaime Fabregas; Cast: Fernando Poe Jr., Vic Vargas, Marianne dela Riva, Imelda Ilanan, Dencio Padilla, Subas Herrero, Bert Olivar, Rene Hawkins, Manjo del Mundo, Paquito Diaz, Charlie Davao, Robert Talabis, Ali Sotto, Robert Ortega, Ernie Zarate

Gubernatorial candidate Vic Vargas wants to tie up any loose ends during his political campaign, and so wants to be rid of his mistress. He asks old friend Fernando Poe, Jr. to take an envelope full of cash to her in an attempt to buy her off, but she angrily refuses it and sends Poe away. Vargas then goes to see her himself, and during a heated exchange, he accidentally knocks her through a glass door and kills her. The whole thing is caught on videotape by two freelancers hoping either to blackmail Vargas or sell evidence of his affair to his political rival. But no sooner does Vargas leave than Poe returns, and with the camera still running, finds the woman's dead body. After a woman comes forward to say that she saw Poe leaving the dead woman's apartment on the night she was killed, Poe is arrested, and he is represented by Vargas' attorney (Subas Herrero). Although Herrero assures Poe that there isn't enough evidence to convict him, Vargas receives an offer to buy the videotape, which he does. With a little nifty editing, Poe comes off looking very guilty in the video, which is enough to convict him and send him to prison. But Poe manages to escape from prison and then goes on a quest to find the complete videotape and clear his name, which prompts Vargas to send Paquito Diaz and an army of goons after him. In a climactic shootout, Poe wipes out everybody, including his erstwhile friend Vargas.

Poe gives his usual stern, unwavering performance, and there are plenty of fistfights to go along with all of the gunplay, so fans were no doubt placated. There is also a very good performance from Vargas as the conflicted heavy. (In Tagalog)

Mad Doctor of Blood Island

1968 Hemisphere Pictures; 88 minutes/color
Directors: Gerardo de Leon, Eddie Romero; Screenwriter: Rueben Canoy; Cinematographer: Justo Paulino; Filmscore: Tito Arevalo; Cast: John Ashley, Angelique Pettyjohn, Ronald Remy, Ronaldo Valdez, Alicia Alonzo, Tita Munoz, Bruno Punzalan, Alfonso Carvajal, Tony Edmunds, Johnny Long, Edward Murphy, Paquito Salcedo, Felisa Salcedo, Quiel Mendoza, Ricardo Hipolito, Cenon Gonzalez

On his second trip to Blood Island, John Ashley portrays a pathologist sent to investigate the discovery of a green-blooded corpse on the island. Accompanying him on the trip are Angelique Pettyjohn, who is looking for her wayward father (Tony Edmunds), a former stockbroker who dropped out of sight and somehow wound up on the small island where he crawled inside of a bottle, and Ronaldo Valdez, who grew up on the island and is hoping to convince his mother (Tita Munoz) to return to the mainland with him. They are not there long before horrendous happenings transpire (Pettyjohn is terrorized by a monster that disembowels a hunter that comes to her aid, two young lovers are dismembered, and Ashley tries to treat a disfigured native with a green complexion). Valdez, whose father is said to have died seven years earlier, finds his mother living with Ronald Remy, the doctor who had tried to treat his father for leukemia. After witnessing his mother's murder (in which she is literally torn to pieces by the hideous monster), Valdez learns from Remy that the monster is, in fact, his father, whose death was faked by Remy and Munoz in order to hide what he had become as a result of being the guinea pig for Remy's experimental leukemia treatments. Ashley also puts it all together, and after discovering Remy's secret laboratory, he confronts the good doctor. But Remy's folly (the monster) shows up and goes berserk, attacking Remy, trashing the lab, and setting it ablaze. While Ashley, Valdez and Pettyjohn (now reunited with her sobered-up father) manage to escape, Remy is presumed dead, as is the beast. But the monster would return in a sequel, *Beast of Blood* (1970), as would Remy's character Dr. Lorca, though the role would be assumed by Eddie Garcia.

The film has been heavily criticized (justifiably so) for the over-indulgent use of the zoom lens during the more horrific moments, and more than a little surprisingly for a Gerardo de Leon film, there doesn't seem to have been a great deal of care taken, the impression being that of a very hurried shoot. But behind the sometimes crude execution is a fairly intriguing screenplay by Rueben Canoy, unfurling in stages to reveal various family skeletons. There is a peculiar familial arrangement at the center of the drama, with Munoz sharing her mansion with her lover Remy, who has turned her husband into a monster, and also allowing her husband's young mistress (Alicia Alonzo) to live there and seduce her son Valdez as well. It is an odd mix, to say the least, which the film makes no attempt to explain. Both Valdez and Alonzo were little more than kids when they appeared here; both still active, they are among the more respected actors working in the Philippines today. They both perform well here, even if Valdez's English delivery sounds a bit choked.

Having worked together since 1941's *Ang Maestra*, this appears to have been the final collaboration between directors de Leon and Eddie Romero. Romero would complete the Blood Island saga, both writing and directing *Beast of Blood*, in which he dropped the weird familial and perverse sexual subtexts of the previous Blood Island films, delivering a more straightforward tale of mad science. (In English)

Madonna ... Babaeng Ahas
(Madonna ... Snake Woman)

1991 Regal Films; 111 minutes/color
Director/screenwriter: Artemio O. Marquez; Cinematographers: Vic Anao, Jimmy Baer; Editor: Edgardo Vinarao; Filmscore: Demet Velasquez; Cast: Snooky Serna, Tirso Cruz III, Eric Quizon, Rose-

marie Gil, Luis Gonzales, Caridad Sanchez, Johnny Wilson, Mario Escudero, Anthony Taylor, Subas Herrero, Lucita Soriano, Odette Khan, Harvey Vizcarra, Judy Anne Santos, Luis Benedicto, Eddie Infante, Dante Castro, Jess Vargas, Jeff Hernandez, Angie Rosa, Raul Salvador

As the result of a curse put on her by her own mother, a young woman (Snooky Serna) develops an alarming skin condition. She is further disturbed to find that she is pregnant, and the combined shame of her appearance and her pregnancy sends her off into the wilderness, where she gives birth to a daughter; exiting the birth canal with the child is a large serpent. A passing hunter, hearing the cries of a baby coming from a cave, enters and, after finding the mother dead, takes the baby home where he and his wife raise it. Eventually the child grows into a beautiful young woman (Serna again), apparently normal and healthy in every way, until an attempted rape by her drunken adoptive father causes her to transform into a serpentine beast. Thus begins a series of transformations and killings of would-be rapists, as men are frequently forcing themselves on Serna. She is finally freed from the curse when she marries her true love.

It is not unusual—one might suggest that it is the norm—to find strong religious motifs within the horror genre, but it is to be expected all the more in a country as devoutly Catholic as the Philippines. Here this religious faith finds expression first when Serna attempts to enter a church and is prevented from doing so by a strong wind that literally blows her away. What is particularly interesting is that Serna, whose character was spawned as the result of an evil curse, finds salvation nonetheless; on her wedding day she is again buffeted by a strong wind as she attempts to enter the church. On this occasion she is able to overcome and enters the church to be married. Significantly, she is freed from her curse upon entering the church.

The transformation scenes are handled reasonably well, though the end result of the transformation is less than impressive. Never shown beyond the head and shoulders, the serpent beast is obviously a rubber mock-up, and not a terribly good one. Serna also starred in the bizarre serpent-themed horror film *Zuma* (1987). (In Tagalog with some English)

Maestro Toribio: Sentensyador
(Master Toribio: Judge)

1994 Octo Arts Films; 106 minutes/color

Director/screenwriter: Jose N. Carreon; Cinematographer: Johnny Araojo; Editor: Joe Solo; Filmscore: Nonong Buencamino; Cast: Eddie Garcia, Tirso Cruz III, Lito Legaspi, Jimmy Fabregas, Patrick dela Rosa, Ramon Christopher, Toby Alejar, Marco Polo (Garcia), Aira Ariza, Lovely Rivero, Ramon Recto, Mikee Villanueva, Teresa Loyzaga, Jenette Fernando, Don Pepot, Nanding Fernandez, CJ Ramos, Ben Tisoy, Ernie Forte, Archie Adamos, Cris Daluz, Romy Romulo, Eddie Nicart, Pocholo Montes, Tony Tacorda, Telly Babasa

One night while partying at a disco, Eddie Garcia gets into a scrape with Marco Polo. The police show up and haul Polo out, allowing him just enough time to vow to get even with Garcia. When Polo is killed later by some gang rivals, Garcia is initially questioned as the prime suspect, but with no evidence to hold him on, he is released, infuriating Polo's father (Jimmy Fabregas). Anxious to avenge his son's murder, Fabregas sends some hit men after Garcia, and after surviving a number of attempts on his life, Garcia seeks refuge by hiding out with drinking buddies in a carnival. But Fabregas' goons eventually find him there too, and Garcia is again forced to run. In time, Garcia learns that his friend Tirso Cruz III, who has strong underworld ties, was responsible for Polo's death. Garcia shows up at Polo's memorial service and drags Fabregas off at gunpoint. After explaining the truth to him, Garcia takes Fabregas to see Cruz, and Fabregas opens fire in a rage and is quickly cut down by Cruz's men, but not surprisingly, Garcia is able to overcome Cruz and his men.

This is pretty standard Garcia action fare, casting him as a lovable and irascible rogue and a brawler. The notable exception to the formula here is that he plays a grandfather, which is an uncommon acknowledgement of his age. (In Tagalog with some English)

Magandang Hatinggabi
(Good Midnight)

1998 Star Cinema; 101 minutes/color

Director: Laurenti Dyogi; Screenwriter: Ricky Lee; Cinematographer: Joe Tutanes; Editor: Kelly M. Cruz; Filmscore: Greg Caro; Cast: Marvin Agustin, Diether Ocampo, Mylene Dizon, Bojo Molina, Laura James, Noni Buencamino, Eula Valdes, Allan Paule, Angelica Panganiban, Alwyn Uytingco, Lorena Garcia, Jaclyn Jose, Angelika de la Cruz, Jericho Rosales, Miguel de la Rosa, Wilson Santiago, Mary Kaye de Leon, Rigor Ferrer, Jay de los Reyes, Ray Flores

Five teenagers driving down a desolate stretch of rural road at night encounter an old crone who suddenly walks out in front of their van. They appear to hit her, but when they stop the van and get out, they find no trace of her. They do, however, spot a roadside attraction called "Midnight Express," and curious about the ramshackle attraction out in the middle of nowhere, they go in. They are greeted inside by a grotesque, obese man in a wheelchair (a heavily made-up Noni Buencamino), who invites the kids to sit down to dinner with him, and then proceeds to tell them a pair of creepy tales.

In the first, a family of four purchases a van with a very unfortunate past: a killer (Buencamino again) shot and killed the woman who owned the van and then drove off with the woman's young daughter. Buencamino and the girl both died when the van drove over a cliff and into the ocean. The current owners then find that the van is haunted.

The second story is far more substantial, and stars Angelika de la Cruz as a hunchbacked schoolgirl who is mercilessly tormented by her classmates. But popular Jericho Rosales takes a liking to her and pursues a relationship with her, until meeting her mother (Jaclyn Jose), who turns out to be an aswang (a kind of variation on the vampire myth) who tells Rosales that de la Cruz was conceived as a result of a rape perpetrated on Jose by another aswang (Buencamino yet again). With this news Rosales runs away, and a heartbroken de la Cruz leaves school and returns with her mother to their creepy old mansion in the woods. But Rosales finds himself unable to stay away from de la Cruz, and so he follows her there. Buencamino shows up and a battle of aswangs ensues between he and Jose. But Jose is no match, and before she dies, she passes her power on to de la Cruz, who transforms into a hideous beast and defeats Buencamino. But the horrified Rosales then stakes and kills de la Cruz, sitting despondently by her body afterwards.

After hearing these two stories, the five teenagers find that they are unable to leave, and their corpulent host shocks them by rising from his wheelchair and peeling away his blubbery exterior skin to reveal an even more grotesque under skin. He then chases the kids around the building, which suddenly becomes a large, labyrinthine maze of perilous rooms; but the kids escape by preventing the clock's hands from striking midnight, upon which Buencamino perishes and the kids find that, once they get outside, the "Midnight Express" collapses into a pile of rubble and disappears into a hole in the ground.

While the film opens interestingly, particularly with the appearance of the bizarre and blubbery character portrayed by Buencamino, the first story seems very inconsequential, providing only a little suspense, while the closing segment with the teens pursued through the building basically plays like one overlong gag. Far more interesting is the middle segment, a tragic romance that is at its most interesting while chronicling the unremitting cruelty of the school children. (In Tagalog with some English)

Magdalena S. Palacol Story

1991 Omega Releasing Organization; 92 minutes/color

Director: Junn P. Cabreira; Screenwriter: Jun Lawas; Cinematographer: Rudy Dino; Editor: Joe Solo; Filmscore: Mon del Rosario; Cast: Alma Moreno, Tobi Alejar, Gardo Versoza, Allan Paule, Robert Arevalo, Orestes Ojeda, Roldan Aquino, Alicia Alonzo, Ernie Ortega, Tony Carrion, Ernie Zarate, Pocholo Montes, Mike Austria, Eruel Tongco, Rico Gallego, Rafael Romero, Valarie Valdez, Bumbee Arenas, Paola Salonga

In this violent revenge melodrama, Alma Moreno's family is murdered and she herself is gang raped, stabbed repeatedly and left for dead. Of course she survives, and after recovering she sets out to avenge her family and her honor. Guns being her weapon of choice, she becomes an expert shot and off she goes. Moreno gives a strong performance, but the material is fairly routine. (In Tagalog with some English)

The Maggie dela Riva Story: God ... Why Me?

1994 Viva Films/Golden Lions Films; 126 minutes/color

Director/screenwriter: Carlo J. Caparas; Cinematographer: Ernesto Dominguez; Editor: Abelardo Hulleza; Filmscore: Demet Velasquez; Cast: Dawn Zulueta, Ricky Davao, Michael de Mesa, Miguel Rodriguez, John Regala, Boots Anson-Roa, Tonton Gutierrez, Robert Arevalo, Liza Lorena, Lito Legaspi, Marita Zobel, Philip Gamboa, Mia Gutierrez, Ali Sotto, Ana Rivera, Zoraya, Laurice Guillen, Maggie dela Riva, Gen. Romeo Pena

Carlo Caparas once again mines the vein of the true-crime genre, here tackling one of the most celebrated criminal cases in the history of the Philippines, the story of actress Maggie dela Riva, a young film star in the 1960s. At the age of 25, and at the height of her fame, dela Riva was abducted by four men who tortured and raped her; it turned out that she was not their only victim. Over a period of several years, the foursome had similarly assaulted many other women, although the other victims did not come forward and press charges due to both shame and fear, and the four young men, who were from prominent families, came to be referred to in some circles as "The Untouchables." But it was the courageous dela Riva who ended their reign of terror by going public and pressing charges. The four men were convicted, and when the full range of their crimes became known, they were given the death penalty.

This may be Caparas' best work within the genre (a genre which he practically owns), aided tremendously by a strong performance by Dawn Zulueta as dela Riva. Caparas, while not being overly-graphic, does not skimp in portraying dela Riva's ordeal, spending half of the film's running time depicting how she was repeatedly raped, beaten, burned with cigarettes and degraded in various ways. Dela Riva appears briefly herself at the film's conclusion, greeting her daughter who comes home from school in tears asking her mother if what the children in school said about her was true. The film concludes with dela Riva walking with her daughter and telling her the truth about what had happened to her years before. (In Tagalog with some English)

Magic Temple

1996 Star Cinema; 106 minutes/color
Directors/screenwriters: Peque Gallaga, Lorenzo Reyes; Cinematographer: Joe Tutanes; Editor: Danilo Gloria; Filmscore: Archie Castillo; Cast: Jason Salcedo, Junell Hernando, Jun Urbano, Anna Larrucea, Jackie Lou Blanco, Marc Solis, Sydney Sacdalan, Gina Pareno, Aljon Jimenez, Koko Trinidad, Tito Arevalo, Rudy Meyer, Cholo Escano, Chubi del Rosario, Mae-Ann Adonis, Tess Nichelena, Carlo Aquino, Christopher Peralta, Aldrin Hernando, Manny Parcon, Jubal Gallaga, Eugene Enriquez

In this fantasy feature, the mythical world of Samadhi is kept in harmony by a set of scales containing a magic stone, which is guarded by a group of wise men. When evil sorceress Jackie Lou Blanco destroys that stone, all hell breaks loose—literally. With Samadhi in chaos, three young boys are sent by their teacher (Jun Urbano) to defeat Blanco and restore the scales of balance. The three boys are each gifted with special talents, which they have honed under Urbano's tutelage. Jason Salcedo has mastered gravity and telekinesis; Junell Hernando is able to communicate with nature (talking to plants and animals); Marc Solis has the peculiar talent of causing explosions by spitting fruit seeds from his mouth. So, the three boys set off to find and confront Blanco. Along the way, they have no shortage of adventures and are forced to deal with all manner of monsters and netherworld beings. They receive periodic help from a pint-sized martial artist, and eventually succeed in their quest, bringing peace to Samadhi once more. In the end, they learn that the mysterious martial arts master who had occasionally showed up in their time of need was a manifestation of their teacher Urbano.

The production values are high and the special effects often striking, yet despite winning various awards in 1996, this was nowhere near being the best Filipino film of the year. Originally the maker of more adult-oriented films—some very adult—Gallaga's work with partner Lorenzo Reyes seems more and more reliant on young children in central roles. *Batang X* and *Baby Love* (both in 1995) both featured children as protagonists, and even what were largely more adult-oriented works, like *Aswang* (1992) and *Halik ng Vampira* (1997) used children in very prominent comic relief roles. It's tempting to conclude that Reyes had a negative effect on Gallaga as a filmmaker. While their work together has had moments of inspiration, too much of it seems frivolous, unlike Gallaga's earlier work, i.e. *Oro, Plata, Mata* (1982) and *Virgin Forest* (1984). It seems odd that a maker of arty sex films would wind up so blandly commercial, but in this respect, Gallaga would hardly be the first person to abandon artistic merit to commercialism. (In Tagalog)

Magkaribal (Rivals)

1979 Regal Films; 103 minutes/color
Director: Elwood Perez; Cast: Vilma Santos, Christopher de Leon, Alma Moreno

In this standard love triangle melodrama, good friends Vilma Santos and Alma Moreno are both in love with wealthy horse breeder Christopher de Leon. He winds up choosing Santos and the two get married, but as time passes they begin to drift apart and de Leon starts spending more time away from home as he worries about business. When Santos and de Leon run into Moreno again she has become a successful businesswoman, owning her own restaurant. As his marriage is now full of tension, and seeing that Moreno is still carrying a torch for him, de Leon takes the opportunity to begin an affair with her, but it doesn't take Moreno long to feel as neglected as Santos, and de Leon begins to feel boxed-in on all sides. The film concludes with Santos showing up at Moreno's apartment, finding de Leon there and storming out; de Leon chases after Santos, Moreno chases after de Leon, and they all wind up by a swimming pool where, having had enough, de Leon shoves both women into the pool and walks out. As Moreno can't swim, Santos swims to her aid and the two women embrace and break out in laughter. The film is very bland. (In Tagalog with some English)

Magkasangga sa Batas
(Partners in Law)

1993 Harvest International/Golden Kay International; 93 minutes/color

Directors: Philip Ko, Erwin Lanado; Screenwriter: Erwin Lanado; Cinematographers: Peter Li, Baby Cabrales; Editors: Tony Sy, Philip Ko, Ever Ramos; Filmscore: Jaime Fabregas; Cast: Edu Manzano, Cynthia Luster (Yukari Oshima), Gabriel Romulo, Shiela Ysrael, Rachel Lobangco, Charlie Davao, Lovely Rivero, King Gutierrez, Johnny Wilson, Stella Mari, Edwin Reyes, Marita Zobel, Monsour del Rosario, Lani Lobangco, Boy Fernandez, Telly Babasa, Naty Santiago, Louie Catana, Paolo Conti

Hong Kong director Philip Ko brings his rough and rowdy brand of martial arts cinema to the Philippines with this fast paced crime film. Japanese Interpol agent Yukari Oshima (billed as Cynthia Luster, as she would be in all of her subsequent Filipino films) travels to the Philippines to help NBI agents Edu Manzano and Monsour del Rosario smash the Manila branch of the Japanese crime syndicate, the Yakuza. Maniacal Yakuza hit man Gabriel Romulo kills del Rosario and leads an assault on Manzano's home that kills Manzano's mother, prompting Manzano and Oshima to raid the mansion headquarters of the Yakuza boss. When they do, the bullets, fists and feet all fly at a furious pace. Manzano chases the fleeing Romulo, and having run out of bullets, lights him ablaze, burning him to a cinder.

This is certainly a more rambunctious affair than any of Manzano's other action films and the frenzied pace of the martial arts is certainly exhilarating; it's also very unrealistic. While watching Oshima change direction in mid-air in order to kick an opponent does strain credibility beyond the breaking point, it needs to be understood that this is cartoon violence, and good cartoon violence at that. Oshima would continue to work in the Philippines, turning up next in Ko's even more outlandish (and far less entertaining) *Magkasangga 2000* (1993). (In Tagalog and English)

Magkasangga 2000
(Partners 2000)

1993 Harvest International/Golden Fortline; 100 minutes/color

Directors: Philip Ko, Johnny Wood, Joe Mari Avellana; Screenwriter: Joe Mari Avellana; Cinematographers: Raymond Chang, Rey Lapid; Editors: Rudy Tabotabo, K Philip Ko; Filmscore: Jaime Fabregas; Cast: Ricky Davao, Cynthia Luster (Yukari Oshima), Monsour del Rosario, Eddie Gutierrez, Gabriel Romulo, Charlie Davao, Philip Ko, Melvin Wong, Bernardo Bernardo, Jaime Fabregas, Eleonor Academea, Larissa Ledesma, Jimmy Ko, James Hermogenes, Boy Fernandez, Rando Almansor, Rommel Valdez, Ruel Vernal, Tony Vernal, Jim Rosales, Tsing Tong Tsai, Joey Padilla, Ernie David, Ace Espinosa, Telly Babasa, Blandino

In this remarkably bad follow-up to *Magkasangga sa Batas* (1993), Yukari Oshima and Ricky Davao play Metropol partners in the year 2000 (it must've seemed so far away at the time). They are trying to bring down warring drug syndicates when a sword-wielding space alien (Gabriel Romulo) arrives, followed by alien Monsour del Rosario: Romulo is a fugitive from another planet and del Rosario's mission is to capture him and take him back. Romulo is a kind of space vampire, who drains the life from people. He also has an odd way of showing up whenever there is a shootout between opposing crime factions, or between the police and the syndicates; why this is so is apparently unimportant. Romulo manages to kill del Rosario, but Oshima retrieves del Rosario's sword and uses it to defeat Romulo in an overly comedic conclusion.

The abundant comedy (which is really quite awful) is the main killer here. For instance, there is a running gag involving a typically flamboyant homosexual who tries to commit suicide after receiving news that he is HIV-positive. Romulo, who is forever turning up out of the blue, drops in on the roof of the building that the man is contemplating jumping from, but when he tries to drain the man's life force, Romulo has a violent reaction, presumably to the man's HIV. Thereafter, whenever Romulo encounters this man, he flees in terror. In fact, the police use the gay man to hold Romulo at bay during the concluding battle. And the alien is not the only one terrified of him: when Oshima and Davao bring the man down to police headquarters to question him about his encounter with the alien, police chief Eddie Gutierrez shakes the man's hand, but then quickly withdraws it and begins to cower when told that the man is HIV-positive, and then berates Oshima and Davao for bringing such a person into the office. The next time Oshima and Davao enter the precinct some of their co-workers literally flee, while others, like Gutierrez, wear gloves, surgical masks and gowns. Of course, this is supposed to be funny, but frankly, it's just lame.

There is also a very unsubtle comedic performance by Jaime Fabregas, whose musical score is another minus here. Screenwriter Joe Mari Avellana seems unsure of whether he wanted to write a science fiction, action, or comedy film; the elements needn't be exclusive, but Avellana might have done better to pick one path and follow it, since combining all of the disparate elements resulted in such a convoluted mess. As for the action, that much is handled well (though the sight of Romulo suspended by a cable and flying through the air wears thin), and there is plenty of director Philip Ko's usual high-flying martial arts approach, with Oshima defying gravity almost constantly. Normally, this would be worth a few laughs, but when the material is this bad everything just seems to fall flat. In short, the whole thing is done-in by Avellana's horrible screenplay. (In Tagalog and English)

Mahal Ko ang Mister Mo
(Your Husband, My Lover)

1991 Regal Films; 108 minutes/color
Director: Junn P. Cabreira; Screenwriter: Jose Javier Reyes; Cinematographer: Rudy Dino; Editor: Joe Solo; Filmscore: Demet Velasquez; Cast: Joey Marquez, Alma Moreno, Cristina Gonzales, Anjo Yllana, Paquito Diaz, Sylvia Sanchez, Vanessa Escano, Michelle Bautista, Roldan Aquino, Gina Leviste, Romy Blanco, Olive Madridejos, Marlon Rozano, Rene Camba, Rudy Villar, Bimbo Bautista

In this mind-numbingly witless "comedy," Joey Marquez plays an incompetent, constantly bungling police officer. Though he is married to beautiful Alma Moreno, Marquez is a compulsive womanizer who cannot abstain from cheating on his wife. The bulk of the film is little more than Marquez sneaking out of places in his underwear to dodge jealous boyfriends of his conquests, or hustling half-naked women out of his bedroom window to escape the wrath of his wife. What little else there is involves Marquez infuriating his commanding officer (Roldan Aquino) with his incessant foul-ups. This is without question as bad as it gets. (In Tagalog with some English)

Manananggal in Manila
(Vampire in Manila)

1997 MAQ Productions; 98 minutes/color
Director: Mario O'Hara; Screenwriter: Floy Quintos; Cinematographer: Rey de Leon; Editor: George Jarlego; Filmscore: Nonong Buencamino; Cast: Angelika, Tonton Gutierrez, Alma Concepcion, Aiza Seguerra, Eric Fructuoso, Mike Magat, Poppo Lontoc, Jasmin Mendoza, Bella Flores, Edwin O'Hara, Idda Yanesa, Tony Angeles, Dante Balois, Mon Confiado, Edward Belaro, Allan Angeles, Janice Mendoza, Sammy Vencio, Edwin Castillano

Pregnant Angelika lives in a high-rise apartment building with her younger sister (Aiza Seguerra). She befriends a neighbor, fashion model Alma Concepcion, but Angelika's brother (Mike Magat), who is a police officer, begins to suspect Concepcion of involvement in a series of gruesome murders in which the victims have had their hearts torn out. The press and the city residents alike are blaming the killings on a vampire, and they are correct; and Magat is correct too in his suspicions regarding Concepcion, who turns out to be the fearsome, winged beast. Angelika begins to have bizarre visions of being seduced by a man with the head of a wild pig, which turns out to be Tonton Gutierrez, Concepcion's demonic companion. As she is given to hysterical fits, it becomes necessary to exorcise Angelika (the film employing all the usual exorcism trappings, like green bile, for instance), but things are only resolved when Concepcion is staked and then set ablaze by Magat.

Directed by Mario O'Hara, the film was a big box office success, and features enough weirdness to satisfy anyone. Among the film's more bizarre elements are a bubbling cauldron of internal organs (collected by Concepcion from her victims), which rises up and transforms into Gutierrez, and an excellent scene in which Concepcion chases Magat's car, continually landing on top of it and blinding Magat's view with her rather impressive wingspan. Still, the film is more style than substance, though within the horror genre this is most often a plus. (In Tagalog with some English)

Mananayaw (Dancer)

1997 Four Aces; 88 minutes/color
Director/screenwriter: Celso Ad. Castillo; Cinematographer: Isagani F. Sioson; Editor: Abelardo

Hulleza; Filmscore: Rey Ramos; Cast: Rita Magdalena, Emilio Garcia, Rod Rodrigo, Eddie Gutierrez, Criselda Volks, Angie Ferro, Romy Diaz, Tony Carreon, Rolando Tinio, Lou Veloso, Lucas Valdez, Paolo Ramirez, Phillip Henson, Jiego Malvar, Bino Garcia Jr., Benjie Felipe, Raymond Vargas, Danny Labra, Max Umali Jr., Jaime Bandolino

Wealthy paraplegic Eddie Gutierrez is living in his mansion with only three servants—a husband and wife and their daughter (Criselda Volks)—to keep him company. Gutierrez's younger brother (Emilio Garcia) shows up with his stripper girlfriend (Rita Magdalena), and Gutierrez correctly surmises that the reason for Garcia's visit is merely to hide away for a while. As the result of some double-dealing with underworld figure Romy Diaz, Garcia needs a place to lay low for a while. Gutierrez reluctantly allows them to stay, but Magdalena's sexual teasing drives Gutierrez beyond control, and he soon forces Volks to perform sexual favors for him. After a while, Magdalena becomes bored with being cloistered away, and she sneaks off and returns to her stripping job, which turns out to be a big mistake, as Diaz forces her to reveal Garcia's whereabouts. Diaz shows up at Gutierrez's house with a compliment of well-armed goons, and although he manages to gun them all down in the ensuing shootout, Garcia is injured and Gutierrez is killed. The film closes with Garcia, now trapped in his brother's wheelchair, abandoned and alone until the rather unexpected arrival of Magdalena, bag in hand and ready to move in.

The arrival of Magdalena at the conclusion of the film is an improbable—even somehow odd—inclusion by director Celso Ad. Castillo, who is not known for particularly upbeat endings (or, in this case, semi-upbeat). It somehow seems against the nature of Magdalena's character, unless her decision to return was merely the result of guilt for having revealed Garcia's location to his pursuers. While Castillo's direction is top shelf, his screenplay here fluctuates. (In Tagalog)

Manila by Night

1980 Regal Films; 151 minutes/color
Director/screenwriter: Ishmael Bernal; Cinematographers: Sergio Lobo; Editor: Augusto Salvador; Filmscore: The Vanishing Tribe; Cast: Charito Solis, Alma Moreno, Lorna Tolentino, Rio Locsin, Cherie Gil, Gina Alejar, Orestes Ojeda, William Martinez, Bernardo Bernardo, Johnny Wilson, Jojo Santiago, Sharon Manabat, Maya Valdes, Rolly Lapid, Rey Tomenes, Bong Benitez, Roger Saulog, Dante Castro, Tony Angeles, Perry Fajardo, Lucy Quinto, Pinky Shotwell, Vangie Labalan, Aida Carmona, Abbo dela Cruz

Ishmael Bernal's compelling and fascinating, if overlong, expose chronicles the Manila nightlife of a diverse group of city residents whose lives are all linked in one way or another. Bernal depicts a mix of characters searching for love and purpose, but whose lives seem to often gravitate toward the opposite, each one seeming to ultimately live a shallow, deceptive and purposeless existence. Bernal's direction is inspired, but occasionally lacks subtlety, as when Charito Solis discovers drugs in her son's room and drives him from the house in a rage, battering him with anything and everything she can get her hands on, Bernal all the while inter-cutting the scene with various images of Christ throughout the house (paintings, statuettes, and even rugs). Though the running time seems excessive, the variety of characters and constant shifting of the narrative to portrays each one's individual circumstance makes the film move along at such a pace that it passes easier than many Filipino films which, while shorter, often seem to drag on interminably. The film's most interesting performance is given by Cherie Gil as a lesbian street tough. (In Tagalog with some English)

Manila: Open City

1968 Nepomuceno Productions; 82 minutes/color
Director/screenwriter: Eddie Romero; Cinematographers: Dik Trofeo, Ricardo Periodica, Loreto Isleta; Editor: Elsa Abutal; Filmscore: Leopoldo Silos; Cast: Charito Solis, James Shigeta, Alex Nicol, John Ashley, Ric Rodrigo, Mario Montenegro, Lauro Delgado, Oscar Roncal, Nova Villa, Eddie Garcia, Cachupoy, Vic Diaz, Ben Perez, Norma Blancaflor, Rosa Mia, Rebecca Gonzales, Minda Morena, Cristina Scott, Ben Rubio, Pete Herazo, Abelardo Cortez

Director Eddie Romero had previously shown a partiality toward the WWII genre with films like *The Walls of Hell* (1964) and *The Ravagers* (1965), and he further indulged that interest here with this story of the American liberation of the Philippines. Top-billed Charito Solis plays a nun and James Shigeta is a sympathetic Japanese officer who helps hide Solis and a group of orphans. Eddie Garcia appears briefly as a not-so-sympathetic Japanese commander, Ric Rodrigo portrays a Filipino soldier and Mario Montenegro gives a fiery performance as a Filipino patriot. Former American teen idol John Ashley appears sparingly as a

U.S. Army medic. The film is of particular interest to some because it is the forgotten Ashley/Romero collaboration. Unlike Romero's films for Hemisphere Pictures, Nepomuceno Productions apparently allowed him a fair budget, resulting in some impressive battle scenes, in particular the climactic sequence in which the Americans overrun the Japanese. (In English)

Manolo en Michelle: Hapi Together (Manolo and Michelle: Happy Together)

1994 Octo Arts Films; 102 minutes/color
Director/screenwriter: Mike Relon Makiling; Cinematographer: Ben Lobo; Editor: Rudy Tabotabo; Filmscore: Jessie Lasaten; Cast: Ogie Alcasid, Michelle Van Eimeren, Patrick Guzman, Michael V., Jenette Fernando, Jaime Fabregas, Malu de Guzman, Gary Lising, Lou Veloso, Jan Rivera, Jennifer Mendoza, Ernie Baron, Ramon Zamora, Lucita Soriano, Beverly Salviejo, Don Pepot, Bert Mansueto, Danny Pansalin, Ben Sagmit

Michelle Van Eimeren, Miss Australia 1994, traveled to the Philippines to star in this comedy in which she is cast as a mermaid plucked from the sea by fisherman Ogie Alcasid. Capable of transforming her lower torso into human form, Van Eimeren begins to spend a lot of time on land where she is spotted by a vacationing perfume manufacturer who, impressed by her statuesque beauty, offers her a modeling contract. Taking Alcasid as her manager, Van Eimeren travels to Manila, but once there, she is pursued by nutty professor Jaime Fabregas, who is out to prove the existence of mermaids. Van Eimeren is also pursued romantically by Patrick Guzman. Though Van Eimeren throws Alcasid over for Guzman, it is Alcasid who comes to her rescue (with buddy Michael V.) when Van Eimeren is captured by Fabregas. Van Eimeren and Alcasid make good their escape and live happily ever after together in the sea.

Ramon Zamora puts in a cameo, challenging Alcasid to a martial arts duel, but Alcasid confounds him by performing a stage magician's act. Van Eimeren would return to the Philippines to star in *Siyempre, Ikaw Lang, ang Syota Kong Imported* (1995). (In Tagalog and English)

Marami Ka Pang Kakaining Bigas (You've Got a Lot of Rice to Eat)

1994 Viva Films; 121 minutes/color
Director: Jun Aristorenas; Screenwriter: Amado Lacuesta; Cinematographer: Johnny Araojo; Editor: Rene Tala; Filmscore: Nonong Buencamino; Cast: Eddie Garcia, Rustom Padilla, Gloria Diaz, Michelle Aldana, Paquito Diaz, Jaime Fabregas, Janine Barredo, Luz Valdez, Sylvia Sanchez, Zandro Zamora, Dexter Doria, Lito Garcia, Romy Romulo, Danny Labra, Junar Aristorenas, Jun Aristorenas, Teresa Loyzaga, Manjo del Mundo, Joey Padilla, Oliver Osorio, Angie del Carmen, Eddie Tuazon, Bert Garon, Kim Laurel, Nonoy de Guzman, Ernie David, Bong Gatos, Diding Andres, Rey Big Boy, Wilson Go

After the death of his partner (Jun Aristorenas), veteran policeman Eddie Garcia is teamed with younger officer Rustom Padilla. Though their relationship is playfully adversarial, they learn to depend heavily on one another after crossing a group of corrupt officers headed by Zandro Zamora. It happens that the corruption reaches all the way up to commanding officer Paquito Diaz, and Garcia and Padilla are forced into hiding, staying with a string of Garcia's girlfriends, including sexy house madam Dexter Doria. But even Garcia, ladies man that he is, runs out of girlfriends after a while, and with crooked cops beating the pavement looking for them, they go to stay with Padilla's mother (Gloria Diaz). From the reactions of both Garcia and Diaz upon seeing each other, it is obvious that they share a past, and any discerning viewer knows where this is leading. Still, it takes Gloria Diaz some time to reveal to Garcia that he is Padilla's father. Things wind down with a shootout in Doria's brothel, where Garcia and Padilla kill the corrupt officers, and Padilla finally finds out that Garcia is his father when Garcia cries out "Anak" (or "Son!") upon seeing Padilla fall wounded. The film ends with Garcia and Gloria Diaz finally marrying.

It may not win many points for originality, but the film is very entertaining just the same, with Garcia and Padilla being well matched, Garcia again cast as the amusingly irrepressible rogue. Aside from playing a cameo at the beginning of the film, director Aristorenas also sings the film's theme song. (In Tagalog)

Mariano Mison ... NBI

1997 Star Cinema; 95 minutes/color
Director: Joey del Rosario; Screenwriters: Humilde "Meek" Roxas, Ricky Lee, Joey del Rosario; Cinematographer: Johnny E. Araojo; Editor: Danny Gloria; Filmscore: Nonong Buencamino; Cast: Eddie Garcia, Ricky Davao, Gardo Versoza, Daniel Fernando, Kier Legaspi, Elizabeth Oropesa, Bojo Molina, Bob Soler, Rez Cortez, Conrad Poe, Zandro Zamora, Dindo Arroyo, Orestes Ojeda, Manjo del

Mundo, Marithez Samson, Anna Capri, Jordan Castillo, Romano Vasquez, Edwin Reyes, Robert Rivera, Ernie Zarate, Ray Ventura, Vangie Labalan

Chronicling the career of NBI agent Mison, this film runs through a series of busts (kidnappers, illegal gambling, etc.) and eventually winds up with the kidnapping of Mison's wife and a climactic shootout in a cemetery where Mison rescues her. Eddie Garcia is good as Mison, and Elizabeth Oropesa gives a good performance as his wife. The material, however, is only fair. (In Tagalog with some English)

Maricris Sioson: Japayuki

1993 Regal Films; 102 minutes/color
Director: Joey Romero; Screenwriter: Lualhati Bautista; Cinematographer: Ricardo Jacinto; Editor: George Jarlego; Filmscore: Nonong Buencamino; Cast: Ruffa Gutierrez, Janice de Belen, Monsour del Rosario, Joel Torre, Isabel Rivas, John Estrada, Karla Estrada, Cheska Diaz, Shirley Tesoro, Onnie Sioson-Pacheco, Johnny Vicar, Rudy Meyer, Robert Natividad, Mon Confiado, Mhalouh Crisologo, Princess Reymundo, Louie Katana

In this true crime film, Ruffa Gutierrez portrays the title character, a young woman who travels to Japan to work as a dancer and winds up being shipped home in a crate. Troubled by the number of young Filipino women who have likewise returned from Japan in boxes, activist Janice de Belen travels to Japan with government investigator Joel Torre to uncover the truth. They suspect that Filipino women working in Japan are being drugged and forced into prostitution, but in the end they are unable to definitively pin anything on Gutierrez's Japanese employer, nightclub owner Monsour del Rosario. Despite the fact that Gutierrez's body was covered with bruises, gashes, cigarette burns and grievous injuries that include a cracked skull and genital mutilation, the Japanese government maintains that she died of hepatitis, and the Philippine government placidly accepts the explanation. Director Joey de Leon is the son of internationally known Philippine director Eddie Romero. (In Tagalog with some English and Japanese)

The Marita Gonzaga Rape-Slay: In God We Trust

1995 Golden Lions Films/Regal Films; 118 minutes/color
Director/screenwriter: Carlo J. Caparas; Cinematographer: Boy Dominguez; Editor: Abelardo Hulleza; Cast: Sunshine Cruz, Jinggoy Estrada, Maggie dela Riva, Tommy Abuel, Royette Padilla, Brando Legaspi, Manjo del Mundo, Anthony Cortez, Rustica Carpio, Philip Gamboa, Jon Ilagan, Irene Riosa, Gen. Romeo Pena, Ernie Reyes, Naty Santiago, Mila Montanez, Arnel Carrion, Tony Tacorda, Tina Rivera

Again, director/producer Carlo Caparas pursues his passion for true-crime sensationalism. Marita Gonzaga was a young woman who was gang-raped and brutally bludgeoned to death with a brick by three psychotic drug addicts. Caparas spends a good deal of the first half of the film portraying the drug addicts and their increasingly violent behavior, while a cursory attempt is made to portray Gonzaga herself (young, happy, looking forward to the future). Following the murder, Caparas makes short work of the police investigation and subsequent arrests, and moves on to the trial, as well as portraying the family's grief. The guilty verdict comes as no surprise, and the trial itself, as portrayed, is something of a non-event. (In Tagalog)

Masikip na ang Mundo Mo (Your World Is Crowded)

1990 Horizon Films; 89 minutes/color
Director: Lito M. Nocon; Screenwriter: Lito N. Mena; Cinematographer: Danny Bustos; Editor: Segundo Ramos; Filmscore: Demet Velasquez; Cast: Sonny Parsons, Tetchie Agbayani, Michael de Mesa, Isadora, Lito Legaspi, Gino Antonio, George Estregan Jr., Rodolfo "Boy" Garcia, Lucita Soriano, Eddie Arenas, Vic Varrion, Naty Santiago, J.R. Perez, Rommel Valdez, Bamba, Amanda Amores, Tony Martinez, Boy Sta. Maria, Bert Cayanan, Roger Moring, Rey Solo, Boy Gomez

Allegedly based on a true story, Sonny Parsons stars here as a police officer who is trying to nab a quartet of hooligans for raping a young woman and killing her boyfriend. Led by Michael de Mesa, the rapists/murderers really cross the line when they abduct and rape stripper Tetchie Agbayani, who happens to be Parsons' love interest. De Mesa's father is a police officer himself, and after finding out that Parsons is on the case, he tries to buy him off. Naturally, that goes nowhere, and de Mesa and company are forced to deal with Parsons themselves. Wounded in an attempt on his life, Parsons goes into hiding, but de Mesa flushes him out by killing Parsons' mother and once more abducting Agbayani. Parsons manages to avenge his mother's murder and saves Agbayani's life, though not before the sadistic de Mesa has blinded her.

The story is certainly routine, but the efficiency of the running time helps avoid putting a strain on the patience, and the film moves briskly toward its pay-off. Playing one of the gang members, George Estregan, Jr., does his usual mugging, over-acting deplorably. (In Tagalog)

Massacre Files

1994 Regal Films; 98 minutes/color
Director: Joey Romero; Screenwriter: Ricky Lee; Cinematographer: Jun Pereira; Editor: George Jarlego; Filmscore: Nonong Buencamino; Cast: Zoren Legaspi, Chuck Perez, Monsour del Rosario, Jacklyn Jose, Amy Austria, Gina Pareno, Alma Concepcion, Joanne Quintas, Rochelle Barrameda, Jess Lapid Jr., Ronnie Lazaro, Daniel Figueroa, Nonie Buencamino, Ernie Zarate, Pocholo Montes, Naty Mallares, Dante Castro, Ronald Barrameda

NBI agent Monsour del Rosario tries to uncover the identity of a gang responsible for a series of rape/murders. Though Jacklyn Jose survives the attack on her, she is too frightened to cooperate with the police. But after attending a wake for a subsequent victim, and seeing the pain and grief it has brought, she finally decides to do what she can to help. Further help comes del Rosario's way when one of the gang members, haunted by ghastly nightmares of the victims crying out to him for help from beyond the grave, finally comes forward. After a shootout with the killers, who are led by Jess Lapid, Jr., the gang is arrested and Jose is able to face her attackers. Del Rosario then puts them away.

Aside from del Rosario, Jose, and to a lesser extent Lapid, the film wastes its cast, in particular the beautiful and talented Amy Austria. The most interesting performance, however brief, comes from "Macho Man" Chuck Perez, of all people: after the murder of his wife he continues to return to the restaurant where she worked as a waitress, still expecting to see her. (In Tagalog)

Matalino Man ang Matsing, Naiisahan Din! (Although the Monkey Is Clever, You Can Still Outsmart Him!)

2000 Viva Films; 104 minutes/color
Director: Jun Aristorenas; Screenwriters: Humilde "Meek" Roxas, Jun Aristorenas; Cinematographer: Ver Dauz; Editor: Nonoy Santillan; Filmscore: Willie Yusi; Cast: Eddie Garcia, Willie Revillame, Patricia Javier, Joanne Quintas, Rez Cortez, Rico J. Puno, Eddie Arenas, Jun Aristorenas Jr., Nelcy Benedicto, Dinky Doo Jr., Danny Labra, Kuhol, Jose "Kaka" Balagtas, Nonong de Andres, Rico Miguel, Jun Aristorenas, Richard Merck, Pinky Rose, Bong Vargas, Rey Solo

This is familiar ground for Eddie Garcia, once again cast as a veteran police officer with an eye for the ladies (and much younger ladies at that). Garcia goes after wily con man Willie Revillame, and after catching him, decides to put Revillame's skills to good use, teaming up with him to infiltrate the stronghold of effeminate crime boss Rez Cortez. Garcia and Revillame defeat Cortez and his men in the end during the standard shootout. Equal parts action and comedy, the film is passably entertaining, though some of the comedy is childish and overstays its welcome. Director Jun Aristorenas appears briefly as one of Garcia's informers. (In Tagalog)

Matinik na Kalaban
(Tough Foe)

1995 EDL Productions; 115 minutes/color
Director: Leonardo L. Garcia; Screenwriter: Humilde "Meek" Roxas; Cast: Ronnie Ricketts, Tony Ferrer, Julio Diaz, Cristina Gonzales, Mariz, Jess Lapid Jr., Rez Cortez, Bing Davao, Nick Romano, Renato del Prado, Dinky Doo Jr., Jojo de Leon, Mila Montanez, Usman Hassim, Dong Serrano, Robert Miller, Christopher Ricketts, Ver Rodriguez, Max Alvarado, Joy Samson, Jayson Ricketts, Falcon Ferrer Jr., Telly Babasa, Joe Lapid, Boy Garcia, Kim Laurel, Rudy Lapid

Policeman Ronnie Ricketts knocks heads with corrupt congressman Tony Ferrer, but Ferrer has some of his own men inside the police force, including Rez Cortez and Jess Lapid, Jr. With the help of his partner, Ricketts is able to root out the corrupt officers and defeat them—and Ferrer too—in a climactic shootout. This is an unexceptional film in pretty much every category, the only notable feature being the fact that the final shootout takes place in a modern sports complex rather than the standard warehouse or abandoned old villa. Ricketts gives a good enough performance, as do most of the cast, but there is a thoroughly annoying and unfunny turn by Dinky Doo, Jr. as Ricketts' whiney, clumsy brother, which is completely out of place given the tone of the film in general. There is also an entirely arbitrary appearance by Cristina Gonzales as a TV reporter. (In Tagalog with some English)

Matira ang Matibay
(Strong and Able)

1995 Omni Films/My Way Films; 104 minutes/color

Directors: Philip Ko, Teddy Chua, Artemio Marquez; Screenwriters: Mike Cassey, Rey Atalia; Cast: Ronnie Ricketts, Cynthia Khan, Anthony Alonzo, Philip Ko, Melanie Marquez, Luis Gonzales, Winston Ellis, Nog-Nog, Dinky Doo Jr., Louie Katana, Jojo de Leon, Jonathan Gabriel, Rando Almanzor, Mike Cassey, Warren Escudero, Shema Yamamoto, Telly Babasa, Ernie David, Alex Legaspi

In this Philippine/Hong Kong co-production, syndicate boss Luis Gonzales hires sleek fashion model Melanie Marquez to steal a priceless medallion from a Chinese monastery. She succeeds in eluding a throng of monks, and so begins a series of double-crosses by various underworld figures, including co-director Philip Ko and Philippine gangster Anthony Alonzo. Interpol agent Cynthia Khan is sent to the Philippines to track the medallion and gets some assistance from goofy cabbie Ronnie Ricketts. All sides wind up in an old airfield for the exchange, and a wild shootout, martial arts kick-up and airplane chase ensues in which just about everyone dies, save Khan and Ricketts.

There are considerable differences between the Philippine and Hong Kong versions: while the Hong Kong version (titled *Angel On Fire*) is much shorter at 82 minutes, it does earn points for eliminating some of the unnecessary Filipino characters, most especially two auto mechanic brothers who are presumably intended for comic relief. The Hong Kong version also ads another female agent for good measure, and the brevity of the running time helps give it a livelier pace, with the martial arts scenes coming at a more furious tempo. The Hong Kong version also features a more appropriate Filmscore. (In Tagalog and English)

Maynila, Sa mga Kuko ng Liwanag (Manila, In the Claws of Neon)

1975 Cinema Artists; 120 minutes/color
Director: Lino Brocka; Screenwriter: Clodualdo del Mundo, Jr.; Cinematographer: Mike de Leon; Editor: Ike Jarlego, Jr.; Cast: Rafael (Bembol) Roco, Hilda Koronel, Tommy Abuel, Lou Salvador Jr., Jojo Abella, Lily Gamboa-Mendoza, Joonee Gamboa, Pio de Castro III, Joseph Jardinoza, Spanky Manikan, Danilo Posadas, Pancho Pelagio, Bobby Roldan, Jerry O'Hara, Rudy Hermano, Rikki Jimenez, Tommy Yap, Chiqui Xerex-Burgos

In this grim and intriguing melodrama, Bembol Roco travels to Manila to find Hilda Koronel, a girl from his rural village who he is still very much in love with. He finds work briefly in construction, but when he is let go, Roco finds himself sleeping out on the street. He is taken in by a street hustler who leads him into the sleazy world of male prostitution, but after just one experience in that capacity Roco feels degraded enough to abandon that path. Having located the building where Koronel lives by way of a return address on a letter she had sent to her family back home, Roco tries to see her but is turned away by her landlord. Roco then spends much of his time staking out Koronel's building, watching for hours from across the street, hoping to see her emerge. After a number of false identifications, he finally sees Koronel face-to-face. He finds her desperately unhappy, poverty-stricken and prostituting herself with her landlord as pimp. After spending the day with Roco, Koronel agrees to return home with him, but she fails to show up at the appointed time for their departure. Confused and hurt, Roco then learns from Tommy Abuel that Koronel has been killed. The film takes a bizarre turn in concluding as the emotionally distraught Roco goes to Koronel's apartment building and confronts and fatally stabs Koronel's landlord. The screaming of the landlord's wife draws a crowd and Roco flees the building and is chased through the streets by a mob, which eventually corners him in an alley. The film ends with Roco screaming as the mob apparently prepares to beat him to death. (In Tagalog)

Mayor Latigo: Ang Barakong Alkalde ng Baras (Mayor Latigo: The Macho Mayor of Baras)

1990 Octo Arts Films; 104 minutes/color
Director: Jose N. Carreon; Screenwriter: Jojo M. Lapuz; Cinematographer: Rey de Leon; Editor: Pepe Marcos; Filmscore: Mon del Rosario; Cast: Eddie Garcia, Marianne dela Riva, Jess Lapid Jr., Johnny Delgado, Lani Lobangco, George Estregan Jr., Ruben Rustia, Jaime Fabregas, John Gaddi, Rez Cortez, Mario Escudero, Jose Romulo, Joey Padilla, Michael Angelo, Jackielyn Samonte, Jane Zaleta, Zandro Zamora, Ros Olgado, Nanding Fernandez, Ernie Zarate, Arnold Ringor, Robbie Donato, Lucy Quinto, Susan Quinto

Eddie Garcia has the lead in this true account of the political career of Baras Mayor Meliton Geronimo, a career law enforcement officer who later moved into politics. He is strongly opposed in his run for office by incumbent mayor

Jaime Fabregas, who twice sends hit men to assassinate Garcia; both attempts fail, and the popular Garcia wins election. Upon the swearing-in of the mayoral winners, Garcia finds himself snubbed by provincial governor Ernie Zarate, who intentionally neglects to call out Garcia's name during the swearing-in ceremony: furthermore, Garcia arrives at his office to find it boarded up. After taking office he survives still more attempts on his life, all masterminded by Fabregas, who is still scheming behind the scenes. Garcia shakes up the status quo, making plenty of enemies in the process, and political loopholes are used to nullify his election and force him out of office. But he refuses to vacate his position, and in an extraordinary show of support, the people rally behind him, camping outside of his office building and refusing to allow the police to remove him from office. Reluctantly, military officer Rez Cortez, who served under Garcia in the police force, sends in riot police to remove Garcia, whatever the consequences. In a strong finish, the people are confronted by the military, who fire tear gas canisters into the building to try and bring Garcia out, but the rioting persists and Garcia is able to last the night. The next morning, however, while trying to help a wounded friend outside to get medical help, Garcia is surrounded and forced to surrender. As he is led away in handcuffs, the crowd outside chants his name as Garcia defiantly raises his hands in the air.

The film concludes by noting that Meliton Geronimo served 17 days in jail following the siege before he was ordered released. Several years later, after the ousting of President Ferdinand Marcos in 1986, Geronimo again ran for Mayor of Baras and won a landslide victory. Aside from the expected good performance from Garcia, there are many others, among them Jess Lapid, Jr. as Garcia's younger brother, who forsakes his job as a police officer to stand alongside his brother. (In Tagalog with some English)

Melencio Magat: Dugo Laban sa Dugo (Melencio Magat: Blood Against Blood)

1995 Regal Films; 105 minutes/color
Director: Toto Natividad; Screenwriter: Humilde "Meek" Roxas; Cinematographer: Johnny Araojo; Editor: Ruben Natividad; Filmscore: Jaime Fabregas; Cast: Eddie Garcia, Zoren Legaspi, Jeric Raval, Jun Aristorenas, Dick Israel, Rochelle Barrameda, Jasmin Reyes, Beverly Vergel, Melissa Mendez, Marco Polo Garcia, Odette Khan, Danny Labra, Alex David, Romy Romulo, Pocholo Montes, Cris Daluz, Robert Miller, Rommel Valdez, Earl Ignacio, Rando Almanzor, Nemie Gutierrez, Dax Rivera, Bebeng Amora, Nonoy Gates, Alex Cunanan, Freddie Ondra, Oscar Moran, Boy Gomez

In this well crafted crime drama with Shakespearean overtones, Eddie Garcia plays Melencio Magat, an organized crime boss embroiled in a struggle with rival crime boss Jun Aristorenas. After a gangland shootout in which a good many men are killed, Garcia and his partner (Dick Israel) are arrested and sent to prison. During his incarceration Garcia's wife gives birth to a son, but Aristorenas takes the infant and kills Garcia's wife. Raised by Aristorenas, the boy grows up believing that Garcia is the man who killed his mother. When Garcia and Israel are eventually released from prison, Garcia's now adult son (Jeric Raval) comes gunning for him to avenge his mother's murder. Garcia is also relentlessly pursued by young policeman Zoren Legaspi, another son of his by a long ago love affair. After Garcia kills Aristorenas, the film climaxes with a shootout (naturally) between Garcia's men and Raval's. They are joined by the police, led by Legaspi, and after the truth comes out regarding the parentage of Garcia's sons, Garcia is shot by both of them in the conflict. There is some familial resolution, however, as Garcia and his sons share a tender moment in the ambulance ride to the hospital. The film does not reveal whether Garcia lives or dies, but given his injuries, one can safely assume he expires.

Well helmed by director Toto Natividad, and not surprisingly, given the cast, well played, the only drawback here is some ill-advised humor early on when Garcia is forced into a literal shotgun wedding by his future father-in-law. (In Tagalog)

Minsan pa nating Hagkan ang Nakaraan (Kiss the Past Once More)

1983 Viva Films; 105 minutes/color
Director: Marilou Diaz-Abaya; Screenwriter: Racquel Villavicencio; Cinematographer: Manolo Abaya; Editor: Marc Tarnate; Filmscore: George Canseco; Cast: Vilma Santos, Christopher de Leon, Eddie Garcia, Mona Lisa, Baby Delgado

Successful building contractor Eddie Garcia is too busy to spend much time with his younger wife (Vilma Santos), so she winds up finding affection elsewhere. She has an affair with struggling young architect Christopher de Leon, and though she tries to end the affair, she is unable to make a clean break. She soon finds it all but impossible when de Leon is hired by Garcia for a new building project. The three of them end up spending a lot of time together, and when Santos finds out that she is pregnant, de Leon becomes an almost constant presence in Garcia's home: he is even there when Santos goes into labor, and accompanies Santos and Garcia to the hospital where he paces the waiting room floor with Garcia. Though Garcia is overjoyed by the birth of a son, both Santos and de Leon are sure that de Leon is the real father. Santos begins avoiding de Leon, and eventually Garcia gets wise to the situation. One night at a party in Garcia's home, de Leon sneaks into the baby's room and smuggles the child out of the house, prompting the drunken and enraged Garcia to grab his gun and set off for de Leon's apartment to confront him. Garcia finds de Leon and guns him down, and at the same moment Santos, who has been trailing behind in her own car, loses control of the vehicle and is killed. The film closes with Garcia silhouetted against the rising sun, cradling his child, gun still in hand. Garcia won the FAMAS Best Supporting Actor award for his performance. (In Tagalog with some English)

Minsa'y Isang Gamu-gamo (Once There Was a Moth)

1976; 99 minutes/color
Director: Lupita Aquino-Kashiwahara; Screenwriter: Marina Feleo Gonzalez; Cinematographer: Joe Batac; Editor: Edgardo Vinarao; Filmscore: Restie Umali; Cast: Nora Aunor, Jay Ilagan, Eddie Villamayor, Perla Bautista, Gloria Sevilla, Paquito Salcedo, Luz Fernandez, Lily Miraflor, Leo Martinez, Nanding Fernandez, German Moreno, Carlos Padilla Jr., Michael Sandico, Ricky Sandico

Although she isn't generally mentioned as being among the more prominent Filipino directors of the Second Golden Era of Philippine cinema, Lupita Aquino-Kashiwahara's work here is regarded by many as being one of the significant works of the period: in fact, it won the FAMAS Best Picture award (though it wasn't even close to being the best Filipino film of 1976). Nora Aunor stars as an idealistic Filipina nurse who dreams of traveling to America to further her education. Her high regard for the U.S. begins to unravel, however, due to a series of incidents involving the U.S. military, including the shooting death of a fisherman who is gunned down by a U.S. soldier, and a U.S. fighter jet that sprays a field near Clark Air Field with bullets during a test maneuver and injures a young boy. Finally, it is the death of her younger brother, shot dead while playing near the air field by an apparently bored U.S. soldier, which causes Aunor to decide against traveling to America. (In Tagalog with some English)

Mission Order: Hulihin si ... Avelino Bagsic ang Rebelde (Mission Order: Get ... Avelino Bagsic, the Rebel)

1984 RSL Filmovie Productions; 119 minutes/color
Director: Roland S. Ledesma; Screenwriters: Roland S. Ledesma, Alfredo A. Joson; Cinematographer: Rudy Quijano; Editor: Rodel Capule; Filmscore: Roki; Cast: Rhey Roldan, Tony Ferrer, Donna Villa, Janice Jurado, Ada Alberto, George Estregan, Philip Gamboa, Nick Romano, Jose Romulo, Ruben Rustia, Johnny Vicar, Rudy Dominguez, Johnny Caranza, Alex "Boy" Sevilla, Jim Rosales, Ricky Roger, Mike Cohen, Lauro Flores, Danilo Jurado

Rhey Roldan stars as Avelino Bagsic in this true life account of the life of the notorious rebel. As the story begins, he is a trusted and valuable employee working in the office of an American businessman (Mike Cohen). He is set up by a jealous co-worker and accused of robbing the boss. Dismissed from his job, Roldan confronts the co-worker and stabs him to death in the ensuing scuffle. He is sent to jail, but manages to escape and finds refuge among a band of rebels. Taking the name Kumander Zaragosa (from his favorite radio serial, it seems), Roldan quickly advances in rank within the rebel outfit and soon becomes one of the government's most wanted individuals. He is pursued by General Tony Ferrer and has to take to the jungles to hide, where he meets his end by way of a surprise attack from a rival rebel outfit led by Johnny Vicar. The late-arriving Ferrer and his government troops show up just in time to watch Roldan expire. Though there are occasional directorial flourishes, for the most part Roland Ledesma's direction is too bovine to support a two-hour running time. (In Tagalog)

Moises Arcangel: Sa Guhit ng Bala (Moises Arcangel: In the Line of the Bullet)

1996 MAQ Productions; 105 minutes/color
Director: Toto Natividad; Screenwriter: Humilde

"Meek" Roxas; Cinematographer: Ramon Marcelino; Editor: Ruben Natividad; Filmscore: Mon del Rosario; Cast: Eddie Garcia, John Regala, Ricky Davao, Alma Concepcion, Rosemarie Gil, Melissa Mendez, Beverly Vergel, Orestes Ojeda, Johnny Vicar, Alex David, Rando Almanzor, Mon Confiado, Romy Romulo, Richard Duran, Dante Castro, Shirley Palma, Nemie Gutierrez, Ace Baylon, Dinky Doo Jr., Boy Rivera

A happy domestic scene is predictably shattered when retired military man Eddie Garcia's family is killed by assassin John Regala while on their way to the airport. The day before Garcia buries his family, he begins to receive cruelly taunting phone calls from Regala. In time Garcia discovers the identity of his tormentor: it turns out that, after martial law had been declared in the 1970s, Garcia had presided over the execution of Regala's father by firing squad for the crime of drug trafficking, and Regala spent the intervening years planning his revenge. Garcia eventually gets his man, killing Regala in a final showdown. The screenplay by Humilde Roxas, and the direction by Toto Natividad manage to maintain the suspense most of the way, but as usual, the film does run a bit overlong, which tends to dampen enthusiasm for the climax. Garcia gives his usual excellent performance, but Regala is a bit over-the-top ... again. (In Tagalog with some English)

Moro

1991 FLT Films International; 123 minutes/color
Director: Jose Mari Avellana; Screenwriter: Diego C. Cagahastian; Cinematographer: Ricardo Remias; Editor: Rudy O. Montecajon; Filmscore: Mike Loanzon; Cast: Ricky Davao, Jackie Lou Blanco, Dante Rivero, Maila Gumila, Tommy Abuel, Maritoni Fernandez, Ernie Zarate

Ricky Davao has the lead in this true story based on the life of Lieutenant Colonel Mandangan P. Domato. The main struggle here is with a counterfeit operation run by Dante Rivero, a former race car driver now confined to a wheelchair as a result of a crash during competition. It turns out that Rivero doesn't actually need a wheelchair, as Davao finds out when he confronts the racer-turned-crime boss. The film climaxes with a spectacular car chase through city streets with both Davao and Rivero in turbo-charged racers, before Rivero makes a switch and tries to make a getaway by helicopter; Davao shoots him down, something that would be more exciting if it weren't so common in Filipino cinema. Otherwise, the film's lengthy running time consists largely of Davao's relationships with Muslim Jackie Lou Blanco, his Muslim marriage to Maila Gumila, and his adulterous affair with Maritoni Fernandez, as well as a brief opening passage depicting his affiliation with a Muslim rebel group. Though the film includes an opening commentary on the plight of Filipino Muslims and calls for an end to discrimination and more understanding, the screenplay itself does not seem particularly designed to further that end. Its opening statement notwithstanding, this plays very much like any ordinary police saga, except that the lead character just happens to be a Muslim. (In Tagalog with some English)

Multo in the City
(Ghost in the City)

1994 Regal Films; 106 minutes/color
Director: Don Escudero; Screenwriter: Jose Javier Reyes; Cinematographer: Ricardo Jacinto; Editor: George Jarlego; Filmscore: Nonong Buencamino; Cast: Manilyn Reynes, Zoren Legaspi, Herbert Bautista, Jaclyn Jose, Aiko Melendez, Maritoni Fernandez, Nanette Inventor, Cherrie Pie Picache, Ai-Ai de las Alas, Mae McGlaughlin, Vangie Labalan, Cita Astals, Ogie Diaz, Monte Tirasol, Benjie Felipe, Mae Anne Adonis, Romy Romulo, Myrna Rosales, Pocholo Montes, Pen Medina, Johnny Vicar, Mon Confiado, Mhalouh Crisologo, Angel Confiado, Tanya Iwakawa

Accused of witchcraft by her neighbors, Jaclyn Jose's house is attacked by the usual angry, torch-wielding mob, which burns her house down. Jose is not there during the attack, however, and only her daughter (Tanya Iwakawa) suffers the wrath of the locals. When she returns to find her daughter dead, Jose buries her and plants a tree at her gravesite. Many years later, the tree has grown up nicely and is adjacent to an elementary school where some children unearth Iwakawa's skeleton. Shortly afterward, the school is plagued by strange occurrences (children getting sick, the killing of the gardener, who is found hanging from the tree), and schoolteacher Aiko Melendez is possessed by Jose's spirit. She becomes the protector of Mae McGlaughlin, a young girl suffering abuse at the hands of her sadistic mother (Maritoni Fernandez). With the sudden death of Fernandez, McGlaughlin is then possessed by the spirit of Iwakawa, and things come to a head at the school's Founders Day celebration when school principal Nanette Inventor tries to dispose of Iwakawa's skeleton, invoking Jose's wrath. The tree marking Iwakawa's gravesite becomes lethal, its branches reaching out and strangling people and dragging Inventor into an opening in the tree, which then closes and seals her up. Things are resolved when school employees Manilyn Reynes and Herbert Bautista promise to bury Jose and Iwakawa side-by-side at the foot of the tree.

Though principally comedy actors, Reynes and Bautista do a good job in serious roles, but the same cannot be said of Inventor and Ai-Ai de las Alas (playing a teacher), both comedic actresses who apparently thought this was a comedy, thus giving their usual over-the-top performances, so out of place here that they effectively sabotage the film, nullifying what atmosphere director Don Escudero is able to generate. Why Escudero allowed them to run hog wild is perplexing, but it sinks what could have been an impressive film. (In Tagalog with some English)

Murder in the Orient

1973 Ilocandia Productions/World Wide Films Corporation; 72 minutes/color

Director/screenwriter: Manuel G. Songo; Cast: Ron Marchini, Leo Fong, Eva Reyes, Leila Hermosa, Danny Rojo, Raymond, Jim Delon, Gil Guerrero, Mary Diaz, Robert Talabis, Rodolfo "Boy" Garcia, Jose Villafranca, Mario Escudero, Bien Juan, Josephine, Edgar Garcia, Baldo Marro, Ben Manalo, Boy Caoili, Alex Reyes, Jing Caparas, Ben Romano, Jay Grama, Marlene Sison, Flor Antonio, Greg Rocero, Mel Arca

In this very low-grade martial arts film, American Ron Marchini is in Manila when he happens across a young woman being chased by a gang of thugs: he tries to help her, but unfortunately she is stabbed. Before dying, she gives Marchini a key to a treasure map. The woman's brother (Leo Fong) flies to Manila, and he and Marchini team up with a female Interpol agent to get the map. All along the way they do battle with a criminal gang also out to retrieve the map, which is said to give the location of a fortune in gold buried by the Japanese during WWII. Marchini and Fong find the location of the map, but after digging, what they find is a skeleton with a samurai sword. Drawn on the sword is half of yet another map that, when laid alongside a second sword in the government's possession, reveals the location of the gold. Marchini and Fong turn the sword over to the government and then go their separate ways.

The film has obvious camp value, but serious martial arts fans will be sorely disappointed by the lackluster fight sequences. Manuel Songo does a terrible job as director (as screenwriter too, for that matter), and consequently, the performances are very amateurish. Both Fong and Marchini would periodically return to work in the Philippines, Fong in *Enforcer from Death Row* (1975) and *The Last Reunion* (1978), and Marchini in *Forgotten Warrior* and *The Wolf* (both in 1986). (In English)

Muro-Ami (Reef Hunters)

1999 GMA Films; 99 minutes/color

Director: Marilou Diaz-Abaya; Screenwriters: Ricardo Lee, Jun Lana; Cinematographers: Marissa Floirendo, Manolo Abaya; Editor: Jess Navarro; Filmscore: Nonong Buencamino; Cast: Cesar Montano, Pen Medina, Jhong Hilario, Amy Austria, Rebecca Lusterio, Jerome Sales, Walter Pecatang, Teodoro Penaranda Jr., Ranilo Boquil, Cris Vertido, Gigi Agustin, Erwin Sevilla, Policarpio Araula

After the grandiose historical epic *Jose Rizal* (1998), director Marilou Diaz-Abaya followed up with this much less ambitious melodrama, which casts Cesar Montano as the surly captain of the Aurora, a rusted-out tub that he uses to run an illegal fishing business. The film concerns itself with the Aurora's ill-fated last trip at sea as Montano employs over one hundred muro-ami, or reef divers, most of them underage boys who share their quarters with rats and twice a day must jostle one another for position to eat rice out of large, dirty old basins. In what amounts to slave labor conditions, the divers work frantically to meet Montano's quota, diving eight times a day and scaring the fish into nets by banging on the coral reef. Eventually Jhong Hilario, the keeper of Montano's accounts, stages a mutiny. Having been caught pilfering money, Hilario kills the young boy who finds him out, and then convinces the adult members of the crew that the gruff Montano is responsible. Both Montano and first mate Pen Medina are bound and thrown overboard, and though Medina drowns, Montano manages to free himself and climb back aboard the Aurora, where he confronts Hilario. During the ensuing scuffle, Hilario tosses a lantern and fire spreads quickly, causing the crew to abandon ship as Montano goes down with the sinking vessel. The film features some beautiful underwater photography by Marissa Floirendo and Manolo Abaya (who won the FAMAS award for Best Cinematography), which presents quite a striking contrast to the dank, bleak ship. (In Tagalog)

The Muthers

1976 Dimension Pictures; 82 minutes/color
Director: Cirio H. Santiago; Screenwriter: Cyril

St. James; Cinematographer: Ricardo Remias; Editor: Gervacio Santos; Cast: Jeanne Bell, Rosanne Katon, Trina Parks, Jayne Kennedy, John Montgomery, Ken Metcalfe, Sam Sharroff, Rocco Montalban, Bill Baldridge, Robert Miller, Carlo Varca, Antonio (Tony) Carrion, Dick Piper, Bert Olivar, Alfonso Carvajal

Jeanne Bell and Rosanne Katon lead a band of pirates on the high seas, hijacking and robbing pleasure boaters. When they return to home base, Bell is upset by the disappearance of her younger sister, and she and Katon set off looking for her. Along the way, they meet a Secret Service agent (Gee, they're everywhere) who tells Bell that her sister has been incarcerated, and maybe worse. The authorities are aware of a sex slave ring being run by prison warden Tony Carrion from his prison deep in the jungle, and the authorities are prepared to forgive Bell and Katon's piracy if they will go undercover into the prison and get to the bottom of things. Since Bell will also have the opportunity to locate her sister, they accept the deal. Once inside the prison, Bell learns that her sister has already escaped and has been two days in the jungle. Conditions in the prison camp are predictably deplorable, and when her sister is brought back from the jungle dead Bell goes ballistic, kung fu-ing prison guards (well, at least her diminutive, athletic male double does) until she and Katon are thrown in "the box." Eventually, Bell and Katon escape with fellow inmates Trina Parks and Jayne Kennedy, and they are pursued by Carrion and his guards. The girls then meet up with their band of pirates in the jungle and have a climactic shootout with Carrion and his men, as well as with a rival band of pirates led by John Montgomery.

Director Cirio Santiago entered the women-in-prison genre somewhat late with this film, since production of this type of picture peeked in the early 1970s. Nonetheless, the film obviously did well enough for Santiago to feel compelled to periodically return to the genre for years to come, directing *Women of Hell's Island* in 1978, *Caged Fury* in 1980, and as late as 1993 he was still at it with *Caged Heat 2: Stripped of Freedom*. (In English)

My Pretty Baby

1990 Regal Films; 114 minutes/color
Director: Leroy Salvador; Screenwriter: Mauro Gia Samonte; Cinematographer: Ding Austria; Editor: Ferren Salumbides; Filmscore: Blitz Padua; Cast: Aiko Melendez, Eddie Gutierrez, Gloria Diaz, Eddie Garcia, Aga Muhlach, Eric Quizon, Jeffrey Santos, Paquito Diaz, Larry Silva, Manny Castaneda, Gammy Viray, Kim delos Santos, Buddy Dator, Kim Laurel, Noli Villar, Eddie Villa

In this tawdry and tragic melodrama Aiko Melendez lives in a country village with her father (Eddie Gutierrez) when her long-lost mother (Gloria Diaz) comes calling. Melendez is thrilled to meet her mother, whom she has no memories of, and wanting to get to know her, she agrees to go with her to the city. Though he tries, Gutierrez is unable to stop her, and so he follows, traveling to the city in hopes of finding his daughter and convincing her to come home. Diaz owns a nightclub, and a compliment of thugs to go with it, who try to dissuade Gutierrez in his search. They even hire policeman Eric Quizon to run Gutierrez out of town, but as he has a young daughter himself, Quizon sympathizes with Gutierrez and becomes something of an ally. Meanwhile, Melendez is surprised to find her mother living with young Aga Muhlach, who she is putting through law school in exchange for sexual favors. Knowing that there is nothing but trouble ahead for Melendez, Muhlach tries to get her to return home, but is thrown in jail for his trouble since a number of police officers on the take are also in Diaz's employ. Eventually, Gutierrez is gunned down while attempting to retrieve Melendez, and incredibly, Diaz shows up at the funeral with a court order granting her custody of Melendez, who she drags off in the middle of the funeral. It turns out that Diaz does have evil plans for Melendez: in hock up to her eyeballs to shady businessman Eddie Garcia, Diaz agrees to Garcia's terms—he will cancel her debt in exchange for a night with Melendez. In a protracted and disturbing scene, Garcia rapes Melendez while Diaz sits downstairs listening to her daughter's harrowing screams. Afterward, Diaz tries to comfort her daughter, but Melendez kills Diaz by slitting her throat with a broken champagne bottle. Melendez is then forced to stand trial and is defended by Muhlach, who has by then graduated from law school and is a practicing attorney. Melendez is acquitted and returns to her home village and Jeffrey Santos, her childhood sweetheart. (In Tagalog with some English)

The Myrna Diones Story: Lord Have Mercy!

1993 Golden Lions Films/Regal Films; 128 minutes/color
Director/screenwriter: Carlo J. Caparas; Cinematographer: Ernesto Dominguez; Editor: Abelardo

Hulleza; Filmscore: Demet Velasquez; Cast: Kris Aquino, Boots Anson-Roa, Eddie Rodriguez, Gina Alajar, Joel Torre, Monica Herrera, Almira Muhlach, Robert Arevalo, Marita Zobel, Bert Olivar, Renato del Prado, Manjo del Mundo, Fred Moro, Danny Labra, Benjie Felipe, Miguel Romero, Nonoy de Guzman, Tony Tacorda, Rey Fabian, Ernie David, Joey Galvez, Rowena Enriquez

In this true crime film Kris Aquino portrays the title character, who is accused of shoplifting by two police officers and is taken to jail along with her sister and two cousins in the town of La Union. Later that night they are taken from their jail cell by six police officers, who drive them out to the country and brutally rape and murder them—or so they thought. Aquino winds up surviving the attack, and gets assistance from newspaper editor Boots Anson-Roa in pressing charges against the men, all of whom have friends in high places. Filmmaker Carlo Caparas' work lacks polish, but his films in the true crime genre always pack a punch because of the appalling nature of the events depicted. (In Tagalog with some English)

Nagmumurang Kamatis ... Kumakasa Pa! (Over the Hill ... Still Fighting!)

1996 Premiere Entertainment Productions; 113 minutes/color

Director/screenwriter: Luciano B. Carlos; Cinematographer: Odigario Dalawis, Jr; Editor: Jess Aning; Filmscore: Jaime Fabregas; Cast: Eddie Garcia, Boots Anson-Roa, Wendell Ramos, Bob Soler, Cita Astals, Sharmaine Suarez, Michelle Parton, Via Veloso, Criselda Volks, Denise Joaquin, Theresa Aldea, Conrad Poe, Lou Veloso, Pocholo Montes, Whitney Tyson, Dang Cruz, Joshua Zamora, Dindo Macarena, Valentin Simon, Thelma Crisologo, Lalane Edson, Pamela delos Santos

In this comedy Eddie Garcia is a dance instructor who decides to change professions. He becomes the lead singer of a rock band, but business is slow and he has a hard time making ends meet. Feeling the wrath of his landlady (Boots Anson-Roa), he is compelled to return to his former vocation and starts dancing up a storm with wealthy Cita Astals, who rewards him handsomely for his, uh, time. Anson-Roa becomes suspicious as to the source of Garcia's sudden cash surplus, and she embarks on a not-so-subtle sleuthing excursion to discover the truth about Garcia's change of fortune. Along the way, she inadvertently crashes in on a group of terrorists led by Conrad Poe, and she is taken prisoner. She is in the process of being interrogated by the terrorists when an NBI raid nabs everyone, including Anson-Roa, who is assumed to be one of the antigovernment outlaws. Garcia comes along to clear Anson-Roa, and the two of them begin dating, Anson-Roa's gratitude towards Garcia having softened her heart. But their relationship enrages Astals, who turns out to be the elusive Dragon Lady heading up a drug syndicate. Some of her thugs beat Garcia severely, landing him in the hospital, but the film ends quickly with Astals being captured by the police and Garcia and Anson-Roa kicking up their heels on the dance floor.

Garcia and Anson-Roa—both seasoned dramatic actors—are also very good comedy players, but the film does feature a number of annoying and entirely irrelevant supporting players. As usual in Filipino comedy, there is a stereotypical, flamboyantly gay character whose presence is in no way necessary to the story. (In Tagalog)

Nasaan ang Puso (Where the Heart Is)

1997 MAQ Productions; 99 minutes/color

Director: Chito S. Rono; Screenwriter: Roy Iglesias; Cast: Christopher de Leon, Maricel Soriano, Judy Ann Santos, Spencer Reyes, Gina Pareno, Ronaldo Valdez, Efren Reyes Jr., Dexter Doria, Mandy Ochoa, Manny Distor, Archie Adamos, Winnie Cordero, Luis Gonzales, Gammy Viray, Vic Belano, Mon Confiado, Jerry O'Hara, Elaine Lozano, Pewee O'Hara

Though it took most of the awards at the 1997 Manila Film Festival, this is a pretty standard piece of work, the kind of over-ripe melodrama that seems to never go out of style in the Philippines. Centering on the turbulence within Maricel Soriano's family, the film shows (via flashback) the messy separation of her parents (Ronaldo Valdez and Gina Pareno) years earlier, with Valdez taking Soriano and leaving the two younger siblings with their mother. Now, years later, Pareno dies and the two younger siblings (Judy Ann Santos and Spencer Reyes), now teenagers, must go and live with Valdez. Soriano herself is pregnant and married to an attorney (Christopher de Leon). Valdez seems to have no affection for Santos and Reyes, and soon succumbs to a heart attack while angrily rebuking his children. After Valdez dies, Soriano and de Leon make arrangements for Santos and Reyes to go and live with another couple (Dexter Doria and Efren Reyes, Jr.), with Soriano and de Leon providing financial support. But they don't know that the couple who have taken the kids in are crooks. One day while cleaning the house, Santos knocks over a jar of stolen diamonds, and while she is picking them up, wouldn't you know the police bust in. Santos is arrested along with Doria and Reyes, and is accused of being involved in the funny business that the pair has been up to. Since she was caught red-handed with the goods, Santos is also charged, and de Leon takes over as her defense attorney, but to no avail. Santos is convicted, and Soriano goes berserk in the courtroom and suffers a miscarriage. Soriano somehow manages to blame de Leon for Santos' conviction, and the subsequent miscarriage, and she becomes withdrawn, eventually snapping out of it by pitching a massive tantrum. All the while, de Leon has been working hard to have Santos' conviction overturned, which he succeeds in doing, and everyone is reunited in a teary conclusion.

This overblown soap opera was dreamed up by Regal Films matriarch Lily Monteverde, and swept the Manila Film Festival, winning Best Actress (Soriano, whose weeping and histrionics apparently paid off), Best Actor (de Leon, who is comparatively subdued) and Best Film. Director Chito Rono also won, and he does a good job, but the problem here is that the material is so hackneyed. (In Tagalog)

Nimfa

1990 Regal Films; 121 minutes/color
Director/screenwriter: Eduardo Palmos; Cinematographer: Felizardo Bailen; Editor: Joe Solo; Filmscore: Demet Velasquez; Cast: Cristina Gonzales, Gabby Concepcion, Aiko Melendez, Ricardo Cepeda, Sylvia Sanchez, Dexter Doria, Gino Antonio, Loli Mara, Michelle Bautista, Ernie Zarate, Dinky Doo Jr., Archie Adamos, Nonoy Gates, Janine Reyes

Seeking relief from her sadistic husband (Ricardo Cepeda), Cristina Gonzales begins a tempestuous affair with Gabby Concepcion, who is himself married to Aiko Melendez, with whom he has a child. Both of their spouses discover the affair, and Concepcion separates from his wife. When Gonzales attempts to leave her husband, however, he commits suicide. Ultimately, Concepcion returns to his wife and child, and in a bittersweet and somewhat improbable ending, Gonzales becomes godmother to Concepcion's child.

Director/screenwriter Eduardo Palmos has an obvious tendency toward soap opera, but it may never have been worse than here, where he produces a weepy, overly sentimental piece of tripe that almost refuses to end. The softcore sex scenes between Gonzales and Concepcion, while probably considered obligatory in this type of "romance" saga, are surprisingly monotonous. (In Tagalog)

Ninja Kids

1986 Viva Films; 111 minutes/color
Director: Pablo Santiago; Screenwriters: Tommy David, Jose Javier Reyes; Cinematographer: Ding Austria; Editor: Ike Jarlego, Jr.; Filmscore: Ricky del Rosario; Cast: J.C. Bonnin, Francis Magalona, Ramon Christopher, Keno, Ricky Rivera, Dennis da Silva, Herbert Bautista, Leo Salonga, Yani de Veyra, Mia Prats, Elizabeth Oropesa, Ernie Ortega, Protacio Dee, Lito Garcia, Victor Bravo, Manjo del Mundo, Liza Lorena, Paquito Diaz, Max Alvarado, Marissa Delgado, Mario Escudero, Lito Anzures, Mely Tagasa, Bomber Moran, Joaquin Fajardo

In this youth-oriented comedy/fantasy, seven high school buddies go camping in the wrong forest. They are terrorized by a winged monster in the trees above their tent at night, and by day they must dodge boulders hurled at them by a giant ogre. They decide to explore a cave and meet a wizard who tells them that Dragon Lady Elizabeth Oropesa has swiped his magic sword. The wizard transforms the group of youths into ninjas, and off they go to retrieve the sword. After battling a tribe of hostile natives, the boys return to the city where they become instant celebrities after apprehending a gang of criminals. They then face-off with Oropesa's henchmen, and after making short work of them, duel with Oropesa herself, who breathes fire at them and shoots fireballs out of her eyes before resorting to transforming into a monster. The kids triumph by stabbing her with the magic sword. (In Tagalog)

Nunal sa Tubig
(A Speck In the Water)

1976 Crown Seven Productions; 115 minutes/color
Director: Ishmael Bernal; Screenwriter: Jorge Arago; Cinematographer: Arnold Alvaro; Editor: Augusto Salvador; Filmscore: The Vanishing Tribe; Cast: Elizabeth Oropesa, Daria Ramirez, George Estregan, Ella Luansing, Ruben Rustia, Pedro Faustino, Tony Carreon, Carlos Padilla, Leticia de Guzman, Tita de Villa, Ven Medina, Rustica Carpio, Al Garcia

This ponderously paced melodrama takes

its sweet time to even work up to any discernible storyline, eventually settling in to a standard love triangle, with George Estregan becoming romantically involved with both Elizabeth Oropesa and Daria Ramirez. Oropesa winds up pregnant and when she goes into labor, Ramirez—a midwife—births the baby, but then kills it. Ramirez departs to ponder whether or not her actions were deliberate, while the traumatized Oropesa is left to be consoled by Estregan. Otherwise, the tedious narrative moves at a snail's pace, following the daily lives of the residents of the small fishing village, and delves into environmentalism when the people of the village find thousands of dead fish floating offshore, evidence of the encroachment of industry, which, of course, kills everything in its path—hardly a bold statement, and in no way as poignant as the filmmakers obviously had wished.

Regarded by many as director Ishmael Bernal's "art film," *Nunal sa Tubig* sinks under the weight of the director's own self-indulgence. It may have been passably entertaining had Bernal trimmed it to roughly 90 minutes, but like so many Filipino filmmakers who seem determined to pad their films to reach a two-hour running time, Bernal goes the extra mile, and the entire enterprise suffers for it. The film's major attribute is the Filmscore provided by the group The Vanishing Tribe, which is occasionally interesting enough to make one forget how dull the narrative is. All of that notwithstanding, the film somehow managed to win Best Picture from the Catholic Mass Media Awards in 1976. Go figure. (In Tagalog)

Obsesyon (Obsession)

1998 Taurus Films; 96 minutes/color
Director/screenwriter: Rolly Bernardo; Cast: Rita Magdalena, Brandon Ramirez, Von Serna, Shiela Sanchez, Susan Reyes, Susing Yason, Jimmy Concepcion, Ariel Reyes, Emil Cristobal, Judd Cauntay, Joe Anao, Ric Pinal, Rolly Aquiza, Elpa Anastacio

Rita Magdalena made her name in softcore sexploitation films like this one, where she is abducted by a young man who, true to the title, is obsessed with her. He kidnaps her and keeps her bound and gagged in a stable, occasionally taking the time to rape her. But when his mother finds out, Magdalena's captor is forced to move her to the woods. Once there, they have some time to talk and get to know one another, and having grown compassionate toward her abductor, Magdalena lets go by a number of opportunities to escape.

Meanwhile, Magdalena's boyfriend is agonizing over her disappearance, recalling his own sexual escapades with her in flashbacks. He gets over her absence easily enough, however, by bedding various other women who are fighting over him. Eventually Magdalena's captor allows her to return home, and he is arrested after being reported to the police, not by Magdalena, but by one of his own friends. Magdalena returns to her boyfriend, but finds that things just aren't the same. Her boyfriend is then stabbed in the stomach by another jealous girlfriend, but he recovers and gets together with the young woman who stabbed him, obviously feeling that it must be true love. For her part, Magdalena refuses to press charges against her abductor, and he is therefore released. The film concludes with Magdalena being joyously reunited with her lover/rapist.

Okay, so it isn't exactly politically correct, but then, sex films rarely are. The threadbare narrative is heavily padded by plenty of softcore sex scenes, and nudity in general, not only through flashbacks of Magdalena and her boyfriend, but also her boyfriend with various other women as he passes the time anxiously awaiting her return. There's also a catfight in a mud puddle in which one of the participants is totally nude, and director/screenwriter Rolly Bernardo allows the camera (thus the viewer) to ogle Magdalena at length in the shower. The conclusion of the film offers the following acknowledgement: "We would like to express our deepest gratitude to our friend, JESUS, WHO is with us—Always!" Curious for a sex film. (In Tagalog)

Once Upon a Time in Manila

1994 M-Zet Films/Harvest Films; 108 minutes/color
Director: Tony Y. Reyes; Screenwriters: Marvic (Vic) Sotto, Tony Y. Reyes; Cast: Vic Sotto, Cynthia Luster (Yukari Oshima), Gloria Sevilla, Val Sotto, Larry Silva, Yoyong Martirez, Ritchie Reyes, Romy Diaz, Charlie Davao, Protacio Dee, Ever Etafo, Rio Diaz, Augusto Victa, Babalu, Ruby Rodriguez, Yoyoy Villame, Tiya Pusit, Mely Tagasa, Larissa Ledesma, Edna Sarmiento, Hiro Kawaguchi, King Kong, Ernie David, Danny Labra, Nonong de Andres, Rommel Valdez, Rene Hawkins, Romy Romulo, Turko Cervantes, Pong Pong, Torling Pader, Roger Moring, Ernie Forte, Jett Sahara

This action/comedy finds Hong Kong police lieutenant Yukari Oshima traveling to the

Philippines to locate some documents detailing underworld business dealings. The documents had fallen into the hands of Vic Sotto's mother, who fled Hong Kong with a crime boss hot on her trail. Once in Manila, the crime boss hooks up with Philippine cohorts Charlie Davao and Romy Diaz, who point him in the direction to go. Sotto sends his mother into hiding and then teams up with Oshima, who needs to take the documents back to Hong Kong to smash the syndicate. Sotto leads her to the province where his mother is hiding, and the following morning as Oshima is preparing to leave with the documents, the criminals show up, having beaten the location of the house out of Sotto's buddy Larry Silva. The hoods manage to get the documents, but Oshima and Sotto follow them to the airport, and in a final showdown they kill the syndicate boss and his henchmen in another shootout.

The film is moderately entertaining, though there are definite detracting elements, principally the gratingly unsubtle playing of Sotto's pals Yoyong Martirez and Ritchie Reyes. Oshima's posturing during her fight scenes also tends to wear thin. (In Tagalog and English)

The One Armed Executioner

1980; 89 minutes/color
Director: Bobby A. Suarez; Screenwriter: Ray Hamilton; Cinematographer: Jun Pereira; Editors: David Hung, Joseph Zucchero; Filmscore: Gene Kauer; Cast: Franco Guerrero, Jody Kay, Pete Cooper, Nigel Hogge, Mike Cohen, Brian Smith, Joe Zucchero, James Gaines, Joe Sison, Leopoldo Salcedo, Odeth (Odette) Khan, Danny Rojo, Joe Cunanan, Nestie Mercado, Telly Babasa, Ave Sullano, Celso Lindaya, Jimmy Reyes, Edoy Patalino, Ernie David

In this malodorous piece of cheese from director/producer Bobby Suarez, Franco Guerrero plays an Interpol agent in Manila who goes up against a drug smuggling operation. The drug lord responds by sending some thugs around to Guerrero's place: they kill Guerrero's wife and then cut off Guerrero's left arm with a sword. Despite the admonitions of his boss (Leopoldo Salcedo) to let the agency handle the matter lawfully, Guerrero is bent on revenge. An old friend, who just happens to be a martial arts expert, takes Guerrero in and puts him through a grueling training program, teaching him how to be an effective martial artist despite his handicap, as well as how to quickly load and handle a gun with just one hand. The training period itself takes up a hefty chunk of the film's running time, but once completed, Guerrero quickly tracks down his wife's killers, brutally killing them and eventually getting the drug gang's leader while thwarting a planned drug shipment. Though he had disobeyed Salcedo's orders, Guerrero's boss finds it hard to argue with the results and welcomes him back.

While Guerrero does actually give a fairly good performance—in fact, one of the better ones in his career—this is still, after all, a Bobby Suarez film, and there's no getting around the bad supporting roles and general impoverishment, both budgetary and creative, which are Suarez's trademark. Worst of all is seeing the distinguished Salcedo slumming in what must surely have been a career low point. (In English)

One Day Isang Araw
(One Day, One Day)

1988 Regal Films; 115 minutes/color
Director: Pablo Santiago; Screenwriters: Tony Pascua, Fred Navarro; Cinematographer: Ver P. Reyes; Editor: Augusto Salvador; Filmscore: Jaime Fabregas; Cast: Fernando Poe Jr., Matet de Leon, Dawn Zulueta, Dencio Padilla, Paquito Diaz, Bayani Casimiro, Odette Khan, Johnny Wilson, Balot, Larry Silva, Flora Gasser, Malu de Guzman, R.R. Herrera, Atong, Rudy Meyer, Jose Romulo, Rene Hawkins, Rachel Ann Wolfe, Lawrence Pineda

Cute little Matet de Leon is living with her wealthy grandfather (Bayani Casimiro) when she is kidnapped, lifted from her grandfather's mansion by helicopter no less. But in the chaos of the getaway, she falls from the helicopter onto the roof of small-time crook Fernando Poe, Jr. and his partner Dencio Padilla. Fortunately, the fall was not from a great distance, but the force of her landing causes amnesia, and de Leon cannot remember where she lives or how she came to land on Poe's roof. Poe and Padilla take the little girl in, and she is happy living with the two poverty-stricken crooks, but one day she spots Paquito Diaz, one of her kidnappers, and her memories begin to return. It turns out that the kidnapping was actually orchestrated by de Leon's aunt and uncle (Odette Khan and Johnny Wilson), and after Poe and Padilla uncover the kidnapping gang, Diaz rolls over on Khan and Wilson.

Being the number one box office draw in the Philippines, Poe did not really need to reach a broader audience, but that would seem to be the aim here as the film is much more family-oriented, teaming Poe with a cute little kid (which has occasionally happened before), and even giving him several musical numbers to perform with her, in which Poe reveals a passable singing voice: and all of this without a single shot being fired. It's light, but fair entertainment. (In Tagalog)

Orapronobis

1989 Pathé Europa/Giancarlo Parretti Production; 94 minutes/color

Director: Lino Brocka; Screenwriter: Jose F. Lacaba; Cinematographer: Rody Lacap; Editors: George Jarlego, Sabine Mamou; Filmscore: Herbert Bougis, Hugo Crotti; Cast: Phillip Salvador, Dina Bonnevie, Gina Alajar, Bembol Roco, Ginnie Sobrino, Abbo de la Cruz, Pen Medina, Joel Lamangan, Gerard Bernschein, Ernie Zarate, Jess Ramos, Obby Castaneda, Pocholo Montes, Bon Vibar, Raquel Villavicencio, Joe Taruc, Dodie Lacuna, Thea Cleofe Salvador, Archie Adamos, Fred Capulong, Rene Hawkins, Esther Chavez, Estrella Kuenzler, Ruben Rustia, Apo Chua, Tess Dumpit, Roger Moring

One of the film industry's more outspoken opponents of the Marcos regime, director Lino Brocka was no less outspoken in his opposition to Corazon Aquino's administration, as this effective and very grim melodrama attests. Phillip Salvador stars as a dissident priest jailed under Marcos' rule, but freed with the advent of the Aquino presidency. After his release, Salvador leaves the priesthood and marries Dina Bonnevie, a television reporter who championed his cause in the press. Two years later, Salvador is very involved with a human rights organization and travels to a province outside Manila where eight years earlier he had a love affair with Gina Alajar. Upon seeing her again, Salvador meets the eight-year-old son he didn't know he had fathered. He also finds that the province is being terrorized by the Orapronobis, a ruthless band of anti-communist vigilantes led by sadistic Bembol Roco. Hiding their atrocities behind both religious and patriotic rhetoric, the vigilantes are seemingly immune to the law, and Salvador decides that the only solution is to evacuate the local residents to Manila, where they are given refugee status. Manila turns out to be no refuge, however, as the publicly outspoken Salvador narrowly survives a attempt on his life that claims the life of his brother-in-law. As for the refugees, many of them are accused of involvement with communist rebels and are hauled off, including Alajar and her son. Salvador is unable to locate them at any of the local police precincts, and the authorities deny any involvement in the arrests. Those who were taken eventually do turn up, all slaughtered by Roco, and as Salvador arrives and mourns his dead son, the military are holding an impromptu press conference denouncing the victims as communist rebels. The film concludes with Salvador phoning his old friend Pen Medina, a rebel fighter during the Marcos regime, who has returned to the underground to reorganize his rebel friends to fight the Aquino Administration.

As he had with his film *Bayan Ko: Kapit sa Patalim* in 1985, Brocka turned to the French to help get this film made, and the film opens with a statement attesting to the authenticity of the events depicted. It is widely considered the last significant work by Brocka, the Philippines' most significant filmmaker. He died in a car accident in 1991. (In Tagalog with some English)

Oras Oras, Araw Araw
(Every Hour, Every Day)

1989 Viva Films; 115 minutes/color

Director: Emmanuel H. Borlaza; Screenwriter: Armando Lao; Cinematographer: Charlie Peralta; Editor: Ike Jarlego, Jr.; Filmscore: Willy Cruz; Cast: Sharon Cuneta, Rowell Santiago, Eric Quizon, Gloria Romero, Dante Rivero, Vic Vargas, Rey "PJ" Abellana, Helen Gamboa, Alicia Alonzo, Gil de Leon, Suzanne Gonzales, Dexter Doria, Vicky Suba, Tina Loy, Larry Silva, Augusto Victa, Aida Carmona, Tito Arevalo, Gamaliel Viray, Rina Reyes, Gina Perez, Ester de Jesus, Rene Matias, Rod Samson, Simon Soler, Ryan Soler

Adapted from a komiks serial, this grand melodrama casts Sharon Cuneta as a TV show hostess who befriends lounge singer Helen Gamboa. Cuneta becomes curious about a scar on Gamboa's cheek in the shape of an 'X,' and after Gamboa relates a sad tale of how, years earlier with a husband and young son, she had an illicit affair that resulted in the birth of a baby girl. When her husband (Dante Rivero) learned the truth, he took a knife and carved an X on her face. Afterward, Gamboa's lover tried to take the baby, and she was only able to stop him by stabbing him to death. Convicted of murder, Gamboa was sent to prison and felt that she had no alternative but to give the baby up for adoption to a couple who could provide well for her. After serving her sentence, Gamboa tried to reconcile with her son, but found the going rough. Sensing a heartwarming story that would make good television, Cuneta seeks out Gamboa's son and attempts to orchestrate a reunion. Any discerning viewer will not be surprised by the revelation that Cuneta is actually Gamboa's long-lost daughter. No longer finding it such a heartwarming story, Cuneta has a hard time dealing with this revelation and withdraws from the situation, but Gamboa's son picks up the ball and seeks out Gamboa in an attempt to bring reconciliation between his parents. Gamboa begs forgiveness from Rivero, but just as he begins to reciprocate, Gamboa is overcome by emotion and suffers a heart attack. She is rushed to the hospital, and her son sends for Cuneta, who arrives just in time for everyone to reconcile before Gamboa dies.

The film is well handled within its genre, the problem being that the genre thrives so much on clichés, but fans of this type of sentimentality obviously didn't mind; with superstar Cuneta leading the cast, and a hit theme song sung by her and Gamboa, the film was enormously successful. Cuneta began her career as a singer. (In Tagalog and English)

Order to Kill

1985 Amazaldy Film Productions; 117 minutes/color

Director/screenwriter: Augusto Buenaventura; Cinematographer: Freddie Conde; Editor: Edgardo Vinarao; Filmscore: Ernani Cuenco; Cast: Joseph Estrada, Vivian Velez, Eddie Garcia, Fred Montilla, Bomber Moran, Sonny Erang, Fanny Serrano, Suzanne Gonzales, Angelo Castro Jr., Nona Herrera, Ernie Ortega, Mon Godiz, Luis Benedicto, Ben Canlas, Tinoy Evasco, Noel Uy, Romy Nario, Mel Arca, Eddie Gicoso, Jing Caparas, Avel Morado, Big Boy Gomez, Ernie David, Robert Miller, Robert Talby

In this standard crime story, policeman Joseph Estrada makes a show of barging into mob boss Eddie Garcia's home and putting Garcia on notice that he plans to bring him down. Garcia responds by sending his men out gunning for Estrada, and though they miss their intended target, hit man Robert Talby does gun down Estrada's wife. Ten years later, Estrada has worked his way up to captain, and has in no way forgotten Garcia; as it turns out, both he and Garcia are vying for the affections of lovely Vivian Velez. Eventually, Estrada wins the girl, and gets his man too in a climactic shootout in which Garcia and all of his henchmen (including a hulking mute named "Golem") are killed.

Typically formulaic, the film is appealing nonetheless, even if Estrada looks over-the-hill. Estrada would only make one more film before leaving show business for politics, becoming a senator. He thrived there as well, and would go on to become President of the Philippines. His luck ended there, and he would resign in disgrace in 2001 after being accused of taking bribes, among other things; in short, he was the type of crook that he spent a career fighting against in films. (In Tagalog and English)

Oscar Ramos: Hitman

1987 Viva Films; 111 minutes/color

Director: Efren C. Pinon; Screenwriter: Fred Navarro; Cinematographer: Sergio Lobo; Editor: Augusto Salvador; Filmscore: Nonoy Tan; Cast: Ramon Revilla, Vic Vargas, Marianne de la Riva, Bong Dimayacyac, Carlos "Sonny" Padilla Jr., Paquito Diaz, Mon Godiz, Baldo Marro, Louella de Cordova, Larry Silva, Eddie Ynfante (Infante), Angelo Ventura, Eric Francisco, Joseph de Cordova, Perry Baltazar, Rudy Meyer, Grace Robles, Lucy Quinto, Crystal Pinon, Alex Bolado, Carlos Diaz, Rusty Santos

Ramon Revilla runs afoul of corrupt Barangay police captain Paquito Diaz. After being arrested on trumped-up charges and being tortured, Revilla manages to shoot his way out of jail with the help of a friend posing as his legal counsel. After his dramatic escape, Revilla becomes a local hero to the citizens, who are only too aware of the corruption in the police department. With the police on his trail, Revilla turns the tables on them and begins killing his pursuers. This brings government troops to the region, from whom Revilla is rescued by communist rebels. The rebels take Revilla to their jungle hideaway, and it isn't long before he becomes their assassin, knocking off various corrupt politicians; but Revilla winds up becoming an adversary to the rebels after they stage a raid on a small village, slaughtering every man, woman and child. Disillusioned with both sides, Revilla puts together his own band of fighters and attacks the rebel camp to quash the commies. But after this triumph, the government forces catch up with him, and in yet another exchange of fire, Revilla meets his end.

It's difficult to know just who to pull for here; though Revilla is the protagonist, it's very difficult to warm up to a hit man working for communist rebels, and while he has the obvious sympathy of the viewer early on, the savage cruelty of his retribution (hanging policeman Baldo Marro upside-down from a tree and beating him to death with a stick, slicing Larry Silva's stomach open and spilling his guts on the ground, tying Paquito Diaz over a box of dynamite and blowing him to pieces) is likely to make many—

hopefully most—less sympathetic toward him. Director Efren Pinon's work here is adequate, though he doesn't seem to have developed any particular flair for his craft. There is also the comical sight of the aging Revilla outrunning machinegun fire to contend with. (In Tagalog)

Over My Dead Body

1986 Sunfilms International; 111 minutes/color
Director/screenwriter: Arsenio "Boots" Bautista; Cinematographer: Fortunato Bernardo; Editor: Edgardo Vinarao; Filmscore: Ernani Cuenco; Cast: Tony Ferrer, Bembol Roco, Efren Reyes Jr., Raoul Aragon, Anna Marie Gutierrez, Lolita Ayala, Arsenio "Boots" Bautista, Jing Abalos, Dave Brodette, Charlie Davao, Romy Diaz, Baldo Marro, Bomber Moran, Boy Padilla, Bobby Talabis, Vic Varrion, Zandro Zamora, Nick Romano, Philip Gamboa, Larry Silva, Bing Davao, Rey Sagum, Robert Miller, Robert Talby, Danny Riel, Nonoy de Guzman

Policeman Bembol Roco and his partner Efren Reyes, Jr. are engaged in trying to topple a crime syndicate headed by Arsenio "Boots" Bautista when they get the break they've been waiting for. They pressure syndicate man Larry Silva into turning state's witness, and hide him away in a safe house. But Roco makes the mistake of telling too much to his brother-in-law (Tony Ferrer), unaware that Ferrer is a secret syndicate hit man. Ferrer knocks off Silva, but also kills policeman Bing Davao, who gets in the way, and an unfortunate fisherman, who just happens along at the wrong time. When Ferrer learns that Davao was Roco's best friend, he becomes desperate to keep his profession a secret more than ever, and so kills the only person who can expose him, that being the syndicate man who contracted his services. But what Ferrer doesn't know is that he has now killed Bautista's most trusted confidant. Now both the syndicate and the police are determined to uncover Ferrer's identity, which the syndicate accomplishes first. Bautista sends a hit squad (headed by Baldo Marro) to get Ferrer, but they only manage to kill his girlfriend, and Ferrer responds by running around knocking off Bautista's top men. Roco also becomes a thorn in Bautista's side, and the syndicate bombs Roco's house, killing his son and seriously wounding his wife. Roco, Ferrer and Reyes raid Bautista's fortress, wiping out everyone, but although Roco had wanted to take Bautista alive, Ferrer guns him down, fearing that Bautista will finger him as Davao's killer. Now suspicious, Roco runs a ballistics test and confirms that Ferrer's gun also killed Silva and Davao. Roco arrives at Ferrer's house, and the two are prepared to draw arms on one another when the police arrive and gun Ferrer down.

As an action film, the narrative is engrossing and it manages to get a melodramatic boost from Ferrer's familial conflict. Unfortunately, the film's English dubbing is horrible, as always. (Dubbed into English)

Oxo vs Sigue Sigue

1991; 99 minutes/color
Director: Dante Pangilinan; Screenwriters: Jesse Pangilinan, Leleng Ubaldo; Cinematographer: Caloy Salcedo; Editor: Nap Montebon; Filmscore: Demet Velasquez; Cast: Sonny Parsons, George Estregan Jr., Carol Dauden, Dick Israel, Nick Martel, Rhey Roldan, Bobby Benitez, Robert Talby, Danny Riel, Marilyn Monteverde, Martin Parsons, Eric Enriquez, Nonong de Andres, Ross Rival, Rene Balan, Robert Miller, Naty Santiago, Usman Hassim, Vic Varrion, Tony Bagyo

Opening with a violent street brawl resulting in bloody mayhem, dismemberment and murder, the story here finds rival gang leaders Sonny Parsons and George Estregan, Jr. being sent to the same prison, where they continue their violent rivalry. While the film occasionally stops and pauses to show flashbacks as Parsons and Estregan look back on their respective paths to destruction, it is basically little more than one violent act of retribution after another, culminating in a prison uprising. While the majority of the prison population is preoccupied with escape, the two rival gangs take the opportunity created by the mass chaos to kill off one another. But rather than kill each other, Parsons and Estregan instead murder warden Danny Riel and chief guard Robert Talby. The film closes with a split screen of Parsons and Estregan each being led to their executions. Despite his prominent billing, Dick Israel has a fairly brief appearance as a prison gang leader who is promptly dispatched by Estregan via impalement with a pickaxe. (In Tagalog)

Paano Ba ang Mangarap? (How Do You Dream?)

1983 Viva Films; 112 minutes/color
Director: Eddie Garcia; Screenwriters: Orlando Nadres, Andrea Benedicto; Cinematographer: Romeo Vitug; Editor: Ike Jarlego, Jr.; Filmscore: George Canseco; Cast: Vilma Santos, Christopher de Leon, Amy Austria, Armida Siguion-Reyna, Vic Silayan, Jay Ilagan, Perla Bautista, Robert Campos, Moody Diaz, Ester Chavez, Augusto Victa

When her lover (Jay Ilagan) is killed in a motorcycle accident, pregnant Vilma Santos decides that it is time to introduce herself to Ilagan's wealthy parents. She is met with considerable hostility by Ilagan's mother (Armida Siguion-Reyna), but Ilagan's father (Vic Silayan) is more levelheaded. Silayan and Siguion-Reyna offer to adopt the baby, and given their financial advantage, and wanting what is best for her child, Santos agrees to the offer. In the meantime, Santos is asked to stay at Silayan's home to be properly cared for during her pregnancy. She gives birth to a healthy baby boy, and all would be well but for the fact that Santos has second thoughts about giving up her baby. A solution presents itself when Ilagan's younger brother (Christopher de Leon), who has taken quite a liking to Santos, drops his girlfriend (Amy Austria) and proposes marriage to Santos. She accepts and they are married in a hasty civil ceremony, infuriating Siguion-Reyna, who refuses to let Santos be mother in any way to the baby. In fact, when Santos tries to hold her own child, Siguion-Reyna goes berserk, physically attacking Santos. The ailing Silayan tries to subdue his wife and suffers a heart attack in the process. Silayan dies, and Siguion-Reyna becomes even nastier to the point that she takes the baby and leaves the country. Santos and de Leon go through a very rocky stretch, which includes de Leon running off with his ex for the holidays, but after patching things up, Santos and de Leon decide to track Siguion-Reyna down and regain custody of Santos' baby, which they accomplish.

The screenplay, which was adapted from a komiks serial, is typical Filipino soap opera, with the expected stream of tragedy, and it is customarily lengthy. The performances are good, though Siguion-Reyna is something of an evil caricature. The brightest spot is Eddie Garcia's direction: one of the top actors in the Philippines for many years, Garcia is also an accomplished director and has an artist's eye for composition. It's too bad that the material he had to work from here was more-or-less routine. Ironically, Ilagan, whose character dies in a motorcycle accident in the film's opening moments, really did die in a motorcycle accident in 1992. (In Tagalog with some English)

The Pacific Connection

1975 Nepomuceno Productions; 89 minutes/color

Director: Luis Nepomuceno; Screenwriters: Jacques Ehlen, Cesar Amigo, Robert Ursui; Cinematographer: Loreto Isleta; Editors: Emil Haviv, Eli Haviv, Jacques Ehlen; Filmscore: Yuri Haviv; Cast: Roland Dantes, Nancy Kwan, Guy Madison, Alejandro Rey, Dean Stockwell, Gilbert Roland, Hiroshi Tanaka, Cole Mallard, Gloria Sevilla, Fred Galang, Elizabeth Oropesa, Nonet Lagdamed, Vic Diaz, Joaquin Enrique, Teddy Benavidez, Robert Saez, Mark Le Buse

Set in the Spanish colonial period, Roland Dantes stars here as a young man living on a farm with his parents. He has been trained by his father (Gilbert Roland) in the art of the arnis sticks (Filipino stickfighting), and when the governor's tax collector's come calling, Dantes takes exception to the way in which his parents are treated and both he and his father use their skills with the arnis sticks to run the tax collectors off. But they are later paid a visit by the governor himself (Alejandro Rey), who kills Roland and proceeds to rape Dantes' mother. During the rape, however, she grabs a knife and emasculates Rey, who then stabs her to death. Dantes is arrested and scheduled for execution, but when the ship transporting him sinks, he washes ashore an island and is taken in by the resident tribe. There he meets and falls in love with Nancy Kwan, as well as meeting blind martial arts master Guy Madison. After his sons (Dean Stockwell and Cole Mallard) inform him of Dantes' presence on the island, Rey arrives with Samurai Hiroshi Tanaka to avenge himself on the son of the woman who robbed him of his manhood. Tanaka soundly beats Dantes in a duel, and Dantes is left for dead, but of course he manages to survive, and after two years of training in the hills with Madison, Dantes emerges ready to get his own revenge on the man who killed his parents. He pays Rey a visit disguised as a sultan, and kills Stockwell, Mallard, Tanaka and Rey.

With the international explosion in martial arts films in the 1970s, Dantes was the most prominent Filipino entry in the genre at the time, though he was not much of an actor. This is not much of a consideration for the genre overall, however, and he is helped out here by an unusually strong supporting cast, though aside from Roland, who appears only briefly, none of them give particularly strong performances. Dantes and his arnis sticks next turned up in *Sultan Ben* (1975). (In English)

Pacific Inferno

1979 Nathaniel Productions/Arbee Productions; 89 minutes/color

Director/screenwriter: Rolf Bayer; Cinematographer: Mars Rasca; Editors: Richard C. Meyer, Ann Mills; Cast: Jim Brown, Richard Jaeckel, Tim Brown, Tad Horino, Dindi Fernando, Vic Diaz, Vic Silayan, Butz Aquino, Wilma Reading, Rick Von Nutter, Dick Adair, Jimmy Shaw, Sonny Batacan, Pedro Faustino

Set during WWII, the story here concerns the use by the Japanese of captured U.S. Navy men (Jim Brown, Richard Jaeckel and Tim Brown) to retrieve $16 million in silver pesos dumped in Manila Bay to keep the Japanese from getting them. The Americans conspire with Filipino resistance fighters until Japanese commander Vic Silayan discovers the plot, but the Americans pull off a bold escape, except for Jim Brown and Jaeckel, who stay behind to blow up the Japanese prison camp, both perishing in the process. (In English)

Padre Amante Guerrero

1992 FLT Films; 111 minutes/color
Directors: Ruben de Guzman, Edgardo Vinarao; Screenwriter: Humilde "Meek" Roxas; Cinematographer: Romy Vitug; Editor: Edgardo Vinarao; Filmscore: Jaime Fabregas; Cast: Eddie Garcia, Ronaldo Valdez, Dennis Roldan, Maritoni Fernandez, Lara Melissa de Leon, Roldan Aquino, Edwin Reyes, King Gutierrez, Dencio Padilla, Manjo del Mundo, Vic Varrion, Vic Felipe, Jess Olmedo, Rey Solo, Danny Riel, Roger Moring, Romy Romulo, Bobby Oreo, Tito Arevalo, Orestes Ojeda, Eddie Arenas, Lucita Soriano, Jaime Fabregas, Ernie Zarate, Eva Ramos, Ben Datu, Randy Pimentel, Luis Benedicto, Cynthia Carriedo, Edwin Arenas, Tony Tacorda, Leo Padilla, Jerry Martin, Rene Pascual, Ernie David, Danny Labra, Jimmy Reyes, Fred Esplana, Roland Montes, Roger Moring, Abel Morado, Alex Tan, Renato Morado, Ronald Asinas

In this effective action film, Eddie Garcia portrays a Catholic priest whose brother, police lieutenant Dennis Roldan, is in a struggle to destroy a drug cartel headed by Ronaldo Valdez. During a raid on one of the cartel's warehouses, Roldan is badly wounded and must go into hiding while recovering. Meanwhile, Garcia has an interesting visitor in the confessional: Maritoni Fernandez confesses to two cold-blooded murders. In the first, for which she was a paid assassin, she shot a man in the head during an intimate moment. After receiving payment for the hit, Fernandez then inexplicably shot the payoff man, and is therefore now running for her life. Garcia takes her in, but when her pursuers show up at the church with automatic weapons, he smuggles her out in the trunk of his car. As Garcia and Fernandez travel in hopes of eluding the underworld thugs, Fernandez delights in trying to seduce Garcia, which she eventually succeeds in doing. It all turns out to be an attempt to gain Garcia's trust in an attempt to get him to divulge the whereabouts of his brother, and that Fernandez is actually working for Valdez. Valdez eventually resorts to having Garcia abducted in order to flush Roldan out, which succeeds as Roldan shows up with a formidable force of officers for a showdown with Valdez.

The performances are all good, with Garcia the standout, and the direction by Ruben de Guzman and Edgardo Vinarao is accomplished with a sure hand. Vinarao also serves as editor, which is his usual vocation. Garcia does his share of fighting and shooting in the film, and the concept of a two-fisted, shoot 'em up priest is different, to say the least. Garcia would again play a rough and tumble priest in the 1997 film *Padre Kalibre*. (In Tagalog with some English)

Padre Kalibre

1997 Regal Entertainment; 102 minutes/color
Director: Val Iglesias; Screenwriter: Al Marcelo; Cinematographer: Vic Anao; Editor: Edmund Jarlego; Filmscore: Marita Manuel; Cast: Eddie Garcia, Monsour del Rosario, Aya Medel, Eddie Gutierrez, Dan Fernandez, Orestes Ojeda, Val Iglesias, Archie Ventoza, Shundrey Jimenez, Frank Ocampo, Renato Morado, Richard Benoza, Manuel Montemayor, Pol de la Cruz, Cesar Iglesias, Blandino Guban, Greg Rocero, Frank Lapid, Jet Ocampo, Rudy Lapid, Fred Ondra, Edgar Serillo, Rey Flores, Freddie Abisia

Thoroughly corrupt and sleazy congressman Eddie Gutierrez seeks to possess a piece of land in his district which is occupied by the Church, but when he finds priest Eddie Garcia is unwilling to sign over the deed, he hires hit man Monsour del Rosario to do some persuading. Taking along three of Gutierrez's men, del Rosario abducts Garcia from the church, dragging him from the confessional, but has a change of mind afterward, and winds up gunning down Gutierrez's three lackeys instead, and then flees with Garcia. Gutierrez basically rules the small town, and has checkpoints set up at all roads leading out of town. Forced to find a place to hide, they go to the house of del Rosario's girlfriend (Aya Medel), but it turns out that she too is working for Gutierrez, and when she tries to shoot del Rosario, he is forced to kill her. Del Rosario and Garcia manage to escape before their enemies arrive, and the film then presents a number of chases as the duo attempt to elude various hit men and police at points around the city. At the conclusion, Garcia and del Rosario confront Gutierrez in front of a large gathering at a prayer rally where Gutierrez is speaking, and when the incensed Gutierrez pulls out a gun and shoots del Rosario, policeman Orestes Ojeda shoots Gutierrez. Neither shot is fatal, and Gutierrez is arrested while del Rosario would presumably also face some legal repercussions for his earlier actions.

Pretty standard in most respects, the film is well directed by Val Iglesias and is given a lift by Garcia, leaning heavily on his sharp comedic abilities. It was during this period that Garcia had signed on for a three-year run on a Filipino television sitcom, a decision he later regretted, claiming that it prevented him from taking more film roles. His popularity as a film star remained undiminished, however, and *Padre Kalibre* was the number one box office draw at the 1997 Metro Manila Film Festival. If the film has a shortcoming, it would be one common to modern Filipino cinema, that being the cheesy synthesized score (in this case provided by Marita Manuel) which lends the film an impoverished tone. (In Tagalog)

Ang Pagbabalik ni Pedro Penduko (The Return of Pedro Penduko)

1994 Viva Family Entertainment; 110 minutes/color
Director: J. Erastheo Navoa; Screenwriter: Ely Matawaran, J. Erastheo Navoa; Cast: Janno Gibbs, Chiquito, Vina Morales, Leo Martinez, Donita Rose, Jun Aristorenas, Malou de Guzman, Rez Cortez, Romy Diaz, Cloyd Robinson, Cris Daluz, Danny Panzalin, Ace Espinosa, Bing Angeles, Beverly Salviejo, Ross Rival, Boy Roque, Lester Salansang, Danita Paner, Arnel Ignacio, Fernando Poe Jr., Robin Padilla, Rudy Fernandez, Bing Loyzaga, Robert Miller

In this comedic fantasy, Janno Gibbs finds a magic amulet, which gives him heroic powers (well, marginally, anyway). Pursuing him for the amulet is Chiquito, and when Gibbs is sucked into a vortex created by the amulet, Chiquito follows. They are spit out into a strange world where mythological monsters are not myth at all. While trying to outrun Jun Aristorenas and his bandits, Gibbs must also fight all manner of netherworld creatures, including a cave full of winged batmen, a trio of flaming fire demons, and finally Satan himself (in the person of Leo Martinez). Gibbs defeats them all with the help of superheroine Darna (Vina Morales), and there is even a surprise visit by the King himself, Fernando Poe, Jr., who shows up wielding Panday's magic sword. After being thanked by Aristorenas for his assistance in defeating an army of zombies, Gibbs is thrust once more back into his own world.

The film manages to stay afloat largely on the strength of the bizarre fantasy elements. While Gibbs is a passable comedic actor, the film has the usual over-the-top performances that are so common to Filipino comedy, including a predictably unrestrained turn from Chiquito, and the usual flamboyant gay stereotype (here given by Rez Cortez). Aside from Poe, there are also uncredited cameos by action stars Robin Padilla and Rudy Fernandez. (In Tagalog)

Pagputi ng Uwak ... Pag-itim ng Tagak (The Heron Turns White, The Seagull Turns Black)

1978 V.S. Film Company; 120 minutes/color
Director: Celso Ad. Castillo; Screenwriters: Celso Ad. Castillo, Iskho Lopez, Lando Perez Jacob, Ruben Arthur Nicdao; Cinematographer: Romeo Vitug, Ricardo Remias; Editor: Abelardo Hulleza; Filmscore: George Canseco; Cast: Vilma Santos, Joonee Gamboa, Bembol Roco, Mario Escudero, Fred Panopio, Angie Ferro, Abdul de Leon, Lito Anzures, Miniong Alvarez, Andres Centenera, Carpi Asturias, Feling Cudia, Yolanda Luna, Mervyn Samson, Dolores Pobre, Johnny Ramirez, Joe Baltazar, Robert Talby

Vilma Santos portrays a classical violinist who returns to her small home village where she meets and falls in love with Bembol Roco, much to the dismay of Santos' two aunts, who consider Roco too common and therefore beneath them. Although Santos and Roco elope, Santos winds up leaving him when her aunts force her to choose between Roco and the family wealth. Humiliated, Roco runs off and joins the Huks, a communist rebel group whose members inhabit the nearby hills. While he is away, the pregnant Santos gives birth to his child, and the film concludes when Roco sneaks into Santos' home for his first glimpse at his child. Then, as Santos and Roco make love, unseen government assassins open fire on the house from outside killing everyone inside, except for the child, which is last seen crying in its crib.

The film is absorbing and very well directed by Celso Ad. Castillo, until the final fourth, in which the director comes close to squandering all of his efforts with a series of weepy, tediously lengthy monologues by Santos which draw the film out and threaten to drag it down. Even so, the film won the FAMAS Best Picture award, and Castillo won the FAMAS for Best Director. The film also took FAMAS awards for Supporting Actress (Angie Ferro), Cinematography (Romy Vitug) and Filmscore (George Canseco). (In Tagalog)

Pahiram ng Ligaya
(Borrowed Happiness)

1984 Golden Productions; 115 minutes/color
Director/screenwriter: Ed Palmos; Cinematographer: Carding Herrera; Editor: Rene Tala; Filmscore: Cecilio Gas; Cast: Eddie Rodriguez, Liza Lorena, Maricel Soriano, Albert Martinez, Luis Gonzales, Marissa Delgado, Isabel Rivas, Chichay, George Estregan, German Moreno, Ruben Rustia, Pia Moran, Aurora Boulevard, Marivi Santos, Ricky Yuson, Lena Lara

After twelve years of marriage and still no children, Liza Lorena and Eddie Rodriguez are overjoyed when Lorena gets pregnant; their joy is short-lived, however, when Lorena is taken to the hospital and the child is stillborn. But as fate would have it, a young poverty-stricken woman gives birth to a daughter in the same hospital that night, and as she is incapable of properly caring for the child, arrangements are made for Lorena and Rodriguez to adopt the girl. Though she is initially happy to have a child to raise, Lorena becomes increasingly distant as the girl grows up. By the time the girl reaches the age of seventeen and has blossomed into a beautiful young lady (played by Maricel Soriano), Lorena seems to be going through some sort of mid-life crisis, and she becomes more and more jealous of the very close relationship between her husband and their daughter, and seems to feel like something of an outsider within her own family. There is also some suggestion that she fears that something improper is developing (or perhaps has already begun) between Rodriguez and Soriano. About that time, Soriano's birth mother (Marissa Delgado) shows up, and Lorena pays her off to keep her from coming around and intruding in Soriano's life (which doesn't work). Inevitably, Lorena's jealousy and irrational behavior causes an ever-widening rift between her and Rodriguez, and Rodriguez feels compelled to move out. He spends his time in nightclubs getting drunk, and a pretty, young dancer takes pity on him and takes him home, consoling him with sex.

Meanwhile, left at home alone with the ever-difficult Lorena, Soriano is likewise compelled to leave home, and she seeks out her birth mother. She finds Delgado living in a slum with a surly, abusive drunk (George Estregan), and winds up living in cramped quarters with three ill mannered half-siblings. The film ends with a surprise birthday party for Lorena, which is interrupted by the arrival of the police, who bring news of the death of Rodriguez in an accident, and through their shared grief, Lorena and Soriano are brought back together again.

Though it gets off to an interesting start, the film bogs down considerably in the second half as the viewer is forced to sit through a succession of weepy attempts at reconciliation. (In Tagalog and English)

Palabra de Honor
(Word of Honor)

1984 Viva Films; 107 minutes/color
Director: Danny Zialcita; Screenwriter: Mike Vergara; Cinematographer: Felizardo Bailen; Editor: Ike Jarlego, Sr.; Filmscore: George Canseco; Cast: Eddie Garcia, Gloria Diaz, Hilda Koronel, Ronaldo Valdez, Elizabeth Oropesa, Dindo Fernando, Beth Bautista, Tommy Abuel, Amy Austria, Jackie Lou Blanco, Mark Gil, Suzanne Gonzales, Virginia Montes, Mario Escudero, Augusto Victa, Tony Angeles, Bert Asuncion, Lucy Quinto, Rolly Papasin, Bert Dizon, Lilian Laing

This sudsy melodrama from director Danny Zialcita is an interesting mishmash of jealousy, greed, infidelity, politics, murder and, true to its title, one man's word of honor. Wealthy family patriarch Eddie Garcia lights a fuse when he announces his intention to marry Gloria Diaz. Belittled as a "nobody" by Garcia's daughter Jackie Lou Blanco, Diaz is seen by most as a fortune hunter (it turns out that she is). Meanwhile, Garcia's other daughter (Hilda Koronel) is sleeping with Dindo Fernando, while her husband (Ronaldo Valdez) is having an affair with Amy Austria, whose boyfriend (Tommy Abuel) is trying to ignite sparks with Beth Bautista, whose husband Mark Gil is ... well, he's pretty straight and narrow, aside from past communistic views which threaten to prevent his getting a teaching job at a university where Garcia serves on the board of directors. Also serving on the board are Abuel and Elizabeth Oropesa. Though married to Fernando, Oropesa has romantic feelings of her own for Garcia, and vents her frustration over his remarriage by opposing Gil's hiring, and organizing demonstrations outside of Gil's home. Things take a nasty turn when Valdez has a run-in with Austria's jealous husband Abuel, and when Valdez is murdered, Abuel is charged. As for Garcia, he discovers that his beloved Diaz is not the woman that he thought she was, and he informs her that she has no place in his life. Yet, wanting to keep his promise to her of a grand wedding, Garcia goes through with the ceremony, and the film ends with Garcia and Diaz exiting the church, getting into separate cars and each going off their own way. The pointlessness of the wedding ceremony may make it seem more than a little ridiculous on its face, but given the wanton infidelity throughout the film, it can be viewed as the ultimate extension of what seems to be a running commentary on the perceived shallowness of matrimony which the film spends a healthy portion of its running time highlighting.

The film does, however, offer a glimmer of hope for the romantic at heart through Gil's character: having started his teaching job, Gil delivers an idealistic, almost nauseatingly flowery lecture, partly to his class, partly to his wife, who stands listening in the doorway, in which he speaks about marriage being "two hearts; two loves united, mounted in music, every moment a melody." Gil's idealism is in stark contrast to the rest of the characters (Garcia excepted), and it's not exactly clear which view the film favors, but this ambiguity helps make the film interesting. (In Tagalog and English)

Pambato
(Most Valuable Player)

1993 EDL Productions; 105 minutes/color
Director: Leonardo L. Garcia; Screenwriter: Tony Tacorda; Cinematographer: Jun Dalawis; Editor: Edgardo Vinarao; Filmscore: Nonong Buencamino; Cast: Ronnie Ricketts, Tony Ferrer, Mariz, John Regala, Charlie Davao, Romy Diaz, Nick Romano, Ruel Vernal, Ramon Christopher, Marita Zobel, Onchie dela Cruz, Marco Polo Garcia, Rey Sagum, Ramon D'Salva, Bernie Fabiosa, Max Alvarado, Karen Timbol, Don Umali, Tony Tacorda, Jojo de Leon, Vic Belaro, Efren Lapid, Rex Lapid, Dong Serrano, Marie Grace Laxa, Joy Samson, Nanding Fernandez, Nog-Nog

Wealthy Charlie Davao covets a piece of land inhabited by squatters, and so sends his men out to bulldoze the shantytown and chase the squatters out. But local residents Ronnie Ricketts and Tony Ferrer have been teaching the people how to fight back, and when the bulldozers arrive the people are defiant. All hell breaks loose, and when Ricketts sees that his mother and sister have been injured by the toppling of their dwelling, he loses control and jumps in one of the bulldozers and crushes the legs of Davao's son (the ever-sadistic John Regala) under the dozer's blade. Doctors are forced to amputate Regala's legs, and Ricketts is sent to prison. Ricketts has a hard time in prison, getting on the wrong side of a jailhouse gang led by Ruel Vernal, but he manages to survive, do his time and then get released. Once out, Ricketts finds the embittered Regala determined to avenge himself from his wheelchair, and Ricketts' sister is raped and killed by Marco Polo Garcia, another of Davao's demented sons. Ferrer, who is the father of Ricketts' girlfriend, is then murdered, and Ricketts has some of the local boys arm themselves and engage in a shootout with Davao's men. Ricketts kills Regala (and a good many others) and the film ends with him once more being led away to prison.

There are no surprises here, but the film is well made and reasonably suspenseful, and Ricketts, one of the best of the young action stars who emerged in the 1980s, gives his usual intense performance. But for the most part, this is the expected rationing out of revenge and familial tragedy. (In Tagalog)

Papunta Ka Pa Lang Pabalik na Ako (You Are Going to the Place That I Have Just Returned from Alone)

1996 Viva Films; 102 minutes/color
Director: Jun Aristorenas; Screenwriters: Humilde "Meek" Roxas, Jun Aristorenas; Cinematographer: Ver Dauz; Editor: Rene Tala; Filmscore: Nonong Buencamino; Cast: Eddie Garcia, Joko Diaz, Jennifer Sevilla, Ricardo Cepeda, Glydel Mercado, Michelle Parton, Berting Labra, Ernie Zarate, Amado Cortez, Paquito Diaz, Junar Aristorenas, Angel Baldomar, Turk Cervantes, Gino Illustre, Glenn Almonte, Danny Labra, Danny Ramos, Ruffa Mae Quinto, Mia Gutierrez, Ernie David, Robert Miller, Rey Solo

Police sergeant Eddie Garcia's arrest of a powerful drug lord leads to trouble (doesn't it always?): he narrowly escapes an attempt on his life, which claims the lives of his wife and two of his three children. Garcia eventually defeats the drug syndicate with the help of younger officer Joko Diaz. Director Jun Aristorenas does a good enough job, and Garcia is more than capable, of course. The problem here is that the screenplay seems to merely rehash the storyline of any number of other Garcia action films (or a good many action films in general). Other than the distinct feeling of déjà vu, the film is more than adequate. (In Tagalog with some English)

Para Sa'yo ang Huling Bala Ko
(My Last Bullet Is for You)

1990 Regal Films; 98 minutes/color
Director: Toto Natividad; Screenwriter: Fred Navarro; Cinematographer: Ricardo Herrera; Editor: Toto Natividad; Filmscore: Demet Velasquez; Cast: Richard Gomez, Louella de Cordova, Ruel Vernal, Subas Herrero, Dencio Padilla, Dick Israel, Dindo Arroyo, Ruben Rustia, Roldan Aquino, Zandro Zamora, Johnny Vicar, King Gutierrez, Eric Lorenzo, Apple Bautista, Vic Varrion, Usman Hassim, Turko Cervantes, Robert Miller, Ernie David, Jimmy Reyes

Police officer Richard Gomez is in the right place at the right time to stop a supermarket hold-up by a drugged-out gang of psychotics. He guns down the entire gang, but in the heat of the furious gunplay he accidentally shoots and kills a young girl. Unable to overcome his feelings of guilt, Gomez resigns from the force and returns to his family's farm in the country. Living on his father-in-law's farm with his wife and young son, Gomez seems to find happiness, and the family is very excited by the prospect of oil on their land. Word of their impending good fortune spreads quickly, and local tycoon Subas Herrero offers to by the land, but is turned down. Unaccustomed to not getting his way, Herrero sends the usual band of thugs (led by the ubiquitous Dick Israel) to persuade the family to sell, but Israel and company wind up shooting and killing Gomez's father-in-law, and when Gomez's wife (Louella de Cordova) resists Israel's sexual advances, he stabs her through the stomach with a large knife, literally pinning her to a tree. Meanwhile, Herrero has local policemen Roldan Aquino and Johnny Vicar on his payroll, and has them throw Gomez in jail. Gomez escapes, and after killing Aquino, Vicar and a number of other members of the corrupt local police department, heads of on the expected quest for vengeance. Ultimately, he triumphs after a river of bloodletting.

This is an extremely violent piece of work, from the opening supermarket massacre to the climactic bloodbath in Herrero's mansion. Director Toto Natividad chooses to show many—maybe even most—of the shootings in slow motion to make the most of the blood spurting, splashing and splattering in every direction. With Gomez's wife dispatched relatively early on, and no subsequent love interest to fill the void, Natividad frees himself up to focus on the visceral thrills resulting from Gomez's violent retribution. In this respect, Gomez, who is most often a romantic lead of the teen idol variety, may have seemed an odd choice for a role of this type, but he fares quite well. Natividad outdoes himself here as regards the film's reveling in the violence of the vengeance of its protagonist, surpassing even the considerable carnage of *Durugin ng Bala si Peter Torres* (1989), in which Natividad had the advantage of a leading character whose moral inhibitions had been consumed by the brutality of prison life. (In Tagalog)

Parola

1991 ATB-4 Films; 105 minutes/color
Director/screenwriter: Jett C. Espiritu; Cinematographer: Rosendo Buenazeda; Editor: Nap Montebon; Cast: Sarah Gomez, Marco Polo Garcia, Isadora, Romy Diaz, Dick Israel, Rhey Roldan, Philip Gamboa, Lucita Soriano, Robert Talby, Edmon Ramos, Albert Garcia, Eric Enriquez, Marlyn Marquez, Joe Baltazar

Sarah Gomez portrays the title character, a young woman living with her grandmother on the island of Tilaw Taw. Through flashbacks it is revealed that Gomez was conceived as a result of the rape of her mother, who left the island after giving birth. After the death of her grandmother, Gomez decides to seek out her mother, and lusty fisherman Romy Diaz agrees to take her off the island. But once he gets her aboard his boat, Diaz and his incorrigibly demented buddy Dick Israel keep Gomez imprisoned below deck as a sex slave. Gomez escapes with the help of young boat mate Marco Polo Garcia, and after the two of them arrive in the city, they discover that Gomez's mother is in prison, having been convicted—wrongly as it turns out—of her lover's murder. Gomez goes undercover as a prostitute in order to catch the real killer, which she accomplishes, and then returns to Tilaw Taw with her vindicated mother. But upon returning, Gomez and Garcia must confront Diaz and Israel, who are bent on revenge, and the film closes with a shootout in which everyone dies except Gomez and her mother.

Jett Espiritu's direction, while occasionally inventive, is a bit too coy at times, particularly for a film that stakes itself largely on sexual motifs. Regarding the ending, the reappearance of Diaz and

Israel seems much too contrived toward providing a shoot 'em up finale, and Espiritu (who also wrote the screenplay) would have been better off ending things with the exoneration of Gomez's mother. As it is, the film drags on unnecessarily only to come to a perplexingly abrupt and screeching halt. As for Gomez, aside from being very beautiful, she shows herself to be a more than capable actress, yet her film career doesn't seem to have taken off. The film also boasts of being Garcia's first starring role. For that matter, it may very well have been his last. (In Tagalog)

Patapon (You Are Garbage)

1993 EDL Productions; 106 minutes/color

Director: Leonardo L. Garcia; Screenwriter: Oden Amurao; Cast: Ronnie Ricketts, Tony Ferrer, Cristina Gonzales, Roi Vinzon, Mariz, Delia Razon, Jon Hernandez, Romy Diaz, Dick Israel, Berting Labra, Rez Cortez, Rommel Valdez, Mario Escudero, Nick Romano, Mila Montanez, Mary Grace Laxa, Jay Jay Gonzales, Rey Sagum, Tony Tacorda, Frank Lapid, Arabel Caducio, Alex David, Eddie del Mar Jr., Vic Felipe, Jess Ramos, Nanding Fernandez, Mike Vergel, Jojo de Leon, Vic Velaro, Ver Rodriguez, Jess Vargas

This run-of-the-mill action film stars Ronnie Ricketts as a soldier called home from fighting rebels on Mindanao after the murder of his father. Upon his return, Ricketts finds that his father was killed while en route to a town meeting to speak out against a large chemical company moving into town. Ricketts is quickly put off by the lack of interest on the part of the police, and it comes as no surprise that police commander Tony Ferrer is tied in with crooked chemical plant honcho Roi Vinzon and his cronies (the usual assortment of offenders, like Romy Diaz and Dick Israel). Things follow the usual path, with Ricketts stirring up trouble and dodging bullets, and the thugs kidnapping his wife, mother and sister, leading to the standard showdown where Ricketts charges in to rescue his family and gun down all the bad guys. Director Leonardo Garcia does a competent job, and there are some good action sequences, in particular a shootout on the subway, but the problem here, as is common in the action genre, is the extreme familiarity of the material. (In Tagalog with occasional English)

Patayin sa Sindak si Barbara (Kill Barbara with Panic)

1995 Star Cinema; 93 minutes/color

Director: Chito S. Rono; Screenwriter: Ricardo Lee; Cinematographer: Joe Batac; Editor: Jess Navarro; Filmscore: Jessie Lasaten; Cast: Dawn Zulueta, Lorna Tolentino, Tonton Gutierrez, Amy Austria, Antoinette Taus, Anita Linda, Angie Ferro, Nonie Buencamino, Eva Aquino, Ernie Zarate, Augusto Victa, Nestor Escano, Cris Daluz

In this remake of Celso Ad. Castillo's 1973 horror classic *Patayin Mo sa Sindak si Barbara*, Dawn Zulueta commits suicide after learning of an affair between her husband (Tonton Gutierrez) and her sister (Lorna Tolentino). Immediately after the funeral, the household is disturbed by manifestations of Zulueta's presence (apparitions, flickering lights). When the haunting turns violent, priest Ernie Zarate is called in to exorcise the house, but when that doesn't work, a medium is brought in to perform a séance, during which Zulueta's spirit takes possession of her daughter (Antoinette Taus) and stabs the medium. Deciding that Taus has been traumatized by the death of her mother, the police allow the family to take her away for a change of scenery. They head for the country to stay with relatives, but the spirit of Zulueta follows, intent on killing Tolentino. After materializing in physical form, Zulueta leads Tolentino through the forest to a lake of fire (some vacation spot) and attempts to throw her in, but Gutierrez arrives in time to save her by jumping Zulueta, plunging both she and himself into the flames.

Like a good many horror films, this film is at its best early on while maintaining a degree of subtlety, and director Chito Rono fills the first half of the picture with some excellently eerie moments. The film's highlights include a mysterious woman in the cemetery seen from a distance by Tolentino during Zulueta's funeral, Gutierrez observing from his bedroom window as Taus frolics through the yard by moonlight with Zulueta's unseen spirit, and in particular, a scene where the dollhouse in Taus' bedroom comes to life, lit up inside, dolls animated, and while watching all of this through the dollhouse window, Taus sees Zulueta's face peering through a window on the opposite side of the dollhouse. There is also a pleasingly creepy moment when Gutierrez finds one of Taus' dolls rocking in front of the television, as if watching the cartoons that are playing. Gutierrez picks up the doll and is horrified when its face contorts in a demonic scowl. Unfortunately, as Zulueta's appearances become more frequent, and her interaction with the rest of the cast more common, the unsettling aura of mystery dissipates, and all that is left is blood and thunder. Still, the film is impressive, and is a cut above the norm. (In Tagalog with some English)

Pati Ba Pintig ng Puso
(Even the Beat of the Heart)

1985 Viva Films; 111 minutes/color
Director: Leroy Salvador; Screenwriter: Orlando Nadres; Cinematographer: Joe Batac, Jr.; Editor: Ike Jarlego, Jr.; Filmscore: Willy Cruz; Cast: Sharon Cuneta, Gabby Concepcion, Charito Solis, Eddie Garcia, Dina Bonnevie, Edu Manzano, Rey "PJ" Abellana, Joel Alano, Jobelle Salvador, Naty Santiago, Evelyn Vargas, Vicky Suba, Danny Cruz, Vangie Labalan, Alex Dona, Tony Pascua, Charlie Ordonez, Rosemarie Gil, Romeo Rivera

Gabby Concepcion leaves America to return to the Philippines after receiving word that his sister (Jobelle Salvador) has suffered a nervous breakdown and is hospitalized in a mental institution. Upon returning, Concepcion finds Salvador to be completely withdrawn and in a near vegetative state. Concepcion had left the Philippines in order to escape his domineering grandfather (Eddie Garcia), whom he had always blamed for the deaths of his parents. In a flashback it is revealed that Concepcion's father (Romeo Rivera) was driven to suicide, the result of feelings of failure and extreme stress brought on by Garcia's demanding expectations and low tolerance for imperfection. Concepcion's mother (Rosemarie Gil) was accidentally shot and killed while trying to prevent Rivera's suicide.

Once back home, Concepcion takes a liking to Sharon Cuneta, one of the household maids, and after a whirlwind romance, the two are married. This infuriates Garcia, and while Concepcion is away on business, Garcia seeks to return the meek Cuneta to her position as a servant, making her scrub the toilet, and even having her put on her maid's uniform again to serve his guests at a dinner party. In time Salvador is jarred out of her withdrawn state by a traumatic memory of Garcia having stopped her from running off with her boyfriend by having her beau shot, which permanently disabled him. Finally, their disgust for Garcia sends Concepcion, Cuneta and Salvador packing, at which time they are joined by the entire household staff of maids and various other employees who, suitcases in hand, depart in one grand show of contempt and rebellion, leaving Garcia bellowing at them from the front drive.

The screenplay, which was adapted from a komiks serial, is pretty sudsy stuff, very high on melodrama, if not presented with any particular artistic flair. More interesting to consider is the possibility that the domineering patriarchal motif may have been, like many other films during the martial law era, motivated out of contempt for the Marcos regime. (In Tagalog and English)

Pedrito Masangkay: Walang Bakas na Iniiwan
(Pedrito Masangkay: Gone Without a Trace)

1994 First Films; 99 minutes/color
Director: Francis "Jun" Posadas; Screenwriter: Erwin T. Lanado; Cinematographer: Rosendo Buenaseda; Editor: Rogelio Salvador; Filmscore: Marita Manuel; Cast: Ian Veneracion, Cristina Gonzales, Andy Poe, Beth Tamayo, Subas Herrero, Perla Bautista, Karen Timbol, Dick Israel, Dexter Doria, Odette Khan, Mikee Villanueva, Danny Labra, Michael Alano, Royce Subida, Francis Baun, Ben Sagmit, Ernie Zarate, Robert Talby, Leleng Ubaldo, Penggot, Leo Lazaro, Gerry Roman, Jeric Vasquez, Ben Romano, Dave Moreno, Kiko Palmos, Pol Bermundo, Conrado Belen, Frank Young, Robert Miller, Usman Hassim, Rene Balan

In his determination to shed his baby-faced appearance, Ian Veneracion may have finally turned the corner with this psycho thriller, in which he plays a greasy serial killer who manages to turn part of Manila's population and a number of its police detectives into unwitting cannibals. Working as a cook and a busboy at a Manila eatery, Veneracion falls in love with Beth Tamayo, the daughter of his boss (Subas Herrero). His feelings for Tamayo are reciprocated, which infuriates Herrero, who gives Veneracion a sound beating and sends him packing. But when he returns that night to see Tamayo, she isn't there, and Veneracion is treated to another beating at the hands of Herrero. This time, however, Veneracion fights back, hacking Herrero to pieces with a cleaver, along with Herrero's wife and Tamayo's two bratty, young siblings. With the disappearance of Herrero, Veneracion stays on at the eatery under the new management, while the police discover a garbage bag full of hands and feet washed up on the beach, and an examination of the fingerprints taken from one of the hands helps identify Herrero as one of the victims. When another employee at the eatery turns up missing, policemen Andy Poe and Dick Israel pay a call to interview Veneracion. While there, they freely partake of the food Veneracion is preparing, unaware that the kabobs they are enjoying are actually the remains of the recently murdered employee that they are looking for. After their visit, the police decide to try and keep an eye on Veneracion, but it does Cristina Gonzales no good: also employed at the eatery, Gonzales discovers the bloody clothing of her slain co-worker one night after closing, and Veneracion is forced to kill her as well. Afterwards, he decides to leave, but when he is accosted by the police outside he attempts to flee and is captured and arrested. In prison, he attempts suicide, and is transferred to the hospital, where he confesses the truth to the police. Haunted by memories of his own birth (!), when his insane mother tried to kill him, Veneracion tells the police of how he murdered Herrero and his family, and when asked what he did with the bodies, he owns up to using them as food for the eatery. This sends the policemen present running for the bathroom to vomit since many of them had eaten there, and Veneracion is then able to grab one officer's gun and make another escape attempt, but he is shot and killed outside the hospital.

Director Francis Posadas may have turned in his best work here, eschewing his usual straightforward approach for a somewhat more stylistic tack more appropriate for the bizarre subject matter. It's a shame that he doesn't often spread his wings artistically, since this film clearly shows a creativity not expressed in much of his other work. Perhaps he should deal with the macabre more often since he clearly has a flair for it. Among the many grisly moments is a scene in which a policewoman, trying to identify the remains found on the beach, goes to fingerprint a severed hand and is appalled when, in the process, a rotting finger breaks off in her hand. Aside from the gruesome subject matter and the lively presentation by Posadas, the film is also given a boost by the score provided by Marita Manuel, and there is some full-frontal nudity from Gonzales, though the way in which it was shot suggests the use of a body double. Incidentally, as incredible as it may sound, the film was allegedly based on a true story. (In Tagalog)

Pepeng Agimat

1972 Imus Productions; 119 minutes/color
Cast: Ramon Revilla, Gloria Romero, Alona Alegre, Rosemarie Gil, Aurora Salve, Etang Discher, Chiquito

In this bizarre fantasy, Ramon Revilla portrays the title character, a man bestowed with magical powers and called on to defend his rural neighbors against a reign of terror instigated by witch Etang Discher. Revilla finds himself combating all manner of creatures, including green monster dwarfs, a giant ogre, and a horse-headed demon. With the help of Discher's daughter (Rosemarie Gil), Revilla finds Discher's lair and defeats her in a magic duel. The film's presentation is rather plain, and the special effects primitive, but the weird fantasy elements manage to make it somewhat interesting. (In Tagalog)

Pepeng Agimat

2000 Millennium Cinema; 116 minutes/color
Director: Felix E. Dalay; Screenwriters: Felix E. Dalay, Jojo M. Lapuz, Jerry Tirazona; Cinematographers: Ely Cruz, Pablo Bautista; Editor: Renato de Leon; Filmscore: Jaime Fabregas; Cast: Ramon "Bong" Revilla Jr., Dennis Padilla, Princess Punzalan, Jess Lapid Jr., Gladys Reyes, Vanessa del Bianco, LJ Moreno, Joonee Gamboa, Al Tantay, Ramon "Jolo" Revilla III, Ramon Revilla (Sr.), Christopher Roxas, Roldan Aquino, King Gutierrez, Gerald Ejercito, Boy Roque, Danny Riel, Archie Ventoza, Jesette Prospero, Dea Reyes, Paeng Giant, Gilbert Bautista, Jaime "Pango" Cuales, Allan Medina, Larry Correa, Rico Orbita, Sonny Tuazon

Ramon "Bong" Revilla, Jr. plays the title character in this remake of a film that had originally starred his father, Ramon, Sr. Playing a Metro Manila policeman, Revilla becomes convinced that Manila is under attack by Satanic forces, and he fingers Gladys Reyes for a number of killings. Feeling that Reyes is possessed, Revilla seeks to take her to exorcist Joonee Gamboa, but tries to do this by kidnapping Reyes, for which he is arrested and thrown in jail. Revilla manages to break out of jail and flees to Gamboa's rural home. After tangling with various monsters in the forest, Revilla is drawn into a cavern where he is visited by the apparition of Ramon, Sr., who gives him an amulet, which bestows Ramon, Jr. with special powers and makes him impervious to bullets. Targeted by the forces of darkness, Revilla battles the evil Madam Sophia (Princess Punzalan) and her various henchmen, in particular a nasty, demonic Jess Lapid, Jr. Punzalan also raises a graveyard full of zombies that storm Manila causing panic and chaos, but Revilla saves the city, defeating Punzalan and blowing up her temple. The film's special effects range from quite impressive to not so impressive, but it's entertaining enough in its own way. It's particularly interesting to see Ramon Revilla, Sr. put in a cameo, having walked away from his film career after being elected to the senate in the early 1990s. (In Tagalog with some English)

Pepeng Kuryente: Man with a Thousand Volts
(Electric Pepeng: Man with a Thousand Volts)

1987 Imus Productions; 117 minutes/color
Director/screenwriter: Jose Yandoc (Ramon Revilla); Cinematographer: Ramon Marcelino; Editor: Tony Sy; Filmscore: Mon del Rosario; Cast: Ramon Revilla, Dante Rivero, Marissa Delgado, Ramon Zamora, Melissa Mendez, Ramon "Bong" Revilla Jr., Gwen Avila, Alicia Alonzo, Cecille Inigo, George Estregan Jr., King Gutierrez, Rodolfo "Boy" Garcia, Palito, Lito Anzures, Bomber Moran, Lucita Soriano, Marco Polo Garcia, Edwin Reyes, Renato del Prado, Ingrid Salas, Johnny Delgado, Robert Talby, Ernie David, Baldo Marro, Danny Riel

Once again Ramon Revilla is cast as a populist hero with supernatural powers. As the film opens, Ramon "Bong" Revilla, Jr., gets into a scrape with a local gang of thugs, which quickly leads to the murder of his parents (Ramon Revilla and Alicia Alonzo). Ramon, Jr., retaliates by killing several of the gang members, for which he is arrested and sentenced to 15 years in prison. He serves his sentence and is released, and with the part now being assumed by Ramon, Sr., he finally marries his sweetheart (Marissa Delgado). After being struck by lightning, he becomes charged with electricity, and his touch has the ability to heal all manner of ailments. After healing a man in a wheelchair, word of his abilities spreads quickly, and his house is soon visited by busloads of ailing people. He is sidetracked for a time when his sister spots Johnny Delgado and recognizes him as the leader of the gang that killed their parents, and Revilla charges into Delgado's house and kills him and all of his gang. After meandering a while, the film concludes with Revilla killing Dante Rivero and his gang, which has been terrorizing the local fishing village.

The film has points of interest, including early in the story when, prior to being struck, Revilla seems to be followed by lightning which tends to strike trees in his vicinity, and the concluding showdown with Rivero in which Revilla hurls coconuts which burst into flames and explode upon impact. But Revilla's screenplay (written under the pseudonym Jose Yandoc, under which he also directed) seems to lose focus, and his direction is too mundane, which tends to make the excessive running time exasperating. (In Tagalog)

Perlas ng Silangan
(Pearl of the East)

1969 FPJ Productions; 120 minutes/color
Director: Pablo Santiago; Screenwriters: Ruben Rustia, Fred Navarro; Cinematographer: Sergio Lobo; Editor: Augusto Salvador; Filmscore: Ariston Avelino; Cast: Fernando Poe Jr., Susan Roces, Vic Vargas, Jose Padilla Jr., Carlos Padilla Jr., Ruben Rustia, Jose Vergara, Bert Olivar, Pedro Faustino, Manolo Robles, Vic Varrion, Van de Leon, Andres Centenera, Vic Silayan, Lito Anzures, Nello Nayo, Bruno Punzalan, Letty Ojera, Zernan Manahan, Larry Dominguez, Jessie Velasco, Pablo Guevarra, Paquito Salcedo, Miguel Lopez, Johnny Long, Vic Feranz, Nita Carmona

In this epic Filipino historical adventure/melodrama, Fernando Poe, Jr. is cast as a slave aboard a Spanish galleon who manages to escape and washes ashore an island where he is taken in by the resident Muslim tribe. He falls in love with tribal princess Susan Roces, but must do battle with neighboring tribesman Vic Vargas for the right to wed her; Poe wins, of course, and then joins with the tribe in their struggle against the invading Spanish, but the natives are overwhelmed by the enemy and are inevitably forced to surrender to Spanish rule.

This may well be director Pablo Santiago's best work, and it features some impressive cinematography by Sergio Lobo. (In Tagalog and Spanish)

Pieta

1983 Amazaldy Films; 114 minutes/color
Director/screenwriter: Carlo J. Caparas; Cinematographer: Joe Batac, Jr.; Editor: Edgardo Vinarao; Filmscore: George Canseco; Cast: Ace Vergel, Vivian Velez, Charito Solis, Luis Gonzales, Mario Montenegro, Bomber Moran, George Estregan, Max Alvarado, Rodolfo "Boy" Garcia, Vic Diaz, Deborah Sun, Johnny Wilson, Lucita Soriano, Ernie Ortega, Janette Zervoulakos, Scarlet Hansen, Manning Bato, Rusty Santos, Steve Alcarado, Marco Polo Garcia, Mira Montes, Arthur Cervantes, Danny Labra, Leon Pajaron, Nery Santos, Ernie Forte, George Henson, Boy Santa Maria, Roger Moring, Eddie Gicoso, Boy Antiporda, Nonoy de Guzman, Eddie Tuazon, Bobby Oreo, King Gutierrez

Playing the title character, street tough Ace Vergel is getting himself tossed around by a gang of thugs led by Max Alvarado when Luis Gonzales, fresh out of prison, jumps to his aid. Gonzales has a job waiting for him, and he takes Vergel along to meet his boss, organized crime figure Vic Diaz. After pummeling Diaz's toughest man, Vergel secures a job in the organization pulling heists, but when he rapes Gonzales' daughter (Vivian Velez), things go sour for Vergel. Now an outcast from Diaz's gang, and with Gonzales out to get him, Vergel kills Diaz by tossing a hand grenade into his living room, and then shoots and kills Gonzales. Well, he gets sent to prison for all of this, but escapes with the help of fellow inmate Bomber Moran, who then takes Vergel to meet his boss (Johnny Wilson). Vergel enjoys the good life working in Wilson's criminal gang, but after learning that his rape of Velez has resulted in a child, he decides to pay her a visit. With the help of Vergel's mother (Charito Solis), Velez takes the baby and flees into the forest, but they are pursued by Vergel, who is himself pursued by the police. With the police closing in on him, Vergel takes Velez and the baby hostage, but he is then shot and killed by police sharpshooter George Estregan.

The film is helped by a strong cast of veteran performers, and an interesting score by George Canseco, but there is no counteracting the thoroughly unpleasant nature of its central character, whom the viewer spends the entire movie waiting to see get his comeuppance, and director Carlo Caparas' screenplay seems directionless at times. There is certainly nothing here to justify the excessive running time (then again, there seldom is), but Caparas seems incapable of brevity, surrendering to self-indulgence wherever possible. Still, the film was successful enough to prompt Caparas to immediately follow it up with a sequel, *Pieta: Ik Alawang Aklat* (1985). (In Tagalog)

Pilya (Naughty Girl)

1997 Taurus Films; 83 minutes/color

Director/screenwriter: Neal "Buboy" Tan; Cinematographer: Boy Anao; Editor: Nap Montebon; Filmscore: Boy Alcaide; Cast: Rita Magdalena, Jorge Estregan (George Estregan, Jr.), Sara Gomez, Ursula Ortiz, Rey "PJ" Abellana, Erwin Montes, Robert Martin, Rey Roldan, Jinky Oda, Bea Lorena, Miguel Moreno, Vic Santos, Jeric Vasquez, Gabina, Jimmy Concepcion, Carling Conge, Emil Cristobal, Linda Caceres, Reny Nicandro, Ver Lang, Vic Gabion, Ludy Caintoy

In this low-grade exploiter, Rita Magdalena plays a young woman in an apparently arrested state of childhood who lives in the slums with her sister and brother-in-law. She spends her days playing hopscotch with the neighborhood children and skipping through the streets with her hair in pigtails, sucking on a lollipop and toting her rag doll. When stud Robert Martin moves into the neighborhood, he awakens Magdalena's dormant sensuality. A number of other women are likewise attracted to Martin, including Sara Gomez, who angers Magdalena by making a play for Martin at a neighborhood dance party. Gomez's beau (George Estregan, Jr.) gives Martin a pretty sound beating, and a catfight erupts between Magdalena and Gomez. The following day Estregan, still fuming, tries to rape Magdalena, and when Martin comes along and intervenes, another fight ensues. Not in the mood for another beating, Martin pulls a knife and stabs Estregan, killing him. Magdalena is heartbroken when Martin is led away to jail in handcuffs, but still more trouble lay ahead: she returns home where her drunken brother-in-law and two of his buddies rape her. The police arrive to find Magdalena traumatized, and her three assailants dead and foaming at the mouth. Magdalena's sister confesses that, after her husband and his friends had raped her too, she dumped poison into their jug of liquor after they had passed out (shades of Marilou Diaz-Abaya's 1980 film *Brutal*). For this she is sent to prison, leaving the now thoroughly retarded Magdalena alone to fend for herself.

Neal Tan's direction is pretty nondescript, and Magdalena gives what has to at least place on the list of all-time worst performances in the history of world cinema. It's difficult to convey how bad she really is, but the word "abomination" does come to mind. The film's only attribute is the lovely Gomez. (In Tagalog)

Pilyang Engkantada (Mischievous Fairy)

1978 Tropical Films/S.Q. Studios; 110 minutes/color

Director: Jose Miranda Cruz; Screenwriter: Artemio Marquez; Cinematographer: Eduardo Cabrales; Editor: Joe Solo; Filmscore: Angel Cruz; Cast: Dondon Nakar, Winnie Santos, Ike Lozada, Luz Fernandez, Mar Quijano, Allan Valenzuela, Anthony Segovia, Vanessa Lopez, Romy Reyes, Beth Madrid, Rodolfo Pakipot, Irene Paleleo, Tony Lacson, Mar Guerrero, Victor Lee, Irma Padilla, Eddie Killer, Lolita Sarmento, William Go, Jun Concepcion, Roy Padilla, Silvio Ramiro, Jean Santos, Max Rojo

In this bizarre and schizophrenic fantasy, a teenage girl rescues an old hag from a drooling, machete-wielding maniac, and the old hag in return uses her powers of witchery to save the girl from her cruel, drunken father. The witch then takes the girl to a jungle hideaway inhabited by fairies and gnomes, and feeds her some fruit which endows the girl with magic powers. From there, the film shifts gears rather drastically with the teenage girl going to live in the mansion of corpulent TV variety show host Ike Lozada. She passes her time in the opulent mansion by using her magic to play various pranks on the hired help. When Lozada hears the girl's angelic voice crooning "The Way We Were" with some hippie street singers, he puts her on his television program. She falls in love with her co-star, a young man with whom she sings syrupy love ballads. Eventually, it falls on her to thwart a gang of bandits by flying through the air, chasing down their van, and kung fu-ing them into submission. Obviously a film with an extreme identity crisis, it would have fared much better if the entire midsection dealing with teenage love, TV stardom and childish hijinx had been excised. As it is, it's a mess. While the musical numbers are bland and more than a little somniferous, the incidental score is occasionally inspired. The film's highlight is the moment when the old witch conjures a giant to frighten away the girl's abusive father. (In Tagalog with some English)

Pintsik

1994 Viva Films; 109 minutes/color
Director: Jun Aristorenas; Screenwriters: Humilde "Meek" Roxas, Jun Aristorenas; Cast: Cynthia Luster (Yukari Oshima), Dennis Padilla, Kempee de Leon, Donna Cruz, Smokey Manaloto, Roi Vinzon, Andy Poe, Jenny Roa, Ace Espinosa, Junar Aristorenas, Mykell Chan, Gene Padilla, Robert Villalon, Robbie Donato, Ronald Asinas, Allan Quimbo, Danny Labra, Johnny Vicar, Manny Samson, Rolan Montes, Steve Alcarado, Pong Pong

In this very ordinary comedy, Yukari Oshima arrives in the Philippines from Japan after learning that her father has been taken hostage by a terrorist group led by Andy Poe. For some reason, NBI agent Johnny Vicar's assistance basically consists of hooking Oshima up with bungling crook Dennis Padilla, whom Vicar explains has the right connections to find the group holding Oshima's father for ransom. Padilla brings in some of his friends, who are every bit as inept as he is, but they still manage to locate Oshima's father and make good their rescue. But on their way back from the terrorists' jungle hideout, they are all picked up by yet another bunch of thugs, who will only release them if Oshima's father comes up with $5 million. This he does, but by then Oshima, Padilla and company manage to break free for the climactic rumble, which of course they win. The only surprise here is that Jun Aristorenas, who both directed and concocted the story and screenplay with Humilde Roxas, would be bothered with something this vacuous. "Pintsik" is a term for Filipinos of mixed Chinese heritage. (In Tagalog with some English and Japanese)

Portrait of My Love

1965 Sampaguita Pictures; 86 minutes/black & white
Director/screenwriter: Luciano B. Carlos; Cinematographer: Amaury Agra; Filmscore: Restie Umali; Cast: Susan Roces, Eddie Gutierrez, Shirley Moreno, Nori Dalisay, Etang Discher, Matimtiman Cruz, German Moreno, Tita de Villa

This romantic comedy/drama stars Susan Roces as a young woman who, after a run of bad luck with a series of boyfriends, is set up by a friend on a blind date with Eddie Gutierrez. But when Gutierrez playfully chases after Roces, he finds himself arrested and charged with attempted rape. Roces drops the charges, and feeling that her problems with men may indicate a problem within herself, she undergoes a round of hypnotherapy. The results are dramatic, as she becomes much more outgoing and begins to romantically pursue Gutierrez. After falling in love, Gutierrez must next contend with his scheming grandmother (Etang Discher), who tries to reunite Gutierrez with his ex-flame. Fortunately, true love triumphs in the end, and Gutierrez and Roces remain a couple. The story and execution are very ordinary, and the film is somewhat awkward in transitioning from the comedic first half into the tear-jerker second half. (In Tagalog with occasional English)

Pretty Boy Segovia

1978 Essex Films; 95 minutes/color
Director: Danny L. Zialcita; Cinematographer: Felizardo Bailen; Editor: Enrique Jarlego, Sr.; Filmscore: Demet Velasquez; Cast: Rudy Fernandez, Chanda Romero, Tina Monasterio, Imelda Ilanan, Anita Linda, Mario Escudero, Ernie Ortega, Paolo Baron, Avel Morado, Johnny Vicar, Johnny Madrid, Dick Israel, Mary Walter, Yolanda Luna, Rolly Papasin, Louie Florentino, Cesar Esguerra, Enrico Villa, Dodie Ramirez, Edna Diaz

In this revenge opus, Rudy Fernandez is

living with his disabled mother and sister when his older brother returns home, bringing with him a wheelchair for mother. He also has a troubling tale to tell about how he stole a significant amount of cash from a wealthy, powerful man, and it's not long before someone comes around to collect. While Fernandez is on the beach making love to Chanda Romero, Johnny Vicar shows up with some friends back at the house and proceeds to murder not only Fernandez's brother, but his mother and sister as well. Predictably, this prompts Fernandez to go on a quest for vengeance. Along the way, he recruits would-be thief Dick Israel to assist him. He eventually succeeds in avenging his family, but is mortally wounded in the process.

Director Danny Zialcita's juxtaposition of the murder of Fernandez's family members with Romero's writhing in ecstasy on the beach lacks subtlety and gives the impression of being a deliberate aping of Celso Ad. Castillo's 1970 film *Nympha*, in which Castillo inter-cut shots of a girl praying with those of a young couple having intercourse; but whereas Castillo chose the more controversial mingling of sex and religion, Zialcita here takes the more conventional path of juxtaposing sex and violence. The film offers no screenwriting credit. (In Tagalog with some English)

Ang Probinsyano

1996 FPJ Productions; 118 minutes/color
Director: Ronwaldo Reyes (Fernando Poe, Jr.); Screenwriters: Pablo S. Gomez, Manny Buising; Cinematographer: Ver Reyes; Editors: Augusto Salvador, Rene Tala; Filmscore: Jaime Fabregas; Cast: Fernando Poe Jr., Dindi Gallardo, Amanda Page, Amado Cortez, Bob Soler, Zandro Zamora, Berting Labra, Romy Diaz, Marita Zobel, Rudy Meyer, Vic Varrion, Joey Padilla, Nonoy de Guzman, Jim Rosales, Rene Matias, Robert Rivera, Dante Castro, Melisse Santiago, Janus del Prado, Dindo Arroyo, Renato del Prado, Ernie Zarate, Telly Babasa, Tom Olivar

Policeman Fernando Poe, Jr. calls for back-up before going into Bob Soler's illegal drug plant, but when he is spotted, a shootout ensues in which Poe guns down a good many of Soler's men, but is drastically outnumbered and ultimately shot. A colonel is the first on the scene, and upon finding Poe's bloody, unconscious body, he takes the curious step of hiding him. The late-arriving back-up comes and finds plenty of dead bodies, but no Poe. The colonel hustles Poe to an out-of-the-way region to recover from his wounds, and meanwhile he tells Poe's wife and young son that his whereabouts are unknown. When Poe does eventually return, he has partial amnesia, and his wife and son are strangers to him. In his confusion, Poe begins frequenting bars where he meets an exotic dancer with a young daughter, whom he had known before, and he begins a relationship with her. When Soler gets word of Poe's return, he sends some men gunning for him, but with Poe not there, they take his girlfriend hostage. While Poe arrives and manages to kill the would-be hit men, his girlfriend is killed in the shootout, orphaning her daughter, whom Poe takes in. Poe then finds the location of Soler's new drug lab and again goes storming in, only to find that his police buddy Zandro Zamora is involved in Soler's operation. This time Poe is helped out by promptly arriving back-up. In the end, Poe leaves his wife and son behind to go off and raise his girlfriend's daughter. But he would return in a sequel, *Ang Pagbabalik ng Probinsyano* (1998).

This is fairly standard Poe fare, with plenty of fisticuffs, and Poe going through his trademark windmill wind-up before delivering some of his punches, which, frankly, may provide more chuckles than excitement. Still, directing under the name Ronwaldo Reyes, Poe shows himself to be maturing as a filmmaker. There is also a scene right out of an old John Wayne western in which Poe enters the equivalent of a roadside tavern, and with an exceptionally quick draw and dead aim guns down twenty men. (In Tagalog)

Proboys

1995 Mahogany Pictures, Inc.; 104 minutes/color
Director: Ike Jarlego, Jr.; Screenwriters: Jake Tordesillas, Romer Gonzales, Owen Bobaoilla, Ony Cargamo, Chris Martinez; Cinematographer: Clodualdo "Ding" Austria; Editor: Marya Ignacio; Filmscore: Jimmy Antiporda; Cast: Ruby Rodriguez, Beth Tamayo, Giselle Sanchez, Joanne Pascual, Sharmaine Suarez, Nino Muhlach, Brando Legaspi, Jojo Abellana, Emilio Garcia, Paco Arespacochaga, Liza Lorena, Rez Cortez, Jaime Fabregas, Gamaliel Viray, Pocholo Montes, Cecille Inigo, Anthony Taylor, Jason San Pedro, Chris Llanes, Kuhol, Ramon "Bong" Revilla, Jr.

This comedy follows the hijinx of a snobby and typically mischievous group of high school girls, with the emphasis, naturally, being on their romantic pursuits and rivalries. Certainly nothing groundbreaking, but the film can be counted an artistic success of sorts purely by virtue of its comparative restraint when measured against the average Filipino comedy. The exception to that would be Giselle Sanchez who, as a repressed Catholic girl, is encouraged by her friends to come out of her shell. Still, the film is lightly entertaining, particularly if viewed with low expectations. (In Tagalog with some English)

Quezon Massacre

1989 Alpha Films International; 100 minutes/color

Directors: Tata Nel, Ariel Antonio; Screenwriter: RG-1; Cinematographers: Popoy Orense, Ike Orense; Editor: Joe Ramirez; Cast: Dhouglas Veron, Sonny Parsons, Conrad Poe, Rhey Roldan, Nick Romano, Rex Lapid, Robert Talby, Charlie Davao, Ramon Boy Bagatsing, Olga Miranda, Shirley Tesoro, Jay-Arr Veron

In this average action/jungle warfare film, Sonny Parsons is leading a platoon into the mountainous terrain of Quezon to do battle with anti-government rebels, when five military officials are taken hostage, Dhouglas Veron among them. One of the girls in the rebel camp takes a liking to Veron and helps him escape under cover of night, prompting the rebels to execute the rest of the hostages. Veron returns with government forces to wipe out the rebels, and Parsons also returns to participate in the government assault.

Despite prominent billing, this is not a starring vehicle for Parsons, who puts in token appearances at the beginning and end of the film. Early on, he also manages to get into a barroom brawl, which, while completely irrelevant to the story, seems somehow expected (after all, what's a Sonny Parsons film without a good fistfight?). The real star here is Veron, who frankly doesn't have the charisma to carry a whole film. Charlie Davao also makes a token appearance as an army general in two brief scenes where he basically sits at his desk drinking coffee and barking over the phone. With such brevity in the appearances of its big name performers, one can assume a budget-consciousness at work, but on the positive side, some of the pyrotechnics are fairly impressive. (In Tagalog)

The Raiders of Leyte Gulf

1963 Hemisphere; 80 minutes/black & white

Director/screenwriter: Eddie Romero; Cinematographer: Felipe Sacdalan; Editor: Eddie Romero; Filmscore: Tito Arevalo; Cast: Leopoldo Salcedo, Michael Parsons, Efren Reyes, Jennings Sturgeon, Eddie Mesa, Liza Moreno, Oscar Keesee

In the early 1960s, filmmaker Eddie Romero sought to break into the U.S. market with a string of WWII films, among them this being a notable example. Michael Parsons portrays a U.S. Lieutenant who parachutes onto a small island near Leyte in order to rescue captured U.S. Major Jennings Sturgeon. Parsons quickly makes contact with guerrilla leader Leopoldo Salcedo, but finds him less than enthusiastic about the assignment. Having lived under an unspoken truce with the Japanese for some time, Salcedo is not eager to stir up trouble and give the Japanese a reason to come gunning for his guerrilla army. He does agree, however, to have his men participate in the rescue mission, but when it fails, Salcedo's fears come to pass. Not only do the Japanese engage the guerrillas in combat, but Japanese commander Efren Reyes also blames the local townspeople. In an attempt to get Sturgeon to divulge the nature of his mission, Reyes begins a daily ritual of executing civilians. He also allows Sturgeon to freely roam the town, but with people dying daily on his account, Sturgeon becomes a pariah. Salcedo and Parsons plan a raid to save the entire village from Reyes' tyrannical rule and retrieve Sturgeon, but while the Japanese are defeated, Sturgeon is killed by Oscar Keesee, a local tavern owner who blames Sturgeon for the town's tribulations.

The film offers some very interesting characterizations, including Salcedo's guerrilla leader, pragmatic to the point of being accused of cowardice by one of his underlings (Eddie Mesa), and Keesee's tavern owner—a two-face always looking to earn favor with Reyes, yet killing Sturgeon after accusing him of being a traitor. Romero offers a fascinatingly complex screenplay here. (In English with some Tagalog)

The Ravagers

1965 Hemisphere Pictures/Filipinas Productions; 79 minutes/black & white

Director: Eddie Romero; Screenwriters: Cesar J. Amigo, Eddie Romero; Cinematographer: Mars Rasca; Editor: Jovan Calub; Filmscore: Tito Arevalo; Cast: John Saxon, Fernando Poe Jr., Bronwyn Fitzsimons, Robert Arevalo, Mike Parsons, Vic Diaz, Vic Silayan, Kristina Scott, Josie Sancho, Vic Uematsu, Angel Buenaventura, Pedro Navarro, Paquito Salcedo, Jose Dagumboy, Minda Moreno, Louie Alba, Richard Ray

In this standard WWII melodrama, the Japanese take control of a convent in the Philippines, where they store a fortune in gold, unaware that the nuns are hiding American Bronwyn Fitzsimons inside the convent. American John Saxon is working with Filipino guerrillas, and he sends Fernando Poe, Jr., and Vic Diaz to sneak into the convent and plant some explosive charges in preparation for an assault on the Japanese, and while there, Poe and Fitzsimons begin to fall in love. The attack on the Japanese fails, but the guerrillas follow-up a day later by attacking the Japanese at a dock as they are preparing to load the gold onto a boat. But the guerrillas are double-crossed by some of their own as Vic Diaz and some others flee into the jungle with the gold. The film climaxes with a three-way battle as both the Japanese and the guerrillas follow Diaz and his men into the jungle. The guerrillas manage to surround and kill the Japanese, as well as killing Diaz and his men, and the film ends on a somber note as Mother Superior Kristina Scott leads the nuns in a funeral procession for a fallen sister, who died in the conflict at the convent.

Capably directed by Eddie Romero, the film is most interesting as an example of one of the young Poe's early starring roles (and, yes, he has just as much, if not more, screen time as top-billed Saxon), while he was in the early stages of his emergence as the Philippines' greatest action hero. It is also interesting seeing a young Robert Arevalo, cast as one of the guerrillas. (In English with some Tagalog and Japanese)

Raw Force

1981 American Panorama/Ansor International; 86 minutes/color

Director/screenwriter: Edward Murphy; Cinematographer: Frank Johnson; Editor: Eric Lindemann; Filmscore: Walter Murphy; Cast: Cameron Mitchell, Geoff Binney, Jillian Kessner, John Dresden, Jennifer Holmes, Hope Holiday, Rey King, Carla Reynolds, Carl Anthony, John Locke, Mark Tanous, Ralph Lombardi, Chanda Romero, Britt Helfer, Vic Diaz, Camille Keaton, Tony Oliver, Jewel Shepard, Don Gorden (Bell), Tony Beso

In this horror/martial arts hybrid, Cameron Mitchell and the Burbank Karate Club travel to Warrior Island, where legend has it that disgraced ninjas are buried. Little do they know that the island is inhabited by cannibal monks who dine on young women, which they usually acquire from a band of thugs in exchange for jade. The Burbank Karate Club members battle the monks, the thugs, and risen zombie ninjas, and emerge victorious in the end, making off with enough jade to make them all rich. The film is played tongue-in-cheek, but it's mostly hit-or-miss. Mitchell is responsible for most of the hits. (In English)

Rebelyon (Rebellion)

1987 D'Scorpion Films; 96 minutes/color

Director: Willie Dado; Screenwriter: Leleng Ubaldo, Jr.; Cinematographer: Jimmy "Baer" Corpuz; Editor: Oscar Dugtong; Filmscore: Caloy Rodriguez; Cast: Vic Vargas, Dante Varona, Rommel Valdez, Melissa Mendez, Romy Diaz, Eden Bautista, Peping Escueta, Billy Gill, Mar Abalavan, Ado Geronimo, Badong Trinidad, Ading Noche, Alita Gallego, Carol Richer, Jun Delgado, Danny Rojo, Charlie Davao, Martha Sevilla, Rammil Rodriguez, Andrew Young, John William, Michael Deaver, Amy Lopez

Set at the beginning of the 20th century during the U.S. colonial period, this film stars Vic Vargas as a private commissioned to go into a particular region and eradicate a rebel insurrection. It seems strange that a lowly private should be put in charge of such an operation, but stranger still is the fact that when Vargas follows orders by stopping off to acquire soldiers to carry out the assignment, commanding officer Charlie Davao only gives him two men! The rebel insurrection is a particularly lawless pack of followers of Filipino freedom fighter Emilio Aguinaldo: murder, rape and looting are the normal course of events, and it becomes necessary to send in undercover Filipino enlisted men in civilian garb. The U.S. Army stages an assault on the area, with an American officer leading the mostly Filipino troops into battle.

This is a somewhat confused piece of work, partly due to poor editing, partly due to a scattershot screenplay, but mostly accountable is the haphazard direction of Willie Dado, which frequently borders on incompetence. Nonetheless, there are fleeting moments when Dado's amateurish direction can almost pass as merely unorthodox, and thereby almost comes across in some odd way as inspired—just not enough. (In Tagalog and English)

Reputasyon (Reputation)

1996 Re-Ichi Films International/Nolasco Visual Arts; 111 minutes/color

Director: Elwood Perez; Screenwriters: Iskho F. Lopez, Diego F. Recto, Dennis C. Evangelista; Cinematographer: Ricardo F. Jacinto; Editor: George Jarlego; Filmscore: Ernie Magtuto; Cast: Miya Nolasco, Amalia Fuentes, Romeo Vasquez, Gloria Diaz, Miguel Salveron, Roy Alvarez, Richard Bonnin, Mitch Valdes, Romano Vasquez, Nanette Inventor, Liza Lorena, Lisa Macuja, Bon Vibar, Ernie Zarate,

Raquel Villavicencio, Tony Mabesa, Joji Isla, Flora Gasser, Ogie Diaz, Marga Milano, Jason Calma, Karla Gutierrez, Jinky Oda, Adriana Agcaoili, Victor Valbuena

After a ten-year absence from film, Amalia Fuentes returned in this standard soaper wherein she plays a nutty lounge singer with a teenage daughter. Fuentes' daughter (Miya Nolasco) has a chance encounter with her father (Romeo Vasquez), a successful businessman in the process of running for political office. Nolasco tries to orchestrate a reunion between her parents, but Vasquez is already married to Gloria Diaz. Nolasco's relationship with Fuentes hits a rocky period, and so she goes to live with Vasquez and Diaz, but years of buried pain resulting from being the product of a broken home begins to surface. Nolasco's subconscious desire to turn her pain back on her parents manifests itself, and she runs away and becomes a stripper. Vasquez's political opponent sees an opportunity to trash Vasquez in the media, and so sends his son to photograph Nolasco on stage in the strip club, but when he does, a brawl ensues in which Nolsaco winds up getting shot. After undergoing surgery and hovering near death in the hospital, Nolasco eventually recovers and leaves for America with Vasquez and Diaz after saying a tearful farewell to Fuentes.

Those who remember Fuentes from her prime in the 1960s will likely be taken aback upon seeing how heavy she has gotten—something the film's promotional campaign sought to prepare people for by announcing that Fuentes "is back—bigger and better than ever." The film also seeks coinage from the reuniting of Fuentes and Vasquez, who had been a popular screen team in the 1960s, as well as real life sweethearts. (In Tagalog with some English)

Rizal sa Dapitan
(Rizal in Dapitan)

1997 Movpix International/Independent Cinema Association of the Philippines/Philippine Long Distance Telephone Co.; 98 minutes/color

Director: Tikoy Aguiluz; Screenwriter: Jose F. Lacaba; Cinematographers: Nap Jamir, Romeo Vitug; Editor: Myrna Medina-Bhunjun; Filmscore: Jaime Fabregas; Cast: Albert Martinez, Amanda Page, Candy Pangilinan, Rustica Carpio, Tess Dumpit, Roy Alvarez, Noni Buencamino, Chris Michelena, Junell Hernando, Jimmy Fabregas, Soliman Cruz, Paul Holmes

One of a number of Rizal films produced with the centennial of Philippine independence, director Tikoy Aguiluz's rendering focuses on Jose Rizal's time in Dapitan, where he was banished by the Spanish for involvement in the *Liga Filipina*, a nationalist organization. It portrays Rizal's turbulent relationship with his common-law wife Josephine Bracken, with whom he was denied a proper Christian wedding by the Church, which branded him a heretic for his unflattering portrayal of the friars in his novels. The film chronicles Rizal's activities in Dapitan, including setting up a school and opening a medical clinic, and follows through to Rizal's execution by the Spanish in 1896 after being accused of being the mastermind of a failed uprising on the mainland. (In Tagalog and English)

Robin Good: Sugod ng Sugod
(Robin Good: Attack and Attack)

1991 Viva Films; 100 minutes/color

Director: Tony Y. Reyes; Screenwriters: Joey de Leon, Tony Y. Reyes; Cinematographer: Oscar Querijero; Editor: Renato de Leon; Filmscore: Mon del Rosario; Cast: Jimmy Santos, Dawn Zulueta, Herbert Bautista, Gelli de Belen, Cherry Pie Picache, Dennis Padilla, Ruby Rodriguez, Jaime Garchitorena, Panchito Alba, Romy Diaz, Jinky Oda, Tony Carreon, Jojie Isla, Charlie Arceo, Ben Tisoy, Errol Dionisio, Joaquin Fajardo, Ernie David, Danny Labra, Bing Angeles, Maning Bato, Jess Santos, Dinky Doo Jr., Feling Cudia, Boy Ranay, Robert Talby, Minnie Aguilar, Mina Nicolas, Rommel Valdez, Turko Cervantes, Boy Salvador, Cris Aguilar, Pong Pong, Torling, Nemy Gutierrez, Boy Gomez, Roger Moring

This parody of the Robin Hood story stars Jimmy Santos as Robin Good, the King of the Forest. As expected, he falls in love with Maid Marian (Dawn Zulueta), and disguised in a suit of armor, he wins the right to marry her after defeating villainous Romy Diaz in a jousting match. But his identity is exposed by jealous Cherry Pie Picache, a member of Santos' own camp who is herself in love with Santos. After being taken prisoner, Santos is helped in his escape by Zulueta, and together they make their way back to Santos' camp. Knowing that Zulueta is in love with Santos, the king (Tony Carreon) approves of their marrying, which forces Diaz's hand. Diaz takes Carreon prisoner, and with his men, he then raids Santos' camp, but of course Santos and his merry men prevail, and the film ends happily when Santos and Zulueta wed. The film is marginally entertaining; comedian Joey de Leon co-wrote the screenplay, and one can't help but think that the project may have fared somewhat better had he appeared in the lead. (In Tagalog with some English)

Rosang Tatoo
(Rose Tattoo)

1991 Eureka Films; 110 minutes/color
Director: Dan Ilagan; Screenwriter: Humilde "Meek" Roxas; Cinematographer: Ramon Marcelino; Editor: Rene Tala; Filmscore: Vehnee Saturno; Cast: Monica Herrera, Ronaldo Valdez, Patrick dela Rosa, Beth Bautista, King Gutierrez, Jograd dela Torre, Evelyn Querubin, Allan Paule, Shirley Fuentes, Smokey Manaloto, Quila Alvarez, Rando Almanzor, Ruther Batuigas, Crispin Ngo, Renato del Prado, Dante Javier, Dino Espiritu, Rez Cortez

In this absurd, convoluted crime saga, Monica Herrera is set-up for a murder rap by crime boss Ronaldo Valdez (explaining why is not really worth the time and effort), but after a brief jail stay, she is released when the charges don't stick. Her brief incarceration certainly changes her, however, and upon her release Herrera joins a street gang and runs around threatening and fighting people, committing cold-blooded murder by shooting and stabbing. In time, Herrera meets and falls in love with Patrick dela Rosa, a hit man with a heart of gold (he only kills people in order to pay for quality medical care for his gravely ill kid sister), but when she finds out that he was the one hired by Valdez to kill her brother, Herrera ends up killing dela Rosa too (then weeping inconsolably over his corpse). The truth is that Herrera looks foolish playing a hardened criminal, and the screenplay is every bit as foolish. (In Tagalog with some English)

Rubia Servios

1978; 88 minutes/color
Director: Lino Brocka; Screenwriter: Mario O'Hara; Cinematographer: Conrado Baltazar; Editor: Jose Tarnate; Filmscore: Freddie Aguilar; Cast: Vilma Santos, Phillip Salvador, Mat Ranillo III, Estrella Kuenzler, Esther Chavez, Carpi Asturias, Jess Ramos, Leah de Guzman, Mark Versoza

Vilma Santos portrays the title character, a medical student who is abducted and raped by Phillip Salvador, a jilted suitor. After escaping from him, Santos goes to the police and Salvador is arrested, convicted and sent to prison. But as a result of the rape, Santos winds up pregnant, and her beau, fellow medical student Mat Ranillo III, proposes marriage and wants to raise the child as his own. Six years later, Santos and Ranillo are married and raising two children, having also had one of their own, when Salvador is released from prison. He immediately begins stalking Santos, and knowing that her daughter is his child as well, Salvador kidnaps the girl and takes her to an island hideaway. Salvador treats the child affectionately, and father and daughter do form something of a bond, but with the girl pining for her mother, Salvador contacts Santos and she agrees to meet with him. Their meeting quickly turns sour, however, and Salvador winds up abducting Santos at gunpoint. On a boat ride to the island Salvador tearfully professes his love for Santos, but she takes the opportunity to whack him with an oar, and after grabbing his gun, shoots Salvador and he falls into the sea. Santos then proceeds to the island where she is reunited with her daughter. Based on a true story, the film closes with post-script informing the viewer that the real Rubia Servios moved to America with her husband and children. (In Tagalog with some English)

Run Barbi Run

1995 Moviestars Productions/Cinemax; 104 minutes/color
Director: Tony Y. Reyes; Screenwriters: Rosauro de la Cruz, Tony Y. Reyes; Cinematographer: Sergio Lobo; Editor: Eduardo Jarlego; Filmscore: Jaime Fabregas; Cast: Joey de Leon, Maricel Laxa, Roldan Aquino, Subas Herrero, Nanette Inventor, Richard Merck, Noel Trinidad, Eraserheads, Lou Veloso, Rolando Tinio, Gary Lising, Archie Adamos, Inday Garutay, Allan K., Vangie Labalan, Mely Tagasa, Winnie Cordero, Amy Coronel, Prospero Luna, Robert Talby, Danny Labra, Nonong de Andres, Rene Hawkins, Ernie Forte, Jun Encarnacion, Giovanni Calvo

Returning to a character he had previously played in 1991's *Barbi (Maid in the Philippines)*, Joey de Leon again dresses in drag. This time, pizza deliveryman de Leon walks into a gang shooting when he makes a delivery to the house of Robert Talby. The shooters are members of Roldan Aquino's Scorpion Gang, who the police are anxious to get. Thanks to de Leon's identification, the police are able to arrest the gang, except for Aquino himself, who manages to elude them. With Aquino at large, the police set de Leon up in a new apartment to keep him hidden away until the trial, but when tabloid TV reporter Archie Adamos blows de Leon's cover, de Leon flees and seeks to hide his identity by dressing in drag.

While not one of de Leon's better efforts, the film is passably entertaining; it should be noted, however, that de Leon makes one ugly drag queen. (In Tagalog with some English)

Sa Kabilugan ng Buwan
(On the Full Moon)

1997 MAQ Productions/Available Light Productions; 96 minutes/color

Director: Manny Castaneda; Screenwriter: Jose Javier Reyes; Cinematographer: Romulo Araojo; Editor: Danny Gloria; Filmscore: Nonong Buencamino; Cast: Gladys Reyes, Christopher Roxas, Assunta de Rossi, Gabby Eigenmann, Giorgia Ortega, Spencer Reyes, Richard Bonnin, Cita Astals, Boyong Baytion, Archie Adamos, Gary Lising, Jon Archaval, Mon Confiado, Chris Daluz

In an upper-class neighborhood, a group of teenagers become curious about their beautiful and mysterious new neighbor. Well, they should be, as her arrival coincides with a series of brutal murders. It turns out that the charming young woman next door occasionally turns into a winged demon who flies about at night looking for prey. Of course, the kids eventually find a way to destroy her. The transformation scenes are handled via computer effects, which may look impressive to today's computer-enamored culture, but for some the novelty of such effects has no doubt long since worn thin. So has the teen-oriented horror film, in which children save the world, or in this case the neighborhood. (In Tagalog)

Sa Kuko ng Agila
(In the Claw of the Eagle)

1989 Rich Film, Inc.; 118 minutes/color

Director: Augusto Buenaventura; Screenwriter: Ricky Lee; Cinematographer: Freddie Conde; Editor: Edgardo Vinarao; Filmscore: Jimmy Fabregas; Cast: Joseph Estrada, Nikki Coseteng, Maria Isabel Lopez, Tommy Abuel, Paquito Diaz, Laurice Guillen, Ruben Rustia, Subas Herrero, Lara Melissa de Leon, Dexter Doria, Nick Nicholson, Ilonah Jean, Bomber Moran, Freddie Aguilar, Jinggoy Estrada, George Estregan, Jr.

As he continued to pursue a political career (he was by then a senator), Joseph Estrada made his final film appearance here, starring as a bus driver who finds a girl lying in an alley and takes her to the hospital. Upon receiving treatment, the girl reveals that she was raped by American soldier Nick Nicholson, and the enraged Estrada can't help becoming personally involved in seeking justice for the crime. But prominent local businessman Subas Herrero, reaping the benefit of commerce brought by the U.S. military presence, pulls some strings and manages to help Nicholson avoid prosecution. Bus driver Estrada continues to push for justice and organizes demonstrations against the U.S. military bases, and Herrero responds by targeting him for assassination, sending his expected band of goons after Estrada. Estrada survives: big deal. Estrada was too over-the-hill to be taken seriously in such a tough guy role. (In Tagalog with some English)

Sa Piling ng Aswang
(In the Midst of the Vampire)

1999 MAQ Productions/Serafim Productions; 99 minutes/color

Directors: Peque Gallaga, Lorenzo Reyes; Screenwriters: Lorenzo Reyes, Gabriel Fernandez; Cinematographer: Richard Padernal; Editor: Jess Navarro; Filmscore: Marc Araman; Cast: Maricel Soriano, Gina Alajar, Gardo Versoza, Manilyn Reynes, Jason Salcedo, Junell Hernando, Janus del Prado, Justin Simoy, Gigette Reyes, Cogie Domingo, Gary Marzo, Rommel Martin, Bea Lopez, Joan Aguas, Pilar LaFontaine, Dolly Sinai, Jomari Uy, Adonna Valle, Allan Pia

Once again directors Peque Gallaga and Lorenzo Reyes return to the horror genre, with mixed results. Maricel Soriano plays a young woman who travels south to Panay where her brother was killed while hiking. Soriano hopes to discover the truth about her brother's death, and she is accompanied on the boat ride to Panay by a group of high school students on a field trip to learn about the aswang, a mythological beast. But Soriano and the school kids soon find that the small village they are staying in is entirely populated by people who change into such creatures when the moon is full. When the locals transform into fanged monsters, Soriano and the kids flee into the forest with two soldiers stationed in the area. Soriano helps one of the village women give birth in a cave, and when the woman dies, Soriano keeps the baby and eventually uses it to barter freedom for her and the high school kids by giving the child back to the villagers.

The most interesting character is a village elder portrayed by Gina Alajar: with her hair dyed gray, her eyebrows and lashes white, and wearing strange contact lenses, the character is made even more bizarre by the fact that the dialogue was dubbed by actor Michael de Mesa. The film is more than a little similar to *Aswang*, the closing tale in Gallaga and Reyes' anthology film *Shake Rattle & Roll 2* (1990), though it is far less effective. While there are moments that exhibit a sense of style and atmosphere, the film suffers under the weight of the directors' most unfortunate tendencies, including an over-reliance on humor (which is at least largely subdued here) and a preoccupation with juvenile characters. All in all, one would be better off watching the segment from *Shake Rattle & Roll 2* for a more effective rendering of the same basic premise. (In Tagalog)

Sabado Nights
(Saturday Nights)

1995 Neo Films; 112 minutes/color

Director: Romy V. Suzara; Screenwriter: Frank Rivera; Cast: Michelle Parton, Pia Pilapil, Ina Raymundo, Lander Vera Perez, Anthony Cortes, Matt Mendoza, Shintaro Valdes, Paolo Abrera, Jessica Rodriguez, Dexter Doria, Bobby Andrews, Gino Ilustre, Eddie Mercado, Melissa Buencamino, Maybelle Cruz, Danna dela Cruz, Jayboy Samson, Oyee Barro, Manggie Cobarrubias

"The women of the 90s, the new generation. This is their story." So says the opening of *Sabado Nights*, a kind of half-baked moralistic tale of the sexual mores (or lack thereof) of three women, and the impact it has on their lives. On Saturday nights Ina Raymundo, Pia Pilapil and Michelle Parton hit the dance clubs with the motto "To each her own, never alone, tonight we'll be lucky." With such an inauspicious beginning, one might have hoped that the film would coast along on camp value, but it soon switches gears from kitsch and settles in to overripe melodrama. Pilapil, being the eldest of the trio, hears her biological clock ticking, and is not so much looking for companionship as she is looking for a sperm donor. She finds him in a visiting stranger from Thailand, and on a night when all three of the women are entertaining their respective gentlemen for the night, two of Raymundo's beaus show up (Matthew Mendoza and Lander Vera Perez) and cause a scene. Much to the amusement of Raymundo's stud of the evening, both Mendoza and Vera Perez storm out. Raymundo's true affections being for Mendoza, she chases after him imploring "Let me explain!" Unfortunately, Mendoza doesn't wait around for an explanation; it might have been interesting to hear.

With all of their wanton sexual escapades, the gals begin to worry and decide to all get HIV tests. Happily, they are all negative, and the girls then decide to settle down. Parton winds up with Anthony Cortes, whom she somehow took to be only a cab driver, but who actually comes from a very wealthy family (Oh, happy day!); Pilapil, who is now pregnant, winds up with one of Raymundo's discarded lovers (Vera Perez), who fortunately doesn't mind that she is carrying a complete stranger's baby (Oh, happy, happy day!). As for Raymundo's fortunes, they are longer in coming—four months, to be exact—as her love (Mendoza) is still reeling from her various sexual peccadilloes, and needs time to sort out his feelings. In a predictable ending, he comes to his senses and returns to Raymundo.

And the message here is ... what? Apparently that loose girls finish on top, so to speak, provided they get their wild oats sown and settle down. Oh, and let's not forget those HIV tests. As a moralistic tale, the film is far too obvious and ultimately falls flat. As a sex film it's even flatter: in one lengthy montage, we see the girls, each with their respective sex partners, all having wild, passionate sex, *though no one even bothers to undress!* Basically, we get a lot of pseudo-erotic shots of people dripping ice cubes on each other (Oooooooh, baby!).

The film's high water mark comes towards the end when Raymundo tells her two friends that she has learned to be intimate with Mendoza "from a distance." "That's my girl," says Pilapil, after which Parton chimes in with "Profound." Indeed. (In Tagalog and English)

Sabina

1963 Sampaguita Pictures; 110 minutes/black & white

Director: Jose de Villa; Screenwriter: Medy Tarnay; Cinematographer: Felipe S. Santos; Editor: Jose Tarnate; Filmscore: Restie Umali; Cast: Susan Roces, Eddie Gutierrez, Lito Legaspi, Bella Flores, Etang Discher, Charlie Davao, Boy Alano, Boy Garcia, Matimtiman Cruz, German Moreno, Nonita Navarro, Jaime Javier, Max Taeza, Serafin Sika

In this light drama, Susan Roces has dual roles as twin sisters separated at birth and adopted into different families. Both grow up in the poorer part of town, where their paths occasionally cross in the marketplace, always on bad terms. One of the sisters frequently rats out the other for thieving, not wanting to be accused herself since they are dead ringers. The two eventually find out that they are sisters when their wealthy, ailing grandmother (Etang Discher) sends her attorney to find them. The sisters are invited to come and live with Discher, but soon after their arrival spooky events begin to occur as Discher is terrorized by frightening masked figures. The culprits turn out to be greedy relatives in Halloween masks, who are trying to scare the old lady to death before she is able to write the twins into her will. The twins eventually uncover the truth with the help of their boyfriends (Eddie Gutierrez and Lito Legaspi). With the sisters being assisted by an assortment of oddball friends (including bungling German Moreno), whom they convince Discher to hire in various domestic positions, the film at times has something of a Dead End Kids feel, particularly during the latter portion, which basically turns into a parody of the old dark house motif. (In Tagalog)

Sagad Hanggang Buto
(Bad to the Bone)

1991 Moviestars Productions; 108 minutes/color
Director: Ricardo "Bebong" Osorio; Screenwriters: Humilde "Meek" Roxas; Cinematographer: Rafael Accion; Editor: Renato de Leon; Filmscore: Jaime Fabregas; Cast: Ace Vergel, Edu Manzano, Efren Reyes Jr., Rachel Lobangco, Paquito Diaz, Christina Gonzales, Perla Bautista, Dencio Padilla, Willie Revillame, Johnny Vicar, Dindo Arroyo, Carlos Salazar, Eddie Arenas, Ernie Forte, Polly Cadsawan, Vic Belaro, August Pascual, Albert Garcia, Joey Padilla, Mike Vergel, Nonoy de Guzman, Joe Baltazar, Boy Gomez, Alan Garcia, Ernie David

In this violent but unexceptional action film, our hero is drug-dealing gang member Ace Vergel (yes, that's right, our hero the drug dealer). Both Vergel and policeman Edu Manzano are vying for the affections of Christina Gonzales. Manzano turns out to be a sleazy, corrupt officer, which is necessary in order to put the viewer in Vergel's corner. Manzano kidnaps Gonzales, but Vergel rescues her and they take to hiding in an abandoned building. Manzano locates them, and then comes the climactic shootout in which Vergel is badly wounded, but still manages to kill Manzano.

The story is convoluted with an abundance of unnecessary subplots in which Vergel has an ongoing struggle with rival gang leader Paquito Diaz (whom he kills), fights with surly, abusive adoptive father Johnny Vicar (whom Diaz kills), and kills the man responsible for the murder of his real parents many years earlier, which causes a feud with the man's son (Efren Reyes, Jr.), who also participates, and is killed, in the concluding gunfight. If it all sounds a little confusing, it is. Though Vergel survives to be arrested in the end, screenwriter Humilde Roxas would have done better to just kill everyone off at the climax since none of the characters are especially worth saving. The action sequences are handled well enough, though like everything else here, nothing really stands out. (In Tagalog)

Salisi Gang (Rival Gang)

1989 Teejay Films; 106 minutes/color
Director/screenwriter: Leonardo "Ding" Pascual; Cinematographer: Apolinar Cuenco; Editor: Rodel Capule; Filmscore: Rey Valera; Cast: Sonny Parsons, Glenda Garcia, Berting Labra, Dick Israel, Robert Talabis, Robert Talby, Johnny Vicar, Vic Varrion, Robert Miller, Telly Babasa, Alex Bolado, Joe Baltazar, Nemie Gutierrez, Jess Bernardo, Marithez Samson, Allan Garcia, Turing Pader, Gerry Roman, Jeric Vasquez, Edward Luna, Freddie Suyangco, Alfred Enriquez, Zaldo Cruz, Ariel Araullo

Sonny Parsons is in the wrong place at the wrong time and is wrongly accused of a theft and sent to jail. While in jail he is befriended by irrepressible Dick Israel, and when they both get out Parsons joins Israel's gang. Parsons quickly emerges as the gang's leader, and they pull off a number of burglaries (including the brazen robbery of a congressman's home), relying more on finesse rather than violent methods. They are not adverse to using violence to eliminate rival gangs, however, and they become a priority to the police department because of their high profile targets. In the end, Parsons is chased by the police and cornered in a shipyard, where he is gunned down.

This is an above average vehicle for Parsons, which unfortunately still only makes it an average film. Berting Labra makes a brief appearance as a friend of Parsons' who is stabbed to death by a gang of drunks. (In Tagalog)

Sambahin ang Ngalan Mo
(Your Name Is Revered)

1998 Regal Films; 107 minutes/color
Director/screenwriter: Jose N. Carreon; Cinematographer: Johnny Araojo; Editor: Joe Solo; Filmscore: Nonong Buencamino; Cast: Eddie Garcia, Christopher de Leon, Jomari Yllana, Alice Dixson, Efren Reyes Jr., Mon Confiado, Robert Aviles, Alicia Alonzo, LJ Moreno, Isabel Miely, Pinky Amador, Charlie Davao, Ernie Zarate

This is an excellent crime drama wherein Eddie Garcia portrays Don Ramon Zorilla, patriarch of a family crime empire. His son (Christopher de Leon) narrowly survives a hit attempt in a shopping mall, but de Leon's pregnant wife is not so lucky. After the death of his wife, de Leon seeks retribution by knocking off Charlie Davao, head of the rival crime family and the one who ordered the hit on de Leon. But de Leon then shocks Garcia by renouncing his role as heir of the family empire, and turning himself in to the police. Convicted of Davao's murder, de Leon is sent to prison, leaving his young son to be raised by Garcia. By the time de Leon gets out of prison, he finds out that his now-grown son (Jomari Yllana) has been groomed as Garcia's new heir. Garcia does leave the door open for de Leon to return, however. Though reluctant, de Leon does return to fight by his father's side when Efren Reyes, Jr., the heir of Davao's dynasty, launches a series of attacks on the family. Garcia, de Leon and Yllana all attack Reyes' stronghold, and though de Leon manages to kill Reyes, he loses his own life in the process. In the aftermath of de Leon's death, Yllana decides that his father had the right idea after all, and he tells Garcia that he too is leaving the family empire behind.

Jose Carreon does a good job as both director and screenwriter, and all of the performances are sharp, the action robust, and there is a good filmscore by Nonong Buencamino. (In Tagalog)

Sambahin Mo ang Katawan Ko (You Worship My Body)

1995 Moviestars Productions/Mahogany Pictures; 103 minutes/color

Director: Francis "Jun" Posadas; Screenwriters: Francis "Jun" Posadas, Salvador Royales; Cast: Stella Ruiz, Tonton Gutierrez, Emilio Garcia, Janet Diaz, Lito Legaspi, Ramil Rodriguez, Perla Bautista, Alicia Alonzo, Pen Medina, Ray Ventura, Pocholo Montes, Annabelle Calupitan, Keena Zaide, Clarisse Ocampo, Bernard Atienza, Jimboy Salazar, Francis Enriquez, Marissa de Guzman, Theresa Paron, Terence Baylon, Noli Villar, Mardie Fuentes

Stella Ruiz returns to the island of her childhood and the small fishing village where as a child she witnessed her mother fall to her death from a lighthouse while trying to flee a group of local men who were trying to rape her. Returning to seek vengeance for her mother's death, Ruiz does not have the violent retribution in mind that one might expect. Instead, she uses her feminine charms to disrupt the lives of those she holds responsible for her mother's death. She uses the sons (Tonton Gutierrez and Emilio Garcia) of her targets, luring Gutierrez away from his plans of a future in the priesthood (thereby greatly upsetting his parents), and causing strife between Garcia and his fiancée. On Garcia's wedding day, Ruiz lures him away to the lighthouse where her mother died, and there they have a steamy liaison, leaving the wedding party fuming. When word gets back to the chapel that Garcia was seen stealing away with Ruiz, the infuriated wedding party forms a mob and goes marching off to the lighthouse. In a strange and almost surrealistic climax, the mob arrives at the lighthouse and Ruiz flees in terror. She is pursued through the forest and is eventually trapped on the beach, where she stands atop a large stone and tearfully screams accusations at the men who forced her mother to fall to her death. The silenced mob somberly disperses, and Garcia apologizes to his fiancée while Gutierrez consoles the weeping Ruiz. The storyline and presentation are interesting, though the retribution theme is strangely left hanging, more than a little unresolved. (In Tagalog)

Santiago

1970 Lea Productions; 123 minutes/color

Director/screenwriter: Lino Brocka; Cinematographer: Conrado Baltazar; Editor: Felizardo V. Santos; Filmscore: Doming Valdez; Cast: Fernando Poe Jr., Dante Rivero, Boots Anson-Roa, Hilda Koronel, Jay Ilagan, Caridad Sanchez, Mildred Ortega, Mary Walter, Ruben Rustia, Mario O'Hara, Joonee Gamboa, Lorli Villanueva, Angie Ferro, Corazon Noble, Cecilia Bulaong, Lily Gamboa, Celeste Legaspi, Luis Benedicto, Pons de Guzman

Set during WWII, this early directorial effort by Lino Brocka stars Fernando Poe, Jr. as a patriot fighting in a resistance army commanded by Ruben Rustia. They stage an attack on the village of Santiago, thinking it to be occupied by the Japanese, but Poe is appalled to find that their victims in the attack consist entirely of Filipino citizens. Poe's conscience forces him to leave the resistance force, and upon returning to the burned-out remains of Santiago he finds the badly wounded Hilda Koronel, apparently the only survivor. He takes her to a neighboring village, and after being taken in by Boots Anson-Roa, nurses Koronel back to health. To a point, anyway, as Koronel has been left blinded and mute by the attack. Anson-Roa falls in love with Poe, upsetting her former beau (Dante Rivero), and when Rivero spreads word that Poe was a part of the group that firebombed Santiago, Poe finds himself ostracized by the rest of the village. But when the Japanese show up, Poe becomes a hero to the people by teaming up with Rivero, as well as with Rustia and his men, to fight the Japanese. Poe gives a strong performance, as do the rest of the cast, and Brocka showed himself to already be ahead of the pack as a director. (In Tagalog)

Savage!

1973; 77 minutes/color
Director: Cirio H. Santiago; Screenwriter: Ed Medard; Cinematographer: Felipe Sacdalan; Editor: Richard Patterson; Filmscore: Don Julian; Cast: James Iglehart, Lada Edmund Jr., Carol Speed, Sally Jordan, Rosanna Ortiz, Ken Metcalfe, Vic Diaz, Harley Paton, Marie Saunders, Andres Centenera, Eddie Gutierrez, Subas Herrero, Aura Aurea

In this sleazy 70s exploitation time capsule piece from director/producer Cirio Santiago, James Iglehart plays a mercenary who collects a bounty for bringing in an anti-government rebel leader in the usual non-descript third world banana republic. But when he hears that his bounty has been executed without benefit of trial, Iglehart blows his stack. Being a black man, Iglehart knows all about suffering oppression at the hands of "the Man," and he flies into a drunken rage, confronting a government official and killing him by breaking his neck. Iglehart is then arrested and scheduled for execution, but he manages to escape and seeks help from American showgirls Carol Speed and Sally Jordan (well, who would *you* go to?). Iglehart joins up with the rebels, eventually becoming their leader, and although they fail to topple the government in the climactic battle, they manage to elude U.S. shadow government man Ken Metcalfe to fight another day.

As Santiago films go, this is not as bad as some, which admittedly isn't saying much, but the film does move along briskly, never stopping to pause, and is filled with enough T & A, jive lingo, T & A, bad performances, and T & A to make it a contender in the 70s kitsch classic sweepstakes. (In English)

Savage Justice

1988 Eastern Film Management/FGH; 82 minutes/color
Director: Joey Romero; Screenwriters: David Howard, Parker Bratel; Cast: Julia Montgomery, Steve Memel, Chanda Romero, Ruel vernal, Esther Chavez, Millicent Bautista, Rey Big Boy, Ken Metcalfe, Liz Shepherd, Anthony East, Willy Williams, Hero Bautista, Mykell Chan, Gally Sayson, Ronaldo Ledesma, Carlo Morris, Frank Campbell, David Giberson, Jean del Rosario, Eddie Gaerlan, George Geynes, Ray Wolfgram, Geodefrey Hazelton, Bryan Walterhall

Set in a fictitious republic, the story here begins with a violent revolution in which U.S. ambassador Ken Metcalfe is killed while trying to escape the country, and his daughter (Julia Montgomery) is taken prisoner by rebel leader Ruel Vernal. One year later, Montgomery has been reluctantly assimilated into the rebel group, to the chagrin of Chanda Romero, who resents being replaced by Montgomery as Vernal's woman. Vernal plans an attack on a local village and feels confident that Montgomery is now one of their own, and so allows her to participate. During the chaos of the raid, Romero takes the opportunity to shoot Montgomery, and when Vernal inquires as to her whereabouts afterward, Romero tells him that Montgomery ran off. But Montgomery is nursed back to health by doctor Anthony East, and she teams up with Steve Memel, an ex–Green Beret who lost his wife in the rebel raid. They set out to score some weapons to help the village prepare for another assault by Vernal's rebels, and along the way, Montgomery puts together a fighting force consisting of five Buddhist monks (notoriously aggressive fighters, those) and a group of children she finds living on a derelict ship ruled by dictatorial dwarf Rey Big Boy. Montgomery does come back with weapons for the townsfolk, and Vernal, obsessed with getting Montgomery back, does indeed storm the town again. But his forces perish, and Vernal himself is killed by Montgomery.

Joey Romero—the son of filmmaker Eddie Romero—is a good enough director, but there's only so much one can do with material this feeble. On top of everything else, there is a tinny filmscore by Marita Manuel that reeks, but the film's theme song is a highlight, and includes the memorable verse "the world gets rough, 'cause things get tough, when you fight back, they beat you up." The song itself is too short to accommodate the closing credits, and so is played over twice until the crawl is finished. On the plus side, Vernal and the beautiful Chanda Romero—director Joey Romero's cousin—have good roles. (In English)

Savage Sisters

1974 Cinema Projects International/American International; 81 minutes/color
Director: Eddie Romero; Screenwriters: H. Franco Moon, Harry Corner; Cinematographer: Justo Paulino; Editor: Isagani Pastor; Filmscore: Bax; Cast: Gloria Hendry, Cheri Caffaro, Rosanna Ortiz, John Ashley, Sid Haig, Eddie Garcia, Rita Gomez, Leopoldo Salcedo, Vic Diaz, Dindo Fernando, Angelo Ventura, Romy Rivera, Alfonso Carvajal, Robert Rivera, Subas Herrero, John Plater, Bruno Punzalan, Joonee Gamboa, Max Rojo, Johnny Long

This is another exploiter set in the usual fictitious banana republic, with the story here involving several disparate groups trying to do each other out of $1 million stolen from the government by Dindo Fernando and his revolutionary army. The anti-government rebels make the mistake of enlisting the aid of a band of cutthroats led by Sid Haig, and the irrepressibly sadistic Haig kills Fernando and his men and begins making plans to leave the country with the money. Meanwhile, Fernando's girlfriend (Cheri Caffaro) is arrested and thrown in prison with fellow revolutionary Rosanna Ortiz; they are set to be interrogated by prison guard Gloria Hendry, but affable conman John Ashley convinces Hendry to help him break the two rebel gals out of prison, the idea being that Caffaro and Ortiz can lead them to the money. Hendry agrees to the plan, and after successfully pulling off the prison break, they are all pursued by military officer Eddie Garcia. During a madcap shootout on the docks involving all parties, our three heroines run Garcia down with their jeep and then chase after Haig and his henchman Vic Diaz. With Ashley to show them the way, they catch up with Haig and Diaz on the beach, where they are preparing to make a getaway by boat, and the girls bury Haig and Diaz up to their necks and allow the tide to do the rest of the job. They then stiff Ashley of his fourth of the loot, giving him a paltry $10,000.

The film is played strictly for laughs, and there are some amusing performances, some expected (Haig, Diaz, Garcia, and Ashley), and some unexpected (Leopoldo Salcedo as the republic's dictatorial general, Rita Gomez as a sexpot prison warden, and Alfonso Carvajal as Garcia's photographer, following his subject around and documenting every moment of Garcia's career, including his demise). The film is something of a who's who of Filipino cinema of the era, including appearances by Bruno Punzalan, Angelo Ventura, Subas Herrero, Joonee Gamboa and Max Rojo. There is also an unbilled cameo by director Eddie Romero, who plays a brief scene with long time collaborator Ashley. (In English)

Scorpio Nights

1985 Regal Films; 122 minutes/color
Director: Peque Gallaga; Screenwriter: Rosauro Q. dela Cruz; Cinematographer: Ely Cruz; Editor: Jess Navarro; Filmscore: Jaime Fabregas; Cast: Anna Marie Gutierrez, Orestes Ojeda, Daniel Fernando, Eugene Enriquez, Amanda Amores, Mike Austria, Crispin Medina, Arbie Antonio, Carlas Balasbas, Angelo Castro Jr., Rosauro Q. dela Cruz, Lorenzo A. Reyes, Rafael Solonga

In his dingy upstairs poverty row apartment, Daniel Fernando masturbates while peering through the rickety floorboards and watching the couple below (Orestes Ojeda and Anna Marie Gutierrez) having sex. Ojeda works nights as a security guard, and his routine is to come home from work at 4:00 A.M., sit down at the table to eat the meal that Gutierrez has left out for him, wash up, and then climb into bed and have sex with his wife. Fernando takes notice of the fact that Gutierrez, who is always asleep when Ojeda gets home, barely stirs from slumber as her husband makes love to her, and so one night Fernando creeps in while Ojeda is still at work. Leaving the lights off, Fernando makes a little noise to simulate Ojeda's routine (moving some dishes around, turning on the tap) before cautiously climbing into bed with Gutierrez and proceeding to have sex with her. True to form, Gutierrez hardly notices, merely pulling her nightgown down and rolling over after Fernando withdraws. Emboldened by his first success, Fernando tries it again one night, and things go as scripted until he attempts to get out of bed and leave, at which point Gutierrez springs to life, pulling him back into bed for a considerably more participatory romp. From then on the two have a lively and often dangerous affair, with Fernando creeping downstairs nightly. Suddenly, Gutierrez's once stifling, suffocatingly dull life is fraught with peril, with Fernando sometimes barely managing to creep back upstairs before Ojeda returns home, and in one instance, having to hide beneath the bed, where he winds up having to spend the night.

Eventually, Ojeda becomes aware of the affair, and comes home from work early one morning. Entering the apartment during a particularly raucous session between Gutierrez and Fernando, Ojeda shoots Fernando, and as he lies dying on the floor beside the bed, then shoots Gutierrez. With his wife bleeding and gasping for life, Ojeda strips and proceeds to mount her, and continues to have sex with her even after she has expired. Then, when he reaches climax, Ojeda puts the gun to his own head and kills himself.

If one accepts film as a basically voyeuristic medium (and I have no intention of arguing the pros and cons of that particular viewpoint), then it certainly stands to reason that pornography is the height (or, more appropriately, depth) of artistic voyeurism. Director Peque Gallaga certainly straddles the fence between soft and hardcore sex, and comes up with two hours of voyeurism ostensibly about a peeping tom. While the ending is an almost unparalleled downer, the film was hailed by some as the most "sensual" Filipino film ever. Gutierrez has undeniable sex appeal, but her charms are so overwhelmed by the squalidness of the setting that her sexual attributes are fairly buried in all the seamy, depressing and ugly surroundings and circumstances. Unless one is aroused by Peeping Toms, masturbation, sex in filthy communal bathrooms, watching two people literally spitting into each other's mouths (in slow motion, no less), and sex with bloody corpses, then this will possibly be nothing but an endurance test. None of this is to suggest that the film is without any merit (Gallaga is, after all, a talented director), but ultimately, this is an extreme exercise in voyeurism on a pornographic level. (In Tagalog)

Search for Vengeance

1984 Cinex Films/Twin Dragon/F. Puzon Film Enterprises; 86 minutes/color
Director: Raymond Malonzo; Cinematographer: Ver Dauz; Editor: Joe Mendoza; Filmscore: Snafu Rigor; Cast: Reginald King (Rey Malonzo), Charlie Davao, George Estregan, Johnny Wilson, Fred Param, Liz Allen, Anne Marie, John Reed, Ricky Moreno

The well-worn premise of this crime saga sees policeman Rey Malonzo kill the son of crime boss Charlie Davao during an altercation in a discotheque. Though Davao's son had pulled his gun first and Malonzo merely fired in self defense, Malonzo is suspended pending an investigation. Unsatisfied, Davao seeks revenge and has an assassin kill Malonzo's wife, which sends Malonzo on his own, uh, search for vengeance. Malonzo runs around knocking off Davao's men, and even becomes a latter-day Robin Hood, robbing from Davao and giving the money to the unfortunate citizenry, but he is only the darling of the people for a short time. Davao turns the tables on Malonzo, sending his men out to steal from the people and having them claim to be doing so on Malonzo's orders (and they're dumb enough to believe that?). Well, the gullible townspeople buy it, and Malonzo is soon sought by the police, Davao *and* the moronic citizenry. When the townspeople manage to capture Malonzo, they tie him to a cross and are prepared to stone him to death, but Malonzo is saved by the arrival of his police buddy George Estregan. The film climaxes with the police defeating Davao's men in a shootout while Malonzo chases Davao into a nearby cemetery and kills him. (Dubbed into English)

Secrets of Pura

1991 Regal Films; 111 minutes/color
Director: Joey Gosiengfiao; Screenwriter: Ricky Lee; Cinematographer: Charlie Peralta; Editor: Edmond Jarlego; Filmscore: Lutgardo Labad; Cast: Alma Moreno, Eddie Rodriguez, Carmina Villaroel, Carmen Barredo, Lorenzo Mara, Ricardo Cepeda, Christopher Llanes, Lou Bunyi, Emily Artadi, Marguey Rodriguez, Bong Regala, Bernard Banares, Rose Tiu, Angela Figueras, May Nadayag, Daisy Romualdez, Rosemarie Gil, Laurence Pineda

Producer Joey Gosiengfiao takes the directorial duties on this tawdry tale of a good girl gone bad. Alma Moreno is Pura, a young woman who leaves her small hometown and travels to Manila to seek fame and fortune. She quickly finds a slot in a nightclub, but unfortunately it's as a prostitute (albeit a classy one). She meets the man of her dreams and has that old hooker's dilemma of hiding her true profession from her beau. Eventually, she comes clean with him, and he is very willing to overlook her means of support until he discovers that his father (Eddie Rodriguez) is one of her clients. Rodriguez's wife also finds out, and plans to shoot Moreno, but when Rodriguez intervenes, the gun goes off killing Rodriguez's wife. Rodriguez quickly frames Moreno for the shooting, but her lover exonerates her, turning on his own father in the process. The film then ends happily with Moreno marrying her sweetheart.

Moreno has a unique beauty, and is a very good actress as well, but this is basically just another soaper. Gosiengfiao also produced *Isang Gabi Tatlong Babae* the same year, which chronicled the sexual misadventures of three beautiful young women. (In Tagalog and English)

Selosa (Jealous Woman)

1997 Octo Arts Films; 91 minutes/color
Director: Mel Chionglo; Screenwriter: Ricky Lee; Cinematographer: Jorge Tutanes; Editor: Ferren Salumbides; Filmscore: Nonong Buencamino; Cast: Rosanna Roces, Patrick Guzman, Lara Morena, Emilio Garcia, Alicia Alonzo, Evangeline Pascual, Susan Africa, Patricia Perez, Randolf Reyes, Roy Rodrigo

In this overblown bit of softcore fluff, Rosanna Roces tires of boyfriend Patrick Guzman's constant philandering and ends her relationship in a huff. Guzman takes up with Lara Morena, and in an attempt to make him jealous, Roces has friend Emilio Garcia pose as her new boyfriend. Before too long Roces and Garcia become lovers in reality, but Roces breaks that off too, since she still has hopes of getting Guzman back. In time she does, and Garcia and the now discarded Morena commiserate together by beginning their own love affair. But Garcia is unable to let go of his feelings for Roces, and he phones her constantly; he also reveals to Guzman the fact that he and Roces had been intimate. Guzman throws a tantrum and again ends his relationship with Roces, a curious thing to do since he himself had been intimate with Morena. The film ends with everybody apologizing to each other and making nice. Stripped of the sex scenes, there's little else here. Alicia Alonzo has yet another motherly role, which seems to be all she ever gets anymore. (In Tagalog with some English)

Sensual

1985 Regal Films; 102 minutes/color
Director: Marilou Diaz-Abaya; Screenwriter: Jose Javier Reyes; Cinematographer: Conrado Baltazar; Editor: Marc Tarnate; Filmscore: Jaime Fabregas; Cast: Barbara Benitez, Charito Solis, Chanda Romero, Lito Gruet, Lara Jacinto, Hero Bautista, Vangie Labalan, Cris Daluz, Arvie Antonio, Josie Galvez, Rolando Tinio, Sarah Alonzo, Romeo Enriquez, Ella Luansing, Tony Mabesa, Crispin Medina

This interesting erotic melodrama stars Barbara Benitez as a teenage girl having a lesbian love affair with her best friend and schoolmate Lara Jacinto. They are spotted in an intimate moment one afternoon by Lito Gruet, who is out for a day's hunting. Taken with Benitez, Gruet follows her home to find out where she lives, and continues to pursue her until she relents, beginning a relationship with Gruet that leaves Jacinto tormented by jealousy. Benitez becomes conflicted, unsure of where her true affections lie, but in the end she is not required to make a decision as she leaves her hometown of Nueva Ecija with her mother (Chanda Romero) after the death of her grandmother (Charito Solis). Benitez gives a very good performance, but the sexual content (as well as some full frontal nudity on her part) may have hindered her breaking into more mainstream work (the same may be true of Jacinto). There are also excellent performances by established actresses Romero (as Benitez's somewhat dour mother) and Solis (as the daffy grandmother). Director Marilou Diaz-Abaya does a superb job, particularly in the handling of some interesting dream sequences, one in which Benitez sees herself fleeing through a field while being literally hunted by Gruet with his rifle. (In Tagalog)

Sgt. Ernesto Baliola: Tinik sa Batas (Sgt. Ernesto Baliola: Thorn in the Law)

1992 Moviestars Productions; 93 minutes/color
Director: Ricardo "Bebong" Osorio; Screenwriter: Amado Lacuesta; Cinematographer: Val Dauz; Editor: Renato de Leon; Filmscore: Demet Velasquez; Cast: Sonny Parsons, Efren Reyes Jr., Aurora Sevilla, Dindo Arroyo, Shirley Tesoro, Eric Francisco, Oliver Osorio, Gilda Aragon, Fred Moro, Joey Padilla, Fernando "Chinkee" Tan, Melissa Sosa, Martin Parsons, Bebeng Amora

Soldier Sonny Parsons tries to defend the people of his poverty-stricken area by fighting against greedy developers who want to bulldoze their slum dwellings. He manages to drive the demolitionists off on a couple of occasions by way of two lively brawls, but thug Dindo Arroyo returns with the police, who open fire on Parsons. Some of the locals join Parsons in returning fire, and Parsons winds up in hot water with his military commander (exchanging fire with law enforcement officers does tend to complicate one's military career). Realizing that the residents are in desperate need of money, Parsons forms some of the locals into a group and leads them on a bank robbing spree (also guaranteed to play havoc with one's military record). After a while, Parsons becomes Public Enemy Number One, and the film ends (as so many of his films do) with Parsons' favorite closing shot as he is caught in a shootout with the police and we are treated to yet another freeze-frame of the defiant Parsons, bloody but unbowed, still firing while caught in a hail of bullets.

No surprises here, other than a bigger than normal role for the thuggish Arroyo. The film also seeks comic relief from Parsons' romantic peccadilloes and the frequent squabbles they cause with his wife, Aurora Sevilla. Ha ... ha ... ha. (In Tagalog)

Sgt. Melgar

1989 Regal Films; 101 minutes/color
Director: Arturo San Agustin; Screenwriter: Tony Tacorda; Cinematographer: Vic Anao; Editor:

Edgardo Vinarao; Filmscore: Emil Losenada; Cast: Lito Lapid, Tetchie Agbayani, Jean Garcia, Monica Herrera, Perla Bautista, Phillip Gamboa, Romy Diaz, Dick Israel, Roi Vinzon, Jim Rosales, Danny Riel, Marie Fuentes, Alex de Leon, Robert Talabis, Eddie Tuazon, Vic Varrion, Robert Miller, Renato del Prado, Joe Andrade, Willie Dado, Lucita Soriano, Fred Panopio, Tanya Torre, Rona May Juralbal

In this true-life account of a Filipino national hero, Lito Lapid plays the title role, as the film chronicles his life from brawling street thug to dedicated constabulary and fighter of insurrectionists. The film runs through a number of battles with rebel groups, variously led by Dick Israel, Romy Diaz and even Tetchie Agbayani. In the concluding battle Lapid is badly wounded by gunfire that rips his stomach open to the point that his entrails begin to spill out. Lapid has the presence of mind to catch them in a helmet and then sprints through the field of fire to reach cover, where he promptly passes out. This seems more than a little hard to swallow, but then, this is a supposedly true story. It is also true that the Filipinos are very big on their national heroes, and so this may well be a case of aggrandizement of an already storied career.

The question of license is also an issue in a curious scene in which Lapid, leading his men through the jungle in search of a rebel camp, comes across a small hut inhabited by a woman and her baby, bearing more than a passing resemblance to traditional renderings of the Madonna and Child. After a successful battle with the rebels, Lapid and his men pass by the hut once more on their way back but find it empty, at which time a picture falls from the wall. Lapid picks the picture up and finds that it is a depiction of Mary and the baby Jesus. True or not, it is an interesting moment. (In Tagalog with some English)

Sgt. Patalinghug: CIS—Special Operations Group

1991 Harvest International; 120 minutes/color
Director: Jerry O. Tirazona; Screenwriters: Erwin T. Lanado, Major Stanley Urong; Cinematographer: Apolinar Cuenco; Editor: Rodel Capule; Filmscore: Willie Yusi; Cast: Eddie Garcia, Efren Reyes Jr., Aurora Sevilla, Beverly Vergel, Lani Lobangco, Charlie Davao, Nick Romano, Orestes Ojeda, Dick Israel, Gabriel Romulo, Jesse Delgado, Apple Punzalan, Nathaniel Rivera, Honey Policarpio, Dexter Doria, Renato del Prado, Fred Moro, Robert Talby

This gritty crime thriller from director Jerry Tirazona showcases an outstanding performance by Eddie Garcia as an officer in the Central Intelligence Service who goes undercover to infiltrate a holdup gang headed by Charlie Davao. After a rambunctious shootout, the gang is vanquished, and Garcia arrests Davao. While Davao stews in prison, Garcia has his own problems, being shot in the face while pursuing another gang of criminals. After a lengthy hospital stay and recovery period, Garcia returns to work battling a vicious gang of crooks led by the ubiquitous and thoroughly psychotic Dick Israel. Garcia and his fellow officers likewise bring this bunch to justice in another rough and rowdy shootout, during which one of Israel's men has his arm shot off. In time Davao manages to get out of prison, and naturally comes gunning for Garcia. Getting word over his police radio that there is a large group of heavily armed men gathering outside of his house, Garcia races home and arrives to the chatter of automatic weapons fire coming from his house. Sneaking in the back door, he finds his wife and son using his home arsenal to hold Davao's men at bay, and in a gripping climactic confrontation, both Garcia and his son are wounded, but still manage to wipe out Davao's formidable force, and Garcia uses a grenade launcher to explode Davao's fleeing car.

Most often employed as a screenwriter, there is nothing in Tirazona's career—either before or since—to suggest that he would be capable of such a taut directorial job, but his work here is excellent, and the film features several highly dramatic and enthusiastically violent shootouts. Willie Yusi's musical score also deserves mention: with all of the mundane, droning synthesized scores used in the action genre, it is refreshing that Yusi eschews any attempt at bombast, using his synth instead to provide simplistic, yet highly dramatic and foreboding—even occasionally eerie—notes that almost seem to be straining to cry out with urgency. Excellent in every respect, *this* is how it's done. (In Tagalog with some English)

Sgt. Victor Magno: Kumakasa Kahit Nag-iisa
(Sgt. Victor Magno: Will Continue to Fight, Even Alone)

1988 Serres Films; 94 minutes/color
Director: Nilo Saez; Screenwriter: Humilde "Meek" Roxas; Cinematographer: Bhal Dauz; Editor: Segundo Ramos; Filmscore: Vehnee Saturno; Cast: Ronnie Ricketts, Roland Dantes, Nadia Montenegro, Robin Padilla, George Estregan Jr., Ruel

Vernal, Philip Gamboa, Dick Israel, Val Iglesias, Ernie Forte, King Gutierrez, Mercy Dizon, Renato del Prado, Christopher Paloma, Johnny Wilson, Edward Luna, Larry Esguerra, Boy Salvador, Rolan Montes, Jet Sahara

Police sergeant Ronnie Ricketts tangles with a drug gang led by Roland Dantes, and Dantes has his men tie Ricketts to a railroad track. They leave him to his fate, but a young boy comes along to free him. With a train bearing down on them there isn't even enough time to loose the bonds on his right hand, and though he was able to roll his body out of the way, Ricketts loses his right arm under the train. He allows everyone—even his wife—to believe that he is dead, telling only friend George Estregan, Jr. where he is. Estregan helps nurse Ricketts back to health, and after learning to shoot left handed, Ricketts goes off shot gunning Dantes' men. Word gets around that Ricketts is still alive, and Dantes and company come after him, but Ricketts ends up killing all of his enemies in a shootout in an old rail yard. He is then reunited with his wife (Nadia Montenegro) ... who sings him a song!

It's interesting to see one time martial arts hero Dantes as the heavy, and future superstar Robin Padilla as one of his goons. Also of interest is Estregan in one of his earlier roles, which he plays straight, his mugging mode a few years from kicking into overdrive. There is also Dick Israel in a brief appearance as a police buddy of Ricketts,' who gets killed early on. As for Ricketts himself, he plays things with his usual intensity. (In Tagalog)

Shake Rattle & Roll 2

1990 Regal Films; 120 minutes/color
Director: Peque Gallaga, Lorenzo Reyes; Screenwriters: Peque Gallaga, Don Seducers, Lorenzo Reyes; Cinematographer: Eduardo F. Jacinto; Editor: Rene Tala; Filmscore: Toto Gentica; Cast: Janice de Belen, Eric Quizon, Isabel Granada, Caridad Sanchez, Eddie Gutierrez, Joey Marquez, Carmina Villaroel, Sylvia Sanchez, Joey Reyes, Jinky Laurel, Daisy Romualdez, Manilyn Reyes, Ana Roces, Rez Cortez, Aljon Jimenez, Anjo Yllana, Vangie Labalan, Mae Anne Adonis, Romy Romulo

In this late-arriving follow-up to the 1984 horror anthology *Shake Rattle & Roll*, Peque Gallaga and Lorenzo Reyes share the directing credit on all three stories. In *Multo* (Ghost), Janice de Belen and Eric Quizon spend their honeymoon in a house with a dark past. Years earlier, a young woman (Isabel Granada) was brutally murdered by a crazed abortionist (Eddie Gutierrez), an event which begins to haunt de Belen's dreams. All hell breaks loose when Quizon finds a ring that belonged to Gutierrez, and after putting it on he becomes possessed by the spirit of the maniac abortionist. Unable to remove the ring, Quizon cannot control himself, and he eventually attempts to kill de Belen, who can only save herself and her husband by cutting his finger off and throwing the ring in the fireplace. The story is quite gruesome (perhaps too much so for mainstream Western tastes) but very effectively presented.

The second story, *Kulam* (Witchcraft), is the apparently obligatory comedy segment, and not too funny at that. Ladies' man Joey Marquez (that part *should* be funny) is laid up in the hospital in an almost complete body cast, but he still takes the opportunity to start a fling with his nurse. His doctor (Daisy Romualdez) takes exception to this since she has her own designs on Marquez. Romualdez is also a witch, so she rigs up a voodoo doll of Marquez and delights in sticking pins in the doll's crotch. Young Carmina Villaroel also has a crush on Marquez and helps him escape. While fleeing through the hospital they run into a maternity ward full of monster babies (the same ones used in Gallaga and Reyes' 1988 film *Tiyanak*, in which de Belen played mother to a demon child; in the only amusing moment in the segment, Marquez sees the hellish children, looks into the camera and gasps "Oh, my God! A child of Janice!"). Lotlot de Leon appears in footage cribbed from *Tiyanak*, in which the baby goes on a murderous rampage through the hospital. Marquez and Villaroel also come across a morgue full of zombies (de Belen makes a brief appearance as one of the zombies). Eventually, Marquez and Villaroel turn Romualdez's black magic back on her and change her into a frog, which is last seen in a jar marked for dissection. Har har har.

Since the final segment, *Aswang* (Vampire), stars former child star and frequent comedy actress Manilyn Reynes, one might have expected that this too would be played for laughs, but it's actually a no-holds-barred barnstormer of a horror tale. Traveling to a remote village with a friend, Reynes is made somewhat ill at ease by the strange stares from some of the locals. Her suspicions continue to build, and she soon witnesses a bizarre midnight ceremony in which a young man is hacked to pieces and devoured by the villagers, who transform into hideous beasts with enormous fangs. When her presence is discovered, she flees into the misty forest and a harrowing chase ensues. All told, this may be the best *Shake Rattle & Roll* segment of all. The film itself is marred only by the lame second segment. (In Tagalog)

Shake Rattle & Roll 3

1991 Regal Films; 126 minutes/color
Directors: Peque Gallaga, Lorenzo Reyes; Screenwriter: Jerry Lopez Sineneng; Cinematographer: Joe Tutanes; Editor: Danny Gloria; Filmscore: Toto Gentica; Cast: Janice de Belen, Manilyn Reynes, Kris Aquino, Ogie Alcasid, Rosemarie Gil, Eva Ramos, Mae Ann Adonis, Lilia Cuntapay, Joel Torre, Armida Siguion-Reyna, Subas Herrero, Gina Alejar, Joey Marquez, Ricardo Cepeda, Ai-Ai de las Alas, Vangie Labalan, Inday Badiday, Pen Medina, Lucy Quinto, Cris Daluz, Joey Reyes, Manny Castaneda

The third installment in Regal's horror anthology series begins with a tale called *Yaya* (Nursemaid), about an evil spirit that snatches infants and appears as an old hag (Lilia Cuntapay). Kris Aquino tries to protect the baby, but ultimately loses the battle. The segment has some effectively chilling scenes, not the least of which is the delirious moment when Aquino locks herself in a car as the evil entity/old hag terrorizes her, shaking the car and popping up at one window, then another.

The second segment, *Ate* (Sister), concerns Janice de Belen's attempt to discover the truth about her sister's death. When she goes to view her sister's body, she finds the coffin empty and her sister (Gina Alejar) roaming the grounds. Alejar seems to have become involved with some sort of cult whose members succeeded in raising her from the dead. In the end, she returns to the grave as de Belen manages to escape sinister cult leaders Subas Herrero and Armida Siguion-Reyna, with the help of Joel Torre. The story has some uniquely bizarre moments, as when Alejar, instinctively yearning for the grave, transforms her longing into a love for the dust of the earth and begins ravenously devouring the dirt from a potted plant as de Belen struggles to restrain her.

With both Manilyn Reynes and TV comedienne Ai-Ai de las Alas in the closing segment, *Nanay* (Mother), it was a safe bet that it would tend more toward comedy (particularly since neither of the preceding stories had, and the filmmakers seem determined to tarnish the series with a levity quota). Reynes plays a schoolgirl rooming at a girl's boardinghouse where she is constantly targeted for ridicule by the older girls (including de las Alas). Reynes comes home from the beach one day with a slimy little sea monster whose bile dissolves human flesh, and the creature goes on a rampage through the house, drooling over Reynes' tormentors, thereby eliminating her source of misery. Reynes then affectionately returns the little beast to the sea. With its considerably longer running time and special effects (human bodies dissolving into bubbling, bloody masses of flesh and bone), this segment is obviously intended to be the film's showpiece, but from an artistic perspective, it is far and away the weakest in the trilogy. The unfortunate tendency toward comedy would regrettably dominate the next installment in the series. (In Tagalog with some English)

Shake Rattle & Roll 4

1992 Regal Films; 113 minutes/color
Directors: Peque Gallaga, Lorenzo Reyes; Screenwriter: Jerry Lopez Sineneng; Cinematographer: Joe Tutanes; Editor: Danny Gloria; Filmscore: Archie Castillo; Cast: Manilyn Reynes, Edu Manzano, Aljon Jimenez, Sunshine Cruz, Nida Blanca, Janice de Belen, Al Tantay, Aiza Seguerra, Phillip Gamboa, Gina Alajar, Miguel Rodriguez, Ai-Ai de las Alas, IC Mendoza, Aiko Melendez, Bella Flores, Pen Medina, Rey Solo, Lilia Cuntapay, Malou de Guzman, Mae Anne Adonis, Vangie Labalan, Mely Tagasa, Romy Romulo

Another three tales in Regal's popular horror series, this time largely comedic. In the first story, *Ang Guro* (The Teacher), Manilyn Reynes is a high school student given to fantasizing about marrying her chemistry teacher (Edu Manzano). Her feelings toward him quickly change, however, when she witnesses him change into a hideous monster and brutally murder her best friend (Sunshine Cruz). Manzano's transformation results from his concocting a Jekyll/Hyde formula that brings out his bad side. Naturally, no one believes Reynes, and the story climaxes with her being chased around the campus by Manzano before being rescued by a boy with a crush on her.

Ang Kapitbahay (The Neighbor) concerns a number of disappearing children in a public park. A young girl (Aiza Seguerra) witnesses a bizarre creature drop down from a tree, snatch a dog, and then leap back up into the tree, but she cannot get anyone to believe her. Knowing that its presence is no longer a secret, the creature pays a night visit to Seguerra's home, but is unable to find her and carry her off. Seguerra winds up going to the park one night and climbing the tree, where she finds the missing children caged. She confronts the monster and is able to awaken its tender side, at which time it lowers the children down from the tree and into the waiting arms of their mothers. The story has the feel of a modern Aesop fable, and the monster make-up is very inventive. Janice de Belen portrays Seguerra's mother.

The concluding story, *Ang Madre* (The Nun), again features a child as its protagonist. A series of shantytown slaughters is blamed on a vampire, and a young boy (IC Mendoza) witnesses a nurse (Aiko Melendez) from the local hospital sprout bat wings and split in two at the waist, the top half flying off to search for prey while the bottom half remains on the ground with the inner organs exposed. This gives Mendoza an idea, and he steals some hot sauce from a local disco. The next night, when he again witnesses Melendez transform, he pours hot sauce into the lower half of the torso, causing the top half to shriek in agony as it is flying about. The appearance of a male vampire poses another problem, but Mendoza enlists the aid of disco DJ Ai-Ai de las Alas, and they are able to defeat the vampires with ... hot sauce. The use of hot sauce as a lethal weapon against vampires seems a bit too contrived an attempt at humor. The story does have one truly effective moment, however, when an angry mob gathers outside the house of an old woman (Lilia Cuntapay), whom they mistakenly believe to be the vampire, and when she placidly walks outside she is assaulted and staked by the mob. (In Tagalog with some English)

Shake Rattle & Roll 5

1994 Regal Films; 103 minutes/color
Directors: Don Escudero, Jose Javier Reyes, Manny Castaneda; Screenwriter: Jose Javier Reyes; Cinematographer: Jun Pereira; Editor: Danny Gloria; Filmscore: Nonong Buencamino; Cast: Sheryl Cruz, Manilyn Reynes, Ruffa Gutierrez, Chuck Perez, Monsour del Rosario, Jaclyn Jose, Tom Taus Jr., Don Pepot, Cita Astals, Bong Regala, Ogie Diaz, Ding Dong Dantes, Archie Adamos, Eva Darren, Rustica Carpio, Aida Carmona, Nonong de Andres, Angel Confiado, Romy Romulo, Michelle Ortega

This is somewhat different than the rest of the series in that the three stories are presented by way of a linking story in which three young people visit a carnival mystic to have their fortunes told. In the first story, directed by Don Escudero, Ruffa Gutierrez and Bong Regala vacation on a remote island and are temporarily stranded when the boat scheduled to pick them up fails to arrive due to mechanical problems. Regala becomes deathly ill when his body is invaded by a fearsome parasite, while Gutierrez is lured into the jungle by strange flute music. She meets mysterious Monsour del Rosario and follows him back to a house, which, while somewhat quaint on the outside, is surprisingly elaborate and lush in its interior. In any event, it definitely looks out of place in the middle of the jungle. It transpires that del Rosario is some kind of demonic entity out to steal Gutierrez's soul. She manages to escape and the house crumbles and falls into a crack in the earth, after which Regala recovers and he and Gutierrez finally leave.

The second story, *Anino* (Shadow), is directed by Jose Javier Reyes (who wrote all three segments), and features Sheryl Cruz and Jaclyn Jose as sisters who move into a new apartment with their brother and a friend. They quickly discover that the apartment is haunted by a malevolent spirit that appears at first only as a shadow. Eventually, the entity manifests itself physically and begins brutalizing the foursome. While they do manage to escape the apartment, there is no resolution to the haunting.

The final story, *Impakto* (Demon), is directed by Manny Castaneda, and with Manilyn Reynes and Tommy Taus, Jr. heading the cast, is not surprisingly a comic segment. Reynes and Taus are siblings kidnapped by a criminal gang intending to hold them for ransom. While transporting their captives, the kidnappers experience car trouble and are forced to walk to a rundown, derelict hotel, which turns out to be occupied by vampire Chuck Perez, who chases everyone throughout the building all night. While Perez is busy killing the kidnappers, Reynes, Taus and the hotel's only other occupant (hobo Nonong de Andres) manage to stake Perez. Although played for laughs, the story is quite gruesome. (In Tagalog with some English)

Shake Rattle & Roll 6

1997 MAQ Productions; 100 minutes/color
Directors: Maurice Carvajal, Frank G. Rivera, Anton Juan; Screenwriters: Luna Lopez, Tony Perez; Cinematographers: Romulo Araojo, Eduardo Cabrales; Editor: Edmund "Bot" Jarlego; Filmscore: Jesse Lasaten; Cast: Camille Pratts, Joanne Quintas, Daniel Pasia, John Apacible, Bobby Benitez, Theresa Jamias, Aiza Seguerra, Matet de Leon, Tom Taus Jr., Ara Mina, Lelissa Mendez, Kiko Villamayor, Tonton Gutierrez, Giorgia Ortega, Raymond Keannu, Roy Alvarez, Toffee Calma

Reviving the series after several years, the anthology this time kicks off with a story called *Ang Telebisyon* (The Television), directed by Maurice Carvajal, in which cute little Camille Pratts finds refuge from loneliness through television. Neglected by her constantly quarrelling parents (Joanne Quintas and Daniel Pasia), Pratts receives companionship from Mr. Boo, a clown-faced jester on a children's television program. Pratts falls asleep in front of the TV one night, and is awakened by Mr. Boo beckoning to her from inside the set. She is reluctant to answer, though, and Mr. Boo's tone then becomes menacing. When Pratts flees the room Boo hops out of the television set and proceeds to chase her through the house, eventually getting hold of her and dragging her into the TV set with him. Quintas and Pasia arrive home to find their daughter screaming for help from inside the TV. Pratts manages to reach her arms out of the set, and her parents then pull her out, after which the television explodes. The segment ends on a sugary note with the happily reunited family all smiles as they embark on a trip together. Well, maybe that's all Mr. Boo wanted in the first place.

The second segment, *Ang Tulay* (The Bridge), is an abbreviated version of a feature directed by Frank Rivera, and involves the efforts of three young girls to lay to rest the spirit of a young boy (Tom Taus, Jr.) who drowned beneath a bridge. They eventually succeed with the help of a spiritist who, during a séance, brings out a host of drowning victims who appear beneath the bridge solemnly carrying candles, who then disappear.

The concluding story, *Ang Buwan* (The Moon), is directed by Anton Juan, and stars Tonton Gutierrez as a college student who falls in love with bewitchingly beautiful Giorgia Ortega; but she turns out to be responsible for the deaths of a number of young men on campus who each had their hearts ripped out. With the help of professor Roy Alvarez, Gutierrez discovers that Ortega is cursed by some sort of malevolent moon demon long worshipped by a pagan cult, and she transforms into a hideous beast when the moon is full. Gutierrez witnesses this transformation one night, but despite her horrid appearance, he professes his love to Ortega, and this seems to release her from the curse. They do not wind up together, however, as Ortega's release from bondage manifests itself in a number of white doves which fly away blissfully free.

The use of a condensed feature for the second segment, and the fairly inconsequential nature of the opening segment, suggest a lack of inspiration. As for the closing tale, though the story itself is not especially creative, it does contain a number of atmospheric moments. However, all in all, the series may have been better left alone at that point. (In Tagalog with some English)

Sinasamba Kita
(I Worship You)

1982 Viva Films; 118 minutes/color
Director: Eddie Garcia; Screenwriter: Orlando Nadres; Cinematography: Romy Vitug; Editor: Ike Jarlego; Filmscore: George Canseco; Cast: Vilma Santos, Christopher de Leon, Phillip Salvador, Lorna Tolentino, Ramil Rodriguez, Irene Celebre, Luz Fernandez, Moody Diaz, Lolita Abesamis, Demy de Cordova, Norma Blancaflor, Kristina Paner, Fanny Serrano, Larry Leviste, Yvonne, Eddie Garcia

In this melodramatic soaper, businesswoman Vilma Santos is in love with business associate Christopher de Leon, but he only has eyes for Santos' younger sister (Lorna Tolentino). While de Leon is discreet in pursuing Tolentino, she resists his advances owing to her loyalty to Santos, but the truth is that Tolentino has strong feelings for de Leon, although she soon enough has a suitor of her own in Phillip Salvador. This infuriates de Leon, and Santos is hardly oblivious to his true feelings. Well, there's your romantic conflict—now the tragedy: Tolentino is in a car accident that leaves her in a vegetative state, though doctors can detect no actual brain damage. When de Leon tries to visit her, Salvador flies into a rage and takes Tolentino away to an isolated country house. While Santos searches high and low for Tolentino, de Leon slips into an alcoholic haze, spending his nights in cheap bars with cheap women. When Tolentino regains her senses, she enrages the volatile Salvador by calling out for de Leon, and out of his mind with jealousy, Salvador rapes her and holds her captive. Eventually, Santos finds Tolentino, and Salvador comes to his senses long enough to allow them both to return home, where Tolentino and de Leon are finally united, Santos having learned to put her own feelings aside.

Eddie Garcia is a very capable director, and he has a keen cinematic eye; it would be interesting to see him direct something more stylistically suited to his directorial approach. But as a director, anyway, romantic soaps seem to be his genre of choice. Santos and de Leon were a popular screen team during the 1970s and '80s, being romantically paired in many films. Given that, it is interesting that it is Tolentino who is the object of de Leon's affections here, and Santos the odd one out. (In Tagalog and English)

Sisa

1998 Good Harvest; 106 minutes/color

Director/screenwriter: Mario O'Hara; Cinematographer: Rey de Leon; Editor: Ike Jarlego; Filmscore: Blitz Padua; Cast: Gardo Versoza, Patrick Guzman, Marcus Madrigal, Aya Medel, Evangeline Pascual, Ogie Juliano, Frank Rivera, Jerry O'Hara, Alex Jimenez, Lilia Cuntapay, Master Dem, Romy Morales, Janice Mendoza, Edward Orbito, Samuel Reyes, Orlando Reyes, Ruben O'Hara

In this intriguing, surrealistic account of Joe Rizal's final hours while awaiting execution, the national hero is haunted in his prison cell by taunting phantasms, but is comforted by Sisa, a beautiful mystery woman from his youth. Through flashbacks, Rizal recalls Sisa, a beautiful girl who liked to entertain people with her singing (though she was apparently tone deaf), and fighting with another young man for Sisa's affections. The film also recounts abuses Rizal both personally experienced and witnessed under Spanish colonial rule. On a lighter note, he is also visited in his cell by the apparition of a portly magician (Master Dem), whom he apprenticed under as a young man. Filmmaker Mario O'Hara chooses a more unique approach to the subject of the Philippines' greatest national hero, unlike other films marking the centennial of Philippine independence by the likes of Tikoy Aguiluz and Marilou Diaz-Abaya. O'Hara's more surrealistic approach seems to have been an attempt to explore Rizal's state of mind during his last hours. (In Tagalog)

The Sisters

1987 Seiko Films; 117 minutes/color

Director: Emmanuel H. Borlaza; Screenwriter: Mia Concio; Cinematographer: Romeo V. Vitug; Editor: Edgardo Vinarao; Filmscore: Nonoy Tan; Cast: Rita Avila, Stella "Pinky" Suarez, Joel Alano, Ricky Davao, Barbara Perez, Charito Solis, Jestoni Alarcon, Michael Locsin, Manjo del Mundo, Rusty Santos, Rina Reyes, Noella Arana, Ken-Ken Lacia, Maritess de los Reyes, Romeo Enriquez, Alma Lerma, Fren Gonzales

Rita Avila is stood up on her wedding day and left at the altar by Joel Alano, but as bad as it is for her, her mother (Charito Solis) takes it much worse: Solis goes on a drinking binge and quickly descends into complete insanity. One night while Avila's sister (Stella "Pinky" Suarez) is entertaining her beau (Jestoni Alarcon), Solis creeps up and shoots him, and then puts the gun to her own head and kills herself. This traumatic event lands Suarez in a mental hospital where she is treated by doctor Ricky Davao. While treating Suarez, Davao falls in love with Avila, but problems arise when Alano tries to worm his way back into Avila's life. Though initially hostile toward Alano, Avila eventually relents, realizing that she still loves him. Suarez gradually comes out of her withdrawn state and is well enough to go home to be cared for by Avila and aunt Barbara Perez, but her state of denial leads to dementia, and she believes that Alano is Alarcon. The devious Davao convinces Avila to play along, claiming that it may be therapeutic for Suarez to believe that Alarcon is still with her, and Avila in turn gets a very reluctant Alano to indulge Suarez in her fantasy. Despite the obvious heartache that it causes Avila, and the strong distaste of Alano, Davao is pleased, believing that he is now free to romance Avila. When Suarez seduces Alano, and winds up pregnant in the bargain, there's nothing for them to do except get married, which the self-sacrificing Avila endorses. Though it creates a house full of unhappy people, Davao couldn't be more pleased with the situation, berating Alano by telling Avila what a "jerk" he is for taking advantage of the deluded Suarez.

One day well into her pregnancy, Alano takes Suarez to a bluff where she and Alarcon used to steal away together, and being there brings back memories of her time with Alarcon, snapping Suarez back to reality. Meanwhile, drunken, pistol-wielding Davao shows up at the house and tries to force himself on Avila. While Avila struggles to defend herself, Alano and Suarez arrive, and when Alano and Davao mix it up, Davao's gun goes off, seriously wounding Suarez. Davao then drops the gun and the wounded Suarez retrieves it and shoots Davao. Alano and Avila rush Suarez to the hospital where she gives birth to her baby before dying. The film ends with Avila and Alano together again and raising the child.

Mia Concio's screenplay is fairly absorbing, and the direction by Emmanuel Borlaza occasionally (though too infrequently) slips the bounds of convention, as in the rather spirited moment when Solis kills Alarcon. (In Tagalog and English)

Smith and Wesson

1988 Viva Films; 111 minutes/color

Director: Tony Y. Reyes; Screenwriters: Tony Y. Reyes, Joey de Leon, Vic Sotto; Cinematographer: Rody Lacap; Editor: Ike Jarlego, Jr.; Filmscore: Jaime Fabregas; Cast: Joey de Leon, Vic Sotto, Beverly

Vergel, Panchito Alba, Paquito Diaz, Mon Alvir, Angela Luz, Jimmy Fabregas, Rene Requiestas, Vangie Labalan, Esther Chavez, Spanky Rigor, Minnie Aguilar, Bomber Moran, Tsing Tong Tsai, Ned Hourani, Tito Sotto, Val Sotto, Ruben Rustia, Karen Santo Domingo, ER Canton Salasar, Bert Cayanan, Polly Cadsawan, Adonis Montemayor, Nemie Gutierrez, Ernie Forte, Romy Romulo, Danny Rojo

In this spoof of *Miami Vice*, Vic Sotto and Joey de Leon are the title characters, two detectives working on the Muyami Vice squad, assigned to bring down a syndicate headed by Paquito Diaz. The drug situation has become particularly problematic on the local college campus, so the boys take to hanging out there, where they meet Beverly Vergel and Angela Luz, who they begin relationships with. In order to thwart Sotto and de Leon, Diaz resorts to kidnapping the girls, but the boys are able to rescue them. Diaz manages to escape, however, and Sotto and de Leon continue to pursue him and his gang. The film then shifts to a parody of *Bloodsport* (1987), when the boys get word that Diaz and company will be attending a martial arts tournament, and the only way for Sotto and de Leon to gain access to the secretive event is for them to enter the competition. Sotto enters and miraculously wins the competition by defeating Ned Hourani, after which they chase down and arrest Diaz.

The screenplay, by Sotto, de Leon and director Tony Reyes, has its share of amusing gags, and Sotto and de Leon do a good job of sharing the spotlight. There is also an amusing performance by Rene Requiestas as one of Diaz's men. Sotto and de Leon also co-produced. (In Tagalog and English)

Smokey Mountain: Mga Banyaga sa Sariling Lupa
(Smokey Mountain: Strangers in Our Own Country)

1989 Maharlika Films; 102 minutes/color
Director: Arturo San Agustin; Screenwriter: Eddie Joson; Cinematographer: Tony Pacheco; Editor: Edgardo Vinarao; Filmscore: Emil Losenado; Cast: Joel Torre, Jim Rosales, Star Querubin, Rey "PJ" Abellana, Rez Cortez, Leni Santos, Philip Gamboa, Romy Diaz, Digna Moreno, Atong Redillas, Tony Bernal, Robert Talby, Jose Romulo, Vic Varrion, Danny Riel, Joe Andrade, Randy Ronquillo, Danny Labra, Franco Mateo, Jeric Vasquez, Bebeng Amora, Joeseph Serra, Pons de Guzman, Michelle Dungca, Bert Vivar, Boy Mediavillo, Eddie Mapili, Tony Beso, Alex Nevado, Eddie Montalban

After being driven from their home by a new government land reform policy, Joel Torre travels to the city with his wife (Star Querubin) and cousin (Jim Rosales). They find the going tough in the city, and the only work Torre is able to get is making deliveries and collecting payments for a drug trafficking gang. Rosales finds out and tries to persuade Torre to drop that line of work, but when his efforts fail, Rosales goes to the police and leads them to the warehouse where the drug gang is operating. After the raid, gang member Romy Diaz and some of the other members not present at the time of the raid abduct Rosales, torture him mercilessly (burning his eyes with an acetylene torch), and kill him. After finding Rosales dead, Torre goes berserk, killing his fellow gang members (he drowns one in a public toilet), his bloody rampage culminating in his killing of Diaz, whom he ties to a column, battering his knees with a sledgehammer and eventually pummeling him to death. Torre then dumps Diaz's body at the front gate of his former drug lord boss along with a scrawled message of warning, but his vengeance strangely ends there, and the film concludes with Torre rallying residents of Smokey Mountain, a garbage dump populated by squatters, with the cry "Mabuhay Smokey Mountain!"—"Long Live Smokey Mountain!" It seems that Torre was determined not to be driven out of another dwelling, but in truth, the government eventually did close the dump.

The film follows the usual pattern of gang violence and retribution, but is somewhat more interesting than the norm, particularly during the film's early portion when the rural residents try to resist government dislocation, and when the trio of stars arrives in the city, walking the streets of a considerably different environment with a fair amount of trepidation. While the film's opening and closing tries to make some sort of commentary, it is unfortunately lost in the clichéd pattern taken by the rest of the narrative. (In Tagalog)

South Seas Massacre

1976 Montage Films; 85 minutes/color
Director: Pablo Santiago; Screenwriters: Tommy C. David, Leo Martinez; Cinematographer: Joe Batac; Editor: Segundo Ramos; Filmscore: Tito Arevalo; Cast: Troy Donahue, Junero Jennings, Vic Vargas, Eddie Garcia, Vic Silayan, Eva Reyes, Daria Ramirez, Lito Anzures, Ding Salvador, Dagul Se, Johnny Rio, Rene Roque, Tony Viray, Diego Viernes, Douglas Cruz, Fil Lizarondo, Benny May, Edwin Perry, Dante Rivas, Eddie Albert, Vic Varrion,

Johnny Long, Rudy Meyer, Ben Sanchez, Jojo Lapuz, Nestor Brillantes

While working in a coal mine, Troy Donahue uncovers the identity of a saboteur responsible for the deaths of some miners. When confronted, the saboteur draws a gun, and while struggling with Donahue, the gun goes off: the saboteur is killed and Donahue flees. Unfortunately for Donahue, the saboteur's brother is an Interpol agent who relentlessly pursues him. After capturing Donahue, the agent is in the process of transporting him by ship to the proper authorities when they are hijacked by a sadistic band of pirates led by Eddie Garcia. Handcuffed to one another, Donahue and the Interpol agent jump ship and wash ashore on an island where they are taken in by peaceable natives. It isn't long before Garcia and his cutthroats show up and take over the island, raping women and slaughtering men. The Interpol agent is enslaved with the natives while Donahue, in an apparent betrayal of his benevolent hosts, seems to join up with the pirates. But it is all part of Donahue's plan, and he eventually helps the natives stage an uprising in which Garcia and his men are killed. Donahue and his erstwhile pursuer then depart the island as friends.

This seems to be the only film by director Pablo Santiago to see release, however limited, in the West. Unfortunately, it is not one of his better works. Strangely, many of the more prominent Filipino actors receive no screen credit, including Garcia, and also Vic Silayan, who portrays the native chief. (In English)

Sparrow Unit: The Termination Squad

1987 Davian International; 85 minutes/color
Director: Ben Yalung; Screenwriter: Tony Capo; Cinematographer: Dominic Blacksmith; Editor: Stephen Soul; Cast: Ramon "Bong" Revilla Jr., Ronnie Ricketts, Debbie Miller, Sonny Parsons, Dick Israel, Allen Balman, Ernie Ejercito, King Gulliver, Bomber Moran, Vic Diaz, Mario Kasser, Romeo Rivera, Robert Tame, Ernest Forte, Fred Moro, Jimmy Reyes, Johnny Vicar, Jose Romulo, Ernie David, Rey Tomenes, Ernie Zarate, Lito Francisco

The unit of the title is a group of seven assassins from the communist NPA (National People's Army), who are sent to Manila to kill a number of top officials in the military and the Metro Police Department. After knocking off some of Manila's top lawmen (including Vic Diaz and Johnny Vicar), the commies (led by Ramon Revilla, Jr.) wind up running around the city murdering traffic cops. To stop them, the government sends in captain Sonny Parsons, who forms a group with the more masculine appellation of the Eagle Unit. The Eagles are able to whittle away at the Sparrows until only Revilla and Ronnie Ricketts are left, and the two of them perish in a final showdown with Parsons and the military. Actually, Revilla kills Ricketts himself when the badly wounded Ricketts tries to surrender after questioning whether or not they've been doing the right thing in running around killing innocent people. No kidding!

The narrative is a bit awkward in as much as the murderous communist terrorists fill the bulk of the running time, shown agonizing over their fallen comrades and comforting one another, while the deaths of the police officers are pretty summarily passed over. Ad to that the fact that middling action star Parsons gets the good guy role while more popular stars Revilla and Ricketts (who both give very good performances) play the murderous communist vermin, and it's enough to make you wonder who exactly the filmmakers intended for the audience to pull for. Violence is robust with many bloody gunshots to the head. (Dubbed into English)

Stomach In, Chest Out

1988 Cinesuerte; 108 minutes/color
Director: Junn P. Cabreira; Screenwriters: Junn P. Cabreira, Tony Calvento; Cinematographer: Rudy Dino; Editor: Segundo Ramos; Filmscore: Demet Velasquez; Cast: Eddie Garcia, Joey Marquez, Lara Melissa de Leon, Mercy Dizon, Debraliz Valasote, Daphie Garcia, Beth Yalung, Dexter Doria, Monica Herrera, Janice Jurado, Arsenio Bautista, Rudy Meyer, Rochelle Alfaro, Emil Cabanlig

In this mildly amusing comedy, a group of inept female military recruits are assigned training under Major Eddie Garcia and Sergeant Joey Marquez, both of whom spend time ogling the girls, including spying on them in the shower. But when the married Garcia attempts to romance some of the girls, it leads to a string of humiliating experiences, and Garcia begins to suspect that Marquez is constantly setting him up. Garcia proposes to get even by threatening to send Marquez and the girls to Mindanao, a hotbed of rebel activity. To thwart this plan, Marquez and the girls make an audiotape of Garcia in a compromising situation, which they use to blackmail him. The two sides agree to resolve things with a war game: if Marquez and the girls win, they do not go to Mindanao; if Garcia wins, he gets the tape. During the game, Garcia is captured and held hostage by anti-government rebels, and Marquez and the girls wind up having to rescue him.

The film is entertaining enough to get by (if only just), but Marquez looks like a hopeless amateur next to Garcia, and his constant whimpering is the film's major detraction. (In Tagalog with some English)

Stop Abortion

1986 Gintong Ani Productions; 117 minutes/color

Director/screenwriter: Leonardo Q. Belen; Cinematographer: Vic Anao; Editor: Oscar Dugtong; Filmscore: Gabby Castellano; Cast: Mishelle Zobel, Delia Razon, Greggy Liwag, Anthony East, Didith Romero, Lampel Cojuangco, Joe Andrade, Ben Morro, Tony Martinez, Boy Sanggol, Alma Miller, Cora Santiago, Marieta dela Cruz, Hanna Reyes, Maria Shiela Larracochea, Mercedes Guitila, Beth Gonzales, Cesar Lilleza, Salvador Suerte

In this odd, though somehow fascinating film, Anthony East portrays a gynecologist who also teaches courses at the local university, where he is involved in an affair with one of his students. Reporter Greggy Liwag is writing a piece on abortion (which is illegal in the Philippines) and wants to interview East on the subject. In an unlikely coincidence, the night before interviewing East, Liwag finds the doctor's daughter (Mishelle Zobel) passed out drunk on the side of the road. He drives her home and returns to see her the following day, and soon after begins a romance with her. But before the relationship is consummated, Zobel discovers that she is pregnant, the result of her night of drunkenness when she passed out and was taken advantage of. East's young mistress is also pregnant, and so East performs an abortion on her, as he will occasionally do for some of his patients. At the same time, hearing of his daughter's pregnancy, he refuses to perform an abortion on her, citing the illegality of it. Ultimately, East's mistress dies as a result of complications from her abortion, but not before telling Liwag the truth. Zobel resorts to performing an abortion on herself and winds up in the hospital. Liwag turns East in to the authorities, which naturally complicates things between he and Zobel, and when he is eventually able to find her again, she has become a nun and is working in an orphanage.

It's difficult to know exactly what to make of this film. Early on, one suspects it of being a softcore sex film masquerading as an anti-abortion message piece. During the first third of the narrative there is a good deal of sex and nudity (even full frontal), as in the scene where Zobel and her two girlfriends are raped, and also in the depiction of East's tryst with his student/lover, and there are even vaginal close-ups when East performs an abortion on a wealthy woman (for an exorbitant fee), even showing close-ups of East inserting his fingers into the woman's vagina. All of this causes one to wonder what director/screenwriter Leonardo Belen is really up to, but eventually the film lives up to its title by settling in to show the hypocrisy of the abortionist, who is perfectly willing to perform abortions for wealthy women or to cover up his own infidelity, but does not feel compelled to risk his own daughter's physical or mental health. East also takes the curious position that abortion is a moral responsibility in cases where the child is unwanted, thereby sparing the child from living an unhappy life, a view commonly expressed by pro-abortionists, who seem to have no problem prejudging the quality of the lives of others, even as they are just beginning. But East obfuscates this belief by simultaneously maintaining that life begins *outside* the womb when the first words of love are spoken between a man and a woman. Belen seems to present the pro-abortion position as convoluted and, finally, immoral. The film's moral posturing is at its most obvious when Belen seeks to make parents responsible for even the actions of their young adult children. Zobel blames her unwanted pregnancy on the fact that her parents are too busy to spend time with her, thinking no more of her than to leave her money in the mornings as they rush off to their important jobs. It is a view supported by every character in the film save East. Zobel also suffers a series of nightmares in which she is alone in a field, desperately calling out to her parents in time of crisis, but is unable to find them. Even less subtle is the dream in which she hears the cries of her aborted baby only to find them coming from a mound of earth. East's dying mistress is also shown envisioning herself being sacrificed by a tribe of primitive pagans.

But, ultimately, all of Belen's moralizing is undone by the fact that he is attempting to make a moralistic point by way of the morally dubious method of pandering to the softcore sex market, rendering the film an exercise in hypocrisy. (In English)

Stupid Cupid

1987 Regal Films; 134 minutes/color

Director: Maryo J. de los Reyes; Screenwriters:

Armando Loa, Jake Tordesillas, Jose Javier Reyes; Cinematographer: Ely Cruz; Editor: George Jarlego; Filmscore: Jaime Fabregas; Cast: Snooky Serna, Richard Gomez, Nadia Montenegro, Alicia Alonzo, Rosemarie Gil, Ruby Regala, Maricel Soriano, William Martinez, Lani Mercado, Pops Fernandez, Martin Nievera, Manilyn Reynes, Janno Gibbs, Caridad Sanchez, Bella Flores, Dencio Padilla, Lito Pimentel, Flora Gasser, Lou Veloso, Balot, Matimtiman Cruz, Cloyd Robinson, Jograd de la Torre, Evelyn Vargas

This is a trilogy of romance stories, all directed by Maryo de los Reyes. The opening story stars the popular screen romance team of Snooky Serna and Richard Gomez. One day while riding horses with his girlfriend, Gomez spots Serna and is completely smitten, as is she. Later, Gomez's girlfriend falls from her horse and injures her leg, and while she is laid up recuperating, Gomez seizes the opportunity to steal away and meet Serna down at a picturesque babbling brook. But after recovering, Gomez's girlfriend rides down to the brook and catches the two lovers together, and Gomez returns home to find his mother (Rosemarie Gil) furious over his indiscretion, and Gil pays Serna's mother (Alicia Alonzo) a visit. The two mothers have it out, and both wind up forbidding their children from seeing one another. Serna receives a letter from Gomez informing her that he is going through with his marriage to his girlfriend, and Serna then falls into despair, wasting away and becoming deathly ill; but on his wedding day, Gomez receives word from his intended that she cannot go through with the wedding since she knows that Gomez is not truly in love with her, but with Serna. Gomez excitedly rushes to Serna's house, but finds that she is missing. As everyone is frantically searching for her, Gomez rushes to the scene of their previous rendezvous and finds Serna there, gravely ill. The two lovers embrace, and the story then concludes with them exchanging wedding vows in front of the water fall in the glen where they first fell in love. Pure soap.

The second story is a comedy that finds William Martinez taking his whiney, bitchy bride (Maricel Soriano) to a quaint little country inn, which turns out to be haunted. While the initial haunting they experience is perpetrated by a couple determined to drive off the inn's business, it soon becomes apparent that the inn is truly haunted by the ghost of an ill-fated bride and a host of zombies. The segment is at its most impressive toward the end when de los Reyes momentarily puts the lame humor aside, and Martinez and Soriano are pursued by the once beautiful specter, which now appears as a grotesque, rotting corpse. It makes one long for a serious Filipino rendering of the old dark house motif.

The concluding story is a musical comedy that finds brothers Janno Gibbs and Martin Nievera returning to the Philippines from America. Gibbs falls in love with Manilyn Reynes, a relationship discouraged by both Nievera and Reynes' sister (Pops Fernandez). Gibbs and Reynes decide to run away together, prompting Nievera and Fernandez to go off searching for them. During their search for their siblings, the hostility between Nievera and Fernandez turns to feelings of love, and the story concludes with a double wedding topped with a musical number. It's trite but occasionally amusing. (In Tagalog and English)

Sudden Death

1975 Topar Films/Caruth C. Byrd Productions; 82 minutes/color

Director: Eddie Romero; Screenwriter: Oscar Williams; Cinematographer: Justo Paulino; Editor: Edward Mann; Filmscore: Johnny Pate; Cast: Robert Conrad, Don Stroud, Felton Perry, John Ashley, Thayer David, Aline Samson, Larry Manetti, Caruth C. Byrd, Chuck Courtney, Ken Metcalfe, Jenny Green, Jess Barker, Nancy Conrad, Angelo Ventura, Eddie Garcia, Conrad Poe, Tony Gosalvez, Rocco Montalban, Robert Rivera, Angie Ferro, Joanna Ignatius, Vic Diaz

In this somewhat convoluted action yarn, sugar company president Ken Metcalfe survives an assassination attempt that claims the lives of his wife and children. The authorities believe it to be an act perpetrated by a group of revolutionaries upset about the recent merger of the sugar company with an American company (you know, the rape of the country and all that). Since U.S. government man John Ashley doesn't seem to have any luck finding out who is responsible, Metcalfe turns to outside help: he approaches retired covert operations man Robert Conrad, but Conrad declines to get involved, since he is rather enjoying his leisurely life in his beach house with his girlfriend and his daughter (real life daughter Nancy Conrad). But his good buddy Angelo Ventura, who also seems to live in the house, senses an assignment in the offing and so calls Felton Perry in Los Angeles, another old buddy from Conrad's covert operations days. Perry, excited by the possibility of another dangerous assignment, leaves his karate schools behind and flies to the Philippines. Upon arriving,

Perry finds Conrad still reluctant to get involved in Metcalfe's troubles, but when Metcalfe is killed, Conrad changes his mind. He sends his daughter and girlfriend into hiding with Ventura, and then he and Perry set out to get to the bottom of things. When shady government man Ashley (probably C.I.A.) finds Conrad and Perry nosing around, he sends for renowned hit man Don Stroud to handle the situation. Eventually, Conrad and Perry wind up killing everyone from corrupt sugar company executives to C.I.A. man Ashley, and ultimately Stroud as well. But the film has a surprise ending in store, and it is one of director Eddie Romero's most inspired moments as a filmmaker.

The following year, both Romero and Ashley would serve as associate producers on Francis Ford Coppola's *Apocalypse Now*, which, though not released until 1979, began shooting in the Philippines in 1976, but *Sudden Death* was the swan song of the Romero/Ashley partnership. Ashley returned to America to become a successful television producer, including producing a number of television films starring Conrad, and Romero returned to making more serious films for the domestic market, like *Ganito Kami Noon, Paano Kayo Ngayon?*, which returned him to the forefront of Philippine directors in 1976. (In English)

Suicide Force

1984 Atlas International/Emperor Films International; 77 minutes/color

Director: S.C. Ramos; Cinematographer: Danny Bustos; Editor: S.C. Ramos; Filmscore: Derek (Demet Velasquez); Cast: Johnny Wilson, George Pallance, Bill James, Vic Vargas, George Regan (George Estregan), Ray Malonzo, Archer Vergel, Rex Lapid, Efraim (Efren) Reyes Jr., Ramon Zamora, Suzy Garret, Jimmy Santos, Freddi Yance, Ray Tomenes, Danny Riel, Tony Tacorda, Buddy Lanusa, Elly Perez, Nestor Brillantes, Danny Amador, Matt Fullosa, George Tormida, Paquito Diaz, Max Alvarado, Baldo Marro, Boy Santa Maria

When the U.S. ambassador to the Philippines is abducted by a rebel army led by Paquito Diaz, a rescue team is sent consisting of nine men, led by Vic Vargas, and including womanizing corporal George Estregan, Efren Reyes, Jr. and Baldo Marro. The rescue squad manages to find the rebel camp, and in a protracted chase and battle, they rescue the ambassador, though they lose many of their own squad in the process. Vargas returns only to find that the man he has rescued is not the ambassador at all, but rather the ambassador's personal secretary. The real ambassador is already safely back in America, and his secretary merely continued to pose as the ambassador in order to prevent his abductors from killing him. After learning this, and thinking back on all of his fallen comrades, Vargas loses his composure, and the film ends on a freeze-frame as he attacks the secretary and has to be restrained. Gee, some people's lives are obviously more important than others.

While Estregan is billed as "George Regan," and Efren Reyes, Jr., receives billing under the first name "Efraim," other cast members are unbilled altogether, including Diaz, Marro and Max Alvarado, who plays the leader of a band of rebels encountered by the rescue mission along the way. One of the film's good points is a curious score credited to Derek Velasquez. Given the other misnamings in the credits, it seems likely that this was actually "Demet Velasquez." (Dubbed into English)

Sumigaw Ka Hanggang Gusto Mo (Scream as Much as You Like)

1998 Viva Films/Kaizz Ventures; 99 minutes/color

Director: Enrico S. Quizon (Eric Quizon); Screenwriter: Ian Victoriano; Cinematographer: Romeo Vitug; Cast: Eric Quizon, Carmina Villaroel, Bobby Andrews, Onemig Bondoc, Gladys Reyes, Red Sternberg, Rufa Mae Quinto, Ciara Sotto, Ryan Eigenmann, Bernadette Allyson, Assunta de Rossi, Berwin Meily, JP Plata, Genesis, Quinto Mirasol, Mel Kimura, Errol Dionisio, Danny Ramos, Ida Yanesa, Sunshine Dizon

This is a throwback to the slasher films of the 1980s, which opens with six college students hiking in the woods and being killed by a mysterious figure in a long dark raincoat. One young man survives the attack and describes the assailant who came at them with garden shears. Not long afterward, three young co-eds disappear in turns from the local university, and it comes as no surprise that mild mannered biology professor Eric Quizon turns out to be behind it all. The three missing girls are tied up and being held prisoner by Quizon in the basement of his isolated, rundown two-story house. After tearfully recounting his troubled childhood to the girls, including telling them how he killed his abusive mother by setting her on fire, Quizon turns the girls loose and chases them around the house. About that time, everyone seems to put it all together, and Quizon's house is beset by students, the detective investigating the case, and guidance counselor Carmina Villaroel. Villaroel does the unexpected and shoots the detective, and she then confronts Quizon, who it turns out is her twin brother. When they were children, Quizon had pushed Villaroel from a bridge into a river, and somehow Villaroel wound up in a psychiatric ward. Still mentally unbalanced, Villaroel shoots Quizon as student Bobby Andrews enters the room, and with no one to witness the confrontation between Villaroel and Quizon, or Villaroel's shooting of the detective, she is proclaimed a heroine by the press for having ended Quizon's reign of terror.

The revelation of Quizon as being the killer is true to form within the genre, and the twist of having Villaroel reveal herself as Quizon's twin is only slightly better. In fact, the film so faithfully follows the slasher genre formula that if it weren't for the cast of new, young Filipino actors, one could easily be convinced that the film was shot in the mid-1980s. Even still, it is reasonably entertaining for what it is, though also true to its genre, the ending is needlessly drawn out. The main things here worth commenting on are the superb cinematography by Romeo Vitug, and Eric Quizon's impressive directorial job, nicely atmospheric at times. (In Tagalog with some English)

Super Inday and the Golden Bibe (Super Girl and the Golden Goose)

1988 Regal Films; 106 minutes/color
Director: Luciano B. Carlos; Screenwriter: Jose Javier Reyes; Cinematographer: Gener Buenaseda; Editor: Efren Jarlego; Filmscore: Jaime Fabregas; Cast: Maricel Soriano, Eric Quizon, Manilyn Reynes, Janno Gibbs, Aiza Seguerra, Melanie Marquez, Nova Villa, Jimmy Santos, Mel Martinez, Ramil Rodriguez, Evelyn Vargas, Michael Roberts, Ray Alvarez, Flora Gasser, Palito, Jack Fajardo, Bomber Moran, Big Boy Gomez, Ernie David

In this comedic superheroine fantasy, little Aiza Seguerra is booted out of what seems to be Heaven after eating an apple from a tree (hmmm, that sounds familiar). She is sent down to earth in the form of a goose and is taken in as a pet by young washerwoman Maricel Soriano. When the local villagers are terrorized by an army of netherworld monsters led by the weird Melanie Marquez, Soriano's goose becomes her mentor. The talking goose lays an egg and instructs Soriano to drink its contents; when she does, Soriano is magically transformed into Super Inday, and is gifted with various magical abilities, including flight, and she endears herself to the locals by saving them from a giant spider. In search of a career-boosting scoop, reporter Eric Quizon arrives, and Soriano is immediately smitten; but Quizon only has eyes for Super Inday. In the end, the town's safety all comes down to a duel between Soriano and Marquez, which Soriano wins with the help of goose Seguerra. There is even a victory parade for Soriano, and Seguerra (once more in human form) flies back to Heaven on the back of a giant dove. The special effects are exceptionally cheesy, but since the entire premise is likewise, it really can't be counted too heavily against the film. The most interesting moment comes when Soriano faces-off against lizard man Palito, who continually confounds her by changing his image to that of people she loves.

Quizon's role is pretty embarrassing since it can only be described as that of the traditional damsel in distress. Both heroine and villainess fight over Quizon, and when he finds himself in Marquez's clutches, Quizon falls into a dead faint. He then awakens to find himself being carried off by her, not unlike Julie Adams by the *Creature from the Black Lagoon*, and he again screams like a girl and passes out cold. Melanie Marquez can carry me off anytime. (In Tagalog)

Ang Syota Kong Balikbayan (My Balikbayan Girlfriend)

1995 FPJ Productions; 118 minutes/color
Directors: Pablo Santiago, Tony Cruz; Screenwriters: Pablo S. Gomez, Manny Buising, Jaime Fabregas; Cast: Fernando Poe Jr., Anjanette Abayari, Maritoni Fernandez, Paquito Diaz, Max Alvarado, Dencio Padilla, Boy Alano, Jaime Fabregas, Romy Diaz, Rudy Meyer, Eddie Arenas, Bomber Moran, Chiquito, Randy Santiago, Janno Gibbs, German Moreno, Odette Khan, Doreen Bernal, Dindo Arroyo, Naty Santiago, Gamaliel Viray, Dexter Doria, Dedes Whitaker, Angie del Carmen, Lily Rose, Gem Castillo, Edna de Leon, Dawlyn Petiete, Jennifer Mindanao, Rene Hawkins, Nonoy de Guzman, Jimmy Reyes

Anjanette Abayari returns to the Philippines from America to visit her uncle (Jaime Fabregas), and after rear ending Fernando Poe, Jr.'s jeepney, she soon falls in love with him. Meanwhile, crooks Paquito Diaz and Max Alvarado, while trying to elude the police, hide a cache of stolen diamonds in Poe's jeepney, and when Poe drives off, they find it very hard to retrieve them. Knowing that Poe and Abayari have become an item, Diaz and Alvarado abduct Abayari in order to lure Poe into an exchange. They take Abayari to an old mansion for safekeeping, unaware that the house is haunted, and they spend the night being terrorized by a vampire, a werewolf and a primitive ape man. Poe shows up to rescue Abayari, which he does after slugging it out with the werewolf. Diaz and Alvarado work for crime boss Romy Diaz, and Poe has a climactic shootout with their gang (which seems like little more than a concession to Poe's action genre fans), and we last see Paquito Diaz and Max Alvarado in a jail cell where they are terrorized by one of the vampires from the haunted house.

With the way in which it jumps around through its various storylines, the film is more than a little disjointed; but, since this is down to the writing, it's not likely that the change of directors can be held accountable. This was director Pablo Santiago's last picture—he apparently died during filming, and director Tony Cruz finished the picture. Aside from German Moreno's brief appearance, there are a number of other star cameos, including a musical number featuring Randy Santiago and Janno Gibbs, who help Poe serenade Abayari. Overall, this is a very sub-par Poe film. A balikbayan is a Filipino living abroad. (In Tagalog and English)

Tabi Tabi Po!
(Look Behind You!)

2000 FLT Films International; 117 minutes/color

Directors: Jose N. Carreon, Tata Esteban, Joven M. Tan; Screenwriters: Jose N. Carreon, Mike V. Loanzon, Joven M. Tan; Cast: Wowie de Guzman, Bernadette Allyson, Izza Ignacio, Berting Labra, Antonette Taus, Onemig Bondoc, Cita Astals, Joanne Quintas, Gladys Reyes, Angelica Pangilinan, Elizabeth Oropesa, Piel Morena, Raymond Bagatsing, Melissa Mendez, Cris Daluz, Bella Flores, Mely Tagasa, Richard "Ebong" Joson, Alvin Anson, Josette Prospero, Boy Roque, Alex Cunanan, Nonong de Andres, Boy Gomez, Stefano Mori, Michael Roy Jornales, Jefferson Long

Picking up the tradition of the horror anthology, which was carried along for years by Regal Films with their *Shake Rattle & Roll* series, as well as films like *Regal Shocker* (1991), this feature offers three stories from three different directors. Director/screenwriter Jose Carreon contributes *Vampira 2000*, the opening segment, wherein reporter Wowie de Guzman is covering a series of murders when he discovers that the killer is sexy vampire Bernadette Allyson; but rather than turn her in, de Guzman falls in love with her. Allyson, who chooses to live a normal life among humans (as normal as possible anyway) is hunted as a traitor by three vampire assassins, whom she manages to defeat by sprinkling them with holy water given her by Berting Labra. The segment is very stylish in its presentation, but is a textbook example of style over substance.

The second story, *Engkantada* (Enchanted), is a fairly lighthearted tale directed by Tata Esteban, and concerns the efforts of some woodland fairies to stop a greedy developer from ravaging their habitat. Gee, there wouldn't be a message in this, would there? Message or no, the story is vacuous.

The concluding segment, *Demonyita* (Little Devil), is the most atmospheric tale in the trilogy. Written and directed by Joven Tan, the story concerns two demonic sisters, spawned as a result of their mother's dabbling in black magic. One sister is happily evil, while the other longs to live a normal human existence, putting the sisters at odds with one another. In time the sibling rivalry runs amok, but the good sister wins in the end. (In Tagalog)

Tadtarin ng Bala si Madelo
(Riddle Madelo with Bullets)

1988 Regal Films; 105 minutes/color

Director: Arturo San Agustin; Screenwriter: Joe R. Ranay; Cinematographer: Vic Anao; Editor: Boy Vinarao; Filmscore: Emil Losenada; Cast: Lito Lapid, Monica Herrera, Melissa Mendez, Amanda Amores, Charlie Davao, Romy Diaz, Jose Romulo, Alex de Leon, Eddie Tuazon, Rene Hawkins, Robert Miller, Nonoy de Guzman, Willie Dado, Pons de Guzman, Philip Gamboa, Mario Escudero, Tony Bernal, Robert Talabis, Danny Riel, Vic Varrion, Danny Labra

Army sergeant Lito Lapid leaves his wife and young daughter behind to head into the hills and do battle with Romy Diaz's formidable rebel force. After a number of battles, Lapid emerges a highly decorated hero and sets his sights on the drug empire of Charlie Davao, which he also manages to bring down. Despite the impressive cast, the film makes too little use of most of its name performers. Danny Riel is killed off in the first 20 minutes, and Davao, typecast again as a crime boss, doesn't show up until the final third. There is also a thoroughly routine screenplay to contend with, but the action sequences are well done and manage to make things salvageable. With all of the shooting, brawling and explosions, Lapid's fans were likely satisfied. (In Tagalog)

Tag-Araw, Tag-Ulan (Stormy Summer)

1992 Viva Films; 113 minutes/color
Director: Celso Ad. Castillo; Screenwriters: Amado La Cuesta, Ronald Garballo; Cinematographer: Loreto Isleta; Editor: Edgardo Vinarao; Filmscore: Jaime Fabregas; Cast: Dina Bonnevie, Gary Estrada, Jenny Roa, Suzanne Gonzales, Chuckie Dreyfuss, Jigo Garcia, Mutya Crisostomo, Mark Gil, Michelle Ann Lopez, Jennifer Ann Durr, Roy de Guzman, Vincent Berba, Rusty Ramirez, Lennon Serrano, Alma Lerma, Joseph Serra

After a four-year hiatus, director Celso Ad. Castillo returned to work with this embarrassingly trite melodrama wherein Dina Bonnevie catches her fiancé (Mark Gil) in bed with another woman, and seeks to recover from the shock by running off to spend the summer with friends at a beach resort. While there, she befriends 18-year-old virgin Gary Estrada, who has been trying to romance Jenny Roa, without success. Roa does have feelings for Estrada, but is simply not prepared to go all the way yet. Given the amount of time that Estrada has been spending with Bonnevie, Roa begins to suspect that something is going on, and she throws quite a tantrum one evening. It seems to spoil the summer for everyone, and Estrada and his friends leave. Roa leaves soon after, and before too long Bonnevie is the last one left at the resort. But Estrada returns, and being disappointed at not having lost his virginity, begins simpering and eventually drops to Bonnevie's feet weeping and wailing and pleading for some affection. It's revoltingly embarrassing, but hey, it works—Bonnevie obliges, and the two of them have a passionate night on the beach. The next day, Estrada thanks God that Bonnevie was his first lay (hmmmm), to which Bonnevie replies, "Don't mention it," and adds, "If it's any help, I also like you a lot." Bonnevie tells Estrada that he is now a man, and the two part company. Keep your hanky handy.

Given Castillo's reputation, this is a surprisingly frivolous work, and he followed it with the even more disappointing *Kapag Iginuhit ang Hatol ng Puso* (1993), again starring Bonnevie. In both cases, Castillo seems to have merely been hired as director and was not involved with the conceptual side of these films, and so cannot really be held accountable for the lackluster scenarios. Afterward, the director would again become more involved in his projects, and his work would once more take on a certain relevance. But this? This is crap. (In Tagalog and English)

Tagos ng Dugo (Bloodstain)

1987 V.H. Films; 117 minutes/color
Director: Maryo J. de los Reyes; Screenwriter: Jake Tordesillas; Cinematographer: Ely Cruz; Editor: Jess Navarro; Filmscore: Jaime Fabregas; Cast: Vilma Santos, Richard Gomez, Michael de Mesa, Miguel Rodriguez, Lito Pimentel, Mark Joseph, Joey Hipolito, Joey Marquez, Francis Arnaiz, Tony Santos Sr., Caridad Sanchez, Lucita Soriano, Bing Davao, Dante Castro, Anna Feliciano, Alicia Alonzo, Ross Rival, Mia Gutierrez, Aida Carmona, Kristel Romero, Vic Belaro, Rene Balan, Emil de Guzman, Emma Mendoza, Archie Adamos, Nemie Gutierrez, Joe Lapid, Pong Mercado, Alex Toledo, Gil Zaldaga

In this fascinatingly weird psychodrama, Vilma Santos portrays a young woman with an unfortunate past, having been raped as a child by the man who also killed her parents. She experienced further sexual abuse while growing up in an orphanage where she killed an orderly who had been renting out some of the girls by night. As an adult, she begins a rapid descent into madness. Haunted at night by the grotesque visage of the murdered orderly, and unduly traumatized by her menstruation, Santos begins dressing as a common hooker, picking up men by night and murdering them with a switchblade. Along the way, she falls in love with a young police officer whom she mistakenly believes to be her brother. She attempts to consummate her incestuous love for her brother through the police officer, but when he rejects her she stabs him too. Several policemen kick in the door and find their fellow officer bleeding to death and Santos raving like a lunatic. The film ends on a lingering shot of Santos, huddled in a corner, spattered in blood and babbling insanely.

Working with enough perverse motifs for a dozen films, director Maryo J. de los Reyes handles things fairly tactfully without sacrificing any of the emotional punch within the respective story elements. While opting to avoid gratuitous displays, de los Reyes offers a stylized approach that is enhanced by a better than average score by Jaime Fabregas. In most respects—style, content, execution—this is a cut above the norm. (In Tagalog)

Tahan Na ... Heto na ang Ligaya! (Stop Crying ... Here Is Happiness!)

1998 Taurus Films; 84 minutes/color

Director/screenwriter: Rolly Bernardo; Cast: Rita Magdalena, Anthony Cortez, Ria Alonso, Von Serra, Ariel Reyes, Alyssa Alvarez, Erwin Montes, Jeck Chavez, Jimmy Concepcion, Susan Reyes, Susing Yazon, Emil Cristobal, Ariel Henson, Judd Cauntay, Joanna

Rita Magdalena portrays a young woman who works as a domestic servant for tyrannical Ariel Reyes. A large part of her day consists of fending off advances—and rather strong ones at that—from Reyes' son (Anthony Cortez). With her living quarters on the grounds, Magdalena is always at risk, and sure enough, Cortez rapes her one night. When Magdalena winds up pregnant, Reyes angrily dismisses her and runs her off the property. After the child is born, however, Reyes becomes excited by the idea of having a grandchild, and she convinces Cortez to snatch the child and bring it home to mother to raise as her own. Though she tries, Magdalena is unable to retrieve her baby afterward, but in the days that follow Cortez is filled with remorse, and after he and mother have it out, Reyes too has a dramatic change of heart and happily returns the baby to Magdalena. The film then ends rather oddly with Magdalena and Cortez marrying.

Given the extremely nasty nature of Reyes' character, her sudden change of heart is so unlikely as to make the ending a joke. It is also very improbable that Magdalena would marry Cortez, who first raped her, then swiped her baby! Director/screenwriter Rolly Bernardo had likewise had Magdalena marrying her rapist in the film *Obsesyon* (also in 1998). One cannot help but wonder if this pattern on the part of Bernardo represents a dismissive attitude toward rape, or otherwise considers women as being irresistibly drawn to men who have staked them out as personal property via forced sex. Bernardo (who worked for years as a production designer) seems to have found a place at Taurus Films directing and writing tawdry melodramas, though he doesn't show any particular skill in either endeavor. (In Tagalog)

Takot Ako sa Darling Ko!
(I'm Afraid, My Darling!)

1997 Neo Films; 100 minutes/color
Director: Leo Valdez; Screenwriters: Ely Matawaran, Jose Baktolome; Cinematographer: Oscar Querijero; Filmscore: Mon del Rosario; Cast: Joey de Leon, Jenny Syquia, Dennis Padilla, Ericka Fife, Richard Merck, April Boy Regino, Pocholo Montes, Gloria Diaz, Nonong de Andres, Beverly Salviejo, Philip Supnet, Ena Garcia, Jay Garcia, Bea Patricia Bueno, Shintaro Valdes, Sylvia Rigon, Chris Daluz, Lucy Quinto, Pong Pong, Boy Gomez, Jojo de Leon

In this screwball comedy, schoolteacher Joey de Leon falls in love with Jenny Syquia and proposes marriage, unaware that he is marrying into a family of vampires. Meanwhile, a developer seeks to acquire the vampire family's estate, intending to tear it down to put up a condominium. Unable to drive the family out, the developer abducts local children, knowing that the citizens in town will blame the vampire family and destroy them, but de Leon discovers the truth and exposes the scheme. The film has fun playing with horror genre conventions, leaving out few of the old dark house staples (creepy servants, and Gloria Romero as a family matriarch with a passion for eerie organ music). It's very silly, but also quite fun. (In Tagalog with some English)

Ang Tangi Kong Pagibig
(My Only Love)

1954 Sampaguita Pictures; 143 minutes/black & white
Director: Mar S. Torres; Screenwriter: Conrado Conde; Cinematographer: Cesar Silos; Filmscore: Constancio C. de Guzman; Cast: Carmen Rosales, Rogelio dela Rosa, Luis Gonzales, Rosa Mia, Horacio Morelos, Herminia Carranza, Marcela Garcia, Apolonio Aguilar, Leleng Isla, Elena Adorable, Nenita Jana

Though occasionally harkening to the Hollywood musicals of the 1930s and '40s, Filipino musicals of the Golden Era seem to have had more in common with opera, the emphasis being on heartbreak and tragedy. Such is the case here, as popular co-stars of the day Carmen Rosales and Rogelio dela Rosa are teamed. Rosales plays a popular but unhappy nightclub singer who tries to leave her job, but is prevented from doing so by the tyrannical club owner, who keeps her there by force since business has never been better. Rosales resorts to knocking her employer over the head in order to flee to the rural village where her family lives. Once there, she meets dela Rosa after being chased by his dog, which bites her on the leg. Rosales and dela Rosa fall in love and plan to marry, but with his business failing since her departure, the nightclub owner shows up and tries to drag Rosales back to the city on her wedding day. Dela Rosa gives the villainous club owner a sound beating in a slugfest that looks like it came right out of a 1940s Hollywood serial, and one would expect all to be resolved.

Truth is, though certainly nothing spectacular, the film would have been just fine had it ended there, but at this point, the unnecessarily traumatized Rosales runs off and disappears. Eventually learning that Rosales has become a nun (!) and gone to the city, dela Rosa and his pal Luis Gonzales set off to find her. They have no luck though, and after a night of heavy drinking they get into a serious car accident. While Gonzales mends quickly, dela Rosa's injuries are more severe, requiring surgery and a lengthy hospital stay. During his recovery dela Rosa is tended by Rosales, who has learned of his accident and come to his aid, but dela Rosa is frustrated by his inability to convince her to forsake her vows as a nun and return to him. Finally, after a number of teary-eyed scenes, Rosales runs back to dela Rosa, and all ends happily.

The film's execution is fine, for its era, but what is often exasperating about Filipino films is how even the most ordinary of stories are made to drag on interminably, sometimes leaving the viewer feeling that there is no end in sight. Sadly, that is the case here. (In Tagalog with occasional English)

Tanikalang Apoy
(Chain of Fire)

1959 Sampaguita Pictures; 120 minutes/black & white

Director: Jose de Villa; Screenwriter: Tommy C. David; Cinematographers: Higino J. Fallorina, Amaury Agra; Filmscore: Danny Holmsen; Cast: Lolita Rodriguez, Paraluman, Rita Gomez, Eddie Arenas, Eddie Garcia, Carlos Salazar, Etang Discher, Van de Leon, Bella Flores, Matimtiman Cruz, Pablo Raymundo, Jaime Javier, Santiago Duenas, Sabas San Juan, Wilfrido Dado, Jimmy Evangelista, Art Morado, Rafael Jimenez

Adapted from a komiks serial by Pablo Gomez, this vintage melodrama finds Eddie Arenas marrying Lolita Rodriguez and taking her to live in his family's ancestral mansion; but Rodriguez quickly finds that she has married into a family of borderline lunatics. After receiving a frosty reception from Arenas' domineering mother (Etang Discher), aloof sisters (Paraluman and Rita Gomez), and weasely brother (Eddie Garcia), Rodriguez catches Gomez going through her things and trying to steal some lipstick, and when the rest of the family is attracted by the confrontation, Discher forces Gomez to lie facedown on the floor and then proceeds to give her a brutal lashing with a whip. Even more disturbing than that, Rodriguez soon finds out that Discher has murdered Paraluman's lover. As for Gomez, she turns out to be a drug addict, and when she is unable to pay her pusher, she sneaks him into the house one night and points him the way to the family safe. Rodriguez discovers the man trying to get into the safe and a struggle ensues, with the entire household showing up in time to see Rodriguez in a dark room with a man leaping through the window. Accused of sneaking the man in for an illicit liaison (something that, incredibly, even Arenas believes), Rodriguez finds herself chained in the basement as punishment. Later, Garcia tries to force himself on Rodriguez, and when her screams bring the rest of the family rushing into the room, Garcia claims that Rodriguez had tried to seduce him. Remarkably, although it was Rodriguez's screams that had brought everyone there, the jug-headed Arenas again chooses to believe the worst about his wife. Rodriguez gives everyone a piece of her mind—finally!!—before packing up and leaving, and eventually Arenas finds the guts to stand up to his insane mother, and he too leaves in a pique. The film climaxes with the deranged Paraluman locking the sleeping Discher, Gomez and Garcia in their respective rooms and then setting the house ablaze, after which the film ends hastily with a tearful reunion between Rodriguez and Arenas. Though much of the plot is ridiculously contrived, it manages to be entertaining as an absurd soap opera. Garcia won the FAMAS Best Supporting Actor award for his performance. (In Tagalog)

Tanzan the Mighty

1962 Sampaguita Pictures; 88 minutes/black & white

Director: Carlos Vander Tolosa; Screenwriter: Ben Feleo; Filmscore: Pastor de Jesus; Cast: Dolphy, Eddie Gutierrez, Jean Lopez, Josephine Estrada, Panchito (Alba), Venchito Galvez, Herminia Carranza, Cora Maceda, Nena Perez Rubio, Naty Santiago, Naty Mallares, Santiago Duenas, Fausto Tolentino, Sabas San Juan, Clara Yumul, Lydia Correa, Meldy Corrales, Nori Dalisay, Amparo Lucas, Aurita Sanchez

Dolphy is Tanzan (not to be confused with Tarzan, of course), a jungle man on a tropical island. Wealthy adventurer Panchito Alba arrives on the island looking for his two long-lost granddaughters (Jean Lopez and Josephine Estrada), who both went down in a plane crash when they were toddlers, and were each found and raised by separate tribes on the island. Accompanying Alba in his search is Eddie Gutierrez, but it is Dolphy who brings the two girls together and reunites them with their grandfather. Alba repays Dolphy by taking him prisoner and shipping him back to civilization where he is put on display in the circus as a jungle wild man. This is very upsetting to Estrada, who has become Dolphy's girl, and when Dolphy manages to escape, he somehow manages to make his way back to the island. Shortly thereafter, Estrada and Lopez decide that they have both had their fill of civilization, and with Gutierrez (now Lopez's beau), they too return to the island to join Dolphy, and presumably all live happily ever after. Aside from Dolphy's comedic shenanigans, the film features a fair number of musical numbers. As proof that Tanzan is *not* Tarzan, the film was followed by a sequel, *Tanzan vs Tarzan* in 1963. (In Tagalog)

Tapang sa Tapang
(Courage for Courage)

1995 Star Cinema; 104 minutes/color
Director: Francis "Jun" Posadas; Screenwriters: Humilde "Meek" Roxas, Jerry O. Tirazona; Cinematographer: Vic Anao; Editor: Tony Sy; Filmscore: Mon del Rosario; Cast: Lito Lapid, Cynthia Luster (Yukari Oshima), Jess Lapid Jr., Efren Reyes Jr., Bob Soler, Philip Gamboa, Dick Israel, Ruel Vernal, Ernie Zarate, Mansueto Velasco, Ben Sagmit, Noel Nuqui, Protacio Dee, Honey Policarpio, Jason San Pedro, Royce Subida, Perla Bautista, Dan Fernandez, Edgar Santiago

When her father is murdered in Manila, Yukari Oshima leaves Japan and flies to the Philippines. She goes to Cebu to take over her father's company, a toy manufacturer and exporter, unaware that her father's top employees are using the company as a front for an arms smuggling operation (handguns hidden inside the bellies of Teddy bears and the like). Manila policeman Lito Lapid discovers the operation, but being outside of his jurisdiction, he cannot make an arrest. He tells Oshima what he has discovered, and the two of them soon enough find that they cannot trust the local police to handle the situation, many of them being involved in the smuggling operation as well, but after finally finding one trustworthy local cop, Lapid and Oshima get the force to join them in shooting it out with the smugglers on the dock.

After a number of films in the Philippines where, for the most part, she spoke only English, Oshima (who is Japanese) seems to be easing into Tagalog use here, using it to a surprising degree. The film is considerably different from her work for Hong Kong director Philip Ko—for starters, Oshima's martial arts scenes are more conventional; while still fast-paced, and more than a little lively, there are none of the outlandish, comical, gravity defying leaps here. In fact, the martial arts showdowns are much less a centerpiece, with director Francis Posadas relying instead on more conventional action genre mainstays, like car chases (and some pretty good ones, too). But in the spirit of things, Lapid does a lot more high-kicking than usual. So too, Oshima is required to do more actual acting than usual. (In Tagalog and English)

Target: Central Luzon Bank Robbery

1988 Triple A Films/Chiba Fareast Films; 88 minutes/color
Directors: Arturo San Agustin, Antonio Jose Alonzo; Cinematographers: Apolinar Cuenco, Rudy Ramos; Editors: Pat Ramos, Xavier Ramos; Filmscore: Marita Manuel; Cast: Anthony Alonzo, Maria Isabel Lopez, Jon Jon Hernandez, John Regala, Zandro Zamora, Amanda Amores, Robert Lee, Nonoy de Guzman, Fred Panopio, Rex Lapid, Vic Santos, Robert Miller, Usman Hassim, Larry Silva, Vic Varrion, Alex Bolado, Bobby Henson, Roland Montes, Belo Borja, Eddie Tuazon, Boy Mediavillo, Ben Chavez

Down-on-his-luck Anthony Alonzo leaves his wife behind and travels to the city to find work. He very quickly meets up with old friend Zandro Zamora who is prospering as the leader of a hold-up gang. Zamora offers Alonzo a job with his organization, and in desperate need of money, Alonzo accepts. The abusive Zamora beats his girlfriend and she seeks comfort via an affair with Alonzo, which causes problems between the two old pals once Zamora discovers the affair. As a result, the hold-up gang is split into two factions, with half choosing to follow Alonzo. Angeles City not being big enough for two separate hold-up gangs, a violent feud erupts between the two groups, and when one of his men is abducted, brutally tortured and killed by Zamora's loyal right hand man (John Regala), Alonzo retaliates by killing Regala and sending him back to Zamora in a coffin. Zamora responds by ambushing each of Alonzo's gang members in turn until, with no one left, Alonzo packs up his money and returns home to his wife. But Zamora is waiting there when Alonzo arrives home, and everybody dies in a climactic shootout. As Alonzo lay dying, his wife rushes out of the house to help him, clutching their baby, which Alonzo had yet to see. After seeing the child, Alonzo dies. The rival gang premise of the film is pretty tired, and the direction (by Alonzo and Arturo San Agustin) is very plain. (In Tagalog)

Task Force Habagat
(Task Force Monsoon)

1993 J&R Films; 106 minutes/color

Director: Romy V. Suzara; Screenwriters: Diego Cagahastian, Henry P. Nadong; Cinematographer: Isagani Sioson; Editor: Rene Tala; Filmscore: Jaime Fabregas; Cast: Edu Manzano, Paquito Diaz, Bomber Moran, Jing Abalos, Emily Loren, Edgar Mande, Monica Herrera, Jorge Estregan (George Estregan, Jr.), Nikki Martel, Dexter Doria, Romy Romulo, Manjo del Mundo, Jim Rosales, Eddie Nicart, Maita Sanchez, Eddie Tuazon, Aries Bautista, Polly Cadsawan, Vic Belaro, Ernie Forte, Joey Padilla, Gerald Ejercito, Rudy Meyer

Edu Manzano is handpicked by the Vice President to head up a task force assigned to clean up the city, in particular ridding it of organized crime. The film runs through a number of busts (bank robbers, drug traffickers, and a number of kidnapping cases) before settling into its main struggle, which is Manzano's efforts to bring down the Red Scorpion Group, a criminal organization headed by George Estregan, Jr. The gang proves a formidable foe for Manzano and his men, which leads to a familiar tale of urban warfare. Romy Suzara's direction is pretty straightforward, without frills, until the ending when he makes the decision to use slow motion in depicting Estregan's demise. The results are awkward at best, as Manzano, having given orders for his men to take Estregan alive, rushes across a creek to where Estregan's body has fallen. Turning a corner to get to the body, Manzano has a hard time getting his footing, the effect being that the slow motion photography basically brings everything to a momentary standstill, the climax hanging in mid-air for what seems like an awful long time. Presumably, the intention of the slow motion was to draw out and heighten the suspense, but Manzano's slow progress through the water, only to stumble and struggle to keep his balance tends to have more of a comic effect, and makes director Suzara look like an amateur. (In Tagalog with some English)

Tatak ng Kriminal
(The Mark of the Criminal)

1993 FLT Films; 103 minutes/color

Director: Edgardo Boy Vinarao; Screenwriter: Amado Lacuesta; Cinematographer: Jun Rasca; Editor: Edgardo "Boy" Vinarao; Filmscore: Nonong Buencamino; Cast: Eddie Garcia, Tetchie Agbayani, Johnny Delgado, Jean Saburit, Berting Labra, Elizabeth Tamayo, Fred Moro, Manjo del Mundo, Romy Romulo, Rey Solo, Edwin Reyes, Nonoy de Guzman, Eddie Tuazon, Vangie Labalan, Butch Bautista, Ester Chavez

Ex-con Eddie Garcia is having a hard time finding work, or even a place to stay, until he helps thwart a couple of hold-up men who are trying to rob cabbie Berting Labra. In gratitude, Labra puts Garcia up and gets him a job with the cab company. Garcia falls in love with Elizabeth Tamayo, one of his fares, and when he learns that Tamayo is hiding out from casino owner Johnny Delgado, he resolves to help her. Garcia goes crashing onto Delgado's estate with a battalion of his cabbie buddies who engage in a big donnybrook with Delgado's flunkies, while Garcia himself takes care of Delgado, killing him in a shootout. Now if that doesn't win Tamayo over, one wonders what in the world would. In comparison with some of Garcia's other action films, this is fairly lightweight, but not without points of interest, particularly the endearing moment when the love struck Garcia agonizes over whether Tamayo could ever fall for an ex-convict cab driver. (In Tagalog)

Tatlo, Dalawa, Isa
(Three, Two, One)

1974 Cinemanila Corporation; 129 minutes/color

Director: Lino Brocka; Screenwriters: Tony Perez, Mario O'Hara, Orlando R. Nadres; Cinematographer: Romeo Vitug; Editor: Augusto Salvador; Filmscore: Minda D. Azarcon; Cast: Jay Ilagan, Perla Bautista, Hilda Koronel, Anita Linda, Lolita Rodriguez, Mario O'Hara, Mary Walter, Bembol Roco, Socrates (Soxy) Topacio, Roger Mariscal, Rolly Papasin, Laurice Guillen, Jojo Abella, Bey Vito, Claude Wilson, Barbara Browne, Estrella Kuenzler, Manny Ojeda, Lily Miraflor, Mely Mallari, Melvy Pacubas, Dante Balois, Edwin O'Hara, Pio de Castro III

This is a trio of unrelated stories all directed by Lino Brocka. In the first story, Jay Ilagan plays a troubled teen committed by his mother to a drug rehabilitation program, an ordeal which he manages to survive and emerge a new person. In the second story, Hilda Koronel sends a letter to her U.S. serviceman father, prompting him to fly to the Philippines and offer to take her back to America. Although she very much wants to go, in the end she finds herself unable to leave her alcoholic mother. The final story stars Lolita Rodriguez as a middle-aged woman living in a gothic home with her domineering mother (Mary Walter). When Rodriguez becomes infatuated with Mario O'Hara, she hires him as gardener, and soon begins an affair with him, inviting the judgmental wrath of Walter. (In Tagalog with some English)

Tatlong Taong Walang Diyos (Three Godless Years)

1976 NV Productions; 120 minutes/color and black & white

Director/screenwriter: Mario O'Hara; Cinematographer: Conrado Baltazar; Editor: Efren Jarlego; Filmscore: Minda Azarcon; Cast: Nora Aunor, Christopher de Leon, Rafael (Bembol) Roco Jr., Orlando Nadres, Peque Gallaga, Mario Escudero, Yolanda Luna, Edwin O'Hara, Joey Galvez, Dante Balois, Soxy Topacio, Liverio Tabalon Jr., Tommy Yap, Nina Lorenzo, Estrella Antonio, Melvin Flores, John Arino, George Atutubo, Peachy Callo

Generally regarded as one of the more significant Filipino films of the 1970s, this tragic WWII melodrama stars Nora Aunor as a young woman who is raped by a Japanese soldier (Christopher de Leon). It soon becomes obvious, however, that de Leon has more than a passing interest in Aunor, and he continues to visit her and shower her with gifts. Though Aunor steadfastly rejects him, her parents are won over by de Leon, who brings them food and other supplies scarce to the rest of the village during the Japanese occupation. This ostracizes the family from their neighbors, and they are further made outcasts when Aunor turns out to be pregnant as a result of her rape. After giving birth, Aunor begins to let go of her hatred for de Leon and the two are married, which breaks the heart of Bembol Roco, a former beau of Aunor's who has returned from two years service in the Philippine military. With the Japanese now in control of the country, Roco no longer has a military to serve, but upon finding Aunor married to a Japanese soldier (and her having given birth to his child as well), Roco goes off and joins the Philippine resistance. In time, Aunor's parents are accused of complicity with the rebels and are executed, but Aunor finds a way to blame Roco and the resistance for making her life a hell. When the Americans return, the Japanese flee the village, and Aunor and de Leon take to the forest with their baby, where they are set upon by a band of Filipino rebels who kill de Leon. Likewise, upon returning to her village, Aunor is chased by an angry mob that recognizes her as the wife of a Japanese soldier, and she is killed by Filipino resistance fighters. The film concludes with Roco arriving in town and frantically searching for Aunor, who he finds lying dead in the streets with a good many other corpses awaiting burial.

Initially the film was criticized widely as being overly sympathetic in its portrayal of the Japanese, a reaction that, given the record of the Japanese during the occupation, was only to be expected. In hindsight, however, this response does seem overly sensitive, since the only sympathetic Japanese character in the film is de Leon, who is, after all, a rapist. (In Tagalog)

T-Bird at Ako (T-Bird and I)

1982 Film Ventures; 111 minutes/color

Director: Danny Zialcita; Cinematographer: Felizardo Bailen; Editor: Enrique Jarlego, Jr.; Cast: Vilma Santos, Nora Aunor, Tommy Abuel, Suzanne Gonzales, Odette Khan, Dindo Fernando, Liza Lorena, Rosemarie Gil, Leila Hermosa, Baby Delgado, Rustica Carpio, Angie Salinas, Johnny Wilson, Subas Herrero, Tony Carreon, Mario Escudero, Joe Garcia, Dick Israel, Rolly Papasin, Dodie Ramirez, Johnny Vicar, Josie Shoemaker, Anita Linda, Olive Hilario, Alvin Enriquez

This courtroom drama stars Nora Aunor as an attorney who volunteers to defend exotic dancer Vilma Santos, who is accused of murder after having shot and killed her abusive boyfriend (Dick Israel) during a fight. Having just successfully defended a lesbian who was accused of murdering her lover's husband, Aunor has begun to question her own sexuality, and she finds herself attracted to Santos. The case is being prosecuted by Tommy Abuel, who has proposed marriage to Aunor, but when Aunor tells him that she is attracted to another woman, Abuel becomes irate. Abuel begins to take out his frustration on Aunor in the courtroom, to such an extent that judge Tony Carreon openly questions whose trial he is presiding over. Aunor has invited Santos to stay at her home during the trial, but finds her advances rebuked, and Santos once again starts seeing her old flame (Dindo Fernando), by whom she bore a child out of wedlock. Despite a bitterly fought court case, all seems to end well, as Santos is acquitted and reunites with Fernando, prompting Aunor to reevaluate her flirtation with lesbianism and return to Abuel.

Director Danny Zialcita never seems to rate a mention among the better Filipino film directors, but he has a sophisticated sense of composition, which occasionally veers into a stylish mode, and while his films by-and-large fall into the category of standard, sudsy melodrama, it is his stylish consideration that sometimes sets them apart. It was quite a coup here to cast major stars Aunor and Santos together in a film dealing with a controversial subject, although the film never really approaches anything particularly racy. Still, it is superior to the stars' other significant team-up, Ishmael Bernal's tedious *Ikaw ay Akin* (1978), in which the stars were wasted in standard romantic love triangle drivel. (In Tagalog and English)

Ten Little Indians

1984 Good Harvest Productions; 105 minutes/color

Director/screenwriter: Tony Pascua; Cinematographer: Baby Buenaseda; Editor: Ruben Natividad; Filmscore: Vicente Sotto III; Cast: William Martinez, Chatty Ramirez, Herbert Bautista, Hero Bautista, Harlena Bautista, Peewee Quijano, Eric Francisco, Bebong Osorio Jr., Roderick Martinez, Love Sandoval, Joy Pobre, Gay Pobre, Mila Ocampo, Moody Diaz, Peter Corpuz, Tessie Mendoza, Vincent Dafalong, Ross Rival, Bebeng Amora, Totsie Magcalas, Amado Arevalo, Roger Santos, Eduardo Ching

In this odd little film, William Martinez plays a deranged young man with a cowboy fixation. While running around town imagining himself to be the Lone Ranger, Martinez comes across a busload of school children dressed as Indians for a musical number that they are to perform at a scout function. Using a toy six-shooter, Martinez hi-jacks the bus and takes the children and their scoutmaster (Chatty Ramirez) out into the woods. After being bitten by a snake, Martinez is saved by Ramirez and the children, who administer first aid, and a day later, in gratitude, Martinez tries to lead the children out of the forest. Unfortunately, they encounter five criminal fugitives who beat Martinez into unconsciousness and drag Ramirez into the brush and rape her. The children flee further into the forest and are pursued by the criminals, with Martinez and Ramirez following once they have gathered themselves. The police find the fugitives, killing some of them in a shootout, but not before three of the children have been killed while trying to elude their pursuers. The film ends with a lengthy, weepy funeral for the children.

It's a little hard to get a handle on this one. The bizarre behavior of Martinez early on would suggest that the film is going to be a comedy, but it shifts gears rather drastically, becoming a genuine tragedy in the final third of the running time, with the rape of Ramirez, the shooting of two of the children and the drowning of a third. It certainly concludes on a downbeat note. There is also the fact that the execution is rather bland. (In Tagalog)

Terror Is a Man

1959 Lynn-Romero Productions/Valiant Films; 89 minutes/black & white

Director: Gerardo de Leon; Screenwriter: Harry Paul Barber; Cinematographer: Emmanuel Rojas; Editor: Gervacio Santos; Filmscore: Ariston Avelino; Cast: Francis Lederer, Greta Thyssen, Richard Derr, Oscar Keesee, Lilia Duran, Peyton Keesee

Director Gerardo de Leon's early experiment in doing an international film stars Richard Derr as the only survivor of a shipwreck who washes ashore Blood Island and is taken in by the reclusive scientist Francis Lederer. Lederer's wife (Greta Thyssen) desperately wants to leave the island, partly stifled by the isolation and partly frightened by her husband's bizarre experiments: Lederer is trying to expedite the evolutionary process by turning a panther into a man. His monstrous hybrid creature periodically escapes and frightens all of the natives into fleeing the island. Eventually, the beast escapes and kills its creator before falling from a cliff to its death. The film is equipped with a warning bell prior to the depiction of a surgical procedure to alert more squeamish viewers to avert their eyes during what, at the time, was considered by some to be a shocking sight.

Working with American producer Kane W. Lynn, this film opened up the lucrative American market to both de Leon and the film's co-producer Eddie Romero, both of whom would continue to work with Lynn throughout the 1960s, producing war films like *The Walls of Hell* (1964) and *The Ravagers* (1965) before returning to the horror genre with a string of further Blood Island films. (In English)

Tigasin (Hard)

1999 Star Cinema; 98 minutes/color

Director: Ike Jarlego, Jr.; Screenwriter: Mel Mendoza-del Rosario; Cast: Eddie Garcia, Victor Neri, Alma Concepcion, Lito Legaspi, Peque Gallaga, Alvin Anson, Roldan Aquino, Rez Cortez, Manjo del Mundo, Ogie Diaz, Amy Perez, Ester Chavez,

Augusto Victa, Dexter Doria, Jean Saburit, Archie Adamos, Gino Paul Guzman

Well, it had to happen, and now it has—a movie where people are being killed by ... Viagra. Eddie Garcia is back doing what he does best—playing a wily veteran of the police force, teamed once more with a young hotshot cop, in this case Victor Neri. Together they must find out who is distributing bootleg Viagra pills that are killing middle-aged and elderly men in the city. Their investigation leads them to restaurant manager Alma Concepcion, but Neri falls in love with her and refuses to believe that she is involved. He turns out to be wrong, as their surveillance of Concepcion leads them to the criminal gang of Roldan Aquino, and Garcia and Neri gun down one-and-all in the concluding shootout, including Concepcion. There are plenty of car chases and shootouts, and given the subject matter, some expected humor, most of which is very tacky. As for Garcia, despite his age he shows no signs of slowing down, and is as entertaining as ever. (In Tagalog with some English)

A Time for Dying

1983 Nepomuceno Productions; 109 minutes/color

Director: Luis Nepomuceno; Screenwriter: Cesar J. Amigo; Cinematographer: Loreto Isleta; Filmscore: Tito Arevalo; Cast: Charito Solis, Pancho Magalona, Fred Galang, Rod Webb, Miguelito, Eddie Garcia, Eva Darren, Yoshindri Mori, Teddy Benavidez, Norma Blancaflor, Ben Perez, Mary Walter, Rick Baeker, Angel Esmeralda, Robert Arevalo, Rebecca Rocha, Max Rojo, Dino del Valle, Alex Romeo, Sammy Sarmiento, Jun Sanchez, Jun Garcia, Rod Francisco

In this ambitious WWII melodrama from director/producer Luis Nepomuceno, the arrival of the Japanese sends a Philippine ROTC unit into the hills to hide. Once there, they team up with a Philippine guerrilla army, which turns out to be a big mistake since the guerrillas, as incredible as it seems, make the Japanese look like sweethearts. The brutal guerrilla leader kills the Philippine ROTC leader and rapes his daughter (Charito Solis). The guerrillas also keep a pen of Filipino female prisoners on hand as sex slaves (something that, as it happens, the Japanese actually did during the war). Meanwhile, down in the village, surprisingly subdued Japanese Captain Pancho Magalona tries to rule compassionately over the people, and even forms a close friendship with a young Filipino boy (Miguelito). But Magalona's command is called into question when he is unable to locate and capture a downed U.S. pilot who is being hidden in the hills by the guerrillas. Brutal Japanese Major Eddie Garcia arrives and gets a break when one of the guerrilla army's sex slaves (Eva Darren) escapes, and upon arriving in town rats the guerrillas out to the Japanese, revealing the location of the guerrilla camp. Garcia leads an attack on the camp, but somewhat surprisingly, the Japanese are overcome and forced to flee. Garcia having died in battle, Magalona takes the remnant of his forces back to town where they are prepared to die in battle. But with Miguelito having gone to be by Magalona's side, the Filipinos are reluctant to attack, and offer to allow Magalona and his men to leave if he returns Miguelito over to them. Since he was not holding the boy by force to begin with, Magalona readily complies and he and his men are permitted to board their boat and leave.

For a country that suffered so appallingly under the Japanese occupation, it seems odd that a Filipino filmmaker would make the Japanese captain the most level-headed and philosophical character while the Philippine guerrilla leader is the primary villain (after having killed Solis' father, the guerrilla leader proceeds to rape Solis atop her father's grave).

Nepomuceno takes a page out of Sam Pekinpah's book, filling the film with bloody, slow motion shootings, and he throws any pretense toward tact to the wind during the battle sequence in which he hires real amputees, dousing them in stage blood to portray people who have just had their limbs blown off. Solis gives a good performance, and Magalona's sensitive portrayal is impressive, but the film's best performance is given by Darren as the guerrilla sex slave, who escapes her degrading and brutal captivity, reveals the location of the guerrilla camp to Garcia and is then killed by him for her trouble. (In English)

Tingga ng Katarungan
(Lead Justice)

1990 Harvest International; 115 minutes/color

Directors/screenwriters: Jerry O. Tirazona, Erwin T. Lanado; Cinematographer: Apolinar Cuenco; Editor: Rene Tala; Filmscore: Rey Ramos; Cast: Jess Lapid Jr., John Regala, Tirso Cruz III, Mayleen Zapanta, Honey Policarpio, Marithez Samson, Nick Romano, Philip Gamboa, Dick Israel, Gabriel Romulo, Bobby Benitez, Jessie Delgado, Odette Khan, Rey Sagum, Allan Rogelio, Joe Baltazar, Rene Matias, Kaka Balagtas, Mark Tiongson, Clyde Maturan, Jeric Vasquez, Gerry Roman, Boy Ranay, Jun de la Paz

This is a somewhat convoluted action film in which police officer Jess Lapid, Jr., is relieved of duty after engaging in a shootout while off duty. Nonetheless, he is drawn into a struggle between warring gangs. Petty drug dealer John Regala seeks vengeance against a more powerful and sadistic gang for the chainsaw killing of his parents and siblings. Unfortunately, the more powerful gang also has more powerful friends in sleazy cops Tirso Cruz III and Dick Israel. Lapid and Regala join forces and eventually emerge victorious. There is the standard warehouse shootout, which is better here than the usual (and is lifted by Rey Ramos' somewhat offbeat score), and as expected, it is followed by a sort of post-climax climax, in which Lapid and Regala finish off the rest of the heavies in another shootout, this time at an airfield.

Though he receives top billing, Lapid's role seems somewhat subordinate to Regala's. As for Regala, his hair is curiously flecked with gray for the role, and he employs his customarily over-exertive style. The film is more than a bit on the sadistic side, not only due to the chainsaw killings, but also includes violent rape and straight razor killings, along with the normal high body count by way of gunplay. (In Tagalog)

Tinimbang Ka Nguni't Kulang (You Have Been Weighed and Found Lacking)

1974; 120 minutes/color
Director: Lino Brocka; Screenwriters: Lino Brocka, Mario O'Hara; Cinematographer: Joe Batac; Editor: Augusto Salvador; Filmscore: Lutgardo Labad; Cast: Lolita Rodriguez, Christopher de Leon, Eddie Garcia, Mario O'Hara, Hilda Koronel, Laurice Guillen, Lilia Dizon, Joonee Gamboa, Jerry O'Hara, Joseph Sytangco, Bey Vito, Ernie Zarate, Rolly Papasin, Nina Lorenzo, Melvi Pagubas, Paz Brosas, Dante Balois, Lito Cruz, Fred Alvarez, Erning David, Edwardo Montez, Robert Miller, Chito Ponce Enrile

This excellent and compelling melodrama from filmmaker Lino Brocka is said to have initiated what has been called the Second Golden Era in Philippine cinema. Lolita Rodriguez portrays a mentally disturbed homeless woman who is largely shunned by the people in her town, but she finds acceptance with another of the town's outcasts, leper Mario O'Hara, who lives in a shack near the local cemetery. O'Hara takes Rodriguez in, and they are both befriended by teenager Christopher de Leon. The son of wealthy Lilia Dizon and ne're-do-well ladies man Eddie Garcia, de Leon is disturbed by the turbulent marriage of his parents, as well as having troubles with his fickle girlfriend (Hilda Koronel), and seems to find comfort in the deeply committed relationship he sees between O'Hara and Rodriguez. But when Rodriguez is revealed to be pregnant, the townspeople take her from Rodriguez, and her attempts to return to him lead to tragedy. Rodriguez won the FAMAS Best Actress award, and young de Leon won the Best Actor trophy. (In Tagalog)

Ang Tipo Kong Lalake (My Kind of Guy)

1995 Viva Films; 102 minutes/color
Director: Efren "Lodging" Jarlego; Screenwriter: Dwight Gaston; Cinematographer: Oscar Querijero; Editor: Edgardo Jarlego; Filmscore: Ricky del Rosario; Cast: Joey de Leon, Dennis Padilla, Rita Avila, Michelle Aldana, Cheska Diaz, Michelle Parton, Glydel Mercado, Tony Carreon, Daniel Fernando, Bomber Moran, Errol Dionisio, Teroy de Guzman Jr., Don Pepot, Beverly Salviejo, Jon Achaval, Jessica Cortez, Val Sotto, Danny Panzalin, Ric Arellano, Bella Flores, Ruffa Mae Aquino, Tony Bagyo, Nonong de Andres, Pong Pong

In this comedy, Joey de Leon and Dennis Padilla portray cat burglars who are sentenced to a ten-year prison term. After their release they find employment as handymen at a boarding school for young ladies (nice work if you can get it) where de Leon tries romancing Rita Avila and Padilla pursues Michelle Aldana. Eventually some of de Leon and Padilla's underworld buddies turn up requesting their services for a safe cracking job, but having grown happy with their current lawful situation, the boys refuse. But they are finally persuaded when the underworld boss who approached them abducts the entire boarding house population and holds them hostage. Though they pull off the job, de Leon and Padilla wind up returning the money after rescuing the girls from the bad guys during a madcap climactic fight. The material is pretty slight, but de Leon is always amusing, and Avila is certainly easy on the eyes. (In Tagalog with some English)

Tiyanak (Goblin)

1988 Regal Films; 123 minutes/color
Directors: Peque Gallaga, Lorenzo Reyes; Screen-

writers: Peque Gallaga, Don Escudero, Lorenzo Reyes; Cinematographer: Eduardo F. Jacinto; Editor: Augusto Salvador; Filmscore: Dionisio Buencamino, Jr.: Cast: Janice de Belen, Lotlot de Leon, Ramon Christopher, Mary Walter, Chuckie Dreyfus, Carmina Villaroel, Rudolph Yaptinchay, Smokey Manaloto, Bella Flores, Betty Mae Piccio, Eva Ramos, Suzanne Gonzales, Mae Ann Adonis, Bonafe, Zorayda Sanchez, Crispin Medina, Romy Romulo, Bernard Canaberal, Ray Ventura, Sam Brillantes

Still mourning the loss of her infant, Janice de Belen is only too happy to take in a baby found abandoned in a derelict old house. While the rest of the family senses something is wrong with the child, grandmother Mary Walter declares the baby evil and seeks to destroy it—something for which she pays with her life. The baby, which transforms into a little monster, goes on an all-out rampage, first in a hospital, and then, in a scene reminiscent of the 1958 film *The Tingler*, in a movie theater. The monstrous baby is finally destroyed in the standard climactic conflagration.

Obviously inspired by Larry Cohen's *It's Alive* (1974), *Tiyanak* is superior to its model, largely due to directors Peque Gallaga and Lorenzo Reyes' tendency to fill the film with traditional horror genre trappings (dilapidated, cobweb-ridden, creepy old houses, ominous winds, violent thunderstorms, and the somewhat gothic flavor to at least the interior of the family home), but while there is much to recommend it, there is just not enough to justify a running time of over two hours. In that respect, Gallaga and Reyes seem determined to sink their own ship, for just when you think the movie has reached its climax, it meanders on for another twenty minutes, limping along until reaching its real climax. (In Tagalog)

TNT Jackson

1974 New World Pictures; 72 minutes/color
Director: Cirio H. Santiago; Screenwriters: Dick Miller, Ken Metcalfe; Cinematographer: Felipe Sacdalan; Editors: Gervacio Santos, Barbara Pokras; Cast: Jeanne Bell, Stan Shaw, Pat Anderson, Ken Metcalfe, Chiquito, Max Alvarado, Percy Gordon, Imelda Ilanan, Chris Cruz, Leo Martin (Martinez), John Gamble, Ramon D'Salva, Ruben Rustia, Paquito Salcedo

Jeanne Bell travels to Hong Kong to find out the truth about the murder of her brother. It turns out that he was killed by Stan Shaw, a member of drug kingpin Ken Metcalfe's organization. Bell infiltrates Metcalfe's gang and brings down the syndicate, with the help of Chiquito, who was one of her brother's friends. Falling in love with Shaw was not a part of Bell's plan, but she does anyway. After learning that he was the one who killed her brother, however, she resolves the dilemma pretty definitively. Bell is comically unconvincing as a martial artist, though that's what the script requires her to be, and her most acrobatic moves are performed by an obvious male double in an afro wig. Like virtually all of director Cirio Santiago's work, the film is unexceptional, though it was successful enough for New World Pictures that Santiago and screenwriter Metcalfe reworked it for their 1981 film *Firecracker*. (In English)

Tondo Girl

1983; 119 minutes/color
Director: Manuel "Fyke" Cinco; Screenwriter: Antonio S. Mortel; Cinematographer: Arnold Alvaro; Editor: Edgardo Vinarao; Filmscore: Ernani Cuenco; Cast: Amy Austria, Vic Silayan, Joonee Gamboa, Lito Anzures, Juan Rodrigo, Cynthia Gonzales, Rustica Carpio, Mary Walter, Joey Aquino, Rey Tuazon, Amay Bisaya, Tetchie Agbabani, Eddie Garcia, George Estregan, Fanny Serrano, Arturo "Bomber" Moran, Alma Bonnevie, Angie Salinas, Ernie Zarate, Tino de Lara, Ria Villareal, Tessie Cervantes, Susan David, Cindy Meliza, Francis Zorres, Bonnie Paredes

Feisty Amy Austria lives with her parents in Tondo, a slum of Manila. Her father supports the family working as a cab driver, but when he is hospitalized after being in an accident, Austria tries to pick up the slack. She works a series of short-lived jobs, with varying degrees of disaster, before marrying a well-to-do young man. With Austria being young, inexperienced, and apparently afraid of intimacy, the marriage remains unconsummated however. In time one of Austria's former suitors hears of her good fortunes (marrying into a wealthy family), and he hatches a plot: after getting Austria's father drunk, he deposits him in a hotel room to awaken with a young woman crying rape. Austria agrees to pay the requested amount of money to hush things up, but when she arrives at the blackmailer's apartment, she is rendered unconscious and is in the process of being undressed when her husband barges in and attacks the would-be rapist. Unfortunately, Austria's husband—who had been showing signs of a heart condition—suffers a fatal heart attack when grappling with Austria's attacker. At the reading of the will, Austria's mother-in-law (Mary Walter) is outraged to learn that her son has left everything to Austria, and with her husband's family all bickering over the money, Austria angrily berates them and relinquishes her right to her husband's estate before storming out of the office and returning to her family and the modest life that she left behind. (In Tagalog)

Totoy Buang: Mad Killer of Maynila (Crazy Totoy: Mad Killer of Manila)

1992 Octo Arts Films; 112 minutes/color
Director: J. Erastheo Navoa; Screenwriter: Humilde Roxas; Cinematographer: Danny Bustos; Editor: Joe Solo; Filmscore: Mon del Rosario; Cast: John Regala, Mark Gil, Aurora Sevilla, Rina Reyes, Francis Magalona, Kevin Delgado, Sharmaine Arnaiz, Bob Soler, Daria Ramirez, Zandro Zamora, Johnny Vicar, Romy Diaz, Lollie Mara, Jordan Castillo, Gerald Estregan, Mikko Manson, Mike Castillo, Mike Vergel, Ernie Zarate, Jimmy Reyes, Vic Belaro, Danny Labra, Edgar Santiago, Howard Zaleta, Bernard Atienza, Eddie Tuazon, Bobby Hernandez, Romy Romulo, Nonoy de Guzman, Nonong de Andres

Police in Manila are seeking a homicidal maniac dubbed the Straightjacket Killer, so-named because of the position that he poses his victims in. The killer is a young supermarket stock clerk (John Regala) with resurfacing memories of his abusive father. The memories begin to return after Regala witnesses a man physically abusing his son. Though he is a homicidal maniac, Regala still somehow manages to be the film's protagonist, killing only unsavory characters (albeit in unsavory ways), and ends the film by saving a group of children from a gang of kidnappers before being gunned down by a virtual army of policemen led by Ernie Zarate. The film seems to have no problem in making a hero out of a crazed killer, though it does go to some lengths to limit Regala's victims to villainous types (although the murder of a transit worker who expels a woman from a bus for not having a ticket is a bit dubious). Regala, who is somewhat prone to overacting, seems more suited to these types of roles, where his lack of restraint is more appropriate to the character. (In Tagalog)

Tubog sa Ginto (Dipped in Gold)

1970 Lea Productions; 122 minutes/color
Director/screenwriter: Lino Brocka; Cinematography: Steve Perez; Editor: Felizardo Santos; Filmscore: Doming Valdez; Cast: Eddie Garcia, Lolita Rodriguez, Luis Gonzales, Hilda Koronel, Jay Ilagan, Marissa Delgado, Mario O'Hara, Joonee Gamboa, Veronica Palileo, Joe Avelino, Lorli Villanueva, Angie Ferro, Tony Carrion, Glen Bernardo, Josie Perez, Baby Jimenez, Inday dela Cruz, Lito Franquelli

Eddie Garcia won the FAMAS Best Actor award for his performance here as a successful middle-aged businessman undergoing a sexual identity crisis. Frustrated by his inability to make love to his wife (Lolita Rodriguez), Garcia tries his luck with his secretary (Marissa Delgado) with the same disheartening results. Feeling emasculated, he experiences a sexual reawakening after succumbing to his increasing homosexual desires. After a number of encounters with male partners he meets in bars, Garcia begins a more substantial relationship with Mario O'Hara, a seemingly naïve and somewhat reluctant young man who gives in to Garcia's advances. Garcia hires O'Hara as a chauffeur, giving himself an excuse to have O'Hara live in quarters in the family home, but Rodriguez spies one of their liaisons through the window of O'Hara's room. Stunned by this revelation, Rodriguez begins an affair of her own, which is discovered by her teenage son (Jay Ilagan). Having grown up idolizing his father, Ilagan is deeply stung by his mother's infidelity, but in time he also discovers Garcia's secret. Not only is Garcia in jeopardy of losing his family, but also virtually everything he has worked for when O'Hara turns out not to be the malleable young man Garcia thought he was, but a conniving con man. Having paid someone to photograph one of his intimate nights with Garcia, O'Hara begins blackmailing his erstwhile lover, driving Garcia to the brink of bankruptcy as well as despair. The drama concludes with O'Hara, having gambled away the money that Garcia had already paid him, showing up drunk at Garcia's home. Garcia arrives to find O'Hara attempting to rape Rodriguez, and he is forced to shoot O'Hara. Rodriguez then watches in horror as Garcia tenderly kisses O'Hara's corpse before putting the gun to his own head and taking his own life.

With all apologies to those who will find the statement homophobic, the jarringly frank portrayal of the relationship between Garcia and O'Hara is considerably discomfiting to a heterosexual viewer. Garcia definitely deserved the FAMAS for his performance. (In Tagalog with some English)

Tubusin Mo ng Bala ang Puso Ko (Ransom My Heart with Bullets)

1996 Octo Arts/Cinemax; 95 minutes/color
Director: Toto Natividad; Screenwriters: Humilde

"Meek" Roxas, Jake Tordesillas, Henry Nadong; Cinematographer: Ramon Marcelino; Editors: Toto Natividad, Joyce Bernal; Filmscore: Nonong Buencamino; Cast: Edu Manzano, Anjanette Abayari, Mark Gil, Bembol Roco, Ronaldo Valdez, Jenette Fernando, Roldan Aquino, Archie Adamos, Perla Bautista, Dexter Doria, Pocholo Montes, Danny Labra, Judy Teodoro, Cristy Portugal, Bobby Henson, Nemie Gutierrez, Alex Toledo, Roger Belaro, Kim Laurel, Edward Belaro, Rey Fabian, Senen Cantor

Edu Manzano stars here as an NBI agent who tries to topple the crime empire of gangster Ronaldo Valdez. He manages to arrest Mark Gil, Valdez's right hand man, but when the charges don't stick and Gil is released, Manzano becomes very disillusioned with the system and resigns from the NBI to pursue a career as a lawyer. His marriage is strained by the demands on his time, and eventually his wife (Anjanette Abayari) leaves him. Several years later, Manzano has succeeded in becoming an attorney, though curiously, he has chosen to become a defense attorney. Even more curious is the fact that Abayari has become Valdez's girlfriend (How did *that* happen?!). Valdez treats her horribly, however, and when the two of them fight, Valdez falls to his death from a second story balcony. Abayari is charged with killing him, and Manzano is appointed as her attorney; but despite his best efforts, Abayari is convicted. Resorting to drastic measures, Manzano takes Abayari from the authorities at gunpoint and speeds away in a car. The two are sought not only by the police, but also by Gil, who has taken over Valdez's criminal organization and considers Abayari a loose end. Manzano turns to his old NBI buddy Bembol Roco for help, but that proves to be a big mistake as Roco is on Gil's payroll (gee, what a surprise). Though Manzano and Abayari manage to kill Gil and all of his men in a climactic shootout, the film ends with no word on how they plan to deal with Abayari's conviction. The action sequences are well handled, though the film in general is nothing out of the ordinary. (In Tagalog with some English)

Tumakbo Ka ... Hanggang May Lupa (Run ... While There Is Land)

1990 ATB-4; 102 minutes/color
Directors: Leonardo "Ding" Pascual, Baldo Marro; Screenwriter: Leonardo "Ding" Pascual; Cinematographer: Rosendo E. Buenaseda; Editor: Nap Montebon; Filmscore: Rey Valera; Cast: Baldo Marro, Isadora, Rey Roldan, Dick Israel, Robert Talby, Danny Riel, Robert Miller, Johnny Vicar, Bobby Benitez, Ben Sagmit, Carol Dauden, Armando Arce, Marla Limlingan, Rene Matias

Soldier Baldo Marro returns to his home village only to find it controlled by Robert Talby's protection racket. Marro quickly sets himself up as an adversary to Talby's bunch, with the expected results—his family is killed, and so Marro goes gunning for Talby's goons, which lands him in jail. The local police are on Talby's payroll as well (who could've guessed?), and they take Marro down a lonely stretch of road intending to kill him, but Marro manages to escape. Returning home for his weapons, Marro is ambushed by a combination of the police and Talby's men, but again he manages to escape and flees into the jungle. He is pursued, but is able to kill off all of Talby's men, the police, and finally Talby himself; but he has no time to rest since government troops arrive, led by Marro's own commanding officer, and though they try to get him to surrender, one of the government soldiers disobeys the cease fire command and Marro is killed.

Marro gives a good performance, and there are some impressive pyrotechnics in the climactic battle (as well as some gore, as Marro literally blows police chief Danny Riel to pieces), but none of it compensates for the extremely formulaic material. There is also the fact that Dick Israel, in his usual drugged-out gang member role, gets killed off a bit too early, which deflates things in a hurry, long before the climax. (In Tagalog)

Tupang Itim (Black Sheep)

1989 Patricia Films; 102 minutes/color
Director/screenwriter: Joe "Kaka" Balagtas; Filmscore: Marte de la Paz; Cinematographer: Jimmy Baer; Editor: Cornelio Crisostomo; Filmscore: Marte de la Paz; Cast: Jess Lapid Jr., Eddie Garcia, Tetchie Agbayani, Marissa Delgado, Lucita Soriano, Dexter Doria, Jun King Austria, Glaiza Herradura, Dick Israel, Rez Cortez, Bobby Benitez, Rodolfo "Boy" Garcia, Renato del Prado, Ben Moro, Ben Pinoy, Robert Miller

Having lost his mother when he was still a child, Jess Lapid, Jr. has grown up supporting himself as a pickpocket. With years to perfect his craft, Lapid has gotten quite good at it, and he attracts the attention of a local gang who ask him to join up with them. Lapid accepts the offer, and after a string of big robberies, he emerges as the leader of the group: he also becomes the most wanted man in Manila when he turns killer. One night while robbing a house, Lapid shoots and kills an unarmed man and woman in their bed. With his name—Vergel de Diyos, Jr.—all over the news, Lapid becomes a major source of embarrassment to Eddie Garcia—Vergel de Diyos, Sr.—who is a very prominent businessman. Eventually, Lapid is arrested by thuggish cop Dick Israel and is brought to trial. Convicted of multiple homicides and robberies, Lapid is about to be led away when he commands the attention of the courtroom and reveals that he truly is the illegitimate son of Garcia, the result of an affair between Garcia and Lapid's mother (Dexter Doria), whom Garcia abandoned to poverty. In a superb climax, Lapid grabs the gun of the police officer next to him and shoots Garcia as Israel and his men open fire on Lapid. Lapid falls dead, and the wounded Garcia, with his weeping legitimate son and daughter to help him, crawls to his fallen son and dies embracing him.

While his screenplay does have some flaws, Joe Balagtas does an excellent job directing. Foremost among the flaws is the attempt to generate sympathy for Lapid—a cold blooded killer many times over—by making his nemesis, Israel, the personification of the clichéd goonish cop. There is also the thoroughly unnecessary plot device of having Garcia's wife (Marissa Delgado) wind up being the judge presiding over Lapid's case, which could obviously be seen as a conflict of interest. Among the many positives is a strong performance from Garcia, and a bizarre musical score by Marte de la Paz that especially adds punch to an already punchy climax. Though not without its flaws, this is a very good film. (In Tagalog and English)

Turing Gesmundo, Kapitan Langgam (Captain Ant, Turing Gesmundo)

1992 ATB-4 Films; 104 minutes/color

Director: Robert Talvy; Screenwriters: Leonardo "Ding" Pascual, Ariel Antonio; Editor: Nap Montebon; Filmscore: Nap Montebon; Cast: Sonny Parsons, Rhey Roldan, Tony Bernal, Bobby Benitez, Danny Riel, Marilyn Monteverde, Alexander David, Rubi Rosa, Allan Gilbert, Matuk Astorga, Vic Varrion, Vic Felipe, Berty Cayanan, Ariel Antonio, Susing Yason

When a group of rebels terrorize a remote village, local farmer Sonny Parsons joins in driving them out and becomes a hero to the area residents. To show their gratitude, the people vote him their leader, but Parsons has a zero tolerance for most any kind of impropriety, whether it be public drunkenness or trying to steal a kiss from a young lady. Parsons dispenses a disturbingly cruel punishment, stripping the offenders and tying them to a post while forcing them to stand atop an anthill. Nonetheless, the people seem happy with him in charge. The film finishes up with the rebels returning and Parsons gathering the men in the village together to try and help repel them. During the conflict, the rebels are clearly getting the better of the local militia when government troops arrive and wipe out the rebels.

This is a fairly middling effort. Though cast as the hero of the film, Parsons' stern brand of justice will seem fairly sadistic—even criminal—by Western standards. (In Tagalog)

The Twilight People

1972 Four Associates/Dimension Pictures; 80 minutes/color

Director: Eddie Romero; Screenwriters: Jerome Small, Eddie Romero; Cinematographer: Fred Conde; Editor: Ben Barcelon; Filmscore: Tito Arevalo, Ariston Avelino; Cast: John Ashley, Pat Woodell, Jan Merlin, Charles Macaulay, Pam Grier, Ken Metcalfe, Tony Gosalvez, Kim Ramos, Mona Moreno, Eddie Garcia, Angelo Ventura, Johnny Long, Andres Centenera, Letty Mirasol, Max Rojo, Cenon Gonzalez, Romeo Mabutol, Roger Ocampo, Vic Unson

After a series of women-in-prison sexploiters, the production team of John Ashley and Eddie Romero returned to the horror genre with this film. Not far removed from their Blood Island series, and borrowing heavily from *The Island of Dr. Moreau*, the film stars Ashley as a soldier of fortune abducted by Jan Merlin while scuba diving and taken to the island laboratory of scientist Charles Macaulay, who is trying to create a race of super beings by combining humans and animals. Macaulay feels that Ashley is somehow the ideal subject for his genetic experiments, but runs into a major stumbling block when his daughter (Pat Woodell) falls in love with Ashley. Woodell helps Ashley escape, taking with them Macaulay's dungeon full of animal/human hybrids, Pursued through the jungle by Merlin and his army of men, the monsters do their share in eliminating Macaulay's forces while Ashley kills Merlin. As for Macaulay, he meets his fate at the hands (or limbs, as the case may be) of his wife: half woman/half tree, she is the bitter result of one of the doctor's earlier experiments. No kidding.

Looking like an amateur rush job, the film's time and budgetary restraints are particularly obvious in Tony Arteida's make-up jobs for the various monsters. Arteida had provided the inspired monster make-up for Romero's *Beast of Blood* (1970), but his creatures here do not even come close to his work on that film, though Tony Gosalvez is a hoot as the batman, and Pam Grier makes a sexy panther woman. But by far the best beast here is the one with the least amount of screen time, a man with a wild boar's head, who unfortunately is immediately shot and killed. Ashley and Romero would stay within the fantasy genre for their next collaboration, *Beyond Atlantis* (1973), which would prove to be their only financial loser. (In English)

Mga Uhaw na Bulaklak, Part 2 (The Flower Thirsts, Part 2)

1975 Iyra Ventures; 92 minutes/color

Director: Danilo Cabreira; Screenwriter: Franklin Cabaluna; Cinematographer: Clodualdo Austria; Editor: Rogelio Salvador; Filmscore: Demet Velasquez; Cast: Alona Alegre, Ernie Garcia, Nympha Bonifacio, Trixia Gomez, Marlon Ramirez, Max Laurel, Freddie Quizon, Cloyd Robinson, Tony Santos Sr., Fortunato "Atoy" Co, Brenda del Rio, Bonsie Floro, Mona Lisa, Nemie Velasco, Jojo Santiago, Archie Corteza, Rudy Dino, Gregorio Mercado, Peter Perlas

This sloppy and largely ineffectual melodrama tells the story of a number of slum dwellers and the degrading things they must resort to in order to maintain even their low-level of existence. It happens that they are all driven to stripping and prostitution. One young man works as a male stripper, but earns most of his money by prostituting himself with nasty old women. But when he becomes ill and starts wasting away, he is unable to keep earning to support his wife and child, and he becomes furious when his wife picks up the slack by becoming a prostitute herself. Eventually, driven to despair, the young man commits suicide. Alona Alegre is likewise prostituting herself to support her young son, but she too sickens and dies. The film's only winner is a young woman whose shrewish mother encourages her to become a stripper, and even a prostitute, in order to earn money for them both. But the young lady rises up against her mother and runs off with her boyfriend. The film ends as she stops by to see her old friends and happily shows off the fact that she is pregnant.

Danilo Cabreira's direction is uninventive, and the editing by Rogelio Salvador is irredeemably slipshod, but the film does have one amusing attribute, that being the obnoxious fashions and music that make the 1970s look so riotous in retrospect—it's hard to believe that those fashions made a comeback! One can only hope that *Mga Uhaw na Bulaklak, Part 1* had more going for it than that. (In Tagalog)

Ultimatum

1994 Viva Films; 102 minutes/color

Director: Cirio H. Santiago; Screenwriter: Humilde "Meek" Roxas; Cinematographer: Joe Batac, Jr.; Editor: Gervacio Santos; Filmscore: Nonong Buencamino; Cast: Eddie Garcia, Dina Bonnevie, Vernon Wells, Bob McFarland, Manjo del Mundo, Archie Adamos, Tony Carreon, Ernie Zarate, Joe Sabatino, Jim Broome, Joe Zucchero, Henry Strzalkowski, Ken Metcalfe, Bobby Greenwood, Ramon D'Salva

Policeman Eddie Garcia bids farewell to his girlfriend (Dina Bonnevie) when she accepts a job overseas with Chemco, an American pharmaceutical company. Years later she returns to the Philippines with a group of businessmen to tour the company's new plant near Manila, and Garcia is assigned to work plant security during the tour. He has little time to enjoy his reunion with Bonnevie, however, as the plant is taken over by a virtual army of terrorists led by Vernon Wells, who gains access to the plant by posing as a journalist. Wells demands a $50 million ransom for his hostages or he will use the chemical company's newest product: unknown to the Philippine government, or U.S. ambassador Ken Metcalfe, the chemical company has been developing a new nerve gas. Garcia and the other hostages manage to get loose within the plant, and Wells is infuriated by the number of his men gunned down by the spry Garcia. While Garcia distracts the terrorists, Bonnevie and the only other surviving hostage, Chemco executive Bob McFarland, are supposed to make their escape. It turns out that McFarland is in cahoots with Wells though, and Bonnevie is recaptured. Feeling that his plans are going awry, Wells escapes the plant via helicopter with Bonnevie as hostage, taking a supply of the nerve gas with him. Wells has a ship waiting which is full of well-armed men, but Garcia follows and is able to sneak aboard the ship, where he again causes Wells no end of problems. Eventually, Garcia kills Wells and rescues Bonnevie.

Seeing director Cirio Santiago's work on a Filipino film proper, one is struck by how much more competent his work is here than on the shoddy American co-productions he has been churning out for years for the likes of Roger Corman. Here, unhindered by the brief running time of his work in co-productions, Santiago actually has time to develop his characters, and he stages his action sequences competently. He is also helped considerably by actors the caliber of Garcia, as opposed to Corman's low-rent, no-name players. Though Corman was not involved with this version of the film, his Concorde Pictures simultaneously shot an American version, titled *Stranglehold*, which replaced Filipino stars Garcia and Bonnevie with Americans Jerry Trimble and Jillian McWhirter. As something of a gag, Trimble has a cameo in *Ultimatum* as one of the men aboard Wells' ship, while Garcia takes the same cameo in *Stranglehold*. Humilde Roxas is credited here with the screenplay adaptation, having largely embellished the screenplay of the U.S. version. (In Tagalog and English)

Urban Terrorist

1988 South Cotabato Films; 103 minutes/color
Director: Dante Javier; Screenwriter: Lito Mena; Cinematographer: Rocky; Editor: Joe Ramirez; Filmscore: Gabby Castellano; Cast: Mark Gil, Ronnie Ricketts, Dick Israel, Dhouglas Veron, Juan Rodrigo, Kristel Romero, Tom Olivar, Charlie Davao, E.R. Ejercito, Alex de Leon, Nel de la Ysla, Eva Rica, Vivian Foz, Flora Cristobal, Ariel Antonio, Vic Felipe, Robert Talby, Gerlie Javier

In this very low budget actioner, a group of communist terrorists headed by Mark Gil stage various hits on police officers in the city. Colonel Charlie Davao assigns Lieutenant Dhouglas Veron to head up the task force designated to quash the commies. At the conclusion, the communists all perish in a shootout, culminating in Veron's killing of Gil. While the running time largely consists of the communists planning, then enacting, their hits, or Davao berating Veron's lack of progress in bringing the terrorists to justice, the screenplay makes room for a love triangle within the terrorist group as two of the female members vie for the affections of Gil. There is not much worth mentioning here, other than the casting of popular actors like Gil and Ronnie Ricketts as communist terrorists, while the good guys are represented by pudgy, rather plain Veron. (In Tagalog)

Utol ni Ben Tumbling
(Brother of Ben Tumbling)

1991 Rica Films International; 105 minutes/color

Directors: Diego Cagahastian, Eddy Pajarillo; Cinematographers: Max de la Pena, Roger Baruello, Felizardo Bailen, Jun Rasca; Editor: Francis Vinarao; Filmscore: Demet Velasquez; Cast: Mark Joseph, Paquito Diaz, Conrad Poe, Zandro Zamora, Raoul Aragonn, Dick Israel, Myrna Castillo, Lucita Soriano, Mario Escudero, Vic Varrion, Danny Riel, Eddie del Mar Jr., Naty Santiago, Jack Palomar, Paolo Roces, Efren Abelardo, Boy Cabron Ibanez, Bert Cayanan, Rudy Maningas, Rod Arganosa, Charo Solis, Eruel Tongco, Col. Felix Simon, Romy Llanza

Opening with Lito Lapid's demise at the denouement of 1984's *Ben Tumbling*, this film goes on to chronicle the exploits of Tumbling's brother (Mark Joseph), who joins up with a gang of hold-up artists, making a monkey of Paquito Diaz, whose protection racket is powerless to stop the robberies. Diaz succeeds in abducting Joseph, and his men torture him mercilessly before throwing him from a car and leaving him for dead in the wilderness. Of course, Joseph survives, and embarks on a quest for vengeance. He begins killing off Diaz's men, surpassing their cruelty, until meeting up with and dispatching Diaz himself in a rail yard shootout, after which the police arrive and kill Joseph.

The film is not without its good points, but is seriously flawed: the editing, for instance, is slipshod, and the action sequences are more than a little laughable, with gunmen frequently jumping out from around corners only to stand there seemingly waiting to be shot. Curiously, the film provides no screenwriting credit. (In Tagalog)

Uzi Brothers 9mm

1989 Urban Films; 118 minutes/color
Director: Francis Jun Posadas; Screenwriter: Bert Mendoza; Cinematographer: Ver Dauz; Editor: Nap Montebon; Filmscore: Rey Valera; Cast: Ronnie Ricketts, Sonny Parsons, Perla Bautista, Jaime Fabregas, Renato Robles, Fred Moro, Ruel Vernal, Larry Silva, Leo Lazaro, Val Iglesias, Ben Dato, Griego Gavino, Maritess Suarez, Mercy Dizon, Tony Tacorda, Robert Miller, Job Gavino, Nonong de Andres, Telly Babasa, Eddie Nicart, Dante Javier, Ernie David

Policemen brothers Ronnie Ricketts and Sonny Parsons make some powerful enemies when they mess with the mob: first, the bad guys murder Parsons' fiancé, then, before he even has time to recover from the loss, he and Ricketts have to deal with the murder of their mother (Perla Bautista). Forsaking their calling as peace officers, the two brothers decide to seek vengeance irrespective of the law. They eventually get their revenge, though both are badly wounded in the climactic shootout.

While it probably seemed like a good idea to team Ricketts and Parsons (both popular young action stars at the time), and both of them give good performances, the material is routine. Ricketts' career as an action star would only grow stronger and continued to thrive a decade later, whereas Parsons' popularity seems to have waned in the early 1990s with all of the competition from a plethora of action stars. Before too long, Parsons would leave films for a time to pursue a musical career. (In Tagalog)

Vampira (Vampire Woman)

1994 Regal Films; 115 minutes/color
Director: Joey Romero; Screenwriter: Wali Ching; Cinematographer: Charlie Peralta; Editor: Danny Gloria; Filmscore: Jaime Fabregas; Cast: Maricel Soriano, Christopher de Leon, Jayvee Gayoso, Nida Blanca, Joanne Quintas, Patricia Ann Roque, Caridad Sanchez, Boy 2 Quizon, Lorli Villanueva, Ray Ventura, Ernie Zarate, Eva Darren, Chiqui Xerex Burgos, Pocholo Montes

In this unique take on the vampire theme, a woman distraught over the shooting death of her husband curses her husband's killer, turning him into a vampire. While the man's wife (Nida Blanca) remains free of the curse, their offspring inherit it. Years later, eldest son Jayvee Gayoso has developed into quite a malicious bloodsucker, and with the death of the father, youngest son Boy 2 Quizon begins to show signs of the violent onset of the curse. As the middle child and only daughter (Maricel Soriano) has yet to show any symptoms, Blanca sends her away in the hope that the family curse will bypass her. Soriano arrives at an orphanage run by Catholic priest Ernie Zarate, and Zarate finds a position for her as nanny to widower Christopher de Leon's precocious young daughter. A relationship begins to develop between Soriano and de Leon, to the dismay of Joanne Quintas, who has her own romantic designs on de Leon. Eventually Soriano experiences the onset of the curse and violently attacks and kills a purse snatcher in an alley. From then on she tries to keep her vampiric tendencies in check by killing only chickens. In time, she and de Leon marry, but on their wedding night, as de Leon attempts to make love to his bride, Soriano feels the onset of another vampiric episode and flees the house. In a wonderfully bizarre moment, de Leon follows Soriano into the forest and is shocked to find her gnawing on the neck of a freshly killed deer. Horrified, de Leon flees back to the house. Coincidentally (perhaps too much so), Quintas is also on hand, hiding in the bushes, to witness the strange event, and in a state of shock, she rushes to the authorities. Meanwhile, Soriano's brother Gayoso invades the local church, kills two people and wounds Zarate. In light of this assault, the police begin to take Quintas' story more seriously, and the next day, with an angry mob gathered outside de Leon's house, the police show up and take Soriano to jail. She is set free when de Leon, having recovered fairly well from the shock of seeing his wife gnawing on freshly killed game, goes down to the police station to give Soriano an alibi. He is accompanied by Zarate, who confirms that Soriano was not his attacker, but when Gayoso creeps into the room of the catatonic Quintas and drinks her blood, the locals, knowing of the romantic rivalry between Quintas and Soriano, lay the blame on Soriano, dragging her from the church and proceed with burning her at the stake. Soriano uses her supernatural powers to break free of her bonds and then flees back to the church with de Leon, where they find Gayoso. A battle of vampires ensues, and when Gayoso perishes in flames, somehow the family curse is lifted and both Soriano and younger brother Quizon are freed from their vampirism.

The Filipino perspective on vampirism has always been somewhat unique. Whereas vampire films around the world tend to portray vampires as sexually parasitic creatures that can only be freed through death, Filipino filmmakers frequently use vampires as heroes (or, usually, heroines), who find freedom from their affliction through the power of love and the forgiveness of Christ and the redemption he offers. This can be seen in Teddy Chiu's *Impaktita* (1989) and Peque Gallaga and Lorenzo Reyes' *Halik ng Vampira* (1997). Here, the filmmakers are careful to limit Soriano's killings to animals (with the exception of one petty crook) so as not to lose audience sympathy for the film's star. (In Tagalog)

Vampire Hookers

1978 Cosa Nueva; 79 minutes/color
Director: Cirio H. Santiago, Screenwriter: Howard R. Cohen; Cinematographers: Ricardo Remias, Johnny Araojo; Editor: Herb Bass; Filmscore: Jaime Mendoza-Nava; Cast: John Carradine, Bruce Fairbairn, Trey Wilson, Vic Diaz, Leo Martinez, Karen Stride, Lenka Novak, Katie Dolan, Lex Winter, Mark Campbell, Irving Glick, Ruben Rustia

Director Cirio Santiago's hopelessly unfunny softcore sex/horror comedy follows the exploits of two American sailors (Bruce Fairbairn and Trey Wilson) spending a couple of days' shore leave in Manila. After being conned by local pranksters and going to a bar where they mistake men in drag for women, they eventually wind up in a cemetery where Fairbairn is seduced into staying by three sexy vampire women, who are under the control of vampire John Carradine. The following night Wilson returns to rescue his buddy. The distinguished Carradine should be out of place here, but for the fact that he spent so much of his career appearing in garbage, and Vic Diaz has a very undignified role as Carradine's flatulent, hunchbacked manservant. The softcore sex scenes, which were shot in slow motion, somehow manage to be monotonous and ultimately fail to deliver, which leaves Wilson's occasional Texas colloquialisms as the only bright spot. (In English)

Victim No. 1: Delia Maga (Jesus, Pray for Us!)

1995 Golden Lions Films; 117 minutes/color
Director/screenwriter: Carlo J. Caparas; Cinematographer: Rey de Leon; Editor: Abelardo Hulleza; Filmscore: Boy Alcaide; Cast: Gina Alajar, Joel Torre, Elizabeth Oropesa, Val Victa, Celso Ad. Castillo, Ronnie Lazaro, Fred Moro, Marita Zobel, Tony Tacorda, Nards Belen, Mia Gutierrez, Dexter Doria, Ester Chavez, Danny Labra, Benjie Felipe

Gina Alajar plays the title character in this true crime story about a Filipina maid who is murdered in Singapore. Though her husband (Joel Torre) is a hard worker, the family (which includes three young sons) has a hard time making ends meet, and Alajar accepts a position as a domestic worker in Singapore. Once there she meets and befriends Flor Contemplacion (Elizabeth Oropesa), a fellow Filipina domestic. Oropesa turns out to be mentally disturbed, however, and she murders both Alajar and the young Singaporean boy in her charge—or so the story goes. Torre spends four years trying to discover the truth, but it eludes him. The best he can do is to learn that, although Oropesa was hanged by the Singaporean government for Alajar's murder, an alternative theory had Alajar murdered by her employer, who was enraged upon returning home to find his young son drowned in the bathtub. The film concludes with real footage of authorities exhuming Maga's corpse (with Maga's husband present) in a vain attempt to uncover the truth. There are also tasteless, disturbing real crime scene photos of Maga's corpse lying on the bathroom floor. (In Tagalog)

Victor Meneses: Dugong Kriminal (Victor Meneses: Bloody Criminal)

1993 Octo Arts Films; 103 minutes/color
Director: Jose N. Carreon; Screenwriters: Jose N. Carreon, Jojo M. Lapus, Franklin Osorio; Cinematographer: Felizardo Bailen; Editor: Joe Solo; Filmscore: Nonong Buencamino; Cast: Jeric Raval, Jun Aristorenas, Ogie Alcasid, Tetchie Agbayani, Mikee Villanueva, Shirley Fuentes, Dante Rivero, Perla Bautista, Roldan Aquino, Bomber Moran, Rez Cortez, Ronnel Victor, Lucita Soriano, John Gaddi, Jason Roman, Gerald Ejercito, Berting Labra, Rudy Meyer, Danny Labra, Rommel Valdez, Renato del Prado

Young Jeric Raval follows the lead of his mentor (Jun Aristorenas) and becomes involved in the underworld, warring with Aquino's syndicate. All the while, Raval is also seeking to discover the identity of his father, and he learns that his father (Dante Rivero) is one of Aquino's men (wouldn't you know it?), who has just rejoined Aquino's organization after serving a prison term. Raval begins working with policeman Rez Cortez to bring down Aquino's gang, and during the climactic shootout he is forced to shoot Rivero, wounding him in the leg. Aquino shoots Raval in the shoulder, and the wounded Rivero then saves Raval's life by shooting and killing Aquino. Rivero is then finished off by Cortez. Knowing that his father has saved his life, Raval rushes to Rivero's side as he lay dying, and father and son share a tender moment. The film ends with Raval visiting Rivero's grave. (In Tagalog)

Virgin Forest

1984 Regal Films; 123 minutes/color
Director: Peque Gallaga; Cinematographer: Conrado Baltazar; Editor: Jess Navarro; Filmscore: Jaime Fabregas; Cast: Sarsi Emmanuelle, Miguel Rodriguez, Abel Jurado, Arbie Antonio, Jed Arboleda, Ama Quiambao, Turko, Crispin Medina, Carlos Balasbas, Bruce Fanger, Abbo Q. de la Cruz, Mario Taguiwalo, Ray Ventura, Leo Martinez, Rolando S. Tinio, Romeo Igloria, Bobby Kraut, E.A. Rocha, Cris Daluz, Roy Lachica, Peque Gallaga, Roger Moring

Set in 1901, this is basically an erotic tale centered around a love triangle between Sarsi Emmanuelle, Miguel Rodriguez and Abel Jurado, set against the backdrop of the U.S. capture of Filipino rebel leader Emilio Aguinaldo. Director Peque Gallaga does an excellent job, and the beautiful Emmanuelle proves to be a very capable actress, yet her career doesn't seem to have had any staying power beyond erotica. In terms of dramatic power, cinematic execution and overall content, this film can certainly be considered one of the masterpieces of Filipino cinema, making Gallaga's subsequent career not only perplexing, but his increasing descent into frivolity is a genuine artistic tragedy. Jaime Fabregas won a FAP award for his musical score. (In Tagalog with some English)

Virgin People

1996 Four Aces; 114 minutes/color
Director/screenwriter: Celso Ad. Castillo; Cinematographer: Isagani F. Sioson; Editor: Edgardo Vinarao; Filmscore: Joey Ayala; Cast: Sunshine Cruz, Tonton Gutierrez, Sharmaine Suarez, Anna Capri, Ronaldo Valdez, Roldan Aquino

As he had done with his 1996 film *Isla: The Young Version*, director Celso Ad. Castillo here remakes one of his earlier films. Ronaldo Valdez plays a man living in a remote, mountainous region with his three daughters (Sunshine Cruz, Sharmaine Suarez and Anna Capri). After Valdez is killed by the bite of a cobra, the three sisters find themselves alone, but not for long as a young traveler (Tonton Gutierrez) succeeds in bedding each of the sisters in quick succession. This creates a good deal of friction between the girls, particularly the two older siblings, Cruz and Suarez. It all eventually leads to a fury that results in the deaths of everyone save Capri.

Since the 1970s, Castillo has consistently been one of the most interesting of Filipino directors. The filmmaker got back on track in 1996 after a four-year hiatus and a disappointing return in the early 1990s with a couple of very disappointing features. (In Tagalog)

The Vizconde Massacre: God Help Us!

1993 Golden Lions Films; 119 minutes/color
Director/screenwriter: Carlo J. Caparas; Cinematographer: Ernesto Dominguez; Editor: Abelardo Hulleza; Filmscore: Demet Velasquez; Cast: Romeo Vasquez, Aurora Salve, Kris Aquino, Lady Lee, John Regala, Eddie Fernandez, Tommy Abuel, Marco Polo Garcia, Robert Arevalo, Renato del Prado, Dick Israel, Odette Khan, Jojo Acuin, Fred Moro, Lariza Ledesma, Alex Dona, Nonoy de Guzman, Richie Ylaya, Boy Caparas, Ed Bernardo, Mia Moran

Carlo J. Caparas pretty well found his niche when he made this true crime film that seemed to start a trend in the 1990s of films based on gruesome murders that shocked the nation: Caparas quickly became the king of the genre. This film is about a mother and her two daughters who were brutally murdered and the investigation that went on for years to find the killers. The case was still unsolved at the time of the film, and would be for a decade after: there are those who claim that the police eventually convicted the wrong persons. (In Tagalog with some English)

Wala Akong Binuhay na Kaaway! Ako ang Sasagupa 2 (I Did Not Spare the Life of the Enemy! I Will Prevail 2)

1992 Solid Film International/Jeddfecar Film International; 95 minutes/color
Director: Johnny Wood; Cinematographer: Roger Baruelo; Editor: Ben Samson; Filmscore: Joey Elvina; Cast: Raul "Boy" Fernandez, Franco Guerrero, Honey Policarpio, Ernie Ortega, Lyn Madrigal, Boy Ranay, Rene Balan, Randy Ronquillo, Alex Cabodil, Al Nangka, Eddie Tagalog

This seems to have been an attempt to make a martial arts star of Raul "Boy" Rodriguez by giving him the starring role in what is no more than a standard revenge saga. Fernandez sets out to avenge the murder of his martial arts teacher at the hands of crime boss Franco Guerrero and his thugs. The final third of the film sees Fernandez creeping onto Guerrero's property and slicing up Guerrero's men with a samurai sword (as well as doing away with some of them by the more conventional method of tossing hand grenades), and the film concludes with two protracted showdowns: first, a fairly well choreographed samurai sword fight between Fernandez and Guerrero's last remaining guard, and then a duel to the death with Guerrero himself in which both men die. Technically, Fernandez can be considered the winner, since Guerrero dies first. Though the fight scenes are well handled, the film is badly marred by some very sub-par cinematography, and Johnny Wood's direction is very, uh, wooden. (In Tagalog)

Walang Awa Kung Pumatay (No Mercy Killing)

1990 Omega Releasing Organization; 92 minutes/color
Director: Junn P. Cabreira; Screenwriters: Enrique Mariano, Jun Lawas; Cinematographer: Rudy Dino; Editor: Segundo Ramos; Filmscore:

Demet Velasquez; Cast: Robin Padilla, Rita Avila, Conrad Poe, Dick Israel, Zandro Zamora, Val Iglesias, Bomber Moran, Dexter Doria, Danny Riel, Claudine Gomez, Jenny Ariola, Eddie del Mar, Romy Romulo, Eddie Nicart, Johnny (Boy) Ramirez, Bernard Atienza, Vic Velaro, Jun Hidalgo, July Hidalgo, Erning Mariano, Roger Beraro, Ernie Forte, Roger Moring, Rudy Ramirez

Bad boy Robin Padilla, perhaps the most popular action star among younger Filipino filmgoers, stars in this more-or-less standard revenge/crime saga. He joins up with crime boss Zandro Zamora's organization and is made bodyguard to Zamora's attractive daughter. Padilla begins a brief affair with her (of course), but when she is raped and murdered by one of Zamora's own men, Padilla is fingered for it. Zamora sends a hit squad to get Padilla during a get together with his family, but while the spray of bullets results in a massacre, Padilla is only wounded in the left flank and is patched up by buddy Dick Israel. After recovering, Padilla joins Israel on a crime spree, robbing busses and cabs, but during one hold-up they are confronted by two police officers and are forced to flee, taking Rita Avila as a hostage. They hide out in the country, still holding Avila, and after a while Padilla and Avila begin a romance (which comes as no surprise). Hearing through the grapevine that Padilla is still alive, Zamora sends his men out to try and discover his whereabouts, and so they pay a visit to Padilla's mother (Dexter Doria). They have no luck in getting her to reveal Padilla's location, however, and when Padilla goes home to see his family he finds both his mother and younger sister dead of gunshot wounds to the head. From there, Padilla goes on a rampage, killing Zamora and his gang, wiping most of them out with a double-barreled shotgun. The film concludes with Padilla and Israel attempting to rob a bank, but when the police arrive and surround the building, they are forced to hold the bank's employees hostage. When Padilla and Israel attempt to make their escape, Padilla is shot multiple times and dies.

The film is well executed on just about every level, but does have one glaring continuity error. Padilla's hairstyle changes from very short to long and braided while robbing the bank, which is particularly perplexing at the climax when Padilla has his hair braided while robbing the bank, and even when he is shot, but by the time Avila rushes to cradle his body, he once more has his hair clipped. Such reckless disregard for detail definitely takes the edge off things, damaging an otherwise competent piece of work. Otherwise, there are the usual fisticuffs, and the film is replete with bloody gunshots to the head. (In Tagalog)

Walang Matigas na Buto sa Gutom na Aso (There's No Hard Bone to a Hungry Dog)

1995 Mahogany Pictures/Ultimate Films International; 113 minutes/color

Director/screenwriter: Alex "Boy" Sevilla; Cinematographer: Max dela Pena; Editor: Nonoy Santillan; Filmscore: Jun Garlan; Cast: Palito, Franco Guerrero, Shiela Ysrael, Bob Duran, Berting Labra, Bella Flores, Don Pepot, Ben Sagmit, Alec Loren, Joanna Arriola, Cholo Fernandez, Mayor Boy Estrella, Lily Barbaza, Baby Arriola, Vic Varrion, Danny Riel, Robert Talby, Garry Gallardo, Eric Samonte, Benjie Corpuz, Joker

In this starring role for comedic actor Palito, he travels to Manila with a young boy whose grandfather has just died (yes, it's another country bumpkin in the big city opus), and after getting involved in a community watch program, winds up helping policeman Franco Guerrero bring down a criminal organization led by Berting Labra, of all people. The film climaxes with the police raiding Labra's mansion to rescue two kidnapped girls, resulting in a zany confrontation in which Palito, strangely enough, brings his young friend and a seven-year-old girl along to help. Most of the running time is devoted to the attempts by Palito and his young friend to feed themselves via a number of witless scams. As for Guerrero, he doesn't get much opportunity to employ his martial arts skills, and there is a scene in which he attends a beach party in what is likely the most embarrassing bathing suit of all time. (In Tagalog)

Walang Matigas na Tinapay sa Mainit na Kape (There's No Hard Bread in Hot Coffee)

1994 FPJ Productions; 120 minutes/color

Director: Tony Cruz; Screenwriters: Jose Bartolome, Manuel Buising, Emmanuel Palo; Cinematographers: Ver P. Reyes, Ben Lobo; Editors: Augusto Salvador, Rene Tala; Filmscore: Jaime Fabregas; Cast: Fernando Poe Jr., Alice Dixson, Vandolph, Paquito Diaz, Dencio Padilla, Romy Diaz, Toby Alejar, Dindo Arroyo, Lucita Soriano, Rudy Meyer, Odette Khan, Mely Tagasa, Ernie Zarate, Max Alvarado, Ernie David, Bernie Fabiosa, Rene Hawkins, Nonoy de Guzman, Tony Bernal, Dante

Castro, Zernan Manahan, Kathleen Go Quieng, Boy Santa Maria, Eddie Gicoso, Joed Dawal, Ernie David Jr., Melvin Malbog

Again, Fernando Poe, Jr., lightens the tone by teaming with a young child (in this case Vandolph) for this action/comedy/musical/drama. Vandolph lives with his abusive, alcoholic mother and her equally abusive boyfriend (Ernie David), but when his mother runs off with David and leaves him behind, Vandolph struggles to get along with the other street urchins. He is beaten by the rougher kids, however, and Poe becomes Vandolph's mentor, teaching him to fight so that he can teach his tormentors a lesson. Poe likewise deals with local gang members Romy Diaz and Dindo Arroyo, while also wooing Alice Dixson away from her beau. It's all reasonably entertaining in an odd way, and as in *One Day Isang Araw* (1988), which saw Poe sing a number of tunes with child star Matet de Leon, here he also croons a number. Vandolph sings a few as well, and there is one ensemble number featuring the unlikely musical trio of Paquito Diaz, Max Alvarado and Dencio Padilla. (In Tagalog)

Walang Susuko
(No Surrender)

1988 Teejay Films; 104 minutes/color
Director: Francis "Jun" Posadas; Cinematographer: Apolinar Cuenco; Editor: Rodel Capule; Filmscore: Gabby Castellano; Cast: Jess Lapid Jr., Charlie Davao, Danny Riel, Johnny Vicar, Ronald Nepomuceno, Eric Borbon, Eddie Gicoso, Ben Romano, Boy Macasaet, Clyde Maturan, Alfred Enriquez, Glenda Garcia, Joe Baltazar, Turko Cervantes, Nonong de Andres, Andy Durango, Gerry Roman, Jeric Vasquez, Jun Mendoza, Ros Olgado, Dave Moreno

After a physical altercation with superior officer Danny Riel, army sergeant Jess Lapid, Jr., is thrown in the brig. He and some of his fellow detainees escape and Lapid goes A.W.O.L. Meanwhile, anti-government rebel Johnny Vicar and his army in the mountainous region of Mindanao have kidnapped the daughter of prominent judge Charlie Davao. Unsatisfied with the government's plan of action, Davao seeks out Lapid and has him put together a team of men to go on a rescue mission. Lapid locates Vicar's camp and succeeds in retrieving Davao's daughter, but while making their escape they run into Riel's troops. Seeing that Vicar and his army are bearing down on them, Riel and Lapid reluctantly join forces. They are still outnumbered, however, and find themselves pinned down and surrounded on all sides. What ensues is a two-day battle which, for Riel, Lapid and their men, looks hopeless. But just when things look bleakest, two government helicopters arrive and all but wipe out Vicar's troops. While the final third of the film, devoted to the ongoing battle, is occasionally gripping, overall the film offers nothing special. (In Tagalog)

Walls of Hell

1964 Hemisphere Pictures/Filipinas Productions; 88 minutes/black & white
Directors: Gerardo de Leon, Eddie Romero; Screenwriters: Ferde Grofe Jr., Cesar Amigo, Eddie Romero; Cinematographer: Felipe Sacdalan; Filmscore: Tito Arevalo; Cast: Jock Mahoney, Fernando Poe Jr., Mike Parsons, Oscar Roncal, Paul Edwards Jr., Ely (Kim) Ramos Jr., Fred Galang, Cecilia Lopez, Arsenio Alonzo, Vance Skarstadt, Claude Wilson, Pedro Navarro, Carpi Asturias, Paquito Salcedo, Tommy Romulo, Andres Centenera, Angel Buenaventura (Angelo Ventura), Alex Swanbeck, Willie Salcedo, George Kramer

This grim, much overlooked film chronicles the last days of the Japanese occupation during WWII, as thousands of Japanese marines refuse to surrender, taking refuge in the walled city of Intramuros, where they are also holding some 20,000 Filipino citizens prisoner. The U.S. Army tries to dislodge the Japanese, battering the city walls with mortar fire day and night, but despite the constant barrage, the Japanese hold the city for three weeks. Jock Mahoney plays an embittered U.S. captain and Fernando Poe, Jr., co-stars as an angry Filipino sergeant who convinces him to storm the walled city and free the civilian captives. In a fierce battle, the Japanese fight to the last man, but are finally defeated.

Excellently directed by Gerardo de Leon and Eddie Romero, the film features an impressive climactic battle sequence, and fine performances by Mahoney and Poe. While in the Philippines, Mahoney also starred in Romero's *Moro Witch Doctor* (1964). (In English)

Wanted: Pamilya Banal
(Wanted: Banal Family)

1988 FPJ Productions; 127 minutes/color
Director: Pablo Santiago; Screenwriter: Pablo S. Gomez, Fred Navarro; Cinematographer: Ver P. Reyes; Editor: Augusto Salvador; Filmscore: Jaime Fabregas; Cast: Fernando Poe Jr., Charo Santos, Armida Siguion-Reyna, Rosemarie Gil, Zandro Zamora, Dranreb Belleza, John Regala, Cristina Gonzales, Ann Kimper, Paquito Diaz, Lito Anzures, Vic

Varrion, Tony Carreon, Mario Escudero, Ernie Zarate, Nanding Fernandez, Marco Polo Garcia, Nonoy de Guzman, Jose Romulo, Charlie Davao

In this story of greed and familial feuding, Fernando Poe, Jr., is voted out of the family business by half-brother Zandro Zamora and stepmother Armida Siguion-Reyna. As a result, Poe is forced to move his family out of their spacious upper-class home and into a more modest dwelling. The bitter feelings within the two factions of the family spill over into the younger generation, as Poe's son (Dranreb Belleza) and Zamora's son (John Regala) brawl and engage in a rivalry that ends with a tragic drag race in which Regala is killed when his car plows into a passing truck. The family feud then kicks into overdrive, and Poe finds that he and his family are not welcome at Regala's funeral. Not long after, Belleza is stabbed and killed, and Zamora hires Paquito Diaz and a group of thugs to kill Poe and his entire family. Poe sees this coming and is able to hustle his family out of the house and to safety, but when Diaz discovers their rural safe house, Poe and his family (wife, two teenage daughters and a young son) are forced to flee into the forest. Over a period of a day-and-a-half, Poe is able to wipe out Diaz's men with his rifle, and then captures Diaz himself, dragging him back to Zamora's house and disrupting the family dinner. The police arrive, and when Poe explains things, Zamora pulls out a gun with the intention of shooting Poe, but accidentally shoots Siguion-Reyna instead before he is gunned down by the police. The film closes happily with Poe and his family sitting down to dinner, having been restored to their former prestige.

This is a somewhat different type of Poe film: for starters, though he is obviously the film's main star, there is much more of an ensemble cast made up of prominent performers. The film also has somewhat of a youthful bent, chronicling the lives of the children of both Poe and Zamora (beach parties, brawling, drag racing), which tends to push Poe out of the story for surprising stretches of time. There is also the fact that the film's first hour is given over to melodramatics driven by the family feud, without a single shot being fired. Poe has only one fight scene, and the gunplay is basically saved for the final half-hour.

Pablo Santiago's direction is solid, and the performances are good, with Belleza giving a pretty fiery turn as Poe's ill-fated son. Regala gives his usual manic, wide-eyed characterization, and Siguion-Reyna, whose face lends itself to sour-puss roles, is typecast again as a thoroughly despicable matriarch. Overall, as Poe films go, this is a cut above the norm. (In Tagalog)

Warden

1992 El Nino Films; 108 minutes/color

Director: Cesar Sb. Abella; Screenwriters: Ruben Rustia, Humilde "Meek" Roxas; Editor: Tony Sy; Filmscore: Crispin Sarmiento; Cast: Baldo Marro, Ali Sotto, Harlene Bautista, Carol Dauden, Ruben Rustia, Romy Diaz, Roldan Aquino, Ernie Forte, Rocco Montalban, Manjo del Mundo, Hero Bautista, Joed Serrano, Cesar Sb. Abella, Jose Romulo, Edward Salvador, Bebeng Amora, Danny Labra

In this extremely downbeat prison melodrama, Baldo Marro assumes the job of warden of a prison after his predecessor (Roldan Aquino) is killed by an inmate. Marro reforms the corrupt prison system, much to the chagrin of the guards, who long for the good old days when their brutality was the norm. Marro goes berserk after returning home one night to find his wife with another man, whom he kills during the ensuing struggle. As a result, he is then incarcerated in his own prison, as sadistic guard Romy Diaz becomes the new warden. Diaz makes a point of making things tough on Marro, and when Marro's son comes to visit, the guards accuse him of trying to smuggle a knife in to his father. Upon hearing that his son has been brutalized by the guards, Marro murders Diaz and two of the guards, which gets him transferred to a federal penitentiary. The film ends by jumping years into the future as an elderly Marro returns home to his son and daughter on Christmas Eve and sees his granddaughter for the first time.

Marro gives a good, if relentlessly dour, performance, and there is also a superb performance from co-screenwriter Ruben Rustia as an elderly inmate destined to die in prison. (In Tagalog)

Wating (Street Smart)

1994 MAQ Films; 84 minutes/color

Director: Ishmael Bernal; Screenwriters: Floy Quintos; Cinematographer: Charlie Peralta; Editor: Danny Gloria; Filmscore: Jaime Fabregas; Cast: Richard Gomez, Janice de Belen, Cherie Gil, Carmina Villaroel, Bembol Roco, Celeste Legaspi, Dave Brodett, Pen Medina, Cita Astals, Frannie Zamora, Mike Gayoso, Leo Rabago, Jun Palattao, Danny Rojo

Carmina Villaroel escapes from a women's rehabilitation center and takes up with petty crook Richard Gomez. Before long, they both join up with the car theft ring of socialite Cherie Gil. But they cross Gil, and wind up having to escape amid a hail of gunfire from both the police and Gil's goons. Despite receiving Urian nominations for Best Director, Best Picture, Best Actor (Gomez, who won), and Best Actress (Villaroel, who didn't), this is a pretty uneven work. Though sometimes visually striking, and stylishly directed by Ishmael Bernal, the film is somewhat marred by the director's tendency toward overstatement, particularly regarding the filmmaker's pet peeve of religious hypocrisy, here rather glaringly represented by a character who prides herself on her charity work and lives in a house full of religious icons and paraphernalia, yet treats her servant (Janice de Belen) like a sub-human slave. The film also expresses a very pronounced scorn for power and high society in general (aside from Gil's unsavory character, there is also the fact that Villaroel is raped by a prominent politician at a glitzy social gathering). But amid all of the feigned religiosity, Bernal ends the film with a sincere Christian overture as Gomez and Villaroel, stranded on a country road, accept a ride from a distinctly Christ-like figure who silently gestures for them to climb into the back of his rickety truck. The driver bears an unmistakable resemblance to the pictures and icons of Jesus that are prominent throughout the film, and the way in which he silently gestures for Gomez and Villaroel to accept his charity calls to mind traditional renderings of Christ. Bernal is obviously juxtaposing religious pretense with true Christian spirit, but aside from that, the film is conceptually flimsy. (In Tagalog with some English)

Whiteforce

1988 Eastern Film Management Corp./FGH; 86 minutes/color

Director: Eddie Romero; Screenwriter: Henry Tefay; Cinematographer: Joe Batac; Editor: Garvacio Santos; Filmscore: Ryan Cayabyab; Cast: Sam Jones, Kimberly Pistone, Timothy Hughes, Raoul Aragonn, Jimmy Fabregas, Vic Diaz, Ruben Rustia, Ken Metcalfe, Mike Monty, Tsing Tong Tsai, Tony Ogumsanya, Eric Romero, John Falch, Mauricio Go, Raymond, Algini, Luisa Catanea, Pong Pong, Eric Khan, Frank Juhasz, Jun Juban, Tracy Tuazon

After his production partnership with American actor John Ashley had ended in the mid-1970s, director Eddie Romero continued to occasionally dabble in international co-productions with pictures like the 1983 film *Desire*. In this effort, co-produced with Australia and the U.S., Sam Jones plays an American agent after a computer chip that contains details and names pertaining to an international drug trafficking network run by Australian Timothy Hughes and involving crooked U.S. government agent Mike Monty. Originally thinking that Jones is responsible for the death of her father, U.S. agent Ken Metcalfe, Kimberly Pistone at first seeks to kill him, but she winds up joining forces with Jones and his eccentric computer wiz buddy Jimmy Fabregas. Together they eventually bring down the drug syndicate and win over Jones' nemeses, gruff Manila policeman Vic Diaz. Played with an emphasis on humor, the film is slight, but surprisingly entertaining and inoffensive, although it is hampered somewhat by a customarily feeble score, in this case provided by Ryan Cayabyab. Still, it is good to see Romero free of the obnoxiousness of some of his early '70s co-productions, which tended to express their artistic freedom merely through excess vulgarity. (In English)

Wild

1979 J.P.M. Productions; 91 minutes/color

Director: Danilo P. Cabreira; Screenwriter: Sandy Garcia; Cinematographer: Vic Anao; Editor: Joe Solo; Cast: Lorna Tolentino, Gina Alajar, Ricky Belmonte, Manny Luna, Anna Gonzales, Johnny Wilson, Michael Sandico, Joe Fabregas, Sandy Garcia, Romano Kristoff, Dante Javier, Marissa del Mar, Lily Miraflor, Alma Lerma, Bing Hinson, Ed Villafol, Jeffrey Cruz

Lorna Tolentino portrays a young lass living in a rural area where she earns a meager living working in the tobacco fields. The old woman who raised her is ailing, and unable to afford to buy her medicine, Tolentino goes to a local merchant for assistance. He agrees to help her, but only if Tolentino will sleep with him. Though she initially refuses, Tolentino soon enough relents, but just as soon tires of the arrangement. She hatches a plan, stealing all of the man's cash, then tearing her dress and screaming rape (ah, that old standby). We last see the man being beaten to a pulp by angry locals while Tolentino watches with a self-satisfied look. Tolentino leaves a goodbye letter for the old lady, which includes some of the money she stole, which she leaves to keep the old lady in medicine, and she takes the rest of the cash and hops a bus for the big city. Once there, she makes connections quickly, and she begins a romance with Ricky Belmonte. She ends things with him, however, after finding out that he has been unfaithful, and she moves on to a relationship with a young film director who puts her in adult films: unfortunately, Tolentino's popularity wanes and the director moves on to another girl. So what's Tolentino to do? Well, she finds a new partner in Johnny Wilson, a wealthy older man. He also turns out to be Belmonte's father (gee, how's that for a coincidence?), and after seeing Belmonte again, Tolentino rekindles things with him as well. Upon hearing of the death of the woman who raised her, Tolentino returns home briefly to attend the funeral, and afterward she takes the time to go through the old lady's belongings, thereby finding documentation revealing the identity of her real mother. Would you believe that her natural mother is currently married to Wilson? Wow, another astounding coincidence! Tolentino meets her real mother, but finds her to be a very cold woman; she also discovers that her mother is carrying on an affair with a younger man. So what does Tolentino do? She seduces her mother's boyfriend, of course. Why? Well, why not? After all, he's one of the few male cast members that she hasn't already been to bed with. She then has another big idea and sets up a video camera to record her mother in a tryst with her young lover. She then calls everyone together—her mother, her mother's lover, Wilson, and Belmonte—and after announcing that she has had enough of games-playing, proceeds to shock them all by screening the tape. Pretty self-righteous for a tobacco road whore, huh? Tolentino then returns to her hometown and the boyfriend she left behind.

This is a soap so irredeemably stupid that it is impossible to see it as anything more than a bad joke with a punch line much too late in coming. Wild, indeed. (In Tagalog)

The Woman Hunt

1972 Four Associates/New World; 75 minutes/color

Director: Eddie Romero; Screenwriter: David Hoover; Cinematographer: Justo Paulino; Editors: Ben Barcelon, Joe Zucchero; Filmscore: Jerry Dadap; Cast: John Ashley, Pat Woodell, Sid Haig, Laurie Rose, Charlene Jones, Eddie Garcia, Lisa Todd, Alona Alegre, Ken Metcalfe, Liza Belmonte, Lotis Key, Alfonso Carvajal, Ruben Rustia, Don Lipman, Tony Gosalvez, Paquito Salcedo

In this rehash of *The Most Dangerous Game* (1932), insane millionaire Eddie Garcia hires John Ashley, Sid Haig and Ken Metcalfe to kidnap women for him and bring them to his isolated island mansion in the jungle. The idea is to turn them loose in the jungle so that Garcia and his invited guests (wealthy corporate types and foreign dignitaries) can hunt them down. Feeling the pangs of conscience, Ashley helps the women escape, and flees with them, with Garcia and his hunting party in hot pursuit. Of the escapees, only Ashley and Laurie Rose survive, while Pat Woodell and Liza Belmonte are shot, and Charlene Jones succumbs to a cobra bite.

Garcia manages to rise above the material and has no trouble standing out among all of the other bland performances, though Haig is good too, giving another of his playfully obnoxious performances. Among the many disappointing aspects, Ruben Rustia—a fine actor—is given shamefully little to do, while Lisa Todd, playing Garcia's sadistic lesbian housemate, is an abomination. Ashley and director Eddie Romero would also collaborate on *The Twilight People* that same year. (In English)

Women in Cages

1971 New World Pictures; 81 minutes/color

Director: Gerardo de Leon; Screenwriters: James H. Watkins, David R. Osterhout; Cinematographer: Felipe Sacdalan; Editor: Ben Barcelon; Filmscore: Tito Arevalo; Cast: Jennifer Gan, Judy Brown, Roberta Collins, Pam Grier, Bernard Bodine (Bonnin), Charles Davis (Davao), Johnny Long, Holly Anders, Roberta Swift, Paquito Diaz, Ramon D'Salva, Andres Centenera, Ruben Rustia, Paquito Salcedo

Director Gerardo de Leon's entry in the women-in-prison genre is considerably darker than the works of directors like Jack Hill and Eddie Romero. Jennifer Gan stars as a naïve young woman who takes the fall for her boyfriend, sleazy drug dealer Charlie Davao, and is sent to prison after being caught with a purse full of heroin. The police try to get Gan to roll over on Davao, but being very much in love with him, she follows Davao's instructions to keep silent while he has his lawyers try to free her. Once in prison, Gan survives a number of attempts on her life by one of her cellmates (junkie Roberta Collins, who has been paid in heroin by Paquito Diaz, one of Davao's men, to eliminate Gan and thereby keep her quiet). Along with her other cellmates—including Judy Brown, who like Collins had just completed serving time in Hill's *The Big Doll House* (1971)—Gan endures maltreatment at the hands of the sadistic lesbian head matron Pam Grier, who has a particular hatred for Americans, which she vents by taking them to "the Playpen," a gothic torture chamber that conjures up images of the Inquisition. Gan and her cellmates manage to escape, taking Grier as hostage, and after Grier is raped and killed by some bandits in the jungle, Brown is rescued by police, who keep her from the clutches of Davao's men. The film climaxes aboard Davao's ship, a floating bordello called the *Zulu Queen*, when two undercover cops board her and rescue Gan, shooting and killing Davao in the process. As for Collins, she is left to live out her life as a drug-addicted prostitute aboard the *Zulu Queen*, and the film closes with a grim shot of her, strung-out and perspiring, lying beneath another faceless john.

The screenplay doesn't stray far from genre conventions (catfights, shower scenes, torture, and the inevitable breakout), but what manages to set the film apart from similar works is de Leon's interesting sense of cinematic composition. Art director Ben Otico also deserves mention for the interiors of the prison, which occasionally—and somewhat surprisingly—call to mind the sets of the German expressionist cinema of the silent era.

The film's credits include a number of bogus names (Dwight Howard, Paul Sawyer, Jeffrey Taylor), any one of which could be pseudonyms for the otherwise unbilled Filipino actors Paquito Diaz, Ruben Rustia, Ramon D'Salva and Andres Centenera. This was apparently the last co-production for de Leon and therefore, sadly, his last film to see distribution in the Western market. (In English)

Women of Hell's Island

1978; 72 minutes/color
Director: Cirio H. Santiago; Screenwriters: Ken Metcalfe, Cirio H. Santiago; Cinematographer: Ben Lobo; Editors: Willy Asuncion, Gervacio Santos, Rufino Cabrales; Filmscore: Nonong Buencamino; Cast: Ingrid Greer, Nanette Martin, Kerry Nichols, Bernadette Williams, Ken Metcalfe, Rosemarie Gil, Sherry Greenwood, Bill Baldridge, Jose Mari Avellana, Nigel Hogge, Victor Ordonez, Bob Hood, Easy Black, Helen McNeely

A prostitution ring abducts women, taking them to a jungle prison camp where they are taken out in groups by night to earn money. There are the usual women-in-prison elements, including catfights, torture, the by then stereotypical tough, cynical, streetwise black woman, and the film concludes with the inevitable breakout. The script (by director Cirio Santiago and Ken Metcalfe) is sleazy, but surprisingly devoid of nudity. Metcalfe is featured in one of the more substantial roles, playing the heavy in the jungle prison camp; as usual, Santiago's direction is drab. (In English)

Wonder Vi

1973 JE Productions; 113 minutes/color
Cast: Vilma Santos, George Estregan, Marissa Delgado, Romy Diaz, Angelo Ventura, Ely Roque, Avel Morado, Paquito Salcedo, Jesse Lee

In this entertainingly campy '70s vehicle for Vilma Santos, a U.S. space capsule comes back down to earth, landing in a jungle in the Philippines. On board is a little black poodle, which the U.S. Government would like to retrieve for study. Toward that end, the U.S. offers a $200,000 reward for the dog, which sends all manner of profiteers into the jungle to hunt for it. Aside from a Filipino military unit, the jungle is also besieged by a group of bandits and an outlaw biker gang led by Romy Diaz. But cute jungle girl Santos has already found the pooch and adopted it as her pet. Diaz's gang eventually teams up with the bandits to try and get the dog away from the spunky jungle girl, but Santos is aided by scrawny tough guy George Estregan, as well as receiving assistance from Marissa Delgado and her boyfriend, who had initially planned to take the dog and collect the reward themselves. Together, the group put up a good fight against the bad guys, but they are hopelessly outnumbered and seem to be defeated when the Filipino military shows up. The military arrests all of the bad guys and they confiscate the dog, but upon seeing Santos heartbroken, the military commander turns the dog loose and it runs back into Santos' arms.

This is pure hokum, which is really where its entertainment value lies. Santos was in the process of emerging as one of the superstars of Filipino cinema, and it's easy to see why she has always been so popular: here we get to see her as a young cutie in a leopard skin outfit, kicking and thumping the bad guys (she sings a song too!). There is also the spectacle of the usually thuggish Angelo Ventura as a very gay member of the group of bandits. There is all of this and a cheesy filmscore too. This is good stuff. (In Tagalog)

Working Boys

1985 Viva Films; 114 minutes/color
Director/screenwriter: Mike Relon Makiling; Cinematographer: Ben Lobo; Editor: Ike Jarlego, Jr.; Filmscore: Tito Sotto; Cast: Tito Sotto, Vic Sotto,

Joey de Leon, Herbert Bautista, Chichay, Eula Valdez, Yayo Aguila, Cheska Inigo, Dindo Fernando, Gina Pareno, Rio Locsin, Carmi Martin, Bomber Moran, Max Alvarado, Paquito Diaz, Ruel Vernal, Joaquin Fajardo, Manjo del Mundo, Palito, Ben David, Larry Silva, Balot, Matimtiman Cruz, Jimmy Santos, Julie "Piling" del Mar, Ben Dato, Evelyn Vargas, Malou de Guzman

Herbert Bautista goes to stay with his uncles (comedy trio Tito, Vic and Joey) and they put him to work with them. Making their living doing odd jobs, the film meanders for an hour-and-a-half as the boys bungle one repair job after another, including repairing cars, televisions, phones and alarm clocks. Vic even accepts a job babysitting a bratty little boy, and the guys also perform an exorcism (!), one of the few assignments they succeed at. Otherwise, the film chronicles the romantic escapades of young Bautista. Most of the film's gags fall pretty flat, but things at least—and at last—come to life at the conclusion when the angry locals, tired of the shoddy work done for them by our heroes, form a mob and converge on the trio's workshop. They are interrupted, however, by news that a gang of thugs has taken some schoolgirls hostage, and Tito, Vic, Joey and Herbert go charging to the rescue. Arriving in S.W.A.T. uniforms (and accompanied by the theme song from the 1970s U.S. TV series *S.W.A.T.*), the boys defeat bad guys Paquito Diaz, Max Alvarado, Bomber Moran and Ruel Vernal in a slapstick showdown worthy of the Three Stooges, becoming town heroes in the process.

The enormous box office popularity of Tito, Vic and Joey insured a steady stream of product, but as fast as they were cranking them out, quality material doesn't seem to have been a major consideration. From here the trio went on to do *Good ... Ah!* And *Naku ... Ha!* (both in 1985) for director Junn Cabreira before re-teaming with director Mike Relon Makiling again for the unspectacular *Give Me Five!* (also in 1985). It is interesting that Makiling had written the screenplay for director Celso Ad. Castillo's classic 1973 horror film *Patayin Mo sa Sindak si Barbara*, because his subsequent career has been devoted almost entirely to comedy. (In Tagalog)

Wow ... Multo
(Wow ... Ghost)

1997 MAQ Productions; 103 minutes/color
Director: Tony Y. Reyes; Screenwriters: Al Marcelo, Woodrow Serafin, Tony Y. Reyes; Cinematographer: Baby Buenaceda; Editor: Eduardo Jarlego; Filmscore: Boy Alcaide; Cast: Joey de Leon, Alma Concepcion, Judy Ann Santos, Wowie de Guzman, Daniel Pasia, Paquito Diaz, Yoyong Martirez, Rez Cortez, Don Pepot, Lou Veloso, Danny Cruz, Bing Angeles, Manny Castaneda, Penggot, Subas Herrero, Jimmy Fabregas, Palito, Rey "Aminin" Pumaloy, Vangie Labalan, Maning Bato, Danny Labra, Nonong de Andres, Aisha Galon, Ronel Guadania, Rene Requiestas

Despite re-teaming with Tony Y. Reyes, director and co-screenwriter of some of Joey de Leon's more satisfying work, this may be de Leon's worst offering. Playing an outspoken radio show host, de Leon enrages crooked Paquito Diaz by turning down a bribe and exposing the use of street children as slave labor by Diaz's company. Diaz has de Leon killed, but Joey returns from the grave, and after playfully haunting his friends and former co-workers, he takes possession of his girlfriend, TV hostess Alma Concepcion, while she is on the air, and rails against the exploitation of street urchins, causing Diaz and his thugs to target Concepcion. But by then de Leon has made himself known to Concepcion and helps her defeat the bad guys.

There is an interesting, albeit brief, reunion with de Leon's former comedy sidekick Rene Requiestas, but even by the standards of Filipino comedy in general, which at its best has always had an over-reliance on slapstick, this film manages to be singularly obnoxious, spilling over with annoying characters, almost nonstop screaming, shameless overacting, witless physical humor and an abundance of flamboyantly gay stereotypes. In short, this is just dreadful. (In Tagalog with some English)

Zuma

1986 Cinesuerte; 130 minutes/color
Director: Jun Raquiza; Screenwriter: Manny Rodriguez; Cinematographer: Alfonzo Alvarez; Editor: Serafin Dineros; Filmscore: Marita Manuel, Demet Velasquez; Cast: Max Laurel, Snooky Serna, Mark Gil, Dang Cecilio, Charlie Davao, Rey "PJ" Abellana, Racquel Monteza, Ella de Cordova, Maria Montes, Maria Blanca, Manny Rodriguez, Mark Joseph, Vicky Ramos, Pat Centenera, Ross Molina, Tony Carreon, Sheila Talabis, Philip Pascual

Adapted from a Filipino komiks serial, Zuma is a nasty, green-skinned demon with a large two-headed snake wrapped around his neck. Portrayed by Max Laurel, Zuma is set free from his tomb by an archeological team headed by Mark Gil, who unwittingly frees the demon while excavating an ancient temple. Once free, Zuma rapes a young woman who then becomes his accomplice, luring young women to him so that he can rip their hearts out and eat them. After terrorizing the population for a while, Zuma is lured into a trap and captured in a steel cage, while his accomplice is thrown in prison where she is beaten to death by a prison guard. Since she was pregnant at the time of her death, doctors seeking to study the fetus extract it for their research and are shocked when it leaps out and terrorizes the surgical team. The child—a girl—also has a two-headed serpent draped around her neck, but being half human, she does not share her father's green complexion. The baby is adopted by Gil and his wife (Dang Cecilio), and years later grows into a pretty teenager (Snooky Serna), who hides her serpentine appendage in her long braids, thereby appearing to be a normal human girl. When Zuma breaks free and embarks on another reign of terror, Serna takes it upon herself to stop him, and she follows him down to his subterranean crypt where they are both buried by a cave-in. Both Zuma and daughter would return in a sequel, *Anak ni Zuma*, the following year, though Serna would not reprise her role.

Unlike a good many horror films (mainly from the West), which over-exert themselves in the pursuit of the bizarre, the weirdness flows effortlessly here. The effects are good, with enough gruesomeness to likely satisfy any fan of the genre. Though the running time is customarily excessive, director Jun Raquiza keeps things moving at a good pace most of the way: unfortunately, the final twenty minutes—while the film is building to its climax, no less—tend to drag on and on as Serna, Davao and young soldier Rey "PJ" Abellana (who has fallen in love with Serna) sweat out their time trapped in Zuma's lair while the military frets over what to do next. Even still, overall this is a fairly good horror film. The same cannot be said of the film's sequel, which derives most of its entertainment from its camp value. (In Tagalog)

Chapter Notes

Chapter 1

1. Although this is an oft-quoted remark, its origins are obscure.
2. Bautista, Arsenio "Boots." *History of Philippine Cinema*. (http://www.ncca.gov.ph/culture&arts/cularts/arts/cinema/cinema-history1.htm)
3. Hernando, Mario A. "A History of Philippine Cinema." *The Golden Years: Memorable Tagalog Movie Ads, 1946–1956*. Danny Dolor, Manila: 1994. p. 24.
4. Bautista.
5. Bautista.
6. Bautista.
7. Karnow, Stanley. *In Our Image: America's Empire in the Philippines*. Ballantine, New York: 1989. p. 78.
8. Hernando. P. 24. Hernando cites Philippine film archivist Agustin L. Sotto as the source of this information, though he does not cite its publication.
9. Bautista.
10. Hernando, P. 24.
11. Bautista; also Hernando, p. 27.
12. Bautista.
13. Bautista.
14. Bautista.
15. Cabagnot, Ed. "Notes on the History of Philippine Cinema," *Focus on Filipino Films: A Sampling, 1951–1982*. p. 4.
16. Bautista.
17. Biographical information regarding Jose Rizal comes from Karnow.
18. Hernando, P. 27. Hernando again cites Sotto.
19. Bautista. *History of Philippine Cinema* (Part 2). (http://www.ncca.gov.ph/culture&arts/cularts/arts/cinema/cinema-history2.htm)
20. Bautista;
21. Hernando, p. 27; also Bautista makes mention of Teague and Goulette opening the Cine Anda on August 8, 1909.
22. Hernando, p. 27.
23. Hernando, p. 27.
24. Historical data is again drawn from Karnow.
25. Andrade, Pio, Jr. "Chinese Filipinos Producer of First Filipino Movie." (http://www.tsinoy.com/Roots/TheBeatenPath.cfm?ID=711)
26. Karnow.
27. Karnow.
28. Hernando, p. 28, again citing Sotto.
29. de Vega, Guillermo C. *Film and Freedom: Movie Censorship in the Philippines*. Manila: 1975. p. 7.
30. Bautista (2).
31. Hernando, p. 28.
32. Karnow, pp. 14–15.
33. Lumbera, Bienvenido. *Keynote Address, Silliman University Symposium on Film and Literature*. November 22, 2002. (http://www.geocities.com/icasocot/lumbera_film lit.html)
34. Hernando, p. 28.
35. Hernando, p. 28.
36. White, Timothy. *Politics, Art and Bomba Queens: The Cinema of the Philippines*. (http://www.nus.edu.sg/NUS info/CFA/arts/13.htm)
37. Garcia, Roger. *Mission Impossible: Filipine Filmmaking 1896–1986*. (http://www.spaziocultura.it/gallery/cecu dine/fe_2001/ENG/filippine_s_eng.htm) also; Hernando, p. 21.
38. Cabagnot, p. 4.
39. Lumbera, Bienvenido. *Philippine Cinema Beginnings*. (http://www.filipinoheritage.com/arts/phil-cinema/beginnings.htm)
40. Luzentales, Benny. "Quezon film pioneer 'kisses' career goodbye," *The Manila Times*, Saturday, November 29, 2003. (http://www.manilatimes.net/national/2003/nov/29/yehey/prov/20031129pro13.html)
41. Giron, Eric S. "Gregorio Fernandez," *Focus on Filipino Films: A Sampling, 1951–1982*. pp. 30–31.
42. Information regarding Cooper's affair with MacArthur was drawn from a number of sources. Aside from Karnow's previously cited work, the author also made use of William Manchester's *American Caesar: Douglas MacArthur 1880–1964* (Dell paperback edition, 1983), and Carol Morris Petillo's *Douglas MacArthur: The Philippine Years* (Indiana University Press, 1981).

Chapter 2

1. Lumbera, Bienvenido. *Philippine Cinema Beginnings*. Filipino Heritage.com. (http://www.filipinoheritage.com/arts/phil-cinema/beginnings.htm)
2. Hernando, Mario A. "A History of Philippine Cinema," *The Golden Years: Memorable Tagalog Movie Ads, 1946–1956*. Danny Dolor, Manila: 1994. p. 28.
3. Giron, Eric S. "Gregorio Fernandez," *Focus on Filipino Films: A Sampling, 1951–1982*. p. 31.
4. The information regarding the December 8, 1932 edition of *Graphic* was taken from Arsenio "Boots" Bautista's *History of Philippine Cinema* (http://www.ncca.gov.ph/culture&arts/cularts/arts/cinema/cinema-history1.

htm). The premiere date for *Ang Aswang* comes from the afore-cited Hernando piece (p. 28).

5. The premiere date for *Punyal na Ginto* comes from the afore-cited Bautista piece. In his introductory chapter, "Notes on the History of Philippine Cinema," published in the book *Focus on Filipino Films: A Sampling, 1951–1982*, Ed Cabagnot is either unaware of *Ang Aswang*, or chooses to ignore it, and lists *Punyal na Ginto* as the first Filipino sound film (p. 5).

6. Hernando, pp. 30–31.
7. Hernando, p. 30.
8. The Capra and Lubitsch quotes come from the *Zamboanga* promotional press kit issued in 1937.
9. Server, Lee. "Our Man in Manila," *Film Comment*, March 1999.
10. Cueto, Eric. "Rosa del Rosario Interview" (http://www.marsravelodarna.com/id37.html)
11. All of the reviews quoted are taken from clippings provided in the *Zamboanga* press kit.
12. Erece, Dinno. "The Man They Call Da King!" *S Magazine*, February 2005, Vol. 4, No. 41. p. 12.
13. "tall, strong and practical," *Popular Movie News*, December 1941. p. 31.
14. "tall, strong and practical," *Popular Movie News*, December 1941. p. 14.
15. "tall, strong and practical," *Popular Movie News*, December 1941. p. 31.
16. "tall, strong and practical," *Popular Movie News*, December 1941. p. 31.
17. Giron, Eric S. "Gregorio Fernandez," *Focus on Filipino Films: A Sampling, 1951–1982*. pp. 30–31.
18. Lo, Ricky. "A Close Encounter with FPJ," *S Magazine*, February 2005, Vol. 4, No. 41. p. 40.
19. de Vega, Guillermo C. *Film and Freedom: Movie Censorship in the Philippines*. Manila: 1975. pp. 7–8.
20. de Vega, p. 8. De Vega does not cite his source for the censors' quoted objection to the film's title.
21. Hernando, p. 32.
22. Hernandez, Eloisa May P. "The Spanish Colonial Tradition in Philippine Visual Arts." (http://www.ncca.gov.ph/culture&arts/cularts/arts/visual/visual-spanish.htm)
23. Biographical data regarding Dona Narcisa de Leon came from the article "Mga Kababaihan sa Daigdig ng Pelikula," published in the September 1964 edition of *Movie Confidential*. No author is credited.
24. "Mga Kababaihan sa Daigdig ng Pelikula," *Movie Confidential*, September 1964.
25. Lim, James Alfred L. and Sy, Arlene Bonniebelle A. "The golden age of the silver screen." (http://www.theguidon.com/?get=2004010300)
26. Karnow, Stanley. *In Our Image: America's Empire in the Philippines*. Ballantine, New York: 1989. (p. 18)
27. Karnow (p. 18).
28. Server.
29. Rodriguez, Jose F. "The Decade of Growth," *Literary Song-Movie Magazine*, July 1, 1959, Vol. 21, No. 21. p. 42.
30. Lim, Rolando B. "Pilar Pilapil," *Movie Confidential*, May 1969, Vol. XIV, No. 7.
31. Cueto, Eric. "Rosa del Rosario Interview" (http://www.marsravelodarna.com/id37.html)
32. Castillo, Lilian. "Information, Please," *Popular Movie News*, December 1941.
33. Giron, p. 31.
34. "Rogelio dela Rosa." (http://www.senate.gov.ph/senators/former_senators/rogelio_dela_rosa.htm)
35. Henares, Ivan Anthony. "From Farm Boy to Matinee Idol." *Kapampangan Homepage*. (http://www.geocities.com/balen_net/ivan12.htm)

36. "Si Carmen Rosales-Ang Dorothy Lamour Ng Silangan," *Sinag Tala*, September 1941.
37. Pareja, Lena Strait. "Carmen Rosales Remembered." (http://www.inq7.net/globalnation/sec_sho/2005/mar/21–02.htm)
38. Sotto, Agustin V. "Manuel Silos," *Focus on Filipino Films: A Sampling, 1951–1982*. p. 62.
39. Sotto, Agustin V. "Lamberto V. Avellana," *Focus on Filipino Films: A Sampling, 1951–1982*. p. 14.
40. Hernando, p. 32.
41. "Isinakdal Sa Hukuman Si Rogelio De La Rosa," *Sinag Tala*, September 1941.
42. "Bakit Umalis Si Roger Sa Sampaguita?" *Sinag Tala*, September 1941.
43. "Isinakdal Sa Hukuman Si Rogelio De La Rosa," *Sinag Tala*, September 1941.

Chapter 3

1. The information regarding George and Brereton's opinions comes from William Manchester's *American Caesar: Douglas MacArthur 1880–1964* (Dell paperback edition, 1983) p. 225.
2. Manchester, p. 230.
3. Manchester, p. 236.
4. Karnow, Stanley. *In Our Image: America's Empire in the Philippines*. Ballantine, New York: 1989. p. 296.
5. Karnow, p. 297.
6. Karnow, pp. 206–207.
7. Sotto, Agustin V. "Manuel Silos," *Focus on Filipino Films: A Sampling, 1951–1982*. p. 62.
8. Karnow, p. 309.
9. Jose, Ricardo T. "Accord and Discord: Japanese Cultural Policy and Philippine National Identity during the Japanese Occupation, 1942–1945." (http://nias.ku.dk/Neighbours/Josepaper.htm)
10. LaMont, John. "The John Ashley Interview, Part 2: 1966–1990," *Trash Compactor*, Vol. 2, No. 6, summer, 1992.
11. Biographical information regarding de Leon, as well as titles from his filmography, were drawn from T.D. Agcaoili's chapter "Gerardo de Leon," published in *Focus on Filipino Films: A Sampling, 1951–1982*. p. 45.
12. From the afore-cited Jose piece.
13. Karnow, p. 294.
14. From the afore-cited Jose piece.
15. Biographical data about Salcedo is drawn from "Pol the leading man" by Carl Kuntze (http://www.manilatimes.net/national/2004/feb/20/yehey/enter/20040220ent1.html), "Leopoldo Salcedo-The Great Profile" (http://www.freewebs.com/leopoldosalcedo/) and "Leopoldo Salcedo, Dead at 86" by Sol Jose Vanzi (http://www.newsflash.org/199806/sb/sb000434.htm)
16. Lo, Ricky. "A Close Encounter with FPJ," *S Magazine*, February 2005, Vol. 4, No. 41. p. 43.
17. Karnow, p. 315.

Chapter 4

1. Karnow, Stanley. *In Our Image: America's Empire in the Philippines*. Random House, New York: 1989. p. 324.
2. del Rio, Purificacion. "Alfredo Gomez: Hero of Fort Santiago," *Stars of the Stage & Screen*, September 1946. p. 5.
3. Ocampo, Hernando R. "Red Is the Color of Life," *Stars of the Stage & Screen*, September 1946. p. 7.
4. Rodriguez, Jose F. "The Decade of Growth," *Literary Song-Movie Magazine*, July 1, 1959. pp. 42–43.

5. Information on Agana's effect on Sampaguita's fortunes came from Mario A. Hernando's chapter "A History of Philippine Cinema" in the book *The Golden Years: Memorable Tagalog Movie Ads, 1946–1956*. Danny Dolor, Manila: 1994 (p. 38) and from the Sampaguita Pictures, Inc. website (http://www.sampaguitapictures.com/history.html). Further information on the fire at the Sampaguita facilities came from "The Golden Age of the Silver Screen" by James Alfred L. Lim and Arlene Bonniebelle A. Sy (http://www.theguidon.com/?get=2004010300).
6. Carreon, Julie R. "Carol Varga: Has She Lived Down Her Past?" *Movie Confidential*, July 1959.
7. Sotto, Agustin V. "Lamberto V. Avellana," *Focus on Filipino Films: A Sampling, 1951–1982*. p. 15.
8. Karnow, p. 346.
9. Karnow, p. 346.

Chapter 5

1. "Dela Rosa Move," *The Manila Chronicle*, July 7, 1957.
2. Curaming, Camilinio A. "Political Fever Hits Movie Land," *Movie Confidential*, July 1959, Vol. IV, No.2. p. 16.
3. Curaming, p. 17.
4. de Manila, Quijano. "The 'Untimely Withdrawal' of Roger de la Rosa," *Philippine Free Press*, November 1961.
5. de Manila, Quijano.
6. de Manila, Quijano.
7. de Manila, Quijano.
8. Snooper. "Screen Sidelights," *Literary Song-Movie Magazine*, July 1, 1959, Vol. 21, No. 21. p. 5.
9. "Hail Movie Films Exemption!" *Movie Confidential*, July 1959, Vol. Iv, No. 2. p. 3.
10. "The State of Philippine Movies Today," *Songs & Stars Home Magazine*, September 1959, Vol. 3, No. 1. p. 10.
11. Server, Lee. "Eddie Romero: Our Man in Manila," *Film Comment*, March/April 1999.
12. Hemisphere Pictures press release included in the 1970 pressbook for the film *Beast of Blood*.
13. Snooper. "Screen Sidelights," *Literary Song-Movie Magazine*, July 1, 1959, Vol. 21, No. 21. p. 8.
14. "The State of Philippine Movies Today," *Songs & Stars Home Magazine*, September 1959, Vol. 3, No. 1. p. 10.
15. Snooper. "Screen Sidelights," *Literary Song-Movie Magazine*, July 1, 1959, Vol. 21, No. 21. p. 5.
16. "The State of Philippine Movies Today," *Songs & Stars Home Magazine*, September 1959, Vol. 3, No. 1. pp. 10, 58.
17. Much of the biographical information on Fernando Poe, Jr. came from Dinno Erece's article "Fernando Poe, Jr: The Man They Call da King," in *S Magazine*, February 2005, Vol. 4, No. 41. Other information came from the Philonrise website (http://www.philonrise.com/whoswho/entertainment/fernandopoejr.htm) and GoPinoy.com (http://www.gopinoy.com/specials/who/fernando_index.htm).
18. "Ronnie & Joseph: How Do They Compare," *Movie Confidential*, September 1964. p. 16.
19. Molina, Hilario C. "The FAMAS award story," *Movie Confidential*, September 1964. p. 22.
20. Molina, Hilario C. "The Men Behind the Movies," *Movie Confidential*, September 1964. p. 28.
21. de Vega, Guillermo C. *Film and Freedom: Movie Censorship in the Philippines*. De Vega, Manila: 1975. p. 26.
22. de Vega. p. 27.

Chapter 6

1. Salao, Andy. "On the Spot," *Movie Confidential*, May 1969, Vol. XIV, No. 7. p. 3.
2. de Vega, Guillermo C. *Film and Freedom: Movie Censorship in the Philippines*. Guillermo C. de Vega, Manila: 1975. p. 31.
3. de Vega. p. 33.
4. Karnow, Stanley. *In Our Image: America's Empire in the Philippines*. Ballantine, New York: 1989. p. 359.
5. de Vega. pp. 42–43.
6. de Vega. p. 43.
7. de Vega. p. 46.
8. de Vega. pp. 50–51.
9. de Vega. p. 50.
10. Weaver, Tom. *Interviews With B Science Fiction and Horror Movie Makers*. McFarland, North Carolina: 1988. p. 42.
11. Sherman made the comment on the audio commentary track of the 2003 DVD release of the film by Image Entertainment.
12. Martillo, Letty. "Three Lucky Bicolanos," *Literary Song-Movie Magazine*, July 1, 1959, Vol. 21, No.21. p. 34.
13. Server, Lee. "Our Man In Manila," *Film Comment*, March/April 1999.
14. This information came from a New World Pictures press release included in the pressbook for the film *Beast of the Yellow Night*.
15. Nebbs, Adam. "Vic Diaz: The Face of the Philippines," *Shock Cinema*, No. 27, Winter 2005.

Chapter 7

1. Sotto, Agustin V. "Lino Brocka," *Focus on Filipino Films: A Sampling, 1951–1982*. p. 24.
2. Server, Lee. "Our Man in Manila," *Film Comment*, March/April 1999.
3. Hernando, Mario A. "Ishmael Bernal," *Focus on Filipino Films: A Sampling, 1951–1982*. p. 17.
4. Hernando. P. 18.
5. del Mundo, Clodualdo, Jr. "Conversations with Mike de Leon." (http://www.bayaning3rdworld.com/full a1.htm)
6. Tan, Abbv. "Pornography and the First Lady: The Marcoses Invest in Sleaze," *New Internationalist*, 153, November 1985.
7. Mosura, Amy. "Myra Manibog finds her second chance." *Philippine Daily Inquirer*, November 19, 2004.
8. Caruncho, Eric S. "The 'SO-BAD-IT'S-GOOD' cinematic world of Cirio H. Santiago," *Philippine Daily Inquirer*, December 4, 2005.

Chapter 8

1. San Diego, Bayani, Jr. "All About Eva," *Philippine Daily Inquirer*, July 3, 2006. pp. A2–4.
2. Robles, Raissa. "Terrorists Choice," *Hot Manila*, May 9, 2000. (http://www.hotmanila.ph/esp/robin.html)
3. "Robin and the Rebels," *Asiaweek.com*, April 28, 2000. Vol. 26, No. 16. (http://www.pathfinder.com/asiaweek/magazine/2000/0428/as.people.html)
4. Vanzi, Sol Jose. "Vizconde Massacre Trial Ends with Guilty Verdict," *PHNO: Headline News Philippines*, January 7, 2000. (http://www.newsflash.org/2000/01/hl/hl011801.htm)
5. Vanzi, Sol Jose. "Jessica Alfaro Movie Flops," *FCCS Newsflash*, September 25, 1997. (http://www.newsflash.org/199709/sb/sb000021.htm)

6. Tenorio, Bum D., Jr. "Hubert Webb innocent, says FBI agent," *Manila Standard Today*, February 19, 2004. (http://www.manilastandardonline.com/mnlastd/?page=police01_feb19_2004)

7. Vanzi, Sol Jose. "Vizconde Massacre Trial Ends with Guilty Verdict," *PHNO: Headline News Philippines*, January 7, 2000. (http://www.newsflash.org/2000/01/hl/hl011801.htm)

8. Paras, Wilhelmina. "Sarah's Reel Life," *Asiaweek.com*, March 28, 1997. (http://www.pathfinder.com/asiaweek/97/0328/feat1.html)

9. Paras.

Chapter 9

1. Lim, Bliss Cua. "Crisis or Promise? New Directions in Philippine Cinema," *IndieWire*, August 14, 2000. (http://www.indiewire.com/onthescene/fes_00Filipino_000814_wrap.html)

2. Tariman, Pablo A. "Edgardo Reyes' novel sizzles in Chito Rono's latest film," *Inq7.net*, May 20, 2000. (http://www.inq7.net/saturday/may2000wk3/spc_4.htm)

3. Vanzi, Sol Jose. "Armida Stays Erap," *PHNO Showbiz Chatter*, October 31, 1999. (http://www.newsflash.org/1999/10/sb/sb001003.htm)

4. Sicam, Gloria P. "Armida Siguion-Reyna reviews her first year with MTRCB." July 17, 1999. (http://www.inq7.net/saturday/jul99wk3/spc_2.htm)

5. Sicam.

6. Lacaba, Jose F. "Notes on Film Censorship," *Forum*, December 8, 1999.

7. Marfil, Martin P., Javellana, Juliet L., Aning, Jerome. "Film Board's Foes March But Armida Not Quitting," *Philippine Daily Inquirer*, November 9, 1999.

8. Nisid, Hajari. "Sound and Fury," *Time Asia*, October 30, 2000, Vol. 156, No. 17. (http://www.time.com/time/asia/magazine/2000/1030/philippines.html)

9. Guinto, Joel Francis. "Ex-solon admits to kidnapping boy after arrest—police," *INQ7.net*, February 21, 2005. (http://news.inq7.net/breaking/index.php?index=2&story_id=28225)

10. Vanzi, Sol Jose. "Roldan's Girlfriend in Suicide Attempt," *Philippine Headline News Online*, February 24, 2005. (http://www.newsflash.org/2004/02/hl/hl101844.htm)

11. Echeminada, Perseus, Mendez, Christina and Laude, Jaime. "Nida Blanca murdered," *Asian Journal*, November 8, 2001. (http://www.asianjournalusa.com/default.asp?sourceid=&smenu=77&twindow=&mad=&sd)

12. Dacanay, Barbara Mae. "Blanca's Husband, Driver not suspects," *Gulf News*, Friday, November 9, 2001. (http://www.gulfnews.com/Articles/news.asp?ArticleID=31947)

13. "Nida's husband tagged in slay," *Visayan Daily Star*, Tuesday, November 20, 2001. (http://www.visayandailystar.com/2001/November/20/topstory5.htm)

14. Mendez, Christina. "Nida Blanca Case: Strunk Compelled to Face Charges in RP," *Philippine Headline News Online*, August 30, 2002. (http://www.newsflash.org/2002/08/sb/sb002369.htm)

15. Tubeza, Philip C. "Nida Blanca murder: DOJ questions US judge," *inq7.net*, June 3, 2003. (http://www.inq7.net/ent/2003/jun/04/text/ent_2-1-p.htm)

16. McGirk, Tim. "'He Tried to Get Me to Ban the Film': The country's top censor tells why he quit in protest," *Time Asia*, April 3, 2001. (http://www.time.com/time/asia/arts/magazine/0,9754,104823,00.html)

17. "Philippine Cardinal Welcomes Ouster of Movie Censor," *Catholic World News*, March 22, 2001. (http://www.catholicworldnews.com/news/viewstory.cfm?recnum=15122)

18. Fabros, Aya. "Live Show controversy simmers: Concerned Artists, other groups rally at Mendiola," *CyberDyaryo*, March 28, 2001. (http://www.cyberdyaryo.com/features/f2001_0328_02.htm)

19. Fabros.

20. McGirk, Tim. "The President's Scissors," *Time Asia*, April 2, 2001. (http://www.time.com/time/asia/arts/magazine/0,9754,104662,00.html)

21. Valerio, Ariel. "Former MTRCB chair condemns censorship," *UP Forum Online*, March 2001. (http://www.up.edu.ph/forum/2001/3/tiongson.html)

22. Fabros.

23. McGirk, Tim. "The President's Scissors," *Time Asia*, April 2, 2001. (http://www.time.com/time/asia/arts/magazine/0,9754,104622,00.html)

24. "PGMA's Statement on the Movie Live Show," March 27, 2001. (http://www.opnet.ops.gov.ph/speech-2001mar27.htm)

25. Ligalig, Mike Ortega. "ICM cinemas to ban sexy films," *The Bohol Chronicle*, October 6, 2004. (http://www.theboholchronicle.com/oct062004/fpage/front3.htm)

26. "Actors to get their cut from foreign film-makers," *Sun Star*, Tuesday, August 31, 2004. (http://www.sunstar.com.ph/static/net/2004/08/31/actors.to.get.their.cut.from.foreign.film.makers.(4.00.p.m.).html)

27. de Castro, Isagani, Jr. "Fernando Poe Jr.: Unqualified or Underestimated?" *Philippine Headline News Online*, January 17, 2004. (http://www.newsflash.org/2003/05/sb/sb003227.htm)

28. de Castro.

29. Dalangin-Fernandez, Lira. "Poe says he will run for president in 2004," *Inq7.net*, November 26, 2003. (http://www.inq7.net/brk/2003/nov/26/brkpol_9-1.htm)

30. Dalangin-Fernandez.

31. de Castro.

32. "Crowds flock to film star funeral," *BBC News*, Wednesday, December 22, 2004. (http://news.bbc.co.uk/2/hi/asia-pacific/4116719.stm)

33. "PGMA's Statement on the Movie Live Show," March 27, 2001. (http://www.opnet.ops.gov.ph/speech-2001mar27.htm)

Bibliography

"Actors to Get Their Cut from Foreign Filmmakers." *Sun Star*, Tuesday, August 31, 2004. (http://www.sunstar.com.ph/static/net/2004/08/31/actors.to.get.their.cut.from.foreign.Film.makers.(4.00.p.m.).html)

Agcaoili, T.D. "Chat Gallardo." *Focus on Filipino Films: A Sampling, 1951–1982*. N.p., 1983.

——. "Gerardo de Leon." *Focus on Filipino Films: A Sampling, 1951–1982*. N.p., 1983.

Alano, Ching M. "Postwar Memories of Manila." *The Golden Years: Memorable Tagalog Movie Ads, 1946–1956*. Manila: n.p., 1994.

"All About the Eddies." *Movie Confidential*, Vol. 4, no. 2, July 1959.

Andrade, Pio, Jr. "Chinese Filipinos Producer of First Filipino Movie." (http://www.tsinoy.com/Roots/TheBeatenPath.cfm?ID=711)

Araya, Alfred A., Jr. "Focus on Construction Sector: Workers' Rights Remain Unprotected." *CyberDyaryo*, Tuesday, September 19, 2000. (http://www.cyberdyaryo.com/features/f2000_0919_01.htm)

"Bakit Umalis Si Roger Sa Sampaguita?" *Sinag Tala*, September 1941.

Bautista, Arsenio. "Boots." *History of Philippine Cinema*. (http://www.ncca.gov.ph/culture&arts/cularts/arts/cinema/cinema-history1.htm)

——. *History of Philippine Cinema* (Part 2). (http://www.ncca.gov.ph/culture&arts/cularts/arts/cinema/cinema-history2.htm)

Beast of Blood pressbook. Hemisphere Pictures, 1970.

Beast of the Yellow Night pressbook. New World Pictures, 1971.

Belen, Crispina Martinez. "Director Further Explains Problem of Film Industry." *Manila Bulletin Online*, Sunday, November 21, 1999. (http://www.mb.com.ph/ENTR/Cworld/1999/cw991121.asp)

"Bertoldo-Balodoy." *Point Cebu: Arts and Culture*. (http://www.ngkhai.com/pointcebu/culture/bertoldo.htm)

Burton, Sandra. "Another Thrilla in Manila." *Time*, Vol. 157, no. 4, January 29, 2001.

Cabagnot, Ed. "Notes on the History of Philippine Cinema." *Focus on Filipino Films: A Sampling, 1951–1982*. N.p., 1983.

Carreon, Jose N. "The First Nine." *The FAP e-Zine*, June 1, 2005. (http://www.filmacademyphil.org/archives/060105arj3.html)

——. "The First Nine (Second of Two Parts)." *The FAP e-Zine*, June 8, 2005. (http://www.filmacademyphil.org/archives/060805arj4.html)

——. "Philippine Cinema: An Overview." *The FAP e-Zine*, October 28, 2005. (http://www.filmacademyphil.org/archives/051028arj1.html)

——. "Philippine Cinema: An Overview (Part 2)." *The FAP e-Zine*, November 4, 2005. (http://www.filmacademyphil.org/archives/110405arj1.html)

——. "A Year After." *The FAP e-Zine*, December 16, 2005. (http://www.filmacademyphil.org/archives/121605arj1.html)

——. "The Year That Was (Part 1)." *The FAP e-Zine*, January 6, 2006. (http://www.filmacademyphil.org/archives/010606arj1.html)

——. "The Year That Was (Part 2)." *The FAP e-Zine*, January 13, 2006. (http://www.filmacademyphil.org/archives/011306arj1.html)

——. "The Year That Was (Part 3)." *The FAP e-Zine*, January 20, 2006. (http://www.filmacademyphil.org/archives/012006arj1.html)

——. "The Year That Was (Part 4)." *The FAP e-Zine*, January 27, 2006. (http://www.filmacademyphil.org/archives/012706arj1.html)

Carreon, Julie R. "Carol Varga: Has She Lived Down Her Past?" *Movie Confidential*, Vol. 4, no. 2, July 1959.

Castillo, Lilian. "Information, Please." *Popular Movie News*, December 1941.

"The Cebuano Movies." *Point Cebu: Arts and Culture*. (http://www.ngkhai.com/pointcebu/culture/cmovies.htm)

"Choose Your Stars." *Songs & Stars Home Magazine*, Vol. 3, no. 1, September 1959.

"Crowds Flock to Film Star Funeral." *BBC News*, Wednesday, December 22, 2004. (http://news.bbc.co.uk/2/hi/asia-pacific/4116719.stm)

Cueto, Eric. "Rosa del Rosario Interview." (http://www.marsravelodarna.com/id37.html)

Curaming, Camilinio A. "Political Fever Hits Movie Land." *Movie Confidential*, Vol. 4, no. 2, July 1959.

Dacanay, Barbara Mae. "Blanca's Husband, Driver Not Suspects." *Gulf News*, Friday, November 9, 2001. (http://www.gulfnews.com/Articles/news.asp?ArticleID=31947)

Dalangin-Fernandez, Lira. "Poe Says He Will Run for President in 2004." *Inq7.net*, November 26, 2003. (http://www.inq7.net/brk/2003/nov/26/brkpol_9-1.htm)

"A Death in the Family." *Asiaweek.com*, December 29, 1995. (http://www.asiaweek.com/asiaweek/95/1229/feat3.html)

De Castro, Isagani, Jr. "Fernando Poe Jr.: Unqualified or Underestimated?" *Philippine Headline News Online*, January 17, 2004. (http://www.newsflash.org/2003/05/sb/sb003227.htm)

de Guzman, Susan A. "Gloria in Excelsis." *Filipinas*, Vol. 14, no. 160, August 2005.

de la Cruz, Rosauro. "Celso Ad. Castillo." *Focus on Filipino Films: A Sampling, 1951–1982*. N.p., 1983.

"Dela Rosa Move." *The Manila Chronicle*, July 7, 1957.

del Mundo, Clodualdo, Jr. *Writing for Film*. Communication Foundation for Asia: 1981.

del Rio, Purificacion. "Alfredo Gomez: Hero of Fort Santiago." *Stars of the Stage and Screen*, September 1946.

de Vega, Guillermo C. *Film and Freedom: Movie Censorship in the Philippines*. Manila: 1975.

———. "Film Ways: Contemporary." *1974 Fookien Times Yearbook*, 1974.

———. "Notes on the End of Censorship." *Men and Issues*, June 1970.

———. "Toward the Day of Self-Censorship." *Weekly Nation*, September 21, 1970.

———. "A Viewpoint on Pornography." *The Sunday Times Magazine*, April 18, 1971.

———. "The Work or Art of Censorship." *Philippines Free Press*, August 1, 1970.

Dizon, David. "Imelda: The Government Owes Me P88 Billion." *abs-cbnNEWS.com*, May 16, 2002. (http://uw.abs-cbnnews.com/images/news/microsites/onddot/dotimelda.htm)

Domingo, Gay Ace. "Lily Monteverde: The Triumphant Mother." *The Manila Times Internet Edition*, Sunday, January 2, 2005. (http://www.manilatimes.net/national/2005/jan/02/yehey/weekend/20050102week1.html)

Echeminada, Perseus; Mendez, Christina; Laude, Jaime. "Nida Blanca Murdered." *Asian Journal*, November 8, 2001. (http://www.asianjournalusa.com/default.asp?sourceid=&smenu=77&twindow= &mad=&sd)

"El Hijo Disobediente." *Point Cebu: Arts and Culture*. (http://www.ngkhai.com/pointcebu/culture/disobediente.htm)

Erece, Dinno. "The Man They Call da King!" *S Magazine*, February 2005, Vol. 4, no. 41.

Fabregas, Jaime. "Peque Gallaga." *Focus on Filipino Films: A Sampling, 1951–1982*. N.p., 1983.

Fabros, Aya. "Live Show Controversy Simmers: Concerned Artists, Other Groups Rally at Mendiola." *CyberDyaryo*, March 28, 2001. (http://www.cyberdyaryo.com/features/f2001_0328_02.htm)

"Festival in Berlin." *Literary Song-Movie Magazine*, Vol. 21, no. 21, July 1, 1959.

Flores, Patrick. "Diminishing Controversy in Local Awards." *Manila Standard Today*. (www.manilastandardonline.com)

———. "Limitations of Philippine cinema." *Manila Standard Today*. (www.manilastandardonline.com)

Garcia, Leonardo, Jr., and Masigan, Carmelita. "An In-depth Study on the Film Industry in the Philippines." (http://www3.pids.gov.ph/ris/taps/tapspp0103.pdf)

Garcia, Roger. "Mission Impossible I: Filipine Filmmaking 1896–1986." (http://www.spaziocultura.it/gallery/cecudine/fe_2001/ENG/filippine_s_eng.htm)

Giron, Eric S. "Eddie Romero." *Focus on Filipino Films: A Sampling, 1951–1982*. N.p.: 1983.

———. "Gregorio Fernandez." *Focus on Filipino Films: A Sampling, 1951–1982*. N.p., 1983.

"Gloria and Mat." *Point Cebue: Personality Profiles* (http://www.ngkhai.com/pointcebu/profile/gloria.htm)

GoPinoy.com (http://www.gopinoy.com/specials/who/fernando_index.htm)

Guerrero, Rafael Ma. *Readings in Philippine Cinema*. Experimental Cinema of the Philippines: 1983.

Guinto, Joel Francis. "Ex-solon Admits to Kidnapping Boy After Arrest—Police." *inq7.net*, February 21, 2005. (http://news.inq7.net/breaking/index.php?index=2&story_id=28225)

"Hail Movie Films Exemption!" *Movie Confidential*, Vol. 4, no. 2, July, 1959.

Henares, Ivan Anthony. "From Farm Boy to Matinee Idol." *Kapampangan Homepage*. (http://www.geocities.com/balen_net/ivan12.htm)

Hernandez, Eloisa May P. "The Spanish Colonial Tradition in Philippine Visual Arts." (http://www.ncca.gov.ph/culture&arts/cularts/arts/visual/visual-spanish.htm)

Hernando, Mario A. "A History of Philippine Cinema." *The Golden Years: Memorable Tagalog Movie Ads, 1946–1956*. Manila: n. p., 1994.

———. "Ishmael Bernal." *Focus on Filipino Films: A Sampling, 1951–1982*. N.p., 1983.

Herrera, Ernesto F. "LVN Studio Packs Up." *The Manila Times Internet Edition*, Tuesday, May 10, 2005. (http://www.manilatimes.net/national/2005/may/10/yehey/opinion/20050510opi2.html)

Hersey, Bill. "PEOPLE, Places & Parties." *Tokyo Weekender*. (http://www.weekender.co.jp/new/030207/partyline-030207-html)

"Isinakdal Sa Hukuman Si Rogelio De La Rosa." *Sinag Tala*, September 1941.

Jose, Ricardo T. "Accord and Discord: Japanese Cultural Policy and Philippine National Identity During the Japanese Occupation, 1942–1945." (http://nias.ku.dk/Neighbours/Josepaper.htm)

"Mga Kababaihan sa Daigdig ng Pelikula." *Movie Confidential*, September 1964.

Karnow, Stanley. *In Our Image: America's Empire in the Philippines*. Random House, New York: 1989.

Kuntze, Carl. "Pol the Leading Man." (http://www.manilatimes.net/national/feb/20/yehey/enter/20040220entl.html)

Lacaba, Jose F. "Notes on Film Censorship." *Forum*, December 8, 1999.

LaMont, John. "The John Ashley Interview, Part 2: 1966–1990." *Trash Compactor*, Vol. 2, no. 6, Summer 1992.

Larmer, Brook. "People Power II." *Newsweek*, Vol. 137, no. 5, January 29, 2001.

"Leopoldo Salcedo—The Great Profile." (http://www.freewebs.com/Leopoldosalcedo/)

"Life History of Marvin Edward Gardner." (http://www.aenet.org/family/hismeg.htm)

Ligalig, Mike Ortega. "ICM Cinemas to Ban Sexy Films." *The Bohol Chronicle*, October 6, 2004. (http://www.theboholchronicle.com/oct062004/fpage/front3.html)

Lim, Bliss Cua. "Crisis or Promise? New Directions in Philippine Cinema." *IndieWire*, August 14, 2000. (http://www.indiewire.com/onthescene/fes_00Filipino_000814_wrap.html)

Lim, James Alfred L., and Sy, Arlene Bonniebelle A. "The Golden Age of the Silver Screen." (http://www.theguidon.com/?get=2004010300)

Lo, Ricky. "A Close Encounter with FPJ." *S Magazine*, February 2005, Vol. 4, no. 41.

Lumbera, Bienvenido. Keynote Address, Silliman University Symposium on Film and Literature, November 22, 2002. (http://www.geocities.com/icasocot/lumbera_filmlit.html)

———. *Philippine Cinema Beginnings*. (http://www.filipinoheritage.com/arts/phil-cinema/beginnings.htm)

Luzentales, Benny. "Quezon Film Pioneer 'Kisses' Career Goodbye." *The Manila Times*, Saturday, November 29, 2003. (http://www.manilatimes.net/national/2003/nov/29/yehey/prov/20031129pro13.html)

Manchester, William. *American Caesar: Douglas MacArthur 1880–1964*. New York: Dell, 1983.

Marfil, Martin P.; Javellana, Juliet L.; Aning, Jerome. "Film Board's Foes March But Armida Not Quitting." *Philippine Daily Inquirer*, November 9, 1999.

Martillo, Letty. "Three Lucky Bicolanos." *Literary Song-Movie Magazine*, Vol. 21, no. 21, July 1, 1959.

McGirk, Tim. "'He Tried to Get Me to Ban the Film': The Country's Top Censor Tells Why He Quit in Protest." *Time Asia*, April 3, 2001. (http://www.time.com/time/asia/arts/magazine/0,9754,104823,00.html)

———. "The President's Scissors." *Time Asia*, April 2, 2001. (http://www.time.com/time/asia/arts/magazine/0,9754,104622,00.html)

Mendez, Christina. "Nida Blanca Case: Strunk Compelled to Face Charges in RP." *Philippine Headline News Online*, August 30, 2002. (http://www.newsflash.org/2002/08/sb/sb002369.htm)

Molina, Hilario C. "The FAMAS Award Story." *Movie Confidential*, September 1964.

———. "The Men Behind the Movies." *Movie Confidential*, September 1964.

———. "Ronnie & Joseph: How They Compare." *Movie Confidential*, September 1964.

Muhammad, Amir. "Smorgasbord: Filipino Films in the Age of Deconstruction." *Kakiseni.com*. (http://www.kakiseni.com/articles/columns/MDE3Mg.html)

"Natatanging Gawad Urian kay Anita Linda." *Manunuri ng Pelikulang Pilipino*. (http://www.manunuri.com/natatanging_gawad_2.asp?year=1982)

"Natatanging Gawad Urian kay Lamberto V. Avellana." *Manunuri ng Pelikulang Pilipino*. (http://www.manunuri.com/natatanging_gawad_2.asp?year=1981)

"Natatanging Gawad Urian kay Luis Nolasco." *Manunuri ng Pelikulang Pilipino*. (http://www.manunuri.com/natatanging_gawad_2.asp?year=1983)

"Natatanging Gawad Urian kay Rosa Rosal." *Manunuri ng Pelikulang Pilipino*. (http://www.manunuri.com/natatanging_gawad_2.asp?year=1987)

"Natatanging Gawad Urian kay Tito Arevalo." *Manunuri ng Pelikulang Pilipino*. (http://www.manunuri.com/natatanging_gawad_2.asp?year=1986)

Nebbs, Adam. "Vic Diaz: The Face of the Philippines." *Shock Cinema*, no. 27, Winter 2005.

"Nida's Husband Tagged in Slay." *Visayan Daily Star*,

Tuesday, November 20, 2001. (http://www.visayandailystar.com/2001/November/20/topstory5.htm)

Noriega, Vincent; Avila, Valeriano; Relatado, Kris; Ranillo, Junius F. "The Visayan Film Industry: A Retrospective." *My Place Under the Sun*, Wednesday, January 5, 2005 (http://benjieordonez.blogspot.com/2005/01/visayan-film-industry-retrospective.html)

Ocampo, Hernando R. "Red Is the Color of Life." *Stars of the Stage and Screen*, September 1946.

Paras, Wilhelmina. "Masters of Mumbo Jumbo or Psychics with a Mission? Whatever the Answer, the Spirit Questors Have Clearly Struck a Spiritual Chord in the Philippines." *Asiaweek.com* (http://www.asiaweek.com/asiaweek/97/1017/feat2.html)

_____. "Sarah's Reel Life." *Asiaweek.com*, March 28, 1997. (http://www.pathfinder.com/asiaweek/97/0328/feat1.html)

Pareja, Lena Strait. "Carmen Rosales Remembered." (http://www.inq7.net/globalnation/sec_sho/2005/mar/21–02.htm)

Petillo, Carol Morris. *Douglas MacArthur: The Philippine Years*. Bloomington: Indiana University Press, 1981.

"PGMA's Statement on the Movie Live Show." March 27, 2002. (http://www.opnet.ops.gov.ph/speech-2001mar27.htm)

"Philippine Cardinal Welcomes Ouster of Movie Censor." *Catholic World News*, March 22, 2001. (http://www.catholicworldnews.com/news/viewstory.cfm?recnum=15122)

Philonrise (http://www.philonrise.com/whoswho/entertainment/fernandopoejr.htm)

"Pio A. 'Piux' Cabajar." *Point Cebu: Personality Profiles*. (http://www.ngkhai.com/pointcebu/profile/cabajar.htm)

Red, Isah V. "Population Explosion!" *Manila Standard Today*, March 21, 2005. (http://www.manilastandardtoday.com/?page=goodLife03_mar21_2005)

"Richard Abelardo: Eksperto sa Visual Effects." *Manunuri ng Pelikulang Pilipino*. (http://www.manunuri.com/natatanging_gawad_2.asp?year=1990)

"Robin and the Rebels." *Asiaweek.com*, Vol. 26, no. 16, April 28, 2000. (http://www.pathfinder.com/asiaweek/magazine/2000/0428/as.people.html)

Robles, Raissa. "Terrorists Choice." *Hot Manila*, May 9, 2000. (http://www.hotmanila.ph/esp/robin.html)

Rodriguez, Joe. "The Triumph of Laziness." *Songs and Stars Home Magazine*, Vol. 3, no. 1, September 1959.

Rodriguez, Jose F. "The Decade of Growth." *Literary Song-Movie Magazine*, Vol. 21, no. 21, July 1, 1959.

"Rogelio dela Rosa" (http://www.senate.gov.ph/senators/former_senators/rogelio_dela_rosa.htm)

Salao, Andy. "On the Spot." *Movie Confidential*, Vol. 14, no. 7, May 1969.

San Diego, Bayani, Jr. "All About Eva." *Philippine Daily Inquirer*, July 3, 2006. pp. A2–4.

Server, Lee. "Eddie Romero: Our Man in Manila." *Film Comment*, March/April, 1999.

"Si Carmen Rosales-Ang Dorothy Lamour Ng Silangan." *Sinag Tala*, September 1941.

Sicam, Gloria P. "Armida Siguion-Reyna Reviews Her First Year with MTRCB." *Inq7.net*, July 17, 1999. (http://www.inq7.net/saturday/jul99wk3/spc_2.htm)

Snooper. "Screen Sidelights." *Literary Song-Movie Magazine*, Vol. 21, no. 21, July 1, 1959.

Sotto, Agustin V. "Lamberto V. Avellana." *Focus on Filipino Films: A Sampling, 1951–1982*. N.p., 1983.

_____. "Lino Brocka." *Focus on Filipino Films: A Sampling, 1951–1982*. N.p., 1983.

_____. "Manuel Silos." *Focus on Filipino Films: A Sampling, 1951–1982*. N.p., 1983.

_____. "Mary Walter and the Early Cinema." *Manunuri ng Pelikulang Pilipino*. (http://www.manunuri.com/natatanging_gawad_2.asp?year=1992)

_____. "Mike de Leon." *Focus on Filipino Films: A Sampling, 1951–1982*. N.p., 1983.

_____. "Mona Lisa: An Actress' Pain and Triumph." *Manunuri ng Pelikulang Pilipino*. (http://www.manunuri.com/natatanging_gawad_2.asp?year=1999)

_____. "Natatanging Gawad Urian kay Gerardo De Leon." *Manunuri ng Pelikulang Pilipino*. (http://www.manunuri.com/natatanging_gawad_2.asp?year=1978)

_____. "Natatanging Gawad Urian kay Manuel Conde." *Manunuri ng Pelikulang Pilipino*. (http://www.manunuri.com/natatanging_gawad_2.asp?year=1979)

_____. "Natatanging Gawad Urian kay Manuel Silos." *Manunuri ng Pelikulang Pilipino*. (http://www.manunuri.com/natatanging_gawad_2.asp?year=1980)

_____. "Natatanging Gawad Urian kay William Smith." *Manunuri ng Pelikulang Pilipino*. (http://www.manunuri.com/natatanging_2.asp?year=1985)

_____. "Susana C. De Guzman, Recipient of 1991 Natatanging Gawad Urian." *Manunuri ng Pelikulang Pilipino*. (http://www.manunuri.com/natatanging_gawad_2.asp?year=1991)

"The State of Philippine Movies Today." *Songs and Stars Home Magazine*, Vol. 3, no. 1, September 1959.

"Tall, Strong and Practical." *Popular Movie News*, December 1941.

Tan, Abbv. "Pornography and the First Lady." *New Internationalist*, 153, November 1985.

Tariman, Pablo A. "Edgardo Reyes' Novel Sizzles in Chito Rono's Latest Film." *Inq7.net*, May 20, 2000. (http://www.inq7.net/saturday/may 2000wk3/spc_4.htm)

Tenorio, Bum D., Jr. "Herbert Webb Innocent, Says FBI Agent." *Manila Standard Today*, February 19, 2004. (http://www.manilastandardonline.com/mnlastd/?page=police01_feb19_2004)

Ting, Gwendalene. "Visayan Performing Arts." (http://www.geocities.com/icasocot/ting_visayan.html?200619)

Tiongson, Nicanor G. "Laurice Guillen." *Focus on Filipino Films: A Sampling, 1951–1982*. N.p., 1983.

Tordesillas, Ellen. "Roldan's Friend." *Malaya*, Saturday, July 29, 2006. (http://www.malaya.com.ph/jul29/edtorde.htm)

Torres, Jose, Jr. "Are Ghosts for Real?" *abs-cbnNEWS.com*, November 1, 2002. (http://uw.abs-cbnnews.com/images/news/microsites/onddot/dotghost.htm)

Tubeza, Philip C. "Nida Blanca Murder: DOJ Questions US Judge." *inq7.net*, June 3, 2003. (http://www.inq7.net/ent/2003/jun/04/text/ent_2-1-p.htm)

Valerio, Ariel. "Former MTRCB Chair Condemns Censorship." *UP Forum Online*, March 2001. (http://www.up.edu.ph/forum/2001/3/tiongson.html)

Vanzi, Sol Jose. "Armida Stays Erap." *PHNO Showbiz Chatter*, October 31, 1999. (http://www.newsflash.org/1999/10/sb/sb001003.htm)

____. "Jessica Alfaro Movie Flops." *FCCS Newsflash*, September 25, 1997. (http://www.newsflash.org/199709/sb/sb000021.htm)

____. "Leopoldo Salcedo, Dead at 86." (http://www.newsflash.org/199806/sb/sb000434.htm)

____. "Roldan's Girlfriend in Suicide Attempt." *Philippine Headline News Online*, February 24, 2005. (http://www.newsflash.org/2004/02/hl/hl101844.htm)

____. "Vizconde Massacre Trial Ends with Guilty Verdict." *PHNO: Headline News Philippines*, January 7, 2000. (http://www.newsflash.org/2000/01/hl/hl011801.htm)

Weaver, Tom. *Interviews with B Science Fiction and Horror Movie Makers*. Jefferson, NC: McFarland, 1988.

Wee, Brandon. "The Decade of Living Dangerously: A Chronicle of Lav Diaz." *Senses of Cinema* (http://www.sensesofcinema.com/contents/05/34/lav_diaz.html)

White, Timothy. *Politics, Art and Bomba Queens: The Cinema of the Philippines*. (http://www.nus.edu.sg/NUSinfo/CFA/arts/13.htm)

Yuson, Alfred A. "Kidlat Tahimik." *Observer*, January 17, 1982.

Zamboanga promotional press kit, 1937.

Index

Aawitan Kita 120
Abalos, Ruben 109
Abaya, Leo 199
Abelardo, Juan 38
Abelardo, Richard 38, 39
ABG Studios 52
Aboleda, Rene 80
ABS 81, 101
Abu Sayyaf 178, 179
Abuel, Tommy 139, 150
Abutan, Elsa 108
Accion, Mike 88, 89
Ackerman, Raymond 7
Act No. 3582 25
Actors' Guild 234
Acueza, Inocencia 77
Acuna-Zaldariaga Productions 59
AD Films International 97
Adamson University 141
Africa 98, 177
Agana, Dr. Adriano 62
Agana, Tessie 62, 214
Agar, John 84, 86, 126
Agee, James 65
Agent X-44 103–105
Agila ng Maynila 173
Agilang Itim 65
Aglipay, Edgar 219
Agra, Amaury 130
Aguila 154
Aguiluz, Amable "Tikoy" 191, 192, 197, 198, 200, 230, 232
Aguinaldo, Emilio 157, 158
Aguirre, Vitaliano 186, 187
Airplane Flight Over Manila 10
Ako ang Batas 174
Ako ang Huhusga 173
Ako ang Sasagupa 110, 111
Ako Raw Ay Huk 74
Aladin 65
Alajar, Gina 143, 192
Alamat, Ang 147
Alamat ng Lawin, Ang 236
Alaminos 72
Alario, Pedro 15
Albay 30, 79, 82
Albert, Joseph 97
Aldecoa Street 124
Alegre, Alona 180

Alfaro, Jessica 186, 187
Alfon, Fernando 20
Alhama de Aragon 7
Ali Mudin 65
Alias the Phantom 104
Alipin ng Palad 32
Aliw, Mansarap na Lason 206
Almario, Virgilio 231
Aloha My Love 130
Alonzo, Alicia 119, 171, 172
Alperson, Edward L. 22
Alturas Group of Companies (ASG) 233
Alvarado, Max 111
Alvarez, Miniong 80
Always in My Heart 132
Alyas Stella Magtanggol 201
Ama at Anak 45
The Amazing Philippine Show 159
Ambassador Productions 97
America 38, 39, 42, 43, 53, 54, 57, 58, 62, 70, 71, 119, 120, 135–138, 140, 141, 163, 173, 222, 226
American Biography and Mutoscope 7
American culture 104, 107
An American Guerrilla in the Philippines 39, 57
American International Pictures 126
American-Philippine War 22
Americans 19, 20 28–30, 33, 40, 42–46, 49, 57, 67, 68, 70, 76–78, 83, 84, 87, 94, 95, 97, 98, 119, 120, 123, 126, 127, 135, 137, 142, 157, 158, 163, 164, 154, 240
Amigo, Cesar 88, 92, 108
Amilbangsa, Grace 152, 154
Amy, Susie, Tessie 62
Anak, ang Iyong Ina 130
Anak Dalita 70
Anak ng Aswang 131
Anak ng Bulkan 120, 121, 165
Anak ni Facifica Falayfay 105
Anak ni Palaris 90
Anak, Pagsubok Lamang ng Diyos 177
Anak sa Ligaw 25
Andolong, Sandy 150
Andress, Ursula 222
Angel of Destruction 165

Angeles City 176
Angeles City Regional Trial Court 176
Angelfist 164
Annabelle Huggins Story: Ruben Ablaza Tragedy 184
Anson, Belen 79
Anson-Roa, Boots 182, 184, 218
Antido, Antonio 111–113
Anti-Drug Abuse Council 224
Antipolo Massacre: Jesus Save Us! 184, 185
Apat na Alas 65
Apocalypse Now 163, 165, 185
Apollo Theater 7
Appeals Committee 169
Aquino, Benigno, Jr. 29, 140–142, 165, 166, 184, 218, 239
Aquino, Corazon 29, 145, 158, 159, 166–169, 176, 184, 201, 203, 206, 211, 212, 218, 228, 239
Aquino, Edgardo 101, 102
Aquino, John 193
Aquino, Kris 176, 182, 184, 188, 212, 218
Aquino, Roldan 148
Aquino-Kashiwahara, Lupita 140
An Arabian Cortege 6
Aragon, Antonio 186
Aragon, Honesto 186
Aragon, Mina 106
Arandia, Ronald 185
Araneta, J. Amando 28, 40
Araw Movies 18
Arceo, Liwayway 46
Arevalo, Robert 171
Arevalo, Tito 48, 89, 108
Arizona Kid 137
Arlen, Richard 84
Armalite 176
Arnaldo, Tony 58, 59
Arong family 61
Arroyo, Gloria Macapagal see Macapagal-Arroyo, Gloria
Arroyo, Mikey 212, 216, 220
Asahar at Kabaong 25
Asedillo 147, 148
ASG see Alturas Group of Companies

413

414 Index

Ashley, John 45, 94, 95, 119, 120, 122–124, 126
Asia 20, 29, 33, 43, 46, 76, 127, 240
Asian Film Festival 70, 84
Asiong Salonga 93, 94
Asistio, Boy 216
Asistio, Luis "Baby" 216, 217
Associated Artists 61
Assumption College 152
Astaire, Fred 36
Aswang, Ang 19, 196
Ateneo de Manila 38, 129, 188, 196, 228
Atlanta Center 220, 221, 223, 224
Atrocities of Fort Santiago see *Fort Santiago*
Atrocities of the Orient 86
Aunor, Nora 131–134, 140–142, 146, 147, 191, 192, 212, 238
Australia 178
Austria, Amy 152
Avellana, Lamberto 28, 37, 38, 47, 48, 52, 69, 70, 76, 132, 145, 231, 240
Avenue Theater 47, 49, 51
Awit ni Palaris 65
Azcarraga Street 7
Azucena Productions 61

Babae sa Bintana 202
Baby Tsina 153, 154
Bacalso, Natalio 61
Back to Bataan 57
Bad Boy 176
Bad Boy 2 176
Badjao 70
Bagong Bayani 191–193
Bagong Umaga 69
Baguio 7, 164
Baguio City 22, 98
Bahay-kubo 45
Bakas ng Kahapon 60
Bakit Hindi Ka Pa Dumarating? 46
Balabagan, Sarah 193
Balian 163
Banahaw Pictures 38
Banaue: Stairway to the Sky 133
Banawe Rice Terraces 7
Barangay Theater Guild 38
Barasoain Church 210
Barcelona 9, 31
Barcelona, Benjamin 111–113
Barri, Mario 78, 98
Barrymore, John 48
Basilan 22, 178, 179
Bataan 42, 45, 46, 50, 100
Bataan Death March 49
Batallon de Cazadores 6
Batang Maynila 92
Batang Tulisan 25, 31
Batang West Side 235
Batangas 10, 102, 238
Batch '81 150, 151
Batch 69 205
Battalion XIII 78
Battle of Baliwag 7
Battle of Mount Arayat 7
Bautista, Arsenio "Boots" 1, 8, 19
Bautista, Butch 91

Bautista, Herbert 218
Bautista, Jose see Revilla, Ramon
Bautista, Monsignor Nico 232
Bautista, Perla 138, 140
Bava, Mario 97
Bayadra Brothers 206
Bayagra Brothers 206
Bayan Ko: Kapit sa Patalim 143, 144, 170
Bayani Pictures 61
Bayaning Third World 200, 201
Bayer, Rolf 70, 87
Bayside 84
BCMP (Board of Censorship for Motion Pictures) 25, 100, 101, 107, 113–115, 117, 129, 158, 160
Beach Red 98
Beast of Blood 120, 122
Beast of the Yellow Night 123, 124
Beasts of the East 57, 86
Because You're Mine 130
Behind Enemy Lines 165
Benguet 164
Benitez, Francisco 43
Benito Bros. Pictures 61
Berdugo ng mga Anghel 67
Berlin 9, 83
Berlin Film Festival 163
Berlin International Film Festival 206
Bernal, Ishmael 133, 134, 140, 145–147, 150, 154, 156–158, 193, 195, 204, 240
Bertoldo-Balodoy 19, 20
Beyond the Call of Duty 165
Bicol peninsula 134
Bicolona 34
BID (Bureau of Immigration and Deportation) 222, 234
The Big Bird Cage 125, 127
The Big Doll House 124, 234
Bikini 95
Biktima: (1972) 131
Bilibid prison 177, 187
Binakayan 48
Bituing Marikit 36, 39
Biyaya ng Lupa 99
Black Mama, White Mama 125
The Black Zoo 222
The Blackbelter 104
Blanca, Nida 37, 38, 77, 78, 220–227
Blancaflor, Norma 45, 46
Bleecker Street Cinema 163, 164
Blind Rage 104
The Blood Drinkers see *Kulay Dugo ang Gabi*
Blood of Bataan 56, 57
Blood Thirst 3
Board of Censors see BCMP; BRMPT; MTRCB
Boatman 197, 230
Bohol 233
Bold films 169, 170, 194, 195, 202, 203, 232
Bolsheviks 76
Bomba Queen 160
Bombas 30, 107–110, 113–115, 119, 130, 136, 149, 156, 159, 194

Bonifacio, Andres 9, 198, 200
Bonnevie, Dina 145
Bonnin, Bernard 172
Borja, Eusebio 14
Borrego, Mary 70
Borromeo, Florentino 15, 20
Borromeo, Max 15
Les Boxers 6
Boys' Town 60
Bracken, Josephine 198, 201
Brain of Blood 95
Brenner, Joseph 57
Brereton, Lewis 41
Brian, David 57
Brides of Blood 94–96, 119, 123
Britain 3, 42, 83
British 42, 43
British Council Grant 197
British Film Institute 144, 197
BRMPT (Board of Review for Motion Pictures and Television) 142–144, 160, 161
Brocka, Danilo 134
Brocka, Lino 105, 127, 133–147, 150, 154, 156–158, 167, 169, 188, 193, 195, 197, 200, 204, 230, 240
Brocka, Regino 134
Broken Marriage 146
Brown, Harry 9–14
Brown Emmanuelle 148
Browne, Barbara 138
Brussels International Film Festival 105, 198
Brutal 152
Buenaflor, Edward 170
Buenaventura, Augusto 216, 217
Buenavista 28
Buencamino, Nonong 199
Buhay ng Pagibig ni Dr. Jose Rizal 67
Buhay Pilipino 63
Bukang Liwayway: film 45; play 47
Bukas, Madaling Bukas 138
Bulacan 38, 45, 60, 80, 99, 160
Bulak sa Lunangan 20
Bunye, Ignacio 220
Bureau of Immigration and Deportation see BID
Bureau of Prisons 99
Burgos, Jose 12, 198
Burlesk Queen 147, 148
Busog 110
Byroade, Henry 116

C. Santiago Film Organization 84
Cabagnot, Ed 1
Cabajar, Justo 20
Cacho, Jesus 27, 68
Cadena de Amor 136
Café los Indios Bravos 98
Caffaro, Cheri 126
Caged Fury 125, 164
Cairo International Film Festival 192
Calauan 184
Calderon, Helen 101, 102
California 8, 23, 168, 186, 222, 224, 225
Calle Crespo 7
Calle Santa Rosa 7

Caloocan 216, 218
Camalig 30
Camarines Sur 175
Cambodia 82
Camp Bagong Diwa 179
Camp Crame 166, 167
Canal, Rogelio 101, 102
Cannes Film Festival 143, 144, 163, 168
Canoy, Reuben 120
CAP (Concerned Artists of the Philippines) 142, 156, 160, 229
Caparas, Carlo 180–182, 184–188, 192, 233, 238
Capra, Frank 22
Card Players 6
Carino, Aida 175
Carino, Eva 175, 177
Carino, Lina 88
Carino, Virgilio 179
Carmines Sur 212
Carnap Gang 176
Carpio, Agnes Reyes 220
Carpio, Antonio 187
Carradine, John 126, 127
Carvajal, Alfonso 57
Castelvi, Jaime 72
Castillo, Cecille 152, 154
Castillo, Celso Ad. 110, 115, 133, 140, 147–149, 154, 160, 185, 192, 194, 195
Castillo, Dominador Ad. 97
Castillo, Myrna 160
Castro, Rosalina 100
Catholic Church 9, 12, 37, 166, 168, 198, 225, 227–232
Catholicism 5, 12, 36, 87, 108, 122, 138, 147, 150, 155, 169, 201, 225, 229
Catmon, Cebu 15
Cavalry Command see *Day of the Trumpet*
Cavite 40, 48, 79, 157, 198, 212, 214
Cayado, Tony 73
CEB see Cinema Evaluation Board
Cebu 10, 11, 15, 19, 20, 61
Cebu City 15, 20, 236
Cebu Stars Productions 61
Cebuano 33, 61
Censorship 12–14, 25, 74, 76, 100, 101, 107–109, 113–115, 117, 118, 130, 134, 144, 156, 158, 160–162, 168–170, 193, 195, 202, 203, 205, 228, 229, 231–233
Centenera, Andres 94, 124
Central Bank 80
Centro Statale di Cinematografia e Film 201
Centro Escolar University 15
Chan, Jackie 194
Chaplin, Charlie 38
Charito, I Love You 74
Chicago International Film Festival 201
China 3, 20, 76, 83, 209
Chinese 35, 37, 74, 87, 150, 194
Chinese mestizos 8, 11–13, 16

Chinese Navy 209
Chiong, Luis 20
Chionglo, Mel 195
Chiquito 106, 137
Christ 67, 81, 147
Christians 12, 108, 158, 179
Christianity 5, 12, 36, 37, 155
Chronicle Broadcasting Network 141
CIA 115
CIDG (Criminal Investigation and Detection Group) 222–225
Cinderella A Go-Go 131
Cine Anda 7, 10
Cine Auditorium 15
Cine Ideal 15
Cine Walgrah 7
Cinema Artists 150
Cinema Evaluation Board (CEB) 234
Cinemanila 137, 142
Cinematografo Electro-Optico Luminoso Walgrah 15
Cinematograpo Rizal 7
Citizens Against Crime 220
Citizens Council for Better Motion Pictures 115
City After Dark 134, 140, 146, 147
Clark Air Base 41, 42, 140, 167, 207, 209, 226
Claveria, Narciso 37
Clemente, Juanito 108
Climax of Love 116
Clinton, Bill 226
"Close to You" 132
Coalition Against Trafficking of Women—Asia Pacific 229
Coalition of Filipino Film and Television Workers 229
Cobb, Andrew 34
Cohen, David 123
Cojuangco, Eduardo, Jr. 209
Colgate 68
Collegian Love 18
Colon Street 20
Colonialism: 87, 154, 200; Spain 5, 9, 11–13, 20, 31, 33, 34, 36, 37, 43, 69, 84, 87, 93, 122, 154, 198; U.S. 5, 13, 20, 27, 33, 43, 46, 51, 84, 87, 154, 157, 164
Columbia Pictures 84
Columbus, Christopher 29
Columbus Quadricentennial Art Contest 29
Comedis Theater 7
Commission of Customs 80
Commission on Elections 214, 216, 237
Concepcion, Gabby 174
Concerned Artists of the Philippines see CAP
Concha, Carmen 29
Conde, Conrado 64
Conde, Manuel 51, 65, 66, 147, 175, 240
El Conde de Monte Carlo 65
Condenado 173
Conference on Memory, Truth-telling and the Pursuit of Justice:

The Legacies of the Marcos Dictatorship 129
La Conquista de Filipinas 11, 12
La Conquista de Filipinas de Legazpi 13
Conrad, Robert 126
Constantino, F.H. 73
Constitutional Commission 167
Contemplacion, Flor 190–193
Cooper, Elizabeth "Dimples" 16, 17
Coppola, Francis Ford 163–165, 185
Corman, Roger 123, 124, 163, 164, 234
Corrales, Pilita 130
Corregidor 42, 45, 46, 50, 98
Cortes, Fred 39
Cortez, Amado 175
The Cory Quirino Kidnap: NBI Files 184
Couples for Christ 228
Court of Appeals 180, 187, 227
Court of First Instance 113
Court of Industrial Relations 59, 60
CR Productions 97
The Crawling Hand 222
Criminal Investigation and Detection Group see CIDG
Criollos 12, 24, 34
Cristobal, Adrian 88
Cromwell, John 84
Cross My Heart 174
Cruz, Jose Esperanza 46
Cruz, Sunshine 185
Cruz, Tirso, III 132–134
Cruz, Tony 91
Cry of Battle 98
Cuba 7, 9, 198
Cubao 219
Cultural Center of the Philippines 155, 228
Cuneta, Pablo 174
Cuneta, Sharon 174
Curacha: Ang Babaeng Walang Pahinga 201, 202
Curse of the Vampires see *Ibulong Mo sa Hangin*
Customs Bureau 212, 214
The Czar's Carriage Passing Place de la Concorde 6
Czechoslovakia 3

Daigdig Ko'y Ikaw, Ang 92
Dalagang Bukid 14, 18, 45
Dalisay Pictures 59, 98
Dalisay Theater 60
Dama de Noche 131
A Dangerous Life 3
Dante, Reynaldo 67
Dapitan 9, 11, 197, 198
Darling Nora 132
Darna 23, 68
Darna (film) 68
Darna and the Giants 68
Darna at ang Babaing Lawin 68
Darna at ang Babaing Tuod 68
Darna at ang Impakta 68
Darna at ang Planetman 68
Darna at Ding 68

Darna vs the Planet Women 68
Darren, Eva 94, 95
Datumanong, Simeon 227
Daughters of Satan 3, 125
Davao, Charlie 173
Davao City 236
Davao Gulf 41
The Dawn 127
The Dawn of Freedom 44–46
Day of the Trumpet 84
Dayrit, Manet 199
Deadly Fighters 104
Dear Heart 174
Dear Uncle Sam 169
Death March 52
The Deathhead Virgin 125
de Belen, Janice 188
de Castro, Ceferina 22
de Castro, Eduardo 20, 22, 37, 44, 54, 57
de Cordova, Joseph 57
Deegar Cinema 61
de Guzman, Susana C. 30, 58, 59
de Izquierdo, Rafael 12
dela Cruz, Rey 159, 160
de la Rama, Atang 18, 29
dela Riva, Maggie 101, 102, 168, 187, 188
dela Rosa, Africa 81
dela Rosa, Gloria 81
dela Rosa, Jaime 52, 65, 81
dela Rosa, Purita 216
dela Rosa, Rogelio 35, 36, 39, 40, 45, 48, 52, 63–65, 72, 79–83, 103, 216
de Legazpi, Miguel Lopez 11–13, 48
de Leon, Casiana 45
de Leon, Christopher 137, 138, 141, 142, 146, 150, 154, 173, 174, 186
de Leon, Dona Narcisa Buencamino 27, 29, 30, 39, 60, 73, 149
de Leon, Gerardo 33, 37, 44–46, 48, 54, 62, 67–71, 74, 83, 84, 86, 88, 89, 94, 95, 119, 120, 122, 123, 125, 126, 132, 133, 200, 231, 240
de Leon, Joey 159, 160, 214
de Leon, Jose 29
de Leon, Manuel 149
de Leon, Mike 133, 139, 149–152, 154, 188, 200, 201
de Leon, Pinky 186
de Leon, Teofilo 88
de Leon, Van 82
Delgado, Johnny 151, 188
Delgado, Lota 36, 81
del Mar, Eduardo 37, 65, 67
Del Monte Avenue 90
Del Monte Films 59
del Mundo, Clodualdo, Jr. 139
del Prado, Renato 113
del Rio, Purificacion 53
del Rosario, Esther 68
del Rosario, Monsour 188
del Rosario, Rosa 23, 24, 34–37, 68
del Sol, Mila 39, 47
Denmark 205
Denver, Colorado 70, 73

Department of Defense (Philippine) 117
Department of Foreign Affairs (Philippine) 193
Department of Justice *see* DOJ
Departure of the Igorots to Barcelona 10
De Paul University 62
Derek, John 222
Derr, Richard 86
de Sana, Saldo 53
Desert Warrior 165
Desperation 34
de Vega, Guillermo 101, 113–115, 117–119, 129
de Villa, Nestor 75, 77
Dewey, George 7
El Diablo 67
Diabolika 113
Dial-M 168
Diaz, Gloria 149
Diaz, Lav 203, 235, 236, 240
Diaz, Teddy 127
Diaz, Vic 84, 98, 123, 126–128, 165, 173
Diaz-Abaya, Marilou 152–154, 188, 198–202
Diego Silang 69
Dinglasan, Mar-Len 231
Diones, Myrna 182, 184
Directors Guild of the Philippines 229
Discher, Etang 73
Diwata sa Karagatan 36
Dixon, Ralph 23
Dixson, Alice 187, 204
Dizon, Daniel H. 45, 46
Dizon, Lilia 28, 37, 90, 137
DJ's Pet 174
D'Musical Teenage Idols 131, 132
Doble Solo 106
DOJ 224–227
Dolphy 64, 73, 104–107, 110, 221
Domingo, Andrea 222, 223
Domingo, Salvador 53
Don't Ever Say Goodbye 130
Dragon's Quest 148
Drakulita 110
Droga: Pagtatapat ng Babaing Addict 194
Dudurugin Kita ng Bala Ko 171, 172
Dugo ng Bayan 52, 104
Dumaguete 83
Duntog Foundation 98
Duran, Tita 52, 62, 63, 72
Durando 114
Dutch 43
Dutch Boy Nalcrete 178
Dyesebel 68
DZRH 141
DZRM 68
DZXL 141

Eagle Lion Films 61
Eat, Bulaga 159
Ebolusyon ng Isang Pamilyang Pilipino 235
Ebony, Ivory and Jade 164
Echague, Isabela 19

ECP (Experimental Cinema of the Philippines) 129, 156, 157, 203
Edgar Loves Vilma 130
Edison Biograph 7
Edmunds, Tony 120
EDSA (Epifanio de los Santos Avenue) 166, 211, 223
EDSA revolution *see* People Power revolution
EDSA II *see* People Power II
Educational Pictures 61
Edwards, Vince 84, 86
Eiga Haikyusha 44
Ejercito, Emilio 93
Ejercito, JV 222
Ekland, Britt 98
Electro-Fotografia-Parhelio 14
Ella, Gregorio 138
Elsa Castillo Story . . . Ang Katotohanan 188–190
Elsa Santos Castillo Story: The Chop Chop Lady 190
EMAR Pictures 94
Emily 74
Emmanuelle, Sarsi 158, 159, 197
Empire Theater 7, 10, 11
England *see* Britain
English language 19, 23, 28, 31, 33, 36, 65, 87, 95, 97, 108, 120, 126, 135, 158, 195, 196
Enriquez, Jean 229
Enriquez, Laarni 211
Enrile, Juan Ponce 116, 166
Equalizer 2000 165
Eruption of Mayon Volcano 10
Escenas Callejeras 7
Escolta Street 5, 6, 19, 48
Escudero, Francis 239
Eskrimador 65
Espetaculo Cientifico de Pertierra 6
Espina, Leonardo 223
Esteban 147
Estella, Ramon 28, 72, 74
Estrada, Gary 218
Estrada, Jinggoy 212, 214
Estrada, John 202
Estrada, Joseph 93, 95–97, 106, 142, 175, 179, 203, 204, 206, 207, 209–212, 215–218, 221, 222, 227, 229, 236, 238, 239
Estregan, George, Jr. 218
Estrella, Linda 62
Estudio Americo-Filipino 19
Ethan 98
Europe 37, 39, 42, 43, 87, 163, 198
Eva at si Adan, Si 74
Everlasting Pictures 61
Excelsior Studios 27, 28, 53, 59
Executive Order No. 640-A 161, 162
Executive Order No. 770 156, 158
Executive Order No. 868 160
Executive Order No. 876-A 161
The Expendables 165
Experimental Cinema of the Philippines *see* ECP
Exzur 68
Eye of the Eagle 165
Eye of the Eagle 2 165
Eye of the Eagle 3 165

Fabregas, Jaime 158, 199, 239
Facifica Falayfay 104
Fajardo, Deo 175
FAMAS (Filipino Academy of Motion Picture Arts and Sciences) 49, 61, 69, 70, 72, 73, 76, 77, 86, 88, 94, 98, 99, 103, 105, 108, 130, 131, 136, 138–141, 147, 148, 150, 152, 161, 173, 199, 201
FAP (Film Academy of the Philippines) 97, 161, 162, 199, 201, 234
Far East Films 61
Far East University 35
Fate or Consequence 16
FBI 186, 187, 225
FDCP (Film Development Council of the Philippines) 234
Fe, Esperanza, Caridad 132
Feleo-Gonzalez, Marina 141
Ferdinand E. Marcos: An Epic 119
Fernandez, Dan 218
Fernandez, Eddie 95, 110–113
Fernandez, Gregorio 18, 25, 27, 34, 35, 52, 109, 175
Fernandez, Maritoni 204
Fernandez, Merle 109, 110, 113, 114
Fernandez, Naty 18, 33
Fernandez, Rudy 175, 218
Fernando, Enrique M. 144
Fernando Poe Productions 61
Ferrer, Tony 103–105, 110, 171
Field of Fire 165
Fiesta de Quiapo 7
Fighting Mad 164
Filcudoma Pictures 61
El Filibusteris: novel 9; film (1916) 13; (1962) 49, 88
Filipinas Pictures 61, 94
Filipino Academy of Motion Picture Arts and Sciences *see* FAMAS
Filipino Cockfight 7
Filipino Theatrical Enterprises 60
Filippine Films 19, 20, 23–28, 34, 38–40, 59, 240
Film Academy of the Philippines *see* FAP
Film and Freedom: Movie Censorship in the Philippines 101, 115, 129
The Film Daily 23
Film Development Council of the Philippines *see* FDCP
Film Institute of India 145
Filmakers Productions 61
Final Mission 165
Firecracker 164
Firehawk 165
First District Court of Manila 40
Fitzsimmons, Bronwyn 92
Flaminiano, Rose 177
Flight to Fury 94, 135
Flor, Celia 57
The Flor Contemplacion Story 191–194
Florante, Vida 53
Florida 186
FLT Films 177
Focus on Filipino Films 146
Fookien Times Yearbook 118
Forbidden Women 57

Forgive and Forget 174
Formosa 41, 42
Fort Santiago 44
Fort Santiago (film) 52–55
Fortress of the Dead 98
Fortune Pictures 61
42nd Street, New York 57, 86, 159
Four Associates 123, 126
FPJ Productions 92, 93
France 3, 5, 9, 15, 43, 143–145, 168
Francisco, Boy 91
Franco, Jess 104
Frankfurt International Film Festival 70
Free the Artist movement *see* FTA
French language 36
Fresno, California 222
Friedgen, Lloyd 57, 86
Friends in Love 174
From Hell to Borneo 98
From the Bottom of My Heart 130
FTA (Free the Artist Movement) 160
Fuentes, Amalia 62, 70, 95, 110, 120, 122, 123
Funston, Frederick 157, 158
El Fusilamiento de Dr. Jose Rizal 11

Gable, Clark 36
Gaity Theater 7
Galang, Fred 108
Galla, Pedro 70
Galla, Tito 109
Gallaga, Peque 156–158
Gallardo, Acuna *see* Revilla, Ramon
Gamboa, Elaine 174
Gamboa, Helen 174, 191, 192
Gamboa, Joonee 98, 148
Gandhi 231
Ganito Kami Noon, Paano Kayo Ngayon? 124, 154
Garces, Octavio 219
Garcia, Carlos 80, 81
Garcia, Eddie 73, 103, 108, 114, 115, 120, 122, 123, 136, 137, 145, 165, 173, 174, 220, 239
Gardner, William Henry 20, 22
Garland, Richard 86
Garrison 13 52
Gary, Indiana 62
Gascon: Bala ang Katapat Mo 172
Gaulberto, Nestorio 222, 223, 225
Gawad Urian 124, 192, 199, 201
Gayuma, Ang 34
Gazzara, Ben 98
Genghis Khan 65, 66, 147
George, Harold 41
Germany 3, 33, 149, 163, 164
Geron Olivar 172
Gerow, Leonard T. 41
A Gift of Love 132
Gil, Cherie 147
Gil, Mark 151
Gil, Rosemarie 148
Giliw Ko 39
Ginoong Patay Gutom 52
Give Me Your Heart 130
GLM Productions 61

GMA Films 198, 199
God Save Me! 146
God's People Coalition for Righteousness 228
Godzilla 39
Golden Era of Philippine Cinema 58–78, 79, 87, 103, 162, 180
Golden Harvest award 70
Golden Harvest Productions 97
The Golden Voice of Nora 132
Gomez, Mariano 12
Gomez, Pablo 182
Gomez, Richard 176, 202
Gomez, Rita 70, 73, 82, 98, 130
Gonzaga, Marita 185
Gonzales, Luis 63, 64, 70, 100
Gonzalez, Jose Antonio U. 144
Gonzalez, Dr. Virgilio R. 19, 20
Gotianquin, Pelagia Mendoza y 29
Goulette, Frank H. 10, 11
Gran Cinematografo Parisien 7
Grand Canyon Suite 98
Grand National 22, 23
Grand Opera House 8
The Grapes of Wrath 135
Graphic 19
Grease Gun Gang 176
Greek 155
Greek Parthenon 155
Green Hills, San Juan 219, 220, 236
Grey Film Atelier 201
Grier, Pam 125, 126
Grofe, Ferde, Jr. 98
Grofe, Ferdinand Rudolph von 98
Gross, Dr. Edward Meyer 9, 11, 13, 14
Groundhog Day 169
Grove, Hattie 33
Guam 167
Guerilyera 53, 63
Guerrillas in Pink Lace 98
Guevara, Jose L. 101
Gugmang Talagsaon 20
Guico, Edgardo 221
Guillen, Laurice 188, 189, 219, 234
Guinness Book of World Records 4
Gumapang Ka sa Lusak 145
Gumbao, Mitchell *see* Roldan, Dennis
Gutierrez, Anna Marie 157
Gutierrez, Eddie 223
Gutierrez, Merceditas 225, 227
Guwapo 69
Guy and Pip 133, 134

The Hague 82
Haig, Sid 126, 127
Hain ang Langit 61
Hamilton, Roy 84
Harris, George F. 19, 20, 23, 25, 27, 28, 240
Harrison, Francis Burton 13
Harvard Street 219
Hawaii 20, 84, 167, 172
Hawaiian Boy 84
He Promised to Return 54
Heafner, Robert 187

Healey, Myron 84, 126
Heidelberg 9
Hellman, Monte 94
Hellow, Soldier 138
Hemisphere Pictures 84, 89, 92, 94, 97, 119, 120, 123, 124
Hermoso Drugstore 58
Hernandez, Eulalia 15
Hernando, Mario A. 1, 13, 146
Herrero, Subas 125, 207
Herzog, Werner 163
Hidalgo, July 175
High Velocity 98
Higit sa Korona 65
El Hijo Disobediente 15, 20
Hill, Jack 124
Hills, Beverly 94, 95
Himala 146, 156
Hindi Ka na Sisikatan ng Araw 173
Hindi Mapigil ang Init 160
Hitman 213
Hodobu 43
Hollows, Gregory 226
Hollywood 4, 5, 14, 16, 20, 23, 35, 37–39, 51, 57, 58, 63, 78, 84, 86, 87, 89, 97, 103, 104, 135, 146, 164, 178, 194
Hollywood Far East Productions 92, 97
The Hollywood Reporter 23
Hollywood Spectator 23
Holmes, Burton 7
Holmes, Paul 198
Home Along da Riles 106
Un Homme au chapeau 6
Hong Kong 84, 98, 127, 194, 198
Hontiveros, Daisy 38
Hoover, Herbert 16
The Hot Box 125
Hot Property 127, 204
Huang, Suzette See 219, 220
Hugis ng Pag-asa, Mga 138
Huk 78, 97
Huks 74, 76–78, 147, 148
Huk sa Bagong Pamumuhay 76
Huling Mandirigma 65
Humanda Ka Mayor! Bahala na ang Diyos 184
Hung, Sammo 194
Hunt, Marsha 57
Hunter, Jeffrey 120
Huston, John 45
Hyderabad, India 114

I Do Love You 130
I Dream of Nora 132
I Spit on Your Grave 165
Iba Field 41
Ibarra, Crisostomo 199
Ibong Adarna 39, 78
Ibulong Mo sa Hangin 120, 122, 123
Ideal Theater 7
"If I Had a Girl" 222
Ifugao 70
Iginuhit ng Tadhana 100, 117
Ignacio, Leon 14
Igorota 108, 109
Igorots 108
Ikaw Ay Akin 146

Ilagan, Hermogenes 14, 45, 48
Ilagan, Jay 136, 138, 140, 150–152
Ilaw ng Kapitbahay, Ang 34
Illinois 106
Ilocano 149
Ilocos Norte 99
Ilocos Sur 210
Imperial, Gloria 39
Imperialism *see* Colonialism
Imus Productions 214
Inang Mahal 39
Independence Day 194
Independent Moving Picture Company 8
India 83, 114
Indiana 62
Indonesia 20, 152
Infante, Eddie 57, 60, 84, 98
Insiang 140–142
Intelligence Service of the Armed Forces of the Philippines 227
International Federation of the Phonographic Industry 235
International Labor Organization 214
Intramuros 7, 49, 70, 89
Intramuros: The Rape of a City 52
Iran 197
Iraq 179
Iriarte, Prudencio 15, 19, 20
Iriga City 131
Irons, Jeremy 155
Isang Halik Lamang 45
Isang Laro 141
Isla 149
Islam 177, 179, 193
Island City Malls 233
Island of Dr. Moreau 86
Isleta, Loreto 108
Isputnik vs Darna 68
Israel, Dick 184, 201
Italy 3, 83
Itanong Mo sa Buwan 201
Itim 150
Ito ang Maynila 96
Iwabuchi, Sanji 49
Iyung-Iyo 63

Jack en Jill 104
Jackson, Michael 218
James, Jesse 181
Jamir, Nap 198
Jansen, William H. 23
Jao, Dr. Rodolfo 62
Japan 3, 34, 40–50, 52, 53, 83, 152, 160, 165, 188
Japan Foundation 152
Japanese 36, 41–47, 49, 50, 52–54, 57, 73, 74, 76, 83, 89, 100, 105, 135, 141–143, 150, 199
Japanese government 188
Japanese occupation 34, 43–51, 73, 74, 76, 104, 105, 141, 142, 154, 157
Jarlego, Ike, Jr. 57, 139
Jaworski, Robert 205, 218
JE Productions 94
Jeepney Drivers' Association 142
Jehovah's Witnesses 177

Jergens, Diane 88
The Jess Lapid Story 171
Jessica Films 97
Jesus Is Lord Movement 205, 228
Jeturian, Jeffrey 203
Jimenez, Jose 7
Jimenez, Mark 226
John D. Rockefeller III Grant 197
John en Marsha 106, 221
Johnson, Don 132
Jolo 16
Jones, John William, II 77
Jose, Jaclyn 201
Jose, Jaime 101, 102
Jose, Jesus 171, 172
Jose, Dr. Ricardo T. 46, 47
Jose Nepomuceno Productions 61
Jose Rizal 198–201
Josef Shaftel and Company 57
Joseph, Albert 103
Joseph, George L. 87
Jourdan, Louis 68
Joyce, James 118
Juan Daldal: Anak ni Juan Tamad 67
Juan Tamad 67
Juan Tamad Goes to Congress 67
Juan Tamad Goes to Society 67
Judgement Day 98
Juezan, Undo 61
Jurado, Abel 158

Kabahar, Piux 19, 20
Kadenang Putik 86
Kahariang Bato 87
Kahit Singko Hindi Ko Babayaran ang Buhay Mo 171, 172
Kakabakaba Ka Ba? 150
Kalapating Puti 59
Kalaw, Teodoro M. 25
Kalbaryo ni Hesus 67
Kamay ng Diyos, Ang 33, 70
Kamay ni Satanas 67
Kampana sa Santa Quiteria, Ang 111
Kandilerong Pilak 93
Kapag Iginuhit ang Hatol ng Puso 148
Kapag Puno na ang Salop 173
Kapitan Bagwis 65
Karate Fighters 104
Karnal 152, 154
Karnow, Stanley 1, 116
Kasintahan sa Pangarap 62, 72
Keesee, Oscar 57, 86, 88, 89
Kelly, Elizabeth 49, 89
Key, Lotis 105
Kidlat . . . Ngayon! 68
Kill Zone 165
Kim 84
King Philip II 11, 12
Kingsley, Grace 23
Kintanar, Galileo 227
Kintanar, Romulo 222, 225, 227
Kisapmata 150, 151
KMZH 41
KNP 236, 238, 239
Ko, Philip 194
Koalisyon ng Nagkakaisang Pilipino *see* KNP
Komiks 31, 37, 38, 62, 68, 95, 130, 136, 147, 174, 180–182, 238

Korea 70, 76, 83, 234
Korea (film) 77
Koronel, Hilda 135–140, 141
Krus na Kawayan 175
Kulay Dugo ang Gabi 95, 97, 120, 122
Kumander Sundang 54
Kundiman ng Lahi 73
Kung Bakit Dugo ang Kulay ng Gabi 148
Kurdapya 73
Kurosawa, Akira 155, 188

Labad, Lutgardo 138
Labor and Human Resources Committee 214
Labra, Berting 57, 91, 110–113
Lacaba, Jose F. 204
Lacaba, Pete 229
Lacap, Rody 199
Lacson, Arsenio 79
Laemmle, Carl 8
Laguardia, Consoliza 232
Laguna 77, 78, 218
Lalake sa Buhay ni Selya, Ang 195
Lamangan, Joel 191–193
Lamour, Dorothy 36, 54
Lana, Jun 199
Lang, Fritz 39, 57
Langit Ko'y Ikaw, Ang 75
Lapid, Jess 171
Lapid, Lito 171–173, 215–218
Lapid, Mark 218
Lapu-Lapu Pictures 61
Larawan ng Buhay 60
Larry Santiago Productions 214
Las Vegas 106, 219, 222, 225
The Last Temptation of Christ 169
Latang Asahar 70
la Torre, Olive 54, 62
Lauchengco, Francis 11
Laurel, Jose 100
Lauren, Rod see Strunk, Rod Lawrence
Lawin Pictures 61
Laxa, Espiridion 97
Laxa, Maricel 172
Lazaro, Ronnie 197
Lea Productions 135
Lean, David 83
Lebran Productions 57, 61, 65, 67, 68
Lederer, Francis 86
Lee, Bruce 104
Lee, Christopher 104
Lee, Ricardo 199
Legaspi, Cielito 84
Legaspi, Lito 109, 201
Leibman 6
Lejano, Antonio, II 186
Lemarr, Heddy 68
Leroy, Bert, Jr. 110
Letrondo, Benny 227
Letter of Instructions No. 13 117, 161, 175
Le Veque, Edward 23
Leyte 50, 89
Leyte Motion Pictures 61
LGS Productions 61
Liberal Party 79, 80, 82

Liberty Theater 61
Libingan ng mga Bayani 210
Lichauco, Faustino 27
Life Theater 62, 99
Liga Filipina 9, 197, 198
Ligaw na Bulaklak: (1929) 34, 35; (1975) 145
Ligaya ang Itawag Mo sa Akin 195
Lihim ni Madonna 149
Lilet 49
The Lilian Velez Story 184
Lim, Peter Ong 199
Lim, Roseller 82, 103
Linda, Anita 60, 65, 69, 72, 138
Lingad, Jose 80
Lingayen Gulf 41
Lipa 54, 102, 218, 238
Lipa City 218, 238
Lipa Massacre: Lord, Deliver Us from Evil 184, 185, 218
Lipenos 54
Lippert 94
Lisa, Mona 54, 57, 140
Literary Song-Movie Magazine 82, 86
Little, Florence 22
Live by the Fist 165
Live Show 197, 206, 228–230, 240
Liwayway Magazine 31, 68
Lo' Waist Gang 90
Lobo, Sergio 93
Lollipops and Roses 132
Lombard, Carol 36
London 83, 235
London Film Festival 197
London International Film School 152
Long, Johnny 122, 124
Lopez, Apolinario 111, 112
Lopez, Cecilia 37
Los Angeles 152, 168
The Los Angeles Times 23
Lost Battalion 88, 89
Lota, Sofia 16, 34
Lou, Barromeo 48
Love, Suzanne 197
Love at First Sight: (1960) 62; (1972) 130
Love Is for the Two of Us 130
Love Letters 130
Loyola Marymount University 152, 168
Lubao 35, 80
Lubitsch, Ernst 22
Lumang Bahay sa Gulod, Ang 78
Lumang Simbahan, Ang 34
Lumbera, Bienvenido 1, 13, 129
Luna, Edna 65
Luneta 12
Luxe Theater 83
Luz Theater 7
Luzon 12, 34, 35, 41, 70, 80, 84, 99, 133
LVN Studios 19, 27, 29, 39, 52, 57–59, 65, 68, 70, 73, 77, 78, 93, 98, 149, 175, 213, 240
Lydia 63, 64
Lynn, Kane W. 84, 86, 94, 95, 119, 120, 124
Lyric Theater 19, 51

Maalaala Mo Kaya?: (1954) 64; (1974) 132
Mababangong Bangungot 163, 164
Mabini, Pangasinan 72
Mabuhay Pictures 61
Macabebes 157, 158
Macao 84
Macapagal, Cielo 216
Macapagal, Diosdado 80–82, 100, 101, 216, 231
Macapagal-Arroyo, Gloria 177, 179, 187, 212, 215, 216, 221, 222, 227–234, 236–240
MacArthur, Arthur 13
MacArthur, Douglas 16, 17, 33, 41, 42, 45–47, 49, 50, 98
Macaso, Flavio 69
Maceda, Marichu 30
Macho Dancer 197, 230
Mad Doctor of Blood Island 119, 120, 123
Mad Max 165
Madame X 72
Madison County 169
Madrid 9, 31, 198
Maestra, Ang 33, 83
Maga, Delia 190, 192
Magallanes Street 15
Magalona, Enrique, Sr. 63, 79
Magalona, Pancho 62, 63, 72, 79, 84
Magdalena, Rita 194, 195
Magdapio 7
Magellan, Ferdinand 11
The Maggie dela Rive Story: God... Why Me? 188
Mag-inang Mahirap 38
Magsaysay, Ramon 76–78
Mahoney, Jock 89, 92, 126
Majestic Theater 7
Makati 100, 159
Makati Regional Trial Court 180
Malacanang 81, 119, 144, 151, 154, 156, 167, 212, 220, 230, 231, 237
Malate 49, 124
Malaya 20
Malaya Films 143, 144
Malayan Motion Pictures 1, 14, 34
Malayan Pictures Corporation 20, 27
Malays 11, 35, 122
Malaysia 127
Mallorca, Spain 24
Malonzo, Gigi 218
Malonzo, Rey 216–218
Man on the Run 84
Mananayaw 149, 194
Mandaluyong City 223
Mang Tano: Nuno ng mga Aswang 34
Manibog, Myra 160
Manicad, Dennis 231, 232
Manila 5, 7–16, 19, 20, 24, 38, 39, 41–48, 53, 59–63, 68, 72, 76, 77, 79, 81, 83, 84, 89, 93, 98, 99, 101104, 112, 113, 122, 124, 127, 131, 134, 135, 137, 139–141, 145, 146, 149, 152, 155, 160, 164, 166, 168, 173, 177, 179, 181, 187,

420 Index

197, 198, 201, 204, 206, 211, 214, 225–227, 230–233, 238, 240
Manila Bay 7
Manila by Night see *City After Dark*
Manila Carnival 10
Manila Chronicle 145
Manila Film Center 3, 155–161
Manila Film Festival 103, 198, 199, 201
Manila International Airport 142, 166
Manila International Film Festival 129, 155
Manila Movies Magazine 28
Manila: Open City 122, 123
Manila Talkaton Pictures 19
Manila Times 8, 69
Manuel Conde Productions 61, 65
Manunuri ng Pelikulang Pilipino 228
Mapa, Placido, Sr. 28
Marcelino, Ricardo 58
Marcos, Ferdinand 76, 82, 99–101, 1–3, 114–119, 128, 129 134, 140, 142–145, 150, 151, 155, 156, 158–162, 165–172, 175, 184, 193, 203, 204, 206, 207, 209–211, 218, 224, 227, 228, 239
Marcos, Imee 156, 218
Marcos, Imelda 100, 116–118, 126, 134, 144, 151, 155, 156, 158, 161, 218, 239
Marcos, Mariano 100
Margheriti, Antonio 234
Maria Clara Awards 67, 69
Maria Clara Pictures 61
Maria Went to Town 63
Maricris Sioson: Japayuki 188
Mariette, Gigi 84
Marita Gonzaga Rape-Slay: In God We Trust 184, 185
Markang Rehas 94
Markova: Comfort Gay 105
Marquez, Artemio 60, 218
Marquez, Joey 218
Marquez, Melanie 218
Marquez, Rosanna 115
Mars, Bud 10
Martial law 115–118, 125, 129, 130, 134, 137, 144, 148, 151, 162, 166, 167, 170, 171, 193
Martin, Carmi 204
Martin, Charles 9, 11, 13, 14
Martinez, Albert 197
Martinez, Mike 223
Masarap Habang Mainit 205
Massacre films 181, 183–185, 187, 188
Master Dem 200
Masters of Karate 104
Mathay, Ismael 218
Matimbang ang Dugo sa Tubig 237
Maton, Ang 120
Matukso Kaya ang Anghel 160
Maynila 52
Maynila, sa mga Kuko ng Liwanag 139, 140, 150
Mayon Photoplay Corporation 27
Mayon Volcano 10

McKinley, William 7
McLaurin Bros. Productions 61
McNutt, Paul 51
Medalyon Films 97
Medel, Philip, Jr. 222–227
Medina, Pen 198
Melendez, Aiko 218
Mendez, Henrietta 169, 203
Mercado, Lani 214
Meredith, Burgess 84, 86
Mesina, Arlene 116
Mestizos/mestizas 33–35, 37, 70, 72, 95, 98
Metro Manila Film Festival 162, 175
Mexico 3, 12, 87, 98, 137
MGM 34, 38
Miami, Florida 33, 226
Milagrosa Productions 61
Milan, Willy 225
Miles, Vera 126
Miller, Beverly 119, 123
Miller, Robert 172
Mina, Ara 178
Mindanao 15, 61, 70, 193, 198
Ministry of Tourism 156
Minsa'y Isang Gamu-gamo 140, 141
Miracles of Love 15, 16
Miss Universe pageant 33, 149
Missing in Action 234
Mr. and Mrs. 70
"Mister DJ" 174
Mitchell, Cameron 126
The Moises Padilla Story 88
Molina, Titay 13
Molokai 138
Monay 205
Monroy, Ramon 39
Mont Productions 97
Montalban, Rocco 116
Montano, Antonio C. 97
Montano, Cesar 185, 198
Montano, Delfin 79
Monteiro, Johnny 37, 65, 120
Montenegro, Mario 65, 94, 95, 150
Montes, Eva 68
Monteverde, Lily 30, 150
Monteverde, Remy 150
Montez, Eva 97
Montgomery, George 78, 97, 98, 126
Monzano, Edu 172, 173
Morato, Manuel 168, 169, 203–205
Morato, Tomas 168
Morena, Leila 28
Moreno, Alma 68, 105, 145, 147, 171, 218
Moreno, Liza 68
Moreno, Oscar 37, 79, 82
Moreno, Rosario 49
Moreno, Virginia 98
Mormons 138
Moro Pirates 34
Moro Witch Doctor 98
Moros 20, 22
Mortal 141
Mortiz, Edgar 133
Motion Picture Casting Corporation 97

Motion Picture Daily 23
Motion Picture Producers Association of the Philippines 40
Mount Banahaw, Holy Mountain 197
Mount Pinatubo 215
Movement for the Restoration of Peace and Order 220
Movie Confidential 33, 58, 82, 103
MPAA (Motion Picture Association of America) 107
MTRCB (Movie and Television Review and Classification Board) 160, 161, 168–170, 193, 195, 203–206, 221, 223, 228, 229, 231, 232, 234, 238
Multo ni Yamashita 54
Munoz, Alfred 99
Munoz, Tita 119
Muntinglupa 177, 187
Murder in the Orient 128
Murray, George 68, 69
The Music Played 131
Muslim 70, 93, 98, 177–179, 181, 193, 226
Muslim Screenwriters Club 193
Musser, George 19
The Muthers 125, 164
My Blue Hawaii 132
My Little Brown Girl 131
My Little Darling 130
My Only Love 174
My Pledge of Love 130
The Myrna Diones Story: Lord, Have Mercy! 182, 185

Nable, Jose 80, 81
Nacionalista Party 81
Nadres, Orlando 138
Nagahama, Colonel 53
Naked Island 160
Naked Vengeance 165
Nam Angels 165
Nanking 46
Nardong Putik 214
NARIC (National Rice and Corn Corporation) 29
Nasaan ang Puso 201
National Artist for Film 231
National Artist for Literature 231
National Broadcasting Network 168
National Bureau of Investigation see NBI
National Council of Churches 204
National Labor Union 60
Navarro, Jess 199
Navarro, Raymundo 27
Navoa, Eleuterio 27
NBI (National Bureau of Investigation) 48, 49, 186, 187, 221, 223–227
Neeson, Liam 169
Negros, Occidental 79
Negros, Oriental 83
Nepa Theater 83
Nepomuceno, Jesus 14
Nepomuceno, Jose 14–16, 18–20, 25, 27, 28, 34–36, 45, 61
Nepomuceno, Luis 1, 108
New Jersey 235

New People's Army *see* NPA
The New Society 117
New World Pictures 123, 126
New York 8, 23, 42, 57, 86, 94, 106, 163, 201
New York Times 163
New York University 197
Nicholson, Jack 94, 126, 127
Nicholson, Nick 207
Nicolas, Coca 159
Night of the Cobra Woman 3, 125
Nina Bonita 73, 74
9 Teeners 131
Niponggo 43
Nixon, Richard 116, 141
No Man Is an Island 120
No Place to Hide 57
Noble, Corazon 39, 40, 52
Nolasco, Luis 27, 52, 53, 70
Nolasco Brothers Pictures 27, 28, 52, 53, 70
Noli Me Tangere: novel 9, 69; film (1915) 13; (1930) 14; (1961) 49, 88
The Nora and Eddie Show 131
Nora in Wonderland 132
Nora, Mahal Kita 132
Norris, Chuck 234
Novales, Ramon 36, 53
NPA (New People's Army) 222, 225, 227
Nueva Ecija 134
Nueva Ecija North High School 135
Nunal sa Tubig 145
NV Productions 132, 141
Nympha 115, 140, 147, 148

Odeon Palace 20
O'Hara, Mario 136–139, 141, 142, 200
O'Hara, Maureen 92
Ohmart, Carol 84, 86
Ojeda, Orestes 157
OK, Fine, Whatever 73
Once Before I Die 222
One Man Army 165
Ongkiko, Mario 220
Oo, Ako'y Espiya 52
Optical Media Board 235
Orapronobis 167, 168
Orasang Ginto 51
Order to Kill 216
Organisation Catholique Internationale du Cinema 229
Oria, Elsa 36
Orient Theater 104
Oriental Pictures 61
Oro, Plata, Mata 157, 158
Oropesa, Elizabeth 192
Orpheum Theater 10
Ortigas Avenue 62
Ortiz, Pilar 134
Ortiz, Rosanna 110–113, 126
Osmena, Sergio 51
Osorio, Consuelo 175
Our Love Affair 130
Outrages of the Orient 54, 86

Paano Ba ang Mangarap 174

Pacific 42, 54, 57, 86
Paco 10
Padilla, Casimiro 60
Padilla, Dennis 218
Padilla, Jose, Jr. 59, 76
Padilla, Jose, Sr. 34, 80
Padilla, Robin 175–179, 215
Padilla, Roy 175
Padilla, Zsa Zsa 105–107
Padre Balaguer 201
Padre Kalibre 175
Padre Pugante 207
Pagbabalik, Ang 45
Page, Amanda 198
Pagputi ng Uwak, Pag-itim ng Tagak 148
Pagsanjan 218
Pagsilang ng Mesiyas, Ang 67
Pakistan 83
PAL (Philippine Artists League) Productions 61
Palanca, Carlos 11
Palanca Bros. Productions 61
Palanan 157
Palapos, Loy 233
Palaris Productions 39, 52, 61
Palmolive 68
Paloma, Pepsi 159, 160
Pampanga 15, 19, 25, 35, 79, 80, 82, 171, 173, 215, 216, 218, 236
Pandacan 10
Panday 182, 238
Panelo, Salvador 219
Panganiban, Rosario 15, 16
Pangasinan 54, 72
Pangilinan, Renato 111, 112
Pangilinan Productions 61
Panorama de Manila 7
PAR Productions 61
Paraluman 64, 82
Paramount Pictures 7, 22, 38, 51, 194
Paranaque 113, 218
Pareno, Gina 68
Paris 9, 163
Parlatone Hispano-Filipino 19, 20, 27, 38
Parsons, Michael J. 89, 98
Parsons, Sonny 181
Partido Bansang Marangal 168
Pasadena, California 22
Pasay 101, 113
Pasay City 102, 174
Pascual, Frisco N., Jr. 97
Pasig 48
Pasig City 180
Pasig regional Trial Court 225
Pasig River 49
The Passionate Strangers 98
Patayin Mo sa Sindak si Barbara 110, 148
Paterno, Adelaida 29
Paterno, Paz 29
Paterno, Pedro 7
Pathé 9
Pauline Productions 97
Paulino, Reynaldo 97
PBA (Philippine Basketball Association) 205, 218, 219

Peace Corps 94
Pearl Harbor 40–42
Pearl Theater 113
Pearson, Drew 16
Pedro Penduko 69
Pedro Vera, Jr. Productions 61
Pendulum of Fate 29
Pennsylvania Syncopation 18
People Power revolution 116, 166, 167, 172, 228
People Power II 211, 228
People's Pictures 61, 68
Peregrina, Eddie 131, 133
Perez, Azucena 99
Perez, Barbara 82
Perez, Gregorio "Cocoy" 30
Perez, Dr. Jose 30, 62, 72, 99, 104, 130, 213
Perez, Tony 138
Perfumed Nightmare see Mababangong Bangungot
Peritz 6
Perkins, Carl 84
Perlas ng Silangan 93, 94
Pertierra 5
PETA (Philippine Educational Theater Association) 137, 141
Peters, Kimwood 7
Pettyjohn, Angelique 120
Phantom Lady 131
Philippine Army 178
Philippine Artists' League 47
Philippine Bill of 1902 238
Philippine Bureau of Science 9
Philippine Centennial 195, 197, 201, 210
Philippine Charity Sweepstakes Office 168, 169
Philippine Court of Appeal 126
Philippine Daily Inquirer 45, 210
Philippine Dental College 24
Philippine Educational Theater Association *see* PETA
Philippine Enquirer 205
Philippine Free Press 15, 83, 193
The Philippine Herald 114
Philippine House of Representatives 211, 212
Philippine Legislature 25
Philippine Mental Health Association 29
Philippine Motion Pictures Producers Association 103
Philippine Movie Pictures Workers' Association 60
Philippine Movie Press Club 199
Philippine National Bank 232
Philippine National Pictures 59
Philippine National Police *see* PNP
Philippine National Red Cross 70
Philippine Paradise Pictures 61
Philippine Pictures, Inc. 52, 61
Philippine Plywood Corporation 168
Philippine Senate 211
Philippine Supreme Court 61, 100, 102, 113, 144, 170, 177, 181, 187, 212, 238
Phipps, Bill 84

422 Index

The Piano 169
Pieta 180
Pietro Barretta 176
Pilapil, Pilar 33, 105, 218
Pilipino Komiks 68
Pimentel, Aquilino, Jr. 232
Pinakamagandang Hayop sa Balat ng Lupa, Ang 148, 149
Pinaysex.com see www.XXX.com
Pineda, Basilio, Jr. 101, 102
Pito-pito films 202, 203
Pizor, Irwin 94
La Place de L'Opera 6
Plaridel Pictures Corporation 59
Plata, Patria 60
Plaza Goiti 6
PNP 176, 219, 221, 223, 239
Poe, Andy 90
Poe, Conrad 239
Poe, Edgar Allan 200
Poe, Fernando, Jr. 89–97, 110, 120, 135, 136, 147, 154, 173, 175, 176, 182, 209, 218, 236–240
Poe, Fernando, Sr. 24, 25, 35, 38, 39, 44, 46, 49, 52, 57, 65, 68, 89, 90, 104
Pons, Jerry 106
Pope John Paul II 177
Porac 171
Pornography 113, 156, 158–160, 169, 194, 203–205, 229, 231
Portes, Gil 229
Portuguese 11, 12
Pou, Lorenzo 24
Premiere Productions 30, 33, 58–61, 65, 72, 77, 78, 84, 90, 92, 120
Presidential Anti-Crime Commission 209
Presidential Appeals Board 195
Presidential Decree 1986 160, 161, 169, 170, 204, 205, 228, 229
Prima Donna 63
Princesa Tirana 61
Principeng hindi Tumatawa 65
Prinsesa at ang Pulubi, Ang 62
Prinsipe Amante 65
Prinsipe Amante sa Rubitanya 65
Prinsipe Don Juan 72
Prinsipe Paris 65
Private Show 197, 201, 230
Probinsyana 59
Protectionism 103, 234
P.S. I Love You 174
Public Forum 154
Puerto Rico 124, 234, 235
Pugo and Togo 47, 54
Pulitzer Prize 33
Punyal na Ginto 19
Punzalan, Bruno 94, 98
Punzalan, Princess 204
Pusong Dakila 45
Puwente de Espana 7

Querida 115
Quezon, Manuel 29, 33, 41, 42, 45, 98, 168, 196
Quezon City 29, 101, 107, 111, 112, 145, 159, 168, 215, 218, 219, 223–225, 227, 231, 233, 238, 239
Quezon City Police Department 111
Quezon Memorial Pictures 61
Quiapo 7, 23
Quilatan, Cortes 212, 213
Quintana, Tessie 45
Quiroz, Alex 225
Quizon, Eric 105, 188
Quizon, Jeffrey 105
Quizon, Jelom Carlo 107
Quizon, Nico 107
Quizon, Rodolfo, Jr. 106
Quizon, Rolly 148
Quizon, Wilfredo "Freddy" 106, 107

Radio Theater 18
Radio Veritas 166, 228
Raiders of Leyte Gulf 89, 98
Raiders of the Sun 165
Rajah Soliman Revolutionary Movement 179
Ramirez, Cesar 72, 97, 180
Ramon Selga 72
Ramos, Antonio 6, 7
Ramos, Ely 52
Ramos, Fidel 166, 169, 178, 190, 191, 193, 209, 215
Ranillo, Mat 61
Rashomon 188
The Ravagers 89, 90, 92, 98, 135
Ravelo, Mars 62, 68, 136, 182
Raw Force 127
Raymundo, Ina 206
Razon, Delia 37, 65
RCA Victor 222
RDR Productions 39, 40
Rebarber, Samuel 7
Rebecca 62
Recto, Ralph 218
Red Cross 29
Regal Films 30, 150, 158, 167, 202
Relasyon 146
Remy, Ronald 37, 95, 97, 119–121
Republic Act 360 160
Requiestas, Rene 184
Return of the Dragon 148
Revilla, Ramon 73, 110, 177, 212–214
Revilla, Ramon "Bong," Jr. 214, 233, 235
Rey, Alejandro 98
Rey, Raquel 223
Reyes, Efren 60, 65, 72, 86, 89, 97
Reyes, Jose Javier 197, 206, 228–230
Reyes, Juan O. 114
Reyes, Luis 89
Reyes, Ramon 139
Reyna Elena 77
Reynolds, Burt 126
Ricketts, Ronnie 175, 181
Rivas, Corazon 37
Rivera, Eva see Carino, Eva
Rivero, Dante 136, 137
Rizal, Jose 8–14, 67, 69, 88, 197–201
Rizal, Paciano 198
Rizal Avenue 49, 60
Rizal Day Celebration 10
Rizal sa Dapitan 187, 198
Rizal Theater 100
Rizalina Film Company 9
Roberta 62
Roces, Alejandro 69, 231
Roces, Rosanna 195, 201, 202
Roces, Susan 62, 70, 73, 82, 92, 93, 182, 239
Roco, Bembol 138, 139, 141, 142, 148, 168
Roco, Raul 205
Rodgers, Ginger 36
Rodrigo, Ric 37, 73, 82, 108, 109
Rodrigo de Villa 65
Rodriguez, Alfredo 224, 227
Rodriguez, Buenaventura 15
Rodriguez, Celestino 15
Rodriguez, Eddie 182, 184
Rodriguez, Lolita 37, 104, 136–139
Rodriguez, Miguel 157, 158, 188
Rojas, Emmanuel 98
Roldan, Arsenio C. 59
Roldan, Dennis 218–220
Rollin, Jean 122
Rome 114, 201
Romeo and Juliet 67
Romero, Cesar 98
Romero, Chanda 192
Romero, Eddie 23, 33, 63, 65, 70, 72, 83, 84, 86–89, 92, 94, 98, 110, 119, 120, 122–125, 127, 134, 135, 142, 154, 157, 188, 231
Romero, Gloria 70, 72, 73
Romero, Joey 188
Romero, Jose E. 83
Romulo, Carlos 33
Rono, Chito S. 195, 197, 201, 203, 230
Roosevelt, Franklin D. 40–42
The Rooseveltodore 7
Rosal, Rosa 28, 37, 69, 70, 72
Rosales, Carmen 36, 46, 53, 57, 59, 63–65, 72, 79
Rosales, Jose 15
Rosales, Nario 72
Rose of the Philippines 8
Rossellini, Roberto 83
Roxas Blvd. 101
Royal Productions 61
Royo, Fernando 57
Rubio, Ben 80
Russia 3, 37, 74
Rustia, Ruben 3, 33, 172
RV Productions 97

Sa Kuko ng Agila 207–209, 216
Sabotage 103
Sacramento County Jail 225, 226
Sagado, Julian 27
Sagur 65
St. Luke's Medical Center 239
St. Theresa's College 101
Saint Louis University 175
Sakay 38
Salao, Andy 103
Salcedo, Juan 48

Salcedo, Leopoldo 26, 35, 45, 47, 48, 52, 53, 57, 65, 67, 68, 79, 88, 89, 98, 148
Salingsing sa Kasakit 61
Salome 188, 219
Salon de Pertierra 5
Salumbides, Vicente 15, 16, 39
Salutin, Rogelio 227
Salvador, Leroy 76, 97, 99
Salvador, Lou 57, 65, 97
Salvador, Phillip 143, 152, 154, 168, 173, 175
Salvador, Rogelio 172
Samar 98
Sampaguita Pictures 19, 27, 30, 32, 36, 38–40, 51, 53, 58, 59, 62, 63, 67, 72, 79, 82, 93, 98, 99, 103, 104, 130, 213, 214
Sampaloc, Manila 53
San Antonio 218
San Francisco, California 38, 120
San Francisco del Monte 239
San Juan 93, 222
San Juan del Monte 206, 212
San Mateo 157
San Miguel, Bulacan 29
San Nicolas 20
Sanchez, Antonio 184
Sanchez, Caridad 223
Sanda Wong 69
Sangang Nangabali 61
Sta. Cecilia Sawmills 168
Santa Cruz 8, 73
Sta. Maria Pictures 61
Santiago 135, 136, 147
Santiago, Adela 30, 58–60
Santiago, Dr. Ciriaco 30, 58, 59, 84
Santiago, Cirio H. 1, 59, 110, 119, 125, 127, 134, 163–165
Santiago, Pablo 93, 94
Santo Domingo 147
Santo Domingo, Rolando 199
Santo Domingo Church 239
Santos, Charo 150–152
Santos, Tony 70
Santos, Vilma 68, 130, 131, 133, 146–148, 150, 154, 173, 174, 185, 203, 218, 238
Sarah Balabagan Story 192
Saravia, Negros Occidental 63
Sarswelas 6, 7, 18, 29, 30, 31, 35, 38, 48
Satur 65
Saudi Arabia 185
Savage! 110
Savage Sisters 110, 125–127
Savoy 16
Sawa sa Lumang Simboryo, Ang 69
Sawamura, Tsutomu 46
Sawing Gantingpala, Ang 65
Sawing Palad 48
Saxon, John 89, 92, 126
The Scavengers 84, 85
Une Scene de Dansa Japonaise 6
Schindler's List 169
Scorpio Nights 156–158
Scorsese, Martin 169
Second Golden Era 129, 131, 133, 134, 140, 141, 152, 162, 165, 167, 193, 197, 200, 203
Secret of the Sacred Forest 98
Secret Witness 104
Seiko Films 167, 194
Selleck, Tom 126
Senate Committee on Illegal Drugs 215
Sendenbu 43, 45
Senswal 206
Sevilla, Gloria 61
Shabu (methamphetamine hydrochloride) 180, 224
Shame: (1984) 159; (2000) 206
Shazam 68
Sherman, Sam 94, 120
Shields, Brooke 155
Shirley, My Darling 70
Shoe Mart 233
Sibal, Jose Flores 88
Siete Infantes de Lara 65, 173
Sigfredo 65
Sigua, Hilario 111, 112
Siguion-Reyna, Armida 151, 203–206, 228
Siguion-Reyna, Carlitos (Carlos) 195, 205
Silayan, Vic 3, 145, 151, 152, 165
Silliman University 13
Silos, Augusto 38
Silos, Cesar 38
Silos, Juan, Jr. 74, 175
Silos, Luis 38
Silos, Manuel 37, 38, 44, 52, 57
Silos, Octavio 38, 51
Siloscope 38
Sin, Cardinal Jaime 158, 166, 211, 227–229
Sinasamba Kita 173
Singapore 190–192
Singson, Luis "Chavit" 210, 211
Siniloan, Laguna 147
Sisa: (1951) 69; (1998) 200
Sison, Jesus 170, 203
Sison, Joe 98
Sister Stella L 150
The Sisterhood 165
Sitting In the Park 131 69 205
SM City 233
SM Malls 232
Smith, Harry 84
Smith, William P. 19, 44, 46, 240
Smith, William (II) 126
Smith and Wesson 176
Smith Sound Systems Laboratories 19
Snake Sisters 148, 160
Snooper 82, 86–88
Snow Games 6
So Long America 62
Social Service Pictures 86
Social Weather Stations 238
Solis, Charito 73–75, 108, 109, 147, 151, 152, 154
Song-Movie Magazine 28
Songs and Lovers 130
Songs and Stars Home Magazine 86, 87
Sonora, Rosemarie 136, 137
Sony Music Philippines 193
Soriano, Maricel 201
Sorsogon 173, 239
Sotto, Agustin V. 1
Sotto, Tito 159, 214, 215, 224, 236
Sotto, Vic 159, 160, 214
Sotto, Vicente *see* Sotto, Tito
Soul of a Fortress 98
The Soul Saver 16
The Sound of Music 135
South China Sea 209
South Vietnam 84
Southeast Asia 235
Southeast Asian Film Festival 99
Southern Winds 152
Spain 3, 5, 7–9, 11, 12, 20, 33, 197–199
Spanish-American War 7, 43
Spanish Inquisition 9
Spanish language 19, 27, 31, 33, 196
Sparrow Unit: The Termination Squad 181
Spielberg, Steven 169
Spirit Questors 155
S-R Productions 61
Sri Lanka 82
Sto. Domingo, Dr. Braulio 206
Star Awards 3, 199, 201, 228
A Star Is Born 132
Star Search 131
Star Talk 195
Stars of the Stage and Screen 53
State of Rebellion 212
The Steel Claw 98
Stephan Films 143
Strada, Stella 159
Strand Theater 22
Stranglehold 165
Strunk, Rod Lawrence 222–227
Stryker 165
Stuart-Santiago, Angela 205
Sturgeon, Jennings 67, 89
Suarez, Bobby 125
Subic Naval Base 207, 209, 226
Sugat ng Puso, Mga 45
Sunset Over Corregidor 54, 57
Superbeast 125
Suzara, Romy 195
SVS Pictures 61
Swanky Hotel 102
Sweet Sixteen 130
Sweet Sweet Love 130
Sweetheart 130
Sweethearts 70, 71
Sword of the Avenger 65
Sy, Henry, Sr. 232, 233
Sycangco, Liezl 176–178

Taal Volcano 10
Taft, William Howard 164
Taga sa Bato 173
Tagalog 19, 31, 33, 36, 43, 54, 61, 87, 126, 163, 196, 206
Tagalog Ilang-Ilang Productions 97
Tagalog-Kislap Pictures 97
Tag-Araw, Tag-Ulan 148
Taglish 196

Tahimik, Kidlat 163, 164
Tait, Edward 19, 20, 23, 28, 240
Takas sa Bataan 54
Takipsilim 36
Tamaraw Pictures 61, 97
Tampuhan, Ang 40
Tanduay 7
Tangi Kong Pagibig, Ang 63
Tanikala 152
Tanikalang Apoy 173
Taong Paniki 39, 67
Taong Putik 68
Tapatan ng Tapang 216
Tarantino, Quentin 2
Tarlac 227
Taruc, Luis 74, 76, 78
Task Force Marsha 221, 224
Tatalon 127
Tatay Kong Nanay, Ang 105
Tatlo 141
Tatlo, Dalawa, Isa 138
Tatlong Hambog 16
Tatlong Maria 46
Tatlong Taong Walang Diyos 141
Tawag ng Tanghalan 131
Taxation 82, 103, 130, 161, 202, 231, 233–235
Taylor, Kent 94, 95
Teague, Eddie 10, 11
Teatro Junquera 15
Teatro Pilipino 196
Teehankee, Claudio 167
Teenage Escapades 132
Teen-age Jamboree 130
Teenage Jamboree 132
Teenage Senorita 130
Tell Nora I Love Her 132
Tennessee 20
10th Battalion sa 38th Parallel, Korea 69
Teongson, Ramon 11
Teotico, Fernando 11
Terrified 222
Terror Is a Man 84–86, 88
Terrorist Hunter 220
Thailand 83, 152
Theater 44, 46–49
The Thirsty Dead 128
Thyssen, Greta 86
Tinimbang Ka Nguni't Kulang 137, 138
Tinio, Rolando 188, 196
Tiongson, Nicanor 228, 229, 231, 238
Tito, Vic and Joey 159, 214
T.N.T. Jackson 164, 165
To Susan, with Love 93
Toho Films 44
Tokyo 199
Tolentino, Amelita 186
Tolentino, Lorna 173, 174
Tolosa, Carlos Vander 19, 37, 54, 68
Tondo 10, 39, 63, 140
Too Hot to Handle 3, 165
Toro see Live Show
Toronto Film Festival 195
Torre, Joel 152, 154, 169, 184, 185, 188, 192, 199

Torres, Dr. Arturo 225
Torres, Katherine "Kaye" 224, 226, 227
Torres, Mar S. 64
Tough Guy 91
Tower Productions 113
Tracy, California 225, 226
A Train's Arrival 6
Tres Muskiteras 67
Tres Sagganos 37
Trimble, Jerry 165
Trinidad, Benjamin 68
Troubador 60
Trozo 130
Trudis Liit 130
Tuason, Luis 16
Tubog sa Ginto 135, 136
Tuko sa Madre Kakaw 39
Tuloy and Ligaya 38
Tupas 11
Turumba 163
Twin Fist for Justice 131

Uhaw 109, 115
Ulila, Ang mga 20
Ulila ng Bataan 62, 213
Ulilang Watawat 51
Ulog Cocktail Lounge 101
Ultimatum 165
Ulysses 118
La Union 182
United Arab Emirates 192, 193
United Artists 65
United States 19, 20, 22, 29, 33, 34, 37, 40, 41–43, 48–50, 51, 58, 62, 74 76, 77, 83, 84, 86, 87, 89, 94, 100, 106, 107, 116, 125, 136, 138, 140–142, 156, 161, 163–165, 166, 169, 182, 186, 187, 194, 179, 197, 207, 209, 222, 224–226, 232, 235
U.S. Army Philippine Scouts 173
U.S. Congress 7, 40, 116
U.S. embassy 186, 187, 225
U.S. First Cavalry 49
U.S. government 115, 225
U.S. Immigration and Naturalization Service 186
U.S. Justice Department 225, 226
U.S. Library of Congress 7
U.S. military 141
U.S. Navy 84
U.S.-Philippine extradition treaty 226
Universal Pictures 8, 38
University of Aix-en-Provence 145
University of Heidelberg 149
University of Madrid 8
University of Santo Tomas 45, 77, 99
University of Sind 114
University of the Philippines 46, 135, 145, 197, 228
University of the Philippines' College of Mass Communication 238
University of the Philippines Film Center 98, 197, 201
The Untold Story of Carmela Vizconde 184

Urban Terrorist 181
Utol Kong Hoodlum, Ang 176
Utol Kong Hoodlum 2, Ang 176

Valdez, Ronaldo 119, 132, 201
Valenciano, Gary 186
Valentino, Rudolph 22
Valenzuela, Ramon 97
Vampire Hookers 127
The Vampire People see *Kulay Dugo ang Gabi*
Van Doren, Mamie 137
Varga, Carol 68, 69
Vargas, Vic 93, 94
Vasquez, Romeo 37, 97, 120, 122, 182
Vatican 179
Vaudeville see Vod-a-vil
The Vengeance of Fu Manchu 104
Venice Film Festival 65, 66, 147
Ventura, Honorio 25
Vera, Dolores H. 30, 31, 72, 82, 99
Vera, Jose O. 27, 30, 35, 62, 99
Vera, Pedro 27, 30, 39, 40, 53
Vera-Perez Enterprises 99
Vergel, Ace 179, 180, 215
Vergel, Alicia 72, 84, 180
Vernal, Ruel 140
Versoza, Gardo 200
Vi and Bot 133
Via Crucis 26
Victim No. 1: Delia Maga (Jesus, Pray for Us!) 184, 192
Victory Joe 52
Victory Song of the Orient 46
Vida de Jose Rizal, La 9
Video piracy 4, 231, 233, 235
Videogram Regulatory Board 235
Vietnam 76, 83, 116
Vietnam War 163
The Village Voice 163
Villanueva, Brigida Perez 29
Villanueva, Brother Eddie 205
Villanueva, Victoria 113, 114
Villar, Manuel 211
Villarino, S. Alvarez 19, 20
Villegas, Monsignor Socrates 228, 229
Villongco, Carmen 27
Vinarao, Edgardo 141
Virgin Forest 157, 158
Virgin Mary 146, 202
Virgin People 148, 149
Visayan film industry 15, 19, 20, 61
Visayas 15, 61, 87, 196
Vision Theater 20
Vistan, Manuel 60
Vistan-Chapman Productions 61
Vitug, Romy 198
Viva Films 167, 177, 187, 191–194
Vizconde, Carmela 182, 186
Vizconde, Estrellita 182
Vizconde, Jennifer 182
Vizconde, Lauro 182
Vizconde, Maria 68
Vizconde massacre 182, 184, 186, 187, 191
The Vizconde Massacre: God Help Us! 182–185

Vizconde Massacre 2 184
VM Productions 61
Vod-a-vil 6–8, 10, 16, 31, 47, 48
Vod-A-Vil (film) 63
VS Productions 133
Vulcan 165

Waggner, George 97
Wainwright, Jonathan Mayhew, IV 45
Walang Kamatayan 52
Walang Sugat 14
The Walls of Hell 89, 92, 98
Walter, Mary 33, 34, 120, 136, 138, 139
Wanted: Perfect Mother 135
War Crimes Commission 52
War History Club of Angeles 45
Warkill 98
Warner Bros. 38, 51
Washington, D.C. 16, 41, 42, 116
Watergate 116
Wayne, John 57, 91
Weaver, Dennis 126
Webb, Freddie 186, 187
Webb, Hubert 186, 187
Wheels of Fire 165
White, Jesse 106

White Plains, Quezon City 223
Wilde, Cornel 98
Williams, Esther 135
Wilson, Claude 138
Wilson, Woodrow 13
Winfield, Paul 98
Winter Holiday 132
The Woman Hunt 125
Women in Cages 125
Women of Hell's Island 125, 164
Wonder Woman 68
The Wonderful World of Music 130
Woo, John 194
Working Girls 204
World Trade Center 179
World War II 28, 34, 36, 40–54, 72–74, 76, 83, 84, 89, 98, 100, 105, 135, 141, 157, 170, 173, 222
Wycoco, Reynaldo 223–227
Wyndom, Herbert 7
Wynn, Keenan 98
www.XXX.com 232

X'Otic Films 25, 27, 54

Yabut, Nemesio 97
Yabut, Rafael 77, 80, 81
Yakuza 160

Yamashita 127
Yamashita, Tomoyuki 49, 52
Ybarra, Antonio 80
Yearsley, Albert 10, 11, 14
Ye-Ye Generation 131
York, Ace *see* Vergel, Ace
The Young at Heart 132
Young Filmmakers of Asia Festival 197
The Young Idol 130
Young Love 130, 132
Yousef, Ramzi 179
Yutaka, Abe 44

Zambales 219
Zamboanga 20–24, 62, 65
Zamboanga City 141
Zamboanga del Sur 82
Zamora, Jacinto 12
Zaragosa, Carmen 29
Zarate, Ernie 137
Zobel, Claudia 159
Zoetrope 164
Zorilla Theater 7
Zshornack (Zschornack), Zaldy 90, 91, 110, 120
Zultana International 97
Zulueta, Dawn 188

www.ingramcontent.com/pod-product-compliance
Lightning Source LLC
Chambersburg PA
CBHW080753300426
44114CB00020B/2722